Virginia Historic Marriage Register

Augusta County Marriages, 1748-1850

compiled by

John Vogt
&
T. William Kethley, Jr.

Iberian Publishing Company
Athens, Georgia

© COPYRIGHT 1986 BY JOHN VOGT

ALL RIGHTS RESERVED. NO PART OF THIS BOOK MAY BE
REPRODUCED IN ANY FORM WITHOUT PERMISSION IN
WRITING FROM THE PUBLISHER, EXCEPT BY A REVIEWER
WHO MAY QUOTE BRIEF PASSAGES IN A REVIEW TO BE
PRINTED IN A MAGAZINE OR NEWSPAPER.

Published by the Iberian Publishing Company.

ISBN 0-935931-23-6

Printed in the United States of America.

CONTENTS

Abbreviations	iv
Introduction	v
Part 1. Surname frequency	1
Part 2. Man's name	29
Part 3. Woman's name	221
Appendix. Ministers performing marriages as reported in Augusta County clerk returns.	408
Figure 1. Origins of Augusta County	414
Map-Virginia counties circa 1850	endleaf

ABBREVIATIONS

```
b........bondsman (party granting surety to the
              clerk that marriage can be held
              without any legal impediment.)
bro .....brother of
col .....colored
con......consent (usually given by a parent
              or guardian)
cty .....county
d .......daughter of
(dec) ...deceased
gd ......granddaughter of
gdn .....guardian of
ggd .....great-granddaughter of
ggs .....great-grandson of
gs ......grandson of
lic .....license, followed by date of
              license when available
min .....minister performing ceremony,
              followed by date of return
ne ......nephew of
ni ......niece of
p,perm- .......permission (to marry), given by
              parent(s) or guardian
q .......Quaker (Society of Friends)
              marriage
s .......son of
sis .....sister of
std .....stepdaughter of
stm .....stepmother of
sts .....stepson of
test.....witnesses in a sworn oath
wit......witness
```

INTRODUCTION

<u>Augusta County Marriages, 1748-1850</u> represents a continuing effort designed to publish a comprehensive finding aid for all marriage records before 1850 for Virginia and its western holdings. Although about forty percent of these pre-1850 Virginia marriages have been published, access to much of this printed material remains difficult. A scholar wishing to conduct in-depth research must perforce visit the Virginia State Library and its fine collection of print, manuscript, and microfilm genealogical materials. Time and distance often precludes such concentrated research.

Designed so that the reader may quickly search by name both husband and wife, this ready reference guide has an additional master frequency listing of all last names to account for variations in spellings by the recording clerks or ministers. The record arrangement should assist in searching through a large volume of marriages with relative facility. Yet, by no means is this guide to be an ending point for inquiry on the particular marriage under search. For the beginning genealogist, an excellent reference is Norman Edgar Wright's <u>Building an American Pedigree</u> (Provo, Utah: Brigham Young University Press). Among current periodical literature, the most extensive source listing may be found in <u>The Genealogical Helper</u> (c/o The Everton Publishers, Inc., P.O. Box 368, Logan, UT 84321). In addition, the authors have published <u>Marriage Records in the Virginia State Library: A Researcher's Guide</u> for a listing of Virginia marriage records.

In the guide's master listing of all last names (Part 1), which also shows the frequency of their occurrence, the researcher must utilize his creativity in searching all the possible variants of a name. County clerks often spelled the names according to their own phonetic whims, and versions of the same family name may occur pages apart in the husband/wife listings. This is particularly true for Augusta County where a number of Pennsylvania Germans migrated. English county clerks were wont to record names phonetically in the absence of literate couuples, and frequently the surnames appear slightly altered in the surname frequency of this volume. Where surnames are at odds between the clerk's recording of the bond and the minister's return, both entries have been retained and a note of the variation has been placed in the marriage record (e.g., 'Minister's return spells name as 'Armontrout' ' or 'Armontrout'?) It is usually clear from the date and other data that this in fact is a single marriage. However, the researcher is left to decide on the proper name spelling. Similarly, where the names are identical, but the year varies, both entries have been retained.

Arranged in double columns for speed in searching, each unique last name is followed by two numbers. These represent the number of husbands and wives respectively by that name occurring in the register. Once the researcher has determined the various names desired, he can proceed to the alphabetical listings of marriages first by husband's last name (Part 2), and then by wife's last name in a separate listing (Part 3).

Both of these listings contain identical information--only the names have been reversed. In all instances, the first names of the two marriage partners are fully spelled out to facilitate indexing. Thus, 'Abm.' was rendered 'Abraham' in all cases and not 'Abram,' which in itself represents an abbreviation. Similarly, 'Eliz.' became 'Elizabeth,' etc. However, names such as 'Polly', 'Eliza', and 'Lucy' were retained. Abbreviated name forms are retained occasionally in the comments section where the bondsman, relatives, or minister performing the ceremony may have been cited.

In most instances the date of the marriage bond varies from the actual return by several days to a week or more, and both are recorded whenever available. Whenever a bondsman is listed, the date following the name of the couple in the record is that of the bond's issuance; if a minister's return was also recorded for that couple and incorporated in the record, the date of the return follows the name of the minister. If only a minister's return is recorded, the date is omitted after the minister's name, and the date following the couple's name is that of the actual marriage ceremony as reported by the minister.

AUGUSTA COUNTY

At its greatest extent in 1738, Augusta County encompassed all that territory from its border with the newly created Frederick County southward to Virginia's limits. Westward, it extended over all territory claimed by Great Britain to the Mississippi. From Augusta's lands ten counties were created directly (see chart) and, ultimately, nearly all of the states of West Virginia, Kentucky, Ohio, Illinois, and portions of Pennsylvania claim derivation from Augusta's further subdivisions.

The first explorations of this new land west of the Blue Ridge Mountains were conducted in the early 1700s. The earliest settlers appeared in the Shenandoah Valley by the late 1720s, and by the 1740s the tide of migration to the area had begun to swell. Scotch-Irish and Germans from Pennsylvania intermingled in this first migration, and by 1750 the population of this new backcountry county was about 2,500. These first settlers found a rich land for hunting, with plentiful game and rich bottomlands for subsistence farming.

Augusta's early history was punctuated by serious Indian incursions during the 1750s and 1760s. Only the deep winter months of late November through early February were relatively safe from marauding bands. The last Indian inroads into the Valley area of Augusta ended about 1764. With little assistance from the Williamsburg government, the backcountry citizenry developed a significant militia for self-protection.

Emigration was another dominant theme for Augusta County during its first century. Younger sons were enticed westward and southward into North Carolina and Tennessee by cheap land prices. Often entire families packed their wagons and made their way along the rough traces that were transformed into interregional roads. The primary route was the 'Wilderness Road.' Beginning at Staunton, it stretched westward to the Falls of the Ohio (Louisville) for a distance of five hundred miles. This road included almost three dozen waystations and communities along its route for stopovers. Settlers from other states linked into this main western thoroughfare. It was unusual for an Augusta family of the eighteenth century not to count at least one descendant who did not migrate westward into the Ohio Valley region.

Another migration was continuing into Augusta at the same time, namely, the influx of German settlers from central Pennsylvania. Thousands of persons of German descent, mostly farmers, filled the ranks of Augustans on the westward migrations. Geography played an important role in this movement. As Pennsylvania Germans migrants moved westward, they were almost inexorably drawn southwestward by the northeast-southwest parallel ridges of the Alleghanies which impeded westerly travel. Cheap lands in the Augusta area also attracted these settlers as land prices in Pennsylvania began to rise.

Augusta County commenced its 'birthing' of new counties from its original territory very early. In 1754 the county of Hampshire (WV) was formed from a northern portion of Augusta. Sixteen years elapsed before the next county broke away (Botetourt- 1770). From this particular separation there later developed forty-eight counties of Virginia, West Virginia, and Kentucky. During the American Revolution all the remaining subdivisions of Augusta save one emerged: Monongalia (WV), Ohio (WV), and Yohogania, all in 1776; and Rockingham, Pendleton, Rockbridge, and Illinois counties in 1778. The last county, Bath, was created in 1791, leaving Augusta County in its present form. In all of the further subdivisions, the lands originally encompassed by Augusta County was the parent territory for eighty-five counties formed prior to separation from Virginia sovereignty.

DEFINITION OF TERMS
Marriage Bond

Augusta County followed the rubrics of regulations for marriages which dated from the colonial period. In 1660/1661 the law requiring a bond was first enacted. Because of a scarcity of ministers, the colony required that all persons wishing to be married by license must go to the county court clerk and give bond with sufficient security (usually $150 by the nineteenth century) that there was no lawful cause to prevent the marriage. The license was then prepared by the clerk and presented to the minister who would perform the ceremony. Because many of the bonds were secured on the same day of the marriage, or else dated by the clerk with the marriage date, a system of conventional notation has been adopted in this volume to avoid unnecessary repetition. When a bondsman is noted with no date for the bond, the date may be presumed the same as the date of the marriage ceremony reported by the minister. Bonds issued with other dates are noted in the comments section following the names and date (e.g. 'bond-29Sep1811').

Another option was to perform the ceremony 'by banns', that is, after publicly announcing or 'publishing' the intentions of the parties at three congregational meetings. Such marriages avoided the necessity of a bond or license from the clerk. This custom predominated in several religious denomination; for example, Abraham Garber, minister of the Church of the Brethren (Middle River) performed every marriage save one which he reported by the device of publishing of banns.

Occasionally, interesting incidents are recorded by the county clerks as addenda to the marriage record. One such case was on the issuance of a bond by the Augusta clerk to Oliver Miller and Margaret Hagerty, otherwise called Margaret Brown, on 9 February 1799. It occasioned a legal opinion which was appended to the bond and which is revealing as to the mechanism and legal requirements of licensing by bond:

> The difficulty with the clerk of Augusta in issuing a marriage license in the case of Oliver Miller and Margaret Brown is: That as it is a matter known to him that a certain Brown got a license some time ago to marry said Margaret, after which they lived together some time as man and wife, when he left her and hath never returned, whether it is the duty of the clerk on the application of said Miller for license to marry her, to have proof, either of the death of the said Brown or of the marriage under the first license never

having been legally solemnized or of the said Brown being a married man at the time of the said pretended marriage, or, in short, whether it is the duty of the clerk to require proof that the said Margaret is a single woman? It appears to me under the law that the clerk discharged his duty by taking the bond and security required by law (which, together with the penalty against bigamy, seems to be th provision in the law to prevent illegal marriages) and to enquire whether the parties are of age. If these requisites are complied with, it appears to me to be at the risque of the parties themselves, if the marriage is illegal, and the clerk cannot withhold the license. (John Coalter, February 9, 1799).

According to the county marriage register, Oliver Miller and Margaret Brown were married by Rev. William King on 10 February 1799.

Consent

Parties seeking a license to marry were required to show evidence of their legal age to enter such a contract or else to have a consent from their parent(s) or guardian if under the age of twenty-one years. Unlike marriage bonds, which were form documents and often printed with appropriate blanks for names to be inserted, a written consent was at the discretion of the writer and therefore a very individualistic document. Most consents were mere scraps of paper with a brief permission signed by a parent. Other surviving consent documents reveal a wealth of information for the researcher. As an example, on 3 November 1800 Sally Poage wrote to the clerk of Augusta County granting permission for her son William to marry Polly Wright:

To the Clerk of Augusta: My son, Wm. Poage, son to the deceased Wm. Page, after having served his apprenticeship with Robert Carson, blacksmith, applied to me for my consent in case of marriage between him and Polly Rite, which I give in presence of Wm. Carson. Robert Carson will also send a certificate in presence of the same witness--Sally Poage. test: Wm. Carson, Wm Roades. (The certificate from Wm. Carson, releasing Wm from his apprenticeship, accompanies this document).

Marriage Records; Marriage Register

During the colonial period, the law required that every marriage be recorded in a true and perfect parish register. After 1780, ministers were required to report all marriages to the county court clerk whose duty it was to see that the returns were entered in a book kept for that purpose. The county record books which have survived, such as that of

Introduction

Augusta County, are sometimes titled "Marriage Records" or "Marriage Registers," although true 'registers' as defined by law did not begin until 1853.

SOURCES

The current volume of Augusta County marriages is compiled from a number of primary and secondary sources available in the Virginia State Library, Archives Division. The original records were consulted whenever available.

Primary sources:
(1). Augusta County Marriage Record, 1785-1813. Unpaged. (Microfilm reel # 98).
(2). Augusta County Marriage Record, 1813-1846. 67 folios. (Microfilm reel # 98). A photostatic copy of this record is available for consultation in the research room of the archives.
(3). Augusta County Marriage Record, 1842-1853. 14 folios. (Microfilm reel # 98).
(4). Miscellaneous Marriages Card File, box 6 [Marriage Licenses, 1828-1839].
(5). Augusta County Marriage Bonds (photostatic copies): vol.1 (1785-86); vol.2 (1787-89); vol.3 (1790-91); vol.4 (1792-93); vol.5 (1794-95); vol.6 (1796-97); vol.7 (1798-99).
(6). Augusta County Minister's Returns (photostatic copies): vol.1 (1785-1820).

Published sources:
(1). Colonel Thomas Hughart Chapter of the Daughters of the American Revolution(comps.). First Marriage Record of Augusta County, Virginia, 1785-1813 (n.d.) This is an abstraction of minister's returns, and is found in the original Augusta clerk's book of returns as well as Chalkley's work below.
(2). Bushman, Katherine G. (comp.). Supplement to First Marriage Record of Augusta County, Virginia, 1785-1813 (Verona, Va.: McClure Press, 1978). These are corrections to the First Marriage Record cited above.
(3). Colonel Thomas Hughart Chapter, DAR (comps.). Second Marriage Record of Augusta County, Va., 1813-1850 (Verona, Va.: McClure Press, 1972). Consists of minister's returns for the period stated in groupings by ministers as transmitted to the county clerk.
(4). Chalkley, Lyman. Chronicles of the Scotch-Irish Settlement in Virginia; Extracted from the original Court

Introduction

<u>Records of Augusta County, 1745-1800</u>. 3 volumes (n.p.: Mary S. Lockwood, 1912-1913; reprinted: Baltimore: Genealogical Publishing Co., 1965). Chalkley appears to have had access to records at the beginning of this century which are no longer extant, particularly for the early period prior to the Revolution.

A total of 5,244 marriages are recorded in this present Virginia Historic Marriage Register for Augusta County.

Augusta County Marriages -- Surname Frequency

-----...3..322
Abernathy...1..0
Abney...3..6
Acker...0..1
Acord...7..5
Adair...1..1
Adams...0..5
Adkins...1..1
Aerion...0..1
Agnue...1..0
Ailer...2..3
Ailor...1..6
Ailshire...1..2
Ailstrop...1..0
Aistrop...0..1
Akerly...1..0
Alderman...1..0
Aldoffer...0..1
Alexander...22..15
Alford...1..1
Alfort...1..0
Alfred...0..1
Alinger...1..0
Alison...2..0
Allason...1..0
Allbright...0..1
Allen...14..22
Allinger...1..0
Allison...11..11
Almarode...1..1
Almenrode...0..1
Almerode...1..1
Almonroade...1..1
Almorode...0..1
Alor...0..1
Althaffer...1..0
Amen...1..0
Amend...1..0
Amon...1..0
Ancell...1..0
Anderson...24..23
Andrew...8..1
Andrews...2..2
Any...1..0
Apley...1..0
Apple...4..4
Appleby...0..1
Arbast...1..0
Arbocast...0..1
Arbogast...1..0
Arbuckle...4..1
Archdaton...0..1
Archdeacon...1..0
Arehart...2..3
Arganbright...0..1
Argebright...0..1
Argenbright...10..8
Arginbright...1..0
Arion...1..0
Arisman...2..0
Armantrout...1..0
Armentrout...1..1
Armintrout...0..1
Armontrout...0..1
Armstrong...24..23
Arnall...1..0
Arnold...1..0
Ashby...0..1
Asherd...0..1
Askins...0..1
Astal...0..1
Asten...1..0
Aston...1..2
Attershall...0..1
Aughe...1..0
Aukes...1..0
Austin...3..3
Aylor...1..2
Bachelor...0..1
Back...1..1
Backenstoe...2..1
Backley...0..1
Badger...1..0
Bagby...0..2
Bailey...7..4
Bailor...2..3
Baily...0..1
Bain...1..0
Bains...0..1
Baird...2..0
Baker...4..4
Balard...0..1
Balbzell...0..1
Baldwin...3..5
Ball...1..0
Ballar...0..1
Ballard...3..3
Ballew...1..0
Balman...1..0
Balmer...1..0
Balsley...2..1
Baltzer...0..1
Balzley...0..1
Bander...0..2
Banes...0..1
Barbour...0..1
Barclay...1..0
Bare...8..4

Augusta County Marriages -- Surname Frequency

Barger...5..2
Barker...1..2
Barkley...1..0
Barley...0..1
Barnes...0..1
Barnet...2..2
Barnett...3..3
Barnhart...2..3
Barns...0..1
Barrett...0..1
Barrigar...0..1
Barry...1..2
Bartley...1..2
Baskin...3..0
Baskins...6..3
Batcheller...1..0
Bateman...2..1
Bates...1..0
Baties...0..1
Batis...2..0
Battow...1..0
Baumgartner...1..0
Bawcutt...1..0
Baxter...1..0
Baylor...9..5
Baynes...0..1
Bazzle...1..1
Beal...1..1
Bealy...0..1
Beam...1..2
Bean...1..0
Bear...8..5
Beard...27..21
Beasley...0..1
Beaten...1..0
Beaty...2..2
Beck...6..2
Beery...0..1
Beeton...1..3
Behler...1..0
Beith...1..0
Bekane...1..0
Bell...50..42
Bengas...1..0
Benner...1..0
Bennett...2..0
Benson...1..1
Berkeley...1..1
Berlin...1..0
Berrier...0..1
Berry...14..10
Berryhill...1..0
Bertrum...1..0
Besse...1..0

Best...1..4
Betty...1..0
Bibb...1..0
Bibe...1..0
Bibee...0..1
Bible...1..0
Biby...0..1
Bickerstoff...1..0
Bickerton...0..1
Bickle...1..1
Bigger...1..0
Bilheimer...0..1
Billheimer...0..1
Billhymer...1..0
Bing...1..1
Bingham...1..0
Bird...1..6
Bishop...1..6
Bittle...2..0
Bitzell...0..1
Black...20..13
Blackamore...0..2
Blackburn...2..1
Blackeley...1..0
Blacker...0..2
Blackmore...1..0
Blackwell...2..2
Blackwood...3..8
Blain...2..0
Blair...11..17
Blake...1..0
Blakely...2..2
Blakemore...2..6
Blakly...0..1
Blane...1..0
Bleaker...0..1
Bleakley...0..1
Bleakly...1..2
Blear...0..1
Blewitt...1..0
Bogas...1..0
Bohannon...0..1
Boils...0..1
Bollar...0..1
Bolls...0..1
Bolsley...1..0
Bolton...1..1
Bookhamer...1..0
Boon...0..1
Boone...0..1
Booz...0..1
Borden...1..0
Boreland...1..0
Borland...2..1

Augusta County Marriages -- Surname Frequency

Borrigar...1..0
Bosang...0..1
Bosserman...3..8
Boswell...1..0
Botkin...4..3
Botkins...1..0
Botram...1..1
Bott...0..1
Bouler...0..1
Bourland...0..1
Bowen...1..2
Bower...1..0
Bowers...4..2
Bowls...0..1
Bowman...5..10
Bowyer...4..2
Boyd...7..7
Boyer...0..2
Boyers...1..0
Boyles...0..1
Boys...2..1
Braden...0..1
Bradshaw...2..1
Brady...3..4
Brafford...0..1
Braford...0..1
Bragg...0..3
Branaman...1..3
Brand...2..3
Braneman...1..0
Branen...0..1
Branham...0..1
Bratten...0..1
Bratton...6..5
Brawford...2..3
Brawley...0..1
Bray...0..1
Breckenridge...0..1
Breckinridge...2..1
Breden...0..2
Bredin...0..2
Breesland...0..1
Breeze...3..0
Breezeley...0..1
Breverd...1..0
Brew...1..0
Brewer...1..0
Brian...0..1
Brians...1..0
Brice...0..1
Bridge...1..4
Bridger...0..1
Bridget...1..0
Bridgett...1..0

Brien...1..0
Bright...5..5
Brightwell...1..0
Brilhart...1..0
Brisco...0..1
Brison...1..0
Brittain...1..1
Britten...1..0
Britton...1..4
Brobeck...1..2
Brocius...1..0
Brockman...0..1
Brodhurst...1..0
Brooback...0..1
Brook...1..1
Brooke...0..1
Brooking...0..1
Brooks...13..6
Broom...1..0
Brosius...2..2
Brothers...0..1
Brower...2..5
Browers...1..2
Brown...55..49
Brownfield...4..0
Browning...2..0
Brownlee...10..8
Bruback...1..0
Brubeck...1..1
Bruce...1..1
Bruffey...2..0
Brukmann...1..0
Brunk...0..1
Bruntain...1..0
Bryan...4..0
Bryans...0..1
Bryant...2..2
Buchanan...14..9
Buckley...1..1
Buckman...1..0
Buckner...0..1
Buks...1..0
Bulcher...0..1
Bull...0..1
Bumgardner...0..2
Bumgarner...4..0
Bunch...1..2
Burch...1..2
Burdett...1..0
Burgentine...1..0
Burges...1..1
Burgess...4..10
Burk...0..2
Burkart...0..1

Augusta County Marriages -- Surname Frequency

Burke...1..1
Burkentine...1..0
Burket...1..3
Burkett...1..3
Burkhart...2..1
Burkholder...1..1
Burner...0..1
Burnes...0..1
Burnett...0..1
Burns...2..2
Burnsides...1..0
Burrus...1..0
Burton...1..2
Burwell...1..0
Bush...4..8
Bushong...3..2
Buster...2..0
Butt...0..3
Byer...1..0
Byerley...0..1
Byers...5..6
Bywaters...0..1
Cail...0..1
Cain...5..0
Calahan...0..1
Calbraith...0..1
Calbreath...0..3
Caldbreath...0..1
Caldwell...10..10
Cale...6..4
Caler...1..0
Cales...0..2
Calhoon...2..1
Call...0..1
Callaghan...0..4
Calleson...0..1
Callison...3..1
Calvert...1..1
Cambden...0..1
Cambell...1..1
Cameron...2..0
Campbell...28..17
Camper...1..0
Cannady...0..1
Canole...0..1
Canote...2..1
Cantley...1..0
Caphart...1..0
Carcofe...0..1
Carden...2..0
Carell...1..0
Carey...1..0
Cargo...1..1
Carhart...0..1

Carico...1..0
Caricofe...0..1
Carlile...1..0
Carlos...1..0
Carlyle...0..1
Carnal...0..1
Carothers...1..0
Carpenter...2..2
Carr...0..2
Carrethers...1..0
Carrico...0..1
Carricof...0..1
Carricofe...1..0
Carrington...2..0
Carrol...3..1
Carroll...0..1
Carson...9..4
Carter...0..2
Cartmill...1..0
Caruthers...3..3
Carwell...1..0
Cary...0..1
Casady...2..0
Cash...2..0
Cashaw...0..2
Casidy...1..0
Caslen...1..0
Cason...1..2
Casper...0..1
Cassady...1..3
Castleman...0..1
Catling...1..0
Caufman...0..1
Caul...0..1
Caulk...1..0
Cave...0..3
Cawley...1..0
Cawly...1..1
Cawthron...0..2
Cease...1..3
Cesterson...0..1
Chambers...4..3
Chandler...1..0
Chaplain...0..1
Chaplin...0..3
Chapman...1..4
Cheatham...0..2
Chesnut...1..4
Chesnutt...1..2
Childers...1..1
Chrisman...2..4
Christian...8..7
Christopher...1..0
Churchman...1..2

Augusta County Marriages -- Surname Frequency

Clark...4..4
Clarke...8..7
Clarkson...1..0
Clayton...4..1
Claytor...2..0
Clemans...1..0
Clemants...0..1
Clemens...0..1
Clements...2..0
Clemer...0..4
Clemmens...1..0
Clemmons...1..1
Clemons...1..1
Click...1..0
Clide...1..0
Cliff...1..0
Clifton...2..1
Cline...6..5
Clinebill...3..4
Clinedinst...3..0
Clinetinch...0..1
Clinginpeel...1..0
Clinon...0..1
Cloverfield...0..2
Cloyd...1..0
Clyne...1..0
Clynes...0..1
Coalter...1..6
Coatney...1..0
Cochran...5..2
Cocke...1..0
Cockran...1..0
Cockrell...1..0
Coffey...1..1
Coffman...8..8
Cofney...0..1
Coger...2..0
Coiner...19..13
Colbreath...1..0
Colbreth...1..0
Coldbreath...1..1
Cole...0..1
Coleman...1..0
Coley...1..2
Collins...8..7
Coltrider...1..1
Coly...1..0
Comerford...0..1
Commens...0..1
Compton...1..0
Conal...1..0
Conell...0..1
Conklin...1..0
Connally...1..1
Connaway...0..2
Connell...0..3
Connelly...4..3
Connely...0..2
Conner...2..3
Connor...1..0
Connoway...1..0
Conova...0..1
Conrod...1..0
Conway...0..1
Cook...3..11
Cooke...2..1
Cooper...17..9
Coorsy...0..1
Copehaver...1..0
Copeland...1..0
Corby...4..1
Cord...0..1
Corry...1..0
Coruthers...1..0
Cosley...1..0
Coughenour...0..1
Coulter...1..0
Coursey...3..6
Cowan...2..2
Cowdon...1..0
Cowger...1..0
Cowman...0..4
Cox...9..9
Coyner...2..4
Craig...16..22
Craine...1..0
Cramer...1..0
Crane...1..3
Crathers...0..1
Craun...2..2
Cravens...1..0
Crawford...24..39
Crawn...1..2
Creek...1..1
Creiner...1..0
Cress...1..0
Cribbins...1..0
Crick...2..1
Crickenbarger...1..0
Crigler...1..0
Crips...0..1
Criser...0..1
Crist...9..15
Criswell...1..0
Croan...0..1
Crobarger...1..1
Croft...2..4
Crombaker...0..2

Augusta County Marriages -- Surname Frequency

Crombick...0..1
Cromer...2..0
Cromwell...1..0
Crone...6..3
Crookshanks...1..0
Croom...0..1
Croome...0..1
Crosby...9..5
Crosen...1..0
Cross...6..2
Crossin...0..1
Crouch...0..1
Crouse...3..0
Croushorn...1..0
Crow...4..1
Crowbarger...1..3
Crown...1..0
Crum...1..3
Crumbacker...0..1
Crumbaker...0..1
Crump...0..1
Crumpacker...1..0
Crumpecker...0..1
Cullen...4..3
Cullon...0..1
Culp...0..3
Culpt...0..1
Culton...3..0
Cumins...0..1
Cummins...3..2
Cundiff...1..0
Cunningham...7..6
Cup...2..3
Cupp...4..4
Cupps...0..2
Cups...2..0
Curby...1..0
Curren...1..0
Curry...23..28
Cury...0..1
Cushing...0..1
Cushingberry...1..0
Cusin...0..1
Dachen...0..1
Dack...0..1
Dacke...1..0
Daft...1..0
Daggey...1..0
Daggy...6..6
Dale...0..1
Dalhouse...0..3
Dalton...1..1
Dameron...1..0
Dane...1..0

Daniels...1..1
Dannell...1..0
Danner...2..1
Danser...1..0
Darrow...0..1
Darst...1..1
Daugherty...3..3
David...1..0
Davidson...1..2
Davies...2..1
Davis...26..16
Davison...3..0
Dawson...1..1
Day...4..0
Deal...3..4
Deam...0..1
Dean...1..4
Deane...0..2
Deary...2..4
Decker...1..2
Decrisen...1..0
Dedamore...1..0
Deeds...1..1
Deemster...1..0
Deitz...1..0
Dellon...0..1
Delly...0..1
Delman...1..0
Delter...1..0
Delzell...1..0
Demasters...2..0
Denison...1..1
Denizen...1..0
Denney...1..0
Dennis...0..1
Dennison...5..2
Denny...0..1
Depriest...2..2
Dequeza...0..1
Derrough...0..1
Despar...0..1
Desper...2..0
Detamore...1..1
Detrick...2..0
Dettemore...0..1
Devenbough...1..1
Devericks...1..1
Deverix...1..0
Devine...0..1
Dice...3..0
Dick...0..1
Dickenson...1..1
Dickerson...0..1
Dickey...0..4

Augusta County Marriages -- Surname Frequency

Dickinson...1..0
Dickson...4..0
Dicky...0..1
Diddle...3..1
Didell...0..1
Dietrick...0..1
Dill...1..0
Dillan...2..0
Diller...0..1
Dillon...0..1
Dinkle...2..3
Dinnison...0..2
Dinsmore...1..2
Dinwiddie...1..0
Dixon...9..6
Doack...1..0
Doage...1..0
Doak...2..6
Doake...0..1
Dobage...0..1
Dobbs...0..3
Dodson...1..0
Dohine...0..1
Dohm...3..0
Doke...0..1
Dold...1..5
Dolino...1..0
Dollen...0..1
Dollhouse...0..1
Dolton...1..0
Donaghe...6..6
Donahe...0..1
Donaho...2..1
Donahugh...1..0
Donaldson...4..1
Donally...0..1
Donalson...0..1
Donaphan...1..0
Donavan...1..0
Donavin...1..0
Donefin...0..1
Donnally...0..1
Donnell...1..0
Donnelly...1..0
Donoho...1..0
Donovan...1..1
Doom...6..3
Dooms...1..0
Doren...0..1
Dorman...1..0
Dougherty...3..1
Douglas...1..2
Douglass...0..1
Douthat...4..1

Dove...1..0
Dowell...0..3
Dowling...1..0
Downey...3..4
Doyle...2..0
Driskell...1..0
Driver...0..1
Drum...1..0
Drumgold...1..0
Drummond...1..0
Dryden...1..0
Dudleston...1..0
Dudley...1..1
Duffield...3..0
Duke...1..0
Dull...10..4
Dun...1..0
Dunahugh...1..0
Dunbar...1..1
Dunlap...12..14
Dunlop...1..0
Dunn...1..4
Dunwiddie...0..1
Duval...1..0
Dyer...2..2
Eagal...0..1
Eagan...1..0
Eagle...8..3
Eagon...0..1
Eakard...1..0
Eakel...1..0
Eakerman...1..0
Eakin...1..0
Eakle...3..6
Earhart...3..8
Earley...0..2
Early...4..2
East...3..3
Eastham...0..1
Eaton...1..0
Eccard...1..0
Eccord...1..2
Echard...1..0
Echord...1..0
Eckard...1..0
Edde...0..1
Edgar...1..1
Edgecomb...0..1
Edmiston...1..1
Edmonds...0..2
Edmondson...2..0
Edmonson...1..0
Edmunds...1..1
Edmundson...1..0

Augusta County Marriages -- Surname Frequency

Edson...0..1
Edwards...1..1
Eeast...0..1
Effinger...2..0
Egnew...1..0
Eidsell...0..1
Eidson...3..3
Eikord...1..0
Ekerson...0..1
Elinger...1..0
Ellery...0..1
Ellet...0..1
Ellinger...1..1
Elliot...2..0
Elliott...8..7
Ellis...3..1
Elmore...1..0
Elsey...1..0
Elstock...0..1
Emmery...0..1
Emmett...0..2
Emmitt...0..1
Engard...1..0
Engleman...7..9
Engleton...1..0
English...0..1
Eppard...1..0
Epply...1..0
Ergebright...0..1
Erinaund...1..0
Ervin...5..0
Ervine...2..0
Erwin...12..23
Erwine...0..1
Eskridge...0..2
Estill...5..7
Estis...1..0
Etter...1..1
Eubank...3..0
Eurick...0..1
Euritt...1..2
Evan...0..1
Evans...10..8
Eve...0..1
Evelsizer...0..1
Everhart...1..0
Eversole...1..2
Evilsiser...0..1
Evy...3..0
Ewell...2..1
Ewin...1..3
Ewing...4..3
Ewings...0..1
⌒ Faber...3..0

Fackler...3..3
Fadely...1..1
Faegely...0..1
Fagus...1..0
Faidley...0..1
Fairbairn...1..0
Fairberman...1..0
Fairburn...2..3
Fall...4..5
Falls...0..3
Fallwider...1..0
Farish...1..0
Farmer...1..0
Farr...1..0
Farrow...2..2
⌒ Fauber...2..12
Faucet...1..1
⌒ Faulber...1..0
Faundree...0..1
Fauver...3..2
⌒ Fawber...2..4
Fawcet...1..0
Fawner...1..1
Faysnight...1..0
Feamster...0..1
Fellers...0..4
Fellows...2..1
Felps...1..0
Fennel...2..1
Fenton...2..4
Fertig...0..1
Fetzer...1..0
Fielding...0..1
Fife...0..1
Fifer...4..5
Fimster...1..0
Finely...0..2
Finla...1..0
Finley...8..10
Finly...1..0
Firebaugh...0..1
Firebough...1..1
Fishburn...5..2
Fishburne...1..0
Fisher...17..15
Fitch...3..2
Fitz...0..1
Fitzgerald...0..1
Fitzpatrick...4..7
Fix...4..5
Fizar...1..0
Flack...1..4
Fleiger...0..4
Fleisher...0..2

Augusta County Marriages -- Surname Frequency

Fleming...3..0
Flemming...1..0
Flesher...1..0
Fletcher...2..0
Flinn...1..2
Flory...1..2
Flowers...0..1
Fogel...0..1
Foglesang...0..1
Foley...2..0
Forber...0..1
Forbes...3..1
Forbish...1..0
Forbush...0..2
Foreman...2..0
Forer...1..0
Forrest...0..2
Forsythe...0..8
Fort...1..0
Fortune...0..1
Foster...3..2
Fouber...0..1
Fourber...0..1
Foutz...1..2
Fowler...1..1
Fowtick...1..0
Fox...4..6
Fraim...0..1
Frainer...0..1
Frame...4..6
France...0..2
Frances...0..1
Francis...2..3
Francisco...2..1
Frankam...0..2
Frankum...0..1
Franzman...0..1
Fraser...1..0
Fravel...1..0
Frazer...6..4
Frazier...3..6
Fream...0..1
Freed...1..1
Freeland...0..1
Freeman...0..2
Frely...1..0
French...2..0
Frenger...1..2
Fretwell...1..0
Frey...1..0
Fridley...5..1
Friel...1..4
Frogg...1..0
Fronsman...1..0

Fry...4..3
Fuchs...1..0
Fudge...1..3
Fuler...1..0
Fulks...1..0
Fuller...1..1
Fulton...8..20
Fultz...3..1
Fulweider...0..1
Fulwider...6..8
Funk...1..0
Funkhoser...0..1
Funkhouser...4..5
Funston...1..0
Fur...0..1
Furr...3..0
Gabart...0..2
Gabbert...1..1
Gabert...0..1
Gabhart...2..5
Gaines...2..1
Galbraith...0..2
Galen...0..1
Galespy...1..0
Gall...1..0
Gambell...1..0
Gamble...4..4
Gamwell...2..0
Garber...10..14
Gardiner...2..0
Gardner...6..6
Garhenour...1..0
Garmen...1..1
Garmon...1..1
Garnes...0..1
Garnett...0..1
Garretson...0..1
Garrison...2..1
Garton...0..1
Garvey...1..0
Garvin...4..2
Gates...1..1
Gatewood...2..1
Gaugh...1..0
Gay...6..0
Gayhart...0..1
Geating...0..1
Geeding...1..1
Geeting...0..1
Gelston...1..0
Gentry...1..0
George...1..0
Geralds...0..1
Gerhart...1..0

Augusta County Marriages -- Surname Frequency

Gette...1..0
Gibbons...0..5
Gibson...7..15
Gilbert...1..0
Gilbraith...1..0
Giles...2..1
Gilkerson...2..2
Gilkeson...6..11
Gillaspie...1..1
Gillaspy...0..1
Gilleat...1..0
Gillespie...2..0
Gillespy...2..0
Gilliam...1..1
Gilliat...1..1
Gillis...0..1
Gillum...1..0
Gilmore...0..2
Gipson...0..1
Given...1..1
Givens...8..5
Givins...0..1
Gladden...0..1
Gladwell...2..0
Glass...1..2
Glassburn...1..0
Glendy...1..0
Glenn...7..5
Glover...1..0
Glutz...0..1
Goah...1..0
Gochenauer...1..0
Gochenour...0..5
Goff...0..1
Goin...3..0
Going...1..0
Goings...2..2
Goins...1..0
Gold...1..3
Golladay...5..4
Golloday...2..1
Gongwer...2..0
Gonwer...0..1
Gooch...1..0
Good...3..8
Goodlink...1..0
Goodnight...1..1
Goodrich...1..0
Goodwin...3..3
Gordan...1..1
Gorden...1..1
Gordon...4..3
Gorrell...1..0
Gowing...1..0

Gragg...1..1
Graham...16..17
Grandie...1..0
Grant...2..6
Grass...7..6
Gratton...0..2
Graves...1..2
Gray...8..3
Greaver...1..2
Green...1..3
Greenwood...0..1
Greer...2..0
Greever...0..1
Gregery...0..1
Gregory...9..11
Greiner...6..7
Greiver...1..0
Greogry...1..0
Gresham...1..1
Grever...1..1
Grice...1..0
Griever...0..1
Griffeth...0..1
Griffey...1..0
Griffin...1..2
Griffith...4..9
Griggs...1..0
Grigsby...1..0
Grill...1..0
Grim...2..2
Grimm...1..2
Griner...1..0
Grinstead...1..0
Grips...1..3
Groah...1..1
Groff...2..0
Groom...1..0
Grooms...4..4
Grose...1..0
Grove...11..14
Groves...1..2
Grow...2..0
Grub...0..1
Guffy...1..1
Guiller...0..1
Guin...2..2
Guinn...3..2
Gully...0..1
Gum...1..0
Gunnell...1..0
Gunning...1..0
Gutherie...0..1
Guthrey...1..2
Guthrie...1..2

Augusta County Marriages -- Surname Frequency

Gutshall...0..1
Guy...3..1
Gwin...1..1
Gwinn...4..1
Haffner...3..5
Hafner...1..5
Hagar...1..0
Hagarty...0..1
Hager...1..0
Hagerty...0..3
Hain...0..1
Haines...1..1
Hains...1..4
Halbert...0..2
Haldeman...1..0
Halderman...1..3
Hale...1..2
Hall...14..22
Ham...2..1
Hamaker...1..0
Hambleton...1..0
Hamd...1..0
Hamer...0..1
Hamilton...20..17
Hamm...0..1
Hammaker...0..1
Hamp...0..1
Hampton...0..1
Hamrick...1..1
Hanah...0..1
Hance...0..1
Handly...1..0
Hanger...28..28
Hanke...0..1
Hankie...0..1
Hanlen...1..0
Hanna...6..5
Hannah...3..2
Hansbarger...1..4
Hansel...1..3
Hansell...1..1
Hanzele...0..1
Hapener...1..1
Hapner...0..1
Harbarger...1..1
Harberger...0..1
Harbison...1..0
Hardbarger...1..2
Harden...1..0
Harding...1..3
Hardshell...0..1
Hardwick...4..0
Hardy...1..0
Hare...0..2

Haring...0..1
Harland...1..0
Harlow...1..0
Harman...3..1
Harmon...2..3
Harner...1..1
Harness...0..1
Harnest...1..2
Harnsbarger...0..2
Harnsberger...1..0
Haroff...1..0
Harouf...1..0
Harouff...0..1
Harper...1..1
Harrigan...1..0
Harris...19..14
Harrison...10..4
Harrow...0..1
Harry...0..1
Harsbarger...0..1
Harshall...1..0
Harshaw...1..1
Harshman...0..1
Hart...10..3
Hartigan...1..3
Hartman...0..1
Hartshooke...0..2
Hartsook...0..1
Hartzo...0..1
Harvey...3..0
Harvie...1..0
Harzog...0..1
Hashaw...0..1
Haskins...0..1
Haslet...0..2
Haslett...1..0
Hassafluck...0..1
Hasterson...1..0
Hatfield...1..1
Hatten...0..1
Hatton...1..0
Haup...0..3
Haupe...2..0
Hawk...1..3
Hawkins...3..0
Hawp...3..2
Hawpe...4..2
Hay...1..0
Haybarger...1..3
Hayes...1..0
Hays...9..4
Hazelip...1..0
Head...1..0
Headly...0..1

Augusta County Marriages -- Surname Frequency

Headrick...1..0
Hearn...0..1
Hearse...1..0
Heatherley...0..1
Heaton...1..1
Hedebough...0..1
Hedrick...1..0
Hedwick...1..0
Heiden...0..1
Heise...1..0
Heiser...1..0
Heisey...1..0
Heiskell...2..3
Heitzer...1..0
Heizer...6..2
Helm...0..1
Helmick...1..1
Helms...6..1
Hemp...2..4
Hempenstall...0..2
Henderson...15..22
Hendren...0..1
Henkel...2..0
Henkle...1..0
Henn...1..0
Henry...9..13
Hensley...1..0
Hepler...1..0
Heppard...0..1
Herdman...1..0
Hering...1..0
Herndon...0..1
Hernsberger...1..0
Heron...1..0
Herpine...0..1
Herren...0..1
Herrin...1..0
Herring...4..2
Herron...2..1
Heslet...1..1
Hess...3..2
Hesterson...1..0
Heyden...1..0
Hibbert...0..1
Hickell...0..1
Hicklin...2..6
Hickok...1..0
Hicks...0..3
Hide...0..1
Hides...1..0
Hiestand...1..0
Higgason...1..0
Higginbotham...1..0
Hight...1..0

Higs...0..1
Hilberd...1..0
Hildebrand...1..2
Hill...2..6
Hillary...1..0
Hillis...2..1
Hiltebrand...2..0
Hincey...1..0
Hind...2..0
Hinds...2..0
Hine...1..0
Hiner...1..0
Hines...0..3
Hiney...2..0
Hinkle...0..1
Hinton...1..2
Hipard...0..1
Hipes...0..1
Hippard...2..0
Hippart...1..0
Hiser...1..0
Hite...6..2
Hively...1..0
Hizer...1..1
Hobock...1..0
Hodge...3..5
Hodges...0..1
Hofe...1..0
Hofert...0..1
Hoff...1..0
Hoffert...1..0
Hog...1..1
Hogan...0..1
Hogg...2..4
Hogsett...3..3
Hogshead...16..23
Holderman...1..0
Holladay...0..1
Hollaway...0..1
Hollis...0..4
Holmes...4..5
Holt...1..1
Holton...1..1
Holtz...1..0
Homes...0..1
Hood...1..0
Hoof...1..1
Hook...7..2
Hooke...2..0
Hooks...0..1
Hoopman...0..2
Hoover...4..7
Hope...1..0
Hopewell...0..1

Augusta County Marriages -- Surname Frequency

Hopkins...1..1
Hopper...0..1
Hopping...2..0
Horn...0..3
Horne...0..2
Hortshough...0..1
Hottle...1..3
Houchins...0..1
Houdashell...1..0
Houdishell...1..0
Houf...1..3
Houff...3..1
Houghobout...1..0
Houser...2..0
Houseright...1..0
Houston...1..3
Howard...1..0
Howdasher...0..1
Howdeshell...0..1
Howell...2..3
Hoye...1..0
Hubard...0..1
Hubbard...0..1
Hudlaw...0..1
Hudlow...1..0
Hudson...4..4
Hueston...1..0
Huff...8..9
Huffer...4..2
Huffert...2..1
Huffman...9..2
Hufford...1..0
Hufman...0..2
Hugart...1..0
Hugghart...1..0
Hughart...1..0
Hughes...0..3
Hughs...1..2
Hulet...1..0
Hulett...0..1
Huling...1..1
Hull...3..6
Hulvey...1..0
Humbert...1..1
Hume...1..0
Humes...0..1
Humphrey...3..5
Humphreys...2..5
Hunley...2..1
Hunter...13..16
Hupman...3..0
Hurst...0..1
Hushour...0..1
Husk...0..1

Huston...3..3
Hutchens...2..2
Hutchenson...1..0
Hutcheson...7..5
Hutchins...0..1
Hutchison...3..0
Hyatt...0..1
Hycarser...0..1
Hyde...3..0
Hyden...1..0
Hyland...1..0
Hynes...0..1
Imboden...3..5
Ingleman...0..2
Ingles...1..0
Ingleton...1..1
Ingram...1..1
Insle...0..1
Irvine...2..7
Irwin...0..1
Isaacs...1..0
Iseman...1..1
Isenhouser...0..1
Jackson...8..16
James...2..2
Jameson...2..1
Jamison...2..6
Jarvis...2..2
Jenkins...1..1
Jennings...1..6
Jewell...0..1
Joh...1..0
John...1..0
Johns...2..1
Johnson...15..7
Johnston...15..14
Jollett...1..0
Jonas...0..1
Jones...23..19
Jordan...4..1
Joseph...2..2
Jourdan...0..1
Journal...0..1
Judd...0..1
Jurtz...0..1
Kaiger...1..0
Kale...1..0
Kanely...1..0
Karahoof...0..1
Karichoff...2..0
Karichoof...0..2
Karicofe...1..5
Karikoff...2..0
Karracofe...0..1

Augusta County Marriages -- Surname Frequency

Karricofe...0..1
Karricoff...1..0
Kasterson...0..1
Kaufelt...1..0
Kayser...2..0
Kearns...1..0
Kee...1..0
Keen...1..0
Keenan...1..0
Keener...0..1
Keenon...1..1
Keeran...1..0
Keeth...0..1
Keiser...1..1
Keith...0..1
Keizer...1..0
Kellar...5..4
Keller...11..9
Kellor...1..1
Kelly...4..2
Kelsey...0..1
Kelso...2..0
Kenady...1..0
Kendall...1..0
Kendle...1..0
Keneday...1..0
Kenedy...1..0
Kennaday...0..2
Kennady...1..1
Kennedy...6..4
Kennerley...2..4
Kennerly...1..5
Kenney...0..2
Kenny...2..0
Kent...0..1
Keran...1..0
Kerr...15..14
Kershe...0..1
Kershner...3..2
Kersner...1..0
Kessecker...1..0
Kesterson...2..4
Keys...1..0
Keyser...0..2
Kiblinger...1..0
Kice...1..0
Kidd...1..0
Kiger...1..0
Kilkenny...3..2
Killian...1..0
Kilpatrick...1..1
Kincaid...1..2
Kinder...0..1
Kindig...3..3
Kindred...0..1
King...17..14
Kinkade...1..0
Kinkaid...3..1
Kinkead...7..3
Kinnear...1..0
Kinney...3..3
Kinny...0..1
Kinsolving...1..0
Kiplinger...3..2
Kiracofe...2..2
Kirby...1..0
Kirchkoff...1..0
Kirchoff...0..1
Kirk...4..4
Kirkland...2..2
Kirkpatrick...1..4
Kirtley...1..0
Kise...1..0
Kiser...2..1
Kisner...1..1
Kister...1..0
Kitch...0..1
Kite...1..0
Kline...1..0
Klingenpeel...2..0
Klingingpeal...1..0
Klingingpeel...1..0
Klutz...0..1
Knave...0..1
Knowles...1..6
Knowls...2..2
Kohler...1..0
Koiner...3..8
Koogler...1..1
Koontz...1..2
Kootz...0..1
Kraun...1..0
Krawn...0..1
Krickenbarger...1..1
Krizer...0..1
Kroll...1..0
Krone...0..1
Krown...1..0
Kuhns...1..0
Kule...1..0
Kunkel...1..0
Kurtz...2..2
Kyger...1..1
Kyle...5..0
LaRue...1..0
Lafland...1..0
Lahman...0..1
Lainey...1..0

Augusta County Marriages -- Surname Frequency

Lair...1..0
Laird...4..3
Lamay...1..0
Lamb...9..8
Lambard...1..0
Lambert...13..5
Lamey...1..0
Lamme...0..1
Lanack...0..1
Lancaster...0..1
Lance...0..1
Lanckton...0..1
Landes...9..10
Landess...1..0
Landis...2..6
Landiss...0..2
Lange...1..1
Langford...1..1
Lankford...1..0
Lansaw...1..0
Lantern...0..1
Lantin...1..0
Laporte...2..1
Larew...7..4
Larner...0..1
Larrick...0..1
Lashbaugh...0..1
Lauks...1..0
Lavel...1..1
Lavell...1..0
Lavender...1..0
Laverty...1..1
Law...2..1
Lawell...1..0
Lawrence...2..2
Lawson...0..1
Laymore...0..1
Layton...1..0
Laywell...1..2
Lea...1..0
Leaguet...1..0
Lear...1..0
Leas...0..2
Leckie...1..0
Leddick...1..0
Ledegay...0..1
Lee...3..0
Leedy...3..1
Leeper...1..0
Leeser...0..1
Leffley...1..0
Lefler...0..1
Lehman...0..1
Lemmon...0..1

Lemmy...0..1
Lemon...2..1
Leonard...7..6
Leopard...1..1
Lerew...2..0
Lesley...0..1
Lessley...2..8
Lessly...0..1
Letcher...1..0
Letshew...1..0
Levick...1..0
Levingston...0..2
Lewis...12..8
Licks...1..0
Life...2..0
Liggett...1..0
Lightner...4..2
Likes...1..1
Lilley...4..4
Linch...2..0
Linck...0..1
Lincoln...1..0
Lindel...0..1
Ling...1..0
Lingsweiler...1..0
Link...11..11
Linn...1..1
Linsey...1..0
Liptrap...3..0
Litten...2..3
Litteral...1..0
Littlepage...1..0
Lively...2..1
Livick...4..4
Livingston...0..2
Lobban...0..1
Lockbridge...1..1
Lockhart...3..1
Lockridge...7..12
Loeffler...0..1
Loetz...0..1
Loffties...0..1
Loftus...1..0
Logan...4..1
Lohr...2..4
Long...18..16
Lookelbough...0..1
Looney...1..0
Loop...0..2
Loots...1..0
Lootz...2..0
Lortz...1..0
Lott...1..0
Lotts...1..4

Augusta County Marriages -- Surname Frequency

Lottz...1..0
Lotz...1..1
Loucks...0..1
Loudermilk...3..0
Louks...1..0
Louney...0..1
Loushback...1..0
Love...1..1
Lovegrove...1..0
Lovel...1..1
Lovell...0..1
Lovingood...0..2
Lowdermilk...1..1
Lowe...1..0
Lowery...1..1
Lowman...4..7
Lowrets...1..0
Lowrey...0..1
Lowry...1..1
Lowtermilk...1..0
Loyd...1..1
Lucas...3..3
Luck...0..1
Luffler...1..0
Lukeden...0..1
Lunsford...0..1
Lushbough...0..1
Lusk...1..0
Lutz...3..6
Lyle...4..3
Lynch...4..0
Lynn...2..1
Lyon...2..0
Lyons...2..0
Mackaby...1..0
Madison...0..1
Mahan...1..0
Mahon...0..1
Mahoney...0..2
Mahony...1..0
Malcolm...1..2
Malcom...0..1
Mandele...0..1
Mansfield...1..0
Manuell...0..1
Mardis...1..0
Mares...1..0
Marks...0..1
Markwood...1..2
Marshall...8..2
Martin...15..9
Marton...1..0
Masincup...0..1
Mason...0..1

Masoncup...0..1
Massey...0..1
Massie...0..2
Masters...0..1
Mateer...0..1
Matheny...3..1
Mathews...10..7
Maupin...3..1
Maury...0..1
May...4..1
Mayes...0..1
Mayfield...1..2
Mayo...1..0
Mays...6..1
Maze...3..0
McAdams...1..0
McAfee...2..0
McAlary...2..1
McAlear...0..1
McAlery...1..0
McBride...2..0
McCLure...0..1
McCaaley...0..1
McCabe...0..1
McCadden...0..1
McCaferty...0..1
McCaleb...1..0
McCames...0..1
McCamey...1..1
McCampbell...1..1
McCan...1..0
McCann...1..1
McCannon...0..1
McCarty...2..0
McCaslin...0..1
McCauley...2..1
McCausland...2..1
McCawley...1..0
McChesney...5..10
McClanahan...2..0
McClaughlin...1..0
McCleland...3..1
McClelland...1..1
McClenachan...7..6
McClentock...1..0
McClintic...1..0
McClintick...2..1
McClune...1..0
McClung...18..2
McClure...10..9
McColley...1..0
McCollins...1..0
McColmick...0..1
McComb...2..1

Augusta County Marriages -- Surname Frequency

McCommis...0..1
McCorgar...1..0
McCorkell...0..1
McCorkle...2..1
McCormack...2..0
McCormick...4..3
McCoskey...1..1
McCown...1..0
McCoy...1..0
McCray...1..2
McCreery...5..0
McCrery...1..0
McCroskey...0..2
McCue...9..10
McCulloch...4..0
McCullock...3..2
McCullough...2..1
McCune...4..8
McCurdy...3..2
McCutchan...5..9
McCutchen...27..21
McCutcheon...2..1
McDade...1..0
McDaniel...1..1
McDead...0..1
McDonald...1..0
McDowell...6..4
McElroy...0..1
McElvanny...1..0
McElwee...1..0
McElwrath...1..0
McFadden...2..1
McFaddin...0..2
McFall...3..3
McFarland...0..2
McFarlane...1..0
McFeeters...1..0
McGaffock...1..0
McGarry...1..0
McGee...1..0
McGill...3..0
McGilvray...1..0
McGlaflin...0..1
McGlamery...1..0
McGlammery...0..1
McGlaughlin...1..0
McGraw...0..1
McGuffin...4..6
McIlree...1..0
McIlvain...1..0
McIntire...1..2
McIntosh...1..1
McKamy...0..1
McKee...4..1

McKemy...4..4
McKenny...2..1
McKensey...2..0
McKenzie...1..0
McKesson...1..0
McKinney...1..1
McKinny...1..0
McKitrick...0..1
McKnight...1..3
McKoskry...0..1
McLaughlin...2..0
McLeas...1..0
McLeer...1..0
McMahon...2..3
McMillen...1..0
McMinn...1..0
McMullan...1..0
McMullen...3..2
McMullin...0..1
McMullins...0..1
McMurtry...1..0
McNabb...1..0
McNair...3..4
McNeil...2..0
McNight...2..5
McNutt...1..5
McPheeters...4..7
McQuain...1..0
McQueen...0..1
McTear...0..1
McWhorter...1..0
McWilliams...1..4
Meade...1..0
Means...1..0
Meck...1..0
Meddings...1..0
Meek...1..3
Meeks...0..5
Mefford...1..0
Mell...0..3
Mellen...1..0
Melrose...1..0
Melton...1..0
Menker...1..2
Menzies...1..0
Merit...1..0
Meritt...1..0
Merrit...0..1
Merritt...2..5
Mesner...1..0
Messersmith...2..5
Messmaker...1..1
Meyers...1..0
Michael...15..19

Augusta County Marriages -- Surname Frequency

Michel...2..1
Michie...2..0
Middleton...1..0
Miely...1..0
Miller...57..51
Milliken...1..0
Mills...6..6
Milsap...1..0
Milton...0..1
Mims...0..1
Mines...7..2
Minga...0..1
Mingo...0..1
Minick...0..2
Minnick...2..3
Minnis...1..0
Miser...1..3
Mitchel...0..2
Mitchell...10..13
Mizener...0..1
Mizer...1..2
Moeler...1..0
Moffet...1..0
Moffett...14..20
Moffette...1..1
Mohler...2..3
Mohr...1..1
Moirs...1..0
Molds...1..0
Moneymaker...0..2
Monroe...0..1
Montgomerie...1..0
Montgomery...6..6
Mood...0..1
Moon...1..0
Mooney...3..0
Moony...1..0
Moor...1..0
Moore...24..14
Moorman...1..0
Moredock...1..0
Morel...1..0
Morgan...5..1
Morrell...1..0
Morris...9..1
Morrison...3..2
Morriss...0..1
Morrow...1..0
Morton...2..0
Mosby...1..1
Moses...2..2
Moss...1..0
Mount...1..0
Mowbray...0..1

Mowrer...0..1
Mowrey...0..1
Mowry...4..12
Moyer...0..2
Moyers...7..5
Muchmore...0..1
Muck...1..0
Mulholland...1..0
Mulinx...1..0
Mulnix...1..0
Mummer...1..0
Muncy...1..0
Murphy...3..0
Murray...3..4
Murry...3..4
Myers...11..9
Mynes...1..0
Myres...0..2
Nabours...1..0
Naher...2..0
Nair...0..1
Nales...1..0
Neal...2..1
Near...1..1
Nebergall...5..2
Neere...0..1
Neighborrgall...1..0
Neighbourgall...0..1
Neill...1..0
Neilson...1..0
Neizer...0..1
Nelson...4..3
Nesbet...1..0
Nesbit...1..0
Ness...1..0
Nest...1..0
Nevins...1..0
New...1..0
Newcomb...2..0
Newell...0..1
Newham...1..0
Newlan...1..0
Newlen...1..0
Newman...2..4
Newton...3..4
Nichol...3..2
Nicholas...0..2
Nichols...1..0
Nicholson...0..2
Nickel...0..1
Nickenson...1..0
Nickey...2..0
Nickle...1..2
Nickoles...0..1

Augusta County Marriages -- Surname Frequency

Nigle...0..1
Nimerick...0..1
Nimmo...1..0
Nixon...0..1
Noffinger...1..0
Noland...1..2
Nolin...1..0
Noll...1..0
Nonyer...1..0
North...1..0
Norton...0..1
Nutty...2..2
Nyman...0..1
O'Kane...1..0
Oakley...0..1
Ocheltree...4..3
Odell...1..0
Oder...1..0
Oehler...1..0
Offlider...1..0
Offlighter...1..0
Offord...0..1
Ohrbough...1..0
Oldham...1..0
Olinger...2..1
Oliver...1..1
Olves...0..1
Ong...2..1
Orbison...0..1
Orbough...2..0
Orebaugh...3..2
Orebough...2..4
Orner...1..0
Orr...0..1
Orrele...1..0
Osborne...1..0
Ott...2..4
Ougheltree...0..1
Overshiner...1..3
Owens...2..1
Owie...0..1
Padget...0..1
Page...2..0
Paine...4..2
Painter...4..4
Palmer...15..16
Pannel...0..1
Pannell...1..0
Panzle...1..0
Papper...0..1
Parent...2..2
Paris...0..2
Parks...1..2
Parmer...1..0

Parr...2..0
Parratt...0..1
Parrent...0..1
Parris...2..5
Parry...1..3
Parson...1..0
Parsons...1..2
Pary...0..1
Pateson...1..0
Patrick...1..5
Patterson...32..25
Patton...7..1
Pauf...1..0
Pauff...0..1
Paul...4..5
Pauley...1..1
Paulus...1..1
Pauss...1..0
Paxton...2..2
Payne...1..0
Peaco...4..3
Pearce...1..0
Pearey...1..0
Pearsen...0..1
Pearson...1..2
Peatt...1..1
Peck...5..12
Pecker...1..0
Pecot...1..0
Peebles...1..2
Peer...1..3
Peerie...1..0
Peery...0..2
Pelter...1..1
Pence...1..1
Pendell...1..0
Pendleton...1..0
Pennell...1..0
Penrose...0..1
Peples...0..1
Pepperley...1..1
Percy...0..2
Perkey...2..1
Perkins...2..1
Perry...6..2
Peters...7..8
Peterson...1..1
Petty...0..1
Peyatt...0..1
Peyton...2..1
Pfifer...1..0
Phagan...1..0
Phifer...1..0
Philips...0..8

Augusta County Marriages -- Surname Frequency

Phillips...1..4
Pickering...3..1
Pickle...1..0
Pickral...0..1
Pifer...2..0
Pillson...0..1
Pilson...3..1
Pine...0..1
Pinkerton...1..0
Piper...0..2
Pirkey...1..0
Pitman...2..2
Pitzer...1..0
Platt...1..0
Plecker...2..1
Plumb...1..0
Plunket...1..0
Plunkett...1..0
Poage...20..13
Pockrott...1..0
Poe...1..0
Poindexter...0..1
Pointer...1..0
Points...1..3
Pollard...1..0
Pollock...2..0
Pool...0..1
Porter...6..2
Porterfield...1..1
Posey...1..0
Potter...3..1
Potts...1..0
Poulas...0..1
Powell...0..3
Powers...4..9
Powlas...0..2
Prewer...1..0
Price...6..8
Printz...0..1
Prior...1..0
Probst...2..1
Props...1..0
Propst...2..2
Pryor...1..0
Ptomey...1..2
Ptomy...1..0
Puckett...1..0
Pue...0..1
Puff...1..0
Puffenbarger...1..1
Puffenberry...1..0
Puffinbarger...0..1
Pugh...1..2
Puls...1..0

Pumphrey...2..0
Pursell...1..0
Quick...4..1
Raab...1..0
Rabb...1..0
Rabern...0..1
Rader...4..2
Radner...0..1
Rady...1..0
Rafferty...1..0
Ragan...1..0
Ragen...1..0
Ragland...1..0
Raidner...1..0
Raines...0..1
Ralston...6..6
Ramsay...2..5
Ramsbottom...2..1
Ramsey...9..4
Ramsy...0..2
Randal...0..1
Randolph...1..3
Ranicks...1..0
Ranken...1..0
Rankin...16..15
Ransbarger...3..1
Ransberger...0..1
Ranson...1..0
Rapp...3..3
Rauch...0..1
Rauly...0..2
Rawley...1..1
Ray...3..1
Rayburn...1..1
Reaburn...3..0
Ready...1..0
Reah...0..1
Reburne...0..1
Red...1..0
Redder...1..0
Redifer...3..0
Rediford...1..0
Redman...1..1
Redmond...1..0
Redner...0..1
Rednour...1..0
Reece...1..0
Reed...12..13
Reese...1..1
Reeser...1..0
Reeves...1..3
Reglor...0..1
Regon...0..1
Reid...3..2

Augusta County Marriages -- Surname Frequency

Reidenour...1..0
Reif...0..1
Reiff...0..1
Reignheart...0..1
Reimensnyder...1..0
Reiser...0..1
Reitenour...1..0
Rennick...1..0
Repetoe...1..0
Resley...1..0
Resors...1..0
Reubush...3..0
Revercomb...3..1
Reyburn...0..1
Reynolds...1..2
Rezer...1..0
Rhea...1..0
Rhinehart...1..1
Rhoades...0..2
Rhodes...4..0
Rhyan...1..1
Rice...2..3
Richards...1..0
Richardson...1..0
Richeson...1..0
Richey...1..1
Rickett...1..0
Riddle...7..4
Rife...2..2
Rigby...0..1
Riley...0..1
Rimel...1..0
Rine...1..0
Rinehart...5..4
Riner...1..0
Ringuson...1..0
Rippetoe...1..0
Ript...1..0
Risk...11..4
Ritchey...1..0
Rittenhouse...1..1
Ritter...0..2
Roach...2..1
Roadcap...2..0
Roades...1..0
Roads...1..0
Roberts...5..5
Robertson...19..12
Robinson...6..2
Robison...1..0
Rodchers...1..0
Rode...0..1
Rodenheizer...1..0
Rodes...2..0
Rodgers...4..3
Rogers...1..3
Roland...2..1
Roler...1..0
Roles...0..1
Rolestone...1..0
Roller...3..1
Rolston...1..0
Roop...2..4
Roople...0..1
Root...1..3
Roots...1..0
Rosenbarger...1..1
Ross...6..5
Roudabush...1..0
Roudenbush...1..0
Rough...0..6
Row...3..1
Rowe...1..0
Rowh...1..1
Rowland...0..1
Rowler...0..2
Royer...1..0
Rozen...1..0
Rubush...1..0
Ruddle...2..0
Ruff...4..3
Ruhl...1..0
Ruket...1..0
Rule...1..0
Rumbough...1..0
Runkel...1..0
Runkle...4..9
Runnels...0..1
Runnolds...1..0
Rupe...0..1
Rupert...2..0
Ruple...2..3
Rush...3..4
Rusht...1..0
Rusk...1..0
Rusmisel...3..8
Rusmisle...2..0
Rusmissel...1..0
Russel...1..1
Russell...9..16
Russmassell...1..0
Rust...1..0
Rutherford...1..0
Rutledge...5..5
Rutlidge...0..1
Rutt...1..0
Ryan...2..2
Ryanhart...0..1

21

Augusta County Marriages -- Surname Frequency

Ryder...1..0
Safley...0..1
Salvage...1..1
Sampson...1..0
Samuels...2..0
Sanders...4..0
Sandy...4..1
Sansebough...1..0
Saufley...0..1
Saunders...0..1
Savage...2..1
Sawyers...2..4
Saxon...1..0
Sayers...1..0
Scantland...1..0
Schnebly...1..0
Scholl...1..0
Schooler...0..1
Schoue...0..1
Scott...16..17
Screle...0..1
Scribner...0..1
Scrogden...1..0
Scull...1..0
Scylor...0..1
Seal...1..0
Searaight...1..0
Searight...0..2
Sears...0..1
Seawright...3..4
Seftle...0..1
Seig...2..3
Seldomredg...0..1
Seldomridge...3..1
Sellers...0..2
Selling...1..0
Sensabaugh...0..1
Sensebaugh...1..1
Sensebough...1..1
Sensibaugh...0..2
Sevier...1..0
Sewall...0..1
Sewell...1..0
Seylor...1..0
Shackelford...1..1
Shafer...1..1
Shaffer...3..2
Shalley...1..0
Shally...1..0
Shaner...1..0
Shank...1..0
Shankland...2..0
Shanklin...3..0
Shannon...4..5

Sharp...4..5
Sharret...0..1
Shaver...8..13
Shaw...2..0
Sheaffer...0..1
Shearley...1..0
Shedden...0..1
Sheets...20..11
Sheetz...9..11
Sheffer...2..1
Sheigis...1..0
Shell...0..1
Shelley...1..1
Shelly...2..5
Shelman...0..1
Sheltman...1..0
Shelton...5..1
Shempe...0..1
Shepard...2..0
Shephard...1..0
Shepherd...3..1
Sherley...0..1
Sherly...1..0
Sherman...0..1
Sherrets...0..1
Sherror...1..0
Shettman...1..0
Shetz...1..0
Shewe...0..1
Shewy...2..0
Shibley...1..0
Shickel...1..0
Shields...14..11
Shiflet...0..1
Shiflett...3..2
Shindler...0..4
Ship...0..2
Shiplet...1..0
Shipman...1..1
Shipton...0..1
Shirer...1..0
Shirey...4..1
Shirfey...1..0
Shirley...1..2
Shoemaker...1..0
Shoemate...1..1
Shonk...0..1
Shore...0..3
Shoritz...0..1
Short...0..1
Shott...0..1
Shotts...0..1
Shotwell...0..1
Shoue...0..1

Augusta County Marriages -- Surname Frequency

Shoults...2..0
Shoultz...0..1
Shover...1..2
Showalter...4..1
Shown...1..1
Shreckhise...1..1
Shreve...1..0
Shriver...1..0
Shroader...0..1
Shropshire...0..2
Shuby...1..0
Shue...2..0
Shuey...4..7
Shull...3..1
Shultz...7..8
Shumate...0..1
Shura...0..1
Shutler...1..0
Shyrigh...0..2
Siddons...1..0
Sieg...0..1
Silings...1..0
Silknatre...0..1
Silknitter...1..0
Silling...7..6
Sillings...1..3
Silor...1..1
Silvers...1..0
Simbro...0..1
Simmerman...1..4
Simmon...0..1
Simmons...1..1
Simpson...0..1
Sims...5..0
Sink...1..0
Siron...0..1
Sisler...1..0
Sites...3..0
Sitlington...1..2
Sively...1..0
Skelton...1..2
Skillern...2..0
Skiner...1..0
Skyles...2..0
Slagel...0..1
Slagle...2..6
Slanker...0..1
Slaten...0..1
Slaughter...1..0
Slaven...3..0
Sligh...1..1
Sloane...0..1
Slone...1..0
Sluser...1..0
Slusher...2..4
Sly...1..0
Slye...0..1
Small...1..2
Smallshoffer...1..1
Smiley...7..2
Smiltzer...1..0
Smily...1..0
Smith...51..46
Snapp...2..0
Snedegar...1..0
Sneders...0..1
Snedicor...1..0
Sneed...1..0
Snell...1..0
Snideman...1..0
Snider...5..4
Snodgrass...1..0
Snyder...9..8
Solleday...1..0
Somer...1..0
Sorrells...0..1
Sorrels...2..3
Sours...2..1
Southard...1..1
Southwood...0..1
Sowers...1..4
Spangler...1..1
Spatts...1..0
Spear...1..1
Spearing...2..0
Spears...1..1
Speck...4..2
Speers...0..1
Spence...1..0
Spencer...2..3
Sperry...0..1
Spicer...1..0
Spindle...1..0
Spinkle...1..0
Spitler...8..7
Sponter...1..0
Spotts...1..4
Sprigs...0..1
Spring...1..1
Springer...0..1
Sprinkle...1..0
Sproul...3..4
Sprouse...1..1
Sprowl...2..1
StClair...1..3
StJohn...0..1
Staggs...1..0
Standforth...0..1

Augusta County Marriages -- Surname Frequency

Stanton...1..5
Staples...2..0
Stark...1..0
Starks...0..1
Start...2..0
Staubus...0..4
Stauffer...0..1
Staunly...0..1
Staunton...2..0
Steel...1..5
Steele...7..23
Steigle...0..1
Stephen...1..1
Stephens...2..0
Stephenson...2..1
Sterlinger...0..1
Sterret...1..3
Sterrett...0..4
Sterrit...0..2
Sterritt...2..0
Stevens...1..0
Stevenson...4..5
Steward...0..1
Stewart...1..0
Sticer...1..0
Stickleman...2..0
Stickley...1..2
Stiegle...0..1
Stiff...1..0
Stiles...0..1
Stockdale...0..2
Stodgall...1..0
Stofer...2..1
Stoffer...0..1
Stokes...1..0
Stombock...1..1
Stone...1..2
Stoner...1..0
Story...1..1
Stoudamire...0..1
Stoutamire...1..0
Stoutamoyer...2..3
Stover...10..11
Strain...2..4
Strane...1..0
Street...1..0
Stribling...2..3
Strickland...1..1
Strickler...4..3
Strine...0..1
Stroader...0..1
Strong...1..3
Stuart...14..17
Stull...1..1

Stulzer...1..0
Stunkard...1..0
Sturm...1..0
Suddarth...0..1
Sullivan...2..1
Summer...0..1
Summers...5..7
Supple...1..0
Surber...3..0
Surface...2..3
Swab...1..0
Swang...1..0
Swank...1..4
Swartsley...1..0
Swartz...0..1
Swartzel...1..0
Swartzley...1..1
Swats...1..0
Swatsley...1..0
Swatzel...1..1
Swatzley...1..0
Swearingen...0..1
Sweed...0..1
Sweetz...1..0
Swick...0..2
Swink...11..9
Swisher...10..8
Switzer...3..5
Swoope...2..2
Swope...1..0
Swords...0..1
Syford...1..2
Syfort...0..1
Syler...0..1
Sylor...0..1
Symmerman...1..0
Syple...1..5
Syrcle...0..1
Tacket...1..0
Tackett...0..1
Talbert...1..0
Taliaferor...1..0
Taliaferro...1..0
Talley...0..1
Tallman...2..0
Tally...3..2
Taner...1..0
Tankersley...3..0
Tankesley...0..1
Tanner...4..2
Tapp...1..1
Tarbert...0..1
Tascott...0..1
Tate...11..16

Augusta County Marriages -- Surname Frequency

Taylor...21..14
Teabo...1..1
Teaford...7..6
Teagle...1..0
Teany...0..1
Tebo...1..1
Teebo...2..1
Teeford...4..1
Tees...1..0
Teese...1..0
Teford...1..0
Teitrick...1..0
Telfair...1..1
Telford...1..0
Temereman...0..1
Templeton...1..0
Teney...0..1
Tennant...1..1
Tenton...0..1
Terrell...1..0
Terrill...2..5
Terry...1..0
Teter...1..2
Tetrick...0..1
Tevenbaugh...0..1
Tevenbough...1..0
Thacker...0..2
Tharp...1..2
Thomas...6..7
Thomason...0..1
Thompson...25..24
Thomson...0..1
Thornton...8..1
Thorp...2..0
Throp...1..0
Thurman...1..0
Tiefenbach...0..1
Tiffany...1..0
Tinkle...1..0
Tisdale...2..1
Todd...4..2
Toeme...1..0
Tole...1..0
Tolmink...0..1
Tomblinson...1..1
Tomlinson...1..0
Toms...0..1
Toole...1..0
Torbet...3..1
Torbett...2..0
Towberman...0..1
Towel...1..0
Towell...1..2
Towerman...0..1

Townsend...2..0
Trainer...1..1
Trainum...1..0
Travis...2..1
Trayer...2..1
Tremper...0..1
Trencher...1..0
Trent...1..0
Trible...0..1
Trimble...8..16
Trobaugh...1..0
Trobough...1..0
Trorabaugh...0..1
Trorebach...0..1
Trorobaugh...1..2
Trotter...10..1
Troughrobaugh...0..1
Trout...4..5
Troxal...0..1
Troxall...1..1
Troxel...1..4
Troxell...2..2
Trump...1..2
Tucker...1..0
Tuening...0..1
Tumbleston...0..1
Tumblin...0..2
Tummins...0..1
Turk...3..5
Turner...4..2
Turnins...0..1
Turnipseed...2..2
Tuttle...2..1
Tutwiler...1..1
Tweedy...1..0
Tyerie...1..0
Ulery...1..0
Ulrick...1..0
Underwood...0..1
Usher...1..3
Ustler...1..0
Utsler...1..0
Utz...1..0
Vachub...0..2
Valentine...0..1
Vance...2..2
Vancent...0..1
Vanfosen...1..0
Vanfossen...1..3
Vanlear...7..6
Vanosdal...1..0
Vanosdale...1..0
Vanpelt...1..0
Vansical...1..0

Augusta County Marriages -- Surname Frequency

Vanstaven...1..0
Vantrump...0..1
Varley...1..0
Varner...1..2
Varnum...0..1
Vauchob...0..1
Vaughn...1..0
Venable...1..0
Vernon...0..1
Vernum...1..2
Via...2..0
Vians...0..1
Vickers...1..0
Vigar...1..0
Vines...3..2
Waddell...3..2
Waddle...3..3
Waddy...0..2
Wade...6..3
Wadsworth...1..0
Wagey...1..0
Waggener...0..1
Waggoner...5..0
Waggy...0..1
Wagner...2..3
Wagoner...0..1
Waid...2..0
Waide...1..0
Wakely...0..1
Wakle...1..0
Walace...0..1
Walch...0..1
Walker...13..8
Walkup...0..1
Wall...1..0
Wallace...13..9
Walls...1..2
Walsh...1..0
Walters...1..1
Walton...2..3
Waltz...1..0
Wandless...1..0
Wanlis...1..0
Ward...3..2
Wardlaw...2..0
Ware...1..1
Warley...1..0
Warner...1..3
Warren...1..0
Warrenburgh...0..1
Warrick...0..1
Warris...1..0
Wartsook...1..0
Warwick...1..0

Waseman...0..2
Waserman...1..0
Washington...1..0
Wason...2..0
Waterman...1..0
Waters...0..1
Watkins...1..3
Watson...1..1
Watts...2..0
Way...0..1
Wayland...4..1
Wayt...3..1
Wead...1..0
Weade...0..1
Weast...0..2
Weathers...1..1
Weaver...9..17
Web...0..1
Webb...7..4
Weckle...0..1
Weed...0..1
Weeks...0..1
Weer...1..0
Wehn...1..0
Weickel...0..1
Weiford...0..3
Weigant...1..0
Weigle...1..2
Weikle...1..1
Weir...1..0
Weirly...1..0
Weitzel...0..3
Weitzell...3..0
Welch...5..2
Weles...1..0
Weller...0..2
Welsh...0..2
Wenger...0..2
Wenner...1..0
Weri...1..0
Werley...0..1
Wesit...0..1
West...2..1
Western...1..2
Weston...1..0
Wetzel...1..0
Wheelbarger...1..0
Wheeler...1..1
Wheeling...0..1
Wherley...1..0
Whetesel...0..1
Whisler...1..0
Whisman...4..2
Whist...1..0

Augusta County Marriages -- Surname Frequency

Whitaker...1..0
White...13..9
Whitemore...0..1
Whitesell...4..4
Whiteside...0..1
Whitesides...1..0
Whitlock...4..2
Whitmore...9..5
Whitsal...1..0
Whitsel...1..1
Whitsell...1..4
Whitzel...2..1
Wickle...2..0
Wicle...0..1
Wiekle...0..1
Wiferd...1..0
Wikel...1..0
Wilds...1..1
Wilen...0..1
Wiles...1..0
Wiley...3..1
Wilfong...0..1
Wilhelms...1..0
Wilkerson...1..0
Will...1..0
Willfong...1..0
Williams...13..8
Williamson...1..0
Willis...0..1
Wills...1..0
Willson...8..5
Wilson...43..26
Wily...1..0
Wimer...1..0
Wims...1..0
Windle...2..0
Windsor...1..0
Wine...3..4
Winefield...0..1
Winegar...1..0
Winegardner...0..1
Wineinger...0..1
Wines...1..0
Wingfield...0..3
Winters...0..1
Wise...5..2
Wisehart...0..1
Wiseman...9..7
Wishart...0..1
Witherow...1..0
Withrow...2..2
Witsal...1..0
Witsel...0..1
Witts...2..1

Woland...0..2
Wolf...3..1
Wolfe...0..1
Woltz...1..0
Wolwine...1..0
Wombledorf...1..0
Wonderlake...0..2
Wonderlick...3..2
Wood...10..5
Woodall...1..0
Wooddell...1..0
Woodell...1..0
Woodram...0..1
Woods...10..7
Woodson...0..1
Woodward...5..5
Woolard...2..0
Woolf...0..1
Woolwine...0..3
Worth...0..1
Woventuery...1..0
Wright...10..12
Wyan...1..0
Wyand...0..1
Wyatt...0..1
Wykle...1..0
Wyms...1..0
Xaupi...1..2
Yager...1..0
Yancey...1..0
Yancy...0..1
Yarberry...1..0
Yates...2..0
Yeagly...1..0
Yeaky...1..0
Yearour...1..0
Yearouse...0..1
Yearout...5..3
Yonas...0..1
Yorkshire...1..1
Yost...4..4
Youel...2..2
Youell...3..0
Young...28..28
Younger...0..1
Younkard...0..1
Yount...1..0
Youstler...0..1
Youtzler...1..0
Zahn...1..2
Zahns...0..1
Zee...0..1
Zeller...1..0
Zimbro...3..2

Augusta County Marriages -- Surname Frequency

Zimmerman...4..7
Zink...1..0
Zumbro...3..0
Zwitchel...0..1

Augusta County Marriages -- Man's Name

----- & ----- ----- 18 Feb 1794; Rev. Charles O'Neil marriage testimonial bond b- Sampson Mathews & William Forbes
Jacob & Margaret Perkey 17 Sep 1804; min- John McCue
Robert & Polly Youel 6 Nov 1800; min- William Wilson- 6Nov1800

Abernathy
John & Lavinia Logan 17 Apr 1823; min- James Morrison

Abney
John & ----- ----- 10 Jul 1769; license only
Shelton R & Martha Jane Davis 3 Dec 1835; min- William G Jackson
William & Elizabeth McClenachan 23 Dec 1794; d Alexander who consents test- John McDowell b- John McDowell min- John McCue- 23Dec1794

Acord
Andrew B & Jane Roberts 11 Jan 1843; min- James Bunting
Andrew J & Eveline Armstrong 28 Mar 1845; min- D F Bittle
Francis & Seelia Stuart 27 Jan 1823; min- Josiah Cole
Jacob & Ann Bowman 29 Mar 1821; min- William W Calhoun
Jacob & Sarah Brooks 25 Dec 1823; min- Josiah Cole
John & Elizabeth Baylor 20 Jun 1816; min- William Calhoon
John & Zaday McFarland 27 Jan 1823; min- Michael Meyerhoeffer

Adair
John & Elizabeth McKnight 10 Jan 1791; Minister's return spells name as 'Addair and McNight' d-in-law of William Burgess b- William Burgess min- Archibald Scott- 11Jun1791

Adkins
Daniel & Mary Livick 7 Jun 1849; min- Samuel Martin

Agnue
James & Margaret Givins 22 Apr 1788; min- William Wilson- 22Apr1788

Ailer
George & Mary Tanner 22 Apr 1791; d John (German) b- John Tanner
James & Sarah Stuart 2 Aug 1831; min- William Calhoon

Ailor
Anthony & Sophia Earhart 4 Apr 1797; min- William Wilson- 4Apr1797

Ailshire
John & Elizabeth Dunlap 2 Nov 1809; min- William King

Ailstrop
Jesse & Susannah Williams 14 Jan 1802; d John wit- John Williams b- Alexander StClair

Akerly
Paul & Sally Miller 27 Nov 1788; b- Stephen Miller (Paul signs as 'Paul Akerlein')

Alderman
James & Catherine Warner 8 Jun 1795; d Henry who consents test- John Boswell b- John Boswell

Augusta County Marriages -- Man's Name

Alexander
----- & ----- ----- 30 Nov 1772; license only
Andrew A & Susannah Hunter 11 Feb 1833; min- James C Wilson
Andrew & Nancy Hamilton 16 Sep 1788; d John who consents
  wit- William Stoner & Philip Brown b- Francis Alexander
  min- William Wilson- 16Sep1788
Cyrus & Sarah Jane McCue 5 Aug 1848; min- Robert L Dabney
David & Margret Wakely 21 Mar 1839; min- J Killian
Francis & Elizabeth McClure 28 Dec 1790; b- Josias McClure
  min- William Wilson- 29Dec1790
James (Jr) & Sarah Shirey 11 May 1843; min- B M Smith
James L & Susan Hughs 24 Nov 1842; min- A G Chenowith
James & ----- ----- 11 Sep 1759; license only
James & Emily Woodson 16 Feb 1843; min- B M Smith
John & Jennet Alexander 10 Mar 1790; b- Francis Alexander
  min- William Wilson- 11Mar1790
John & Dianah Alor 5 Feb 1835; min- Samuel Kennerly
John & Sarah Gibson 27 Nov 1789; min- Benjamin Erwin-
  27Nov1789
John & Rachel Miller 12 Feb 1791; widow b- George Harding
  min- John Montgomery- 13Feb1791
John & Anne Roberts 6 Nov 1823; min- William Wilson Jr
John & Nancy Stuart 19 Jan 1809; min- John McCue
Moses L & Nancy Hamilton 25 Jun 1835; min- Samuel Kennerly
Peter & Jinny Steele 24 Mar 1787; d Samuel who consents
  wit- Samuel Steele & Robert Steele b- Samuel Steele min-
  Archibald Scott- 27Mar1787
Robert & Jane Beard 28 Jan 1796; min- Archibald Scott-
  28Jan1796
Robert & Janetta Scott 14 Nov 1831; min- James C Wilson
William W & Jane B Henry 7 May 1833; min- James Morrison
William & Sarah Henry 19 Nov 1794; min- John Brown-
  19Nov1794
Alford
Robert & Melvina Rogers 26 Feb 1850; min- John Garber
Alfort
John & Caty Coughenour 4 Oct 1830; min- Abraham Garber-
  publication of banns
Alinger
Peter & Sarah Rusmisel 24 Mar 1842; min- D F Bittle
Alison
John & Elizabeth Bratten 9 Mar 1807; min- William King
William & Jane Caldbreath 9 Oct 1816; min- Wright Burgess
Allason
William & Jane Martin 29 Nov 1797; Minister's return
  spells name as 'Allison' widower & widow (of David) b-
  Andrew Alloson min- William Wilson- 30Nov1797
Allen
Francis & Margaret Irvine 7 Dec 1826; min- John Hendren
George P & Sarah Ann Miller 18 May 1847; min- J A Van Lear
George W & Lucy Ann Coyner 10 Sep 1835; min- William Scull
Hugh & ----- ----- 6 Nov 1765; license only
James & Frances Erwin 1 Apr 1793; sis to John Erwin who
  consents, and affirms Frances over 21 b- David McNair min-
  William Wilson- 2Apr1793

Augusta County Marriages -- Man's Name

Allen (cont.)
  James & Hannah Hanger 10 Nov 1808; min- William Wilson
  James & Elizabeth Tate 3 Sep 1793; d Robert & Margret Tate
    who consents test- Ibby McClung & Polly Tate b- Peter
    Hanger Jr min- John McCue- 5Sep1793
  James & Polly Young 21 Feb 1788; min- William Wilson-
    21Feb1788]
  John & Ann McCue 5 Jun 1821; min- John Hendren
  John & Eleanor Steele 29 Sep 1790; d Robert b- Robert
    Steele min- Archibald Scott- 16Oct1790
  John & Jane Sterret 16 Mar 1815; min- John D Ewin
  Joseph & Jane Walters 6 Feb 1845; min- T T Castleman
  Monticue & Evy M Shore 10 Oct 1795; Minister's return
    spells name as 'Montique' Evy (of age) b- Francis Huff
    min- John McCue- 13Oct1795
  Robert & ----- ----- 23 Apr 1762; license only
Allinger
  Henry & Sarah Grant 23 Aug 1834; min- Augustus Babb
Allison
  Andrew & Martha B Calbreath 19 Apr 1823; min- James C
    Willson
  Andrew & Elizabeth Hall 21 Mar 1786; Minister's return
    spells name as 'Holt' bond min- William Wilson- 26Mar1786
  James & Abigail Churchman 23 Mar 1812; min- Wright Burgess
  James & Mary Givens 4 Jun 1798; d John Givens, dec. b-
    James Givens min- William Wilson- 6Jun1798
  John G & Margaret Brown 20 May 1823; min- John Hendren
  John & Nancy Cummins 15 Apr 1799; d Charles b- Charles
    Cummins John of age
  John & Polly Frame 4 Sep 1806; min- John McCue
  Thomas L & Elizabeth Reed 3 Mar 1831; min- Conrad Speece
  William & Margaret Blackwood 14 Jun 1790; Margaret gives
    own consent, stating she has no friends in these parts b-
    John Steven
  William & Margaret Eakle 30 Oct 1828; min- Conrad Speece
  William & Jean Young 9 Feb 1788; d James who consents b-
    William Anderson min- Archibald Scott- 21Apr1788
Almarode
  John & Sarah Bosserman 6 Nov 1837; min- J C Hensell
Almerode
  Frederick & Jane Benson 22 Aug 1799; d William who
    consents and gives bond wit- Charles B Rhoades test as to
    Frederick- John Brown test as to Jane- Andrew Crawford b-
    John Lotz
Almonroade
  Philip G & Margaret S Zimmerman 22 Mar 1849; min- Alonzo P
    Ludden
Althaffer
  William M & Margaret C Stover 23 Sep 1847; min- G W Israel
Amen
  Henry & Elizabeth Crane 24 Feb 1795; min- William Wilson-
    24Feb1795

Augusta County Marriages -- Man's Name

Amend
  Henry & Eve Tanner - Sep 1813; min- John Brown
Amon
  Henry & Elizabeth Grove 21 Feb 1795; Minister's return spells name as 'Grone' b- Michael Grove
Ancell
  William & Maria Wingfield 30 Mar 1809; min- William King
Anderson
  Alexander & Esther Crosby 26 Feb 1811; min- William Calhoon
  Alexander & Esther Kirkland 26 Apr 1786; d James bond min- William Wilson- 27Apr1786
  Andrew & Martha Crawford 12 Mar 1788; b- John Miller min- William Wilson- 13Mar1788
  Andrew & Eliza McWilliams 10 Sep 1828; min- John Hendren
  Andrew & Catherine Smith 6 Feb 1812; min- William King
  Charles & Margaret Cave 5 Nov 1792; d Elizabeth, who consents wit- Thomas Story, Agnes Holmes & William Caul b- John Holmes min- John McCue- 8Nov1792
  Eugenio & Jane Philips 14 Feb 1830; min- John Hendren
  George A & Margaret S Sperry 5 Dec 1839; min- P E Stevenson
  George & Mary Bredin 11 Feb 1789; Minister's return spells name as 'Breedon' b- Edward Bredin min- William Wilson- 12Feb1789
  Henry & Aribella Conova 24 Jul 1828; min- Francis McFarland
  James & ----- ----- 2 Oct 1764; license only
  James & ----- ----- 10 Dec 1771; license only
  John & ----- ----- 4 Feb 1774; license only
  John & Eliza Jane Palmer 10 Apr 1845; min- B M Smith
  Richard & Rebecca Strickler 20 Oct 1836; min- James Morrison
  Robert & ----- ----- 4 Nov 1765; license only
  Robert & Christiana Lockridge 24 Mar 1808; min- Joseph Reid
  Robert & Margaret Young 11 Sep 1786; d William bond min- William Wilson- 13Sep1786
  W N & Mary Jane Kerr 9 May 1838; 'Dr.' W N Anderson min- John A Steele
  William & ----- ----- 21 May 1763; license only
  William & ----- ----- 5 Sep 1774; license only
  William & Elizabeth Helmick 8 Feb 1831; min- James Morrison
  William & Jenetta Murry 21 Apr 1836; min- John A Steele
  William & Susanna Vanfossen 1 Jul 1817; min- William King
Andrew
  Daniel & Ann Hashaw 1 Nov 1811; min- Wright Burgess
  David & Elizabeth Stone 25 Apr 1809; min- William King
  Jacob & Margaret Shaver 5 Jun 1839; min- John A Van Lear
  John & Catherine Beery 28 Nov 1800; Minister's return spells name as 'Catherine Rury' d Philip b- Philip Peery ('Biry?') min- William King- 2Dec1800
  John & Anne Rauly 25 Nov 1841; min- John Brower
  Joseph & Rebecca Arehart 9 May 1850; min- Henry Witzel
  Josiah & Catharine Landes 21 Dec 1832; min- G H Reimensnyder
  Samuel & Margaret Weigle 9 Apr 1800; d Philip b- Philip Weigle min- William Wilson- 14Apr1800

Augusta County Marriages -- Man's Name

Andrews
  David & Elizabeth Dull 12 May 1825; min- Josiah Cole
  George & Elizabeth Peery 27 Dec 1790; b- Joseph Lang
Any
  Christopher & ----- ----- 20 Mar 1764; license only
Apley
  John & Elizabeth Derrough - Sep 1817; min- John Brown
Apple
  George M & Margaret Fix 23 Dec 1847; min- J C Hensell
  Michael & Barbara Beard 16 Feb 1824; min- Francis McFarland
  Michael & Elisabeth Roberts 21 Jun 1786; min- Archibald Scott- 21Jun1786
  Paul & Isabella Knowles 27 Apr 1803; min- William King
Arbast
  John & Margaret Miller 6 Jan 1844; min- D F Bittle
Arbogast
  David & Elizabeth Fleisher 4 Jul 1785; d Peter Flaisher bond
Arbuckle
  Alexander W & Julia H Bell 2 Dec 1833; min- Conrad Speece
  James & ----- ----- 11 Jan 1762; license only
  James & Catherine Alexander 1 Jan 1798; d Andrew Alexander, dec. con- Martha Alexander, mother test- Andrew Hunter & Samuel Hunter Jr b- Samuel Hunter Sr James from Greenbrier cty min- John McCue- 2Jan1798
  Mathew & Jane C Bell 18 Nov 1834; min- Conrad Speece
Archdeacon
  Michael & Ann Blair 1 Oct 1807; min- William McPheeters
Arehart
  David C & Barbara C Bosserman 3 Sep 1846; min- J C Hensell
  George L & Frances Spitler 5 Oct 1848; min- J McKendree Reiley
Argenbright
  Asher & Sarah Rusmisel 29 Mar 1839; min- John A Van Lear
  Augustus & Jane Dunlap 16 Sep 1833; min- Augustus Babb
  David & Mary Hull 6 Apr 1848; min- J C Hensell
  Felly & Betsy Hycarser 2 Dec 1802; min- William King- 2Dec1802
  George L & Mary L Bishop 16 Jun 1842; min- D F Bittle
  Jacob (Jr) & Christena Mowry 26 Mar 1798; d Lewis Maurer b- Lewis Mowry
  Jacob & Sidney Jackson 10 Sep 1829; min- Francis McFarland
  Jacob & Sophia Miser 10 Aug 1846; min- P Shickel
  Jacob & Susannah Russell 25 Aug 1803; min- William King
  John & Tina Burket 28 Jun 1827; min- Joseph Smith
Arginbright
  David & Sarah Simmerman 29 Nov 1844; min- William Calhoon
Arion
  John & Mary Garber 15 Dec 1831; min- Abraham Garber- publication of banns
Arisman
  Benjamin & Polly Hipard 1 Apr 1833; min- James C Wilson
  John & Martha Balard - Sep 1835; min- Joshua Webb

Augusta County Marriages -- Man's Name

Armantrout
  James & Polly Shuey 1 Sep 1835; min- William Calhoon
Armentrout
  Peter & Catherine (Leonard) 8 May 1804; min- William King
Armstrong
  Archibald & Elizabeth McCutchen 23 Nov 1824; min- William W Calhoun
  Bennami & Matilda J Armstrong 4 Jan 1849; min- John Bowen
  James & Barbara Brubeck 17 Nov 1831; min- Francis McFarland
  James & Margaret Hogshead 7 Apr 1808; min- William Calhoon
  John C & Susan Crosby 21 Jul 1836; min- Stephen Smith
  John C & Mary A Ramsbottom 17 Feb 1842; min- Jacob Bachtel
  John & Polly Crawford 4 Dec 1790; d William b- James Tallman min- Archibald Scott- 10Dec1790
  John & Hetty Hipes 21 Oct 1823; min- James Morrison
  John & Margaret W McChesney 18 Jan 1844; min- J C Hensell
  John & Nancy Standforth 10 Oct 1821; min- Daniel Stephens
  John & Mary Trout 3 Feb 1820; min- William Calhoon
  John & Martha Wade 29 Aug 1822; min- John Brown
  Mahlon & Jane Weaver 29 Jan 1829; min- John Hendren
  Nehemiah & Acheas English 2 Jun 1815; min- William King
  Richard & Catherine Hansell 7 Sep 1815; min- William King
  Robert & Jane Friel 15 Apr 1794; d Daniel, who gives bond
  Thomas & Isabella Armstrong 22 Jul 1786; d Archibald bond min- Samuel Carrick- 25Jul1786
  Thomas & Jane Burgess 27 Nov 1815; min- Wright Burgess
  William (Jr) & Catherine Friel 23 Feb 1793; 'Catherine Price?' d Daniel who consents test- James Ross & John Friel b- William Armstrong Sr no minister listed; clerk's memorandum cites ceremony date as 26Feb1793
  William J & Mary P McCutcheon 8 Jan 1823; min- William W Calhoun
  William & Elizabeth Bowman 15 Jun 1822; min- John Hendren
  William & Elizabeth Erwin 1 Apr 1788; d Jarred who consents wit- John Armstrong & Andrew Jordan b- John Armstrong min- Archibald Scott- 1Apr1788
  William & Catharine Fellers 26 Dec 1833; min- Samuel Kennerly
  William & Margaret Kirkpatrick 20 Apr 1809; min- William Calhoun
Arnall
  John T & Elizabeth Steele 10 Oct 1836; min- James C Wilson
Arnold
  Emmanuel & Magdaline Garber 19 Oct 1819; min- Abraham Garber- publication of banns
Asten
  John (Jr) & Sally Moffette 3 Jun 1806; min- William McPheeters
Aston
  James & Jane Hatten 15 Dec 1825; Bond gives name as 'Staton' min- Francis McFarland
Aughe
  Abraham & Jane Imboden 20 Mar 1806; min- John McCue

Augusta County Marriages -- Man's Name

Aukes
  Jacob & Elizabeth Culpt 21 Nov 1805; min- William King
Austin
  Alexander M & Mary L Hunter 4 Mar 1829; min- William Wilson
  James A & Caroline M Murray 22 Feb 1846; min- William Calhoon
  Morris & Lettitia W McClenachan 5 Oct 1797; d Alexander McClenachan, dec con- William Chambers, gdn b- Chesley Kinney min- Archibald Scott- 7Oct1797
Aylor
  John & Polly Michael 17 Jun 1825; min- G H Reimensnyder
Back
  James & Isabella Fairburn 25 Sep 1834; min- John A Steele
Backenstoe
  Frederick & Elizabeth Malcom 13 Feb 1812; min- William King
  John & Polly Fleiger 22 Dec 1790; d John b- John Fleiger min- William Wilson- 23Dec1790
Badger
  Alexander & Margaret Bird 16 Jul 1787; b- Alexander Thompson & William Shields min- Archibald Scott- 17Jul1787
Bailey
  Fleming & Catherine Argenbright 4 Dec 1834; min- Augustus Babb
  George & Elizabeth Karracofe 5 Oct 1848; min- John A Van Lear
  John & Elizabeth Smith 27 Dec 1848; min- B M Smith
  Lewis & Catharine Root 4 Jun 1835; min- Samuel Kennerly
  Lewis & Margaret Shropshire 22 Nov 1822; min- Josiah Cole
  Robert & Elizabeth Bosang 8 Mar 1792; b- William Scott no minister listed; clerk's memorandum cites ceremony date as 8Mar1792
  Samuel & Polly Jewell 9 Mar 1799; 'Mary' d Joseph who consents & Susanna Jewell who consents test- Catherine Lynch both of age b- Ambrose Lee Tinsley & James Lowe min- William King- 9Mar1799
Bailor
  Jacob & Rebecca Rinehart 19 Apr 1822; min- Daniel Stephens
  Martin & Barbara Miser 1 Nov 1796; d Adam b- Adam Miser
Bain
  George W & Jane Gibson 13 Jul 1833; min- George Hildt
Baird
  Peter & Elizabeth Mason 23 May 1816; min- Wright Burgess
  William & Martha Patterson 4 Jan 1786; d James bond min- William Wilson- 5Jan1786
Baker
  George & Eve Long 7 Feb 1797; widower d Henry Long, dec. Alexander Zallinger swears Eve of age, but has not resided in county for six months b- Nicholas Echus
  Isaiah & Lucinda Virginia Burgess 18 Jul 1848; min- J McKendree Reiley
  James & Mary Hill 28 Sep 1785; min- Archibald Scott- 28Sep1785
  William F & Martha Guin 22 Oct 1846; min- Jacob Montgomery

Augusta County Marriages -- Man's Name

Baldwin
  John B & Susan M Peyton 20 Sep 1842; min- F D Goodwin
  Peter & Eve Kellar 12 Sep 1826; min- William Monroe
  Robert S & Lettitia J Speck 4 Aug 1846; min- T T Castleman
Ball
  Amos R & Frances E Gordon 24 Dec 1846; min- James H Brown
Ballard
  John & Elizabeth Smith 10 Nov 1794; 'Eliza'? Own consent
    test- Thomas Wilson J McCue affirms she lived with his
    family for many years and is over 21 test- Jacob Kemp min-
    John McCue- 11Nov1794
  John & Polly Woods 21 Sep 1809; min- William King
  Zephaniah H & Lucy Chaplain 27 Dec 1832; min- Samuel
    Kennerly
Ballew
  Thomas & Dianna Greiner 27 Oct 1842; min- A G Chenowith
Balman
  James & Jane Marks - Nov 1812; min- John Brown
Balmer
  John & Nancy Lange 22 Jan 1838; min- Robert Beers
Balsley
  Jesse & Hannah Pugh 5 Jan 1832; min- John Howell-
    publication of banns
  John & Margaret King 29 May 1818; min- William King
Barclay
  Alexander T & Betty S Moffett 21 Nov 1826; min- Francis
    McFarland
Bare
  David & Sally Ray 10 May 1810; min- John McCue
  Henry & Catherine Bare 19 Apr 1810; min- William Calhoon
  Henry & Jane Kennerley 28 Sep 1820; min- Robert Boyd
  James & Susan Calvert - --- 182-; min- William C. Morrison
  John M & Rachel Crawford 3 Aug 1829; min- William Calhoon
  John & Rebecca Scott 6 Oct 1825; min- Francis McFarland
  Samuel V & Demima Philips 6 Apr 1845; min- B M Smith
  Valentine & Harriet Carrol 1 Oct 1840; min- Samuel Wagner
Barger
  George W & Susan Ann Criser 5 Oct 1847; min- G W Israel
  Jacob & Nancy Cullen 30 Jan 1812; min- John McCue
  Jacob & Susan Ann Glutz 29 Aug 1836; min- Ambrose Henkle
  James P & Martha S Gardner 20 Aug 1846; min- J A Van Lear
  John C & Rachel Engleman 15 Dec 1842; min- J C Hensell
Barker
  Edward & Nancy Dunn 6 Feb 1786; widow bond
Barkley
  John & Catharine Clinebill 3 Sep 1829; min- Francis
    McFarland
Barnet
  James & Ann Dawson 10 Jun 1817; min- Wright Burgess
  Michael & Diana ----- 30 Dec 1786; bond lists Diana as
    'having no relation'
Barnett
  John & Mary C Phillips 6 Jul 1826; min- Daniel Stephens
  Michael & Diana Campbell 4 Jan 1787; min- William Wilson-
    4Jan1787

Augusta County Marriages -- Man's Name

Barnett (cont.)
  William & Caroline Smith 24 Nov 1836; free persons of color min- Isaac Jones
Barnhart
  George & Polly Barnet 27 Jan 1807; min- John McCue
  Gideon & Martha Ann Weade 13 Mar 1845; min- S Wagner
Barry
  Andrew & Polly McCue 18 Aug 1807; min- William Calhoon
Bartley
  Christopher & Catherine Earhart 20 Apr 1805; min- Samuel Monett
Baskin
  Thomas S & Rachel J Bush 12 Nov 1840; min- Benjamin M Smith
  Thomas & Jane Johnston 10 Apr 1815; min- William King
  William W & Margaret Ann Wilson 14 May 1832; min- James C Wilson
Baskins
  Charles A & Elizabeth G Vanlear 6 Mar 1827; min- Conrad Speece
  Charles & ----- ----- 2 Oct 1765; license only
  James H & Lucy M Clarke 24 Apr 1838; min- John A Steele
  James & ----- ----- 28 Sep 1765; license only
  John & ----- ----- 11 Jun 1765; license only
  William & Sarah Vanlear 16 Jan 1829; min- Conrad Speece
Batcheller
  Josiah & Mary Ann Johnson 15 Nov 1821; min- Daniel Stephens
Bateman
  John & Charlotte Allen 19 Aug 1819; min- Wright Burgess
  William & Elizabeth Allen 2 Jun 1813; min- William Wilson
Bates
  William & ----- ----- 15 Jan 1765; license only
Batis
  Charles & Sally Nutty 28 Jan 1819; min- William King
  John H & Julia Ann Croft 26 Oct 1846; min- J A Van Lear
Battow
  Isaac & Lucinda Jane Langford 16 Dec 1845; min- G W Israel
Baumgartner
  Henry & Elizabeth Harzog - Sep 1804; min- John Brown
Bawcutt
  William & Sally Dixon 29 Apr 1803; min- William King
Baxter
  William & Margaret Toms 24 Aug 1788; b- John Dickinson
Baylor
  David & Eliza Hoover 22 Oct 1834; min- George Hildt
  David & Jenetta Powers 24 Apr 1828; min- William Calhoon
  David & Lydia Shuey 10 May 1831; min- Francis McFarland
  George W & Louisa Beard 2 Nov 1837; min- D F Bittle
  George & Lidey Funkhouser 12 Aug 1824; min- William W Calhoun
  Jacob & Eveline E Hanger 2 Oct 1826; min- Michael Meyerhoeffer
  Jacob & Ann Keller 28 Mar 1789; b- George Keller
  John & Susan Daggy 24 Mar 1817; 'Aylor?' min- John McCue
  Samuel & Nancy Falls 10 Apr 1828; min- William Calhoun

Augusta County Marriages -- Man's Name

Bazzle
   John   &   Hannah Paul   5 May 1829;   min- William Wilson
Beal
   John   &   Elizabeth Botram   27 Oct 1811;   min- G H Riemenschneider
Beam
   John   &   Sarah Stover   25 May 1826;   min- John Hendren
Bean
   Mordecai   &   Jane Curry   17 Oct 1795;   Jane nicknamed 'Jenny' d William who consents   test- Benjamin Curry & Alexander Curry   b- Benjamin Curry   no minister listed; clerk's memorandum cites ceremony date as 20Oct1795
Bear
   Andrew   &   Evalina Gibbons   23 Jan 1834;   min- Francis McFarland
   Christian   &   Margaret Trimble   15 Sep 1842;   min- S J Love
   David S   &   Sarah F Taylor   2 Dec 1847;   min- John Bowen
   Harvey   &   Nancy Bell   2 Dec 1841;   min- S J Love
   John   &   Drucilla Jane Beard   13 Oct 1836;   min- J C Hensell
   John   &   Elizabeth Miller   27 Feb 1844;   min- D F Bittle
   Michael   &   Susannah Sieg   4 Feb 1808;   min- William Calhoon
   Paul   &   Mary Kinkaid   30 Jan 1832;   min- William Wilson
Beard
   Daniel   &   Feliska Greiner   12 Jan 1832;   min- John Howell- publication of banns
   Daniel   &   Eliza Jane Taylor   14 Nov 1839;   min- Jacob Bachtel
   David   &   Martha Hunter   17 Jun 1795;   d John   b- John Hunter
   Edward   &   ----- -----   15 Apr 1751;   license only
   Jacob   &   Molly Kootz   9 Apr 1811;   min- William King
   James P   &   Polly Crouch   13 Apr 1820;   min- Robert Boyd
   James   &   Elizabeth G Evans   7 Mar 1833;   min- Francis McFarland
   John   &   ----- -----   16 Jan 1769;   license only
   John   &   Catherine Acord   2 Oct 1817;   min- William King
   John   &   Mary East   11 Sep 1828;   min- James Morrison
   John   &   Barbara Lovingood   14 Nov 1787;   Minister's return spells name as 'Baird'   d Hermon   b- Hermon Lovingood   min- James Chambers- 14Nov1787
   John   &   Harriet W Peaco   9 Nov 1831;   min- John Howell
   Joseph   &   Sidney Sprowl   21 Jan 1799;   Sidney (of age) d William who consents   test- James Clarke   b- William Sprowl Jr
   Noah   &   Mary Stover   15 Jan 1844;   min- C Parkison
   Paul   &   Elizabeth Mandele   - Apr 1809;   min- John Brown
   Peter   &   Catharine Link   1 Sep 1808;   min- William Wilson
   Robert   &   Martha Beard   10 Feb 1801;   d Thomas   b- Thomas Beard
   Robert   &   Sarah Hatfield   16 Aug 1790;   d Hanah, who consents   b- William Richardson   wit- John Hatfield & John Gregg   min- William Wilson- 17Aug1790
   Robert   &   Sarah Mitchell   30 May 1785;   d James   bond
   Samuel   &   Elizabeth Acord   17 Aug 1822;   min- John Hendren
   Thomas   &   Sarah Jameson   16 Apr 1785;   d George   bond
   William   &   Catherine Robertson   1 Jan 1793;   min- William Wilson- 1Jan1793

Augusta County Marriages -- Man's Name

Beard (cont.)
 William & Jane Ewing 8 Mar 1821; min- James Morrison
 William & Margaret Gibson - Apr 1827; min- Joseph Smith
 William & Margaret McNutt 10 Jun 1793; d James who
  consents test- William Sproul & James McNutt Jr b- William
  Sproul min- John Brown- 15Jun1793
 William & Mary McC. Mills 9 Dec 1841; min- Samuel Wagner
 William & Elizabeth Withrow 13 Aug 1837; min- James
  Morrison
Beaten
 Robert & Hannah Rush 1 Aug 1811; min- Wright Burgess
Beaty
 Joseph R & Mildred Herndon 1 Jan 1843; min- D F Bittle
 Joseph & Mary Cason 7 Apr 1824; min- Josiah Cole
Beck
 Andrew & Julia McAlary 24 Oct 1831; min- James Kerr
 Daniel & Elizabeth Summers 9 Dec 1799; d John b- John
  Summers
 David & Nancy Henderson 14 Nov 1833; min- James Kerr
 Jacob & Sarah Summers 22 Dec 1834; min- Augustus Babb
 John & Kitty Fennel 23 Nov 1826; min- Alexander Templeton
 Joseph & Hannah Thomas 28 Dec 1785; bond lists 'next
  friend'(?) as Gilbert Christian min- Archibald Scott-
  30Dec1785
Beeton
 John & Catherine Blakemore 26 Jun 1816; min- William
  Cravens
Behler
 George & Catherine Argenbright 8 May 1797; 'Bailor?' d
  Augustine s Jacob and of age b- Augustine Argenbright
Beith
 William & Sophia Kirk 25 Jun 1807; min- William King
Bekane
 John & Jane Craig 27 Dec 1827; min- William Wilson
Bell
 Abel G & Louisa Virginia Xaupi 24 Nov 1846; min- J A Van
  Lear
 Alexander & Eliza Ann Hogshead 21 Nov 1831; min- John
  Hendren
 David S & Nancy McCue 25 Aug 1842; min- B M Smith
 David & Jane Appleby 27 May 1801; d Robert Appleby, dec.,
  late of Frederick cty con- Margaret Appleby, mother, from
  Frederick test-Samuel Calvert & William Bawcutt b- James
  Edmonston
 David & Mary Christian 18 Feb 1796; d Patrick Christian
  who consents test- James Christian b- Alexander Robertson
  min- William Wilson- 19Feb1796
 David & Nancy Holmes 2 Mar 1809; min- John McCue
 David & Mary Anna Nelson 18 Jun 1800; Minister's return
  spells name as 'Joseph Bell Jr' 'Polly' d Alexander b-
  Alexander Nelson min- William Wilson- 22Jun1800
 David & Rebeccah Patrick 20 Aug 1800; d John who consents
  test- William Patrick & James Gwinn b- William Patrick
 Francis & Sally Bell 21 Apr 1795; d James, dec. b- Samuel
  Bell min- John Montgomery- 22Apr1795

Augusta County Marriages -- Man's Name

Bell (cont.)
Francis & Polly Erwin 25 Jan 1802; d John wit- Charles Penn b- John Erwin min- Benjamin Irwin- 26Jan1802
Harvey & Nancy Beaty 11 Sep 1828; min- James Morrison
Jacob & Virginia McWilliams 10 Apr 1839; min- D F Bittle
James R & Mary Jane Brownlee 7 Apr 1842; min- Francis McFarland
James R & Susan C Smith 22 Nov 1827; min- Francis McFarland
James & ----- ----- 25 Aug 1759; license only
James & Sally Allen 27 Apr 1796; 'Sarah' d James who consents test- James Allen & David Hannah b- Jacob Kinney min- William Wilson- 27Apr1796
James & Sarah Coyner 11 Aug 1831; min- John Hendren
James & Margaret Craig 1 Sep 1807; min- William Wilson
James & Rebeccah Crawford 19 Feb 1818; min- William Calhoon
James & Margaret Curry 14 Sep 1785; d Robert bond min- Benjamin Erwin- 15Sep1785
John H & Elizabeth B Cave 24 Jun 1822; min- John Hendren
John & Elizabeth Brown 19 Jan 1797; Elizabeth (of age) d James Brown, dec con- Jane Brown b- John Brown min- Archibald Scott- 20Jul1797
John & Frances Clemmons 22 Apr 1833; min- Wright Burgess
John & Rachel Foster 2 Apr 1791; orphan of Andrew Campbell b- by next friends, Thomas Carruthers & Andrew Campbell marriage sent to clerk by Samuel Brown and dated 5Apr1791
John & Esther Gamble 23 Jul 1800; widower d James Gamble, dec. b- John Gamble min- William Wilson- 24Jul1800
John & Rebecca Graham 3 Jan 1787; d Elizabeth who consents wit- William Yoall & Robert McDowell b- William Yoall (date of bond uncertain - 1786? 1787?) min- Samuel Carrick- 9Jan1787
John & Elizabeth Griffeth 1 Dec 1812; min- William King
John & Sophia Irvine 19 Apr 1827; min- John Hendren
John & Sarah McCutchen 25 Aug 1800; d Samuel Joseph Bell, s of Samuel, swears that his brother, John, is over 21 b- Samuel McCutchen
John & Mary Young 25 Dec 1787; Minister's return spells name as 'Margaret Young' widow b- James McGonagal min- William Wilson- 27Dec1787
Joseph H & Elizabeth Taylor 22 Aug 1844; min- G W Israel
Joseph Wayt & Ann Archer Robertson 25 Sep 1845; min- B M Smith
Joseph & Jane Downey 26 Mar 1798; Jane (of age) d Philip Downey, dec. b- John Donnelly min- William Wilson- 27Mar1798
Robert & Mary Lessley 7 Aug 1793; Certificate of A. Humphreys, A J.P., that Mary over 21 consent by Samuel McCune Sr, John McCune 7 James McCune b- Archibald McCune min- John McCue- 8Aug1793
Robert & Fanny Smith 4 Jan 1798; Fanny (of age) d John Smith, dec. Joseph Smith swears to Fanny's age b- Andrew Mines
Samuel N & Sally Bowman 26 Dec 1822; min- James Morrison
Samuel & Janet Allison 31 Dec 1805; min- William Calhoon

Augusta County Marriages -- Man's Name

Bell (cont.)
  Samuel & Nancy Bell 20 Jun 1786; Agness? d Nancy bond
    min- Benjamin Erwin- 22Jun1786
  Samuel & Margaret Black 23 Sep 1816; min- John D Ewin
  Samuel & Sarah Cunningham 28 Aug 1804; min- Benjamin Irwin
  Samuel & Margaret Grove 17 Nov 1791; d David, who consents
    wit- John Black & John Hay b- Samuel Miller
  Samuel & Rosanna Smith 3 Jan 1787; b- David Byers min-
    William Wilson- 4Jan1787
  Thomas & Mary Woland 18 Apr 1798; d Jacob b- Adam Bickle
  W J L & Lucy A F Ship 27 May 1834; min- John A Vanlear
  William & ----- ----- 15 Jan 1765; license only
  William & Margaret Allen 27 Feb 1790; min- William Wilson-
    27Feb1790 (See also 'Peggy Allen' under woman's entries
    where Rev. Archibald Scott has sent a return of the same
    date?)
  William & Peggy Allen 17 Feb 1790; 'Margaret' d James, who
    consents b- James Allen wit- David Hanna & James Allen Jr
    min- Archibald Scott- 27Feb1790
  William & Mary Crawford 1 Mar 1796; Mary (of age) d James
    Crawford, dec. b- Alexander StClair Approbation of Jane
    Crawford min- William Wilson- 3Mar1796
  William & Rachel Crawford 17 Sep 1799; widower & widow (of
    Charles) b- Alexander Crawford
  William & Hannah McCutchen 12 Oct 1837; min- Enoch Thomas
Bengas
  George & Elizabeth Towberman 31 Dec 1816; 'Banjay?' min-
    William King
Benner
  Henry & Betsy Frame 8 Oct 1798; d John Fream who consents
    test- William Shields & William Fream b- Archibald Frame
Bennett
  Jesse & Elizabeth Hog 6 Apr 1793; Minister's return spells
    name as 'Betsy Hogg of Rockbridge' Dr. Jesse Bennett
    Elizabeth gives her own consent test- B Kennerly b- James
    Hogg min- William Wilson- 8Apr1793
  Robert J & Sarah W Terrill 12 Nov 1845; min- B M Smith
Benson
  William & Margaret Hunter 6 Aug 1795; Margaret (of age) d
    William b- James Rollins min- Archibald Scott- 11Aug1795
Berkeley
  Absalom & Lavinia H Berkeley 4 Dec 1849; min- T T Castleman
Berlin
  Frederick & Maria F Holt 1 Sep 1844; min- G W Israel
Berry
  Charles & Elizabeth Craig 28 Jul 1819; min- John D Ewin
  George & Polly Connelly 18 Sep 1792; d Thomas, who
    consents wit- Alexander & John Connelly, James Crawford b-
    Thomas Connelly min- James Johnston- 24Sep1792
  Henry & Susan Caroline Shepherd 4 Mar 1845; min- P Shickel
  James & Margaret J Armstrong 25 Nov 1828; min- James
    Morrison
  James & Rebecca K Buchanan 22 Dec 1836; min- James Morrison
  James & Jennie Doak 6 Jan 1787; d David & Jannet who
    consent wit- Robert Doak & John Doak b- John Berry min-
    Archibald Scott- 10Jan1787

Augusta County Marriages -- Man's Name

Berry (cont.)
  John R & Nancy Buchanan 21 Oct 1829; min- James Morrison
  John & Charlotte Berry 23 Oct 1823; min- James Morrison
  John & Isabella Best 15 Apr 1794; affidavit of John Berry that Isabella is over 21 b- James Best min- John McCue- 17Apr1794
  John & Elizabeth Crone 19 Jan 1832; min- William Wilson
  John & Jennat Given 25 Nov 1790; Minister's return spells name as 'Jannet Givens' d William, who consents b- Samuel McClintick wit- J Beal & Robert Given min- John Montgomery- 9Dec1790
  John & Eleanor Jamison 17 Oct 1797; Minister's return spells name as 'Jameson' Eleanor (of age) d John b- Matthew Jamison min- Archibald Scott- 19Oct1797
  Joseph & Frances Garber 15 Nov 1831; min- Abraham Garber- publication of banns
  William & Martha Brown 2 Mar 1845; min- S Wagner

Berryhill
  Alexander & Rachel Thompson 31 Mar 1786; d William bond min- Archibald Scott- 5Apr1786

Bertrum
  Julius & Eave Lanckton 9 Jul 1792; b- Christopher Mantel

Besse
  Jonathan & Elizabeth A Grove 26 Apr 1848; min- W T Richardson

Best
  John & Sally Larew 19 Feb 1807; min- John McCue

Betty
  Andrew & Agness Sitlington 15 Dec 1786; d John bond

Bibb
  Robert F & Margaret Knowles 21 Aug 1841; min- J A Van Lear- publication of banns

Bibe
  Thomas & Elizabeth Harris 6 Mar 1817; min- William King

Bible
  William & Jane C Ritter 15 Sep 1831; min- Benjamin Denton

Bickerstoff
  Edward & Mary Porter 4 Dec 1791; b- William Shields wit- Matthew Gambill no minister listed; clerk's memorandum cites ceremony date as 9Dec1791

Bickle
  Robert G & Mary Jane Rush 26 Oct 1842; min- James Paine

Bigger
  Arthur & Betsey Apple 3 Aug 1826; min- Conrad Speece

Billhymer
  Abraham & Catharine Lutz 28 Mar 1839; min- John J Reimensnyder

Bing
  Samuel & Mary Fulton 18 Jul 1797; d James b- James Fulton min- John Montgomery- 3Aug1797

Bingham
  Thomas & Elizabeth Miller 26 Oct 1818; min- Wright Burgess

Augusta County Marriages -- Man's Name

Bird
  Valentine & Nancy Cheatham 29 Sep 1829; min- Francis McFarland
Bishop
  Thomas & Elizabeth Collins 23 May 1811; min- John McCue
Bittle
  George & Polly Rapp 12 Feb 1798; d Michael Rapp, dec. b- John Fleiger
  William & Nancy Landis 19 Oct 1826; min- John Hendren
Black
  Alexander & Mary Ann Ham 17 Sep 1793; b- Samuel Miller min- John McCue- 17Sep1793
  Andrew H & Mary Jane Jarvis 15 Jun 1848; min- J C Hensell
  Anthony & Catherine Torbet 6 Nov 1798; d Robert con- Hugh Torbet b- John Torbet Catherine (of age) min- Archibald Scott- 10Nov1798
  James & Elizabeth Hulett 26 Apr 1787; min- Archibald Scott- 26Apr1787
  James & Jenny Law 21 Jul 1803; min- William King
  James & Betsy Rice 9 Jun 1800; Betsy (of age) d Margaret who consents b- John Clayton
  James & Jane Sharp 4 Jan 1799; d John Sharp Sr who consents test- Joseph Sharp b- Robert Sharp
  John & Arabella Brown 23 Dec 1841; min- James Paine
  John & Mary Hogshead 17 Oct 1812; min- William Wilson
  John & Rebecca McCutchen 19 Mar 1788; d Robert who consents wit- John McCutchen & John Meck b- James McCutchan min- Archibald Scott- 19Mar1788
  Ralph & Mary Beck 19 Jan 1838; min- John A Steele
  Robert & Sarah Curry 9 Sep 1833; min- Conrad Speece
  Samuel & Eveline Shields 2 Dec 1830; min- William Wilson
  Samuel & Rosanna Wright 23 Apr 1787; Minister's return spells name as 'Rosana' b- Alexander Wright
  William F & Rachel Webb 13 Mar 1834; min- Francis McFarland
  William R & Nancy Ptomey 27 Sep 1825; min- Alexander Templeton
  William & ----- ----- 6 Jan 1764; license only
  William & Margaret Cannady 16 Dec 1809; min- John McCue
  William & Mary Kennaday 20 Nov 1810; min- John McCue
  William & Nancy Tankesley 21 Sep 1826; min- Benjamin Denton
Blackburn
  David R & Margaret Ann Doom 19 Apr 1843; min- E R Veitch
  Samuel & Anna Mathews 17 Aug 1785; 'Ann?' d George bond min- Archibald Scott- 18Aug1785
Blackeley
  George & Margaret P Hogg 17 Feb 1835; min- John A Steele
Blackmore
  William & Catherine Harris 23 Feb 1804; min- William Wilson
Blackwell
  Elijah & Mary Ann Powers 18 Jan 1849; min- George H Martin
  John & Mary Devenbough 15 Jan 1835; min- J J Glossbrenner
Blackwood
  Isaac & Elizabeth Donefin 22 Jun 1818; min- William King
  Joseph & ----- ----- 18 May 1762; license only

Augusta County Marriages -- Man's Name

Blackwood (cont.)
  Samuel & Margaret Humphreys 21 Nov 1797; 'Peggy?' d David
    b- John Davis   min- Archibald Scott- 24Nov1797
Blain
  Isaac & Ann Gutherie 9 Apr 1795; Ann (of age) d William
    sis to Daniel b- Daniel Gutherie min- John McCue- 9Apr1795
  William & Sarah Hopkins 2 Dec 1799; d Samuel who consents
    test- P Thompson b- John Henry
Blair
  Alexander & Elizabeth Nickle 18 Feb 1792; d John, who
    consents wit- William Curry & Matthew Gambell b- John
    Nichol min- William Wilson- 19Feb1792
  James & Ann Eliza Blair 21 Aug 1828; min- Conrad Speece
  John & Elizabeth Hogg 14 Oct 1823; min- Conrad Speece
  Joseph & Elizabeth Harris 29 Apr 1794; d Robert who
    consents and gives bond no minister listed; clerk's
    memorandum cites ceremony date as 1May1794
  Joseph & Jinney Wood 20 Nov 1816; min- Wright Burgess
  Mathew & Mary Cowan 28 Jul 1836; min- John A Steele
  Matthew & Betsy Rankin 23 Sep 1797; d Thomas Rankin, dec.
    b- William Robertson min- William Wilson- 21Sep1797
  Thomas R & Jane Annis Davis 10 May 1838; min- John A Van
    Lear
  William & Mariann Beasley 5 Nov 1829; min- William Wilson
  William & Mary Holmes 26 Sep 1793; d John who consents
    test- Hugh Caul & John Holme b- Hugh Caul min- John McCue-
    26Sep1793
  William & Mary Thompson 20 Dec 1796; Minister's return
    spells name as 'Blane' d Alexander who consents test-
    Alexander Thompson & Peterson Thompson b- Alexander
    Thompson min- John McCue- 20Dec1796
Blake
  Peter & Mary McMahon 3 Sep 1792; d Deborah, who consents
    wit- George Farrel & John Baxter b- John Donaghe min-
    William Wilson- 6Sep1792
Blakely
  James & Margaret Ruff 21 Apr 1789; Minister's return
    spells name as 'Bleakley' b- Smith Thompson min- Archibald
    Scott- 22Apr1789
  Robert & Sarah Cambell - Oct 1817; min- John Brown
Blakemore
  George M & Caroline Coursey 3 Apr 1850; min- George B Rimel
  Joseph & Polly Connell 18 May 1814; min- William Cravens
Blane
  Isaac & Ann Guthrey 9 Apr 1794; min- John McCue- 9Apr1794
Bleakly
  Thomas & Betcey McFall 28 Nov 1805; min- William Wilson
Blewitt
  Samuel & Evaline Hopper 6 Mar 1829; min- William Wilson
Bogas
  Enoch & Elizabeth McCroskey 3 Dec 1790; d Grizel, who
    consents b- John McCrosky s Thomas Baggess wit- Thomas
    Hinds, Henry Venis & Robert Cooper (return sent in by Samuel
    Brown and dated 8Dec1790)

Augusta County Marriages -- Man's Name

Bolsley
  George A & Susanna Irwin 19 Apr 1808; min- William Wilson
Bolton
  Godfrey & Anna Landiss 13 Mar 1817; min- G H
    Riemenschneider
Bookhamer
  Nicholas & Damaris Bird 24 Feb 1845; min- T T Castleman
Borden
  James & Martha Coffman 5 Jan 1847; min- J A Van Lear
Boreland
  William & Mary Dean 14 Feb 1786; bond
Borland
  James & Mary Crawford 17 Sep 1812; min- William Wilson
  William & Sarah Dean 15 Feb 1786; 'Mary Dean'? min-
    William Wilson- 15Feb1786
Borrigar
  Jacob & Susannah Barrigar 15 Dec 1795; Minister's return
    spells name as 'Susanna Barriger (husband's surname missing)
    b- Martin Surface min- John McCue- date of ceremony missing
Bosserman
  Jacob & Elizabeth Switzer 22 Sep 1836; min- J C Hensell
  John & Mary A Rusmisel 12 Mar 1840; min- John C Hansell
  John & Elizabeth Margaret Russell 8 Nov 1837; min- J C
    Hensell
Boswell
  John & Lidia Slusher 24 May 1790; d Coonrod b- George
    Slusher
Botkin
  Richard & Jane Botkin 13 Aug 1789; d John Sr, who consents
    wit- William Botkin & Andrew Jordan Richard is son of Hugh
  Thomas & Margaret Devericks 20 Apr 1786; d Thomas bond
    min- Samuel Shannon- 24Apr1786
  William & Euphemia Botkin 29 Sep 1786; b- Andrew Jordan d
    John s James min- Samuel Shannon- 3Oct1786
  William & Isabella Botkin 1 Sep 1789; d Hugh, who consents
    wit- Richard Botkin & Alexander McQuain s of John, who
    consents wit- Andrew Jordan & Moses Knapp, who gives surety
Botkins
  William & Margaret Shuey 12 Aug 1834; min- E R Veitch
Botram
  John & Elizabeth Daggy 21 Mar 1823; min- G H
    Riemenschneider
Bowen
  William & ----- Humphrey 27 Jul 1835; min- William G
    Jackson
Bower
  James & ----- ----- 16 Aug 1763; license only
Bowers
  David & Betsy Weaver 25 Sep 1826; min- Daniel Stephens
  Henry J & Margaret Wiseman 21 Jan 1847; min- J C Hensell
  Jacob & Mary Cox 28 Jun 1821; min- James Morrison
  John & Jane Blackwell 7 Sep 1843; min- J C Hensell

Augusta County Marriages -- Man's Name

Bowman
  Christian & Hannah Rinehart 19 May 1815; min- William King
  Jacob & Fanny DLiza Clemer 6 Aug 1829; min- James Morrison
  Jacob & Sarah Loop 3 Apr 1828; min- James Morrison
  John & Sally Zahn 14 Jan 1824; min- Josiah Cole
  William & Polly Miller 26 May 1842; min- Alfred G Chenowith

Bowyer
  John & ----- ----- 4 Feb 1754; license only
  John & Elizabeth Hubard 26 Feb 1801; Elizabeth (of age) d Francis b- Jacob Kinney
  Peter & Cathorine Shelman 16 Aug 1793; d Lewis, who gives bond
  William & ----- ----- - Aug 1761; license only

Boyd
  Alexander & Isabella Graham 22 Jun 1793; b- Samuel Wilson min- John McCue- 27Jun1793
  James & Jane Hall 13 Mar 1823; min- John Brown
  John & Mary Graham 2 Nov 1790; Mary 22, d Thomas Sr, who consents b- Solomon Johnson wit- Thomas & Catty Greham
  John & Elizabeth Vernon 18 Jun 1787; Minister's return spells name as 'Vernom' b- George Campbell min- John Brown- 26Jun1787
  Robert & Eleanor Porterfield - Jul 1749; license only
  Thomas & Elizabeth Huston 5 Oct 1795; d Mary who consents test- John Burk b- James Houston min- Archibald Scott- 5Oct1795
  William H & Mary Jane Scott 6 Mar 1849; min- Robert L Dabney

Boyers
  Joseph & Betsy Ewin 30 Jul 1818; min- William King

Boys
  John & Anna StClair 18 Jan 1790; d Alexander, who consents b- Robert Douthat min- William Wilson- 18Jan1790
  William & Jane StClair 9 Jul 1800; d Alexander b- Alexander StClair

Bradshaw
  Thomas (Jr) & ----- ----- 20 Jul 1768; license only
  William & Margaret Coiner 15 Oct 1820; min- John Hendren

Brady
  Andrew H & Sarah Ann Nicholson 10 Apr 1834; min- William G Jackson
  Edward & Elizabeth Erwin 29 Mar 1791; d Richard b- Richard Erwin min- John Montgomery- 4Apr1791
  James & Amanda W Woods 20 Nov 1834; min- George Hildt

Branaman
  David & Mary Halderman 17 Dec 1816; min- William King

Brand
  George & Jane Rutledge 26 Mar 1816; min- William King
  Richard & Frances Brand 3 Apr 1827; min- Francis McFarland

Braneman
  David C & Cynthia Brady 18 Aug 1838; min- J Killian

Bratton
  Adam & Elizabeth Feamster 4 Jul 1788; Minister's return spells name as 'Feemster' d Thomas who consents wit- William Black & John McGummery b- James Lyle Jr min- Archibald Scott- 9Jul1788

Augusta County Marriages -- Man's Name

Bratton (cont.)
  David & Agnes Kirk 14 Dec 1799; d John David of age b- John Kirk
  James & ----- ----- 1 May 1754; license only
  James & ----- ----- 16 May 1774; license only
  Peter & Frances Patterson 22 Sep 1795; d Thomas, dec. b- Mary Patterson min- William Wilson- 24Sep1795
  William & Polly Berry 17 Dec 1812; min- I D Irwin
Brawford
  John & Jane Berry 2 Dec 1788; d Charles b- John Berry min- Archibald Scott- 4Dec1788
  Spotswood & Rebecca Sterrit 13 Aug 1819; min- John D Ewin
Breckinridge
  Robert & ----- ----- 6 Jul 1758; license only
  William & ----- ----- 7 Jun 1797; b- Robert McDowell (remainder of bond blank)
Breeze
  George & Elmira Russell 19 Oct 1845; min- J C Hensell
  William & Sarah Brand 11 Jun 1794; d James b- Robert Stevenson affidavit that Sarah is 21
  William & Francis D Hall 16 Oct 1827; min- William Monroe
Breverd
  John & Jerutia Nelson 6 Dec 1788; Minister's return spells name as 'Beverd' 'McClung informs that Miss Nelson is aged about 30 and about one year from Jersays' b- Thomas McClung min- William Wilson- 7Dec1788
Brew
  Henry & Lovinah Murray 26 Sep 1829; min- William Wilson
Brewer
  Jonathan & Elizabeth B Waddy 8 Oct 1840; min- John C Hensell- publication of banns
Brians
  Thomas & Larina Snyder 5 Mar 1828; min- William C. Morrison
Bridge
  William & Sarah Brown 18 Jan 1816; min- John McCue
Bridget
  James & Ann Eliza Grant 22 Jan 1834; min- Augustus Babb
Bridgett
  George W & Mary Ann Williams 15 Apr 1841; min- J J Reimensnyder
Brien
  Edward & Susana Young 12 Oct 1795; Minister's return spells name as 'Bryan' widow, d of Michael Fackler who consents b- Hugh Paul min- Archibald Scott- 12Oct1795
Bright
  David & Judith Dinsmore 6 Jun 1799; s James Dinsmore, dec. of Amherst George Bright, bro of David, attests to age Samuel Dinsmore, bro of Judith attests to age b- George Bright min- William King- 6Jun1799
  George & Catherine Gochenour 11 Feb 1802; min- William King- 11Feb1802
  Jacob & Polly Grimm 23 Jun 1810; min- William King
  John & Kitty Shott 26 May 1816; min- G H Riemenschneider
  Peter & Caroline Patterson 24 Aug 1843; min- Samuel Wagner

Augusta County Marriages -- Man's Name

Brightwell
  Ptolemy & Malinda Jones 26 Jul 1837; min- Stephen Smith
Brilhart
  John & Catherine Hoof 24 Mar 1801; min- Samuel Garber- 24Mar1801
Brison
  Edward & Charity Hamilton 21 Aug 1787; widow b- Samuel Gray min- James Chambers- 8Jul1788
Brittain
  George & Elizabeth Todd 23 Jul 1823; min- John Hendren
Britten
  William & Mary Hamilton 24 Dec 1801; Mary (of age) d Arthur b- John Hamilton
Britton
  John & Nancy Fisher 18 Jun 1800; b- Hance Calvert min- William King- 18Jun1800
Brobeck
  Joseph & Peggy Thomas 25 Aug 1808; min- William King
Brocius
  George & Dorcas Cullen 27 Jun 1822; min- James C Willson
Brodhurst
  James & Elleanor Ryan 30 Jan 1798; widow John Ryan b- Smith Thompson & William Short
Brook
  Robert S & Margaret S Smith 24 Nov 1835; min- John A Steele
Brooks
  George & Mary Grass 16 Mar 1786; bond (ministers return lists names as Robert Brooks and Polly Grass) min- Archibald Scott- 16Mar1786
  Henry & Elizabeth Mowbray 19 Sep 1825; min- Josiah Cole
  Jacob & Susannah Sheets 23 Sep 1833; min- William Calhoon
  James M & Eleanor T Stuart 7 Aug 1832; min- James C Wilson
  James & Mary McNair 15 Jan 1827; min- John A Gore
  Jonathan & Elizabeth Larew 23 Oct 1792; d Jacob wit- Peter Larew & P Brown min- John McCue- 6Nov1792
  Joshua R & Cynthia Boyd 17 Feb 1834; min- James C Wilson
  Joshua R & Elizabeth Davis 20 May 1845; min- G W Israel
  Pleasant & Sarah Grooms 1 Apr 1840; min- Samuel Wagner
  Robert & Grizey Evans 24 Sep 1794; Affidavit by Robert that Grisez (Crisey?) is over 21 b- William Bell min- John Brown- 26Sep1794
  Samuel & Mary Penrose 9 May 1789; gdn & next friend (?), John Emmitt, who consents and gives surety min- Archibald Scott- 9May1789
  William & Florence Russell 29 Mar 1798; d Joshua Russell, dec., sis of Adam Russell b- Adam Russell min- Archibald Scott- 29Mar1798
  William & Peggy Sheets 2 Jan 1822; min- Josiah Cole
Broom
  Thomas & Sara Galen 28 Jan 1786; min- John Brown- 28Jan1786
Brosius
  George & Elizabeth Minnick 25 Sep 1806; min- William McPheeters
  Jacob (Jr) & Elizabeth Weaver 16 Nov 1833; min- James Morrison

Augusta County Marriages -- Man's Name

Brower
  Enoch & Catharine Landes 30 Nov 1848; min- Daniel Brower
  John & Elizabeth Garber 4 Nov 1841; min- Peter Miller
Browers
  Christian & Sally Miller 21 Feb 1832; min- Abraham Garber-
    publication of banns
Brown
  ----- & Shelly Curry - Sep 1830; min- Gerard Morgan
  Alexander & Margaret Coalter 19 Jul 1799; d David
    Alexander of age b- David Coalter
  Charles Tyree H & Polly Anderson 8 Jul 1808; min- William
    Wilson
  Charles & Mary Woods 28 Nov 1786; d Mary bond min-
    Archibald Scott- 30Nov1786
  Christley & Susanna Wine 12 Dec 1815; min- Abraham Garber-
    publication of banns
  Cyrus & Elizabeth Tummins 22 Aug 1843; min- B M Smith
  Elijah D & Mary L Bush 8 Nov 1832; min- John S Watt
  Francis & Ann Fitzpatrick 16 Dec 1830; min- William
    Calhoon- publication of banns
  Francis & Mary Young 17 Jun 1794; d James b- James Young
    min- John Brown- 19Jun1794
  Henry & Mary S McNutt 10 Feb 1831; min- James Morrison
  Hering & Elizabeth Markwood 28 Feb 1826; min- Abraham
    Garber- publication of banns
  Jacob S & Eleanor B Cowan 16 Sep 1837; min- John A Steele
  James A & Mary A Zimmerman 15 Sep 1841; min- Samuel Wagner
  James A & Mary A Zimmerman 16 Sep 1841; min- Benjamin M
    Smith
  James & Jane Allison 1 Mar 1821; min- Conrad Speece
  James & Rebecca Blackwood 11 May 1798; Rebecca (of age) d
    William Blackwood, dec. b- William Blackwood (sic) min-
    John McCue- 17May1798
  James & Nancy Boyd 6 Feb 1827; widower min- Michael
    Meyerhoeffer
  James & Peggy Boyd 9 Feb 1815; min- John McCue
  James & Rebecca Hogshead 14 Mar 1805; min- Benjamin Irwin
  James & Elizabeth Jones 22 Aug 1816; min- William King
  James & Fanny Newman 11 Jun 1807; min- William Calhoon
  James & Nancy Parry 18 Apr 1826; min- William Monroe
  James & Martha Russell 15 Nov 1786; d Joshua bond min-
    Archibald Scott- 15Nov1786
  John (Jr) & Sarah Brown 7 Nov 1798; d Benjamin b-
    Benjamin Brown min- Archibald Scott- 10Nov1798
  John (Jr) & Elizabeth Carson 22 Sep 1801; d David Adam
    Palmer swears Elizabeth of age b- George Palmer John Brown
    swears as to his age min- William King- 22Sep1801
  John A & Jane Ann Steele 21 Aug 1842; min- James Morrison
  John B & Polly Keyser 7 Feb 1822; min- Conrad Speece
  John H & Amanda Gibbons 27 Jun 1844; min- Francis McFarland
  John H & Eliza Jane Wilson 28 Jun 1849; min- Francis
    McFarland
  John S & Rebecca Ann Taylor 9 Oct 1849; min- Francis
    McFarland

Augusta County Marriages -- Man's Name

Brown (cont.)
 John W & Jane Teaford 11 Sep 1837; min- J C Hensell
 John & Ann Berry 29 Sep 1841; min- John C Hensell
 John & Rosannah Connaway 15 Sep 1800; d Lawrence Connaway, dec. & Elizabeth Connaway who consents test- Moses Rusil & James Allison b- James Allison min- William Wilson- 16Sep1800
 John & Elizabeth Fall 8 Jun 1801; Elizabeth (of age) d George b- Daniel Fall
 John & Margaret Hagerty 1 Apr 1795; Minister's return spells name as 'Hagarty' d John who consents test- Vincent Tapp & Hannah Hagerty b- Vincent Tapp
 John & Ann Keener 20 Apr 1791; John from Shenandoah cty d David b- David Keener
 John & Sarah Moffett 17 May 1836; min- Isaac Jones
 John & Mary Ramsey 5 Apr 1804; min- John McCue
 John & Polly Shields 16 Oct 1823; min- Francis McFarland
 Joseph C & Elizabeth N Campbell 27 May 1847; min- J C Hensell
 Joseph & Mary Richey 19 Jan 1804; min- William King
 Joseph & Kitty Terrill 14 Jul 1814; min- John McCue
 Richard & Mary Curry 12 Apr 1798; Mary (of age) d Samuel b- Isaac Hanna
 Robert P & Nancy B Christian 4 Oct 1842; min- S J Love
 Samuel & ----- ----- 19 May 1774; license only
 Samuel & Eliza Cox 14 Aug 1810; min- William King
 Samuel & Mary Ann Flack 25 Dec 1834; min- William Scull
 Samuel & Margaret Gibson 26 Aug 1797; 'Elizabeth?' d Samuel Joseph Shields swears that Samuel Brown, s William, is of age b- Samuel Gibson min- Archibald Scott- 31Aug1797
 Thomas & ----- ----- 27 Feb 1765; license only
 Thomas & Jean Thompson 21 Aug 1792; Minister's return spells name as 'Mary Thompson' d William b- Robert Wilson Jr min- John McCue- 4Oct1792
 William & Sarah Argenbright 10 Jan 1827; min- John Hendren
 William & Polly Cox 14 Oct 1811; min- William King
 William & Elizabeth Guffy 27 Mar 1804; min- William King
 William & Martha Hillis 25 Apr 1811; min- John McCue
 Wilson & Joanna Hall 5 Sep 1821; min- John Brown

Brownfield
 John & Kitty Fauber 14 Jul 1792; Minister's return spells name as 'Fauver' d Christian, who consents wit- John Stout & Timothy Turner b- James Johnston, Jacob Kinney & Patrick Ryan min- John McCue- 14Jul1792
 John & Susanah Forber 13 Dec 1814; min- William King
 John & Catherine Shover 22 Oct 1829; min- William Wilson
 Thomas & Elizabeth Faegely 19 Dec 1819; min- G H Riemenschneider

Browning
 John & Mary Brown 11 Jul 1832; min- James C Wilson
 William & Rachel P Caruthers 16 Jul 1832; min- James C Wilson

Augusta County Marriages -- Man's Name

Brownlee
Alexander & Catherine Doak 19 Jan 1829; min- Francis McFarland
Alexander & Elizabeth Fulton 4 Mar 1800; d Hugh who consents Elizabeth (of age) test- Robert Fulton & John Fulton b- John Fulton
James & Rebecah Blackamore 28 Sep 1796; widower & widow b- John Gates
James & Mary Eve 28 Jan 1825; min- Josiah Cole
James & Sarah Gardner 14 Apr 1825; min- Francis McFarland
James & Ruth E Heizer 24 Oct 1833; min- William Calhoon
James & Susanna West 11 Jul 1816; min- William Wilson
John (Jr) & Jane B Thompson 12 Jan 1842; min- Francis McFarland
John & Nancy Bell 28 Oct 1819; min- William Calhoon
William & Mary Fulton 10 Nov 1795; d Hugh who consents test- Robert Fulton & John Fulton b- Robert Fulton min- Archibald Scott- 12Nov1795

Bruback
Jacob & Amanda Gilliat 11 Feb 1834; min- Augustus Babb

Brubeck
Abraham & Julia Ann Perkins 2 Jul 1835; min- Henry Brown

Bruce
Charles & Catherine Walton 15 Oct 1793; Minister's return spells name as 'Catherine Walters' b- Moses Jackson min- William Wilson- 17Oct1793

Bruffey
John & Margaret Adams 27 Apr 1785; d Ann Edgecomb bond
Robert & Margaret Conell 1 Apr 1813; min- William Cravens

Brukmann
William & Sophia Yonas 26 Apr 1806; min- William King

Bruntain
Robert & Mary Breezeley 16 Apr 1791; widow b- Isaac Beal

Bryan
Benjamin K & Polly Brawford 20 Sep 1819; min- William Calhoon
James & Eliza Overshiner 20 Feb 1809; min- William King
James & Sally Shown 16 Aug 1815; min- G H Riemenschneider
Reuben & Caroline Swink 2 Sep 1845; min- Francis McFarland

Bryant
Benjamin K & Hardenia W Owens 2 Jul 1833; min- Samuel Kennerly
Wilprey & Agnes Blakely 30 Nov 1791; d Robert, who consents wit- Thomas Call & Lewis Sorrel b- Thomas Call (Caul)

Buchanan
David & Sarah Caldwell 13 Apr 1789; d John b- John Caldwell
David & Rachel Troxel 8 Feb 1827; min- James Morrison
George & Peggy Chambers 3 Feb 1818; min- John D Ewin
James & ----- ----- 23 Aug 1763; license only
James & Peggy Armstrong 6 Sep 1827; min- William C. Morrison- date of ceremony not listed
James & Mary Jane McCutchan 12 Mar 1846; min- W G Campbell

Augusta County Marriages -- Man's Name

Buchanan (cont.)
  John & Margaret Patton 17 Jun 1749; license only
  John & Elizabeth Sensibaugh 27 Apr 1848; min- J C Hensell
  Patrick & ----- ----- 10 Apr 1770; license only
  Robert & ----- ----- - Jun 1761; license only
  Samuel & Rebecca Sawyers 25 Dec 1790; b- Philip North
    min- Archibald Scott- 30Dec1790
  William & Annas Caldwell 12 Aug 1795; Annas (of age) d of
    John, dec. sis to John Caldwell who consents b- Alexander
    Buchanan min- John McCue- 24Aug1795
  William & Martha Dunlap 5 Mar 1835; min- Francis McFarland
  William & Susannah Paine 2 Aug 1827; min- James Morrison

Buckley
  John & Anny Braden 17 Jun 1799; d Edward b- Edward Braden

Buckman
  John & Mary Parratt 1 May 1789; d Henry, who consents b-
    John Mifferd wit- John & Mary Cofman

Buks
  William & Mary Nimerick 27 Oct 1808; min- William Wilson

Bumgarner
  Adam & Mary Gibson 29 May 1800; d David both of age s
    Balzer b- John Sheetz min- William King- 29May1801
  Jacob & Rebecca Patterson - Apr 1812; min- I D Irwin
  Jacob & Mary Waddle 28 Jun 1785; d John bond
  Peter & Sarah Foster 9 Nov 1806; min- William Ki
    publication of banns

Bunch
  George G & Frances A Lawrence 2 Sep 1841; min- Alfred G
    Chenowith

Burch
  Waddle & Harriet Eidsell 26 Mar 1817; min- Wright Burgess

Burdett
  John & Lydia Curry 16 Aug 1816; min- William Wilson

Burgentine
  William P & Mary Ann Adams 15 Jul 1841; min- Alfred G
    Chenowith

Burges
  John & Jane Erwin 15 Jun 1796; 'Burgess?' d Samuel s
    Thomas (con) test- Elisha Price & Robert Gamble Consent
    before William Price, magistrate of Henrico cty b- Samuel
    Erwin min- William Wilson- 16Jun1796

Burgess
  Daniel & Sally Fox 21 Jul 1808; min- William King
  George W & Mary C Rapp 25 May 1843; min- J C Hensell
  John & Hanah McNair 27 Jul 1820; min- Josiah Cole
  Samuel A & Mary Lambert 18 Feb 1847; min- Stephen
    Hildebrand

Burke
  Cunrad & Mary Lance 19 Apr 1787; d Mary who consents wit-
    John Bowman & Absalom Sprun b- John Bowman min- Archibald
    Scott- 19Apr1787

Burkentine
  John & Betsy Henderson 22 Feb 1816; min- William King

Augusta County Marriages -- Man's Name

Burket
David & Elizabeth Sloane 30 May 1813; min- William King

Burkett
Frederick & Rachel Attershall 12 Oct 1786; Minister's return spells name as 'Ottershell' d Heinrich Atterschall bond min- William Wilson- 13Oct1786

Burkhart
Daniel & Polly Sterlinger 20 Jan 1801; Also called Polly Heddebach George Heddebaugh swears Polly of age b- Jacob Bealer ('Behler?')
Peter & Margaret Decker 28 Jul 1794; b- Christian Bomgardner con- Jacob Kinney

Burkholder
Christopher & Hetty Crist 25 Feb 1808; min- William McPheeters

Burns
Frederick & Eliza Dold 10 Mar 1834; min- James C Wilson
Peter & Jane Miller 21 Nov 1789; Minister's return spells name as 'Burnes' d James, who consents b- Francis Huff wit- Robert McClery & William Black min- John Brown- 27Nov1789

Burnsides
Samuel W & Lavina Bull 24 May 1849; min- T A Morgan

Burrus
Edward & Agnes McCann 15 Nov 1798; Minister's return spells name as 'Barras' widow James McCann b- Isaac Hays min- Archibald Scott- 15Nov1798

Burton
Williamson & Sarah Leonard 25 Jan 1837; min- James C Wilson

Burwell
George & Mary Cunningham 6 Jun 1805; min- William King

Bush
James & Rebecca Wilson 30 Nov 1815; min- John McCue
John & Elizabeth Cullon 24 May 1803; 'Elizabeth Collins?' min- John McCue
John & Sarah Steele 3 Nov 1803; min- John McCue
Parker & Elizabeth Spotts - Jun 1814; bond- 2Jun1814 min- William Wilson

Bushong
Abraham & Elizabeth Cox 20 Feb 1845; min- J C Hensell
Jacob & Catharine Cline - Apr 1810; min- John Brown
Solomon & Catherine Halderman 13 May 1829; min- William C. Morrison

Buster
Claudius & Elenor Paul 28 Nov 1815; min- John McCue
John & Polly Shields 2 Mar 1820; min- Robert H Chapman

Byer
Philip & Elizabeth Hynes 17 Jun 1806; min- William King

Byers
David & Elizabeth Horne 10 Apr 1827; min- James Morrison
James & Letty Dixon 29 Apr 1817; min- Conrad Speece, Jr
Joseph & Elizabeth Blair 24 Sep 1791; Minister's return spells name as 'Buyers' d Jane, who consents b- Michael Hermon min- William Wilson- 7Oct1791

Augusta County Marriages -- Man's Name

Byers (cont.)
  Joseph & Elizabeth Blakely 26 Jun 1795; Elizabeth 'Betsey' (of age) d of Thomas who consents b- William Breeze min- William Wilson- 9Jun1795
  Samuel & Nancy Patterson 29 Oct 1823; min- William Wilson Jr

Cain
  Cornelius & Sarah Hyatt 17 Aug 1790; min- William Wilson- 17Aug1790
  Hiatt & Frances Long 23 Mar 1830; min- William Wilson
  Jacob & Catherine Fogel 6 Jun 1785; b- Samuel Runkle wit- Samuel McConkey Jr d Anthony
  James & Lucy Woodward 28 Apr 1812; bond min- Ezra Grover- 30Apr1812
  John & Catharine Frankum 2 Mar 1814; min- William Cravens

Caldwell
  David & ----- ----- 18 Nov 1761; license only
  David & Arabella Vanlear 7 Aug 1806; min- John McCue
  John & Fanny Davis 1 Dec 1789; Minister's return spells name as 'Nancy Davis' b- Zachariah Estill min- Archibald Scott- 2Dec1789
  John & Elizabeth Fulton 1 Dec 1801; d Mary b- William Fulton min- John McCue- 3Dec1801
  John & Elenor Scott 27 Feb 1806; min- John McCue
  Samuel & Elizabeth Alexander 11 May 1813; min- John McCue
  Smith & Antoinetta A Nicholson 5 Nov 1840; min- Frederick D Goodwin
  Thomas & Lettice Ann McClenachan 29 Jan 1800; d Elijah Mrs. Margaret McClenachan swears Letice Ann is of age test- Isaac Tate b- John Tate min- John McCue- 6Feb1800
  William & Esther Buchanan 4 Sep 1787; Minister's return spells name as 'Buchanon d William who consents wit- David Wilson & John Bell b- Alexander Hindman min- John Brown- 10Sep1787
  William & Susan Ellis 23 Dec 1844; min- B M Smith

Cale
  John & Catherine Runkle - May 1827; min- Joseph Smith
  John & Catherine Runkle 17 May 1827; min- Joseph Smith
  Peter & Elizabeth Wiseman 22 Nov 1838; min- John C Hensell
  Preston B & Mary M Funkhouser 15 Nov 1827; min- William Calhoon
  William A & Mary Roberts 4 Oct 1825; min- William W Calhoun
  William & Isabella Hanger 8 Jan 1846; min- J C Hensell

Caler
  Charles & Barbara Smith 20 Apr 1789; (Koehler?) Minister's return spells name as 'Kaylor' b- Michael Apple min- William Wilson- 20Mar1789

Calhoon
  James M & Eliza Jane Thompson 9 May 1837; min- William Calhoon
  James & Mary Lessly 8 Feb 1792; Minister's return spells name as 'Lessley' d Thomas b- David Steel min- John Brown- 8Feb1792

Augusta County Marriages -- Man's Name

Callison
  James H & Isabella P McCutchan 15 Dec 1853; min- Luther Emmerson
  Robert & Elizabeth Mitchel 16 Feb 1793; d James who consents b- Thomas Mitchell affidavit of age of Elizabeth no minister listed; clerk's memorandum cites ceremony date as 19Feb1793
  William & Isabella Harris 12 Apr 1821; min- John Brown

Calvert
  Cary A B & Susan Smith 15 Jan 1844; min- E R Veitch

Cambell
  James M & Margaret A Cupp 4 Aug 1845; min- S Hildebrand

Cameron
  A Warrick & Margaret Miller - Jan 1828; min- Gerard Morgan
  Charles T & Lucy A Edmonds 12 May 1840; min- Frederick D Goodwin

Campbell
  Adam & Sally Steele 19 Dec 1805; min- William Calhoon
  Addison H & Jane Elizabeth Griffith 30 Aug 1849; min- W G Campbell
  Alexander B & Pauline C Hill 16 Sep 1829; min- Conrad Speece
  Alexander & Peggy Brown 20 May 1797; Peggy (of age) d Thomas Brown, dec. con- Elizabeth Brown b- Hugh Paul min- John Montgomery- 22May1797
  Andrew & Rebecca Campbell 28 Jan 1793; d John b- Alexander Humphreys affidavit of age of Rebecca no minister listed; clerk's memorandum cites ceremony date as 28Jan1793
  Archibald & Polly Gregory 21 Aug 1806; min- William King
  Audley & Mary Elliott 26 Oct 1791; b- James Elliott no minister listed; clerk's memorandum cites ceremony date as 28Oct1791
  Charles & Mary Alexander 7 Sep 1785; b- Hugh Campbell wit- Samuel McConkey & John Alexander d James min- Benjamin Erwin- 8Sep1785
  Fountain & Clarinda Collins 16 Oct 1826; min- Francis McFarland
  George W & Sarah Ann Russell 17 Dec 1835; min- Francis A C Mills
  George & Peggy Fowler 22 Jun 1791; d Andrew Certificate that Peggy is over 21 b- James Curtis
  George & ----- Riddle 14 Nov 1789; min- William Wilson- 14Nov1789
  Henry & Polly Shoemate 28 Jul 1814; min- William Wilson
  Hugh & Margaret Erwin 14 Jun 1796; d Samuel Hugh (of age) b- Samuel Erwin min- William Wilson- 16Jun1796
  James & Bridget Devine 21 Dec 1792; Minister's return spells name as 'Divine' widow consent signed by Thomas Greene & Bridget Devin, widow b- John Price min- William Wilson- 24Dec1792
  James & Sally Evans 7 Jan 1800; d Griffin b- John Campbell min- William Wilson- 7Jan1800
  James & Victoire Laporte 14 Oct 1795; Victoire (of age) gives her own consent dated 'Calf Pasture' b- Robert Gamble min- John Montgomery- 19Oct1795

Augusta County Marriages -- Man's Name

Campbell (cont.)
John & ----- ----- 8 Aug 1758; license only
John & ----- ----- 7 Sep 1764; license only
John & Isabella Bleakly 4 Nov 1789; Minister's return spells name as 'Bleackley' b- Thomas Bleakly min- William Wilson- 12Nov1789
John & Mary Early 5 Feb 1795; 'Polly?' d Daniel b- Daniel Early min- William Wilson- 5Feb1795
John & Polly Scott 25 May 1797; Polly from Rockingham cty min- William Wilson- 25May1797
Joseph & ----- ----- 16 Apr 1770; license only
Robert & ----- ----- 13 Jun 1766; license only
Robert & Elizabeth Roople 9 Aug 1813; min- Wright Burgess
Samuel & Martha Rayburn 9 Sep 1806; min- William McPheeters
Theobald John & Sarah Crawford 7 Aug 1792; Minister's return spells name as 'Polly' b- John Campbell Sr min- William Wilson- 9Aug1792
William & Elizabeth McPheeters 9 Aug 1800; d William b- William McPheeters

Camper
Henry N & Elizabeth Ann Bosserman 8 Oct 1834; min- J Hoover

Canote
Jacob & Martha Jones 6 Jan 1798; d Joshua b- Joshua Jones
John (Jr) & Peggy Tumbleston 7 Jun 1798; d Thomas b- Thomas Tumbleston min- John McCue- 7Jun1798

Cantley
Robert & Nancy Johnston 18 Jul 1796; Minister's return spells name as 'Cantly' Nancy (of age) d Robert b- Thomas Turk min- John McCue- 20Jul1796

Caphart
Charles & Dorothy Hansel 31 Mar 1785; b- Adam Calbscop d Philip

Carden
Robert & Mary Clinebill 18 Sep 1813; min- Wright Burgess
Robert & Janet Steele 17 Dec 1799; d James who consents test- William & Polly Steele Robert of age b- Thomas Fulton min- William King- 19Dec1799

Carell
Valentine & Chatrine Weaver 25 Aug 1808; min- William King

Carey
Frederick & Peggy Bush 18 Apr 1816; min- William King

Cargo
Samuel & Sally Malcolm 22 Nov 1814; min- William King

Carico
John & Susan Waddle 3 Aug 1810; min- William King

Carlile
John & ----- ----- 18 Feb 1762; license only

Carlos
Martin & Sarah Mohler 5 Jul 1841; min- S J Love

Carothers
John & Mary Etter 13 Aug 1795; 'Mary Elliott?' min- Archibald Scott- 13Aug1795

Augusta County Marriages -- Man's Name

Carpenter
  John & Elizabeth Weed 27 Mar 1815; min- Wright Burgess
  William & Mary Strickler 9 Jan 1786; min- John Brown- 9Jan1786
Carrethers
  James & Margaret Jackson 17 Dec 1805; min- John McCue
Carricofe
  Jacob & Matilda Collins 17 Jan 1850; min- Peter Miller
Carrington
  Mayo & Anne Adams 28 Sep 1789; Minister's return spells name as 'Carrigton' b- John Hall min- John Montgomery- 30Sep1789
  Paul J & Margaret Augusta Thompson 11 Nov 1845; min- T T Castleman
Carrol
  Charles & Polly Quick 22 Aug 1811; min- John McCue
  Jacob S & Isabella Lehman 18 May 1826; min- William Monroe
  William & Margaret Syler 24 Jun 1794; Minister's return spells name as 'Carrel' d of Jacob Margaret gives own consent test- Daniel Thorp affidavit of Margaret's full age b- Hugh Paul min- John McCue- 24Jun1794
Carson
  Abel & Rebecca Gardner 17 Oct 1832; min- Francis McFarland
  Abraham & Catherine Griffith 2 Jun 1802; min- William Wilson- 2Jun1802
  Addison & Nancy Pickral 7 Jun 1832; min- William Wilson
  Isaac & Elizabeth Shaver 2 Jan 1828; min- John Hendren
  Jacob C & Susan Jane Grant 14 Sep 1848; min- Alonzo P Ludden
  Peyton & Ann Hildebrand 20 Jan 1834; min- John Hendren- publication of banns
  Robert & Sally Poage 9 Dec 1799; d William s Samuel who consents and states Robert of age last spring test- David Carson Sally also of age b- William Carson
  Robert & Catharine Shreckhise 24 Feb 1839; min- John J Reimensnyder
  Samuel & Sarah Harris 28 Feb 1828; min- James Morrison
Cartmill
  John & ----- ----- 29 Jan 1763; license only
Caruthers
  David & Elizabeth Jackson 14 Mar 1786; (Coruthers?) d David min- Archibald Scott- 18Mar1786
  Gimpsey & Jane Gold 3 Dec 1792; 'Carothers?' d Robert b- Samuel Gould no minister listed; clerk's memorandum cites ceremony date as 5Dec1792
  James & Martha P Brooks 20 Dec 1830; min- James C Wilson
Carwell
  John & Sophronia McCutchen 21 Dec 1843; min- J C Hensell
Casady
  John & Sarah Jane Weickel 27 Nov 1845; min- P Shickel
  Washington & Elizabeth Ann Landis 2 Feb 1837; min- John J Riemensnyder

Augusta County Marriages -- Man's Name

Cash
  John & Sally Fawber 18 Nov 1824; min- Luke Collins
  Ready & Mary Hartigan 29 Aug 1823; min- Tobias Riley
Casidy
  Washington B & Elizabeth Andrew 9 Nov 1845; min- J A Van Lear
Caslen
  William & Polly Weiford 26 Sep 1806; min- William King
Cason
  Edward & Sarah Waddy 10 Jun 1824; min- Josiah Cole
Cassady
  Thomas & Sally Towell 26 Jan 1813; min- William Wilson
Catling
  Thomas & Betsey McCue 24 Mar 1814; min- Thomas Bourne
Caulk
  Jacob & Margaret McFaddin 23 May 1792; Bond spells name as 'McFarren' b- John McFaddin min- John Brown- 29May1792
Cawley
  Michael & Jane Shannon 24 May 1785; b- Robert McClenachan
Cawly
  William & Jane Haslet 16 Aug 1808; min- William King
Cease
  Erasmus A & Sarah E Burch 26 Nov 1844; min- G W Israel
Chambers
  David & Isbell Vachub 18 Oct 1794; d John who consents test- William McKee & William Dunlap b- William McKee min- John Montgomery- 23Oct1794
  Thomas (Jr) & Elizabeth Bryans 13 May 1795; Elizabeth (of age) b- Thomas Chambers Sr min- John McCue- 14May1795
  William & Susan Beard 8 May 1828; min- James Morrison
  William & Ann Heatherly 23 Mar 1786; b- Anthony Mustoe min- James Waddle- 26Mar1786
Chandler
  Thomas & Sarah Shropshire 18 Nov 1805; min- William King
Chapman
  Alfred & Mary E Kinney 1 Dec 1837; min- Fred D Goodwin
Chesnut
  William & Mary Gold 23 Mar 1801; 'Chestnut' d Robert Gold & Esther Gold Mary (of age) b- Vincent Tapp min- John McCue- 26Mar1801
Chesnutt
  John & Anne Palmer 19 May 1790; Minister's return spells name as 'Chestnut' d William b- James Spence min- William Wilson- 22May1790
Childers
  John & Mary Huff 9 Jun 1825; min- Josiah Cole
Chrisman
  Thomas & Margaret Cupp 19 Feb 1846; min- Jacob Bear
  Thomas & Martha Jane Sprouse 11 Mar 1847; min- Jacob Bear
Christian
  Ebenezer & Margaret P Bell 14 Aug 1834; min- John Hendren
  Gilbert & ----- ----- 14 Jun 1763; license only
  John B & Jane Finley 26 Jul 1820; min- John D Ewin
  Patrick & ----- ----- 20 Jun 1766; license only

Augusta County Marriages -- Man's Name

Christian (cont.)
  Robert (Sr) & Margaret Christian 22 Feb 1790; s Robert
    sis Robert Christian Jr (both parents deceased) b- Robert
    Christian Jr   min- Archibald Scott- 23Feb1790
  Robert & Sally Bell 18 May 1814; min- William Calhoon
  Robert & Mary Huston 2 Sep 1789; d Wm, who consents wit-
    G Christian Jr & Frances Long b- Gilbert Christian min-
    Archibald Scott- 3Sep1789
  William & Mary G Crump 6 Sep 1843; min- J C Hensell
Christopher
  Robert & Mary Lilley 22 Mar 1838; min- John A Steele
Churchman
  Elijah & Fanny Cawly 2 Jun 1814; min- John McCue
Clark
  Ambrose & Margaret Mahoney 25 Sep 1820; min- Josiah Cole
  Charles & Polly Dequeza 4 Nov 1807; min- John McCue
  Samuel & Jane Mathews 30 Oct 1790; d Sampson, who consents
    wit- John Cooper & Minton Collins b- A Nelson Jr min- John
    Montgomery- 2Nov1790
  William & ----- ----- - Aug 1760; license only
Clarke
  Hatch & Jane Donaghe 22 Dec 1817; min- William King
  Henry & Elizabeth Connaway 30 Jul 1812; min- William King
  James T & Martha M Blakemore 28 Oct 1845; min- S Hildebrand
  Joseph & Elizabeth Dennis 28 Jan 1817; min- William King
  Pleasant A & Isabella Flack 5 Oct 1815; min- William King
  Thomas & Isabella Anderson 8 Apr 1828; min- William C.
    Morrison
  William & Nancy Bilheimer 19 Jan 1832; min- John Howell-
    publication of banns
  William & Sarah Harnsbarger 1 Nov 1821; min- Gerard Morgan
Clarkson
  John & Elizabeth M Harrison 6 Aug 1816; min- William
    Cravens
Clayton
  John & Margaret Rice 20 Dec 1785; widow b- Andrew
    Hamilton min- Samuel Shannon- 2Jan1786
  Thomas A & Mary Ann Fulton 10 Oct 1844; min- James Morrison
  Thomas & Nancy Kinkead 17 Oct 1820; min- John D Ewin
  William & Polly Armstrong 24 Mar 1818; min- William Calhoon
Claytor
  John & Jane Shaver 12 Jun 1828; min- William C. Morrison
  William & Matilda Chaplin 29 Dec 1842; min- Samuel Wagner
Clemans
  Christopher & Mary Nigle 7 Sep 1815; min- John McCue
Clements
  Gersham & Jenny Usher 22 Apr 1791; d Robert, who consents
    wit- David & Francis Bell b- David Bell min- William
    Wilson- 22Apr1791
  John & Elizabeth Eagal 10 Jul 1790; d Christian Eckell,
    who consents wit- Alexander Stuart & J Beal b- Christian
    Eckell

Augusta County Marriages -- Man's Name

Clemmens
John & Susanah Slagle 16 Oct 1815; min- William King
Clemmons
James & Susannah Kennerley 17 Jan 1809; min- William Wilson
Clemons
John C & Elizabeth King 3 Mar 1827; widow min- William W Calhoun
Click
Joseph & Anna Driver 25 Mar 1845; min- T T Castleman
Clide
Solomon & Ellen Burnes 23 Jun 1801; d Richard who consents test- Thomas Burnes & James Burns b- Thomas Bevens Bond signed Solomon Cloyde & Thomas Burns
Cliff
George & Jane Shipman 10 Apr 1803; min- William King
Clifton
Thomas & Betsy Call 1 Jan 1789; Minister's return spells name as 'Caul' d Timothy Caul, who consents wit- Jeremiah Washington & James Rutledge b- Thomas Story min- William Wilson- 1Jan1789
William & Peggy Long 3 Apr 1800; widow and of age b- Lawrence Lynch min- William King- 3Apr1800
Cline
Christian & Rebecca Myers 11 May 1832; min- William Wilson
Jacob & Margaret Black 26 Jan 1790; widow b- Henry Fulwider
Jacob & Susannah Brosius 6 Apr 1803; min- William King
Jacob & Elizabeth Mingo 15 Jan 1822; min- James Morrison
Joseph & Sarah Hartman - Mar 1807; min- John Brown
Peter & Polley Wenger 16 Apr 1816; min- William King
Clinebill
Benjamin & Sarah Lotts 29 Jun 1837; min- J C Hensell
David & Susan Jane Crist 2 Aug 1827; min- James Morrison
Henry & Lea Werley 28 Mar 1833; min- Francis McFarland
Clinedinst
Andrew H & Elizabeth F Weitzel 11 May 1843; min- Samuel Wagner
John & Martha Brady 21 Apr 1835; min- John A Steele
Washington & Sarah Scott Gregory 7 Feb 1828; min- William Monroe
Clinginpeel
Jacob & Isabella Best 6 Feb 1837; min- James C Wilson
Cloyd
James & ----- ----- 20 Nov 1764; license only
Clyne
Peter & Eve Cowman 25 Feb 1793; d John b- John Cowman
Coalter
John & Eleanor McChesney 28 Jan 1808; min- John McCue
Coatney
Edward P & Nancy B Euritt 23 Feb 1843; min- John A Van Lear
Cochran
George & Margaret Henry 30 Sep 1790; d James, who consents wit- David Humphreys & John McCutchan b- Samuel McCutchan
James & Mary Jane Strain 30 Dec 1834; min- Conrad Speece

Augusta County Marriages -- Man's Name

Cochran (cont.)
  John & Margaret Linn Lewis 28 Sep 1826; min- Daniel Stephens
  Robert & Jane Laird 17 Dec 1787; d David who consents b- John Campbell min- William Wilson- 17Dec1787
  William & Eliza McCormick 3 Nov 1824; min- William W Calhoun

Cocke
  Stephen & Margaret Donaldson 9 Sep 1794; 'Donnaldson' d Robert b- Robert Donaldson no minister listed; clerk's memorandum cites ceremony date as 11Sep1794

Cockran
  James & Magdalin Moffett 4 Dec 1792; Minister's return spells name as 'Cochran' d George, who consents b- Matthew Gambill min- John McCue- 10Jan1793

Cockrell
  John W & Elizabeth Mitchell 25 Jan 1825; min- Josiah Cole

Coffey
  Hays & Polly Burket 7 Feb 1815; min- William King

Coffman
  Christian & Ann Garber 19 Oct 1819; min- Abraham Garber- publication of banns
  David & Susannah Mahoney 17 Apr 1820; min- John Hendren
  Jacob & Elizabeth Cooke 16 Apr 1800; min- William Wilson- 16Apr1800
  Jacob & Harriett Hall 14 Sep 1834; min- Wright Burgess
  John & Elizabeth Bell 4 Feb 1806; min- John Bell
  John & Elizabeth Crobarger 6 Jun 1815; min- William King
  Samuel & Hannah Parsons 27 Dec 1832; min- Samuel Kennerly
  Solomon & Eliza Jane Burkett 3 Dec 1846; min- J A Van Lear

Coger
  James & Elizabeth Turk 19 Jul 1797; Minister's return spells name as 'James Conger' d Thomas Turk Sr who consents test- James Turk b- James Johnston min- William Wilson- 20Jul1797
  Michael & ----- ----- 6 Jun 1762; license only

Coiner
  Benjamin & Mary Miller 28 Feb 1833; min- John S Watt
  Christian & Jenney Erwin 3 Aug 1802; min- William King- 3Aug1802
  David D & Celestine Caldwell 11 Oct 1836; min- James C Wilson
  David & Ann Keyser 6 Feb 1829; min- William Wilson
  Gasper & Margaret Berrier 24 May 1788; d Jacob wit- Samuel McCune & David Vence b- Samuel McCune
  George & Susanna Hawp 3 Jun 1794; d Rudolph who consents test- George Almeroth & John Hawpe b- John Hawpe
  Henry & Mary Ann E Smith 4 Aug 1846; min- James H Brown
  Jacob & Mary Byers 18 Aug 1795; d Joseph b- Joseph Byers min- William Wilson- 20Aug1795
  John & Hanna Laywell 19 Jun 1793; Minister's return spells name as 'Cryner' d Andrew b- Philip Ingleman min- John McCue- 20Jun1793
  John & Jane Mowry 4 Dec 1817; min- William King

Augusta County Marriages -- Man's Name

Coiner (cont.)
John & Catherine Spotts 2 Feb 1804; min- William King
John & Anne White 21 Sep 1823; min- John Watson
Jonathan & Mary Swisher 7 Apr 1829; min- William Wilson
Michael A & Elizabeth Kiser 17 Jan 1839; min- John J Reimensnyder
Michael & Sarah Kennedy 12 Sep 1844; min- George H Martin
Philip & Rebecca Crist 16 Mar 1826; min- William Wilson
Philip & Catherine Fawber 5 Mar 1798; d Valentine wit- William Sterrett b- Jacob Swoope min- John McCue- 8Mar1798
Philip & Polly Whitmore 25 Mar 1819; min- William King
Simon & Margaret Miller 2 Jan 1834; min- Ambrose Henkel

Colbreath
William & Mary Hamilton 20 Aug 1787; d John who consents wit- Alexander Kelly & William Gillespie b- John Johnston

Colbreth
John & Elizabeth Hamilton 18 Apr 1785; Minister's return spells name as 'Calbreth' b- James Johnston d John min- John Rodgers- 4Apr1785

Coldbreath
Thomas & Jane Hutcheson 26 Nov 1801; Minister's return spells name as 'Caldbreath' d James b- James Hutcheson min- John McCue- 26Nov1801

Coleman
Samuel G & Diana W Bragg 4 Nov 1824; min- Francis McFarland

Coley
George & Malinda Landes - --- 182-; min- Benjamin Denton

Collins
Calvin & Sarah Link 6 Dec 1827; min- William Monroe
Charles & Betsy Bowman 22 Dec 1814; min- William Wilson
Isaac & Amanda Powers 2 Sep 1847; min- George Huffman
Isaac & Margaret Stockdale 16 May 1826; min- John Hendren- publication of banns
John & Mary Kisner 6 Aug 1788; Minister's return spells name as 'Kizner' b- Martin Miller wit- John Hall min- John Brown- 14Aug1788
Luke & Sarah Miller 7 Aug 1790; Sarah nearly of age d Worttri Moller & Caterine Miller, who consent wit- Alex & James Stuart b- John Collins (return sent by Samuel Brown and dated 9Aug1790)
Luke & Mary Thomason - --- 183-; min- Cornelius Gates- publication of banns
Samuel & Hannah Rupe 9 Sep 1841; min- William Calhoon

Coltrider
Henry & Catherine Overshiner 26 Aug 1807; min- William King

Coly
Alexander & Sarah Smith 7 Jan 1834; min- Samuel Kennerly- publication of banns

Compton
George & Sarah Lewis 5 Sep 1794; Minister's return spells name as 'Mary' Affidavit of Sarah's full age b- James Laird min- John McCue- 10Sep1794

Augusta County Marriages -- Man's Name

Conal
　Francis & Catherine Lohr 8 Oct 1837; min- John A Steele
Conklin
　George H & Mary Brown 27 Dec 1842; min- James Bunting
Connally
　Arthur & Elizabeth Levingston 6 Jan 1787; b- James Levingston
Connelly
　Alexander & Nancy Jackson 3 Jan 1801; Margaret?' d -----
　　Jackson, dec. John Walker swears that Nancy lived with him
　　for eight years since she was fourteen b- John Walker min-
　　Daniel Garber- 5Jan1801
　Arthur & Jane Dale 23 Nov 1785; b- William Johnston d
　　John min- John Brown- 6Dec1785
　Arthur & Hetty Smith 27 Aug 1818; min- William King
　David & Mary Strain 4 Dec 1799; Mary (of age) d James
　　Strain, dec. b- John Strain
Conner
　James & Sarah Philips 3 Aug 1802; 'James Coiner'? min-
　　William Wilson- 3Aug1802
　Thomas & Elizabeth Barnet 29 Apr 1813; min- Thomas Bourne
Connor
　John & Catharine Sheets 2 Dec 1831; min- William Wilson
Connoway
　James S & Betsey Rinehart 19 Jan 1815; min- William King
Conrod
　David & Elizabeth Lamb 5 Nov 1811; min- William King
Cook
　Jacob & Barbary Hull 29 Dec 1795; d Francis b- Francis Hull
　John & Diannah Deary 6 Aug 1829; min- William Wilson
　Thomas & Elizabeth Shaver 5 Oct 1843; min- Henry Wetzel
Cooke
　John & Elizabeth Thomas 7 Apr 1812; min- William King
　William D & Lucy Ann Waddell 27 Sep 1834; min- William Calhoon
Cooper
　Ezekiel & Mary King 28 Apr 1790; d John, who consents
　　wit- Wm Anderson & Isaac White & Wm Bratton b- John Didell
　　& Wm Anderson min- William Wilson- 29Apr1790
　Ezekiel & Margaret Leonard 26 Oct 1826; min- John A Gore
　Henry & Sarah Dickey 5 Aug 1804; min- William King
　Isham & Jinney Lewis 24 Oct 1816; min- Wright Burgess
　James & Polly Barnett 16 Mar 1813; min- William King
　James & Eliza Ott 31 May 1838; min- John C Hensell
　John & Mary Bickle 31 Jan 1801; widow b- Thomas Bell
　　min- William King- 1Feb1801
　John & Elizabeth Coursey 30 Jun 1814; min- John McCue
　John & Polly Craig 22 Sep 1808; min- Joseph Reid
　John & Margaret Edde 16 Apr 1791; d John, of Cowpasture,
　　who consents b- I Beal
　John & Sarah Graham 10 Sep 1793; 'Robert Cooper?'
　　Affidavit of Sarah's full age b- John Lockridge no
　　minister listed; clerk's memorandum cites ceremony date as
　　12Sep1793

Augusta County Marriages -- Man's Name

Cooper (cont.)
  John & Eleanor Wallace 21 May 1832; min- James Kerr
  Joseph & Susanna Harris 30 Dec 1802; min- James Harper- 30Dec1802
  Robert & Martha Steel 2 Oct 1789; Minister's return spells name as 'Steele' b- Robert McCullough min- John Brown- 6Oct1789
  Thomas & Elizabeth Wilson 5 Mar 1798; d Robert b- James McKemy & Robert Wilson min- William Wilson- 7Mar1798
  William T & Mary M Whitesell 5 Jul 1838; min- Thomas Wheeler
  William & Mary Steele McCutchen 25 Nov 1833; min- Francis McFarland

Copehaver
  John & Peggy Varner 29 Jul 1789; b- Henry Verner

Copeland
  Willis & Jane Ong 7 Nov 1795; Minister's return spells names as 'Wellcome Copland and Jane Ongg' widow of Isaac Jane gives her own consent dated Staunton b- William Throckmorton min- Archibald Scott- 6Nov1795

Corby
  Bestor B & Elizabeth Swink 21 Dec 1840; min- John C Hensell- publication of banns
  Jabin B & Elenor McCutchen 16 Jan 1840; min- John C Hansell-publication of banns
  Robert & Jane McCamey 14 May 1820; min- John Hendren
  William & Margaret McKemy 18 Oct 1797; d John McKemy, dec. b- Robert Harris

Corry
  James & Mary Brooking 18 Feb 1795; Minister's return spells name as 'Curry' d Charles Brooking & Ann Brooking who consent test- Robert Curry s Samuel Corry who consents b- William Curry min- William Wilson- 19Feb1795

Coruthers
  John & Mary Elliott 14 Aug 1795; Mary (of age) d William Elliott, dec. b- John Gordan

Cosley
  Dabney & Fanny Tapp 5 Mar 1801; d Vincent b- Vincent Tapp

Coulter
  Michael & ----- ----- 21 May 1763; license only

Coursey
  James & Elizabeth Palmer 31 May 1831; min- Francis McFarland
  John & Polly Donahe 29 Dec 1814; min- William Wilson
  Thomas C & Martha Adline Rankin 20 Sep 1847; min- John L Blakemore

Cowan
  Andrew B & Mary A E Hamilton 23 Aug 1838; min- William Calhoon
  Joseph & Mary Griffin 26 Sep 1799; Mary (of age) b- Thomas Barry

Cowdon
  Samuel & ----- ----- 25 Feb 1762; license only

Augusta County Marriages -- Man's Name

Cowger
  Michael & Catherine Owie 18 Mar 1788; b- Stophel Owie
Cox
  Francis & Rachel Bealy 23 Aug 1804; min- William Wilson
  George & Catharine Bushong 7 Feb 1839; min- John C Hensell
  George & Catherine Dull 31 Jan 1828; min- James Morrison
  George & Mary Fulwider 18 Jun 1846; min- J C Hensell
  George & Nancy Starks 9 Dec 1834; min- Conrad Speece
  Jackson & Eliza Ann Teaford 10 Aug 1844; min- D F Bittle
  Samuel & Hetty Croft 23 Jun 1837; min- Fred D Goodwin
  William & Catharine Faidley 5 Mar 1834; min- Augustus Babb
  William & Amanda Palmer 1 Dec 1836; min- N B Brown-
    publication of banns
Coyner
  Jacob & Elizabeth Coyner 21 Dec 1815; min- John McCue
  Robert & Elizabeth Coyner 25 Dec 1841; min- John A Van
    Lear- publication of banns
Craig
  George & Elizabeth Evans 16 Dec 1790; 'Betsy' d Griffin
    b- James Craig min- William Wilson- 19Dec1790
  George & Kitty Kennerly - Feb 1792; d James b- A Mustoe
    min- John McCune- 1Mar1792
  James (Jr) & Elizabeth Crawford 6 May 1813; min- Thomas
    Bourne
  James & ----- ----- 18 Aug 1772; license only
  James & Susan Bell 4 Jun 1816; min- Conrad Speece, Jr
  James & Ann Gilkeson 26 Jan 1800; d Hugh Archibald Dixon
    swears James of age b- Hugh Gilkeson min- John McCue-
    29Jan1801
  James & Nancy Jones 6 Aug 1822; min- Michael Meyerhoeffer
  James & Elizabeth Mills 9 Mar 1804; min- William Wilson
  James & Elizabeth Shields 13 Mar 1792; d Robert b- Robert
    Shields min- John Montgomery- 20Mar1792
  John & ----- ----- 3 Apr 1771; license only
  John & Sarah Burton 17 Jul 1787; b- John Burton min-
    William Wilson- 17Jul1787
  John & Sally Patterson 23 Jun 1795; d James who consents
    test- William Patterson & William Beard b- William
    Patterson min- John McCue- 24Jun1795
  John & Mary Ann Stickley 19 Dec 1833; min- Samuel Kennerly
  John & Susan Wiseman 11 Oct 1828; min- James Morrison
  Samuel & Elizabeth Bratton 6 Feb 1821; min- John D Ewin
  William & Margaret Shields 23 Aug 1800; d Robert b-
    Robert Shields
Craine
  John & Isabella Grant 15 Nov 1788; b- James Lyle Jr
    Permission from Bull Pasture by Thomas Green & Eleander
    McQuin attesting that they are free people and can marry
Cramer
  Samuel & Sally King 15 Jun 1809; min- William Calhoon
Crane
  John & Nancy Papper 10 Feb 1790; Minister's return spells
    name as 'Pepper' b- James Pepper wit- Samuel Merrit min-
    John Montgomery- 11Feb1790

Augusta County Marriages -- Man's Name

Craun
George & Margaret Swisher 10 Sep 1845; min- P Shickel
Isaac & Sarah Piper 6 Jul 1826; min- William Monroe

Cravens
Joseph & Polly Nickel 26 Nov 1790; Minister's return spells name as 'Nickle' d John, who consents wit- Wm Lang & W Chambers b- W Chambers min- Benjamin Irvin- 30Nov1790

Crawford
Alexander & Mary Hottle 3 Aug 1830; min- William Calhoon
Alexander & Rachel Lessley 20 Feb 1793; 'Lesley?' con- William Bell affidavit of Rachel's full age b- Phillip Dyer no minister listed; clerk's memorandum cites ceremony date as 21Feb1793
Andrew & Rachel Hunter 22 Aug 1799; d William who consents & Mary Hunter who consents test- William Crawford Andrew of age b- William Benson
Benjamin & Magdelin Cochran 20 Oct 1829; min- John Hendren
George & Nancey Clemens 9 Sep 1812; min- William Wilson
George & Nancy Winters 22 Jun 1789; b- Robert Gamble min- Benjamin Erwin- 23Jun1789
Hugh John & Caroline Sidney Sowers 20 Aug 1841; min- S J Love
Hugh & Elizabeth Dickenson 25 May 1820; min- William Wilson
James E & Ellen Welch 19 Apr 1831; min- William Calhoon
James & ----- ----- 30 Oct 1762; license only
James & Margaret Crawford 12 Apr 1823; min- Conrad Speece
James & Mary Crawford 27 Dec 1786; b- George Crawford wit- ----- Urquhart min- Archibald Scott- 18Mar1786 min- Archibald Scott- 30Dec1786
James & Nancy Sawyers 28 Jan 1797; d James Sawyers, dec. con- Hannah Sawyers test- John Thompson b- Thomas Sawyers min- Archibald Scott- 31Jan1797
John & Rebecca Allen 5 Jul 1791; d James, who consents wit- David Hanna & Daniel Early b- James Allen min- John McCune- 5Jul1791
John & Margaret Bell 21 Jan 1819; min- Conrad Speece, Jr
John & Sally Newman 11 Feb 1797; widower Sally (of age) d Leavy b- Joshua Parry min- Archibald Scott- 24Feb1797
Robert & Anne Allen 9 Jan 1787; b- Andrew Anderson certificate by William Craig min- William Wilson- 10Jan1788
Samuel & Elizabeth Craig 9 Oct 1790; d Margaret, who consents wit- Alexander & James Craig b- William Crawford min- Archibald Scott- 12Oct1790
Samuel & Nancy Wilson 21 May 1805; min- Benjamin Irwin
Thomas P & Mary Ann Sellers 30 Mar 1848; min- George H Martin
William B & Nancy J Coalter 17 May 1849; min- B M Smith
William & Eliza A Bell 8 Mar 1832; min- William Calhoon
William & Peggy Bratton 19 Dec 1805; min- John Montgomery
William & Martha Cooper 16 Jun 1786; min- Samuel Shannon- 16Jun1786

Crawn
Jacob & Mary Lamb 12 May 1840; min- John A Van Lear

Augusta County Marriages -- Man's Name

Creek
  Jacob & Barbara Deary 28 Mar 1797; d Ustena b- Jacob Deary
Creiner
  William & Elizabeth Argenbright 14 Jan 1802; d Augustine
    b- John Argenbright
Cress
  Thomas & Catharine Cullen 2 Oct 1834; min- William Scull
Cribbins
  Patrick & Anna Cawthron 4 Aug 1840; min- J J Reimensnyder
Crick
  Jacob & Rosanna Byers 17 Dec 1829; min- James Morrison
  John & Ann C Clemer 9 Feb 1826; min- James Morrison
Crickenbarger
  Peter & Elizabeth M Huff 29 Aug 1841; min- Samuel Wagner
Crigler
  Thomas B & Sarah R Deal 25 Jul 1839; min- Samuel Wagner
Crist
  Abraham & Betsy Golladay 21 Nov 1822; min- John Brown
  Andrew & Barbara Reif 31 Jan 1795; d John b- John Reif
  Daniel & Nancy Burkett 18 Jun 1802; min- William King-
    18Jun1802
  Henry & Sarah Calbreath 10 Oct 1848; min- Robert L Dabney
  Jacob & Polly S McCormick 10 Feb 1825; min- Francis
    McFarland
  Jacob & Lydia Mowry 14 Apr 1800; d Lewis b- Lewis Mowry
    ('Maurer?') min- William Wilson- 14Apr1800
  James & Peggy Crossin 6 Jan 1820; min- Luke Collins
  John & Margret Fauver 14 Jun 1837; min- James Paine
  John & Mary Miller 15 Jan 1807; min- William McPheeters
Criswell
  James & Peggy Cargo 13 Dec 1794; Minister's return spells
    name as 'Chriswell and Mary Carge' b- Jacob Kinney min-
    John McCue- 24Dec1794
Crobarger
  John & Harriet G Hays 17 Nov 1845; min- T T Castleman
Croft
  Jacob & Lidda Browers 7 Jan 1833; min- Abraham Garber-
    publication of banns
  Samuel & Hannah Brower 26 Oct 1825; min- Josiah Cole
Cromer
  Martin & Elizabeth J Golladay 14 Nov 1848; min- W Lee
    Spotswood
  William & Catherine Nebergall 22 May 1800; Minister's
    return spells name as 'Cronser and Nebergale' d Jacob b-
    Jacob Nebergall min- William Wilson- 25May1800
Cromwell
  Oliver & Margaret Roop 16 Nov 1829; min- John Hendren
Crone
  Caleb & Eveline H Woodward 2 Jan 1849; min- John Bowen
  George & Molly Ailor 1 May 1797; (Crown?) Molly (of age)
    d Anthony b- Lawrence Crone & Paul Hinckle
  George & Catherine Shuey 22 Apr 1817; min- William King
  Henry & Phebe Tharp 9 Apr 1806; min- William Wilson
  Levi & Margaret Orebough 16 Jan 1840; min- A B McCorkle

Augusta County Marriages -- Man's Name

Crone (cont.)
Michael & Catharine Woods 1 Nov 1816; min- William King
Crookshanks
John & Mary Cloverfield 27 Aug 1787; b- John Kirk min- Archibald Scott- 30Aug1787
Crosby
Alexander & Mary Dunlap 10 Jun 1813; min- William King
Amos & Mary Anderson 20 Mar 1813; min- William King
George & Patsy Anderson 28 Dec 1824; min- Josiah Cole
George & Margaret Armstrong 17 Jun 1847; min- Stephen Hildebrand
George & Hannah Jones 27 Mar 1817; min- William King
George & Catherine Silling 24 May 1814; min- William King
James & Ann Lucas 2 Feb 1826; min- Francis McFarland
Joshua & Catherine Jones 12 Apr 1827; min- William Wilson
William & Sarah Ann Moyers 25 May 1848; min- J McKendree Reiley
Crosen
Richard & Elizabeth Hartigan 16 Aug 1832; min- James Morrison
Cross
Gabriel & Jane Wood 11 Dec 1838; min- Robert Beers
James & Jane Hunter 19 Nov 1835; min- Francis A C Mills
Jeremiah & Eliza Hunter 15 Apr 1841; min- James Gamble
Jeremiah & Elizabeth Hunter 16 Mar 1809; min- William King
Thomas & Amanda J Cox 27 May 1845; min- E G Jamison
Thomas & Elizabeth Cross 12 Oct 1834; min- George Hildt
Crouse
John & Mary Cail 4 Jul 1816; min- William King
John & Catherine Hill 18 Oct 1814; min- William King
William F & Mary Ann Root 1 Apr 1848; min- W T Richardson
Croushorn
Nicholas & Mary Ann Radner 17 Jan 1839; min- John J Reimensnyder
Crow
Caleb & Susannah Patterson 21 Feb 1837; min- B N Brown
John & Elizabeth Seldomridge 10 Mar 1814; min- William King
Thomas (Jr) & Nancy Donally 13 Mar 1789; d Charles & Mary, who consent wit- John Wayt & Stephen Smith b- Alexander Lewis
William & ----- ----- - Apr 1761; license only
Crowbarger
Henry L & Nancy A Shields 9 Apr 1835; min- Cornelius Gates
Crown
Lawrence & Mary Ailer 3 Jan 1795; 'Ailor'? b- John Rapp min- William Wilson- 6Jan1795
Crum
John & Margaret Ann Orebaugh 28 Jun 1842; min- Henry Wetzel
Crumpacker
Cyrus & Elizabeth Leedy 17 Mar 1825; min- Abraham Garber- publication of banns
Cullen
George B & Martha Ann Terrill 26 Nov 1846; min- S Wagner
Jeremiah W & Margaret Blair 28 Mar 1835; min- William A Coffin

Augusta County Marriages -- Man's Name

Cullen (cont.)
John & Susan Barnhart 27 Jan 1814; min- Thomas Bourne
William & Catharine Barnhart 7 Nov 1816; min- John McCue

Culton
James B & Mary E Gully 25 Sep 1849; min- William T Richardson
Joseph & Jane Moffett 29 Mar 1796; Minister's return spells name as 'Cullen' d James b- James Moffett min- Archibald Scott- 21Mar1796
Robert & Rebecca McPheeters 27 Jun 1796; Minister's return spells name as 'Cullen' d Alexander b- Alexander McPheeters min- Archibald Scott- 31Mar1796

Cummins
Alexander & Abigail Kelsey 18 Apr 1789; widow b- William Knowles
John & Elizabeth Cummins 25 Sep 1803; min- Philip Kennerly
John & Anne McIntire 24 Jul 1811; widower min- John Bell

Cundiff
James & Fanny Phillips 8 Dec 1809; min- William King

Cunningham
James L & Sarah T Doake 3 Mar 1825; min- Francis McFarland
James & ----- ----- 24 May 1765; license only
John & Rachel Kirk 6 Feb 1796; d John b- John Kirk min- Archibald Scott- 9Feb1796
Robert & Jane Kirk 12 Mar 1812; min- William Calhoon
Samuel & Polly Troxel 15 Jun 1826; min- James Morrison
Walter & ----- ----- 4 Jul 1774; license only
William & Agness Young 5 Apr 1825; min- William W Calhoun

Cup
Henry & Susana Baker - Jan 1806; min- John Brown
Valentine & Mary Falls 21 Dec 1793; 'Valentine Crop?'d George b- George Falls no minister listed; clerk's memorandum cites ceremony date as Jan1794

Cupp
Daniel & Elizabeth Blacker - Jan 1807; min- John Brown
Joshua & Catharine Karicofe 12 Aug 1841; min- J A Van Lear
Simeon & Mary Ann Rusmisel 19 Oct 1848; min- George H Martin
Simon & Margaret Karicofe 29 Aug 1838; min- John A Van Lear

Cups
George & Dorothy Runkle 6 Jul 1789; b- Samuel Runkle
Henry & Frances Switzer 13 Feb 1834; min- William Wilson

Curby
Obediah & Nancy Gardner 1 Aug 1844; min- Samuel Wagner- publication of banns

Curren
David & Julian Sullivan 20 Dec 1827; min- Joseph Smith

Curry
Alexander & Elizabeth Curry 6 Oct 1795; Elizabeth (of age) d William b- Benjamin Curry no minister listed; clerk's memorandum cites ceremony date as 9Oct1795
Alexander & Nancy Forsythe 16 Nov 1814; min- William King
Benjamin A & Rebecca G Bell 21 Jan 1842; min- John A Van Lear

Augusta County Marriages -- Man's Name

Curry (cont.)
Benjamin & Polly Snyder   20 Dec 1827;   min- John Hendren
Isaiah & Catherine Trump   24 Jan 1803;   min- William King
James (Jr) & Jane Erwin   3 Feb 1801;   d Edward   b- Edward Erwin   min- Daniel Garber- 5Feb1801
James H & Rebecca Snyder   10 May 1830;   min- Conrad Speece
James R & Martha Jones   29 Mar 1828;   min- John Hendren
James & ----- -----   3 Apr 1772;   license only
James & Rebecca Anderson   1 Jun 1826;   min- John Hendren
James & Sally Curry   8 Oct 1821;   min- John Hendren
James & Mary Erwin   27 Mar 1786;   min- William Wilson- 27Mar1786
James & Margaret Francis   21 Oct 1788;   b- James McKenny   min- Benjamin Erwin- 28Oct1788
John & Polly Curry   28 Jun 1819;   min- John Hendren
John & Frances E Moore   2 Jan 1845;   min- D F Bittle
Nenian & ----- -----   - Jul 1761;   license only
Reuben & Prudence Fifer   5 Sep 1823;   min- John Hendren
Robert & Martha Kennedy   15 Apr 1788;   Minister's return spells name as 'Martha Kenedy'   b- John Stuart   min- William Wilson- 15Apr1788
Robert & Sarah Young   19 Mar 1791;   d Robert, who consents   wit- Andrew & Robert Young   b- Robert Young   min- William Wilson- 22Apr1791
Samuel & Margaret Curry   26 May 1802;   min- Benjamin Irwin- 26May1802
Samuel & Mary Glenn   25 Mar 1800;   Minister's return spells name as 'Glen'   Mary (of age)   d George   b- Hugh Glenn   min- William Wilson- 3Apr1800
Thomas & Eleanor Zwitchel   - Sep 1806;   min- John Brown
William C & Elizabeth Forsythe   25 Aug 1818;   min- William King

Cushingberry
Francis & Elizabeth Teabo   31 Oct 1833;   min- George Hildt

Dacke
Henry & Gerdrant Price   2 May 1785;   d Daniel   b- Gasper Snider   wit- James Preis

Daft
James & Lovey Taylor   24 Oct 1811;   min- John McCue

Daggey
Jacob & Elizabeth Michael   16 Nov 1790;   d Frederick Michael, who consents   b- Richard Roach   wit- Terrence Swiney

Daggy
Adam & May Croom   23 May 1839;   min- George Huffman
Christian & Ann Huffer   18 Jan 1847;   min- George Huffman
Jacob & Eleanor Lockridge   29 Oct 1818;   min- William Calhoon
Jacob & Hana Syple   30 Oct 1816;   min- G H Riemenschneider
John & Catherine Troughrobaugh   20 May 1794;   b- Nicholas Troughrobaugh
Michael & Sybill Syple   21 Dec 1818;   min- G H Riemenschneider

Dalton
William & Susana Harberger   3 Aug 1795;   d Frederick   b- Frederick Harbarger

Augusta County Marriages -- Man's Name

Dameron
  George & Sarah Jourdan 17 Aug 1838; min- George A Leopard
Dane
  Henry & Magdaline Aldoffer 25 Jul 1793; min- William
    Wilson- 25Jul1793
Daniels
  John & Nancy Brown 24 Jan 1825; min- John Hendren
Dannell
  Joseph & Derthy Vancent 24 Sep 1804; min- William King
Danner
  George & Margaret Wilson 11 Aug 1798; Margaret (of age) d
    James b- Henry Amon min- William Wilson- 16Aug1798
  Solomon & Elizabeth Husk 23 Mar 1801; Minister's return
    spells name as 'Hink' s Solomon who consents test- George
    Danner & Leonard Danner b- John Towell min- John McCue-
    23Mar1801
Danser
  Joseph & Susannah Beard 7 Dec 1811; min- G H
    Riemenschneider
Darst
  John & Polly Tarbert 9 Jan 1823; min- A B Davidson
Daugherty
  Hugh & Polly Hanger 16 Apr 1827; min- James Morrison
  Hugh & Jane Young 15 Sep 1808; min- William McPheeters
  John & Elizabeth Byers 10 Oct 1798; d David b- David Byers
David
  William & Mary F Harris 25 Dec 1839; min- John J
    Reimensnyder
Davidson
  Alexander B & Sarah Long 23 Mar 1838; min- John A Steele
Davies
  James & Nancy Haring 8 Jun 1808; min- William Wilson
  Joseph & Mary Ann Estill 17 Oct 1786; Davis? b- Zachary
    Estill wit- Hugh Campbell min- Archibald Scott- 15Oct1786
Davis
  Archibald & Nancy A Lawrence 1 Apr 1841; min- Alfred G
    Chenowith
  Benjamin & Mary Ellen Despar 1 Feb 1849; min- D W Arnold
  Braxton & Betsy Craig 31 Jan 1822; min- James C Willson
  Calvin & Barbara Gillaspie 25 Aug 1842; min- F D Goodwin
  David H & Malinda Rough 10 Mar 1840; min- John C Hansell
  David W & Hanah Bush 23 Feb 1809; min- John McCue
  Henry StJ. & Catharine A Peer 23 Feb 1848; min- John Bowen
  Jacob & Susan Myers 26 Jan 1809; min- William McPheeters
  James F & Eliza Dinkle 28 Jul 1848; min- D W Arnold
  James M & Elizabeth Reese 20 Sep 1845; min- S Wagner
  James P & Charlotte Steel 21 Jul 1836; min- James Paine
  James W & Rebecca Johnson 14 Mar 1839; min- Frederick D
    Goodwin
  James & ----- ----- 21 Nov 1764; license only
  James & Deborah Miller 31 Dec 1787; 'Millar'? d Abraham
    b- Cornelius Ruddle min- Archibald Scott- 3Jan1786(sic)
  Jeremiah & Rosannah Myers 8 Dec 1808; min- William
    McPheeters

Davis (cont.)
  Jesse & Ann Gibson 9 Oct 1827; min- Conrad Speece
  John B & Ann Caroline Seig 20 Apr 1848; 'Rev.' John B
    min- P Shickel
  Joseph & Mary Sowers - Nov 1818; min- John Brown
  Samuel J & Mildred Ann Smith 2 Sep 1847; min- John Bowen
  Thomas & ----- ----- - --- 179-; b- John Crookshank
  William L & Susan Heaton 25 May 1847; min- D W Arnold
  William & ----- ----- - Mar 1760; license only
  William & Anis Caldwell 4 Apr 1791; William the father of
    the late Walter Davis d William b- John Caldwell marriage
    sent to clerk by Samuel Borwn and dated 5Apr1791
  William & Mary Homes 24 Jul 1789; Minister's return spells
    name as 'Holms' d Joseph, who consents b- John Craig wit-
    John Craig & George Davis min- William Wilson- 24Jul1789
  William & Sophia Lovell 24 Apr 1834; min- Joseph Spriggs
  William & Sally Vanlear 30 Nov 1813; min- Thomas Bourne
Davison
  James & Sarah Dinnison 4 Jul 1785; min- Samuel Shannon-
    4Jul1785
  John W & Jane Scott 29 May 1828; min- William Calhoon
  John & ----- ----- 16 Jan 1763; license only
Dawson
  Hamden & Selina M Bagby 27 May 1847; min- T T Castleman
Day
  Isaac W & Elizabeth Brice 11 Jun 1800; Elizabeth 28 Isaac
    belongs to Capt. Grayson's Company and over 21 according to
    Richard Rowland min- William King- 11Jun1800
  Jacob & Mary Neighbourgall 22 Jan 1802; d Jacob s George
    who consents test- William Cromer, John Cromer, & Jacob
    Livergall b- Jacob Neighbourgall
  John & Nancy Freeland 17 Nov 1795; Nancy (of age) b-
    Andrew Jordan
  John & Elizabeth Martin 8 Jan 1800; d David Martin, dec.
    b- William Allison John swears he is of age min- William
    Wilson- 9Jan1800
Deal
  George M & Rebecca Koiner 4 Feb 1836; min- William Scull
  Henry J & Elizabeth Spitler 2 Apr 1840; min- Jacob Bachtel
  John & Eleanor Imboden 13 Sep 1810; min- William King
Dean
  John & ----- ----- 26 Dec 1759; license only
Deary
  Hiram & Margaret Rutledge 3 May 1831; min- Samuel Kennerly
  John & Jenny McMullin 30 Oct 1799; d Michael McMullin b-
    Chesley Kinney
Decker
  Andrew J & Mary Grooms 1 Apr 1840; min- Samuel Wagner
Decrisen
  John & Charlotte Moses 10 Jun 1813; min- William King
Dedamore
  Jacob & Phebe Shaver 26 Jul 1827; min- John Hendren

Augusta County Marriages -- Man's Name

Deeds
  George & Mary Smith 10 May 1788; b- Ludwick Smith min- William Wilson- 11May1788
Deemster
  Gilbert & Betsy Wright 30 Nov 1826; min- William W Calhoun
Deitz
  William & Jane Vauchob 20 Jul 1796; Minister's return spells name as 'William Dietz & Jane Vachub' d Robert b- Robert Wahob min- John Montgomery- 26Jul1796
Delman
  Daniel & Elizabeth Spitler 28 Jul 1799; min- Daniel Garber- 28Jul1799
Delter
  Joseph & Margaret Shultz 13 Oct 1829; min- James Morrison
Delzell
  James & Martha Fulton 16 Nov 1796; d Hugh who consents test- Archibald Murray b- Robert Fulton
Demasters
  Benjamin & Susan Zahn 25 Feb 1840; min- D F Bittle
  Nicholas & Mary Ann Bridge 23 Jun 1837; min- E Joshua Webb
Denison
  Samuel & Nancy Parry 18 Jun 1828; min- John Hendren
Denizen
  John & Sarah Landes 10 Dec 1840; min- J J Reimensnyder
Denney
  Thomas & Polly Hedebough 16 Jan 1806; min- John Emmill
Dennison
  Daniel & Nancy McFall 30 Jun 1813; min- William Wilson
  John (Jr) & Hannah Henderson 23 May 1800; d Jones Henderson b- John Dennison Sr & James Henderson
  John & Martha Parris 27 Jun 1811; min- William Calhoon
  Samuel & Betsy Parris 10 Oct 1816; min- William Calhoon
  Washington H & Rebecca Geating - Dec 1826; min- Joseph Smith
Depriest
  John W & Elizabeth Coffman 21 Mar 1850; min- John Garber
  Robert & Jemima Ramsay 1 Oct 1816; min- William King
Desper
  James & Sarah Trout 12 Jul 1826; min- William Wilson
  John A & Sallie Kesterson 22 Feb 1849; min- J McKendree Reiley
Detamore
  Jacob & Susannah Howdasher 28 Sep 1846; min- P Shickel
Detrick
  Jacob & Mary Anderson 21 Dec 1828; min- William Wilson
  William F & Sarah Elizabeth Roller 18 Mar 1849; min- George Huffman
Devenbough
  John & Elizabeth Hoopman 23 Feb 1804; min- William King
Devericks
  John & Mary Peples 24 Apr 1787; Minister's return spells name as 'Peebles' min- Samuel Shannon- 24Apr1787

Augusta County Marriages -- Man's Name

Deverix
  John & Mary Peebles 16 Apr 1787; d John wit- John Graham
    & William Stuart b- Thomas Deverix
Dice
  George & Jane Hawpe 17 Feb 1820; min- James Morrison
  Jacob & Sarah Creek 8 Aug 1829; min- James Morrison
  William & Margret Seldomredg 26 Dec 1811; min- William King
Dickenson
  Robert & Julia Ann Craig 12 Sep 1832; min- Samuel Kennerly
Dickinson
  John & ----- ----- 7 Nov 1764; license only
Dickson
  John & ----- ----- 15 Jun 1763; license only
  Michael & Janetta M Ramsay 31 Aug 1821; min- John D Ewin
  Richard & Elizabeth Curry 27 Mar 1828; min- John Hendren
  Thomas & Elizabeth Journal 24 Dec 1818; min- Conrad
    Speece, Jr
Diddle
  David & Catharine Pue 5 Jan 1815; min- John McCue
  John & Charity King 29 Dec 1814; min- John McCue
  William & Sally Stuart 5 Dec 1805; min- John McCue
Dill
  Benjamin & Catherine Bailor 9 Mar 1801; Minister's return
    spells name as 'Dile and Baylor' d Jacob b- Jacob Bailor
    min- William King- 12Mar1801
Dillan
  James & Peggy Risk 29 Oct 1801; Minister's return spells
    name as 'Dillen' 'Margaret' d William Sarah Guffie, of
    lawful age and Augusta resident, swears Peggy of age b-
    Govey Stuart min- William King- 29Oct1801
  Peter D & Amanda Porter 29 Jan 1850; min- William T
    Richardson
Dinkle
  John & Sarah Hanna 24 Jan 1849; min- John A Van Lear
  Lewis & Margaret S Hottle 18 Oct 1838; min- John A Van Lear
Dinsmore
  Samuel & Elizabeth Allen 29 Aug 1799; d Ebenezer b-
    Ebenezer Allen min- William King- 27Aug1799
Dinwiddie
  James & Ellenor Lockridge 16 Aug 1785; d Andrew
Dixon
  Andrew & Elizabeth Wilson 19 Mar 1799; widow of Thomas b-
    George Borrel & John Jones s Martin (Morton) Dixon signed
    - 'George Burwell' min- William King- 19Mar1799
  Archibald & ----- ----- 20 Aug 1772; license only
  Archibald & Sally Fisher 13 Mar 1810; min- William King
  David & Rachel Slagle 26 Feb 1830; min- William Wilson
  James & Sally Miller 19 Jul 1814; min- William Wilson
  John (Jr) & Isabella Patterson 24 Dec 1794; d Thomas b-
    John Dixon Sr min- William Wilson- 24Dec1794
  John & Polly Mowry 25 May 1804; min- William King
  John & Rebecca Trotter 22 May 1810; min- William Wilson
  Martin & Margaret McKnight 14 Nov 1785; (McNight?) b-
    William Burgess, father in law of Margaret min- Archibald
    Scott- 15Nov1785

Augusta County Marriages -- Man's Name

Doack
  Robert & ----- ----- 28 Mar 1774; license only
Doage
  David & ----- ----- 30 Oct 1762; license only
Doak
  David & Nancy Best 11 Feb 1812; min- John McCue
  John & Isabella Mitchell 16 Dec 1807; min- William McPheeters
Dodson
  William & Peggy Wiekle 9 Jun 1813; bond- 29Jun1813(sic) min- William Cravens
Dohm
  Jacob & Elizabeth Laywell 24 Jun 1801; widow of Abraham b- Robert McClenachan
  John & Jane Graves 20 Jun 1806; min- William King
  Joseph & Mary Summers 8 Apr 1797; d John b- John Summers
Dold
  Addison & Angelina M Frazier 30 Jul 1834; min- John Hendren
Dolino
  Jacob & Elizabeth Sewall 24 Jun 1801; min- William King- 24Jun1801
Dolton
  James & Mary Jane McFall 4 Oct 1849; min- Peter Miller
Donaghe
  Andrew & Sarah Groves 24 Nov 1823; min- John Hendren
  Hugh & Elizabeth McMahon 7 Mar 1791; d Debora, who consents wit- William Richardson b- James McGongal min- William Wilson- 8Mar1791
  Hugh & Ann Usher 19 Aug 1795; d Robert b- Archibald Stuart min- William Wilson- 21Aug1795
  Samuel & Mary Smith 9 Mar 1810; min- William King
  William & Rebecca Garvin 16 Jan 1810; min- William Calhoon
  William & Catherine Puffinbarger 23 Aug 1821; min- Gerard Morgan
Donaho
  James & Betsey Smith 15 Aug 1816; min- William King
  William & Sarah Sheets 4 Dec 1828; min- John Hendren
Donahugh
  John & Susanna Switzer 14 Jun 1849; min- Jacob Bare
Donaldson
  John & Susanna Kerr 11 Jun 1805; min- John McCue
  Robert & Charity Weaver 9 Jun 1831; min- Francis McFarland
  William & Elizabeth Dold 22 May 1795; d Philip b- Philip Dold min- John McCue- 26May1795
  William & Barbara Walker 6 Sep 1792; wrd of Elizabeth Walker, who consents wit- Robert & John Reed, Hugh & Elizabeth Donaghe, Wm McMahon b- Robert Reed min- William Wilson- 6Sep1792
Donaphan
  Cornelious & Peggy Griffith 26 Oct 1807; min- William King
Donavan
  Dennis & Betsy Cofney 30 Apr 1787; Minister's return spells name as 'Dannavan and Betty Cofney' b- James McGonagal min- William Wilson- 30Apr1787

Augusta County Marriages -- Man's Name

Donavin
  Daniel & Elizabeth Woods 19 Aug 1794; Affidavit as to
    Elizabeth's full age b- Jacob Woods
Donnell
  William & Sarah Austin Reynolds 4 Dec 1833; min- William G
    Jackson
Donnelly
  Andrew & ----- ----- 10 Sep 1766; license only
Donoho
  Thomas & Jane Amanda Almonroade 11 Sep 1845; min- J C
    Hensell
Donovan
  Jeremiah & Elizabeth Dunbar 29 Sep 1790; d Francis, who
    consents wit- William Dunbar & Leroy Newman min- Archibald
    Scott- 16Oct1790
Doom
  George & Sarah Croft 5 May 1835; min- Robert M Lipscomb
  Henry & Elizabeth Cook 31 Jan 1850; min- William T
    Richardson
  Henry & Susan Hanke 14 Aug 1842; min- John C Hensell-
    publication of banns
  Jacob (Jr) & Margaret Lohr 8 Feb 1842; min- P E Stevenson
  John & Sophia Walch 5 Dec 1809; min- William King
  Madison & Peggy McAlear 1 Dec 1836; min- B N Brown
Dooms
  John & Mary Ann Freed 20 Nov 1845; min- S Wagner
Dorman
  David & Catharine Shindler 16 Apr 1817; min- G H
    Riemenschneider
Dougherty
  John & Elizabeth Byers 10 Oct 1796; Elizabeth Burris?
    min- Archibald Scott- 10Oct1796
  John & Agnes Davidson 28 Jul 1790; Minister's return
    spells name as 'Doughady' d John & Sarah, who consent b-
    John Davidson wit- Benjamin Kilborn & James Dougherty
    (return sent by Samuel Brown and dated 31Jul1790)
  William & Mary Bridger 30 Jan 1786; min- Samuel Shannon-
    30Jan1786
Douglas
  Edward & Lavina Meeks 17 Sep 1829; min- Henry S Kepler-
    publication of banns
Douthat
  Robert & Polly Price 26 May 1791; Minister's return spells
    name as 'Dowthat' sis Peter, who consents wit- William
    Austin b- Philip North min- William Wilson- 27May1791
  Robert & Polly Yost 6 Nov 1800; d Henry, sis of Polly (?),
    who swears Polly is of age b- David Greiner
  Thomas & Jean Price 1 Jun 1793; 'Jane?' con- Lewis Price
    (Staunton) wit- Robert Douthat & James Bradshaw min- John
    Brown- 4Jun1793
  William & Anna Lewis 10 Jun 1790; b- Samuel Boys min-
    John Brown- 10Jun1790

Augusta County Marriages -- Man's Name

Dove
  Noah A & Sarah J Ott 18 Jun 1846; min- J C Hensell
Dowling
  Jeremiah & Ann Edgecomb 7 Mar 1795; widow who gives her own consent test-John Bruffey & Margaret Bruffey b- John Bruffey min- John McCue- 12Mar1795
Downey
  Darby & Polley Young 21 Jul 1817; min- Wright Burgess
  Thomas & Mary Robertson 21 Apr 1798; Minister's return spells name as 'Downing' Mary (of age) d William b- Matthew Robertson min- John McCue- 3Apr1798
  William & Ann McPheeters 19 May 1791; d Alexander b- Alexander McPheeters no minister listed; clerk's memorandum cites ceremony date as 24May1791
Doyle
  John W & Josephine Morris 9 Feb 1843; min- F D Goodwin
  Robert & Margaret A Merritt 8 Sep 1836; min- James Morrison
Driskell
  John & Jane Burnett - Aug 1749; license only
Drum
  John & Easther Younkard 26 May 1800; Minister's return omits bride's name b- James Williams min- William King- 26May1800
Drumgold
  Alexander & Ann Balbzell 29 Nov 1809; min- William King
Drummond
  George & Nancy Jordan 20 Dec 1786; widow b- Thomas Davis min- Archibald Scott- 20Dec1786
Dryden
  Thomas H & Manda J Hogsett - Aug 1847; min- Stephen Hildebrand
Dudleston
  Ralph & Catherine Bush 16 Jun 1792; Minister's return spells name as 'Duddleson' d Nicholas b- Nicholas Bush (German) min- John McCue- 19Jun1792
Dudley
  Richard J C & Sarah C Hogshead 26 Mar 1838; min- John Hendren
Duffield
  John & Elizabeth Frame 1 Dec 1790; Minister's return spells names as 'Duffell and Fraim' d David, who consents b- Thomas Duffield wit- Thomas Duffield & Andrew Jordan min- John Montgomery- 9Dec1790
  John & Elizabeth Frame 9 Dec 1790; min- John Montgomery- 9Dec1790
  Thomas & Ann Chesnut 23 Jan 1789; b- John Chesnut, who also consents
Duke
  James & Elizabeth Leopard 7 Jun 1810; min- William King
Dull
  Enos & Sarah Hanger 7 Sep 1843; min- J C Hensell
  Enos & Angeline Stauffer 17 Aug 1848; min- Alonzo P Ludden
  George & Catherine Wiseman 28 Mar 1798; d Peter b- Peter Wiseman

Augusta County Marriages -- Man's Name

Dull (cont.)
  Jacob & Mary Ann Hanger 8 Mar 1832; min- Francis McFarland
  Jacob & Nancy Parks 28 Dec 1826; min- Francis McFarland
  John (Jr) & Elizabeth Higs 7 Mar 1832; min- Francis McFarland
  Michael & Susanah Long 23 Jan 1845; min- Jacob Baer
  Peter & Louisa Bird 15 Mar 1838; min- D F Bittle
  Philip & Catharine Gabhart 7 Apr 1794; d Jacob b- Jacob Gabhart
  William & Margaret Hanger 7 Feb 1837; min- J C Hensell

Dun
  John & Eliza Gilmore - May 1820; min- John Brown

Dunahugh
  Enos & Rosana Wonderlick 7 Oct 1847; min- John Reubush

Dunbar
  Jonathan & Sally Campbell 5 May 1790; Minister's return spells name as 'Peggy Campbell' d James, who consents wit- William Burgess & James Essex b- William Dunbar min- Archibald Scott- 6May1790

Dunlap
  Adam & ----- ----- 29 Dec 1761; license only
  Alexander & Jane Vachub 20 Jun 1791; d John Vachub, who consents wit- Alexander Dod & Joseph Vachub b- William McPheeters min- John Montgomery- 21Jun1791
  Archibald & Margaret Minick 31 Aug 1830; min- Francis McFarland
  Bailey & Sarah Baylor 1 Nov 1825; min- William W Calhoun
  John H & Agnes Philips 23 Feb 1832; min- John Hendren
  John & Darcas Dowell 24 Sep 1802; min- John McCue- 24Sep1802
  Nathaniel & ----- ----- 30 Sep 1765; license only
  Robert & Patsey Graham 10 May 1793; d John who consents test- James Fulton b- Adam Bratton min- John Montgomery- 14May1793
  Robert & Margaret Kerr 29 Oct 1792; 'Kern?' d Robert b- Daniel Kerr no minister listed; clerk's memorandum cites ceremony date as 1Nov1792
  Robert & Eleanor McCutchen 2 Sep 1828; min- Alexander Templeton
  William & ----- ----- 21 Feb 1772; license only
  William & Melvina Curry 9 Nov 1849; min- John Hendren

Dunlop
  John & ----- ----- - May 1761; license only

Dunn
  James M & Mary Ann Peck 19 Aug 1837; min- Stephen Smith

Duval
  John B & Eliza Jane Booz 20 Jan 1848; min- S Hildebrand

Dyer
  Abner & Hannah Lessley 7 Dec 1789; sis of Thomas Lessley, who also gives surety
  William & Grizel McKee 2 Mar 1803; min- William King

Eagan
  Sampson & Rebecca Yost 1 Jun 1796; d Henry b- Henry Yost min- John McCue- 22Jun1796

Augusta County Marriages -- Man's Name

Eagle
Christian & Christina Cook - Oct 1800; min- John Brown
Christian & Jane Cook 20 Oct 1800; Signed Christian Ekel, Paulus Koch & Christian Ekell, the latter two giving surety
Henry & Magdalena Eagle 20 Jun 1799; d Christian b- Christian Eagle
Henry & Susanna Lemmy 24 Jul 1807; min- William King
John B & Melvina Dobbs 4 Aug 1835; min- Samuel Kennerly
John & Elizabeth Barger 26 Jul 1802; min- William Wilson- 26Jul1802
John & Barbara Whitsell 27 Jun 1803; min- William King
Peter & Annette Hanger 17 Feb 1789; Minister's return spells name as 'Agness' d Frederick, who consents b- Augustine Argenbright min- Archibald Scott- 21Feb1788

Eakard
Christian & Barbara Thomas 2 Jun 1792; d John b- John Thomas

Eakel
Philip & Polly Tenton 15 Jun 1809; min- William King

Eakerman
John & M M Reed 1 Feb 1841; min- Benjamin M Smith

Eakin
Alexander & Jane Clinebill 18 May 1829; min- Francis McFarland

Eakle
Christian & Margaret Weller 18 Nov 1845; min- G W Israel
John B & Catherine Kennedy 6 Mar 1818; min- William King
Jonathan & Fanny Allison 14 Mar 1820; min- Conrad Speece

Earhart
Abraham & Susana Burkhart 2 Oct 1794; Minister's return spells name as 'Abraham Yeorhouse and Susanna Burkett' d Nathaniel b- Peter Link min- John Brown- 4Oct1794
John & Elizabeth Staubus 25 Dec 1839; min- Jacob C Killian
Philip & Sarah Collins 8 Jun 1843; min- John A Van Lear

Early
Andrew & Winniford Frazer 26 Jul 1808; min- John McCue
John & Phebe Allison 18 Oct 1809; min- William Wilson
John & Madeline Byerley 1 Aug 1820; min- Abraham Garber- publication of banns
Samuel & Rebecca Campbell 12 Jul 1804; min- William Wilson

East
Charles & Elizabeth Lowdermilk 12 Feb 1791; d Mickle, who consents wit- Isaac White, Balcher Seldoneridge b- John Diddle
Charles & Matilda Mayfield 11 May 1826; min- John Hendren
John H & Mary Whitsell 27 Dec 1849; min- T T Castleman

Eaton
Alben W & Sarah Walker 20 Aug 1835; min- Samuel Kennerly- publication of banns

Eccard
Jacob & Barbara Peck 14 Oct 1790; Minister's return spells name as 'Eccord' d Andrew, who also consents b- Henry Hull min- William Wilson- 14Oct1790

Augusta County Marriages -- Man's Name

Eccord
  Henry & Susannah Bushong 1 Feb 1803; min- William King
Echard
  Christian & Sarah Patterson 13 Dec 1831; min- John Howell
Echord
  Philip & Mary Hale 10 Aug 1841; min- George B Rimel
Eckard
  Jacob & Malinda Stuart 22 Dec 1828; min- William C. Morrison
Edgar
  James & Frances Poindexter 25 May 1826; min- William Monroe
Edmiston
  Robert & ----- ----- 19 Jul 1765; license only
Edmondson
  James & ----- ----- - Mar 1749; license only
  William & Polly McCutchen 18 Aug 1831; min- Francis McFarland
Edmonson
  Thompson & Jane Amanda McCutchen 8 Apr 1828; min- Alexander Templeton
Edmunds
  Thomas & Polly Rife 10 Mar 1803; min- William King
Edmundson
  John & Eliza Calhoon 10 Dec 1822; min- Conrad Speece
Edwards
  Martin E & Fanny Stockdale 8 Nov 1808; min- John McCue
Effinger
  Jacob P & Hester T Mills 4 May 1847; min- Thomas D Bell
  Joseph S & Ann Hogg 14 May 1833; min- Conrad Speece
Egnew
  James & Margaret Givens 21 Apr 1788; d John who consents wit- William Patton, Thomas Givens & James Givens b- Thomas Givens
Eidson
  Henry & Catherine Hanger 17 May 1803; min- William King
  Peter & Eleanor R Moffett 29 Sep 1842; min- S J Love
  William & Agnes Poage 14 Jan 1832; min- William Wilson
Eikord
  Joseph & Polly Golladay 17 Feb 1826; min- Daniel Stephens
Elinger
  George (Jr) & Catherine Griever 20 Apr 1797; d Philip who consents test- Philip Griever b- Andrew Cutler
Ellinger
  Jacob & Elizabeth Palmer 24 Mar 1835; min- Cornelius Gates
Elliot
  John & Nancy Hogshead 8 Mar 1829; min- John Hendren
  Johnson & Jane Clemants 24 Aug 1815; min- William King
Elliott
  Alexander & Nancy Campbell 19 Dec 1786; Alexander from Rockingham cty d Andrew b- John Didall & Alex, son of George Elliott wit- Moras Loyd, Wm Elliott, John Camel min- William Wilson- 20Dec1786
  Archibald & Sarah Clark - Feb 1748; license only
  Archibald & Elizabeth Roop 30 Jan 1840; min- William Calhoon

Augusta County Marriages -- Man's Name

Elliott (cont.)
  George & Florence Bell 28 Sep 1785; b- William Bell
  John & Rebecca Steel 22 Mar 1827; min- Francis McFarland
  Samuel & Mary Lowman 29 Dec 1840; min- D F Bittle
  Thomas & Polly Smith 25 Aug 1803; min- William King
  William & Nancy McCampbell 10 Dec 1785; 'Agness'? d
    Samuel wit- John Bosang min- Archibald Scott- 12Dec1785

Ellis
  Humphrey & Mary Huston 2 Dec 1799; Humphrey from Wythe cty
    widower & widow (of William) b- Joseph Burke
  John & Emila G Fuller 2 May 1850; min- J Killian
  John & Elizabeth Horn 9 Dec 1806; min- William King

Elmore
  Isaiah & Nancy Fitzgerald 15 Jan 1822; min- Josiah Cole

Elsey
  Thomas & Catherine Comerford 19 Jun 1797; d Patrick b-
    Patrick Comerford Thomas a widower

Engard
  William & Nancy Evans 26 Nov 1799; d David Evans, dec. b-
    Jacob Gregory min- William King- 28Nov1799

Engleman
  David & Maria Shell 21 Oct 1833; min- Augustus Babb
  George & Mary Slagle 10 Dec 1812; min- John McCue
  John & Rebecca Strickler 13 Jan 1842; min- John C Hensell
  Michael & Sarah E Hoover 22 May 1845; min- J C Hensell
  Peter & Jane Coiner 11 Apr 1821; min- G H Riemenschneider
  Peter & Elizabeth Engleman 11 Aug 1842; min- D F Bittle
  Philip & Elizabeth Gayhart 31 Dec 1842; min- J B Houck-
    publication of banns

Engleton
  Anthony & Elizabeth Powers 19 Jan 1809; min- William King

Eppard
  John & Elizabeth Landiss 28 Aug 1811; min- G H
    Riemenschneider

Epply
  Jacob & Betsy Raines 19 Nov 1824; min- Michael Meyerhoeffer

Erinaund
  Joseph & Catherine Krickenbarger 30 Nov 1813; min- William
    Wilson

Ervin
  Alexander & Harriet Dean 19 Nov 1835; min- Wright Burgess
  Benami & Jane S Cave 5 Dec 1821; min- John Hendren
  Benjamin & Ferlisha Dean 16 Jul 1835; min- Wright Burgess
  John Hendren & Margaret C Herring 30 Dec 1845; min- J A
    Van Lear
  John & Elizabeth Estill 9 Jul 1835; min- John Hendren

Ervine
  George H & Nancy C Bell 24 May 1849; min- John A Van Lear
  Robertson & Rebecca B Gamble 14 May 1835; min- Conrad
    Speece

Erwin
  Benjamin & Jane Curry 28 Apr 1806; min- William King
  Benjamin & Margaret Wallace 24 Sep 1793; d Robert b-
    Robert Wallace no minister listed; clerk's memorandum cites
    ceremony date as 26Sep1793

Augusta County Marriages -- Man's Name

Erwin (cont.)
Edward & Sarah Percy 31 May 1808; min- William Wilson
Edward & Jane Waddle 2 Apr 1792; Minister's return spells name as 'Wooddell' b- Thomas Wooddell min- Benjamin Irwin- 3Apr1792
Francis & Margaret Blair 9 Mar 1801; d John sis to Mathew Blair Margaret (of age) b- Matthew Blair Francis signs as 'Irwin'
John & Ann Crawford 13 Sep 1821; min- Conrad Speece
John & Rebecca Curry - Feb 1792; d James, who consents wit- Polly & John Curry b- John Curry
John & Jenny Erwin 22 Feb 1791; Minister's return spells name as 'Jane' d Francis, who consents wit- William Erwin & John Bell b- William Irwin min- Benjamin Irvin- 22Feb1791
Joseph & Peggy Montgomery 15 May 1810; min- S Montgomery
Samuel & ----- ----- 25 Jul 1770; license only
Samuel & Polly Wilson 10 Jun 1806; min- William Calhoon
William & Susanah Curry 4 Jul 1785; d James b- Andrew Erwin min- Benjamin Erwin- 7Jul1785

Estill
Ben & ----- ----- - Oct 1764; license only
Boyd & ----- ----- 16 Nov 1773; license only
Henry M & Mary Jane Patrick 6 Dec 1833; min- James C Wilson
Solomon & ----- ----- 8 May 1773; license only
Zachariah Fort & Rebecca Estill 4 May 1785; widow of John Estill b- George Hudson

Estis
Fountain & Mary Mitchell 26 Apr 1831; min- John Howell

Etter
Peter & Catherine Bleaker 14 Jan 1802; d Peter Bleaker, dec. both of age b- John Sheetz

Eubank
Garland R & Elizabeth Chrisman 11 Jan 1844; min- Jacob Baer
Garland & Mary Cease 17 May 1806; min- William King
George & Apalenah McNutt 21 Jun 1832; min- William Calhoon- publication of banns

Euritt
Thomas E & Margaret E Crist 23 Nov 1846; min- Jacob C Spitler

Evans
Calison & Rebecca Ann Decker 31 Jan 1832; min- Francis McFarland
Jesse & Catherine Tumblin 8 Mar 1810; min- Joseph Reid
John & Margaret Jackson 18 Oct 1796; widower & widow b- John Evans Jr min- John McCue- 20Oct1796
John & Jane Trimble 16 Mar 1793; 'Jean?' d Robert b- Robert Trimble no minister listed; clerk's memorandum cites ceremony date as 19Mar1793
Joseph & Jean Blair 4 Aug 1797; Jean (of age) d Joseph Blair, dec. b- Joseph Blair min- Archibald Scott- 8Aug1797
Joseph & Isabella Callison 25 Feb 1801; widower Isabella (of age) d John b- Robert Callison
Joseph & Nancy Steele 17 Aug 1799; both of age d Samuel Steele, dec, sis to William Steele b- William Steele

Augusta County Marriages -- Man's Name

Evans (cont.)
  Joshua & Elizabeth Hanger 29 Apr 1806; min- William Wilson
  Morgan & Agness Lessley 22 Sep 1792; d James (dec)
    consent by John & Sarah Lessley wit- William Johnston &
    William Gamble min- John McCue- 23Oct1792
  Patrick & ----- ----- 28 Aug 1765; license only
Everhart
  Henry & Ann Catharine Tolmink 19 Jun 1845; min- T T
    Castleman
Eversole
  Jacob & Barbara Fisher 25 Nov 1812; min- William King
Evy
  John & Mary Ann Johnston 14 Oct 1847; min- Jacob Bear
  Joseph & Catharine Sweed 22 Feb 1844; min- T T Castleman
  Reuben & Hannah Brunk 10 Jan 1843; min- Samuel Wagner
Ewell
  John & Mary Kennerly 25 Feb 1801; Minister's return spells
    name as 'Kennerley' John from Albemarle cty d James who
    consents test- Philip & Kitty Kennerly b- Philip Kennerly
    min- John McCue- 3Mar1801
  Pleasant & Barbara Fauber 27 Jan 1814; min- William King
Ewin
  Elijah & Amanda Hunter 11 Nov 1830; min- Hezekiah Best
Ewing
  James & ----- ----- - May 1761; license only
  James & Mary Hunter 15 Dec 1795; b- William Patterson
    min- John McCue- 15Dec1795
  John & Sarah Davies 22 May 1787; min- Archibald Scott-
    22May1787
  Robert & Margaret Cunningham 31 Dec 1816; min- William
    Calhoon
Faber
  Christian & Elizabeth Crips 29 May 1821; min- Josiah Cole
  Hiram & Jane Koiner 3 Dec 1840; min- Benjamin Kendig
  Jacob & Elizabeth Warner - Sep 1809; min- John Brown
Fackler
  John M & Amanda P Austin 19 Dec 1839; min- Frederick D
    Goodwin
  John & Nancy Abney 17 Jul 1798; d John Abney, dec. b-
    Robert McClenachan
  Samuel & Elizabeth Fenton 23 Jul 1801; Minister's return
    spells name as 'Fackar' d Enoch b- Enoch Fenton min- John
    McCue- 23Jul1801
Fadely
  John & Keziah Patterson 25 Sep 1837; min- William G Jackson
Fagus
  Henry & Elizabeth Grass 5 Oct 1785; (Fogas?) widow d
    Henry Hawk b- Frederick Hawk min- Archibald Scott- 6Oct1785
Fairbairn
  William & Polley Breesland 25 Sep 1806; min- William
    McPheeters
Fairberman
  George & Catharine Flory 9 Oct 1845; min- T T Castleman

Augusta County Marriages -- Man's Name

Fairburn
  John B & Catherine Jane Hoover 9 Nov 1837; min- J C Hensell
  Samuel & Nancy Snider 6 Jun 1841; min- George B Rimel- publication of banns

Fall
  Daniel & Margaret Crawford 30 Aug 1797; d John who consents test- John Rees b- James Brown min- William Wilson- 31Aug1797
  Daniel & Catharine B Keller 3 Oct 1844; min- J C Hensell
  George & Barbara Kellar - Apr 1806; min- John Brown
  John & Nancy Acord 17 Mar 1818; min- William King

Fallwider
  George & Catherine Carr 25 Oct 1791; b- Valentine Carr (German)

Farish
  Robert & ----- ----- - Apr 1760; license only

Farmer
  John & Christiana Ekerson 10 Feb 1796; widow sis of Jacob Minnick b- Jacob Minnick

Farr
  Leonard & Margaret D Bush 22 Feb 1848; min- J C Hensell

Farrow
  Isaac & Ann Rankin 11 Jan 1820; min- John Hendren
  John & Susannah McWilliams 24 Jun 1822; min- John Hendren

Fauber
  David & Catharine Crist 24 Feb 1831; min- Francis McFarland
  George & Mary Mathews 27 May 1833; min- Conrad Speece

Faucet
  Samuel & Deborah Clarke 23 Feb 1809; min- John McCue

Faulber
  David & Barbara Palmer 27 Jun 1816; min- William King

Fauver
  John & Catharine Hutchens 20 Apr 1826; min- William W Calhoun
  Philip & Mary M Russell 11 Apr 1842; min- John C Hensell
  Samuel & Mary Ocheltree 29 Mar 1833; min- John Hendren

Fawber
  Joseph & Elizabeth Swisher 28 Jul 1798; d John who consents b- John Kaylor test- John Kaler & John Sweitzer
  Samuel & Jane Trout 14 Jan 1819; min- William King

Fawcet
  Charles & Margaret Hodge 25 Aug 1805; min- John Montgomery

Fawner
  Jacob & Jane Weitzel 30 Jan 1799; d Anthony Weitzel, dec. b- John Fawner Jacob was 21 on 10Mar1798 Jane also of age

Faysnight
  George & Barbara Shore 27 Oct 1790; b- Frederick Shore min- William Wilson- 27Oct1790

Fellows
  Jonathan G & Margaret Slagle 8 Jan 1822; min- James C Willson
  Joseph & Sally Fellows 26 Aug 1820; min- Daniel Stephens

Augusta County Marriages -- Man's Name

Felps
  Isaac & Sarah Deane 23 Sep 1788; b- Jacob Warwick
Fennel
  James & Catherine Hanger 11 Jan 1827; min- Alexander Templeton
  John & Eleanor King 19 Jul 1796; b- John Montgomery min- John Montgomery- 3Aug1796
Fenton
  Eleazer & Elizabeth Engleman 3 Aug 1809; min- William King
  Nathan & Mary Jane Deary 5 Apr 1832; min- William Wilson
Fetzer
  George & Susan Kurtz 17 Aug 1837; min- William G Jackson
Fifer
  Addison & Lydia Dickerson 13 Sep 1834; min- John Hendren
  John & Mary Daniels 15 Jan 1827; min- John Hendren
  Peter & Hannah Caricofe 17 Mar 1831; min- John Hendren
  William & Catharine Eversole 23 Jan 1845; min- S Wagner
Fimster
  William & ----- ----- 21 Jun 1763; license only
Finla
  Robert & ----- ----- 19 Mar 1750; license only
Finley
  David & Elizabeth Wilson 9 Mar 1791; d Joseph, who consents wit- Alexander Gibson Jr b- Alexander Gibson Jr min- Archibald Scott- 10Mar1791
  Francis M & Eliza Shura 3 Dec 1840; min- Benjamin M Smith
  James & Prudence Moore 29 Aug 1785; d Samuel who consents test- Arthur Glasgow & Samuel McCorkle b- James Sproul min- Archibald Scott- 30Aug1785
  James & Polly Ramsy 16 Jul 1813; min- Thomas Bourne
  John & Elenor Tate 21 Apr 1807; min- William McPheeters
  Samuel & Elizabeth L Harnest 16 Nov 1841; min- Francis McFarland
  Samuel & Mary Tate 20 Sep 1796; d John b- John Tate min- John Brown- 22Sep1796
  William & Sally Ramsey 15 Jun 1801; d Andrew who consents test- William & Charles Patrick Samuel & William Finley are cousins William (of age) b- Samuel Finley min- John McCue- 16Jun1801
Finly
  James & Patsy Ramsy 2 Oct 1811; min- John McCue
Firebough
  Adam & Elizabeth Kirchoff - Apr 1808; min- John Brown
Fishburn
  Daniel & Margaret Guthrie 19 Oct 1841; min- Samuel Wagner
  David & Catharine Grove 3 Jun 1830; min- William Wilson
  John & Sarah Anderson 3 Jun 1819; min- William King
  Philip & Lydia Silling 4 Jun 1812; min- William King
  William & Catherine Silling 29 May 1820; min- Daniel Stephens
Fishburne
  Henry & Elizabeth Greiner 1 Dec 1812; min- Wright Burgess

Augusta County Marriages -- Man's Name

Fisher
  Absolem & Margaret Rankin 1 Nov 1826; min- James Watts
  Adam & Elizabeth Balsley 17 Dec 1811; min- Wright Burgess
  Adam & Susannah Surface 7 Dec 1801; Minister's return spells name as 'Surfis' d Martin William Fisher, bro of Adam swears latter is of age b- Martin Surface min- William King- 17Dec1801
  Adison K & Sarah A Jennings 27 Feb 1844; min- T T Castleman- publication of banns
  Andrew & Polly Sorrells 8 Aug 1822; min- Conrad Speece
  Anthoney & Polly Huff 5 Feb 1807; min- William King
  Daniel & Elizabeth Carnal 25 Feb 1806; min- William Wilson
  Henry & Polly Culp 1 Dec 1825; min- Conrad Speece
  John & Margaret Brown 29 Apr 1806; min- William King
  John & Polly Long - Aug 1823; min- John Brown
  John & Polly McMullen 30 Nov 1801; 'Mary' d Michael Jane Davey, sis of Polly, swears as to her age b- Charles Page min- William King- 30Nov1801
  John & Merney Sorrels 27 Jan 1803; 'Nancy Sorrells?' min- John McCue
  Lewis & Olivia Loeffler 4 Apr 1843; min- F D Goodwin
  Martin & Rosanna Surface 2 Sep 1805; min- William King
  William & Jane Anderson 30 Sep 1817; min- Wright Burgess
  William & Mary Fifer 12 Oct 1809; min- William King
  William & Catherine Surface 21 Apr 1803; min- William King

Fitch
  James A & Eliza A Givens 12 Dec 1842; min- William H Laney
  Simeon & Melinda Peters 15 Jan 1834; min- Samuel Kennerly
  Stephen & Susan Brown 20 Mar 1825; min- William C. Morrison

Fitzpatrick
  Calib & Polly Lushbough 20 Feb 1810; min- William King
  Clove L & Margaret Merritt 12 Nov 1835; min- J J Glossbrenner
  David & Margaret Powers 11 Jan 1827; min- John A Gore
  Martin & Mary Sheets 8 Dec 1836; min- B N Brown

Fix
  Adam & Jane Heiden 20 Dec 1827; min- William Monroe
  Jacob & Barbara Swink 4 Dec 1786; d Lawrence b- Henry Swink min- Archibald Scott- 4Dec1786
  John H & Sarah Jane Wright 11 Nov 1847; min- Francis McFarland
  Joseph & Mary Humphrey 30 Mar 1848; min- J C Hensell

Fizar
  Henry & Elizabeth Bright 10 Oct 1808; min- William King

Flack
  John & Polly Harmon 29 Apr 1806; min- William King

Fleming
  John & Genetta Davis 26 Jul 1827; min- John Hendren
  Leonard Israel & Mary Bowyer 20 Jun 1787; d William who consents test- William Neeley b- Richard Mathews min- Archibald Scott- 21Jun1787
  William & ----- ----- 6 Apr 1763; license only (listed as 'William Fleming, Gent.')

Augusta County Marriages -- Man's Name

Flemming
  James & Barbara Karicofe 4 Nov 1830; min- Benjamin Denton
Flesher
  John & Betsy B Graham 11 Jul 1831; min- James Kerr
Fletcher
  John & Susannah Fox 7 Oct 1813; min- William King
  Samuel & Sophanna Teaford 12 Jan 1832; min- William Calhoon
Flinn
  John & Sally Blakemore 17 May 1814; min- William Cravens
Flory
  Jonathan & Margaret Ocheltree 4 Mar 1841; min- J J Reimensnyder
Foley
  Isaac & Elizabeth Croome 28 Sep 1841; min- J A Van Lear
  John & Columbia Youstler 9 Jan 1845; min- T T Castleman
Forbes
  John G & Margaret Jane Western 17 Jul 1845; min- T T Castleman
  Michael & Rebecca Brothers 18 Feb 1819; min- William King
  William & Barbara Garber 10 Nov 1787; min- James Chambers- 10Nov1787
Forbish
  William & Barbarah Gabhart 10 Nov 1787; b- Anthony Mustor & William Chambers
Foreman
  Jacob & Elizabeth Paulus 14 Jul 1800; 'Fuehrman?' d Nicholas b- Nicholas Paulus
  Thomas M & Helen W Brooke 30 Aug 1849; min- T T Castleman
Forer
  Jacob & Susannah Whitmore 4 Sep 1840; min- Jacob Killian
Fort
  William & Sarah Weast 8 Oct 1835; min- William G Jackson
Foster
  James & Mary E Taylor 18 Dec 1849; min- B M Smith
  Joshua & Mary Bridge 8 Aug 1836; min- James C Wilson
  William & ----- ----- 14 Dec 1763; license only
Foutz
  David & Polly Imboden 9 Dec 1813; min- William King
Fowler
  James & ----- ----- 27 Jan 1764; license only
Fowtick
  Jacob & Elizabeth Hankie 14 Oct 1786; d Simon b- Thomas Johnson min- Samuel Carrick- 14Oct1786
Fox
  David & Eliza Ann Taylor 28 Oct 1841; min- Alfred G Chenowith
  George & Mary Askins 20 Mar 1793; Certificate both parties are of age b- John Weaver
  George & Elizabeth Burgess 9 Jun 1831; min- William Calhoon
  John & Sally McGlaflin 22 Nov 1827; min- William Calhoon
Frame
  John & Rachel Hogshead 10 Mar 1814; min- William Wilson
  Samuel & Nancy Allen 27 Jun 1792; d James, who consents wit- James Allen b- James Allen Jr min- William Wilson- 29Jun1792

Augusta County Marriages -- Man's Name

Frame (cont.)
  Samuel & Martha Poague Moore 25 Jan 1802; widower & widow
    b- James Bell min- John McCue- 26Jan1802
  Thomas & Mary Walker 3 Jun 1819; min- Conrad Speece, Jr
Francis
  William & Sarah Allen 22 Apr 1801; widower d Ebenezer b-
    Ebenezer Allen min- William King- 23Apr1801
  William & Elizabeth Stiles 24 Oct 1786; Minister's return
    spells name as 'Stile' widow b- John Jenkins min- William
    Wilson- 25Oct1786
Francisco
  Charles & Nancy Miller 29 Mar 1814; min- Conrad Speece, Jr
  George & ----- ----- - Oct 1761; license only
Fraser
  James & Winny Coorsy 10 May 1785; d James
Fravel
  John H & Sarah J Bruce 4 Jul 1848; min- D W Arnold
Frazer
  George & Sally Francisco 29 Sep 1786; Minister's return
    spells name as 'Freyer' 'Capt' George Frazer Sarah? d
    George b- John Francisco min- Samuel Carrick- 14Oct1786
    (Rev. Samuel Shannon also lists marriage on 5Oct1786)
  James A & Patsey Rankin 12 Feb 1809; min- John Montgomery
  James & Polly Fitzpatrick 3 Nov 1814; min- John McCue
  John & Margaret Paul 24 May 1803; min- John McCue
  Thomas & Polly Crist 5 Dec 1797; d Andrew John Crist
    swears to Polly's age b- William Breeze min- Archibald
    Scott- 7Dec1797
  William & Jean Finely 1 Apr 1794; Minister's return spells
    name as 'Finley' d John who consents test- Samuel Finly &
    John McClure b- Samuel Finley min- John McCue- 1Apr1794
Frazier
  James P & Melvina L Frazier 21 Dec 1831; min- John Hendren
  James & ----- ----- 21 Mar 1765; license only
  James & Sarah Powers 10 Sep 1827; min- William C. Morrison
Freed
  Abraham & Sally Fisher 22 Dec 1823; min- Josiah Cole
Frely
  Christian & Elizabeth Harding 20 Sep 1787; Minister's
    return spells name as 'Freley' b- Samuel Harding min-
    Archibald Scott- 22Sep1787
French
  Alexander & Sally Ann Trayer 20 Jan 1835; min- George Hildt
  Hugh & Anne Douthat 14 Jan 1797; widow of William b-
    Robert McClenachan min- John McCue- 15Jan1797
Frenger
  George & Francis McFarland 6 Jan 1848; George a merchant
    min- J C Hensell
Fretwell
  Dabney & Abigail McNight 25 Jun 1840; min- Jacob Killian
Frey
  William & Sarah Witts 12 Feb 1829; min- John Hendren

Augusta County Marriages -- Man's Name

Fridley
  Frederick & Mary C Gilliam 14 Jan 1836; min- Francis A C Mills
  George & Peggy Armontrout 4 Sep 1799; Minister's return spells name as 'Armentrot' wit- Will Loving min- William King- 4Sep1799
  Jacob & Hanah Hanger 26 Apr 1786; d Frederick b- George Hanger (See 'Olinger, Hanah' under Women's listing?) min- Archibald Scott- 27Apr1786
  Jacob & Nancy Hite 3 Feb 1818; min- John D Ewin
  Jacob & Hanah Olinger 27 Apr 1786; min- Archibald Scott- 27Apr1786

Friel
  Morris & Sarah Elliott 1 Aug 1797; 'Freel?' d John who consents test- Reuben Sursell & Joseph Wilson con- Daniel Friel test- Robert Armstrong & James Ross b- James Ross min- Archibald Scott- 3Aug1797

Frogg
  John & ----- ----- 16 Oct 1770; license only

Fronsman
  Jacob N & Salley M Talley 6 Apr 1826; min- Daniel Stephens

Fry
  Cyrus & Lucy Rhyan 3 Apr 1845; min- T T Castleman
  George & Betsey Long 31 May 1791; sis Joseph & orphan of Isaac Long (dec) b- Joseph Long min- William Wilson- 1Jun1791
  John & Catharine Rowh 9 Sep 1841; min- John C Hensell
  John & Polly Young 8 Dec 1815; min- William King

Fuchs
  Mathias & Peggy Rauch 27 Nov 1799; d Peter Rauch (consent given in German) test- John Rauch b- John Mount

Fudge
  Adam & Elizabeth Garmen 1 Sep 1795; Minister's return spells name as 'Garman' d Adam b- Adam Garmen min- John McCue- 1Oct1795

Fuler
  Henry & ----- ----- 15 Apr 1751; license only

Fulks
  Nicholas & Nancy Bott 28 Sep 1790; b- Erasmus Jones, who made his mark because of a hurt arm

Fuller
  Jeremiah & Mary Jane Morrison 4 Jan 1848; min- John Bowen

Fulton
  Harvey & Ellen Smiley 1 Dec 1825; min- James Morrison
  Hugh & Sarah Tate 4 May 1785; widow of James Tate b- John Tate wit- Anthony Mustoe
  James & Sarah Henry 19 May 1836; min- James Morrison
  James & Betsy Mitchel 27 Sep 1809; min- William McPheeters
  Robert & Isabella Brownlee 29 Jan 1799; Isabella (of age) d John b- Alexander Brownlee
  Samuel & Margaret Givens 2 Oct 1795; d John b- John Givens min- John McCue- 13Oct1795
  Thomas & ----- ----- 4 Apr 1751; license only
  William & ----- ----- 2 Oct 1759; license only

Augusta County Marriages -- Man's Name

Fultz
David & Margaret Leas 5 Apr 1825; min- William W Calhoun
Frederick & Hannah Hanger 9 May 1795; d Peter b- Peter Hanger
Peter & Mary Hapner 5 Feb 1801; Minister's return spells name as 'Hepner' d Casper Hepner b- Casper Hapner min- William King- 5Feb1801

Fulwider
David & Palina Beaty 3 Feb 1848; min- J C Hensell
Henry & Ann Cline 6 Jun 1789; d Jacob, who consents wit- Jacob Gochnouer & Jacob Cline Jr
John & Lucinda Craig 4 May 1843; min- J C Hensell
John & Catherine Fulwider 23 Feb 1829; min- Francis McFarland
Joseph & Sarah Houf 10 Apr 1834; min- William Wilson
William & Mary Lowman 6 Oct 1831; min- Francis McFarland

Funk
Henry & Charity Stull 17 Jul 1787; 'Steell?' b- George Givens

Funkhouser
Benjamin & Elizabeth Armstrong 13 Jul 1826; min- William W Calhoun
Daniel & Matilda Miller 27 Apr 1818; min- William King
John & Polly Martin 15 Jun 1826; min- William W Calhoun
William & Sarah Grips 1 Oct 1835; min- William Calhoon

Funston
Isaac & Isabella Sterret 5 Oct 1807; min- John McCue

Furr
Anderson & Polly Fadely 9 Sep 1833; min- George Hildt
Harrison & Sally Forbush 30 May 1831; min- Conrad Speece- publication of banns
James & Jane McCutchen 9 Sep 1841; min- John C Hensell

Gabbert
Jacob & Sally Funkhouser 16 May 1826; min- William W Calhoun

Gabhart
David & Nancy Burgess 1 Nov 1834; min- Augustus Babb
George & Elizabeth Ellinger 24 Aug 1799; d Stoaks b- Stoaks Ellinger s Jacob Gabert who consents test- Philip Palmer & Peter Gabert

Gaines
Abner & Elizabeth Mathews 8 Dec 1792; d William, who consents wit- William Mathews Jr & Ed Rankin b- Joseph Rankin
James & Sarah Jackson 28 Mar 1805; min- William Wilson

Galespy
Alexander & ----- ----- 19 Mar 1771; license only

Gall
John & Margaret Fulwider 10 Mar 1798; John from Rockbridge cty d Jacob Fulwider, dec. b- John Ott

Gambell
James & Salley Ramsey 6 Jun 1815; 'Rev.' James Gambell min- John D Ewin

Augusta County Marriages -- Man's Name

Gamble
James & Salley Ramsay 7 Jun 1815; min- John McCue
John & Rebecca McPheeters 7 Jun 1785; d William b- James Buchanan wit- George Lyburn & John McPheeters
Theophilus & Elizabeth G Irvine 31 Mar 1834; min- John Hendren
William & Polly Poage 15 Jun 1815; min- Conrad Speece, Jr

Gamwell
Joseph & ----- ----- 9 Dec 1768; license only
Robert & ----- ----- 23 Aug 1764; license only

Garber
Abraham & Elizabeth Stover 7 Sep 1830; min- Abraham Garber
Benjamin & Elizabeth Crumpecker 14 May 1846; min- T T Castleman
Benjamin & Nancy Stover - --- 182-; min- Abraham Garber- publication of banns
John & Kitty Miller 9 Apr 1816; min- Abraham Garber- publication of banns
Martin & Elizabeth Brower 16 Nov 1842; min- Peter Miller
Martin & Magdalin Mohler - Sep 1816; min- Abraham Garber- publication of banns
Michael (Jr) & Margaret Smith 11 Oct 1792; d Thomas (dec) & Elizabeth, who consents wit- Sally Smith & Bettey Smith b- Vincent Tapp min- John Montgomery- 11Oct1792
Samuel & Amy Laird 18 Aug 1812; min- Samuel Garber
Samuel & Ann Peters 21 Jun 1838; min- Thomas Wheeler
Solomon & Barbary Long 23 Oct 1805; min- Samuel Garber

Gardiner
James & Margaret Hamilton 27 Nov 1787; Minister's return spells name as 'Gardner' widow b- Anthony Mustoe min- James Chambers- 27Nov1787
John & Rachel Wilson 20 Jul 1789; Minister's return spells name as 'Gardner' d Rachel Willson, who consents b- James Gardiner wit- William Willson & James Willson min- Archibald Scott- 20Jul1789

Gardner
Adam & Elizabeth Russell 23 Jan 1788; con- Robert Russell wit- A Stuart & William Skillern b- Nicholas Spring & Thomas Scott min- James Chambers- 7Jan1788
Alexander & Rebecca H Swink 4 Jan 1844; min- Francis McFarland
James (Jr) & Elizabeth Reed 23 Jul 1792; Minister's return spells name as 'Joseph Gardner and Betsey Reed' d Robert, who consents wit- John Gardiner & Alexander Reed b- Jacob Kinney min- William Wilson- 24Jul1792
James A & Hannah C Fry 15 Sep 1846; min- S Wagner
Samuel & Sarah Bell 19 Feb 1790; d James, who consents b- Robert Bell wit- Robert Bell & Richard Denton min- Archibald Scott- 23Feb1790
Samuel & Ann Fackler 20 Oct 1814; min- William Calhoon

Garhenour
Jacob & Barbara Garber 17 Nov 1836; min- Peter Miller

Augusta County Marriages -- Man's Name

Garmen
John & Nancy Branaman 26 Oct 1802; min- John McCue- 26Oct1802
Garmon
Isaac & Elizabeth Branaman 29 Mar 1804; min- John McCue
Garrison
Bernard A & Dorcas Barger 2 Jan 1845; min- T T Castleman
Joel & Margaret Ann Elliott 16 Jun 1823; min- John Hendren
Garvey
John & Mary Thompson 10 Mar 1788; b- John Lockridge min- John Brown- 13Mar1788
Garvin
John & Sarah Heslet 14 Aug 1808; min- William Wilson
John & Sarah Johnston 25 Nov 1785; d William b- Joseph Garvin wit- Thomas Poage
Samuel & Jane Hutchins 4 Mar 1833; min- John S Watt
Thomas & Elizabeth Young 21 Apr 1789; d James, who consents b- Andrew Young wit- John Dickey & William Hook
Gates
John & Anna Wilen 6 Nov 1786; b- John Ritter min- William Wilson- 6Nov1786
Gatewood
Andrew M & Eliza McCue 24 Nov 1830; min- John Hendren
Andrew & Sarah Moffett 12 Aug 1822; min- John Hendren
Gaugh
Thomas & ----- ----- 1 Oct 1766; license only
Gay
Archibald & Rebecca Greenwood 29 Nov 1798; d ----- Greenwood, dec. James Frasure, gdn, swears Rebecca of age b- James Frazer
Henry & Jane Henderson 15 Apr 1785; d Joanes b- William Galloway
John & Jane Hicks 13 Mar 1817; min- William King
Robert & Rebecca Lockridge 18 Nov 1788; b- Robert Lockridge min- Archibald Scott- 20Nov1788
Thomas & Hamilton Perry 28 Jan 1840; min- A B McCorkle
William & Mary Craig 24 Sep 1785; d Alexander b- William Armstrong wit- John Elliott min- Archibald Scott- 27Sep1785
Geeding
Ephraim & Mary Trimble 27 Mar 1828; min- William Calhoon
Gelston
Samuel & Martha Gray 8 Feb 1787; b- James McGonagal min- Archibald Scott- 8Feb1787
Gentry
Elisha H & Nancy Jones 20 May 1834; min- George Hildt
George
Henry G & Harriet S Kennerly 13 Jun 1834; min- Samuel Kennerly
Gerhart
Leonard & Mary Smith 10 Mar 1787; d Ludwick b- Ludwick Smith
Gette
George W & Elizabeth G Stevenson 19 Dec 1848; min- Robert Nelson

Augusta County Marriages -- Man's Name

Gibson
  John & Catherine Cloverfield 1 Mar 1796; Catherine (of age) d of ----- Cloverfield, dec. b- James King min- William Wilson- 3Mar1796
  Robert & ----- ----- 2 Oct 1769; license only
  Samuel & ----- ----- 3 Jul 1772; license only
  William & Letticia Burns 17 Nov 1808; min- William McPheeters
  William & Isabella Graham 15 Apr 1821; min- Conrad Speece
  William & Polly Rankin 23 Nov 1813; min- William Calhoon
←Zachariah S & Ann Johnson 27 Oct 1808; min- William King

Gilbert
  James & Margaret Hurst 4 Jan 1827; min- William Monroe

Gilbraith
  John & Elizabeth Weiford 7 Nov 1826; min- Daniel Stephens

Giles
→ John & Dicy Hunter 11 Nov 1809; min- William King
  John & Mary A Messmaker 8 Feb 1844; min- Samuel Wagner

Gilkerson
  Hugh & Matilda Hogshead 27 Oct 1825; min- William Wilson
  James & Rebecca Trimble 16 Feb 1833; min- William Calhoon

Gilkeson
  David & Elizabeth Gilkeson 7 Jul 1808; min- John McCue
  David & Polly Humphreys 25 May 1809; min- William McPheeters
  Francis & Polly Hogshead 1 Oct 1799; d James b- James Hogshead
  Henry & Mary Coursey 30 Jan 1806; min- John McCue
  John & Jane Brownlee 6 Aug 1809; min- William McPheeters
  Robert G & Margaret T Shields 11 Nov 1845; min- B M Smith

Gillaspie
  John & Jane Crawford 2 Jun 1807; min- William Calhoon

Gilleat
  John & Eve Joseph 5 Jan 1809; min- William King

Gillespie
  John & Catherine Myres 6 Jan 1810; min- William McPheeters
  Samuel P V & Polley Crawford 4 Apr 1815; min- William Calhoon

Gillespy
  John & Derky Maupin 11 Sep 1805; min- John McCue
  Simon & Agness Black - Feb 1810; min- John McCue

Gilliam
  Alexander & Maria P Peck 8 Mar 1836; min- John Hendren

Gilliat
  William & Mary Teaford 21 Apr 1834; min- Augustus Babb

Gillum
  Pleasant G & Mary L Jackson 24 Jun 1841; min- P E Stevenson

Given
  Samuel & Mary Gibson 18 Mar 1823; min- Conrad Speece

Givens
  James & Jane Lynn 16 Feb 1804; min- Philip Kennerly
  John & Georgiana Tharp 8 Sep 1835; min- Samuel Kennerly
  Robert & Margaret Elliott 17 May 1785; Margaret of age d William b- George Bratton min- Samuel Shannon- 2Jun1785

Augusta County Marriages -- Man's Name

Givens (cont.)
  Robert & Margaret Robinson 29 Mar 1785; d William b- Alexander Robinson wit- Mathew Mathewson & Alexander Robertson
  Samuel & Elizabeth Robertson 19 Mar 1785; b- Alexander Robertson
  Thomas & Betsy Kerr 6 May 1789; Minister's return spells name as 'Givins' d James b- James Kerr min- William Wilson- 8May1789
  William & ----- ----- 21 Mar 1764; license only
  William & Rebecca Kenney 9 Mar 1789; Minister's return spells name as 'Givins and Kennedy' d Matthew, who consents b- Robert Kenny wit- Robert Kenney & William Robertson min- William Wilson- 9Mar1789
Gladwell
  Baird & Nancy Taylor 27 Jan 1823; min- Josiah Cole
  John & Elizabeth Bare 29 Jun 1848; min- Alonzo P Ludden
Glass
  John & Rachel Sawyers 12 Aug 1797; d James Sawyers, dec. b- Hannah Sawyers & John Thompson
Glassburn
  David & Rachel Fox 5 Sep 1805; min- John Montgomery
Glendy
  John & Polly W Larew 2 Jan 1827; min- Francis McFarland
Glenn
  George & Mary Anderson 11 Dec 1823; min- Conrad Speece
  Hugh & Rebecca Anderson 13 Nov 1821; min- Conrad Speece
  Hugh & Elizabeth McCausland 1 Aug 1801; d John b- John McCausland min- Daniel Garber- 28Jul1801
  James & Margaret Young 27 Nov 1785; d Robert b- James Young min- William Wilson- 28Dec1785
  John & Margaret Hartshooke 29 Oct 1819; min- G H Riemenschneider
  Robert C & Janetta Curry 30 Nov 1826; min- Conrad Speece
  William & Ann Curry 14 Jun 1791; d Robert, who consents wit- Samuel & James Curry bride & groom both of age b- Samuel Curry min- William Wilson- 15Jun1791
Glover
  William & Mary E Bowman 13 May 1847; min- J C Hensell
Goah
  George & Mary Headly 19 Dec 1809; min- William King
Gochenauer
  Samuel & Catharine Brower 1 Jul 1835; min- John Gotber
Goin
  Daniel & Frances C Whetesel 11 Mar 1845; min- P Shickel
  John & Aggy Connelly 21 Jan 1815; min- Wright Burgess
  Spencer & Betsy Swink 1 Dec 1825; min- Francis McFarland
Going
  John & Polly King 14 Apr 1823; min- John Brown
Goings
  Mathew & Keziah Goings 5 Mar 1834; coloured persons min- James C Wilson
  Thomas & Frances Goings 20 Sep 1839; coloured min- Samuel Wagner

Augusta County Marriages -- Man's Name

Goins
  John & Margaret Fox 6 Mar 1841; min- D F Bittle- publication of banns
Gold
  John & Elizabeth Coldbreath 26 Mar 1798; Minister's return spells name as 'Galbreath' d Thomas Coldbreath, dec. John of age b- Nicholas Spring Jr min- William Wilson- 27Mar1798
Golladay
  John & Ann Smith 27 Apr 1818; min- William King
  Jonathan & Martha K Bell 2 Jun 1842; min- John C Hensell
  Samuel & Mary Jane Campbell 27 May 1837; min- James Paine
  William K & Perrina Hamilton 5 Oct 1848; min- W T Richardson
  William & Eliza Rankin 23 Oct 1827; min- Gerard Morgan
Golloday
  Abraham & Juliana Smith 28 Mar 1822; min- William Wilson Jr
  Isaac & Eliza Barnes 14 Jun 1826; min- Michael Meyerhoeffer
Gongwer
  George W & Mary A Lutz 8 Jun 1846; min- P Shickel
  Joseph & Jane Patterson 26 Feb 1829; min- William Wilson
Gooch
  Edwin H & Henrietta Sterrett 25 Aug 1849; min- John Hendren
Good
  David & Elizabeth Shaffer - Aug 1825; min- John Brown
  Jacob & Mary Landes 21 Mar 1826; min- Abraham Garber- publication of banns
  Peter & Patsy Cheatham 22 Dec 1821; min- James Sewell
Goodlink
  Michael & Margaret Campbell 30 Apr 1791; Minister's return spells name as 'Goldlink' d Alexander, who consents wit- Robert Porterfield b- John Campbell min- William Wilson- 11May1791
Goodnight
  John & Betsy Weaver - Aug 1825; min- John Brown
Goodrich
  Henry & Margaret Johnson 22 May 1821; 'Hezekiah?' min- Josiah Cole
Goodwin
  John & Sasannah Daugherty 27 Dec 1808; min- William King
  Levi & Mary Thomas 19 Jan 1802; min- William King- 19Jan1802
  Septimus & Jane Reed 6 Feb 1806; min- William Wilson
Gordan
  James & Isabella Kincaid 18 Jan 1838; min- Zach Jordan
Gorden
  Samuel & Martha Kincaid 26 Jan 1836; min- William Calhoon
Gordon
  George & Elianor Knowles 13 May 1807; min- William King
  John & Elizabeth Good 23 Dec 1838; min- P E Stevenson
  John & Sarah Palmer 5 Jan 1843; min- J C Hensell
  Simeon E & Isabella McClung 12 Nov 1844; min- T T Castleman
Gorrell
  Robert & ----- ----- 18 Aug 1762; license only

Augusta County Marriages -- Man's Name

Gowing
  John & Polly Johns 25 Feb 1836; min- William Calhoon
Gragg
  John & Hannah Percy 8 Nov 1792; Minister's return spells name as 'Hannah Perey' d John, who consents wit- Christian & John Percy Jr b- Alexander Robertson min- Benjamin Irwin- 13Nov1792
Graham
  Benjamin F & Susan C Bell 26 Jul 1832; min- Francis McFarland
  Fergus & Elizabeth Trimble 8 Mar 1787; d David s Arthur of Rockbridge cty who consents test- John Stuart & Alexander Hindman b- David Trimble min- Archibald Scott- 13Mar1787
  George W & Edith J Bowers 14 Apr 1840; min- John J Reimensnyder
  Henry Madison & Nancy Houston 10 Jan 1833; min- James Kerr
  James C & Isabella Henderson 27 Dec 1820; min- John D Ewin
  James & ----- ----- 12 Feb 1763; license only
  James & Agnes Young 12 Jun 1804; min- William King
  Jehab & Sarah D Heiskell 20 May 1813; min- Thomas Bourne
  John & ----- ----- - Apr 1761; license only
  Lanty & ----- ----- 22 Jun 1763; license only
  Robert & Sally Brown 11 May 1790; d Thomas b- Stephen Graham
  Robert & Isabella Hogshead 5 Mar 1793; d David sis of David and above 21 b- David Hogshead Jr min- William Wilson- 6Mar1793
  Robert & Rosannah Snyder 10 Oct 1826; min- William Monroe
  William & ----- ----- 24 Mar 1774; license only
  William & Isabella Hellena Baskins 15 Mar 1788; s John who consents test- John Jamison & Joseph Russell b- Christopher Graham min- William Wilson- 20Mar1788
  William & Isabella Patterson 6 Jun 1791; d Robert b- Robert Patterson
Grandie
  Elijah & Polly Reeves 8 Nov 1826; min- Daniel Stephens
Grant
  James W & Jane D Masters 10 Feb 1848; min- J C Hensell
  Jeremiah & Catherine Hemp 31 Aug 1813; min- William King
Grass
  Frederick & Betsy ----- 23 Aug 1785; b- Nicholas Spring
  John & Julia Ann Cox 20 Jan 1842; min- F D Goodwin
  John & Sally Haybarger 30 Jun 1814; min- Conrad Speece, Jr
  John & Polly Masoncup 26 Jan 1802; Minister's return spells name as 'Masincupp' d Jacob Frederick Wear ('Wehr') swears Polly of age John also of age b- Abraham Hawk min- William King- 26Jan1802
  Robert & Susan Grooms 22 Feb 1816; min- John McCue
  William R & Nancy Alexander 25 Nov 1823; min- Conrad Speece
  William & Juliana Cesterson 27 Feb 1834; min- William G Jackson

Augusta County Marriages -- Man's Name

Graves
  Richard & Jane Fielding 28 Feb 1799; widower & widow b- William King min- William King- 28Feb1799

Gray
  Isaac & Elizabeth Kerr 23 Aug 1796; d Robert who consents test- William Koons & David Koons b- William Kerr
  Isaac & Nancy Peck 11 Jun 1835; min- J J Glossbrenner
  James & ----- ----- 23 May 1765; license only
  James & Elizabeth Doren 6 Jun 1787; Minister's return spells name as 'Dooran' b- Abraham McFarland min- Samuel Shannon- 14Jun1787
  James & Emily A Hollis 9 Jan 1845; min- J C Hensell
  John & ----- ----- 26 Feb 1759; license only
  Robert & Salina Armstrong 18 Dec 1828; min- John Hendren
  Solomon & Lavina Forbes 23 Dec 1839; min- John C Hensell

Greaver
  William & Elizabeth Thomas 23 Oct 1826; min- Daniel Stephens

Green
  Daniel & Margaret Ross 15 Nov 1793; d William who consents test- James McGummery & Henry Laywell b- John McClure min- John McCue- 19Nov1793

Greer
  Alexander & ----- ----- 23 Sep 1773; license only
  William & Elizabeth Monroe 11 Oct 1821; min- Josiah Cole

Gregory
  Addison & Sarah Henderson 31 Mar 1842; min- P E Stevenson
  Christian & Jane Shannon 21 Jul 1797; 'Jean?' Jane (of age) d ----- Shannon, dec. b- Jacob Gregory min- Archibald Scott- 23Jul1797
  David & Margaret Warrick 2 Feb 1786; s of Mary d of William b- William Rider wit- John Slavins min- Samuel Shannon- 9Feb1786
  Henry S & Margaret Rough 22 Jan 1846; min- J C Hensell
  Isaac & Sarah Givens 16 Mar 1790; Minister's return spells name as 'Givins' d William, who consents b- Robert Givin wit- Robert Eastham & John Berry min- Samuel Houston- 25Mar1790
  John & Elizabeth Nutty 27 Sep 1833; min- George Hildt
  Samuel & Rachel Hawk 8 Sep 1798; Minister's return spells name as 'Hauk' Rachel (of age) d Henry Jacob Gregory swears Samuel of age b- Thomas Gregory min- Archibald Scott- 15Sep1798
  Thomas & Polly Hawk 4 Jan 1800; d Henry & Catherine Hawk and of age b- William Redford min- William King- 9Jan1800
  Thomas & Jenney Vians 21 Nov 1818; 'Fanny Vines' min- William King

Greiner
  David M & Rebecca Weaver 26 May 1848; min- D W Arnold
  George & Cathorine Whitzel 31 Aug 1797; Cathorine (of age) d ----- Whitzel, dec. b- Abraham Garber
  John D & Jane Terrill 29 Feb 1820; min- Robert H Chapman
  John David & Elizabeth Yost 23 May 1793; d Henry who consents test- John Garber & Edward Burk con- A Mustoe test- Phill North & Charles O'Neil b- Adam Bickle

Augusta County Marriages -- Man's Name

Greiner (cont.)
　John H & Eleanor Hall 9 Sep 1828; min- William C. Morrison
　John & Elizabeth Fishburn 18 Mar 1817; min- William King
Greiver
　George & Catherine Harshaw 16 Feb 1832; min- William Calhoon
Greogry
　Jesse & Elizabeth Chapman 3 Jan 1822; min- James C Willson
Gresham
　Moses & Polly Link 7 May 1807; min- William Wilson
Grever
　Valentine & Sarah Argenbright 8 Jan 1829; min- William Calhoon
Grice
　David B & Susan Moore 2 Jun 1831; min- William Calhoon
Griffey
　Thomas & Catherine Wright 28 Mar 1786; d William b- John Andiddie wit- Robert Caldwall min- Samuel Carrick- 28Mar1786
Griffin
　John & ----- ----- 30 Aug 1773; license only
Griffith
　David & Betsey Wallace 6 Jan 1815; min- William Calhoon
　Elijah & Elizabeth Jamison 2 Oct 1805; min- William King
　Robert & Sally Blair 19 Dec 1809; min- William King
　William & Jemima Jones 29 Jan 1805; min- William King
Griggs
　Thomas & Charlotte Hubbard 15 Jul 1801; Minister's return spells name as 'Hubbord' b- John Bowyer min- John McCue- 16Jul1801
Grigsby
　Peter & Jane Carter 31 May 1808; min- William King
Grill
　Bird & Elizabeth Abney 5 Jan 1820; min- William Calhoon
Grim
　John & Elizabeth Hart 9 Nov 1789; d William b- William Heart min- Archibald Scott- 11Nov1789
　William & Rebecca G Kiracofe 14 Jan 1841; min- Peter Shickel Jr
Grimm
　George & Rachael Slagel 24 May 1827; min- Michael Meyerhoeffer
Griner
　Jacob & Hariet Dixon 1 Nov 1825; min- William Wilson
Grinstead
　James & Mary Shedden 7 Nov 1787; widow b- Nicholas Spring
Grips
　William & Elizabeth Painter 20 Aug 1812; min- William King
Groah
　George & Ann Fitzpatrick 23 Apr 1822; min- James C Willson
Groff
　Christian & Mary Stover 3 Feb 1825; min- Josiah Cole
　George & Polly Shore 2 Feb 1790; b- Francis Huff min- William Wilson- 3Feb1790

Augusta County Marriages -- Man's Name

Groom
William H & Frances Davis 29 Dec 1842; min- Samuel Wagner
Grooms
Arthur & Martha Ann Tally 28 Oct 1824; min- Josiah Cole
John & Catharine Taylor 12 Apr 1847; min- T T Castleman
Robert H & Duretta Ann Johnson 20 Jul 1848; min- J McKendree Reiley
Robert & Polly Chapman 9 May 1814; min- Thomas Bourne
Grose
John & Nancy Corby 25 Apr 1842; min- James Morrison
Grove
Christian & Elizabeth Ritter 26 Jun 1787; Minister's return spells name as 'Groff' b- John Moore min- Archibald Scott- 27Jun1787
Cyrus & Mary Ann Fitch 5 Sep 1849; min- William T Richardson
David & Catharine Bowls 15 Feb 1844; min- T T Castleman- publication of banns
David & Ann Grove 24 Jun 1813; min- William King
Henry & Elizabeth Hoover 8 Aug 1825; min- Michael Meyerhoeffer
Jacob & Margaret Hoover - Oct 1828; min- William Calhoon
Joseph & Nancy Brower 5 Sep 1833; min- Abraham Garber- publication of banns
Joseph & Margaret Clarke 29 May 1817; min- William Calhoon
Martin & Margaret Coiner 7 Feb 1813; min- G H Riemenschneider
Robert & Sarah Jurtz 12 Dec 1833; min- William G Jackson
Windle & Jane Bolls 17 Apr 1806; min- William Calhoon
Groves
Nathaniel & Sarah Ellen Culp 3 Mar 1836; min- Joshua Webb
Grow
Daniel & Catherine Zimbro 16 Sep 1813; min- William King
William & Charity Weaver 7 Sep 1837; min- J C Hensell
Guffy
Alexander & ----- ----- 28 Apr 1763; license only
Guin
Joseph & Nancy Swink 8 Sep 1821; min- John D Ewin
Moses & Betsy Kinkead 21 May 1821; min- John D Ewin
Guinn
Samuel & Margaret Black 29 Mar 1827; min- Alexander Templeton
Samuel & Betsy Henderson 1 Dec 1831; min- James Kerr
Samuel & Elizabeth Henderson 15 Dec 1831; min- James Kerr
Gum
Abraham & Priscilla Wade 8 Jun 1785; d John b- William Slaven wit- William Slaven & John Gum min- Samuel Shannon- 20Apr1785
Gunnell
Nathaniel & Betsey Patterson 31 Mar 1808; min- William Wilson
Gunning
David & Sarah Fulton 17 Sep 1807; min- William McPheeters

Augusta County Marriages -- Man's Name

Guthrey
  John & Margaret Gilkeson 14 May 1794; Minister's return spells name as 'Guthery & Gilkerson' d Hugh b- Hugh Gilkeson min- John McCue- 15May1794

Guthrie
  Hugh G & Elizabeth E Gilkeson 31 May 1849; min- Robert L Dabney

Guy
  James & Elizabeth Hickell 10 Oct 1809; min- John Montgomery
  John & Mary Erwin 19 Nov 1785; d Edward (dec) b- James Guy
  Thomas & Mary Swearingen 14 Feb 1791; Minister's return spells name as 'Swerengin' d Van Robert Guy affirms that Mary is 'reputed' to be 21 b- Robert Guy min- John Montgomery- 23Feb1791

Gwin
  Robert & ----- ----- 20 Feb 1765; license only

Gwinn
  David & Violet Crawford 11 Nov 1790; Minister's return spells name as 'Grim or Ginn' d William, who consents b- J Lyle Jr min- John Montgomery- 11Nov1790
  James & Jane Hicklin 13 Jan 1792; d John, who consents b- John Hicklin min- John Montgomery- 24Jan1792
  Moses & Hannah Hanger 23 Apr 1829; min- Henry S Kepler
  Thomas & Elizabeth Lockridge 8 Apr 1800; d Samuel who consents wit- James Graham test- James Gwinn b- Joseph Gwinn

Haffner
  Daniel & Diana Lutz 24 Sep 1839; min- John J Reimensnyder
  Henry & Margaret Sours - Jun 1818; min- John Brown
  Philip & Catharine Fulweider 9 Mar 1793; d Ulerick Fulwyder Affidavit of Philip that he is 21 b- Ulerick Fulwider

Hafner
  Andrew & Mary Trorebach 6 Jun 1795; d Nicholas b- Nicholas Trorebach

Hagar
  George & Ann Stroader 28 Oct 1785; min- Archibald Scott- 28Oct1785

Hager
  John & Ann Mary Shroader 22 Oct 1785; Minister's return spells name as 'Stroader' d George b- James Basset min- Archibald Scott- 28Oct1785

Haines
  William & Margaret L Strong 4 Nov 1834; min- Conrad Speece

Hains
  Jonathan & Polley Fishburn 17 Sep 1816; min- William King

Haldeman
  Jacob & Mary Earhart 7 Jun 1791; d Nicholas, who consents b- Jacob Eversole

Halderman
  Abraham & Sarah Eastham 9 Jan 1794; min- John McCue- 9Jan1794

Augusta County Marriages -- Man's Name

Hale
John & Mary Swisher 19 Jan 1842; min- George B Rimel

Hall
Abraham & Nancy M Finley 29 Nov 1827; min- Francis McFarland
Cornelius & Susanna Way 13 Dec 1810; min- William Calhoon
Edward & Polly Stuart 20 Jul 1790; b- John Burnsides min- William Wilson- 22Jul1790
Henry & ----- ----- 25 Feb 1771; license only
James A & Susan R Beard 16 Aug 1831; min- Francis McFarland
James & Margret Gibson 30 Jun 1836; min- William Calhoon
James & Nancy Hicklin 15 Nov 1785; d Thomas Hickland b- John Berry wit- Robert Givens
Jefferson & Hannah M Web 11 Apr 1832; min- John Hendren
Nathan & Mary Downey 2 Jan 1800; widow (of William) b- William Short & Judy Price min- William King- 2Jan1800
Nelson & Catherine Crow 26 Nov 1828; min- William C. Morrison
Robert C & Sarah Bosserman 31 Jan 1839; min- John C Hensell
Thomas R & Nancy Martin 11 Aug 1846; min- P Shickel
William & Rebecca Brafford 11 Jun 1787; widow b- Robert McChesney min- Archibald Scott- 16Jun1787
William & Eliza Jane Rusmisel 25 May 1842; min- John C Hensell

Ham
George & Margaret Meeks 8 Sep 1844; min- James Paine
John & Mary Meeks 8 Sep 1844; min- James Paine

Hamaker
Samuel & Elizabeth Croan - Sep 1813; min- John Brown

Hambleton
Charles & Elizabeth Erwin 7 Apr 1809; min- William King

Hamd
William & Mary Evelsizer 25 Dec 1799; Minister's return spells name as 'Ham' d Jacob Evilsizer (Ubelsaueftzer) test- John Lee b- John Armstrong min- William King- 27Dec1799

Hamilton
Alexander & ----- ----- - Nov 1756; 6
Andrew & Nancy Craig 14 Aug 1816; min- William Wilson
Audley & ----- ----- 18 May 1764; license only
Gawin & ----- ----- 1 Nov 1773; license only
Hugh & Elizabeth Clarke 18 Feb 1813; min- William Calhoon
James G & Martha A R Smith 17 May 1842; min- F D Goodwin
James & Polly Erwin 18 Nov 1806; min- William Wilson
James & Belenah Hamilton 26 Mar 1794; min- John McCue?- 26Mar1794
James & Belenah Hamilton 24 Mar 1795; d William Hamilton, dec. b- Charles Baskin min- John McCue- 26Mar1795
James & Rachel Vance 16 Sep 1786; d Samuel b- William Armstrong of Back Creek min- Samuel Shannon- 21Sep1786
John D & Rebecca A S Brown 25 Nov 1834; min- E R Veitch
John & Peggy Baskins 12 Mar 1807; min- John McCue
John & Sarah Craig 3 Mar 1808; min- William Wilson
John & Jane Hamilton 16 Apr 1800; d William Hamilton, dec. & Patience Hamilton who consents test- Fanny Neel b- John Craig Hamilton min- John McCue- date of ceremony missing

101

Augusta County Marriages -- Man's Name

Hamilton (cont.)
John & Barbara Jane Hansbarger 11 Oct 1827; min- William Monroe
John & Rebecca Laverty 10 Aug 1786; min- Samuel Shannon- 10Aug1786
Samuel & ----- ----- 7 Dec 1762; license only
William & ----- ----- 29 May 1771; license only
William & ----- ----- 21 May 1773; license only
William & Nancy Willson 7 Jun 1832; min- William Calhoon

Hamrick
James A & Magdelen O Burgess 5 Oct 1848; min- J McKendree Reiley

Handly
William (Jr) & Catherine Steele 18 Dec 1799; d Samuel Steele, dec. William Steele swears Kitty of age b- John Handly

Hanger
Alexander & Harriet Bare 12 Aug 1833; min- John Hendren
David & Elizabeth Cale 12 Feb 1846; min- J C Hensell
David & Sarah Crosby 15 Sep 1807; min- William Wilson
David & Polly Lesley 4 Jun 1818; min- William Calhoon
Frederick & Peggy Cook 23 Mar 1815; min- William King
Frederick & Elizabeth Guin 11 Apr 1826; min- William Monroe
Frederick & Mary Hull 4 May 1785; d Francis b- Anthony Mustoe wit- Robert Campbell & Samuel Black
George W & Susan C Whitlock 30 Aug 1849; min- Samuel Martin
George & Margaret Coffman 22 Feb 1844; min- J C Hensell
George & Susanna Loop 24 Aug 1822; min- John Brown
Jacob & Hetty Bear 6 May 1833; min- William Calhoon
Jacob & Hannah Fulwider 21 May 1835; min- Cornelius Gates
John (Jr) & Catherine D Reed 18 Mar 1830; min- Francis McFarland
John & Mary Allen 4 Apr 1822; min- Conrad Speece
John & Julian Lanack 25 Mar 1825; min- Josiah Cole
Martin & Jane Kellar 27 Aug 1827; min- William C. Morrison
Peter (Jr) & Susannah Grove 26 Feb 1800; d Windle who consents test- Windle Grove Jr b- John Wise & Henry Grove
Peter (Jr) & Cathorine Link 8 Apr 1785; d Mathias b- Peter Hanger Sr
Peter (Jr) & Margaret Poage 22 Aug 1850; min- W G Campbell
Peter H & Margaret Robertson 25 Jan 1838; min- J C Hensell
Peter & Elizabeth Ann Bare 15 Sep 1834; min- John Hendren
Peter & Patsy Crawford 24 Nov 1818; min- Conrad Speece, Jr
Robert & Nancy Ann Reid 20 Sep 1828; min- James Morrison
Samuel & Nancy Steele 15 Mar 1832; min- Francis McFarland
William A & Rebecca Anderson 17 Jan 1820; min- John Hendren
William S & Margaret S Eidson 2 Sep 1834; min- William Calhoon
William & Eliza Hogshead 11 Oct 1825; min- John Hendren
William & Rebecca Sillings 19 Feb 1829; min- John Hendren

Hanlen
James & Nancy Wheeling 30 Dec 1788; b- John Rhea (Reaugh) min- James Chambers- 30Dec1788

Augusta County Marriages -- Man's Name

Hanna
   Abraham & Mary Carson 9 Mar 1793; b- John Mills min- William Wilson- 15Mar1793
   David & Eliza Mateer 24 Oct 1826; min- Francis McFarland
   Isaac & Rebekah Hogshead 10 Nov 1786; Minister's return spells name as 'Hanah' b- John Mills min- Archibald Scott- 9Nov1786
   Robert & Susan Willson 6 Sep 1825; min- Francis McFarland
   William & Polly Buchanan 13 Mar 1797; Minister's return spells name as 'Hannah' d David Buchanan (Buckwhanen) who consents test- James Hanna b- James Buchanan Jr min- Archibald Scott- 16Mar1797
   William & Amelia Gray 22 Dec 1831; min- John Hendren

Hannah
   Hugh & Elenor Johnston 22 Nov 1788; Minister's return spells name as 'Hanna' d James who consents test- William Wilson b- Thomas Frame Hugh lists trade as shoemaker min- William Wilson- 22Dec1788
   Mefford & Edith Harrison 10 Dec 1823; min- Michael Meyerhoeffer
   Robert & Jane Eveline Berry 2 Aug 1829; min- Francis McFarland

Hansbarger
   Henry & Sally Golloday - Jun 1814; min- John Brown

Hansel
   George & Peggy Funkhouser 10 Sep 1812; min- William King

Hansell
   John & Mary Grips 28 Apr 1835; min- William Calhoon

Hapener
   William & Jane Boyd 19 Jun 1806; min- William King

Harbarger
   Abraham & Jane Vines 3 Aug 1795; d Thomas Thomas Masterson affirm that Jane above 21 and has lived in the county about 12 months b- Roger Sullivan

Harbison
   John & ----- ----- 1 May 1765; license only

Hardbarger
   Thomas & Rachel Spear 3 Jan 1822; min- James C Willson

Harden
   Daniel M & Eliza Ann Gibbons 15 Sep 1836; min- J C Hensell

Harding
   Edward & Margaret Patterson 28 Jun 1790; d Robert, who consents b- George Kirkpatrick wit- William Scott & Thomas Sharp

Hardwick
   Christopher & Jane Bickerton 1 Jun 1820; min- William Wilson
   Gabriel & Mary Allen 10 Jul 1821; min- Daniel Stephens
   James & Sarah Thacker 24 Nov 1828; min- William Wilson
   John & Mary Rodgers 19 Jan 1830; min- Henry S Kepler- publication of banns

Hardy
   Richard W & Martha A Britton 20 Feb 1849; min- T T Castleman

Augusta County Marriages -- Man's Name

Harland
  John & Sarah Hunter 23 May 1837; min- Zach Jordan

Harlow
  Augustine & Agnes Chesnut 17 Jul 1798; Agnes (of age) d
    William b- William Chesnut

Harman
  Henry & Polly Clarke 4 Oct 1825; min- Conrad Speece
  Jacob & ----- ----- 15 Jun 1751; license only
  Michael G & Caroline P Stevenson - --- 184-; min- T T
    Castleman

Harmon
  Henry & Susannah Printz 20 Jan 1801; Susannah (of age) sis
    to Peter Printz b- John McCausland min- William King-
    20Jan1801
  Henry & Mary Weikle 20 Feb 1799; d Philip b- Philip Weikle

Harner
  Henry & Elizabeth Fauber 22 Apr 1823; min- James C Willson

Harnest
  William & Betsy Austin 25 Jan 1819; bond- 17Feb1819(sic)
    min- John D Ewin

Harnsberger
  Ephraim & Rebecca Mowrer - Sep 1808; min- John Brown

Haroff
  Ludwick & Margaret Huffman 6 Feb 1818; min- William King

Harouf
  Jacob & Peggy Keller 12 Mar 1829; min- William Calhoon

Harper
  James & Caroline E Finley 29 Aug 1833; min- Francis
    McFarland

Harrigan
  John & Catharine Merritt 18 Nov 1825; min- Josiah Cole

Harris
  Burr & Milly Bohannon 18 Oct 1785; d James b- Philemon
    Bohannon wit- Charles Donnally
  Clement R & Elizabeth A Gatewood 16 Mar 1845; min- John A
    Van Lear
  George H & Mary Ewin 3 Jul 1820; min- Gerard Morgan
  Henry & Anzaleah Harbarger - --- 183-; min- Conrad Speece
  James & Ann Henry 15 Mar 1822; min- John Brown
  John E & Mary Ellen Reynolds 22 Feb 1849; min- J McKendree
    Reiley
  John & Margaret Frazier 4 Feb 1829; min- William C.
    Morrison
  John & Sally Hansel 7 Aug 1806; min- William King
  Lewis & Patsey Ballard 6 Nov 1818; min- William King
  Robert C & Deborah McCune 9 Aug 1810; min- John McCue
  Samuel C & Elizabeth McCutchan 9 Sep 1847; min- W G
    Campbell
  Thomas & Isabella Dunlap 31 Oct 1841; min- D F Bittle
  Thomas & Mary McClure 16 Jan 1840; min- A B McCorkle
  Thomas & Peggy McCune 10 Jun 1814; min- John McCue
  Thomas & Elizabeth Turk 20 Jun 1814; min- Wright Burgess
  Thomas & Mary Wilson 25 Jan 1816; min- John McCue
  William & Susan Bitzell 24 Sep 1833; min- George Hildt

Augusta County Marriages -- Man's Name

Harris (cont.)
  William & Polly Shull 25 Jul 1830; min- Gerard Morgan
  William & Elizabeth Webb 18 Dec 1792; b- Thomas Tombleston
Harrison
  Benjamin & ----- ----- 8 Aug 1763; license only
  Benjamin & Polly Hall 19 Mar 1791; d John b- John Hall
    min- William Wilson- 22Mar1791
  Daniel & ----- ----- - Jul 1761; license only
  Daniel & Rhoda Brown 14 Apr 1834; min- John Hendren
  Henry & Jane St Clair Cochran 28 Nov 1844; min- T T
    Castleman
  James & Susan Shultz 21 Jan 1841; min- John C Hensell-
    publication of banns
  John & Mary G Berry 15 Dec 1831; min- James Morrison
  Joseph & Polly Boyd 18 Dec 1806; min- John McCue
  Selden & Mary Roberts 9 Jun 1835; min- Conrad Speece-
    publication of banns
  William & Jane Young 25 Aug 1801; d William s Benjamin
    who consents test- Christopher Carman b- Robert Anderson
    min- William King- 25Aug1801
Harshall
  Jacob & Catherine Livick 9 Dec 1820; 'Harshaw' min-
    Josiah Cole
Harshaw
  George D & Elizabeth Moore 25 Mar 1823; min- Josiah Cole
Hart
  David & Elizabeth Wilson 29 Jan 1798; Elizabeth (of age) d
    William Wilson Sr, sis William Wilson Jr b- William Wilson
    Jr
  Jacob & Polly McGuffin 10 Nov 1825; min- James Morrison
  Jesse & Sarah Eakle 20 Apr 1819; min- Conrad Speece, Jr
  Job & Hanna Fix 4 Jan 1794; 'Hannah Swinks?' d Jacob b-
    Jacob Fix (Swinks?) no minister listed; clerk's memorandum
    cites ceremony date as 7Jan1794
  John & Eve Garmon 17 Feb 1800; 'John Horb?' d Adam who
    consents test- John Drumm & John Gorman b- John Garmon &
    John Drum min- John McCue- 20Feb1800
  Silas & Jane Robertson - Sep 1749; license only
  William & Mary Brown 18 May 1789; widow b- Andrew Scott
    min- Archibald Scott- 19May1789
  William & Susan Harris 14 Dec 1826; min- James Morrison
  William & Elizabeth Hinkle 19 Mar 1798; d John b- John
    Hinkle & Stuart Kennedy wit- William Sterritt
  William & Peggy Ramsay 6 Mar 1829; min- William Wilson
Hartigan
  Timothy & Nancy East 9 Jan 1798; d James b- James East
Harvey
  Daniel & ----- ----- 17 Nov 1761; license only
  Joseph & Ann Craig 30 Aug 1791; d Robert (dec) b- Robert
    Craig min- William Wilson- 1Sep1791
  Lyman & Ellen Ann Deal 26 Sep 1844; min- T T Castleman
Harvie
  John & ----- ----- 3 Jan 1772; license only

Augusta County Marriages -- Man's Name

Haslett
Robert & Isabell Thomson 2 Oct 1786; Minister's return spells names as 'Haslett' and 'Thompson' d William min- Archibald Scott- 2Oct1786

Hasterson
Willis & Caty Gregory 9 Oct 1808; min- William King

Hatfield
Andrew F & Catherine Casper 12 Nov 1827; min- William C. Morrison

Hatton
Mark & Jane Kindred 22 Dec 1792; Minister's return spells name as 'Renaered' b- Jacob Swallow no minister listed; clerk's memorandum cites ceremony date as 29Dec1791

Haupe
Henry & Elizabeth Doak 7 Feb 1828; min- Francis McFarland
John T & Eliza Lightner 8 Oct 1840; min- John C Hensell- publication of banns

Hawk
Jacob & Peggy Myres 8 Oct 1792; d Stophel Myers (German), who consents b- Michael Garber

Hawkins
Alexander & Jane Guinn 30 Aug 1832; min- William Calhoon
John & Mary Ann Mohler 12 Mar 1846; min- T T Castleman
William & Nancy Hogg 22 Feb 1787; d Elizabeth Hogge who consents test- Thomas Smythe & Patrick Sharkey b- Patrick Shirkey of Botetourt cty min- William Wilson- 23Feb1787

Hawp
Adam & Catharine Coiner 18 Nov 1794; Minister's return spells name as 'Haup and Corrier'd George b- George Coiner min- John McCue- 27Nov1794
Henry & Elizabeth Teeford 8 Mar 1790; b- Jacob Teeford
John & Pally Neizer 23 Apr 1791; d Adam who consents wit- Adam Hawp b- Jacob Tieport

Hawpe
Henry & Sally Mitchell 30 Nov 1847; min- J C Hensell
John T & Mary S Newton 19 Dec 1832; min- Francis McFarland
John & Catharine Crowbarger 17 Mar 1831; min- Francis McFarland
William & Maria Jane Shultz 15 Feb 1841; min- D F Bittle

Hay
James & Sarah McFaddin 12 Feb 1829; min- James Morrison

Haybarger
Jacob & Elizabeth Shover 17 Aug 1815; min- William King

Hayes
Patrick & Jane Brown 25 Jan 1802; d William b- William Brown

Hays
Andrew & Sarah Mims 19 Sep 1809; min- John Montgomery
David & Nancy Ware 5 Apr 1824; Free persons of color min- John Hendren
Hugh & ----- ----- 28 Apr 1763; license only
John & Betsy Wingfield 20 Jan 1807; min- Benjamin Brughes
Leonard & Sally Mitchell 14 Aug 1823; min- Francis McFarland

Augusta County Marriages -- Man's Name

Hays (cont.)
  Michael & Mary Knowls 26 Jul 1825; min- Josiah Cole
  Richard & Rachel Risk 27 Dec 1792; d Elizabeth Stuart, who consents wit- Charles Stuart (Stewart) & John Risk b- John Risk min- John Brown- 24Jan1793
  William & Polly Gragg 26 Jul 1804; min- William King
  William & Rachel Strong 16 Jun 1841; min- John C Hensell

Hazelip
  Harrison & Mary Bishop 1 Jun 1842; min- F D Goodwin

Head
  John & ----- ----- 27 Jul 1774; license only

Headrick
  Henry & Hannah Breden 11 Mar 1802; min- William King- 11Mar1802

Hearse
  Christian & Mary Lotts 20 Mar 1797; d George Lotts (Loetz) b- Henry Lotts

Heaton
  Amos & ----- ----- 20 Nov 1764; license only

Hedrick
  John & Mary Blair 29 Feb 1792; Minister's return spells name as 'Haduck' d William b- William Blair min- William Wilson- 1Mar1792

Hedwick
  Abraham & Catharine Ledegay 24 Nov 1800; d George b- George Ledegay Signed 'Hetwich' in German Abraham (of age)

Heise
  Joseph & Elizabeth Gabbert 29 Oct 1798; Elizabeth (of age) d Jacob who consents test- Jacob Palmer b- John Gabbert

Heiser
  Jacob & Margaret Patterson 23 Jun 1842; min- Samuel Wagner

Heisey
  Philip & Elizabeth Brady - Mar 1827; min- Joseph Smith

Heiskell
  Henry L & Margaret S Baldwin 11 Nov 1833; min- George Hildt
  Wade H & Susan E Sowers - Sep 1826; min- Joseph Smith

Heitzer
  John & Agness Wright 22 Apr 1800; d Joseph b- Joseph Wright

Heizer
  Edward & Catharine McCutchan 1 Apr 1847; min- J C Hensell
  James & Sarah Jane Brown 19 Jun 1834; min- William Calhoon
  Joseph & Nancy Hanna 2 Sep 1824; min- Francis McFarland
  Nathaniel & Martha Holton 22 Nov 1804; min- John McCue
  Samuel & Eliza Strain 4 Sep 1828; min- Francis McFarland
  William & Susan Brownlee 8 Mar 1832; min- Francis McFarland

Helmick
  Washington & Polly Lotts 18 Jun 1829; min- James Morrison

Helms
  George M & Elizabeth Ransbarger 27 Oct 1830; min- Gerard Morgan
  James & Susan Forbush 1 Nov 1831; min- Conrad Speece
  John & Mary Ann Brown 2 May 1822; min- Conrad Speece
  Joseph & Catherine Brown 19 Jul 1822; min- Daniel Stephens

Augusta County Marriages -- Man's Name

Helms (cont.)
  Richard & Sarah Shelton 17 Apr 1834; min- Conrad Speece
  William B & Rebecca Brown 13 Jan 1820; min- Daniel Stephens
Hemp
  David A & Sarah Nancy Stanton 5 Apr 1849; min- Alonzo P Ludden
  David & Rachel Troxel 28 Nov 1844; min- J C Hensell
Henderson
  Andrew & Margaret McCLure 5 Apr 1796; d John who consents test- James Hutcheson b- George Hutcheson min- John McCue- 7Apr1796
  Charles & Elizabeth Guthrie 18 Sep 1817; 'Harrison?' min- John McCue
  Daniel & Martha Steele 18 Feb 1802; min- John McCue- 18Feb1802
  David & Lucy Hicks 30 Mar 1809; min- John McCue
  James & Ann Caldwell 1 Mar 1792; d William b- John Caldwell min- John McCune- 1Mar1792
  John & ----- ----- 30 Sep 1765; license only
  John & Sarah Lessley 3 Jan 1792; Minister's return spells name as 'Betsy Lofly' d James (dec) b- Alexander Buchanan wit- John McClenachan no minister listed; clerk's memorandum cites ceremony date as 3Jan1792
  Joseph & ----- ----- 24 Sep 1765; license only
  Joseph & Eleanor Hutcheson 1 Apr 1794; d George b- George Hutchison min- John McCue- 3Apr1794
  Joseph & Hannah McCutchen 2 Feb 1799; d Robert Consent test- John Risk b- Jones McCutchen
  Robertus & Catherine Ann Peck 18 Oct 1849; Ceremony performed at the home of Chesley Kinney min- S J Love
  Rodney B & Ruth Ann Wright 21 Oct 1847; min- Francis McFarland
  William & ----- ----- 1 Apr 1765; license only
  William & Mary Beard 29 May 1787; d Edward b- Samuel Beard certificate that Mary 21 yrs old or upwards min- William Wilson- 24May1787
  William & Elizabeth Swisher 9 Sep 1834; min- Joseph Spriggs
Henkel
  Abraham & Maryan Koiner 30 Jun 1835; min- Ambrose Henkel
  Samuel G & Susan Coiner 1 Dec 1832; min- Ambrose Henkel
Henkle
  David & Mary G McCune 24 Oct 1839; min- John A Van Lear
Henn
  John C & Caroline Cease 31 Mar 1845; min- T T Castleman
Henry
  Charles & Agnes Henry 23 Jul 1798; Agnes (of age) d James Charles (of age) b- James Henry
  James & Mary Berry 6 Dec 1787; d George who consents test- Thomas Freeman & Luis Wiseman b- John Berry min- Archibald Scott- 13Dec1787
  John & Polly Fisher 1 Jul 1797; d James Fisher, dec. b- Richard King min- Archibald Scott- 1Jul1797
  John & Amy Sharp 14 Feb 1800; d John Sharp Sr who consents test- Thomas Sharp b- Joseph Sharp

Augusta County Marriages -- Man's Name

Henry (cont.)
  Joseph & Lucy Shumate 8 Sep 1802; min- John McCue- 8Sep1802
  Joseph & Rachel Williams 30 Sep 1800; d John who consents test- William whitesides b- George Williams
  Thomas L & Phebe B Brown 1 Feb 1846; min- J C Hensell
  William B & Isabella Cooper 17 Aug 1833; min- James Morrison
  William & Elizabeth McCune 21 Nov 1787; d Samuel & Elizabeth who consents test- James McCune & Samuel Henry b- Samuel Henry min- James Chambers- 21Nov1787

Hensley
  Enoch H & Ann Maria Bridge 5 Aug 1845; min- G W Israel

Hepler
  David & Margaret Nicholas 2 Apr 1818; min- John D Ewin

Herdman
  George & Polly McKemy 15 Jan 1802; Minister's return spells name as 'McKerny' d James b- James McKemy min- Benjamin Irwin- 26Jan1802

Hering
  Willis & Ann McDowell 31 Mar 1835; min- Samuel Kennerly- publication of banns

Hernsberger
  George & Rebecca Whitmore 21 May 1846; min- J A Van Lear

Heron
  Walter & Margaret Brown 14 May 1798; wit- Benjamin Burgher b- Jacob Kinney

Herrin
  Jacob & Lucy McDaniel 31 Oct 1832; min- James C Wilson

Herring
  Bethuel & Elizabeth Bell 11 Nov 1822; min- John Hendren
  Bethuel & Margaret Erwin 11 Oct 1800; widower Margaret (of age) d John, sis to Thomas Erwin Margaret gives own consent b- Thomas Erwin
  Chilles & Winny Shiflett 13 Feb 1837; min- B N Brown
  William & Hannah Robertson 28 Dec 1786; d Peter b- Randall Givens wit- Thomas & John Robertson William son of Leonard wit- Sarah Herring min- Benjamin Erwin- 8Jan1787

Herron
  Leonard & ----- ----- - Aug 1761; license only
  Robert & Jane Gilkeson 5 Dec 1820; min- William Calhoon

Heslet
  Robert & Polly Reid 5 Feb 1807; min- William Wilson

Hess
  John B & Sarah Ann Earhart 30 Mar 1848; min Henry Wetzel
  John & Mary Sensebaugh 1 Sep 1791; d John s of Christian who consents wit- John Ewing & Jacob Sensibaugh b- John Sensebaugh
  Joseph & Polly Weaver 11 Aug 1826; min- Daniel Stephens

Hesterson
  Hazard & Elizabeth Grass 6 Mar 1807; min- William King

Heyden
  Joseph & Mary Engleman 30 Sep 1828; min- William C. Morrison

Augusta County Marriages -- Man's Name

Hicklin
  James & Jane Stuart 30 Nov 1790; Minister's return spells name as 'Jane Stewart' d William, who consents b- John Stuart min- John Montgomery- 28Dec1790
  Thomas & ----- ----- 10 May 1765; license only

Hickok
  Samuel C & Rebecca Jane Cooper 8 Oct 1833; min- George Hildt

Hides
  William & ----- ----- 8 Mar 1764; license only

Hiestand
  Henry & Susannah Dietrick 12 Jun 1812; min- William Cravens

Higgason
  Garland & Mary Blakly - Dec 1817; min- John Brown

Higginbotham
  William & Polly Shannon 16 Mar 1790; b- John Shannon min- John Brown- 16Mar1790

Hight
  John & Elizabeth Kinder 27 Sep 1810; min- William King

Hilberd
  John & Caty Miller 24 Dec 1833; min- Abraham Garber- publication of banns

Hildebrand
  John & Susannah Leonard 24 Sep 1816; min- William King

Hill
  James & ----- ----- 25 Mar 1762; license only
  Young & Lucinda Luck 2 Dec 1823; min- Josiah Cole

Hillary
  Joseph A & Mary A Wyatt 11 Apr 1822; min- Josiah Cole

Hillis
  Hugh & Judy Grooms 31 Dec 1812; min- William King
  William & Issabella Frazer 25 Oct 1810; min- John McCue

Hiltebrand
  Henry & Susan Grove 9 Jun 1814; min- William King
  Jacob (Jr) & Magdalene Gochenour 22 Aug 1839; min- John J Reimensnyder

Hincey
  Christian & Nancy Stephen 5 Jun 1795; widower & widow (of Robert Stephen b- George Craig

Hind
  Alexander & Martha France 23 Aug 1787; Minister's return spells name as 'Francis' d Mary Francy who consents test- William Alexander & Charles Campbell b- John Allison min- William Wilson- 23Aug1787
  Samuel & Jane Frances 7 Aug 1787; Minister's return spells name as 'Francis' d Mary who consents test- Robert Alexander & Hugh Campbell b- John Alexander min- Benjamin Erwin- 7Aug1788

Hinds
  John & Jean Kerr 28 Jun 1749; license only
  William & Martha Hogshead 3 May 1819; min- John Hendren

Hine
  Daniel & Nancy Graham 16 Sep 1824; min- James Morrison

Augusta County Marriages -- Man's Name

Hiner
  Samuel & Christiena Michael 29 Dec 1839; min- George Huffman
Hiney
  John & Betsy Daggy 17 Jan 1823; min- G H Reimensnyder
  John & Betsy Daggy 18 Jan 1823; min- G H Riemenschneider
Hinton
  Silas & Susan Grimm 15 Oct 1824; min- John Hendren
Hippard
  Adam & Ann Eliza Lawson 30 Mar 1837; min- E Joshua Webb
  Jacob & Susan Jane Speers 12 Oct 1831; min- John Howell
Hippart
  George & Sarah Lowman 22 Jan 1828; min- William Monroe
Hiser
  William S & Sarah M Shultz 11 Jun 1845; min- P Shickel
Hite
  Gabriel & Mary Rankin 19 Jun 1820; min- John Hendren
  George & Betsey Frenger 2 Aug 1808; min- William McPheeters
  James F & Catharine E Lucas 2 Mar 1848; min- J C Hensell
  Michael & Jemima Jones 11 Aug 1798; 'Hight?' d Robert b- Robert Jones min- Archibald Scott- 14Aug1798
  Shepherd H & Malinda Wood 11 May 1839; min- James Paine
  Thomas M & Evelina Ann Sterrett 14 Mar 1836; min- John Hendren
Hively
  John & Susanna Woolwine 20 May 1800; d Philip Woolwine, dec. & Edward Woolwine who consents Both (of age) b- Jacob Woolwine min- William King- 20May1800
Hizer
  George & Esther Lambert 27 Mar 1817; min- William King
Hobock
  John & Mary Orr 11 May 1815; min- William King
Hodge
  Andrew & Isabella McTear 5 Sep 1791; Bond spells name as 'Meteer' d William who consents b- John Hodge, father of Andrew min- John Montgomery- 6Sep1791
  George & Julia A Larner 12 May 1835; min- Robert M Lipscomb
  Joseph & Sarah Rusmisel 22 Nov 1832; min- John Hendren- publication of banns
Hofe
  Peter & Susan Miller 22 Apr 1806; min- Samuel Garber
Hoff
  Samuel & Catherine Mowry 20 Sep 1788; b- Lutwig Maurer
Hoffert
  Henry & Elizabeth Michel - Aug 1806; min- John Brown
Hog
  Peter & Patsy Abney 18 Sep 1798; d John Abney, dec. con- Isabella Abney test- James Hog b- Robert McClenachan min- John Montgomery- 18Sep1798
Hogg
  James & Amy Gregory 20 Aug 1798; Minister's return spells name as 'Hog' 'Ann' con- James Edmondson, gdn of Amy James Edmundson from Staunton test- A Stuart min- William Wilson- 20Aug1798

Augusta County Marriages -- Man's Name

Hogg (cont.)
  Peter E & Sarah Kerr 2 Mar 1829; min- Francis McFarland

Hogsett
  James & Elizabeth Manuell 13 Feb 1815; min- Wright Burgess
  Robert & Obediance Mills 20 May 1847; min- J A Van Lear
  Thomas & Peggy Hogsett 19 Mar 1811; min- William Calhoon

Hogshead
  Charles & Margaret Kerr 22 Mar 1828; min- John Hendren
  Charles & Jane McGlammery 28 Jan 1801; Jane (of age) d John b- John McGlammery
  David B & Susan Jane McChesney 11 Jun 1846; min- W G Campbell
  David & Catherine Graham 16 Nov 1790; b- Thomas Graham min- William Wilson- 19Nov1790
  David & Rebecca Hogshead 27 Nov 1799; Rebecca (of age) d Michael who consents b- Thomas Hogshead
  Gordon & Catherine Knave 16 Dec 1810; min- William King
  James & Nancy Brown 20 Mar 1809; min- William Calhoon
  John G & Sarah W Clark 1 Dec 1842; min- James Bunting
  John & Margaret Francis 20 Jun 1786; d Mary b- John Bell wit- Thomas Bradshaw min- Benjamin Erwin- 22Jun1786
  John & Polly Hogshead 22 Jan 1829; min- John Hendren
  Josiah & Mary Irvine - Mar 1827; min- John Hendren
  Michael & ----- ----- - Nov 1759; license only
  Silas & Jane B Gilkeson 7 Feb 1845; min- John Hendren
  Silas & Peggy Waggener 7 Nov 1816; min- William King
  William & Martha Crawford 5 Nov 1807; min- William Wilson
  William & Sally Nichol 24 Nov 1823; min- John Hendren

Holderman
  Abraham & Sarah Earhart 7 Jan 1794; d Nicholas Affidavit of full age of Sarah b- Thomas Turk Jr min- John McCue- 9Jan1794

Holmes
  James & Jane Aistrop 22 Nov 1791; b- Philip North min- John McCune- 22Nov1791
  John & Patsy Allison 29 Dec 1828; min- William Wilson
  John & Agness Caul 16 Jan 1792; d Timothy, dec. con- Elizabeth Caul wit- H Caul, John Campbell, Thomas Caul b- Thomas Story & Hugh Caul min- William Wilson- 17Jan1792
  Martin & July Ann Vernum 3 Mar 1797; d Daniel b- Daniel Vernum

Holt
  Andrew & Dorcas Fisher 22 Apr 1830; min- William Hank

Holton
  David & Polly Bear 15 Nov 1804; min- John McCue

Holtz
  Jacob & Mary Jane Bosserman 27 May 1841; min- John C Hensell- publication of banns

Hood
  George & Jane Curry 17 Jan 1791; 'Jenney' b- Robert Curry min- William Wilson- 20Jan1791

Hoof
  Frederick & Madlena Fawner 4 Jun 1799; d Christian b- Christian Fawner

Augusta County Marriages -- Man's Name

Hook
Amos & Catharine Fleiger 21 Mar 1801; Marriage bond lists groom's name as John Fleiger' d John b- John Fleiger min- William King- 22Mar1801

Elisha & Jane Forsythe 9 Apr 1820; min- John Hendren

George & Jenny Bleakley 8 Jan 1789; min- William Wilson- 8Jan1789

George & Mary Warner 22 Jun 1791; 'Mary Weaver?' min- William Wilson- 22Jun1791

James & Polly Lewis 20 Jan 1798; Polly gives own consent d Anthony Lewis, dec. test- Thomas Bleakly b- George Hook min- William Wilson- 25Jan1798

Jeremiah & Ally Jackson 19 Apr 1810; min- William King

Robert & Elizabeth Walker 1 May 1817; min- Conrad Speece, Jr

Hooke
George & Jane Bleakly 7 Jan 1789; d Thomas, who consents b- John Campbell

Joseph & Hannah Dobage 4 Jan 1790; Minister's return spells name as 'Hook' widow b- Isaac Beal min- Benjamin Erwin- 19Jan1790

Hoover
Isaac & Margaret Ann Cook 13 Feb 1845; min- Jacob Baer

Jacob & Catharine Peters 2 Dec 1834; min- George Hildt

Jessee & Mary Catharine Eidson 15 May 1834; min- William Calhoon

Samuel & Mary Cassady 23 Jun 1840; min- J J Reimensnyder

Hope
Nicholas & Rachel Christian 21 Apr 1796; widow b- Joseph Burk

Hopkins
John & Jane Irvine 11 Jan 1820; min- John Hendren

Hopping
Ezekiel & Fanny Cunningham 24 Jun 1795; Minister's return spells name as 'Hoffing' d John who consents test- David Cunningham Jr & James Ewing b- John Diddey min- John McCue- 24Jul1795

John & Phebe Norton 14 Jan 1812; min- William King

Hottle
Joseph F & Susan Gibbons 30 Aug 1842; min- John C Hensell

Houdashell
Lorenzo (Jr) & Martha Ann Dudley 3 Apr 1849; min Henry Wetzel

Houdishell
David & Margaret Cook 26 Dec 1827; min- G H Reimensnyder

Houf
William W & Susan C R Link 11 Jan 1846; min- Jacob C Spitler

Houff
Benjamin & Nancy Allbright 10 Dec 1818; min- William King

John & Sally Clarke 15 Mar 1821; min- Conrad Speece

Peter E & Rebecca Link 11 Apr 1845; min- P Shickel

Augusta County Marriages -- Man's Name

Houghobout
  John M & Elizabeth Cease 1 Nov 1838; min- Thomas Wheeler
Houser
  George & Hanna Reignheart 13 Aug 1792; d Owen b- Henry Rinehart
  Peter & Margaret Steele 28 May 1829; min- Francis McFarland
Houseright
  John & Patsey Bouler 25 Jun 1793; d James who consents (Patsey under age) test- J Brooks & Thomas Pannell b- Benjamin Pannell
Houston
  Joseph & Sarah Brownlee 21 Mar 1805; min- John McCue
Howard
  John & ----- ----- - Oct 1764; license only
Howell
  Alfred & Mary Ann Bachelor 28 Aug 1849; min- John Hendren
  Alfred & Polly Riley 18 Sep 1821; min- John Hendren
Hoye
  James & Fanny Tate 5 Jun 1800; Fanny (of age) sis to Mary Shepherd, late Mary Tate James (of age) b- George Grant Mcintosh & David Parry
Hudlow
  Samuel & Margaret Goff 20 Aug 1835; min- Conrad Speece- publication of banns
Hudson
  Charles & Mary Parris 17 Dec 1800; d John b- John Parris
  George H & Mary C Slanker 28 Jun 1848; min- T T Castleman
  Isaac & Sarah Love 18 Aug 1789; s George, who consents b- John Emmitt wit- William Gilkeson & David Williams
  Richard & Elizabeth Rader 5 Sep 1795; 'Reading?' Minister's return spells name as 'Ridden' Elizabeth (of age) d James Raiden b- James Elliott min- Archibald Scott- 6Sep1795
Hueston
  John & Jane Curry 23 Apr 1807; min- William King
Huff
  Francis & Ann Armstrong 28 Oct 1824; min- William W Calhoun
  Francis & Martha Jane Farrow 21 Dec 1848; min- J McKendree Reiley
  Francis & Letitia Jennings 23 Dec 1841; min- F D Goodwin
  Henry & Polly Moore - --- 179-; d John b- John Moore
  Jacob & Easter Beam 12 Jan 1827; min- John A Gore
  John M & Polly Beam 21 Mar 1822; min- Daniel Stephens
  John & Betsey Brown 23 Mar 1813; min- William King
  Vincent & Martha Ann Childers 6 Jan 1825; min- Josiah Cole
Huffer
  David & Polly Pickering 16 Apr 1830; min- William Wilson
  Jacob (Jr) & Margaret Crum 26 Aug 1847; min Henry Wetzel
  Jacob & Susanna Karichoof 27 Apr 1820; min- Daniel Stephens
  John & Hannah Shaver 18 Dec 1845; min- Henry Wetzel
Huffert
  Jacob & Eve Michael 28 Aug 1839; min- George Huffman
  John & Anna Michael 17 Nov 1829; min- G H Reimensnyder

Augusta County Marriages -- Man's Name

Huffman
   Abraham & Catherine Bolton 18 Sep 1836; min- John Hendren
   Christian & Barbary Butt 19 Jul 1790; d Henry, who consents (in German) b- Jacob Sheetz wit- Jacob Sheets (signs in German) & Adam Butt
   Ezra G & Margaret Fauver 29 Oct 1839; min- George B Rimel
   George & Catherine Argenbright 17 Aug 1799; Catherine (of age) d John b- John Argenbright
   James F & Elizabeth Horn 29 Jul 1849; min- George B Rimel
   James H & Sarah Showalter 22 Feb 1838; min- William R Coursey
   John & Ann Bear 7 Aug 1810; min- William King
   John & Polly Daggy - Oct 1825; min- John Brown
   Slyvester & Amelia V Stofer 11 Nov 1847; min- John Bowen

Hufford
   Samuel & Catharine Carricof 12 Jan 1827; min- John Hendren

Hugart
   Thomas & ----- ----- - Mar 1761; license only

Hugghart
   Moses & Mary Elstock 5 Sep 1799; Mary (of age) d Joseph Elstock of Louisa, and a free mulatto woman b- John McCutchen

Hughart
   John & Jenny Thompson 30 Jul 1789; d Edward & Jean , who consents b- Daniel Friel min- John Montgomery- 3Aug1789

Hughs
   Peter & Jane Riddle 14 Nov 1809; min- John McCue

Hulet
   James & Elizabeth McCorkle 21 Apr 1787; d Samuel who consents test- John McCorkell, Benjamin Chapman & Samuel McCorkell b- Jacob Swallow Elizabeth 22 yrs old min- Archibald Scott- 22 Apr1787

Huling
   Andrew & Margaret B Lessley 4 Sep 1834; min- Samuel Kennerly

Hull
   Daniel (Jr) & Mary Ann Eliza Beard 6 Sep 1832; min- Francis McFarland
   Daniel & Barbara Summers 15 Feb 1796; d John b- John Summers
   Jacob & Nancy Sproul 19 Apr 1827; min- James Morrison

Hulvey
   Ephraim & Margaret Cassady 8 Oct 1834; min- William Wilson

Humbert
   Jacob & Elizabeth Humbert 7 Sep 1837; min- John Garber

Hume
   James & Elizabeth Moore 24 Aug 1834; min- William Calhoon

Humphrey
   John & Malinda Lessley 11 Apr 1844; min- J C Hensell
   Patrick & Sally Reed 26 Dec 1805; min- John McCue
   Richard & Catharine Jane Lessley 9 Feb 1844; min- J C Hensell

Augusta County Marriages -- Man's Name

Humphreys
John & Nancy R Sterrett   4 Oct 1827; min- William Calhoon
Spicer & Polly Eversole   26 May 1817; min- William King

Hunley
Austin & Matilda Turner   12 Mar 1835; min- John Hendren
Valentine & Mary Merritt   12 Nov 1835; min- J J Glossbrenner

Hunter
Andrew & Jean Thompson   27 Dec 1791
Elijah & Sarah Ann Cale   27 Mar 1849; min- Alonzo P Ludden
Elijah & Deniza Jane Swink   22 Feb 1842; min- James Gamble
Francis & Margaret McCaaley   24 Mar 1787; Minister's return spells name as 'McCawley' d Margaret McCaly test- William Brown & David McCaly b- James Coulter min- Samuel Carrick- 21Apr1787
James & Jane Didell   19 May 1808; min- William King
John & Barbara Crane   29 Jan 1805; min- William Wilson
Mathew & Catherine Hunter   8 Dec 1790; d Samuel, who consents b- John Hunter min- Archibald Scott- 9Dec1790
Matthew & Mary Hansbarger   18 Nov 1830; min- Gerard Morgan
Robert & Eleanor Fulton   22 Dec 1803; min- John McCue
Robert & Betsy Ann McChesney   31 Aug 1799; d James who consents   test- James McClung s Samuel b- Adam McChesney
Samuel & Sally Dollhouse   7 Jan 1808; min- John McCue
Samuel & Mary Steele   24 Apr 1804; min- John McCue
William S & Catharine M Alexander   2 Mar 1848; min- Robert L Dabney

Hupman
Christian & Mildred Hunley   16 Mar 1833; min- William Calhoon
John & Elizabeth Fourber   4 Mar 1813; min- William King
Valentine & Cyntha Hutchens   29 May 1834; min- Cornelius Gates

Huston
Archibald & Mary Stevenson   20 Jun 1749; license only
James & ----- ----- - Mar 1749; license only
William & Elizabeth Bratton   26 Aug 1790; d-in-law of John Burk, who consents wit- Hance Herron & John Gregory min- Archibald Scott- 2Sep1790

Hutchens
David W & Elizabeth Harris   13 Nov 1832; min- William Wilson
James & Sarah Paris   17 Sep 1835; min- Isaac Jones

Hutchenson
George & Mary Campbell   7 Jan 1786; Minister's return spells name as 'Hutcheson' George from Greenbrier cty d James b- W. Urquhart wit- Samuel Strong min- William Wilson- 2Jan1786

Hutcheson
Isaac & Margaret Hutcheson   10 Nov 1807; min- John McCue
James & Sarah Gregery   9 Sep 1802; min- William King- 9Sep1802
James & Mary Gregory   1 Mar 1804; min- William King
John & ----- -----   25 Jun 1764; license only
John & Margaret Finley   19 Mar 1793; d John b- George Hutcheson min- John McCue- 2Jun1793

Augusta County Marriages -- Man's Name

Hutcheson (cont.)
  Thomas & ----- ----- - Apr 1761; license only
  William & Isabella White 14 May 1812; min- John McCue
Hutchison
  George (Jr) & Elizabeth Stuart 4 Dec 1798; d Benjamin wit- Benjamin Stuart, Chesley Kinney & John Fackler b- George Hutchison Sr
  Robert & Jane Hall 8 Apr 1786; Minister's return spells name as 'Hutcheson' d Robert b- W Urquhart wit- John Berry, Robert Ramsey & James Hall min- Samuel Shannon- 11Apr1786
  Samuel & Jinny McDead 24 Sep 1807; min- John McCue
Hyde
  Addison & Mary Bell 3 Sep 1812; min- John McCue
  Cyrus & Margaret A Crawford 27 Dec 1820; min- Conrad Speece
  John & Sally Crawford 9 May 1811; min- John McCue
Hyden
  Joshua & Martha Chesnut 26 Jan 1796; Minister's return spells name as 'Chesnutt' Martha (of age) d William who consents test- Daniel Good b- Robert Bailey min- John McCue- 2Feb1796
Hyland
  John & Isabella Denison 19 Feb 1835; min- Conrad Speece
Imboden
  George & Isabella Wonderlake 21 May 1822; min- Michael Meyerhoeffer
  Henry & Jane Coiner 14 Apr 1800; Minister's return spells name as 'Impoten' Signed 'Heinrich Imboden' Henry (of age) d George b- George Coiner min- John McCue- 17Apr1800
  John D & Eliza McCue 26 Jun 1845; min- B M Smith
Ingles
  William & Betsy Crawford 22 Sep 1818; min- Conrad Speece, Jr
Ingleton
  William & Jane Fife 7 Aug 1806; min- William King
Ingram
  John & Anne Montgomery 23 Dec 1841; min- James Paine
Irvine
  Andrew & Nancy Gilkeson 28 Sep 1830; min- John Hendren
  Eugenio & Isabella Montgomery 11 Oct 1821; min- John D Ewin
Isaacs
  Peyton & Rachel Lewis 26 Sep 1816; min- William King
Iseman
  Christian & Hannah Wesit 4 Feb 1826; min- Michael Meyerhoeffer
Jackson
  David & Mary Long 8 Apr 1824; min- Josiah Cole
  James & Elizabeth Ann Bowman 11 Sep 1845; min- W G Campbell
  Michael & Barbara Fridley 18 Feb 1817; min- William King
  Peter & Nancy Zahns 26 Mar 1846; min- W G Campbell
  Samuel & Margaret Hall 16 Jan 1797; d William Hall, dec. con- Fanny Allison, mother of Margaret test- Isabella Sterrett & William Sterrett b- William Sterritt min- Archibald Scott- 24Jan1797

Augusta County Marriages -- Man's Name

Jackson (cont.)
　Thomas & Catherine Steele 10 Apr 1807; min- William McPheeters
　William & Margaret Boyles 26 Mar 1785; d Thomas b- Benjamin Yardley
　William & Peggy Conway 27 Nov 1817; min- William King

James
　John Q & Cornelia Smith 18 Oct 1842; min- P E Stevenson
　Thomas & Elizabeth Fauber 30 Jun 1819; min- G H Riemenschneider

Jameson
　William & Margaret Craig 2 May 1789; d Samuel, who consents wit- James Craig & Samuel Crawford b- James Craig min- John Montgomery- 12May1789
　William & Mary McNight 24 Mar 1800; d Timothy b- Timothy McNight min- Robert Wilson- 3Apr1800

Jamison
　Robert & Margaret McCutchen 28 Oct 1795; d John of Calfpasture test- John Meek b- Samuel McCutchen Jr min- John Montgomery- 3Nov1795
　Samuel & Mart Trimble 15 Feb 1821; min- William W Calhoun

Jarvis
　Amos & Nancy Troxell 11 Dec 1834; min- Conrad Speece
　Jeremiah & Elizabeth Tuening 27 Mar 1834; min- Conrad Speece

Jenkins
　William & Nancy Wright 30 May 1810; min- William King

Jennings
　Pollard & Eliza Jane Lowman 4 Mar 1838; min- Stephen Smith

Joh
　Jacob & Betsy Runkle 24 Jan 1804; min- William King

John
　Edward & Sally Baties 20 Jan 1820; 'Batis' min- William Calhoon

Johns
　Allen & Elizabeth C Bishop 29 Oct 1846; min- William Calhoon
　William & Rebecca Fitzpatrick 27 Jan 1825; min- Josiah Cole

Johnson
　Alexander & Salley Sterret 10 Dec 1818; min- John D Ewin
　Andrew & Esther L Alexander 21 Feb 1828; min- James Morrison
　Francis & Mary Jane Hall 4 Jul 1825; min- Josiah Cole
　French S & Betsy Ship 29 Jun 1841; min- P E Stevenson
　Henry A & Frances Coffman 15 Sep 1842; min- Samuel Wagner
　Isom & Catherine Gregory 12 May 1800; d John Gregory, dec. sis to Benjamin Gregory b- Benjamin Gregory min- William King- 12May1800
　James & Isabella Jenkins 3 Jan 1792; Minister's return spells name as 'Joseph Johnson b- John Gorden min- William Wilson- 5Jan1792
　John & Sarah Coltrider 15 Sep 1807; min- William King
　John & Sarah Reed 28 Dec 1826; min- William Monroe
　Lewis & Martha Meek 26 Mar 1826; min- Daniel Stephens

Augusta County Marriages -- Man's Name

Johnson (cont.)
  Lewis & Peggy Montgomery 17 Aug 1826; min- William Monroe
  Martin & Mary A Jackson 24 Mar 1843; min- Samuel Wagner- publication of banns
  Robert & Betsey Jennings 11 May 1831; min- John Howell
  William B & Margaret Sarah Breckenridge 24 Sep 1846; min- T T Castleman
  William & Nancy Robertson 10 May 1828; min- William C. Morrison

Johnston
  Absolem & Margaret Blair 8 Nov 1799; Margaret (of age) d W Blair Samuel King swears Margaret of age b- Robert Reed min- William King- 9Nov1799
  Benjamin & Mary Muchmore 8 Oct 1788; min- William Wilson- 8Oct1788
  James & Esther Turk 19 Dec 1786; d Thomas Sr b- William Robertson s Zachariah min- William Wilson- 19Dec1786
  John & Elizabeth Bell 16 Sep 1794; 'Dr.' John Johnston d Joseph Bell, Gent. b- William Kennerly min- John Brown- 16Sep1794
  John & Mary Greiner 3 May 1797; Mary (of age) sis to David Greiner b- David Greiner
  John & Ruthey Ralston 20 Dec 1804; min- William King
  John & Patsey Walker 29 Dec 1837; min- John J Reimensnyder
  Richard E & Elizabeth Rapp 17 Nov 1840; min- John C Hensell- publication of banns
  Richard & Mary Dickey 23 Dec 1806; min- William Wilson
  Samuel & Catherine Armentrout 6 Apr 1837; min- John J Reimensnyder
  William & Jenny Kirkland 29 Dec 1786; d James b- Arthur Connelly wit- Samuel & James Kirkland min- William Wilson- 4Jan1787
  William & Mary Sheetz - Oct 1825; min- John Brown
  William & Sarah Strickland 27 Jul 1801; d John b- John Strickland
  Zachariah & Polly Brawford 3 Dec 1822; min- James Morrison
  Zachariah & Sarah Walker 23 Dec 1823; min- Conrad Speece

Jollett
  Fielding & Ann Stoutamoyer - Dec 1822; min- John Brown

Jones
  Dudley & Jane McNight 28 Sep 1801; d Timothy b- Timothy McNight
  Enos & Matilda Fenton 23 Aug 1822; min- Josiah Cole
  Enos & Rebecca Fenton 26 Nov 1827; min- William Wilson
  Enos & Catherine Forsythe 31 Oct 1805; min- William King
  Enos & Sarah Kilkenny 26 Mar 1805; min- William King
  Isaac & Maria W Finley 9 Nov 1837; min- A B McCorkle
  Isaiah & Ann Silling 21 Jan 1797; widower d Gasper Silling b- Gasper Silling
  Isiah & Jane Russell 17 Nov 1789; d John, who consents wit- Robert Jones & Henry Swink b- Griffith Evans
  Jacob & Margaret Myers 8 Aug 1797; d Frederick Mauers b- Frederick Myers
  John W & Mary E Valentine 19 Nov 1840; min- Frederick D Goodwin

Augusta County Marriages -- Man's Name

Jones (cont.)
  John & ----- ----- - Feb 1749; license only
  John & Elizabeth Smith 25 Jun 1799; d Thomas Smith, dec. & Elizabeth Smith, his wife who consents test- William Bell Jr b- Micael Garber Jr
  John & Margaret P Teney 27 May 1828; min- William Wilson
  Morris & Elizabeth Yost 31 Jan 1828; min- John Hendren
  Peter & Martha Breden 1 Dec 1792; 'Bredon?' d Edward b- Edward Breden no minister listed; clerk's memorandum cites ceremony date as 5Dec1792
  Peter & Mary Livick 18 Apr 1833; min- William Calhoon
  Preston & Elizabeth Litten 28 Apr 1831; min- William Wilson
  Richard S & Anne Messersmith 19 Nov 1846; min- J A Van Lear
  Robert & Ruth Griffith 9 Apr 1812; min- William King
  Samuel G & Martha M Good 1 Dec 1842; min- F D Goodwin
  William & Susanna Kurtz 12 Feb 1807; min- William King
  William & Isabella Smith 27 Nov 1787; Isabella gives her own consent test- William Henery & William Restill b- Adam Bickel min- James Chambers- 27Nov1787
  William & Sarah Wood 30 May 1787; 'Johns?' d James who consents test- Thomas Duglas & William Killpatrick Wm Jordan swears Sarah 18 on Jan 29 last and Wm is 21 b- William Jordan min- Samuel Shannon- 5Jun1787

Jordan
  Jacob & Elizabeth Shelly 3 Sep 1845; min- P Shickel
  James & Anna Boone 31 Dec 1839; min- John J Reimensnyder
  Lewis & Mary Trible 10 Nov 1785; min- John Brown- 10Nov1785
  William & Maria Hopewell 30 Apr 1843; min- John A Van Lear

Joseph
  Daniel & Annis Jackson 24 Feb 1817; min- William King
  William W & Eliza Jane Spitler 26 Oct 1848; min- J Markwood

Kaiger
  Augustine & Catherine Spring 2 Jan 1786; Minister's return spells name as 'Keiger' d Nicholas b- Samuel Merrit min- William Wilson- 2Jan1786

Kale
  John & Barba Slusher 26 Jul 1804; min- William King

Kanely
  Michael & Margaret Bowers - Jun 1803; min- John Brown

Karichoff
  Christopher & Catherine Tevenbaugh 21 Dec 1795; Minister's return omits Christopher's surname d Baltzer b- Baltzer Tevenbaugh min- William Wilson- 21Dec1795
  Frederick & Eva Ailor 25 Mar 1823; min- G H Riemenschneider

Karicofe
  Benjamin & Elizabeth Earhart 29 Nov 1838; min- John A Van Lear

Karikoff
  Andrew & Sarah Saunders 1 Dec 1831; min- John Hendren
  Frederick & Betsy Haffner 18 Jan 1820; min- G H Riemenschneider

Karricoff
  Jacob & Ann Propst 10 Jan 1835; min- John Hendren

Augusta County Marriages -- Man's Name

Kaufelt
  Augustine & Sarah Bright 10 Mar 1794; 'Coffeld?' d George Bright Sr who consents test- George Bright Jr b- George Bright Jr

Kayser
  Davis A & Sarah A Bell 24 May 1849; min- B M Smith
  W B & E Hall 17 Nov 1847; min- B M Smith

Kearns
  Abraham & Elizabeth Thompson 19 Sep 1795; Minister's return spells name as 'Abraham Coiner' d Andrew b- Andrew Thompson min- Archibald Scott- 29Sep1795

Kee
  John & Peggy Silor 24 Sep 1799; Minister's return spells name as 'Silar' Peggy from Augusta her father, Philip Silor Jr, from Rockbridge Philip consents test- Sarah Silers b- John Acker min- William King- 26Sep1799

Keen
  Samuel A & Elizabeth Summers 25 Apr 1837; min- J C Hensell

Keenan
  Edward & Julianna Hains 6 May 1814; min- William Calhoon

Keenon
  Hugh & Sarah Shackelford 11 Mar 1789; Minister's return spells name as 'Shackleford' d James, who consents wit- James Megongal & Samuel Forsythe min- William Wilson- 12Mar1789

Keeran
  Harrison & Elizabeth F White 8 Jun 1848; min- J C Hensell

Keiser
  Joseph & Elizabeth Bell 12 Apr 1808; min- John McCue

Keizer
  David & Lydia Hill 6 Mar 1801; Lydia (of age) sis to Eleanor Hill b- James Rankin

Kellar
  George & Catharine Beard - Apr 1822; min- John Brown
  John & Susannah Sowers - May 1805; min- John Brown
  Lewis & Nancy Kiplinger 20 Dec 1810; min- William King
  Samuel & Catharine Engleman 2 Oct 1821; min- Michael Meyerhoeffer
  Samuel & Rebecca Harouff 31 Jul 1828; min- William Calhoon

Keller
  Frederick & Barbara Bailor 6 Mar 1787; d Jacob who consents test- Samuel Merrit b- Jacob Bailor
  Frederick & Magdalene Fall 24 Feb 1818; min- William King
  George W & Rebecca Engleman 15 Dec 1842; min- J C Hensell
  Harman D & Susannah Engleman 27 Jul 1847; min- J C Hensell
  Jacob & Louisa Lukeden 1 Sep 1831; min- Samuel Kennerly
  John & Nelly Matheny 13 Nov 1790; Minister's return spells name as 'Kellar' widow b- Jacob Faulkner (note attached that John Keller is a free person & has no relation in this State) min- William Wilson- 19Nov1790
  John & Ann Moyers 15 Apr 1818; min- William King
  Lewis & Elizabeth Coursey 24 Aug 1846; min- James H Brown
  Lewis & Catharine Fall 16 Apr 1818; min- William Calhoon
  Lewis & Susan Landes 27 Sep 1832; min- John Haney

Augusta County Marriages -- Man's Name

Keller (cont.)
 Samuel & Juda Davis 13 Dec 1828; min- William C. Morrison
Kellor
 George & Sophia Mowry 5 May 1786; Minister's return spells name as 'Kellar' d Lewis b- Lutwig Mawrer 'consent personally?' min- William Wilson- 7May1786
Kelly
 James A & Mary W Whitesell 19 Mar 1840; min- P E Stevenson
 John & Elizabeth Lohr 6 May 1803; min- William King
 Peter & Mary Rigby 26 Nov 1788; Minister's return spells name as 'Mary Reyburn' widow b- Robert Burges min- James Chambers- 26Nov1788
 Williamson & Eliza B Bragg 20 Nov 1832; min- Francis McFarland
Kelso
 Charles & May McPheeters 6 Jun 1794; 'Polly?' d William b- William McPheeters no minister listed; clerk's memorandum cites ceremony date as 13Jun1794
 James & Betsy Sitlington 24 Aug 1789; d John, who consents wit- Alexander Crawford & Andrew Sitlington s Hugh, who consents wit- John Walker, John Moore & John Stewart b- Alexander McPheeters min- John Brown- 1Sep1789
Kenady
 Michael & Ellen McCaferty 12 Jan 1786; min- John Brown- 12Jan1786
Kendall
 Jesse & Elizabeth Meeks 19 Feb 1819; min- William Calhoon
Kendle
 John & Mary Dunlap 30 Apr 1818; min- William King
Keneday
 Henry & Elizabeth Sheetz - Dec 1818; min- John Brown
Kenedy
 William & Isabella McKamy 21 May 1828; min- James Morrison
Kennady
 David & Mary McClure 27 Mar 1817; min- John McCue
Kennedy
 George L & Isabella Brown 29 Apr 1828; min- William Calhoon
 Hugh G & Virginia Fulton 16 Mar 1848; min- J C Hensell
 Hugh & Elizabeth Young 25 Nov 1802; min- James Harper- 25Nov1802
 John & Elizabeth Davis 29 Oct 1846; min- James H Brown
 Peter & Elizabeth Stickley 25 Mar 1847; min- George H Martin
 William & Juliann Brown 10 Jun 1801; d William who consents sis to John Brown Juliann (of age) b- John Brown min- William King- 11Jun1801
Kennerley
 James & Lucy Kennerley 3 Apr 1806; min- Philip Kennerly
 John & Sarah Leas 4 Aug 1808; min- William Calhoon
Kennerly
 John & Catherine Herpine 13 Aug 1796; d Thomas Herpine, dec. of shenandoah cty Catherine not of age con- Mary Kennerly, mother & James Kennerly test- Catherine Kennerly b- Mathew Robertson

Augusta County Marriages -- Man's Name

Kenny
  David J & Sarah S Tuttle 28 Mar 1832; min- Samuel Kennerly
  Mathew & ----- ----- 3 Oct 1770; license only
Keran
  Samuel & Sarah Lilley 2 Nov 1822; min- Josiah Cole
Kerr
  Alexander & Sarah Bell 23 Nov 1795; d Samuel b- Samuel Bell min- William Wilson- 24Nov1795
  Amaziah & Jane Rutledge 11 Mar 1825; min- William Wilson
  Benjamin & Elizabeth Myers 24 Jun 1796; d Michael b- Michael Myers min- William Wilson- 26Jun1796
  Daniel & Mary Kirkpatrick 29 Jun 1790; d John, who consents b- John Kirkpatrick min- Archibald Scott- 1Jul1790
  David & Jane Dunlap 29 Mar 1824; min- Francis McFarland
  James & ----- ----- 13 Jan 1762; license only
  James & ----- ----- 17 Feb 1764; license only
  James & Patience Houston 18 Jan 1786; Minister's return spells name as 'Huston' d James Huston s James b- Matthew Kenny wit- Walter Boil, John Mison, John Lewis & John Dogherty min- William Wilson- 16Jan1786
  James & Mary Kerr 24 Nov 1803; min- John McCue
  James & Nancy Thornton 17 Dec 1818; min- William King
  John & Susan Hannah 23 Nov 1815; min- William Calhoon
  John & Elizabeth Hogshead 3 Sep 1792; Minister's return spells name as 'John Then' d James b- Thomas Rutledge & John Watt min- William Wilson- 4Sep1792
  Robert Grove & Cassandra D McCutchan 26 Apr 1830; min- Francis McFarland
  Thomas J & Margaret J Calbreath 22 Apr 1823; min- James C Willson
  William & Mary Grove 20 Dec 1796; Minister's return spells name as 'Mary Windlegrove(?)' d Windle who consents test- Henry Grove b- John Grove min- Archibald Scott- 22Dec1796
Kershner
  Abraham & Deliley Michael 29 Mar 1849; min- George B Rimel
  Jacob & Peggy Gabert 14 Apr 1801; d Jacob who consents test- George Hanger s David b- John Gabert
  Jacob & Mary Haup 10 Nov 1840; min- John C Hensell- publication of banns
Kersner
  John & Lucy Green 1 Apr 1824; min- Francis McFarland
Kessecker
  John & Catharine Dack 26 Dec 1791; d John, dec. b- Henry Deck
Kesterson
  George T & Matilda A Bains 30 Jul 1840; min- Frederick D Goodwin
  John S & Sarah Huff 27 Mar 1835; min- Samuel Kennerly
Keys
  John & Peggy Donaghe 18 Apr 1796; Peggy (of age) d William b- James McGongal
Kiblinger
  Adam A & Mary A Cook 24 Sep 1846; min- Stephen Hildebrand

Augusta County Marriages -- Man's Name

Kice
  Henry & Mary Haybarger 23 Mar 1820; min- Robert H Chapman
Kidd
  Joshua & Sarah Jane Litten 18 Jun 1846; min- James H Brown
Kiger
  John & Sarah Houchins 28 Feb 1812; min- William Wilson
Kilkenny
  James & Peggy Coiner 22 Apr 1801; 'Comer?' d Michael Coiner, dec. Sarah Kilkenny, mother, attests to James's age b- Samuel Long
  James & Elizabeth Imboden 22 Feb 1820; min- Daniel Stephens
  John & Fanny Hines 9 Jul 1812; min- William King
Killian
  Jacob & Julian Koiner 4 Feb 1840; min- Ambrose Henkel
Kilpatrick
  Samuel & ----- ----- 23 Jan 1770; license only
Kincaid
  John & Mary Dunwiddie 7 Jan 1786; Minister's return spells name as 'Dinwiddie' d Robert Dunwoody b- William Dickey min- Samuel Shannon- 17Jan1786
Kindig
  Abraham & Elizabeth Wenger 5 Nov 1846; min- J A Van Lear
  Benjamin G & Delilah Shotwell 21 Oct 1841; min- Benjamin W Kindig
  Elias & Elizabeth Wine 6 Sep 1838; min- John Garber
King
  Adam & Fanny Ann Glass 3 Oct 1805; min- William Wilson
  Adam & Anna Maria Ott 31 May 1796; d John who consents (in German) b- Henry Huffman
  Anthony & Elizabeth Hartzo 3 Aug 1795; d Engelbert b- Engelbert Hartzo
  George & Rebeccah Brown 27 Dec 1790; b- Hugh Brown wit- J Beal min- William Wilson- 29Dec1790
  Henry & ----- ----- 6 Jul 1768; license only
  John & Polly Apple 6 Jul 1820; min- Robert H Chapman
  John & Mary A Frazer 15 Sep 1808; min- John McCue
  Joseph & Elizabeth Ailer 1 Oct 1811; min- John Montgomery
  Richard & Nancy Fisher 9 Mar 1793; 'Margaret Fisher?' b- William Preston Skillern no minister listed; clerk's memorandum cites ceremony date as 18Apr1793
  Robert & ----- ----- 18 Nov 1773; license only
  Robert & Isabella Hanna 30 Nov 1793; b- William King min- William Wilson- 3Dec1793
  Samuel & ----- Garnes 3 May 1797; d Adam b- Adam Garnes
  Thomas & Anna James 1 Apr 1806; min- William King
  William W & Martha Moffett 8 Feb 1827; min- John Hendren
  William & Elizabeth East 5 Oct 1826; min- William Monroe
  William & Nancy Gates 8 Jun 1830; min- William Wilson
  William & Margaret Pence 26 Sep 1792; d Jacob Bentz, who consents wit- Thomas & Robert Poage b- Michael Garber
Kinkade
  Archibald & Sarah Noland 21 Aug 1798; Minister's return spells name as 'Kinkead' d John b- Moses Russell min- John Montgomery- 28Aug1798

Augusta County Marriages -- Man's Name

Kinkaid
  James & Jane Guinn 3 Dec 1829; min- Henry S Kepler
  John & Mary Ptomey 30 Sep 1824; min- Thomas Caldwell
  Morgan & Anny Henderson 14 Mar 1839; min- William Calhoon
Kinkead
  Andrew & Ann Poage 22 Jun 1786; Minister's return spells
    name as 'Kinkade' d John b- Robert Gamble min- William
    Wilson- 22Jun1786
  Charles & Nancy Kinkead 26 Feb 1807; min- John Montgomery
  David & Sally Hodge 14 Oct 1800; d John Hodge, dec. sis
    to William Hodge, and of age b- William Hodge
  Ferdinand & Margaret Fulton 19 Mar 1799; d James b- James
    Fulton
  Robert & Ann Brownlee 12 Jun 1792; b- Robert Rennick no
    minister listed; clerk's memorandum cites ceremony date as
    12Jun1792
  Robert & Peggy Lockridge 22 Apr 1806; min- John Montgomery
  William & Rebecca Lockridge 11 Mar 1806; min- John
    Montgomery
Kinnear
  John & Elizabeth McCune 16 Aug 1793; Minister's return
    spells name as 'Keaner' d John b- John McCune min- John
    McCue- 27Aug1793
Kinney
  Mathew & Jane Smith 28 Jun 1809; min- William Wilson
  Robert H & Rebecca R Wayland 20 May 1841; min- Benjamin M
    Smith
  Robert P & Isabella Stevenson 6 Jun 1844; min- T T
    Castleman
Kinsolving
  Napoleon B & Lavenia Austin 1 Jan 1833; min- Francis
    McFarland
Kiplinger
  John & Elizabeth Carpenter 8 Aug 1788; b- John Pence
  John & Catherine Hudlaw 1 Jan 1788; Minister's return
    spells name as 'Catherine Carpenter' min- William Wilson-
    1Jan1788
  Peter & Sally Carpenter 18 Jun 1791; Minister's return
    spells name as 'Hiplinger and Mary Carpenter d Mary who
    consents b- Frederick Myers wit- Frederick Myers & John
    Kiplinger min- William Wilson- 20Jun1791
Kiracofe
  George & Lucy Ann Messersmith 8 Jan 1839; min- Peter
    Shickle
  Henry & Margaret Fifer 15 Apr 1841; min- Peter Shickel Jr
Kirby
  Henry & Mary Tisdale 19 Aug 1830; min- Gerard Morgan
Kirchkoff
  Frederick & Mary Aylor 27 Mar 1823; min- G H Reimensnyder-
    publication of banns
Kirk
  George & Mary Ann Aston 26 Dec 1801; d John b- John Aston
  James & Jane Powell 18 Jan 1810; min- William Calhoon
  Robert & Martha Moffett 16 Aug 1786; d George b- James
    Lyle Jr min- William Wilson- 16Aug1786

Augusta County Marriages -- Man's Name

Kirk (cont.)
William & Polly Young 31 Aug 1809; min- William Calhoon
Kirkland
James (Jr) & Elizabeth Grub 11 Oct 1787; Minister's return spells name as 'Mary Grub' s James Sr who consents test- James Runken & Thomas Peterson b- William Johnston min- William Wilson- 15Oct1787
Samuel & Becky Blear 11 Oct 1790; 'Blair' d John, who consents wit- James Black & Wm Johnston s James, who consents wit- Arthur & Thomas Connely b- William Johnston min- Archibald Scott- 12Oct1790
Kirkpatrick
Thomas & Jane Hays 31 Jun 1810; min- William Calhoon
Kirtley
John & ----- ----- 10 Feb 1774; license only
Kise
Jacob & Susannah Argenbright 10 Aug 1801; d John who consents test- Wilhem Gruender & Philip Griber b- George Kise
Kiser
Daniel & Polly Coiner 26 Apr 1804; min- John McCue
Jesse & Catharine Messersmith 20 Jun 1844; min- John A Van Lear
Kisner
John & Rachel Weaver 22 Mar 1794; d Peter who consents test- Philip Steigleman & Rebecka Weaver b- Philip Stickleman no minister listed; clerk's memorandum cites ceremony date as 26Mar1794
Kister
Philip & Elizabeth Shonk 2 Feb 1795; b- Henry Deck
Kite
Jacob C & Catharine Slagle 25 Jun 1817; min- Wright Burgess
Kline
John & Mary Mowrey 30 Dec 1793; Minister's return spells name as 'Clyne' d Lewis b- Lewis Mowrey min- William Wilson- 30Dec1793
Klingenpeel
Kilkenney & Sally Fulwider 27 Jul 1826; min- Francis McFarland
Kyle B & Nancy Grove 21 Jul 1842; min- James Bunting
Klingingpeal
John & Sarah Kilkenny 13 Mar 1804; min- William King
Klingingpeel
Jacob & Elizabeth Kennaday 16 Dec 1806; min- John McCue
Knowles
William & Elizabeth Armstrong 1 Apr 1841; min- D F Bittle
Knowls
Robert & Susannah Brooks 13 Feb 1811; min- Regin Hammond
William & Margret Grant 3 Jan 1839; min- D F Bittle- publication of banns
Kohler
Peter & Sally Kyger - Oct 1820; min- John Brown

Augusta County Marriages -- Man's Name

Koiner
  Absalom & Margaret Koiner 16 Apr 1850; min- J Killian
  David C & Maria Long 13 Sep 1842; min- James Bunting
  Martin & Elizabeth Reah 14 Apr 1792; b- Thomas Turke min- John McCune- 20Apr1792

Koogler
  Andrew & Diannah Graham 1 Aug 1837; min- John A Van Lear

Koontz
  Peter & Elizabeth Palmer 28 Sep 1824; min- James Morrison

Kraun
  George & Elizabeth Tetrick 15 Aug 1809; min- William King

Krickenbarger
  Daniel & Sarah Craun 8 Feb 1849; min Henry Wetzel

Kroll
  David & Susannah Minnick 22 Jul 1797; 'Crall?' d Jacob b- Jacob Minnick

Krown
  John & Frankey McQueen 28 Jul 1810; min- William King

Kuhns
  Peter & Elizabeth Jones 2 Dec 1793; d Enos b- Enos Jones

Kule
  Robert M & Catherine Estill 6 Mar 1819; min- John Hendren

Kunkel
  William & Margaret A McCutchen 25 Feb 1833; min- William Calhoon

Kurtz
  Adam H & Amanda C Frazier 16 Jun 1836; min- John A Steele
  Frederick & Catherine Teebo 1 Oct 1820; min- Josiah Cole

Kyger
  Nicholas & Susan E Burke 15 Nov 1845; min- P Shickel

Kyle
  David & Sarah Humphrey 27 Nov 1835; min- Augustus Babb
  Jacob (Jr) & Sarah Cale 6 Aug 1840; min- D F Bittle
  William L & Janetta W McClung 31 Oct 1832; min- Nathaniel W Calhoon
  William P & Mary M Swoope 5 Oct 1843; min- S J Love
  William & Felicia G Points 13 Oct 1846; min- James H Brown

LaRue
  Abraham & Ellen Dickey 30 Mar 1809; min- William Wilson

Lafland
  Dorman & Mary Hogshead 29 Feb 1788; Minister's return spells name as 'Laughlin' b- John McKittrick min- Benjamin Erwin- 10Mar1788

Lainey
  Matthew & Catherine Lamb 6 Jun 1795; Minister's return spells name as 'Laney' d Peter b- Peter Lamb min- William Wilson- 9Jun1795

Lair
  David & Susannah Long 4 Oct 1818; min- Abraham Garber- publication of banns

Laird
  David & ----- ----- 22 Sep 1763; license only
  James (Jr) & ----- ----- 28 Aug 1769; license only
  James & Jane Anderson 15 Aug 1797; d Andrew b- Andrew Anderson min- William Wilson- 15Aug1797

Augusta County Marriages -- Man's Name

Laird (cont.)
  James & Jane Kerr 4 Dec 1799; d James who consents test- Alexander Kerr & Jacob Hershaw b- James McGongal
Lamay
  James & Mary Kasterson 21 Aug 1827; min- William C. Morrison
Lamb
  Abraham A & Louisa Staubus 12 Mar 1846; min- Henry Wetzel
  Adam & Elizabeth Waggy 18 Oct 1803; min- William King
  Andrew & Malinda Gordan 28 Feb 1845; min- P Shickel
  Benjamin & Susan Huff 6 Aug 1818; min- William King
  Jacob & Susana Wise - Apr 1806; min- John Brown
  James R & Sarah J Euritt 7 Sep 1843; min- John A Van Lear
  John & Merry Herring 19 Nov 1846; min- Jacob C Spitler
  Mathew & Keziah Sorrels 8 Oct 1795; d Joseph, late of Augusta cty, sis to Lewis Sorrels b- Lewis Sorrels
  Morgan & Susan Bird 5 Mar 1846; min- Jacob Bear
Lambard
  Abraham & Barbara Hammaker 26 Dec 1795; d David of Shenandoah cty who consents test- John Gets b- Christian Lambard
Lambert
  Christian & Magdalene Hafner 20 May 1795; d Jacob b- Adam Lambert
  David & Peggy Philips 9 Feb 1802; min- William King- 9Feb1802
  Francis & Elizabeth Vanfossen 21 Nov 1801; Minister's return spells name as 'Vanfasson' d Jacob b- Jacob Vanfossen min- William King- 26Nov1801
  Harry & Tirza Blackwood 29 Oct 1834; min- J Hoover
  Harvey & Mary Jane Swink 27 Dec 1844; min- Francis McFarland
  John S & Rebecca Crosby 10 May 1849; min- J McKendree Reiley
  John & Ann Cury 24 Mar 1808; min- William King
  John & Catharine Hartsook - Jun 1826; min- Joseph Smith
  John & Polly Smith 13 Jan 1825; min- Josiah Cole
  Peter & Catharine Wagner 29 Jul 1831; min- John Hendren- publication of banns
  Reuben & Susan Crist 10 Sep 1839; min- A B McCorkle
  Samuel H & Mary Propst 5 Oct 1848; min- George H Martin
  Samuel & Louisa C Link 18 Dec 1845; min- P Shickel
Lamey
  William & Mary Anderson 26 Oct 1833; min- George Hildt
Landes
  Abraham & Susan Kitch 26 Jun 1834; min- William Wilson
  Christian & Polly R Bell 21 Jan 1830; min- Conrad Speece
  David & Catharine A Reeves 17 Dec 1840; min- J A Van Lear
  Henry & Elizabeth Baker - Mar 1808; min- John Brown
  Jacob & Lydia Harsbarger 14 Dec 1843; min- John A Van Lear
  John & Delilah Skelton 11 Feb 1841; min- J J Reimensnyder
  Jonathan & Catharine Landes 20 Dec 1838; min- John J Reimensnyder
  Samuel & Margaret Shaver 3 Jun 1845; min- Daniel Brower

username:
jrplat7417ok

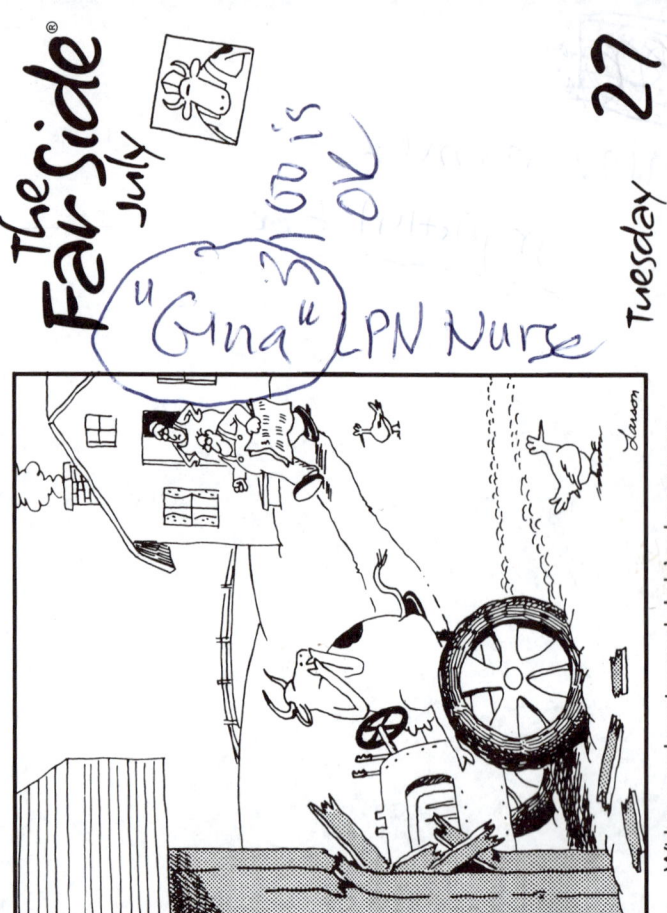

Augusta County Marriages -- Man's Name

Landes (cont.)
Solomon & Elizabeth Detamore   22 Jan 1829;   min- John Hendren
Landess
Samuel & Elizabeth Sheetz   28 May 1816;   min- G H Riemenschneider
Landis
Abraham & Hannah Michael   23 Sep 1830;   min- John Hendren
David B & Mary Seawright   12 Oct 1826;   min- William Wilson
Lange
William & Sarah Hess   1 Aug 1839;   min- John C Hansell
Langford
Robert & Nancy Fisher   7 May 1846;   min- T T Castleman
Lankford
Perry & Mary Parent   30 Nov 1815;   min- William King
Lansaw
William & Elizabeth Sherrets   - --- 179-;   'Landsaw' d Daniel Sharrets b- Daniel Sharrets no minister listed; clerk's memorandum cites ceremony date as 20Jun1792
Lantin
John & Franny Burner   2 Mar 1824;   min- Abraham Garber
Laporte
Alexander & Ambrosia Pauley   6 Jun 1826;   min- Alexander Templeton
Charles A & Harriet D Sheets   15 Nov 1842;   min- Samuel Wagner
Larew
Benjamin & Margaret A Carroll   12 Nov 1840;   min- Frederick D Goodwin
Cyrus S & Julia S Alexander   17 Dec 1839;   min- James Paine
Jacob & Elizabeth Archdaton   12 Sep 1800;   Minister's return spells name as 'Archdain' widow (of Michael Archdalon) Jacob a widower b- Enoch Fenton min- John McCue- 16Sep1800
Jacob & Ann Scott   3 Oct 1815;   min- John McCue
John J & Margaret A B Willson   15 Feb 1844;   min- Francis McFarland
Joseph & Elizabeth Scott   21 Jan 1808;   min- John McCue
Robert S & Mary J L Wilson   14 Dec 1837;   min- A B McCorkle
Lauks
Adam & Mary Rowler   15 Dec 1795;   b- Martin Surface
Lavel
John B & Mary Brown   2 Mar 1843;   min- J C Hensell
Lavell
William B & Catharine G Engleman   6 Aug 1842;   min- D F Bittle
Lavender
Anderson & Catherine Fortune   11 Sep 1826;   min- Daniel Stephens
Laverty
Ralph & ----- -----   20 Nov 1764;   license only
Law
Edward & Catherine Rittenhouse   8 Jan 1799;   Catherine (of age) b- Richard Roach ('Roche, Rotch?')
John & Jane Gwinn   15 Dec 1795;   Jane (of age) b- John Erwin min- William Wilson- 29Dec1795

Augusta County Marriages -- Man's Name

Lawell
 Abraham & Ann Beard 7 Jan 1817; 'Laywell?' min- William King

Lawrence
 John & Catherine Dold 24 Nov 1798; d Philip who consents test- William Dold b- Jesse Dold
 Samuel & ----- ----- 24 Dec 1762; license only

Layton
 Thomas & Salley Massey 24 Apr 1790; b- Smith Thompson wit- James Guy & Isham Ready (note attached:'a girl who has served her time with me- Thomas Smyth') min- John Montgomery- 27Apr1790

Laywell
 Abraham & Elizabeth Sylor 29 Jan 1791; b- John Tennant

Lea
 Martin & ----- ----- - Jun 1785; b- Robert McChesney

Leaguet
 Thomas & Barbara Wine 20 Feb 1817; 'League?' min- William King

Lear
 John Van & ----- ----- 27 Nov 1772; license only

Leckie
 William & Amanda Fitch 24 Aug 1831; min- Samuel Kennerly

Leddick
 Henry & Polly Ballard 4 Apr 1805; min- William King

Lee
 George W & Caroline M Grass 25 Sep 1834; min- Francis McFarland
 Grandison & Catharine Stombock 18 Apr 1847; min- Jacob C Spitler
 John & Anna Emmett 2 Jun 1803; min- William King

Leedy
 Abraham & Catharine Baylor 1 May 1833; min- William Calhoon
 Abraham & Eve Syford 20 May 1803; min- William King
 Samuel (Jr) & Rebecca Crumbacker 21 Oct 1824; min- Abraham Garber- publication of banns

Leeper
 Andrew & ----- ----- 4 Sep 1751; license only

Leffley
 John & Catherine Goodwin 17 Jun 1799; d Joseph Goodwin ('Gooden?') John (of age) b- Joseph Goodwin

Lemon
 John & Nancy Spears 19 Nov 1807; min- William King
 Madison & Catherine Bear 10 Jul 1827; min- Joseph Smith

Leonard
 Abraham & Lucretia Harrison 11 Jun 1822; min- Michael Meyerhoeffer
 Adam & Betsey Hibbert 17 Sep 1816; min- William King
 Daniel & Sarah Fauber 15 Jan 1822; min- James C Willson
 David & Fanny Garnett 28 Aug 1817; min- William King
 J & Catherine Smallshoffer 24 Sep 1835; min- Robert M Lipscomb
 Jacob & Elizabeth Bazzle 21 Oct 1828; min- William C. Morrison

Augusta County Marriages -- Man's Name

Leonard (cont.)
   Samuel & Margaret Coiner 17 Oct 1833; min- William G Jackson

Leopard
   Theophilus & Sarah Goodwin 16 Mar 1826; min- Francis McFarland

Lerew
   John & Elizabeth Doke 11 Mar 1799; d David sis to Samuel Elizabeth (of age) s Jacob who consents test- Benjamin Larew b- Samuel Doke & John McClelland
   Peter & Ann Shields 21 Nov 1795; Minister's return spells name as 'Larew' b- William Wilson min- Archibald Scott- 24Nov1795

Lessley
   James & Polly Crawford 7 Sep 1817; min- William Calhoon
   Samuel & Elizabeth Stuart 24 Jul 1792; Minister's return spells name as 'Lesley' d John, dec. b- Matthew Gambill perm- Arch & Mary Dickson, parents of Elizabeth min- William Wilson- 4Aug1792

Letcher
   John & Mary Pugh 3 Dec 1818; min- William King

Letshew
   William & Mary Rusmisel 19 May 1842; min- D F Bittle

Levick
   Michael & Alizabeth Peer 4 Aug 1837; min- John A Steele

Lewis
   Benjamin & Mary S Crist - --- 1834; min- Luke Collins
   Charles & ----- ----- 19 Jun 1762; license only
   Charles & Ann Hance 15 Mar 1792; Minister's return spells name as 'Ann Hann' b- John Mackall min- William Wilson- 18Mar1792
   David & ----- ----- - Nov 1759; license only
   Edmund H & Margaret C Morgan 14 Apr 1847; min- B M Smith
   Henry & Eliza Ann Painter 13 Aug 1794; Minister's return spells name as 'Elizabeth Ann' d John con- Nicholas Spring b- Joseph Bell & Nicholas Spring min- John McCue- 14Aug1794
   John O & Margaret Ann Fultz 7 Oct 1847; min- B M Smith
   John S & Mary T Stribling 6 Aug 1837; min- Fred D Goodwin
   John & ----- ----- 12 Mar 1772; license only
   John & ----- ----- 2 Feb 1773; license only
   John & Rachel Miller 31 Mar 1789; b- Robert Douthat min- Benjamin Erwin- 1Apr1789
   William & Elizabeth Miller 11 May 1820; min- John Hendren

Licks
   Malachi & Margaret Johnston 25 Dec 1793; Minister's return spells name as 'Malika Lucke' d William b- Andrew Allison min- John McCue- 26Dec1793

Life
   John & Julianna Bumgardner 24 Feb 1823; min- Josiah Cole
   Jonathan & Sally Smith 10 Feb 1815; min- Abraham Garber- publication of banns

Augusta County Marriages -- Man's Name

Liggett
   John M & Mary Margaret Hardshell 26 Nov 1847; min- J A Van Lear
Lightner
   Alexander B & Sarah A B Gardner 15 Nov 1844; min- Francis McFarland
   Christian & Hannah Ingleton 20 Jun 1805; min- William King
   Jacob & Mary W Pillson 18 May 1837; min- William Calhoon
   Samuel & Lucy Ann Darst 7 Feb 1839; min- A B McCorkle
Likes
   William & Mary Ann Branham 11 Jun 1812; min- William King
Lilley
   John & Elizabeth Doak 10 Apr 1797; d Robert John Doak swears John Lilley over 21 b- Robert Doak & Alexander StClair min- Archibald Scott- 11Apr1797
   John & Margaret Swick 12 Oct 1848; min- J McKendree Reiley
   Robert D & Ann Telfair 15 Jun 1824; min- William W Calhoun
   William & Catherine Miller 31 Jul 1815; min- Wright Burgess
Linch
   Hugh & Mary Caldwell 10 Sep 1794; Minister's return spells name as 'Lynch' widow who consents for herself test- William Wilson & John Caldwell b- William Wilson & John Caldwell min- John McCue- 10Sep1794
   John & Mary Best 22 Aug 1795; Minister's return spells name as 'John Lynch and Mary Risk' b- James Best min- John McCue- 3Sep1795
Lincoln
   Abraham & ----- ----- 9 Jun 1770; license only
Ling
   Philip & Christiana Summers 11 Jun 1791; d John, who consents b- John Summers
Lingsweiler
   Nicholas & Margaret Jonas 9 Jan 1797; Margaret (of age) d Daniel b- John Winiger Nicholas a widower
Link
   Daniel W & Catharine Craun 7 Nov 1847; min- P Shickel
   David & Margaret Aylor 28 May 1829; min- G H Reimensnyder
   David & Hannah Mowry 20 Nov 1817; min- William King
   Jacob & Nancy Fouber 7 May 1811; min- William King
   John & Susannah Shindler 5 Nov 1813; min- G H Riemenschneider
   John & Polly Usher 31 Oct 1805; min- William Wilson
   Mathias & Jane Hanger 23 Jan 1826; min- Michael Meyerhoeffer
   Peter & India Burkett 10 Mar 1788; Minister's return spells name as 'Judy Burkitt' d Daniel who consents test- Alexander Moore & John Brumfill b- Dieter Fishborn min- William Wilson- 11Mar1788
   Peter & Mary Landis 26 Oct 1817; min- William King- publication of banns
   Will & Ester Charlott Shindler 10 Jun 1818; min- G H Riemenschneider
   William & Sally Grim 21 Aug 1801; s John Nicholas Link s Jacob Grim, dec, of Shenandoah cty Christian Beard ('Bart') swears Sally is of age b- John Nicholas Link

Augusta County Marriages -- Man's Name

Linn
  Philip C & Eliza Weller 23 Dec 1847; min- S Hildebrand
Linsey
  William & Polly Olves 24 Dec 1802; min- John McCue-
  24Dec1802
Liptrap
  Isaac & Mary Bright 28 Jun 1785; d George b- John Bright
  wit- Henry Lawrence & Elijah Brumfield min- Archibald
  Scott- 29Jul1785
  Isaac & Barbara Lotz 13 Jan 1839; min- John C Hensell
  John & Catherine Lotts 16 Dec 1828; min- James Morrison
Litten
  Abraham & Esther Forsythe 9 Jan 1805; min- William King
  Samuel & Sally Graham 2 Nov 1826; min- William Wilson
Litteral
  Winstead & Peggy Bray 27 Aug 1804; min- William King
Littlepage
  James & ----- ----- 14 Jul 1759; license only
Lively
  Harrison D & Ann V Lamb 4 Feb 1840; min- John A Van Lear
  William & Ann Ross 26 Oct 1790; b- Robert Craig Ann
  served her time with Miss Craig and is now free
Livick
  George & Elizabeth Sheetz 28 May 1823; min- Josiah Cole
  Peter & Matilda Zimmerman 6 Dec 1832; min- William Calhoon
  William & Margaret Plecker 22 Jul 1849; min- Samuel Martin
  William & Harriet Powers 21 May 1835; min- Isaac Jones
Lockbridge
  James & Ann Lockbridge 22 Aug 1788; min- Archibald Scott-
  22Aug1788
Lockhart
  Patrick & ----- ----- 5 Dec 1770; license only
  Randall & ----- ----- - Sep 1760; license only
  William & ----- ----- - Jun 1761; license only
Lockridge
  Andrew & ----- ----- 6 Apr 1762; license only
  Andrew & Christena Youel 20 Mar 1797; Minister's return
  spells name as 'Christiana Youel' d William b- William
  Youel min- John Montgomery- 23Mar1797
  James & Jane Guy 22 Mar 1791; b- James Guy min- John
  Montgomery- 5Apr1791
  James & Ann Lockridge 18 Aug 1788; d Robert who consents
  b- Arthur Walkup min- Archibald Scott- 22Aug1788
  John & Eliza Erwin 29 May 1821; min- John Hendren
  William & Rachael Chambers 1 Jun 1815; min- John D Ewin
  William & Ruth Davis 18 Apr 1820; min- John Hendren
Loftus
  James & Polly Beard 22 Dec 1807; min- William Calhoon
Logan
  James & Jane Clinon 23 Jun 1796; b- Thomas Simpson
  affidavit by Jane that she is 21, has no residence, and is a
  seamstress
  John & Rachel McPheeters 25 Aug 1797; d William b- John
  Coalter min- Archibald Scott- 30Aug1797

Augusta County Marriages -- Man's Name

Logan (cont.)
  William M & Hannah Hudson 16 May 1827; min- William Calhoon
  William & Sarah Wilson 22 Nov 1792; Hugh Wilson certifies before Robert Douthat that Sarah of age and lives in Augusta cty b- Hugh Wilson & Robert Bailey
Lohr
  Christian & Mary Andrews 25 Sep 1795; d John who consents test- Mathias Semet & Alexander Scott b- Alexander Scott
  James & Elizabeth Smith 19 Oct 1848; min- John Bowen
Long
  Adam (Sr) & Catharine Murry 12 May 1840; min- John J Reimensnyder
  Adam & Frances Price 5 Oct 1843; min- E R Veitch
  Alexander & Mary Susan McComb 18 Feb 1845; min- B M Smith
  Edward & ----- ----- 18 Jan 1762; license only
  Emanuel & Amanda K Gordon 24 Oct 1839; min- P E Stevenson
  Emmanuel & Polly Phillips 9 Feb 1809; min- William King
  Jacob & Sally Burket 28 Feb 1791; Minister's return spells name as 'Burkitt' d Nathaniel b- Nathaniel Burket min- William Wilson- 28Feb1791
  Jacob & Louisa Coley 17 Jun 1819; min- William Wilson
  Jacob & Mariah Murry 1 Jan 1843; min- A G Chenowith
  James & Elizabeth Holmes 2 Nov 1810; min- William King
  James & Elizabeth Vance 24 Jan 1839; min- George Huffman
  John & Ardemisia McCauley 2 Feb 1831; min- John Hendren
  John & Elizabeth Sheetz - Jul 1818; min- John Brown
  Joseph & Frany Sheetz 6 Jan 1818; min- G H Riemenschneider
  Nathaniel L & Mary Ann Gorden 24 Dec 1833; min- William G Jackson
  Nathaniel & Mary Argebright 15 Mar 1824; min- Michael Meyerhoeffer
  Peter & Margaret Ewings 28 Jul 1800; Minister's return spells name as 'Peggy Erwin' d Henry b- Henry Ewing, John Allison & Jacob Coyner min- William Wilson- 29Jul1800
  William & Mary Blair 23 Sep 1794; Mary gives own consent d James b- John Campbell William affirms he believes himself and Mary both over 21 min- John Brown- 24Sep1794 ('went to Roanoke'?
Looney
  Joseph & ----- ----- 25 Jun 1764; license only
Loots
  Philip & Susan Cowman 29 Nov 1821; 'Lutz' min- Daniel Stephens
Lootz
  Daniel & Diana Roland - Oct 1818; min- John Brown
  Leonard & Hannah Hagarty 25 Jan 1802; d John b- John Cooper
Lortz
  David & Susan Wiseman 28 Mar 1844; min- J C Hensell
Lott
  George (Jr) & Elizabeth Bright 9 Mar 1795; d George Adam Bright who consents test- John Bright b- John Bright

Augusta County Marriages -- Man's Name

Lotts
  John & Eve Almerode 11 Mar 1799; d George who consents test- Richard Hollis b- John Sensebach
Lottz
  John & Sally Cox 8 Jan 1824; min- James Morrison
Lotz
  Henry & Betsy Cook 20 Oct 1798; d Jacob Cook (Koch) b- Jacob Cook
Loudermilk
  David & Susannah Simmerman 17 Nov 1831; min- William Calhoon
  John & Elizabeth Simmerman 29 Sep 1831; min- William Calhoon
  Michael & Susanna Baynes 25 Jul 1836; min- James C Wilson
Louks
  Adam & Mary Rowler 15 Dec 1795; 'Mary Brownlee?' min- John McCue- 15Dec1795
Loushback
  Martin & Hannah Adams 31 Dec 1791; b- Michael Fackler
Love
  Samuel & ----- ----- 3 Jul 1759; license only
Lovegrove
  William & Elizabeth Pool 14 Oct 1834; min- Peter Miller- publication of banns
Lovel
  George & Caty Shafer 28 Feb 1826; min- Abraham Garber- publication of banns
Lowdermilk
  George & Rosey Huffman 23 Dec 1800; Minister's return spells name as 'Loudermilk and Huff' George (of age) d George b- George Huffman min- John McCue- 25Dec1800
Lowe
  James & Mary Keith 23 Jan 1798; d Andrew Keith, dec. b- Lawrence Lynch & Arthur Ringland
Lowery
  Peter & Susanna Moore 19 Dec 1811; min- William King
Lowman
  David & Peggy Joseph 7 Apr 1812; min- William King
  John & Susan Fulwider 15 Dec 1831; min- Francis McFarland
  Samuel & Lydia Houf 10 Jun 1834; min- William Wilson
  William & Sally Eagon 19 Feb 1835; min- George Hildt
Lowrets
  Andrew & Elizabeth Shaver 20 Dec 1787; widow b- William Trorback
Lowry
  Joseph & Ann Ougheltree 24 Aug 1798; Minister's return spells name as 'Augheltree' Ann (of age) d Michael b- James Lowry min- Benjamin Irvin- 28Aug1798
Lowtermilk
  John & Mary Eccord 23 May 1795; d Francis b- Christian Eccord
Loyd
  Kirkley & Susana Sheetz 24 Mar 1825; min- Josiah Cole

Augusta County Marriages -- Man's Name

Lucas
  Andrew & Margaret Hanger 24 Mar 1842; min- John C Hensell
  David & Elizabeth Strine 29 Nov 1832; min- Francis McFarland
  Jacob & Betsey Lowman 6 Mar 1832; min- Francis McFarland

Luffler
  Edward & Hannah Martin 17 Jan 1792; b- Stephen Martin min- John McCune- 17Jan1792

Lusk
  Robert & ----- ----- 25 Feb 1764; license only

Lutz
  Balser W & Elizabeth Deary 11 Aug 1831; min- William Wilson
  Balser W & Eliza Ellery 14 Apr 1840; min- Jacob Stirewalt
  Leonard & Hannah Hagerty 25 Jan 1802; min- William King- 25Jan1802

Lyle
  James & Margaret Baker 2 Jun 1789; b- William Lyle
  John & ----- ----- 29 Dec 1762; license only
  John & ----- ----- 19 May 1774; license only
  Samuel & Eleanor Finley 18 Sep 1801; d William b- William Finley min- John McCue- 10Sep1801

Lynch
  Andrew & Catharine Keller 12 Aug 1836; min- J C Hensell
  George & Eliza Matilda Jamison 24 Jan 1825; min- Thomas Caldwell
  Lawrence & Kathorine Keeth 1 Oct 1794; widow who consents for herself test- James Welsh & Richard Trater b- Richard Trotter min- John Brown- 5Oct1794
  Robert & Matilda Hall 15 Feb 1827; min- Francis McFarland

Lynn
  Abraham & Matilda Flack 20 Feb 1835; min- William Scull
  Jacob & Fanny Moore 22 Aug 1815; min- Wright Burgess

Lyon
  John & Katty Hook 7 Jan 1794; min- William Wilson- 7Jan1794
  Nathaniel & ----- ----- 29 Oct 1760; license only

Lyons
  Thomas & Jane D Brown 15 Dec 1825; Bond gives name as 'Beam' min- Francis McFarland
  William & Catherine Haup 9 May 1805; min- John McCue

Mackaby
  John & Elizabeth Weigle 10 Mar 1803; min- William King

Mahan
  John & Elizabeth Gibson 3 Mar 1787; min- William Wilson- 3Mar1787

Mahony
  Dennis & Lettice Howell 5 Jun 1793; Minister's return spells name as 'Mehony and Nowell' b- John Campbell min- William Wilson- 24Apr1793

Malcolm
  Alexander & Margaret Hogshead 28 Dec 1798; Minister's return spells name as 'Malcom' d John Hogshead, dec. b- John Hogshead (Jr?) min- William Wilson- 1Jan1799

Augusta County Marriages -- Man's Name

Mansfield
 Thomas M & Casandra P Orbison 1 Jan 1827; min- William Wilson

Mardis
 William & Matty Donaho 4 Nov 1813; min- William King

Mares
 Patrick & Esther Haskins 10 Mar 1798; Esther (of age)

Markwood
 Rufus M & Ann Mills 20 Nov 1845; min- T T Castleman

Marshall
 Charles L & Catherine Ross 19 May 1828; min- William C. Morrison
 Franklin L & Elizabeth Peck 2 Feb 1842; min- Alfred G Chenowith
 George & Margerate Caldwell 27 Feb 1812; min- John McCue
 James & Catherine Caldwell 7 Feb 1805; min- John McCue
 John & Elizabeth Caldwell 12 Jun 1799; Elizabeth (of age) d John Caldwell, dec., sis to Samuel Caldwell b- Samuel Caldwell
 Mansfield & Sarah Parsons 14 Jun 1842; min- Samuel Wagner
 William H & Mary M Eurick 21 Jan 1847; min- J A Van Lear
 William & Susan Gilkerson 15 May 1823; min- James C Willson

Martin
 Alexander & Jane Black 24 Jun 1788; d Henry who consents test- John Black b- John Johnston min- William Wilson- 25Jun1788
 Amos & Susan Barnett 27 Aug 1833; min- William Calhoon
 Archibald & Rebecca Sensabaugh 2 Jun 1825; min- James Morrison
 Austin & Martha Barrett 30 Jul 1835; min- J J Glossbrenner
 Charles H & Mary Margaret Apple 15 Nov 1849; min- Francis McFarland
 Jacob & Agnes Kilpatrick 21 Mar 1787; b- John Kirkpatrick min- Archibald Scott- 5Apr1787
 James J & Ruth Ann Wright 13 Jan 1848; min- James Morrison
 John & Christiana Roop 26 Aug 1823; min- Josiah Cole
 John & Polly Weathers 28 Dec 1820; min- William Calhoon
 Patrick & ----- ----- 13 Dec 1762; license only (signed as 'Pat. Martin, Gent.'
 Robert & Mary Miller 26 Dec 1791; b- John Huggins min- John Brown- 29Dec1791
 Samuel & Catherine Roop 5 Jun 1827; min- William Monroe
 William H & Mary Rosenbarger 24 Sep 1840; min- Benjamin M Kindig
 William & Mary Ann McCormick 27 Jul 1795; b- George Givens
 Woodson & Sally Cusin 17 Sep 1821; min- Josiah Cole

Marton
 John & Elizabeth Steele 13 Dec 1798; Minister's return spells name as 'John Martin' widow of John b- William Sterrett min- Archibald Scott- 13Dec1798

Matheny
 James & Ann S Suddarth 4 Feb 1847; min- W G Campbell
 Lewis & Mary Haslet 5 Jun 1814; min- William Wilson
 Peachy & July Stanton 17 Oct 1825; min- John Hendren

Augusta County Marriages -- Man's Name

Mathews
  George & ----- ----- 13 Sep 1762; license only
  George & Margaret Reed 28 Sep 1790; Minister's return spells name as 'Reid' widow b- Robert Gamble min- Archibald Scott- 29Sep1790
  James & Ann Pollard Gaines 5 Jul 1796; d James Gaines, dec. of Orange cty con- Mildred Gains, mother test- Abner & Elizabeth Gains b- Abner Gains
  James & Patsy Hamm 3 Jul 1827; min- William Monroe
  Joseph & Mary Rhoades 22 Sep 1787; b- Asher Waterman min- James Chambers- 22Sep1787
  Joseph & Mary Vantrump 12 Oct 1811; min- William King
  Joshua & ----- ----- - May 1750; license only
  Nathaniel & Susannah Shoue 28 Dec 1835; min- Joshua Webb
  Sampson & ----- ----- - Sep 1759; license only
  William & ----- ----- 28 Nov 1763; license only

Maupin
  Dabney & Rebecca Johnston 1 Feb 1827; min- James Watts
  J & J R Wood 10 Sep 1835; min- Robert M Lipscomb
  James L & Dorinda Kennerley 26 Dec 1827; min- Gerard Morgan

May
  Abraham & Sarah Long 20 Jan 1820; min- William Wilson
  Adam & Elizabeth Butt 11 Feb 1791; d Henry Bott who consents b- Chaistain Huffman wit- William Patterson
  Fountain & Virginia Young 26 Jul 1848; min- D W Arnold
  George W & Sarah B Peer 12 Jul 1848; min- D W Arnold

Mayfield
  Stephen & Elizabeth Hardbarger 5 Jan 1819; min- William King

Mayo
  Frederick A & Dolly Yearout 29 May 1810; min- William King

Mays
  David & Anna Falls 6 Aug 1828; min- John Hendren
  George & Sarah B Allen 13 Nov 1823; min- Conrad Speece
  James (Jr) & Cinderella Wallace 6 Nov 1839; min- A B McCorkle
  John & Elizabeth Burgess - Jun 1832; min- Samuel Kennerly- publication of banns
  Richard & ----- ----- - Sep 1760; license only
  Robert & Margaret McClenachan 2 Dec 1790; min- Archibald Scott- 2Dec1790

Maze
  Isaac & Ruth Hicklin 6 Sep 1788; d Hugh who consents test- Valentine White b- Joseph Maze
  Joseph & ----- ----- 2 Jun 1750; license only
  Joseph & Agness Hicklin 14 Jun 1787; Minister's return spells name as 'Mays' d Hugh who consents test- Samuel McDonnald & Hugh McDonnald b- John Bosang & James Culbertson min- Samuel Shannon- 18Jun1787

McAdams
  John & Sarah Blackwood 27 Jun 1786; d Samuel b- William Willson wit- Robert Doneldson & I McClanahan min- Archibald Scott- 28Jun1786

Augusta County Marriages -- Man's Name

McAfee
  James & ----- ----- 25 Sep 1762; license only
  James & ----- ----- 17 Sep 1765; license only
McAlary
  Hugh & Savanna Lockridge 7 Jun 1831; min- James Kerr
  Robert & Milley Dowell 24 Sep 1805; min- John McCue
McAlery
  Samuel & Jane Dalhouse 22 Aug 1805; min- John McCue
McBride
  James & Sarah Huff 30 May 1827; min- William Wilson
  William & ----- ----- 17 Oct 1765; license only
McCaleb
  Thomas & Sarah Denny 4 Dec 1804; min- William King
McCamey
  James & Eliza A Cox 1 Nov 1822; min- John Hendren
McCampbell
  John & Ann Buchanan 4 Oct 1797; d William b- William Buchanan
McCan
  Edward & Mary Johnston 16 Jun 1790; widow b- William Downey
McCann
  James & Agness Petty 5 Sep 1785; min- Archibald Scott- 5Sep1785
McCarty
  David & Susanah Yearout 30 Jan 1806; min- William King
  John & Catherine Williams 6 Sep 1808; min- William McPheeters
McCauley
  Garland & Anne Salvage 10 Feb 1822; min- William Wilson Jr
  Garrett & Betsey Herron - May 1828; min- William Wilson
McCausland
  Andrew B & Mary Glenn 16 Jul 1822; min- Conrad Speece
  John & Nancy Whitmore 9 Jul 1835; min- William Scull
McCawley
  Robert (Jr) & Jane Carson 29 Mar 1794; Jane (of age) b- Robert McCawley Sr min- John Brown- 5Apr1794
McChesney
  Adam & Nancy Tate 10 Jan 1800; d John who consents test- Polly Finley b- Isaac Tate
  George W & Evelina Moffett 21 Dec 1826; min- John Hendren
  James & Charlotte Berry 14 Nov 1797; widower d Charles Bery, dec. b- Robert Berry min- Archibald Scott- 16Nov1797
  John & Sarah Cunningham 30 Jul 1803; min- William King
  Zachariah J & Nancy Bell 23 Apr 1822; min- Conrad Speece
McClanahan
  Green & Elizabeth Griffin 10 Jun 1808; min- William Calhoon
  John G & Maria A May 26 Sep 1843; min- P E Stevenson
McClaughlin
  William & Anne Allen 2 Jun 1794; 'McLauhgland?' d Ebenezer b- Ebenezer Allen no minister listed; clerk's memorandum cites ceremony date as 3Jun1794

Augusta County Marriages -- Man's Name

McCleland
  John & Peggy McDowell 20 Jan 1806; min- William Calhoon
  Robert & Elizabeth McCadden 3 Feb 1825; min- Francis
    McFarland
  Samuel & Margaret Minnick 23 Apr 1807; min- William
    McPheeters

McClelland
  John & Peggy McDowell 20 Jan 1806; min- William Calhoon

McClenachan
  Elijah (Jr) & Nancy Moffett 11 Apr 1792; d John, who
    consents b- Jacob Kinney, who also is witness no minister
    listed; clerk's memorandum cites ceremony date as 13Apr1792
  Elijah & Lettice Breckinridge - Sep 1749; license only
  Elijah & Margaret Gilkerson 21 Aug 1799; widower d
    William b- William Gilkerson
  Elijah & Elizabeth Harrison 31 Mar 1803; min- John McCue
  John & ----- ----- 24 Jan 1770; license only
  Robert (Jr) & ----- ----- 15 May 1770; license only
  Robert & Sally Abney 4 Jul 1797; d John Abney, dec. con-
    Isabella Abney test- William Abney b- John McDowell min-
    John McCue- 4Jul1797

McClentock
  Samuel & Susanna King 22 Nov 1793; Minister's return
    spells name as 'McClintock' d Adam b- Adam King min- John
    Brown- 23Nov1793

McClintic
  Thomas M & Nancy Estill 14 Feb 1843; min- John A Van Lear

McClintick
  John & Isabella Cales 16 Nov 1820; min- Robert H Chapman
  Robert & Mary Argenbright 27 Mar 1834; min- William Calhoon

McClune
  Robert & Mary Elizabeth Grove 30 Mar 1848; min- P Shickel

McClung
  Alexander & Elizabeth T Bishop 12 Jan 1841; min- D F Bittle
  Archibald & Elizabeth Walace 27 Jan 1825; min- Francis
    McFarland
  Benjamin S & Maria Wallace 29 Dec 1825; min- Francis
    McFarland
  Charles & Sally Crawford 12 Oct 1815; min- Conrad Speece,
    Jr
  Charles & Sarah Gabhart 7 Aug 1834; min- Augustus Babb
  Charles & Nancy Parris 4 Aug 1836; min- Isaac Jones
  Charles & Rebecca Walker 4 Dec 1834; min- Samuel Kennerly
  James & Mary McChesney 23 Aug 1799; d Robert b- Robert
    McChesney
  James & Elizabeth McPheeters 21 Feb 1791; d John b-
    William McPheeters min- Archibald Scott- 8Mar1791
  James & Matilda Jane Paris 12 Jan 1837; min- Isaac Jones
  John & Anne Borland 6 Dec 1804; min- William Wilson
  John & Mary Stuart 5 Nov 1788; d Benjamin wit- George
    Moore b- Benjamin Stuart min- William Wilson- 12Nov1788
  Joseph & Jane Baily 13 Feb 1812; min- William King
  Robert & Rebecca Ann Crawford 6 Nov 1828; min- Conrad
    Speece

Augusta County Marriages -- Man's Name

McClung (cont.)
  Samuel & Betsy Crawford 29 Jan 1818; min- Conrad Speece, Jr
  Samuel & Mary Haffner 11 Jun 1840; min- J J Reimensnyder
  Samuel & Margaret Hafner 9 Jun 1840; min- John J
    Reimensnyder
  Thomas & ----- ----- 24 Jan 1765; license only
McClure
  Andrew (Jr) & Polly Steele 25 Oct 1800; d Andrew who
    consents test- John McClure & Martin Bush s James b- John
    Steele, son of Andrew Steele
  Andrew & Mary Mitchell 13 Jan 1789; b- Thomas Hall min-
    Archibald Scott- 15Jan1789
  David & Elizabeth Holmes 29 Sep 1795; Minister's return
    omits David's surname d Samuel of Shenandoah cty who
    consents test- Hugh Stuart & James Walker b- David Parry
    min- Archibald Scott- 29Sep1795
  James & ----- ----- 18 May 1773; license only
  James & Betty Strong 26 Mar 1807; min- John McCue
  John & Jane Steel 18 Aug 1808; min- John McCue
  Nathan & Jane McChesney 15 Feb 1821; min- John Brown
  Samuel & Barbara Fauber 14 Feb 1805; min- John McCue
  William & ----- ----- 26 Dec 1769; license only
  William & Mary Shields 20 Jan 1790; d Jane, widow, who
    consents b- Peter Waddel wit- Peter Waddel & John Delacy
McColley
  Joseph & Mary Connely 20 Aug 1789; Minister's return
    spells name as 'McCauley and Connelly' d Arthur wit- James
    & Robert Connely b- Robert Connely min- William Wilson-
    20Aug1789
McCollins
  Micajah & Elizabeth Helms 1 Oct 1809; min- William King
McComb
  James & Susana Henderson 9 Jan 1793; Susana (of age) d
    William sis David b- David Henderson min- John McCue-
    29Jan1793
  Samuel & Sally Woods 22 Oct 1817; min- William King
McCorgar
  Edward & ----- ----- 19 Nov 1763; license only
McCorkle
  John & Lidia Forrest 12 May 1790; d James, who consents
    b- Benjamin Chapman wit- John Bossard & Benjamin Chapman
    min- Archibald Scott- 12May1790
  Robert & Elizabeth Forrest 12 May 1785; d James
McCormack
  George & Jane Steel 21 Jan 1796; d David b- David Steele
  William & Mary Steele 30 Jan 1801; William from Rockbridge
    cty d Robert Steele, dec. Both (of age) b- David Steele
McCormick
  David & Ann Jamison 8 Sep 1794; 'McCormack' d John b-
    James Jamison no minister listed; clerk's memorandum cites
    ceremony date as 9Sep1794
  Henry A & Hannah Ballar 7 Jun 1821; 'Ballard?' min-
    William W Calhoun
  Joshua & ----- ----- 25 Sep 1765; license only

Augusta County Marriages -- Man's Name

McCormick (cont.)
William & Polly McCleland 1 Sep 1807; min- William McPheeters
McCoskey
Joseph & Martha Gillaspy 19 Mar 1790; Minister's return spells name as 'McCoskrey and Gilaspey' d John b- wit- Samuel Bleak & John Thompson b- James Telford min- John Montgomery- 25Mar1790
McCown
Moses & ----- ----- 15 Jan 1765; license only
McCoy
Robert & Margaret Mahon 29 Nov 1791; min- Benjamin Irwin- 29Nov1791
McCray
Samuel & Jane Armstrong 23 Dec 1793; d Archibald who consents test- John Brown & William Armstrong b- William Armstrong min- John Montgomery- 7Jan1794
McCreery
Andrew & Catherine Lamb 1 Jun 1795; Minister's return spells name as 'McCreary' d John b- John Lamb min- William Wilson- 4Jun1795
John & ----- ----- 20 Nov 1762; license only
John & ----- ----- 19 Mar 1771; license only
John & Margaret Black 19 Mar 1787; d William who consents test- John Montgomery & Alexander Black s of Robert who consents b- Charles Donally min- Samuel Shannon- 27Mar1787
Robert & ----- ----- 21 Nov 1764; license only
McCrery
David & Amelia Harris 3 Sep 1829; min- James Morrison
McCue
Franklin & Jane Crawford 16 Sep 1819; min- Conrad Speece, Jr
Franklin & Nancy A Crawford 19 Oct 1830; min- Conrad Speece
James & Margaret Trimble 12 Apr 1808; min- John McCue
John C & Mary J Hansbarger 27 Oct 1842; min- A G Chenowith
John & Ann Barry 20 Apr 1813; min- John McCue
John & Ellen S Douglas 5 Dec 1849; min- B M Smith
John & Hannah Moffett 22 Sep 1819; min- John Hendren
Moses H & Sarah F Steele 6 Sep 1838; min- John A Van Lear
Moses & Sally Smith 17 Apr 1800; Moses from Staunton d Thomas Smith, dec. b- William Chambers of Staunton min- John McCue- 17Apr1800
McCulloch
James & Mary Graham 8 Feb 1805; min- John McCue
John & Nancy Patterson 9 Feb 1804; min- William Wilson
Thomas & Polly McCune 5 Apr 1808; min- John McCue
Thomas & Polly Turk 31 Aug 1802; min- John McCue- 31Aug1802
McCullock
George W & Nancy Miller 9 Apr 1835; min- Samuel Kennerly
Samuel & Elizabeth Varner 4 Feb 1793; d Henry who consents test- John Copenhaver & Andrew Wallace b- Cornelius Odear no minister listed; clerk's memorandum cites ceremony date as 5Feb1793
Thomas & Nancy Black 23 Jun 1824; min- William W Calhoun

Augusta County Marriages -- Man's Name

McCullough
    Lawson & Lidia Varnum 7 Jan 1790; Minister's return spells name as 'Vernum' d Elizabeth, widow wit- John Varnum b- John Varnum min- John Brown- 11Jan1790
    Robert & Jenny Sneders 28 Jan 1789; b- John Hall

McCune
    Archibald & Mary Bell 8 Nov 1792; d James b- James Bell min- John McCue- 4Dec1792
    John L & Julia Ann Willson 2 May 1832; min- James C Wilson
    Joseph & Sarah McCune 27 May 1813; min- Thomas Bourne
    Samuel & Elizabeth Flack 26 May 1808; min- William King

McCurdy
    Andrew & Elizabeth McCutchen 28 Jun 1849; min- W G Campbell
    William & Lucinda H Lyle 7 Dec 1837; min- Enoch Thomas
    William & Jane Thompson 25 Dec 1806; min- William Calhoon

McCutchan
    Cyrus A & Hetty A M Clayton 29 Dec 1846; min- W G Campbell
    John C & Rebecca McCurdy 5 Sep 1844; min- W G Campbell
    Lewis T K & Adaline V McCutchan 23 May 1844; min- W G Campbell
    Samuel & Susanna Mowry 20 Nov 1817; min- William King
    William & Rosanna Lyle 11 Nov 1830; min- Francis McFarland

McCutchen
    Addison & Ann K Buchanan 22 Aug 1833; min- James Morrison
    Albert A & Sarah McCutchen 18 May 1839; min- John C Hensell
    Albert G & Mary Jane Woodward 21 Jun 1836; min- Isaac Jones
    Charles C & Elizabeth Craig 18 Mar 1819; min- William Calhoon
    David & Jane Trimble 17 Dec 1836; min- Isaac Jones (Also a return on file from Isaac Jones for the same couple dated 17Dec1835)
    George W & Sophia Jane Lockridge 25 Oct 1849; min- W G Campbell
    James & Susanna Bollar 31 Aug 1803; min- Philip Kennerly
    James & Susannah Harris 16 Jan 1836; min- James Morrison
    James & Elizabeth Hunter 15 Nov 1786; d William s Ellenor McCutchan b- David Cale wit- Margrit Hunter & Sarah Hunter, John & James McCutchan min- Archibald Scott- 15Nov1786
    James & Elizabeth Kirkpatrick 2 Jul 1811; min- William Calhoon
    John & Sally Cooper 30 Oct 1823; min- James Morrison
    John & Isabella Patrick 11 Nov 1797; Isabella (of age) d John sis William b- William Patrick min- John McCue- 16Nov1797
    John & Dorthula Sproul 13 Oct 1834; min- William Calhoon
    Joseph & Jane Searight 5 Sep 1785; widow of George Searight b- John King d John King wit- James Larid, James Miller, Samuel King min- Archibald Scott- 6Sep1785
    Philander & Rebecca McCutchan 22 May 1844; min- W G Campbell
    Robert W & Rachael Armstrong 17 Jun 1819; min- John D Ewin
    Robert & Elizabeth McCurdy 28 Mar 1844; min- W G Campbell
    Robert & Mary McNight 11 Mar 1799; d Timothy s John McCutchan b- William Morrison

Augusta County Marriages -- Man's Name

McCutchen (cont.)
Samuel & Francis McCutchen 9 Oct 1804; min- John McCue
Samuel & Mary Patrick 16 Jun 1792; d John b- John Patrick
  min- John McCune- 19Jun1792
Samuel & Julia A C Pine 13 Nov 1837; min- Enoch Thomas
Samuel & Elizabeth Ann Seawright 24 Oct 1844; min- J C
  Hensell
William & ----- ----- 2 Aug 1763; license only
William & ----- ----- 10 Sep 1763; license only
William & Peggy Bell 4 Jun 1800; d Samuel who consents
  test- James Bell & John Bell b- Capt. John Bell min-
  William Wilson- 5Jun1800
William & Margaret Cooper 5 Apr 1827; min- James Morrison
William & Jean Finely 13 May 1794; d Robert who consents
  b- Alexander St. Clair Jean of age min- John McCue-
  20May1794

McCutcheon
James & Malinda Hall 12 Jun 1823; min- William W Calhoun
Samuel & Elizabeth Humphreys 16 Feb 1801; d David s
  Capt. Samuel McCutcheon b- David Humphreys & Capt. Samuel
  McCutcheon

McDade
John & Catherine Short 10 Aug 1811; d William min- John
  Bell

McDaniel
Samuel & Bell Craig 29 Jan 1811; min- Joseph Reid

McDonald
Archibald & Elizabeth Knowls 31 Dec 1795; d John b- John
  Knowls

McDowell
James & ----- ----- - May 1760; license only
John & Isabella Lyle 17 Feb 1798; d John Lyle, dec. con-
  Archibald Stuart b- John Bowyer min- John McCue- 17Feb1798
John & Sarah Withrow 13 Aug 1788; John from Staunton d
  William consent for Sarah by Robert Withrow of Mossy Creek
  b- Griffith Evans of Staunton min- Benjamin Erwin- 16Aug1788
Joseph & Sarah McCue 17 Apr 1822; min- James C Willson
Joseph & Mary Moffett 25 Apr 1786; b- Robert Kirk min-
  William Wilson- 27Apr1786
Robert & Patsey Dold 28 Feb 1798; d Philip b- Philip Dold
  min- John McCue- 1Mar1798

McElvanny
Christopher & Mary Powlas 2 Nov 1796; d Nicholas (Paulus)
  who consents b- Jacob Powlas

McElwee
Thomas & Elizabeth Henry 9 Feb 1797; d Samuel b- Samuel
  Henry

McElwrath
John & ----- ----- 17 May 1763; license only

McFadden
Edward & Susannah Rough 16 Oct 1798; d Peter who consents
  b- Christian Lukenbill
William & Margaret Wade 13 Aug 1821; min- Daniel Stephens

Augusta County Marriages -- Man's Name

McFall
  David & Catharine Todd 23 Jul 1842; min- John A Van Lear
  Thomas & Ann Smith 12 Jan 1832; min- William Wilson
  William & Susannah Shirley 16 Mar 1843; min- S J Love
McFarlane
  Andrew & ----- ----- 26 May 1774; license only
McFeeters
  William & ----- ----- - Oct 1764; license only
McGaffock
  James & ----- ----- - Feb 1760; license only
McGarry
  Edward & ----- ----- - Jan 1760; license only
McGee
  Robert & ----- ----- 20 Jul 1765; license only
McGill
  John & ----- ----- - Feb 1749; license only
  John & Jane Edmiston 5 Oct 1785; Edmondson? d Mathew b- William Shires wit- Richard Jones & James McCann min- Archibald Scott- 6Oct1785
  Robert & Mary Craig 16 Dec 1797; d James b- James Craig min- William Wilson- --Dec1797
McGilvray
  Alexander & Sally Bumgardner 16 Mar 1820; min- Robert H Chapman
McGlamery
  John & Margaret Armstrong 18 Sep 1827; min- John Hendren
McGlaughlin
  John & Ann Wiley 27 Oct 1790; d Robert, who consents wit- Thomas Stinson & John McIntire b- Robert Wiley
McGuffin
  James & Elizabeth Erwin 19 Apr 1803; min- William King
  Jamison D & Sarah B Alfred 7 May 1833; min- Conrad Speece
  Thomas H & Eve Elizabeth Shultz 24 Apr 1845; min- J C Hensell
  William & Martha L Fur 27 Sep 1834; min- Samuel Kennerly- publication of banns
McIlree
  Arioine & Sarah Teaford 3 Jun 1828; min- William Calhoon
McIlvain
  John & Elizabeth Hodge 28 Jul 1789; b- John Hodge
McIntire
  James & Ann Dixon 27 Aug 1827; min- Conrad Speece
McIntosh
  George Grant & Sally Whitsell 17 Sep 1796; Sally (of age) d Christopher Whitsell b- Peter Heiskell min- John McCue- 19Sep1797
McKee
  Robert & Ruthey Ross 18 Feb 1794; Minister's return spells name as 'Betsey Ross' b- John Alexander min- John McCue- 25Feb1794
  Samuel & ----- ----- 6 Nov 1762; license only
  William & Rebecca Erwin 12 Aug 1789; orphan, granddaughter of Jane Erwin, who consents wit- Robert Grattan & Mary Erwin b- John Young min- William Wilson- 13Aug1789

Augusta County Marriages -- Man's Name

McKee (cont.)
  William & Peggy Vanlear 1 Feb 1803; min- John McCue

McKemy
  Andrew & Margaret McKemy 27 Oct 1795; d William b- William McKemy no minister listed; clerk's memorandum cites ceremony date as 5Nov1795
  Cyrus & Eleanor Tate Gwin 8 Oct 1834; min- George Hildt
  James & Jane Kirkpatrick 6 Feb 1810; min- William McPheeters
  John & Mary McKemy 27 Oct 1795; d William b- William McKemy no minister listed; clerk's memorandum cites ceremony date as 5Nov1795

McKenny
  Alexander & Mary McClure 27 Dec 1785; 'McKenney?' d Andrew b- William Bell wit- Alexander Stewart & Josias McClure min- Archibald Scott- 27Dec1785
  Nathaniel A & Mary Peebles 29 Apr 1830; min- Gerard Morgan

McKensey
  John & Mary Crane 22 Apr 1800; Mary (of age) b- Cornelius O'dair min- John McCue- 24Apr1800
  William & Elizabeth Clemer 14 Aug 1834; min- Cornelius Gates

McKenzie
  John & Catherine Crick 27 Dec 1827; min- James Morrison

McKesson
  David & Sally Bryant 27 May 1801; d Anderson Bryant, dec., late of Albemarle cty b- William Chambers min- John McCue- 27Mar1801

McKinney
  John & Mary Trimble 8 Sep 1785; d David min- Archibald Scott- 20Sep1785

McKinny
  David & Margaret Wallace 26 Sep 1785; McKenny? d James min- Archibald Scott- 26Sep1785

McKnight
  William & Sarah Meek 28 Feb 1801; d Daniel who consents test- Agness Meek b- Robert McCutchen

McLaughlin
  James & Mary Stuart 30 May 1787; b- Robert Stuart min- Samuel Shannon- 7Jun1787
  James & Elizabeth Woolwine 1 Feb 1787; Minister's return spells name as 'Laughlin' d Elizabeth Wolvine who consents test- G Cordell & John Gorden b- John Moore min- Archibald Scott- 2Feb1787

McLeas
  Charles & Susan Harrow 4 Dec 1837; min- John A Steele

McLeer
  John & Helen Edmunds 4 Sep 1837; min- Fred D Goodwin

McMahon
  James & Polly Frame 20 Feb 1806; min- William Wilson
  Robert & ----- ----- 20 Jul 1758; license only

McMillen
  John & Polly Lefler 7 Mar 1791; Minister's return spells name as 'McMellan [McMiller?] and Leflar' d Jacob who consents b- William Brine & John Hale b- Joseph Lefter min- William Wilson- 7Mar1791

Augusta County Marriages -- Man's Name

McMinn
　Joseph & Elizabeth Linck 28 Feb 1825; min- Josiah Cole
McMullan
　James & Mary Henderson 4 Mar 1800; Minister's return
　　spells name as 'McMillan' d Valentine who consents James
　　(of age) b- James Cochran min- William Wilson- 6Mar1800
McMullen
　Daniel & Mary Rusmisel 8 Jun 1826; min- John Hendren
　Edward & ----- ----- 16 May 1759; license only
　John & Martha Turner 16 May 1788; Minister's return spells
　　name as 'McMullon' b- James Frazer min- Archibald Scott-
　　16May1788
McMurtry
　Samuel & ----- ----- 30 Sep 1762; license only
McNabb
　William & ----- ----- 19 Mar 1750; license only
McNair
　David & Betty Allen 8 Nov 1786; Minister's return spells
　　name as 'McNare' (Elizabeth'?) d James b- Francis Allen
　　wit- Francis Allen, Rebekah & Poley Allen min- William
　　Wilson- 6Nov1786 (sic)
　John & Ann Hogshead 29 Aug 1825; min- John Hendren
　Ward & Catharine Haines 14 Dec 1826; min- John A Gore
McNeil
　Abraham & Margaret Lamme 3 Feb 1795; d James b- James
　　Lamme min- William Wilson- 5Feb1795
　Abraham & Elizabeth Young 20 Dec 1834; min- George Hildt
McNight
　James & Mary Scott 17 Oct 1810; min- John Montgomery
　William & Martha Parris 18 Oct 1832; min- William Calhoon
McNutt
　William & Margaret Stevenson 3 Aug 1843; min- James
　　Morrison
McPheeters
　Archibald A & Mary Jane Brown 25 Oct 1838; min- A B
　　McCorkle
　James & Elizabeth Coalter 23 May 1791; James from
　　Botetourt cty d Michael who consents b- John Coalter no
　　minister listed; clerk's memorandum cites ceremony date as
　　25May1791
　John & Margaret Anderson 22 Dec 1787; (Mary?) b- Robert
　　Donaldson min- Archibald Scott- 25Dec1787
　Robert & Jane Scott 24 Feb 1814; min- William Calhoon
McQuain
　George & Martha Jane Karicofe 29 Aug 1844; min- John A Van
　　Lear
McWhorter
　John & Mary McCorkell 4 Nov 1791; b- John McCorkell no
　　minister listed; clerk's memorandum cites ceremony date as
　　5Nov1791
McWilliams
　John & Isabella Peatt 3 Aug 1826; min- John Hendren

Augusta County Marriages -- Man's Name

Meade
John & Martha Glenn 22 Nov 1798; Minister's return spells name as 'Mead' widower Martha (of age) d George William Glenn swears that his sister of age b- William Morrison min- William King- 28Nov1798

Means
Hugh & Nancy Armstrong 22 Oct 1785; d Robert b- William Chambers wit- Samuel Armstrong min- Archibald Scott- 26Oct1785

Meck
Thomas & Catherine Philips 31 Oct 1807; min- John Montgomery

Meddings
George & Polly Lunsford 9 Mar 1837; min- J C Hensell

Meek
Mathias (Jr) & Keziah Leeser 4 Sep 1786; d Joseph b- Mathias Meek Sr wit- Richard Cain

Mefford
John & Mary Lemon 8 Jan 1787; d George who consents test- John Cofman & Thomas Hannah s Gasper who consents b- Jacob Lemon

Mellen
Patrick & Hannah Fall 25 Jun 1807; min- William King

Melrose
Adam R & Elizabeth C Fisher 11 Jun 1846; min- James H Brown

Melton
William & Elizabeth Paxton 23 Dec 1817; min- William King

Menker
Peter & Barbara Loetz 7 Mar 1796; d George who consents b- John Loetz

Menzies
William A & Elizabeth Garber 17 Oct 1809; min- William Calhoon

Merit
William & Rachel A Fitzpatrick 1 Jan 1838; min- Isaac Jones- publication of banns

Meritt
Valentine & Ann Donaghe 3 Sep 1812; min- William King

Merritt
John & Elizabeth Peters 15 Feb 1816; min- William King
William & Margaret Overshiner 10 Jul 1796; widower & widow (of John) b- George Wiford (Weifford)

Mesner
Christian & Rebecca Insle 15 Jun 1793; Rebecca (of age) b- George Bernard

Messersmith
Elijah & Anna Karichoof 16 Oct 1818; min- G H Riemenschneider
George & Mary Philips 22 Jun 1826; min- John Hendren

Messmaker
Jacob & Susan Chaplin 20 Mar 1828; min- William C. Morrison

Meyers
David & Rebecca Coffman 13 Aug 1840; min- J J Reimensnyder

Augusta County Marriages -- Man's Name

Michael
  Abraham & Eliza Bird 8 Aug 1837; min- J C Hensell-
    publication of banns
  Christian & Catherine Messersmith 11 Sep 1799; d Henry
    Messersmith, dec. Both of age Christian's mother is
    Elizabeth Michael b- George Messersmith
  Christian & Sarah Simmons 19 Sep 1816; min- Wright Burgess
  Daniel & Catherine Hafner 16 Sep 1813; min- G H
    Riemenschneider
  Frederick & Elizabeth Hushour - Dec 1826; min- Joseph Smith
  Henry & Sarah Neere 22 Aug 1819; min- Daniel Garber-
    publication of banns
  Jacob & Susan Shultz 24 Apr 1839; min- George Huffman
  Jacob & Catherine Syple 15 Apr 1813; min- G H
    Riemenschneider
  John & Maria Orebough 21 Jan 1837; min- John J Riemensnyder
  John & Elizabeth Shaffer 10 May 1803; min- William King
  Jonas (Jr) & Polly Moyers 23 Jul 1846; min- Henry Wetzel
  Jonathan & Susanna Huffer 28 Jan 1830; min- G H
    Reimensnyder
  Joseph & Susan Moyers 22 May 1849; min Henry Wetzel
  Peter & Polly Landis 12 Nov 1818; min- Wright Burgess
  William & Susanna Near 18 Aug 1818; min- Daniel Garber-
    publication of banns

Michel
  Jonas & Susana Hofert - Mar 1806; min- John Brown
  Peter & Mary Harness - Jun 1817; min- John Brown

Michie
  John P & Anna Maria Points 13 Oct 1847; min- T T Castleman
  Thomas J & Margaret R Garber - Nov 1826; min- Joseph Smith

Middleton
  John & Elenor Gregory 24 Oct 1833; min- George Hildt

Miely
  Anton & Amanda M Knowles 27 Feb 1845; min- W Kirby

Miller
  Abram & Nancy Moses 13 Apr 1815; min- Conrad Speece, Jr
  Clinton G & Nancy Coiner 25 May 1831; min- Samuel Kennerly
  Daniel & Polly Eakle 20 Jan 1823; min- James C Willson
  Daniel & Rebecca Garber 1 Oct 1846; min- Peter Miller
  George H & Nancy Root 19 Jul 1848; min- T T Castleman
  George W & Hannah Hanger 22 May 1845; min- G W Israel-
    publication of banns
  George W & Elizabeth Jackson 7 Oct 1847; min- W G Campbell
  George & Margaret McCue 27 Dec 1819; min- John Hendren
  George & Sarah Sheaffer 22 Mar 1816; min- William King
  Henry & Mary Hare 26 Mar 1827; min- Michael Meyerhoeffer
  Henry & Elizabeth Weaver 8 Jun 1797; d John Peter Weaver
    who consents test- William Sterritt & Thomas Douthat s
    Martin Moller who consents test- Luke Collins & John Kisner
    b- John Kesner
  Isaac & Agnes Montgomery 27 Apr 1802; min- William King-
    27Apr1802
  Jacob & Martha Groves 23 May 1830; min- Abraham Garber
  Jacob & Jane McIntire 6 Jun 1820; min- Daniel Stephens

Miller (cont.)
Jacob & Polly Mell 5 Sep 1805; min- William King
Jacob & Mary Rhinehart 1 Oct 1794; Mary of age b- George Houser
James C & Eliza B Grove 9 Feb 1832; min- Francis McFarland
James W & Harriet P Allen 5 Nov 1846; min- Francis McFarland
James & Elizabeth M Moffett 30 Apr 1836; min- James C Wilson
James & Elizabeth Moffett 7 Jan 1799; d George who consents b- James Cochran
James & Fanny Powers 4 Nov 1797; widow William b- Thomas Painter
John H & Ellen Kesterson 26 Jan 1836; min- Francis A C Mills
John W & Julia W Heiskell 28 Aug 1810; min- William Calhoon
John W & Betsy Long 27 Oct 1825; min- William Wilson
John & Mary Allen 30 May 1809; widower min- William Wilson
John & Fanny Brower 10 Sep 1840; min- Peter Miller
John & Mary Brown 2 May 1820; min- Abraham Garber- publication of banns
John & Eve Burns 17 May 1791; min- John Montgomery- 17May1791
John & Nancy Crawford 7 Aug 1817; min- Conrad Speece, Jr
John & Catherine Danner 9 Mar 1802; min- William King- 9Mar1802
John & Anna Houston 13 Jan 1810; min- William King
John & Elizabeth Landes 26 Mar 1811; min- Samuel Garber- publication of banns
John & Priscilla Madison 21 May 1788; Priscilla gives her own consent test- James Hogge con- Thomas Miller test- James Anderson, David Anderson, & Phi. Finkle b- Peter Heiskill min- Benjamin Erwin- 21May1788
John & Catherine Miller 19 Nov 1798; d John (Adam? Miller) b- Adam Miller
John & Mary Webb 19 Jul 1827; min- James Morrison
John & Frances Willis 4 May 1842; min- Alfred G Chenowith
Joseph H & Nancy Rough 14 May 1846; min- James Paine
Joseph & Rebecca Biby 1 Jul 1845; min- P Shickel
Joseph & Sarah Hawpe 13 Nov 1813; min- William King
Joseph & Elizabeth Link 26 Nov 1827; min- Joseph Smith
Martin & Susannah Bright 6 Mar 1823; min- James Morrison
Michael & Christian Cline 25 Mar 1791; d Jacob Cline Sr who consents wit- Peter Cline & Jacob Kockanorer b- Jacob Cline marriage sent to clerk by Samuel Brown and dated 7Apr1791
Michael & Molley Sears 25 Mar 1817; min- Abraham Garber- publication of banns
Oliver & Margaret Hagerty 9 Feb 1799; Also known as Margaret Brown (See description of this unusual bond in the Introduction)
Patrick & ----- ----- - Aug 1756; license only
Peter & Barbary Laird 17 Mar 1812; min- Samuel Garber
Robert A & Evalina T Lewis 6 Dec 1827; min- Francis McFarland

Augusta County Marriages -- Man's Name

Miller (cont.)
  Robert & Jennett Ewell 8 Jul 1793; Minister's return spells name as 'Youel' d William Youel b- William Ewell min- John Montgomery- 16Jul1793
  Samuel (Jr) & Priscilla Poage 22 Mar 1828; min- Gerard Morgan
  Samuel & Ann Braford 6 Jun 1786; Minister's return spells names 'Millar & Brawford' d Samuel b- John Braford min- Archibald Scott- 13Jun1786
  Samuel & Elizabeth Fudge 3 Jun 1785; d John b- George Craig wit- William Chambers, Francis Huff, John Black
  Samuel & Mary Gratton 29 Nov 1791
  Samuel & Catharine Wine 28 Nov 1844; min- T T Castleman
  Valentine & Eve France 9 Jan 1794; Eve (of age) b- William Sansebaugh
  Valentine & Sylvia Schooler 22 Aug 1786; Minister's return spells name 'Millar' d Zachariah min- Archibald Scott- 29Aug1786
  William S & Catharine Cupp 29 Feb 1844; min- Jacob Baer
  William & Elizabeth Garretson 12 Jan 1821; min- Robert Boyd- publication of banns

Milliken
  John & Isabella Doak 27 Sep 1786; Minister's return spells name as 'Millihen' b- Robert Torbet min- Archibald Scott- 28Sep1786

Mills
  Alonzo & Mary Bateman 20 Mar 1845; min- S Wagner
  John J T & Polly Holladay 15 Nov 1814; min- Conrad Speece, Jr
  John & Darcus Allison 2 Sep 1811; min- Wright Burgess
  Robert & Polly Emmitt 24 Mar 1807; min- William King
  William & Catherine Hanger 19 Aug 1822; min- John Hendren
  Wilson & Elizabeth Johnston 23 Jul 1818; min- Conrad Speece, Jr

Milsap
  Thomas & ----- ----- 10 Sep 1751; license only

Mines
  David & Mary Jane McNutt 22 Oct 1844; min- J C Hensell
  George & Mary Perry 27 Dec 1827; min- William Calhoon
  George & Sally Walls 25 Mar 1839; min- John C Hensell
  James A & Ellen King 16 Aug 1832; min- William Calhoon
  James & Elizabeth McClelland 21 Feb 1828; min- James Morrison
  Lewis & Hannah Gabart 13 Feb 1810; min- William King
  Samuel & Nancy McWilliams 30 Oct 1821; min- John Brown

Minnick
  Noah J & Mary Jain Whitlock 22 Apr 1845; min- Jacob Baer
  Samuel & Elizabeth Almorode 16 Mar 1802; min- William King- 16Mar1802

Minnis
  Wheeler & Lucy Jane Bunch 5 Aug 1834; min- Samuel Kennerly

Miser
  Frederick & Mary Kiplinger 17 Nov 1790; min- William Wilson- 17Nov1790

Augusta County Marriages -- Man's Name

Mitchell
  George H & Eliza N Campbell 26 Feb 1839; min- Frederick D Goodwin
  James & Mary Brown 23 Jun 1806; min- William McPheeters
  John & ----- ----- 30 Apr 1765; license only
  Thomas C & Isabella Ann Lilley 25 May 1837; min- William Calhoon
  Thomas & Margaret Calleson 28 Mar 1786; Minister's return spells name as 'Margaret Callison' d James s James b- Robert Calleson wit- W Cunningham & William Mitchell min- Archibald Scott- 4Apr1786
  Thomas & Ann Galbraith 9 Jan 1798; Minister's return spells name as 'Caldbreath' d Thomas Galbraith, dec. b- Thomas Galbraith (Coldbreath) min- John McCue- 11Jan1798
  William & ----- ----- 18 Feb 1765; license only
  William & Elizabeth Beard 25 Feb 1801; d Thomas b- Thomas Beard
  William & Agness Brownlee 15 Sep 1785; min- Archibald Scott- 15Sep1785
  William & Sarah Newton 16 Feb 1826; min- Francis McFarland

Mizer
  John & Sarah Spitler 10 May 1831; min- William Calhoon

Moeler
  Christopher & Elizabeth Wolf 29 Nov 1809; min- William King

Moffet
  William & Mary McClenachan 11 May 1791; Minister's return spells name as 'Moffett' d Elijah b- James Moffett wit- David Coalter & Elijah McClenachan Jr min- Benjamin Irvin- 11May1791

Moffett
  George & ----- ----- - Apr 1761; license only
  George & Rebecca Gilkeson 25 Oct 1797; Rebecca (of age) d Archibald Gilkeson, dec. b- Francis Gilkison
  James & ----- ----- 7 Feb 1762; license only
  James & Hannah Miller 19 Sep 1797; d Henry Miller, dec. b- Chesley Kinney
  James & Sarah Mitchell 31 Mar 1831; min- Francis McFarland
  James & Mary Stuart 26 Dec 1789; b- Archibald Stuart min- Samuel Carrick- 29Dec1789
  John (Jr) & Sally Hays 8 Jan 1799; Sally (of age) sis to Patrick Hays b- Patrick Hays
  John & ----- ----- - May 1760; license only
  John & Jane A Edson 21 Feb 1822; min- William W Calhoun
  John & Elizabeth M Tate 5 Nov 1823; min- Francis McFarland
  Robert & ----- ----- 11 Jan 1763; license only
  William & Elizabeth Gamble 28 Jun 1785; b- Robert Gamble
  William & Mary Jones 28 Feb 1820; min- John Hendren
  William & Cynthia Mitchell 27 Dec 1827; min- Francis McFarland

Moffette
  William & Salley McChesney 23 Dec 1806; min- William McPheeters

Augusta County Marriages -- Man's Name

Mohler
  Jacob & Polly Fisher 18 Apr 1822; min- Josiah Cole
  John & Magdalena Ryanhart 16 Apr 1799; min- Daniel Garber- 16Apr1799

Mohr
  John (Jr) & Polly Patterson 3 Feb 1807; min- William King

Moirs
  George & Margaret Michael 22 Sep 1800; Minister's return spells name as 'George Morris' d Frederick Michael, dec. b- John Michael min- John McCue- 23Sep1800

Molds
  Jeremiah & Elizabeth Scott 20 Jun 1801; Elizabeth (of age) d Joseph b- Joseph Paxton min- William King- 20Jun1801

Montgomerie
  John & ----- ----- 22 Nov 1753; license only

Montgomery
  James & ----- ----- 19 Mar 1765; license only
  John (Jr) & Elizabeth Nelson 19 Nov 1813; min- Conrad Speece, Jr
  John & Sarah Hicklin 2 Mar 1785; min- Samuel Shannon- 2Mar1785
  John & Catharine Smith 22 May 1834; min- Joseph Spriggs
  Joseph & ----- ----- 16 Nov 1762; license only
  Thomas & Juliet L Dalhouse 22 Apr 1811; min- John Montgomery

Moon
  Robert B & Mary B Massie 29 Oct 1846; min- Joseph H Fox

Mooney
  Edward & Catherine Hays 23 Dec 1789; Catherine recently from Ireland b- James Curtis
  Edward & Nancy Rankin 11 Jul 1816; min- William King
  Richard & Polly Chaplin 17 Jan 1828; min- William C. Morrison

Moony
  Anderson & Rosanah Chapman 24 Jul 1829; min- William C. Morrison

Moor
  Abner & Rebeckah Barry 26 Sep 1805; min- William King

Moore
  Archer M & Mary E Poage 1 Dec 1833; min- James Morrison
  Daniel & Martha Barnett 16 Oct 1792; Minister's return spells name as 'Burnett' b- Robert Bailey min- John Brown- 17Feb1793
  David & Jane Depriest 13 Aug 1788; d Ann who consents test- William Sterrett & James Elliott b- William Sterratt min- Archibald Scott- 14Aug1788
  David & Polly Marshall 26 Dec 1812; min- Wright Burgess
  Elijah & Priscilla Waters 22 Apr 1822; min- John Hendren
  Isaac & Clary Kesterson 28 Aug 1833; min- George Hildt
  Jacob & Isabella Chesnut 21 Sep 1809; min- William King
  James C & Eleanor Moffett 6 Nov 1823; min- Francis McFarland
  James & ----- ----- 26 Aug 1763; license only
  James & Elizabeth Clifton 21 Aug 1794; Woman's name blank on bond b- Richard Clifton min- John Brown- 21Aug1794

Augusta County Marriages -- Man's Name

Moore (cont.)
  James & Jane Koiner 17 Apr 1823; min- James C Willson
  Jesper & ----- ----- 30 Jul 1759; license only
  John & Elizabeth Boils 12 Dec 1805; min- William Wilson
  John & Margaret Moore 29 Mar 1788; d Moses who consents
    test- John McCutchan & John Black b- James Reaugh min-
    John Brown- 17Jun1787
  John & Jenny Steele 14 Dec 1785; min- John Brown- 14Dec1785
  Joseph & Frances Stuart 11 May 1802; min- William Wilson-
    11May1802
  Moses & ----- ----- 18 Nov 1761; license only
  Moses & Jane Ewing 22 Mar 1786; d James wit- William
    Rankin & Alexander Gibson min- Samuel Shannon- 11Apr1786
  Peter & Jane Humes 8 May 1827; min- James Watts-
    publication of banns
  Robert & Sarah Martin 23 Jul 1828; min- William Calhoon
  Sam & ----- ----- 15 Jul 1757; license only
  Stephen S & Hester Johnston 28 Sep 1847; min- T H Busey
  William & ----- ----- 19 Sep 1763; license only
  William & Mary Palmer 25 Feb 1793; d William b- John
    Hamilton Hodge & John McDowell min- John McCue- 4Mar1793

Moorman
  Edward G & Mary L Crawford 19 Mar 1835; min- Conrad Speece

Moredock
  James & Lucinda Ruff 28 Apr 1850; min- Henry Witzel

Morel
  Henry & Sally Moore 5 Sep 1785; d Benjamin b- Samuel
    Moore wit- Henry Jones & Samuel Moore

Morgan
  Calvin & Sally Fackler 20 Jan 1801; d Michael who consents
    test- H Paul b- John Bowyer
  John & Ann Edmonds 12 Jul 1792; Minister's return spells
    name as 'Edmunds' d George, dec.& Nelly Fillis, who
    consents b- Benjamin Johnston min- John McCue- 12Jun1792
  Luther & Nancy Dold 31 Jan 1798; d Philip who consents
    test- Gideon Morgan b- Robert McDowell min- John McCue-
    1Feb1798
  Samuel D & Matilda McIntosh 2 Nov 1819; min- William
    Calhoon
  William & Eliza A Flinn 29 May 1835; min- Augustus Babb

Morrell
  Jacob & Elizabeth Brooback 26 Oct 1785; b- Lewis
    Geldmecher min- John Brown- 9Nov1785

Morris
  B H & Sarah A Whisman 9 Mar 1843; min- P E Stevenson
  Benjamin D & Sarah E Frainer 10 Jan 1850; min- William T
    Richardson
  Henry & Ann J Nixon 8 Oct 1815; min- William King
  Lindsay & Ann Eliza Coffman 17 Mar 1846; min- T T Castleman
  Rice & Laney Garber 8 Jan 1807; min- William Calhoon
  Richard & ----- ----- 17 Nov 1761; license only
  William & Columbia Jane Burton 14 Jun 1849; min- T A Morgan
  William & Catherine Marshall 26 Jan 1809; min- John McCue
  William & Eliza Palmer - May 1820; min- John Brown

Augusta County Marriages -- Man's Name

Morrison
  James & ----- ----- 24 Mar 1763; license only
  Samuel C & Sarah Collins 16 Feb 1846; min- John Paine
  William D & Elizabeth Clinetinch 19 Apr 1830; min- William Wilson

Morrow
  George & Fanny Rodgers 30 Aug 1787; Minister's return spells name as 'George Muncy & Nanney Rodgers' b- John Elliott min- James Chambers- 30Aug1787

Morton
  Robert & Mary Miller 21 Jun 1792; Cited in bond as 'Robert Merton & Mary Motes' b- James Crawford min- Benjamin Irwin- 21Jun1792
  Robert & Sarah Sorrels 29 Dec 1792; d Joseph, who consents wit- Thomas Beard & Kezzeyar Beard b- Nathaniel Kelley min- William Wilson- 1Jan1793

Mosby
  Armstead & Jane McCullough 29 Mar 1810; min- William Calhoon

Moses
  Isaac & Elizabeth Earley 30 May 1823; min- William Wilson Jr
  Levi L & Elizabeth Rogers 22 Aug 1822; min- William Wilson Jr

Moss
  Alexander & Elizabeth Gibson 20 Jun 1836; min- John A Steele

Mount
  William T & Hannah E Castleman 27 Sep 1848; min- T T Castleman

Mowry
  Abraham & Mary Tiefenbach 19 Mar 1798; d Baltzer b- Baltzer Tevenbaugh
  George W & Sarah Jane Robertson 23 Dec 1847; min- S Hildebrand
  Henry & Mary Gibson 8 Jun 1791; d Alexander b- Alexander Gibson, Jr no minister listed; clerk's memorandum cites ceremony date as 10Jun1791
  Lewis (Jr) & Margaret Coiner 9 Jun 1800; b- George Koiner min- William Wilson- 15Jun1800

Moyers
  Daniel & Barbara Keller 16 Sep 1819; min- William Calhoon
  David & Polly Kellar 11 Mar 1824; min- Josiah Cole
  Jacob & Elizabeth Michael 24 Jul 1848; min- George Huffman
  John & Dolly Cupps 4 Mar 1810; min- William King
  John & Sarah Michael 28 Nov 1833; min- John S Watt
  Lewis & Hannah Michael 2 May 1843; min- George B Rimel
  Peter & Ann Aerion 21 Mar 1850; min- John Wine

Muck
  Joseph & Mary J Koontz 6 Sep 1837; min- James Morrison

Mulholland
  Edward & Isabella Christian 5 Jan 1822; min- John Brown

Augusta County Marriages -- Man's Name

Mulinx
  Archibald & Mary Powell 5 Feb 1786; d Thomas b- William Urquhart wit- John Mulinx & Thomas Cox

Mulnix
  James & Mary Arbocast 10 Apr 1785; min- Samuel Shannon- 4Apr1785

Mummer
  Christian & Betsy Hawp 21 Apr 1790; d Rudolph, who consents wit- John & Susanna Hawp b- Walter Herrin

Muncy
  George & Nancy Rodgers 30 Aug 1787; Minister's return spells name as 'George Morrow & Fanny Rodgers' min- Archibald Scott- 30Aug1787

Murphy
  Daniel & Margaret Aston 7 Mar 1801; d John b- John Aston
  James & Susanah Harper 16 Mar 1785; min- Samuel Shannon- 16Mar1785
  Robert & ----- ----- 18 Mar 1762; license only

Murray
  Archibald & Sarah Fulton 11 Jan 1792; d Hugh b- Robert Fulton min- John Brown- 12Jan1791
  Daniel & Mary Boon 10 Oct 1843; min- S Filler
  Henry & ----- ----- 19 Aug 1758; license only

Murry
  James & Sarah Brownlee 19 Dec 1829; min- Francis McFarland
  James & Sarah Jane Weitzel 10 Sep 1840; min- Samuel Wagner
  Richard & Jane Parent 18 Dec 1823; min- William Wilson Jr

Myers
  Daniel & Elizabeth Crombaker 13 Sep 1806; min- Samuel Garber
  George T & Mary Elizabeth Reed 23 Apr 1850; min- James Morrison
  Henry K & Lucinda Myers 28 Mar 1850; min- B M Smith
  Henry & Elizabeth Trorobaugh 16 Oct 1799; d Nicholas b- Nicholas Trorabaugh Henry was apprenticed until he was of age a year before
  Isaac C & Lucinda Bell 15 Oct 1840; min- J J Reimensnyder
  Isaac & Hannah Crombaker 13 Sep 1806; min- Samuel Garber
  John & Hannah Spitler 2 Oct 1810; min- Samuel Garber- publication of banns
  Joshua E & Anna Seawright 26 May 1829; min- William Wilson
  Lewis & Mary Laymore 23 Nov 1791; b- Michael Garber
  Samuel & Sarah Byers 17 Aug 1844; min- John Hendren
  William & Betsy Michael 15 Apr 1835; min- Wright Burgess

Mynes
  David & Elizabeth King 12 Mar 1796; d William who consents test- Adam King & Robert King b- Thomas Mynes

Nabours
  William & Elizabeth Johnson 27 Apr 1803; min- William King

Naher
  Henry & Catherine Huffert 17 Nov 1827; min- G H Reimensnyder
  John G & Maria Wicle 17 Jan 1834; min- John Hendren

Augusta County Marriages -- Man's Name

Nales
  William & Elizabeth W J Faucet 23 Sep 1808; min- Joel Watson
Neal
  Robert & Fanny Hamilton 23 Jan 1799; Fanny (of age) d William Hamilton, dec., and Patience Hamilton who consents test- John C Hamilton & Hugh Hamilton b- John Hamilton
  William H & Elizabeth M Baskins 28 Jun 1836; min- James C Wilson
Near
  Samuel & Martha Jane Reeves 27 Dec 1849; min- John Harshbarger
Nebergall
  Adam & Rosanah Lutz 28 May 1827; min- Michael Meyerhoeffer
  David & Mary Switzer 10 Apr 1827; min- Michael Meyerhoeffer
  Henry & Nancy McCames 17 Feb 1795; 'McKemy?' b- Jacob Nebergall
  Jacob & Mary Wagoner 17 Nov 1824; min- Michael Meyerhoeffer
  Philip & Mary Lambert 25 Mar 1802; min- William King- 25Mar1802
Neighborrgall
  Adam & Polly Dillon 22 Oct 1802; min- William Wilson- 22Oct1802
Neill
  Samuel & Jane Graham 14 Jan 1793; Minister's return spells name as 'Neal' Jane (of age) b- John Cooper min- John Montgomery- 15Jan1793
Neilson
  Hall & Mary Archer Mitchell 26 Feb 1839; min- Frederick D Goodwin
Nelson
  James & Agness Henry 14 Aug 1787; Minister's return spells name as 'Neilson' d James who consents test- Joseph Nilson & Robert Henery b- James Henry min- Archibald Scott- 16Aug1787
  John & Mary Trimble 10 Dec 1813; min- John McCue
  Joseph & Mary Henry 4 Dec 1786; d James b- Robert Blair wit- Alexander Ramsey
  Robert & Rosa E Points 6 Oct 1848; min- T T Castleman
Nesbet
  John & Sarah Hunter 24 Aug 1787; Minister's return spells name as 'Neisbet' consent for both- Samuel Neisbitt & William Hunter test- John Yeager & James McCutchan b- James McCutchan min- Archibald Scott- 26Aug1787
Nesbit
  John & Phebe Travis 10 Nov 1820; min- John D Ewin
Ness
  William & Elizabeth Welsh - Jan 1809; min- John Brown
Nest
  William & Isabella H Hanna 9 Dec 1824; min- Francis McFarland
Nevins
  Martin & Lavinia B McGuffin 24 Nov 1842; min- James Paine

Augusta County Marriages -- Man's Name

New
  John & Elizabeth Boyer 10 Jun 1807; min- William King
Newcomb
  John H & Mary Eakle 10 Nov 1825; min- Josiah Cole
  William J & Martha Armstrong 22 Sep 1825; min- Conrad Speece
Newham
  John W C & Mary Jane Pelter 18 Jul 1843; min- C Parkison
Newlan
  Benjamin & Catherine Tate 29 Mar 1787; d Samuel who consents test- James Beard & James Sprowl b- Samuel Sprowl min- John Brown- 29Mar1787
Newlen
  Barnabas & Mary Fitz 6 Dec 1804; min- William King
Newman
  Leroy & Nancy Crawford 15 Sep 1825; min- Francis McFarland
  Vincent G & Elizabeth Grips 14 Apr 1836; min- William Calhoon
Newton
  James & Mary Scylor 11 Oct 1797; d Philip Scylor, late of Augusta sis Jacob Scylor b- Jacob Scylor (Silor)
  John & Catharine Hall 23 Jul 1829; min- Francis McFarland
  John & Amanda T Hutcheson 4 Mar 1835; min- George Hildt
Nichol
  John M D & Nancy Burk 4 Sep 1837; min- Stephen Smith
  John & Elizabeth Donaghe 9 Dec 1802; Minister's return spells name as 'Donaho' min- William Wilson- 9Dec1802
  John & Elizabeth Hogsett 14 May 1798; Minister's return spells name as 'Hogshead' d Robert Hogsett, dec. con- Nancy Hogsett test- William Hogsett & James Hogsett b- John McDowell min- Benjamin Irvin- 15May1798
Nichols
  Zephaniah & Rebecca Davis 30 Oct 1790; d James, who consents wit- Osborn Hamilton & Roger Heckman b- Joseph Davis
Nickenson
  Abraham & Mary Simpson 4 Nov 1791; Mary a free mulatto b- James Patterson
Nickey
  Christian & Isabella Cooper 15 Jul 1830; min- Gerard Morgan
  Samuel & Catherine Balzley 30 Jan 1806; min- John McCue
Nickle
  John & Nancy Nickle 18 Apr 1803; min- William King
Nimmo
  David & Elizabeth Peaco 28 May 1844; min- Francis McFarland
Noffinger
  David C & Mary C Grove 4 Apr 1839; min- A B McCorkle
Noland
  Thomas & Margaret McMahon 13 May 1794; Minister's return spells name as 'Nowland & McMahan' Thomas was 21 in October, 1793 b- Moses Russell 15May1794
Nolin
  John & Margaret Bing 20 Nov 1792; Minister's return spells name as 'Mary Bing d John b- John Bing min- William Wilson- 22Nov1792

Augusta County Marriages -- Man's Name

Noll
  Conrad & Peggy Cupp 29 Aug 1826; min- Daniel Stephens
Nonyer
  Thomas & ----- ----- 4 May 1762; license only
North
  Phillip & Margaret Abney 29 Mar 1792; d John, dec b- David Parry min- John McCune- 29Mar1792
Nutty
  James & Elizabeth Hanger 13 May 1841; min- James Morrison
  Samuel & Elizabeth Cales 6 Feb 1845; min- J C Hensell
O'Kane
  John & Martha Bragg 1 Dec 1840; min- P E Stevenson
Ocheltree
  Hamilton E & Mary G Woodward 13 Dec 1832; min- William Wilson
  John & Margaret Young 29 Aug 1836; min- John Hendren
  Michael & Peggy Young 2 Apr 1807; min- William Wilson
  William & Julia A F Sheets 24 Jan 1843; min- Samuel Wagner- publication of banns
Odell
  Silvans & Susanah Neal 7 Feb 1788; Minister's return spells names as 'Silvias O'Dell and Neil' d William Neal (Neill) test- J Underwood & J Slavens b- John Underwood min- Archibald Scott- 10Feb1788
Oder
  Waller & Mary Jane Blakemore 2 Mar 1835; min- William A Coffin
Oehler
  Anthony & Sophia Carhart 3 Apr 1797; widower & widow b- Deter Fischborn
Offlider
  John George & Nancy Lantern 21 Jan 1793; b- William Chambers
Offlighter
  Hamson & Sarah A Whitesell 5 Nov 1840; min- Frederick D Goodwin
Ohrbough
  Henry & Catharina Poulas - Nov 1810; min- John Brown
Oldham
  William & ----- ----- 11 Oct 1769; license only
Olinger
  George & Susanna Troxal 13 Sep 1810; min- William Calhoon
  Jacob & Barbara Downey 1 Jun 1785; d George b- William Cale wit- Thomas Gwin
Oliver
  James & Mary Curry 10 Oct 1788; ni Robert Curry who consents test- James King & William Betman b- Andrew Thompson
Ong
  Isaac & Christiana Fleiger 2 Jul 1789; d John, who consents wit- W Chambers b- John Bosang & Henry Hall
  John & Margaret Allen 26 Mar 1812; min- William King

Augusta County Marriages -- Man's Name

Orbough
  Adam & Elizabeth Safley 3 Jan 1811; min- William Wilson
  John & Barbara Ailer 19 Dec 1816; min- G H Riemenschneider
Orebaugh
  David K & Rebecca E Griffith 27 May 1850; min- John Hendren
  Ephraim & Margaret Bowen 7 Jul 1847; min- J A Van Lear
  George A & Elizabeth Stoudamire 20 Feb 1845; min- John A Van Lear
Orebough
  Adam & Sarah Armintrout 26 Jun 1834; min- Joseph Spriggs
  Michael & Susan Ailor 12 Oct 1818; min- Wright Burgess- publication of banns
Orner
  Jacob & Christinah Miller 24 May 1806; min- Samuel Garber
Orrele
  Mathew & Ann Offord 16 Nov 1826; min- Benjamin Denton
Osborne
  George & Polly Lohr 19 Sep 1807; min- William King
Ott
  David & Nancy Russell 6 Jun 1827; min- Joseph Smith
  John & Susanah Shuey 24 Sep 1835; min- Cornelius Gates
Overshiner
  John & Elizabeth Flowers 5 Apr 1804; min- William King
Owens
  Thompson & Polly Weaver 20 Sep 1830; min- John Hendren
  William & Margaret Peery 2 Apr 1795; b- Chesley Kinney
Page
  William & Molly Burges 25 Oct 1798; Molly (of age) Tamor Elliott swears Molly is of age b- Hance Calvert
  William & Amelia Elliott 31 Jul 1800; widower Amelia not yet 20 d Peter who consents b- David Greiner
Paine
  Daniel & Polly Buchanan 1 Feb 1827; min- William Monroe
  Fountain T & Catherine Susan Grove 17 Dec 1827; min- William C. Morrison
  James & Polly Brittain 12 Jun 1828; min- John Hendren
  Samuel & Maria Craig 7 May 1840; min- D F Bittle
Painter
  David & Elizabeth Mowry 17 Mar 1828; min- Joseph Smith
  George & Susannah Stoffer 26 Jan 1814; min- William King
  John & Elizabeth Frankam - Mar 1828; min- William Monroe
  John & Nancy E Geralds 25 Jan 1849; min- James Paine
Palmer
  Adam & Christiana Kershner 6 Oct 1795; Christiana (of age) d David who consents con- Elizabeth Kershner b- Christian Olinger
  Christian & Mary K Groah 26 Aug 1843; min- James Paine
  Christopher & Elizabeth Dull 11 Mar 1801; d George b- George Dull
  David & Polly Clemer 21 Feb 1822; min- James Morrison
  David & Jane Greaver 1 Jun 1837; min- William Calhoub
  David & Mary Jane Shannon 21 Jan 1847; min- J C Hensell
  George & Peggy Ruple 15 Mar 1816; min- William Calhoon
  Jacob M & Catharine Zimmerman 12 Aug 1841; min- John C Hensell

Augusta County Marriages -- Man's Name

Palmer (cont.)
  Jacob & Barbara Gabhart 21 Feb 1791; d Jacob who consents
    b- John Sharp Jr
  Jacob & Cynthia Sheets 6 Feb 1840; min- D F Bittle
  John & Elenor E A Cambden 28 Aug 1848; min- Alonzo P Ludden
  Peter & Hannah A Hanger 11 Oct 1825; min- Michael
    Meyerhoeffer
  Philip O & Elizabeth Dunlap 8 Mar 1827; min- Francis
    McFarland
  William (Jr) & Jenny Chesnutt 12 Jan 1790; Minister's
    return spells name as 'Chestnut' b- John Chesnutt min-
    William Wilson- 12Jan1790
  William & Nancy Hain 31 Dec 1818; min- William King
Pannell
  William & Jane Small 3 Dec 1836; min- E Joshua Webb
Panzle
  Marshall E & Elizabeth Coley 30 May 1850; min- Daniel
    Brower
Parent
  Levi & Elizabeth Patterson 30 Dec 1830; min- Gerard Morgan
  Samuel & Sarah Jane Cupps 10 Nov 1841; min- Peter Shickel
Parks
  Joseph & Betsy Davis 24 Jul 1795; Betsy 'Elizabeth' d
    Walter who consents test- John Brown b- John Davis min-
    John McCue- 13Aug1795
Parmer
  Samuel & Dolly Ann Moneymaker 30 Dec 1843; min- James Paine
Parr
  Alexander & Jane Bunch 11 Jan 1816; min- William King
  George & Patsey Jamison 5 Dec 1815; min- William King
Parris
  John & Nancy C Henderson 12 Sep 1839; min- Isaac Jones
  Thomas & Mary Hudson 8 Jul 1800; s John Mary (of age) d
    George Hudson, dec. b- Charles Hudson
Parry
  John & Nancy Cassady 11 Apr 1822; min- William Wilson Jr
Parson
  George & Lucy Willson 9 Apr 1829; min- Conrad Speece
Parsons
  Milton & Mahal Newell 22 Jan 1832; min- Samuel Kennerly-
    publication of banns
Pateson
  Joseph & Elizabeth Peters 28 Aug 1835; min- Samuel Kennerly
Patrick
  William & Hetty C Massie 18 Oct 1849; min- William T
    Richardson
Patterson
  Adam & Sophia Jones 26 Mar 1796; d Enos b- Enos Jones
    Adam is 22 years old in January 1796 min- William Wilson-
    25Mar1796
  Adam & Rebeckah Mohr 12 Nov 1805; min- William King
  Allen & Isabella Bartley 18 Feb 1847; min- James Paine
  Elijah & Drusilla Henry 13 Dec 1827; min- James Morrison
  George & Barbara Silling 20 Jan 1798; d Gasper b- Gasper
    Silling

Augusta County Marriages -- Man's Name

Patterson (cont.)
  Israel & Rachel Bell 18 Sep 1806; min- William Calhoon
  James A & Mary A Patterson 25 Dec 1839; min- Jacob C
    Killian
  James F & Maria H Tremper 4 Mar 1828; min- Joseph Smith
  James G & Elizabeth Poage 22 Dec 1842; min- P E Stevenson
  James W & Mariah A Burgess 10 Nov 1842; min- A G Chenowith
  James & ----- ----- 22 Jun 1759; license only
  James & ----- ----- 23 May 1766; license only
  James & Sally Buckner 23 Sep 1827; min- William Wilson
  James & Jenney Craig 24 Jun 1799; d William b- William
    Craig
  James & Anne Hall 16 Sep 1786; d Susannah b- Alexander
    Gibson Jr
  Jameston & Rebecca Vernum 12 May 1796; d Abrahaim sis to
    John Vernum b- John Vernum
  John & ----- ----- 17 Feb 1762; license only
  John & ----- ----- 3 Sep 1770; license only
  John & Susanah Branen 2 Jan 1806; min- William King
  John & Phebe Painter 21 Dec 1848; min- James Paine
  John & Jane Patterson 31 Oct 1794; d John b- John
    Patterson & William Moffett min- William Wilson- 3Nov1794
  John & Catharine Runkle 16 Jan 1845; min- W G Campbell
  John & Polly Welch 8 Feb 1820; min- Daniel Stephens
  Robert & ----- ----- - Mar 1761; license only
  Robert & Jane Anderson 30 Jan 1786; d George b- Samuel
    Armstrong wit- George Anderson, William Brooks s John
    min- William Wilson- 30Jan1786
  Samuel Washington & Margaret Gonwer 10 Feb 1850; min- J
    Killian
  Samuel & Margaret Craig 12 Nov 1816; min- Conrad Speece, Jr
  Samuel & Elenor Tate 6 Dec 1808; min- William McPheeters
  Thompson & Peggy McElroy 5 Jan 1808; min- John McCue
  William & Elizabeth Fulton 1 Dec 1832; min- Francis
    McFarland
  William & Sophia Hughs 15 Jun 1848; min- J C Hensell
  William & Martha Weeks 8 Jan 1846; min- James Paine
Patton
  Charles & Eliza S Fulton 5 Sep 1822; min- Michael
    Meyerhoeffer
  George & Janetta Turnipseed 22 Oct 1835; min- William
    Calhoon
  John & ----- ----- 23 Mar 1754; license only
  John & Elizabeth Gregory 17 Sep 1816; min- Wright Burgess
  Thomas J & Jane McChesney 28 Mar 1844; min- J C Hensell
  Thomas J & Margaret Turnipseed 26 Sep 1839; min- Isaac
    Jones
  Thomas & Jane Swords 16 May 1811; min- William King
Pauf
  John & Mary Hortshough 10 Jan 1798; Mary (of age) d
    Englebert b- Englebert Hartshough
Paul
  Hugh & Eleanor Fackler 22 Dec 1794; Eleanor nicknamed
    'Ally' d Michael, merchant in Staunton who consents test-
    G Christian & Phill North b- Philip North

Augusta County Marriages -- Man's Name

Paul (cont.)
James & Isabella Hillanah Frazer 20 Jul 1801; widower & widow (of Samuel) b- James Frazer min- John McCue- 23Jul1801
Thomas & Matilda Ashby 27 Feb 1812; min- John McCue
Thornton & Charlotte Cawthron 12 Oct 1840; min- J J Reimensnyder

Pauley
Lewis & Betsy Hodges 6 Jul 1824; min- William W Calhoun

Paulus
Peter & Catherine Swoope 3 Mar 1798; d Peter Schwoop who consents b- Jacob Paulus

Pauss
Nicolas & Fanny Wolfe 25 Oct 1786; sis Andrew b- Andrew Wolfe

Paxton
Thomas & Martha Steele 19 Apr 1791; d Robert b- Robert Steele marriage sent to clerk by Samuel Brown and dated 28Apr1791
William & ----- ----- 19 Oct 1773; license only

Payne
Thomas F & Elizabeth Coffman 12 Nov 1846; min- J C Hensell

Peaco
James M & Eliza Keller 24 Dec 1846; min- George H Martin
Samuel (Jr) & Janetta C Keller 9 Jan 1843; min- J C Hensell
Samuel & Elizabeth Powers 11 Sep 1810; min- William King
W W & A M Henderson 26 Dec 1839; min- P E Stevenson

Pearce
William & Nancy Johnston 8 Jan 1833; min- James C Wilson

Pearey
William & Frances O Bywaters 20 Oct 1845; min- P Shickel

Pearson
William & Sarah Lancaster 5 Jan 1802; widower Sarah (of age) b- George Craig min- John McCue- 7Jan1802

Peatt
William & Mary Smith 17 Nov 1814; min- William King

Peck
Jacob & Elizabeth Dachen 9 Mar 1789; Minister's return spells name as 'Daken' d Windel Butt, who consents b- Henry Dill wit- John Clark & Samuel Jimeson min- William Wilson- 9Mar1789
Jacob & Elizabeth Hansbarger 14 Oct 1811; min- Wright Burgess
John Adam & Elizabeth Paul 23 Jan 1823; min- William W Calhoun
Joseph (Sr) & Nancy Hook 18 Nov 1824; min- Josiah Cole- publication of banns
Joseph & Ellen McClure 3 Mar 1814; min- Thomas Bourne

Pecker
Samuel & Barbara Sherley 24 Sep 1791; d Valentine b- Valentine Sherley

Pecot
David & Martha Jane Jennings 26 Feb 1846; min- T T Castleman

Augusta County Marriages -- Man's Name

Peebles
  Robert & Rachel Carlyle 29 Aug 1786; Minister's return spells names as 'Peples' and 'Carlile' d Robert b- John Carlyle s John wit- Robert Peebles, George Carlyle, Robert Carlyle Jr min- Samuel Shannon- 5Sep1786
Peer
  David & Nancy Paul 30 Jan 1817; min- William King
Peerie
  John & ----- ----- - Sep 1760; license only
Pelter
  Sampson & Rebecca Long 2 May 1822; min- James C Willson
Pence
  Henry & Mary Harshman - Dec 1812; min- G H Riemenschneider
Pendell
  Gabriel & Margaret Williams 16 May 1786; Minister's return spells name as 'Pendleton' d Moses b- Zachariah Estill wit- George Hudson, David Williams min- William Wilson- 16May1786
Pendleton
  James & Sarah Bell 28 Jan 1788; d James b- Robert Bell min- William Wilson- 7Feb1788
Pennell
  Zachariah & Catherine Hardbarger 9 Jun 1813; min- William King
Pepperley
  George & Elizabeth Yearout 21 Feb 1801; Minister's return spells name as 'Pepperly' d Charles ('Jahrous?') b- Charles Yearout min- William King- 26Feb1801
Perkey
  E A & Rebecca Jane Teter 1 Oct 1845; min- P Shickel
  Jacob & Sarah L Fertig 16 Feb 1837; min- Stephen Smith
Perkins
  Henry & Elizabeth M Mitchell 8 Mar 1827; min- Francis McFarland
  Thomas & Peggy Ramsay 25 May 1815; min- John McCue
Perry
  Andrew & Rebecca Horn 6 Aug 1848; min- P Shickel
  Caleb & Elizabeth Long 3 Dec 1807; min- John McCue
  James & Lucy Ann Acord 27 Aug 1845; min- P Shickel
  James & Mary Clark 11 Mar 1841; min- J J Reimensnyder
  John M & Martha Jane Riddle 31 Apr 1845; min- P Shickel
  John & Mary Brown 29 Dec 1818; min- William King
Peters
  ----- & Mary Ann Fisher 15 Feb 1831; min- Gerard Morgan
  Conrad & Catherine Hoopman 1 May 1806; min- William King
  George & Mary Parrent 2 Dec 1840; min- Samuel Wagner
  Isaac & Mary Eakle 9 Oct 1828; min- William C. Morrison
  John & Dolly Silknatre 23 Mar 1798; d Jacob b- Jacob Silknatre
  Solomon R & Lidia Gochenour 4 Mar 1847; min- J A Van Lear
  William & Eliza Ann Western 14 Sep 1843; min- Samuel Wagner
Peterson
  Joseph & Catharine W Stanton 18 Jan 1849; min- John A Van Lear

Augusta County Marriages -- Man's Name

Peyton
  Charles L & Margaret A Tate   9 Jul 1835; min- Francis McFarland
  William & Julia A L Moffett   3 May 1836; min- James Morrison
Pfifer
  Jacob & Betsy Hogshead   - Oct 1821; min- John Brown
Phagan
  Philip & ----- -----   20 Feb 1763; license only
Phifer
  John & Agnes Trump   5 Apr 1803; min- William King
Phillips
  William & Dorcas Fisher   10 Jan 1843; min- D F Bittle
Pickering
  Daniel & Susanna Saufley   19 Feb 1811; min- William Wilson
  Johnathan & Polly Bibee   16 Sep 1806; min- William King
  Thomas & Elizabeth Dobbs   31 Dec 1831; min- Samuel Kennerly
Pickle
  Jacob & Susanah Loucks   5 Apr 1794; d George b- John Allison
Pifer
  George & Polly Canole   22 Mar 1804; min- William King
  Joseph & Lydia Lowman   1 Apr 1812; d Bardhard min- John Bell- 24Jun1812
Pilson
  George & Elizabeth Thompson   4 Jan 1795; d Mathew who consents test- John Pilson b- Alexander StClair min- John McCue- 5Jan1796
  Matthew & Lavinia E Finley   5 Nov 1834; min- Francis McFarland
  Samuel (Jr) & Dorcas Alexander   17 Feb 1795; d James b- James Alexander min- John McCue- 19Feb1795
Pinkerton
  Joseph & Sarah McCutchan   27 Apr 1787; d Samuel who consents test- John McCutchan & John Logan b- John Logan
Pirkey
  Jacob & Rachel Billheimer   13 Aug 1833; min- James C Wilson
Pitman
  Jacob & Margaret L Harnest   16 May 1848; min- James Paine
  Philip P & Mary J Tebo   29 Nov 1838; min- Thomas Wheeler
Pitzer
  John & Harriet Ann Taylor   9 Oct 1834; min- George Hildt
Platt
  Henry & Rebecca Craig   3 Jun 1793; b- Robert Craig min- John McCue- 20Jun1793
Plecker
  John & Eliza Crawn   3 Oct 1839; min- John J Reimensnyder
  William & Margaret Adkins   10 Aug 1845; min- P Shickel
Plumb
  William & Mary White   24 Apr 1821; min- William W Calhoun
Plunket
  Benjamin & Elizabeth Russell   25 Jun 1835; min- Augustus Babb

Augusta County Marriages -- Man's Name

Plunkett
John & Mary Hall 26 Mar 1798; widower & widow Mary gives own consent b- James Lowe & Jeremiah Dowling

Poage
Andrew & Polly A Henry 22 Feb 1827; min- James Morrison
Cyrus & Mary Hamilton 8 Mar 1832; min- Conrad Speece
Elijah & Nancy Gratton 31 Jul 1787; min- William Wilson- 31Jul1787
George & ----- ----- 23 Jul 1754; license only
George & Margaret Rankin 9 Apr 1800; George from Bath Cty d Thomas Rankin, dec. perm- Robert Crawford, gdn of Margaret test- Robert Poage & William Poage Jr b- Robert Crawford s William of Bath cty
James & Nancy Brown 31 Aug 1837; min- William Calhoub
James & Sarah Henry 3 Aug 1793; Minister's return spells name as 'Poake' d James b- James Henry min- John Brown- 5Sep1793
John & ----- ----- 3 Jun 1751; license only
John & Rachel Crawford 26 Nov 1792; b- Thomas Wilson min- William Wilson- 27Nov1792
John & Hannah Gillis 9 Oct 1798; d Joseph b- Joseph Gillis
John & Martha Rankin 26 Nov 1798; con- William Crawford, gdn test- Alexander Poage John Poage swears he was 21 last May b- William Poage min- William Wilson- 27Nov1798
Robert G & Sarah Brown 24 Mar 1831; min- William Calhoon
Robert & Martha Crawford 16 Sep 1791; d James who consents b- Robert Crawford & John Robertson b- William Crawford min- William Wilson- 15Sep1791
Thomas C & Gracey Gilkeson 28 Aug 1828; min- John Hendren
Thomas & ----- ----- 27 Apr 1762; license only
Thomas & Nancy Frame 6 Mar 1817; min- Conrad Speece, Jr
William & ----- ----- 17 Apr 1762; license only
William & Peggy Allen 23 Jul 1811; min- William Wilson
William & Elizabeth Anderson 19 Jun 1800; 'Betsey' d Andrew William (of age) and his father living b- William Poage min- William Wilson- 26Jun1800
William & Polly Wright 3 Nov 1800; d William s William (see Introduction for complete information on this bond)

Pockrott
John C & Mary J Deal 24 Aug 1846; min- S Wagner

Poe
Urbane J & Ann Stone 16 Aug 1827; min- Michael Meyerhoeffer

Pointer
John & Sally Larrick - Aug 1815; min- John Brown

Points
Joseph & Sarah Greiner 3 May 1798; d Samuel Greiner Sr, dec. con- Catherine Tennant test- John Johnson & David Greiner b- David Greiner min- John McCue- 3May1798

Pollard
William H & Sarah Lightner 26 Sep 1833; min- Francis McFarland

Pollock
Allen & Susan E Pary 14 Jan 1850; min- William T Richardson
James & ----- ----- - Jul 1761; license only

Augusta County Marriages -- Man's Name

Porter
Charles D & Elizabeth Back 25 Jun 1842; min- Peter Shickel
John & Rachel Berry 21 Dec 1826; min- Alexander Templeton
John & Sally Summers 27 May 1806; min- William King
Robert & Elizabeth Blair 20 Mar 1790; d John, who consents wit- William Young & John Bell b- John Gamble min- William Wilson- 20Mar1790
William B & Elizabeth Thompson 28 Oct 1829; min- William Calhoon
William & Fanny Sharp 30 Sep 1796; Minister's return spells name as 'Fanny Thorp' d John Sharp Sr who consents test- John Sharp Jr b- Joseph Sharp min- Archibald Scott- 5Oct1796

Porterfield
Robert & Sarah A Wayt 17 Nov 1842; min- B M Smith

Posey
Thomas & ----- ----- 30 Nov 1772; license only

Potter
John G & Martha M Maury 7 Jun 1849; min- T T Castleman
John & Polly Miller 23 Apr 1811; min- William King
William J & Eliza Ann Cooper 23 Apr 1849; min- B M Smith

Potts
Amos & ----- ----- 21 Aug 1765; license only

Powers
James & Mary Margaret Peaco 7 Nov 1844; min- Francis McFarland
Moses & Mary Trimble 29 Apr 1803; min- William King
Robert & Susannah Daugherty 20 Nov 1834; min- William Calhoon
William & Fanny Snider 3 Feb 1791; b- James Rutledge

Prewer
John & Hannah Miller 8 Dec 1812; min- Samuel Garber

Price
A H & Harriet Murry 23 Jun 1835; min- Robert M Lipscomb
George & Sophia Bander - Aug 1802; min- John Brown
Jacob & Christina Carrico 25 Jan 1811; min- G H Riemenschneider
N L & Virginia W Smith 21 May 1835; min- Robert M Lipscomb
Samuel & Margaret Black 22 Jun 1797; widower d Samuel Black, dec. b- Samuel Black (Jr?) min- John McCue- 22Jun1797
Thomas & Fanny Halderman 22 Dec 1803; min- Philip Kennerly

Prior
John & Sally Alford 11 Oct 1796; widower & widow John Collins swear Sally of age b- Edmund Wills

Probst
Jacob & Elizabeth Probst 20 Jul 1823; min- G H Reimensnyder
John & Sara Stoutamoyer 29 Mar 1830; min- G H Reimensnyder

Props
Samuel & Catharine Daggy 30 Nov 1819; min- G H Riemenschneider

Propst
Adam & Martha Blackwell 27 Aug 1835; min- J J Glossbrenner
Daniel & Nancy Hooks 21 May 1846; min- J A Van Lear

Augusta County Marriages -- Man's Name

Pryor
  Thomas M & Patsey E Hartigan 16 Aug 1832; min- James Morrison

Ptomey
  William & Catherine Lockridge 22 Sep 1825; min- Alexander Templeton

Ptomy
  Michael & Mary Lockridge 21 Oct 1824; min- Thomas Caldwell

Puckett
  Drury & ----- ----- 4 May 1762; license only

Puff
  George & Ann Myers 3 Dec 1791; b- George Barnhart min- John McCune- 25Dec1791

Puffenbarger
  Henry & Margaret Vanfossen 24 Aug 1815; min- William King

Puffenberry
  Michael & Catherine Yearouse 4 Nov 1793; Minister's return spells name as 'Yearhouse' d Charles b- Charles Yearouse min- William Wilson- 5Nov1793

Pugh
  George & Judith Green 20 Oct 1798; b- Thomas Chinn

Puls
  Henry & Katharine Earhart 17 Aug 1846; min- P Shickel

Pumphrey
  George & Ann Wilfong - --- 183-; min- John Hendren- publication of banns
  Larkin & Frances Swank 25 Jan 1834; min- J Hoover

Pursell
  Benjamin & Eleanor Dunn 10 Dec 1798; Minister's return spells name as 'Pursel' Eleanor (of age) d Walter Dunn, dec. b- John Trimble min- Archibald Scott- 13Dec1798

Quick
  John & Caty Lovel 28 Feb 1826; min- Abraham Garber- publication of banns
  Okey & Rebecca Woodward 27 Feb 1832; min- William Wilson
  William & Peggy Dunn 12 Jun 1811; min- William King
  William & Elizabeth Steigle 12 Oct 1837; min- John J Reimensnyder

Raab
  Jacob & Milly Robinson 6 May 1806; min- William King

Rabb
  George & Elizabeth James 26 Nov 1799; d Thomas b- Thomas James min- William King- 1Dec1799

Rader
  John & Magdaline Hildebrand 16 Apr 1816; 'Rider?' min- William King
  Joseph & Elizabeth Jane Carcofe 25 Mar 1833; min- John Hendren
  Joseph & Mary Sandy 21 Oct 1830; min- John Hendren
  William & Jane Jones 13 Jan 1794; Minister's return spells name as 'Redder' d William who consents test- John Lockridge b- James Trimble min- Bennett Maxey- 16Jan1794

Augusta County Marriages -- Man's Name

Rady
   Patrick & Sarah Rabern 15 Nov 1791; d John Raberen who consents wit- David Fane & Edward Day b- Daniel Fane
Rafferty
   Thomas & ----- ----- 6 Jun 1762; license only
Ragan
   Bartholomew & Margaret Pearson 28 Dec 1793; b- Philip Dyer
Ragen
   Jeremiah & ----- ----- - Oct 1764; license only
Ragland
   John D D & Nancy Markwood 15 Jan 1844; min- C Parkison
Raidner
   Frederick & Catharine Ailor 7 Sep 1817; min- G H Riemenschneider
Ralston
   Henry & Jane Allison 28 Sep 1835; min- James C Wilson
   Moses & Margaret Bell 21 Feb 1805; min- William Wilson
   Samuel & ----- ----- 11 Sep 1766; license only
   Thomas & Nancy Ailshire 22 Mar 1810; min- William King
   William & ----- ----- 1 Nov 1761; license only
   William & Ann Gibson 13 May 1796; Minister's return spells name as 'William Wilson' d David b- David Gibson min- William Wilson- 4May1796
Ramsay
   William S & Martha Ann Finley 19 Mar 1832; min- James C Wilson
   William & Polly Gamble 6 Jan 1824; min- Conrad Speece
Ramsbottom
   Isaac & Jane Chrisman 11 Mar 1847; min- Jacob Bear
   Noah & Anna Chrisman 30 Jul 1846; min- Jacob Bear
Ramsey
   Cyrus & Sarah Hall 2 Jan 1842; min- Samuel Wagner
   James & Margaret Kerr 17 Oct 1794; Minister's return spells name as 'Ramsay and Mary Kerr' d James b- James Kerr min- John Brown- 25Oct1794
   John & ----- ----- - Mar 1749; license only
   John & Elizabeth Downey 2 Dec 1793; Request by John for license test- James Hodge & James Guy b- Adam Bratton
   John & Mary Fairburn 5 Jan 1830; min- William Wilson
   John & Betsey Harner 12 Oct 1807; min- William King
   William & Polly Carter 26 Jul 1798; Polly (of age) b- Samuel Gibson (signed: Sammy Gibson) min- William Wilson- 31Jul1798
   William & Sarah Foutz 17 Mar 1836; min- William Scull
   William & Sarah Fulton 18 Dec 1794; Sarah (Sally) (of age) sis to William Fulton b- William Fulton no minister listed; clerk's memorandum cites ceremony date as 18Dec1794
Randolph
   John & Mary Jane Frazier 4 Jun 1818; min- Wright Burgess
Ranicks
   Robert & Letty Dollen 18 Nov 1794
Ranken
   James & Jinny Russell 17 Sep 1807; min- John McCue

Augusta County Marriages -- Man's Name

Rankin
  Abner G & Ann Fisher 2 Nov 1826; min- James Watts
  Armstrong & Polly Ralston 15 Dec 1801; d Samuel b- Samuel Ralston min- William King- 17Dec1801
  George & Polly Evans 7 Feb 1829; min- William C. Morrison
  George & Polly Rankin 24 Sep 1806; min- William Wilson
  Isaac & Anne Searight 1 Jun 1789; Minister's return spells name as 'Seawright' b- James Searight wit- John Hall min- William Wilson- 2Jun1789
  James S & Katurah Gregory 14 Feb 1837; min- Stephen Smith
  John & Nancy Donaghe 20 Oct 1800; Minister's return spells name as 'Runkel' Nancy (of age) d William Jeremiah Runkle swears his brother, John, is of age b- John Roberts & Jeremiah Runkle min- William King- 22Oct1800
  John & Lucinda Hite 27 May 1813; min- William King
  John & Elizabeth Sheetz 7 Feb 1820; min- John Hendren
  Joseph & Elizabeth Clynes 5 Oct 1804; min- William King
  Richard & Polly Mathews 10 Jun 1789; d William, who consents wit- George Rankin & John Campbell b- John Campbell min- William Wilson- 11Jun1789
  Richard & Eleanor Ralston 11 Jan 1820; min- John Hendren
  Robert & Elizabeth Russell 12 Sep 1805; min- John McCue
  Samuel & Betty Regon 12 Oct 1794; min- William Wilson- 12Oct1794
  Thomas & Jane R Cole 21 Sep 1815; min- William Calhoon
  Thomas & Margaret Dicky 26 May 1807; min- William Wilson

Ransbarger
  Allison & rgaret Ann Hemp 30 Mar 1837; min- J C Hensell
  George & Elizabeth Baker 4 Apr 1796; Minister's return spells name as 'Bambarger' Elizabeth (of age) d Philip Baker, dec. b- John Baker min- William Wilson- 7Apr1796
  John & Nancy Douglas 26 Aug 1793; Minister's return spells name as 'Douglass' b- Garsper Clements min- William Wilson- 19Aug1793

Ranson
  James M & Mary E Baldwin 1 Jul 1841; min- P E Stevenson

Rapp
  Jacob & Polly Heizer 7 May 1807; min- William King
  John & Elizabeth Ailor 1 Feb 1796; 'Ohler?' d Anthony who consents test- George Oehler b- Lawrence Crown min- William Wilson- 2Feb1796
  Joseph & Charlotte Shuey 26 Sep 1806; min- William King

Rawley
  Reuben & Elizabeth Kiracofe 30 Nov 1846; min- P Shickel

Ray
  Daniel & Ann Larew 29 Aug 1816; min- John McCue
  John & Catherine Burch 4 Feb 1800; d William Burch, dec. b- James Buchanan min- John McCue- date of ceremony missing
  Joseph & Lydia Nicholas 14 Oct 1791; b- Gilbert Christian certificate by Daniel Friel & John Sutton that Lydia of age, her parents dead, and no other relatives in the area

Rayburn
  James & Ann Erwine 2 Jul 1807; min- William King

Augusta County Marriages -- Man's Name

Reaburn
 Charles & Mary Hamilton 7 Nov 1805; min- John McCue
 Henry & Jane Blair 22 Dec 1814; min- Conrad Speece, Jr
 John & ----- ----- 16 Feb 1762; license only
Ready
 Patrick & Sarah Reburne 18 Nov 1791; min- William Wilson- 18Nov1791
Red
 Jacob & Sally Beard 22 Feb 1804; min- John McCue
Redder
 Nicholas & Elizabeth Lindel 29 Jul 1793; Elizabeth (of age) b- Thomas Liggett
Redifer
 Andrew J & Casindanete Stuart 17 Apr 1845; min- S Wagner
 David & Peggy Weiford 2 May 1799; Minister's return spells name as 'David Rodefer and Margaret Werferd' d George Wayford b- George Weiford
 William & Jane Masincup 4 Apr 1844; min- Jacob Baer
Rediford
 William & Sarah Grass 30 Dec 1799; Minister's return spells name as 'Rodeford' d Frederick b- Frederick Grass min- William King- 31Dec1799
Redman
 John & Catharine Link 9 Mar 1843; min- Samuel Wagner
Redmond
 Thomas & Nisy Ingram 4 Mar 1786; 'Nancy'? d Joshua b- Robert Wilson wit- Robert Wilson, James McGengal, Joseph Willson min- William Wilson- 4Mar1786
Rednour
 Joseph & Margaret Fox 17 Apr 1793; d Christopher b- Christopher Fox
Reece
 Solomon & Elizabeth Doom 17 Sep 1840; min- Samuel Wagner
Reed
 Alexander (Jr) & ----- ----- 24 Jan 1769; license only
 John K & Liza Spencer 16 Jun 1842; min- James Morrison- publication of banns
 John & Elizabeth Greaver - --- 1835; min- Augustus Babb- publication of banns
 John & Lydia Young 30 Sep 1800; d Robert Young, dec. sis to Andrew of Naked Creek, Augusta cty, who swears Lydia of age b- Andrew Young min- William Wilson- 2Oct1800
 Peter & Sally Miller 5 Sep 1799; d William Miller, dec. b- John Moore & John Reed min- William King- 5Sep1799
 Philip & Mary Taylor 17 Sep 1812; min- William King
 Richard & Nancy Gladden 28 Jan 1829; min- William Wilson
 Robert & ----- ----- - Mar 1758; license only
 Robert & Rebecca Conner 19 Apr 1823; min- William Wilson Jr
 Robert & Isabella Walker 19 Jan 1790; d Elizabeth, widow, who consents b- John Walker min- William Wilson- 19Jan1790
 Sanders & Betsey Crosby 25 Dec 1803; min- Philip Kennerly
 Thomas & Mary Curry 2 Dec 1799; Thomas (of age) d Richard b- Richard Curry min- William King- 2May1799

Augusta County Marriages -- Man's Name

Reese
  Benjamin & Martha Terrill 23 Jun 1823; min- Francis McFarland
Reeser
  Philip & Elizabeth Fauber 15 Jan 1839; min- Isaac Jones
Reeves
  Matthew & Elizabeth J Rogers 27 Jan 1848; min- J A Van Lear
Reid
  Benjamin S & Rebecca C Bell 9 Dec 1830; min- Conrad Speece
  John & Frances Miller 22 Jul 1796; widow William late of Rockbridge cty b- John Kilkainey
  Samuel & Nancy Campbell 30 Nov 1801; widower & widow (of George) b- James Foster
Reidenour
  Joseph & Margaret Tate 18 Apr 1793
Reimensnyder
  John J & Susan M Bryant 3 May 1838; min- D F Bittle
Reitenour
  John & Betsey Apple 16 May 1816; min- William King
Rennick
  Robert & Letty Dalton 17 Nov 1794; Letty (of age) b- Francis Gardiner
Repetoe
  Peter & Mary Eeast 22 Jun 1811; min- Wright Burgess
Resley
  George & Polly Fauber 24 Sep 1811; min- William King
Resors
  Archibald & Margaret Firebough 14 Sep 1826; min- John Hendren
Reubush
  George & Elizabeth Frenger 10 Mar 1829; min- Francis McFarland
  John & Mary Kindig 7 Mar 1848; min- B M Smith
  Peter & Francis Burkholder 30 Mar 1836; min- John Hendren
Revercomb
  George & Rebecca Griffith 25 Sep 1822; min- John Hendren
  John C & Rebecca Ann Hottle 2 Jun 1845; min- P Shickel
  William & Patsy Connell 19 Feb 1816; min- William Cravens
Reynolds
  Joshua (Jr) & Mary Ann Lilley 25 Dec 1845; min- G W Israel
Rezer
  Daniel & Margaret Miller 16 Jun 1796; Margaret (of age) d Jacob Miller, dec., late of PA b- Francis Miller
Rhea
  Archibald & Ann Humphreys 16 Oct 1798; d David b- David Humphreys min- Archibald Scott- 26Oct1798
Rhinehart
  Ulrick & Margaret Minga 6 Mar 1797; d Henry b- Henry Minga
Rhodes
  George & Elizabeth Fleiger 29 May 1792; Minister's return spells name as 'Rodes' d John who consents b- Isaac Ong min- John Montgomery- 29May1792
  Greenberry & Mary K Anderson 3 Nov 1842; min- A G Chenowith
  James H & Rebecca Hess 23 Feb 1841; min- John C Hensell- publication of banns

Augusta County Marriages -- Man's Name

Rhodes (cont.)
  William & Sarah J Smith 24 Oct 1830; min- Francis McFarland
Rhyan
  Henry & Margaret Shuey 15 Dec 1828; min- William C.
    Morrison
Rice
  Taylor & Ann Bishop 28 Sep 1844; min- G W Israel
  Thomas & Esther Scott 25 May 1797; Esther from Rockingham
    cty min- William Wilson- 25May1797
Richards
  Philemon (Jr) & Martha Christian 7 Mar 1793; Martha (of
    age) d Patrick b- Gilbert Christian min- John McCue-
    21Mar1793
Richardson
  William T & Sarah J Patrick 16 May 1850; min- B M Smith
Richeson
  Jacob & Esther Halbert 10 Dec 1807; min- William King
Richey
  Robert & ----- ----- - Oct 1761; license only
Rickett
  Thomas & Mary StJohn 11 Jan 1794; Mary (of age) b-
    William Ridder min- Bennett Maxey- 16Jan1794
Riddle
  Andrew B & Asenath Bush 23 Apr 1835; min- Samuel Kennerly
  George & Fanny Sligh 5 Aug 1805; min- William King
  James R & Amelia Heiskell 21 Jul 1807; min- William Calhoon
  John & Nancy Armstrong 11 Nov 1823; min- John Hendren
  John & Eazy Lowry 4 Jun 1792; b- Matthew Gambill
  Stephen & Catherine Rutlidge 10 Oct 1789; d Thomas, who
    consents wit- Samuel Prier & John Reader b- Jonathan
    Brooks min- William Wilson- 10Oct1789
  Thomas & Jane Campbell 23 Jul 1791; d George wit- Philip
    Hull & George Kuhn b- Philip Hull
Rife
  John & Fanny Crist 28 Feb 1803; min- William King
  Joseph B & Elizabeth D Bridge 13 Sep 1842; min- Samuel
    Wagner
Rimel
  John & Nancy Swisher 23 Dec 1833; min- J Hoover
Rine
  Daniel & Anna Jones 20 Oct 1803; min- John McCue
Rinehart
  Abraham & Mary Ann Wright 30 Jun 1814; min- William Wilson
  Andrew & Christian Shewe 29 May 1803; min- William King
  David & Polly Fellers 14 Oct 1813; min- William King
  Oliver & E M Coursey 28 Feb 1850; min- D W Arnold
  Peter & Barbara Bailor 22 Dec 1797; d Jacob Behler b-
    Jacob Bailor
Riner
  John & Martha Ewin 14 Apr 1800; Minister's return spells
    name as 'Erwin' John (of age) d Henry b- Henry Ervin
    min- William Wilson- 14Apr1800

Augusta County Marriages -- Man's Name

Ringuson
  Jacob & Susan C Franzman - Nov 1824; min- John Brown
Rippetoe
  Porterfield B & Harriett L Livingston 13 Oct 1835; min-
    William Scull
Ript
  Frederick & Mary Savage 7 Jun 1786; b- Dennis Callaghan
    min- Archibald Scott- 14Jun1786
Risk
  Hugh L & Rebecca Ann Weaver 27 Aug 1835; min- Henry Brown
  James & ----- ----- 31 Jan 1763; license only
  James & Rebeccah Henderson 23 May 1799; No bond consent of
    father, Jones Henderson test- Joseph Henderson John Risk
    swears James of age
  James & Elizabeth Risk 14 Dec 1785; d John Risk of
    Rockbridge who consents b- David Risk min- John Brown-
    19Dec1785
  John (Jr) & Patsey Humphrey 21 Nov 1831; min- Conrad Speece
  John & Jannet Brown 23 Aug 1786; 'Jannett?' d John b-
    James Moore wit- James Risk John Brown's wife listed as
    Frankie min- John Brown- 26Aug1786 (in another document
    date listed as 17Aug1786)
  John & Peggy Dougherty 6 Nov 1806; min- William McPheeters
  John & Mary A Good 19 Apr 1845; min- D F Bittle
  John & Sarah Henderson 13 Jun 1796; s Robert d Jones
    Henderson who consents Sarah (of age) John Risk swears
    that his cousin, John is past 21 b- Joseph Henderson min-
    John Montgomery- 16Jun1796
  Joseph & Sicily Miller 30 Apr 1829; min- William C.
    Morrison
  William & Anne Miller 20 Apr 1820; min- William Calhoon
Ritchey
  James & Isabella Crawford 16 Feb 1798; d James Crawford,
    dec. con- Hugh Fulton test- Robert Fulton James Ritchey
    from Rockbridge b- John Fulton min- Archibald Scott-
    22Feb1798
Rittenhouse
  Roland & Margaret Helm 28 Apr 1822; min- Conrad Speece
Roach
  Jacob & Emely Randal 11 Nov 1841; min- Benjamin W Kindig-
    publication of banns
  William & Elizabeth Buchanan 3 Nov 1836; min- James
    Morrison- publication of banns
Roadcap
  Abraham B & Martha S McGuffin 10 Feb 1847; min- J C Hensell
  Stephen & Mary Good 20 Jul 1840; min- J J Reimensnyder
Roades
  John & Lydia Peters 17 Mar 1814; min- William Wilson
Roads
  David & Rebecca Coursey 8 Nov 1821; min- Daniel Stephens
Roberts
  George & Margaret Deal 3 Feb 1848; min- Thomas H Busey
  Isaiah & Nancy Guthrey 11 Jan 1794; Minister's return
    spells name as 'Guthery' Nancy (of age) d William Guthery
    b- John Guthery min- John McCue- 14Jan1794

Augusta County Marriages -- Man's Name

Roberts (cont.)
  John & Margaret Black 17 Sep 1792; d Rebecca who consents
    wit- Joanes Henderson & John McCutchan b- Samuel Black no
    minister listed; clerk's memorandum cites ceremony date as
    19Sep1792
  John & Patsey Hogshead 8 Feb 1793; Patsey (Polly?) (of
    age) d John sis of John b- John Hogshead no minister
    listed; clerk's memorandum cites ceremony date as 8Feb1793
  William L & Mary Gemima Beeton 13 Feb 1838; min- J C
    Hensell
Robertson
  Alexander & Jean Cord 10 Apr 1786; b- James Robertson
    min- William Wilson- 10Apr1786
  Anderson & Mary Lucas 9 Apr 1840; min- John C Hansell
  Andrew & Polly McCabe 14 Feb 1832; min- John Howell-
    publication of banns
  Andrew & Polly Shyrigh 7 Jan 1700; d Jacob Shyrigh, dec,
    sis to Jacob Shirigh b- Jacob Shyrey
  Daniel & Clara Anderson 24 Dec 1822; min- Daniel Stephens
  George C & Ann Harnsberger 23 May 1814; min- Wright Burgess
  James & ----- ----- 3 May 1762; license only
  James & Sarah Evan 12 Oct 1837; min- James Paine
  James & Mary Russell 2 Feb 1789; b- Andrew Russell min-
    William Wilson- 12Feb1789
  John R & Naomi E Fix 3 Jun 1847; min- J C Hensell
  John S & Lucinda Rough 2 Sep 1847; min- J C Hensell
  John & Sarah J Brown 26 Oct 1843; min- James Paine
  John & Margaret Frame 26 Jan 1793; d John Fream who
    consents test- Peter Killy & Henry Kelly b- Andrew Cutler
    min- John McCue- 26Feb1793
  Mathew & Peggy Shultz 5 Oct 1809; min- William McPheeters
  Matthew W & Elizabeth J Coffey 3 Sep 1846; min- James Paine
  Matthew & Catherine Kennerly 19 May 1803; min- William King
  William & Ann Crawford 2 Jun 1788; b- John Crawford min-
    William Wilson- 3Jun1788
  William & Polley Hart 20 Jun 1816; min- William King
  William & Peggy Turk 16 Mar 1808; min- William King
Robinson
  J & Mary Kindig 22 Sep 1842; min- James Morrison
  James & ----- ----- 21 Aug 1764; license only
  James & ----- ----- 19 Mar 1765; license only
  John & ----- ----- 6 May 1763; license only
  Joseph & ----- ----- 8 Apr 1763; license only
  William & ----- ----- 6 Jun 1762; license only
Robison
  John & Martha Watkins 8 Nov 1832; min- William Calhoon
Rodchers
  William & Elizabeth Jackson - Feb 1808; min- John Brown
Rodenheizer
  Henry & Elizabeth B Bartley 19 May 1840; min- A B McCorkle
Rodes
  Frederick & Catharine Stover 7 Sep 1835; min- John Hendren
  Jacob N & Elizabeth Ann Grove 14 Oct 1835; min- John A
    Steele

Augusta County Marriages -- Man's Name

Rodgers
  James & ----- ----- 21 May 1766; license only
  Michaes & Catherine Troxall 24 Jun 1791; sis of Peter who consents (Catherine's parents both deceased) wit- John Moore & Peter Wilson b- Valentine Miller
  Philip & Polly Ryan 28 Dec 1819; min- Daniel Stephens
  William S D & Margaret A Kershner 7 Jun 1842; min- Samuel C Waters

Rogers
  James & Elizabeth Baltzer 27 Dec 1827; min- William Wilson

Roland
  Henry B & Patsy Glenn 18 Mar 1819; min- Conrad Speece, Jr
  John & Elizabeth Allison 3 Jan 1809; min- William Wilson

Roler
  Jacob & Margarett Hide 22 May 1835; min- Samuel Kennerly

Rolestone
  Peter & Catherine Sheetz 25 Mar 1824; min- Josiah Cole

Roller
  John & Montelany Trorobaugh 21 Jun 1799; d Nicholas b- Nicholas Trorabaugh
  Paul & Elizabeth Martin - Feb 1808; min- John Brown
  Slorum & Lydia Swank 2 Jan 1834; min- Augustus Babb

Rolston
  Samuel & Ann Curry 10 Sep 1811; min- Wright Burgess

Roop
  John & Easter Miller 16 Sep 1828; min- John Hendren
  Michael & Caroline Snyder 12 Nov 1829; min- John Hendren

Root
  Abraham & Peggy Levingston 24 Feb 1825; min- Conrad Speece

Roots
  Jacob & Katy Livick 1 Aug 1816; min- G H Riemenschneider

Rosenbarger
  Paul & Eliza Wonderlick 29 Jul 1833; min- J Hoover

Ross
  Andrew H & Julia A Curry 8 Mar 1832; min- Conrad Speece
  David & Mary Allison 17 May 1810; min- William Wilson
  Henry & Frankey Jane Shiflett 17 May 1842; min- F D Goodwin
  James E & Mary Curry 29 Nov 1836; min- Stephen Smith
  John & Catherine Hanger 12 Dec 1821; min- William W Calhoun
  Joseph & Eliza Meeks 14 Aug 1845; min- S Wagner

Roudabush
  Alexander & Caroline Amanda Huff 5 Apr 1849; min- George H Martin

Roudenbush
  Samuel & Rebeca Hufman 15 May 1844; min- D F Bittle

Row
  John & Esabella Row 16 Aug 1832; min- William Calhoon
  Peter & Susan C Jennings 7 Apr 1840; min- D F Bittle- publication of banns
  William & Elizabeth Swick 30 Jan 1840; min- D F Bittle

Rowe
  Henry & Amelia Brooks 2 Dec 1822; 'Rau' min- Josiah Cole

Augusta County Marriages -- Man's Name

Rowh
  John & Lavinia Meek 31 Jan 1839; min- William Calhoon
Royer
  John & Ann Taylor 16 Jun 1792; d Charles of Augusta con- John Taylor Jr b- Dietre Fishburne & John Taylor
Rozen
  Jacob & Peggy Palmer 2 Nov 1829; min- William Calhoon
Rubush
  John & Catharine Cook 12 Jun 1835; min- Francis McFarland
Ruddle
  Stephen & Mary Brooks 6 Oct 1808; min- John McCue
  Thomas & Margaret Hodge 13 Oct 1825; min- Josiah Cole
Ruff
  Jacob & Sarah Anderson 7 Sep 1819; min- Conrad Speece, Jr
  Jacob & Mary McCue 12 Nov 1811; min- John McCue
  John & Lydia Landes 1 Sep 1846; min- P Shickel
  John & Martha Wallace 5 Oct 1804; min- William King
Ruhl
  George & Mary Menker 25 Mar 1799; d Henry Menker who consents b- Henry Rhinehart
Ruket
  Thomas & Christiana McMullen 19 Nov 1792; b- Nicholas Reader
Rule
  George & Mary Menker 26 Mar 1799; 'Minker?' min- William King- 26Mar1799
Rumbough
  George & Elizabeth Britton 5 Sep 18--; min- A B Davidson
Runkel
  Jacob & Catherine Reed 23 Apr 1800; d Christopher & Barbara Reed Barbara consents test- Peter Reed ('Rhead?, Read?') b- Lewis Runkle min- William King- 30Apr1800
Runkle
  James & Frances Shelly 17 May 1796; Minister's return spells name as 'Frances Sherley' d Peter Shally b- Peter Shelly min- William Wilson- 26May1796
  Jeremiah & Christiana Runkle 16 Feb 1796; d Lewis b- Lewis Runkle
  John & Ann Price 25 Jan 1838; min- D F Bittle
  Lewis & Jane Goodwin 17 Nov 1805; min- John Emmill
Runnolds
  Samuel & Mary Clinebill 18 Nov 1847; min- James Morrison
Rupert
  Joseph L & Catharine Coiner 3 Nov 1831; min- Ambrose Henkel
  Paul N & Mary M Koiner 28 Apr 1838; min- J Killian
Ruple
  Jacob & Ann Arganbright 3 Jan 1833; min- William Calhoon
  Jacob & Anne Fawber 20 Mar 1815; min- Wright Burgess
Rush
  Jacob & Elizabeth Ward - May 1811; min- John Brown
  Peter & Barbara Hanger 19 Jun 1789; Minister's return spells Peter's name 'Rusk' Peter from Rockingham cty d Peter Henger Sr b- Carl Rusch min- Archibald Scott- 20Jun1786

Augusta County Marriages -- Man's Name

Rush (cont.)
  Philip & Polly Wishart 10 Mar 1800; 'Weisshart?' d Nicholas b- Nicholas Weisshart

Rusht
  Philip & Molly Shaver 2 Aug 1791; wid b- Valentine Sherley

Rusk
  David & Susan Waseman 5 Jan 1815; min- William King

Rusmisel
  Adam & Eve Margaret Hoover 13 May 1841; min- John C Hensell- publication of banns
  Christian & Patsey Taylor 6 Oct 1831; min- John Hendren
  John & Elizabeth Orebough 31 Oct 1835; min- John Hendren

Rusmisle
  Frederick & Elizabeth Beard 6 Sep 1810; min- William King
  John & Peggy Fifer 27 Sep 1804; min- William King

Rusmissel
  Christian & Ann Shelly 26 Jan 1808; min- William King

Russel
  Isaiah & Catherine Hassafluck 2 Jun 1808; min- William McPheeters

Russell
  Adam & Polly Ross 13 May 1799; d William Ross, sis to John Ross, and of age b- John Ross
  Andrew & ----- ----- 25 May 1762; license only
  Andrew & Elizabeth Graham 2 May 1815; min- William King
  George & Elizabeth Backley 6 Apr 1835; min- John A Steele
  Henry & Peggy Brand 26 May 1810; min- William King
  John & Margaret White 14 Aug 1797; Margaret (of age) d Isaac White, dec. b- James White min- John McCue- 14Aug1797
  Joseph & Sarah Bredin 13 Feb 1797; d Edward b- Edward Bredin
  Joshua & Fanny Gibson 20 Aug 1804; min- William Wilson
  Robert & Catherine Lowman 8 Dec 1817; min- Wright Burgess

Russmassell
  Adam & Sally Sherman 30 Aug 1808; min- William King

Rust
  Philip & Polly Wisehart 12 Mar 1800; widower min- William Wilson- 12Mar1800

Rutherford
  John & Catherine Syfort 10 Apr 1789; d Michael, who consents wit- Michael Garber Jr & Thomas Bratton b- Michael Garber Jr

Rutledge
  Elijah & Rosanna Rutledge 30 Jul 1822; min- Conrad Speece
  George & Mary Calbraith 7 May 1800; Minister's return spells name as 'Caldbreath' Mary (of age) d Thomas Calbraith, dec., sis to Thomas Calbraith b- Thomas Calbraith min- John McCue- 8May1800
  James & Jane Finley 27 Mar 1786; b- Robert Finley min- Samuel Carrick- 28Mar1786
  James & Elenor Ralston 7 Jul 1788; Minister's return spells name as 'Rutlidge' d William who consents test- George Rutledge & James Ralston b- Matthew Ralston min- William Wilson- 14Jul1788

Augusta County Marriages -- Man's Name

Rutledge (cont.)
John & Nancy Ann Fulton 17 Mar 1829; min- Francis McFarland
Rutt
Daniel & Elizabeth Tumblin 22 Jul 1799; Minister's return spells names as 'Daniel Rule and Elizabeth Tumbling' d Thomas b- Henry Huff min- William King- 1Aug1799
Ryan
John & Winey Graham 8 Jul 1824; min- William W Calhoun
John & Nancy Whisman 14 May 1838; min- Z Freeman
Ryder
William & Mary Brisco 2 Feb 1786; widow b- David Gregory min- Samuel Shannon- 21Feb1786
Salvage
Jeremiah & Mary Kelly 18 Oct 1788; min- Benjamin Erwin- 18Oct1788
Sampson
Robert & Hetty Paxton 10 Jan 1835; min- Joshua Webb
Samuels
Samuel & Margaret Reyburn 19 Mar 1785; stepdaughter of John Harper b- Hugh Brown
Shadrach & Margaret Phillips 20 Sep 1824; min- John Hendren
Sanders
Alexander & Margaret Loffties 25 Nov 1794; Minister's return spells name as 'Saunders and Peggy Lofftes' d Ralph of Rockingham Cty who consents test- James Givens & Thomas Givens b- Andrew Moody min- John Brown- 3Dec1794
Daniel & Barbara Simmerman 2 Dec 1800; Minister's return spells name as 'Landus' Daniel swears he is of age d John b- John Simmerman min- William King- 2Dec1800
David & Barbara Summer 2 Dec 1800; min- William Wilson- 2Dec1800
Robert & Elizabeth Huff 15 Jan 1835; min- Samuel Kennerly
Sandy
John W & Martha A Snyder 24 Sep 1845; min- P Shickel
Lewis & Sarah Rauly 13 Sep 1841; min- John Brower
Vincent & Anney Howdeshell - Sep 1842; min- John Brower- publication of banns
William & Susanna Rawley 17 Nov 1836; min- John J Riemensnyder
Sansebough
Adam & Lydia Buckley 1 Apr 1802; min- William King- 1Apr1802
Savage
George & Nancy Peck 2 Apr 1834; min- William Calhoon
Jeremiah & Mary Kelly 16 Oct 1787; Mary gives own consent, having neither parents not guardian test- Henry Black & Thomas Fulton b- John Black of Rockingham cty
Sawyers
Sampson & Mary McCaslin 17 Nov 1790; d John, who consents wit- James Crow b- James Crow of Botetourt Cty min- John Montgomery- 22Nov1790
Thomas & Catherine Allison 5 Jun 1792; d Robert b- Robert Allison no minister listed; clerk's memorandum cites ceremony date as 9Jun1792

Augusta County Marriages -- Man's Name

Saxon
  Joel & Peggy Miller 27 Jul 1804; min- William King
Sayers
  Sampson & ----- ----- - Nov 1759; license only
Scantland
  Charles & Margaret Kerr 25 Mar 1817; min- William King
Schnebly
  John & Catherine Whitsel 7 Jan 1808; min- William Calhoon
Scholl
  Lewis & Magdalena Hanzele - Oct 1808; min- John Brown
Scott
  Anderson & Sarah Ann Cary 8 Dec 1824; min- Luke Collins
  George W & Nancy Moneymaker 19 Jul 1849; min- W W Trimble
  Isaac & Nancy Bell 1 Sep 1790; d James, who consents wit- Josias Anderson & James Penmdleton b- James Pendleton min- Archibald Scott- 2Sep1790
  James & Ann Poage 20 Nov 1834; min- Conrad Speece
  Jesse & Mary Ann Erwin 19 Nov 1816; min- William Wilson
  John & Elizabeth Thompson 5 Jun 1823; min- William W Calhoun
  John & Betsy Ward 25 Aug 1808; min- Joel Watson
  Joseph B & Martha Alexander 5 Feb 1833; min- James C Wilson
  Robert & Mary Blackwood 29 Oct 1785; d Eleanor Haddan b- Mark Haddan min- Archibald Scott- 1Nov1785
  Robert & Ann Campbell 17 Mar 1785; perm- Ann herself b- James Anderson wit- Samuel Black, James O'Neal
  Robert & Elizabeth Harris 22 Nov 1820; min- Luke Collins
  Robert & Hester Q Peck 30 Nov 1843; min- C Parkison
  Thomas & Esther Cashaw 6 Oct 1792; d Benoni Cashaw who consents wit- John Cashaw & John Taylor b- Henry Mace
  Thomas & Catharine Coffman 25 Dec 1845; min- T T Castleman
  Wesley & Elizabeth Williams 25 Jan 1825; min- Luke Collins- publication of banns
  William & Margaret Johnston 26 Jul 1827; min- William Wilson
Scrogden
  George & Lydia Syrcle 14 Jan 1834; min- Samuel Kennerly
Scull
  William & Julia Ann Rush 6 Nov 1833; 'Rev.' Scull min- Augustus Babb
Seal
  Peter & Polly Slye 1 Oct 1807; min- William King
Searaight
  James & Eleanor Hill 26 Nov 1802; min- William King- 26Nov1802
Seawright
  Alexander & Susannah Beard 14 Feb 1822; min- James Morrison
  John & Jenny Louney 3 Jan 1804; min- William Wilson
  William & Mary ann Young 6 Jul 1820; min- James Morrison
Seig
  Jacob & Lydia Hains 3 May 1810; min- William Calhoon
  Paul & Elizabeth Hains 27 Aug 1816; min- William King

Augusta County Marriages -- Man's Name

Seldomridge
  James & Betsey Bailey 11 May 1826; min- John Hendren
  John & Hanah Black 24 Mar 1814; min- William King
  William & Frances McClure 29 May 1832; min- James C Wilson
Selling
  William & Lydia Jones 26 Apr 1804; min- William King
Sensebaugh
  William & Rebecca Miller 25 Apr 1791; d George who
    consents wit- William Sensebaugh & J Beal b- Valentine
    Miller
Sensebough
  John & Catherine Cowman 25 Feb 1793; d John b- John Cowman
Sevier
  Washington & Catherine Chambers 6 Oct 1807; min- William
    Calhoon
Sewell
  Thomas & Anne Shirley 6 Oct 1814; min- Wright Burgess
Seylor
  Jacob & Catherine Goodnight 3 Mar 1814; min- William King
Shackelford
  Reuben & Rebecca Johnston 6 Jan 1790; d Eleanor, who
    consents wit- James Rutledge & Andrew Allison & William
    Shackelford b- Andrew Allison min- William Wilson- 8Jan1790
Shafer
  Charles & Barbara Kellor 7 Jun 1808; min- Z Emmerson
Shaffer
  David & Alcinda Gibson 4 Jul 1841; min- George Huffman
  Jacob & Margaret Andrews 16 Jun 1791
  Peter & Catherine Good   - Mar 1825; min- John Brown
Shalley
  Jacob & Elizabeth Fifer 11 Nov 1820; min- Daniel Stephens
Shally
  Christian & Rosannah Canote 28 Nov 1796; d John b- John
    Canote
Shaner
  George B & Catharine Ann Moore 5 Feb 1846; min- S Wagner
Shank
  Jacob & Polly Stover 5 Sep 1837; min- Fred D Goodwin
Shankland
  Richard & ----- ----- - Dec 1759; license only
  Robert & ----- ----- 21 Aug 1764; license only
Shanklin
  John & ----- ----- - Nov 1767; license only
  Joseph & Phaney Garton 13 Jun 1792; 'Garlon?' daughter in
    law of John Brown who consents d of Phaney Brown who
    consents wit- Joseph Douglas b- Joseph Douglass of
    Rockingham cty marriage dated 23Jun1791
  Thomas & ----- ----- 6 Nov 1765; license only
Shannon
  James & Anne Finley 18 Jan 1802; d John who consents
    Anne (of age) b- Samuel Finley min- John McCue- 21Jan1802
  John (Jr) & Eleanor Fulton 26 May 1800; d James Fulton,
    dec. b- John Shannon Sr
  John & Mary Ann Bosserman 31 Aug 1843; min- George H Martin

Augusta County Marriages -- Man's Name

Shannon (cont.)
John & Ann Boyd 30 Mar 1815; min- John McCue

Sharp
John & Elizabeth Curry 30 Sep 1797; Minister's return spells name as 'John Thorp' d Richard b- Richard Curry min- Archibald Scott- 30Sep1797
John & Ebby McChesney 19 Aug 1796; d James Adam McChesney testifies that his sister, Ebby, is over 21 b- John McDowell
Joseph & Julianna Scott 23 Jan 1812; min- William Calhoon
Thomas & Jean Wilson 20 Nov 1794; 'Mary Willson?' d Mathew b- John Sharp no minister listed; clerk's memorandum cites ceremony date as 3Dec1794

Shaver
Daniel & Rachel Conner 13 May 1834; min- Conrad Speece
George & Frances M Burgess 15 Sep 1841; min- Alfred G Chenowith
Henry S & Anne Houf 28 Jan 1828; min- William Wilson
John F W & Hesther Ann Randolph 30 Mar 1846; min- P Shickel
John & Isabella Jane Wilson 10 May 1842; min- S J Love
John & Rachel Zimmerman 3 Dec 1822; min- G H Riemenschneider
Noah & Eliza Ellet 17 Apr 1850; min- George B Rimel
Samuel & Nancy Conner 23 Aug 1827; min- Conrad Speece

Shaw
George & Nancy Mays 6 Mar 1787; Minister's return spells name as 'Maiss' d Rebecca who consents test- Charles Stewart & Charles Donnelly b- John Griffin min- Samuel Shannon- 16Mar1787
Robert & Elizabeth Boyd 30 May 1799; widower & widow (of John) b- Michael Garber Sr

Shearley
Daniel & Elizabeth Funkhouser 15 Oct 1824; min- William W Calhoun

Sheets
Andrew & Mary Engleman 11 Oct 1841; min- John C Hensell
Daniel & Elizabeth Whitemore 27 Mar 1790; min- William Wilson- 27Mar1790
David & Ann Irvine 28 Jan 1826; min- John Hendren
Elias & Rebecca Fisher 25 May 1827; min- Michael Meyerhoeffer
Elias & Elizabeth Stover 11 Mar 1837; min- George A Leopard
Frederick & Catherine Hines 20 Feb 1812; min- William King
Henry & Polley Waseman 15 Jun 1815; min- William King
Jacob & Elizabeth Butt 2 Jul 1788; Elizabeth gives her own consent test- John Lanahan & Thomas Leanch b- John Heizer
James W & Mary Ann Swatzel 23 Dec 1847; min- Francis McFarland
John & Mary Dyer 22 Feb 1827; min- John Hendren
John & Elizabeth O McNair 4 Sep 1849; min- John Hendren
John & Rebecca Smith - Aug 1825; min- John Brown
Joseph & Caty Temereman 25 Jul 1808; min- William King
Leonard & Polly Lookelbough 2 May 1805; min- William King
Peter & Catherine Eagle 16 Feb 1796; d Christian Ekel b- Christian Eagle

Augusta County Marriages -- Man's Name

Sheets (cont.)
Philip & Catherine Cup 27 May 1791; d Marcus Kopp b- Marcus Kopp
Philip & Mary Shaver 21 Feb 1827; min- G H Reimensnyder
Samuel & Catharine Sheffer 22 Jan 1834; min- John Hendren
Solomon & Margaret Likes 13 May 1834; min- George Hildt
Thomas & Barbara Crist 5 Nov 1805; min- John McCue

Sheetz
Andrew & Catherine Sensebough 23 Sep 1799; d John b- Jacob Sheetz & John Sensibough
Henry & Polly Rice - May 1804; min- John Brown
John & Susana Ergebright - May 1810; min- John Brown
John & Sally Shotts 24 Feb 1814; min- G H Riemenschneider
John & Jane Tomblinson 20 Jan 1831; min- William Calhoon
Michael & Magdalina Syple 25 Nov 1822; min- G H Riemenschneider
Peter & Martha Miller 12 Mar 1840; min- Peter Miller
Samuel & Polly Fisher - Jul 1826; min- John Brown
Simon & Elizabeth Irvine 11 Mar 1841; min- J J Reimensnyder

Sheffer
David & Rachel Shaver 28 Jun 1833; min- George Hildt
William & Catharine Crum 25 Sep 1832; min- G H Reimensnyder

Sheigis
George & Rebecca Reed 28 Mar 1811; min- William Wilson

Shelley
Daniel & Catherine Fauber 15 Jan 1817; min- William King

Shelly
Eli & Julia Ann Elliott 17 Mar 1845; min- Jacob Baer
John & Elizabeth Stover 17 Dec 1804; min- William King

Sheltman
Felix & Eleanor McNair 30 Jul 1814; min- John Bell

Shelton
Dabney & Catherine Shempe 26 Dec 1810; min- John McCue
Henry & Sally Ruple 15 Feb 1824; min- Michael Meyerhoeffer
Thomas W & Mary Wilson 1 Apr 1842; min- B M Smith
William H & Lucy A Campbell 27 Jul 1847; min- J C Hensell
William & Matilda Fauber 30 Dec 1837; min- J C Hensell

Shepard
John & Easther Blakemore 15 Nov 1821; min- Gerard Morgan
William & Mary Warrenburgh 11 Mar 1802; min- William King- 11Mar1802

Shephard
Abraham & Ellen Peck 10 Feb 1813; min- William Calhoon

Shepherd
James & Mary Isenhouser 15 Apr 1794; d Michael b- Michael Isenhouser
Philip F & Sarah Hudson 2 Dec 1824; min- William W Calhoun
William & Peggy Freeman 14 Jan 1808; min- John McCue

Sherly
Balser & Catherine Peters 26 Apr 1808; min- William Calhoon

Sherror
John & Elizabeth Weckle 14 Jan 1805; min- Benjamin Irwin

Augusta County Marriages -- Man's Name

Shettman
John & Elizabeth Moore 14 Jan 1796; 'Skellman?' 'Mohr?' d John b- John Mohr

Shetz
Jacob & Elizabeth Blackburn 9 Jun 1796; min- William Wilson- 9Jun1796

Shewy
George H & Nancy Clark 24 Mar 1836; min- John A Steele
John & Catherine Funkhoser 31 Aug 1809; min- William King

Shibley
John & Eliza Backenstoe 28 Jul 1823; min- James Sewell

Shickel
Peter (Jr) & Julia Ann Mizer 28 Feb 1839; min- D F Bittle

Shields
Adam & Sally Bird 16 Jan 1808; min- William McPheeters
Archibald & Nancy Thompson 7 Nov 1805; min- John McCue
Henry & Elizabeth Haup 14 Nov 1822; min- John Brown
Henry & Elizabeth Mitchell 29 Jan 1790; Minister's return spells name as 'Sheids' d William, who consents wit- Christian Mummer & James Henry b- A Mustae min- Archibald Scott- 4Feb1790
James & Rachel Anderson 10 Mar 1786; d Joseph b- William Black wit- William Shields min- Archibald Scott- 10Mar1786
James & Betsey L Thompson 2 May 1822; min- James C Willson
John & Susannah Crowbarger 23 Apr 1835; min- Cornelius Gates
John & Abigail Kennady 10 Mar 1810; min- John McCue
Joseph & Rachel Fream 24 Nov 1800; Minister's return spells name as 'Frame' widower d John who consents test- William Fream b- Archibald Fream min- John McCue- 27Nov1800
Matthew & Elizabeth Thompson 20 Jan 1822; min- John Brown
Robert & Sarah Bailey 18 Aug 1812; min- William King
William & Eleanor Black 4 Dec 1787; Minister's return spells name as 'Sheids' b- John Black min- Archibald Scott- 8Dec1787
William & Sarah Estill 23 Jun 1792; d John b- James Aston no minister listed; clerk's memorandum cites ceremony date as 28Jun1792
William & Mary Thompson 10 Oct 1797; d Mathew who consents test- William Thompson & William Marshall b- Walter Herring min- John McCue- 12Oct1797

Shiflett
Abraham & Rhoday Ann Shiflet 8 Nov 1842; min- B M Smith- publication of banns
James & Mary Trainer 26 Oct 1825; min- William Wilson
William & Frances Roach 24 Jul 1820; bond- 27Jul1820 min- Josiah Cole

Shiplet
William & Nancy Orebough 9 Nov 1837; min- John J Reimensnyder

Shipman
James C & Nancy Miller 28 Mar 1832; min- John Hendren

Augusta County Marriages -- Man's Name

Shirer
  Charles C & Mary Jane Gutshall 30 Apr 1840; min- John J Reimensnyder
Shirey
  Daniel & Cathorine Shoritz 12 Sep 1793; d Daniel b- Daniel Sheretz
  George & Margaret Hanger 24 Apr 1817; min- William King
  Jacob & Elizabeth M Sellers 21 Nov 1843; min- Samuel Wagner
  Peter & Julia A Keiser 11 Sep 1834; min- William Scull
Shirfey
  Reuben & Susan Nair 3 Feb 1835; min- Wright Burgess
Shirley
  Jonathan & Nancy Reiff 14 Apr 1801; Minister's return spells name as 'Nancy Ruph (Rife?) and omits Jonathan's surname' d John, who signs 'Johann Reiff' as surety min- William King- 9Apr1801 (sic)
Shoemaker
  Christian & Nancy McGraw 27 May 1788; Martin Wolff & Daniel Shirey attest Nancy single and has no relations in this country b- Martin Wolff
Shoemate
  Payton & Polly Adair 11 Feb 1808; min- John McCue
Shoults
  Jacob & Elizabeth Nyman 15 Mar 1804; min- William King
  Valentine & Catherine Hawk 17 Jun 1799; d Henry wit- John Hawk b- Henry Hawk
Shover
  David & Rebecca Dinkle 26 Dec 1847; min- D W Arnold
Showalter
  Erasmus R & Caroline C Johnston 21 Apr 1835; min- Conrad Speece- publication of banns
  Jeremiah & Margaret Bowman 11 Mar 1841; min- J J Reimensnyder
  Nimrod S & Sarah Snider 20 Sep 1846; min- Jacob C Spitler
  Samuel & Mary Catharine Peterson 29 Jan 1846; min- J A Van Lear
Shown
  John & Sarah Crombick 16 Jan 1786; Minister's return spells name as 'Grombick' d George b- Andrew Shown wit- John Donald & William Gregory min- William Wilson- 31Jan1786
Shreckhise
  Jacob & Elizabeth McClure 24 Oct 1836; min- James C Wilson
Shreve
  Martin E & Elizabeth Padget 11 Feb 1850; min- J Killian
Shriver
  Andrew & Elizabeth Krizer 25 Dec 1810; min- John McCue
Shuby
  John & Catherine Cox 7 Sep 1837; min- James Paine
Shue
  George & Elizabeth Mizer 14 Nov 1823; min- Michael Meyerhoeffer
  Jacob & Eve Wagner - Mar 1806; min- John Brown

Augusta County Marriages -- Man's Name

Shuey
  Christian & Catherine Geeding   6 Sep 1814; min- William King
  John & Elizabeth Grass   12 Dec 1835; min- J J Glossbrenner
  John & Lydia Rinehart   2 Jan 1835; min- Henry Brown
  Michael (Jr) & Ann Hogshead   11 Jan 1821; min- William Calhoon

Shull
  Daniel & Margaret Good   25 Aug 1828; min- G H Reimensnyder
  Jacob & Elizabeth Hansel   27 Jan 1806; min- William King
  John & Catharine Good   27 Jun 1850; min- Henry Witzel

Shultz
  Adam & Jane Trimble   23 Oct 1838; min- Isaac Jones- publication of banns
  Cyrus & Mary Jane White   3 Jan 1837; min- Stephen Smith
  George W & Mary A Russel   20 May 1841; min- John C Hensell- publication of banns
  John B & Mary Jane Zimmerman   8 Feb 1843; min- D F Bittle
  John H B & Margaret Fix   21 Oct 1841; min- John C Hensell
  John & Susannah Hull   12 Jan 1829; min- Francis McFarland
  William G & Mary M Black   7 May 1840; min- John C Hansell

Shutler
  Jacob G & Mary Ransberger   23 Dec 1834; min- Samuel Kennerly

Siddons
  James & Sarah Graves   16 Oct 1798; d Richard b- Richard Graves James (of age)

Silings
  Oliver Henry Perry & Rebecca Dinkle   25 Jan 1849; min- P Shickel

Silknitter
  George & Rachael McKitrick   24 Sep 1807; min- William Calhoon

Silling
  Abraham & Priscilla Jones   3 Apr 1790; Minister's return spells name as 'Selling' b- Enos Jones perm-Enos Jones, father & Gasper Seiling (father?) min- William Wilson- 6Apr1790
  Andrew & Ann Jones   4 Jan 1796; d Enos b- Enos Jones
  David & Polly Snider   7 Aug 1806; min- William King
  Enos & Betsy Snyder   28 Dec 1826; min- John Hendren
  George & Barbara Mell   1 Mar 1804; min- William King
  John & Sally Patterson   27 Oct 1798; d John b- John Patterson min- William Wilson- 30Oct1798
  William & Polly Rankin   30 Oct 1820; min- Daniel Stephens

Sillings
  Kinney & Winifred Jones   19 Nov 1829; min- John Hendren

Silor
  John & Mary Price   20 Apr 1843; min- J C Hensell

Silvers
  John & Dolly Wingfield   7 Dec 1804; min- John McCue

Simmerman
  George & Sarah Runnels   4 Aug 1842; min- P E Stevenson

Simmons
  Matthias & Polly Sheetz   17 Nov 1825; min- Josiah Cole

Augusta County Marriages -- Man's Name

Sims
  Edward & Agness Hughes 7 Sep 1785; min- Archibald Scott-7Sep1785
  James P & Sarah Mills 7 Nov 1841; min- Samuel Wagner
  James & Peggy Stuart 11 Nov 1808; min- Joseph Reid
  John & Rebecca Walkup 6 Jan 1806; min- William King
  Miles & Martha Blair 13 Jul 1826; min- Francis McFarland
Sink
  David & Mary Ann Fauber 11 Apr 1822; min- John Brown
Sisler
  Henry & Frances Bowen 2 Nov 1848; min- John A Van Lear
Sites
  Harris & Martha Ann Gordon 11 Jun 1834; min- Samuel Kennerly
  John & Elizabeth Hinton 29 May 1816; bond min- Conrad Speece, Jr--May1816
  Windle & Anne Garber 10 Mar 1846; min- T T Castleman
Sitlington
  Thomas S & Sarah J Hunter 26 Aug 1840; min- Benjamin M Smith
Sively
  George & Mary Lamb 26 Nov 1799; George from Rockingham cty d John b- John Lamb
Skelton
  Samuel & Fanny Wilson 6 Jan 1807; min- William King
Skillern
  George & ----- ----- 2 May 1763; license only
  William & ----- ----- 12 Apr 1763; license only
Skiner
  John & Elenor Underwood 22 Jan 1788; min- William Wilson-22Jan1788
Skyles
  Jacob & Pheby Stoutamoyer 15 Jun 1826; min- G H Reimensnyder
  Samuel & Sara Dettemore 19 Mar 1827; min- G H Reimensnyder
Slagle
  Jacob & Elizabeth Eakle 10 Jan 1822; min- James C Willson
  John & Peggy Erwin 24 Dec 1810; min- William King
Slaughter
  Reuben & Mary Donnally 8 Apr 1791; Minister's return spells name as 'Donally' d Andrew who consents wit- Samuel Merritt b- William Chambers min- John Montgomery- 14Apr1791
Slaven
  Isaiah & Patty Steward 22 Feb 1786; Minister's return spells name as 'Stuart' b- Abraham Ingram min- William Wilson- 22Feb1786
  John & Elizabeth Hodge 30 Jul 1789; min- John Montgomery-30Jul1789
  William & Betsy Gibson 2 Oct 1826; min- Conrad Speece
Sligh
  Henry & Nancy Barker 11 Feb 1808; min- William King
Slone
  Andrew & Barbara Fry 11 Jan 1817; 'Sloan?' min- William King

Augusta County Marriages -- Man's Name

Sluser
  George & Peggy Wineinger 18 May 1795; d John who consents & Caty Wineinger who consents test- Peter Troxell b- David Kershner

Slusher
  George & Ann Baylor 21 Dec 1826; min- William Monroe
  Jacob & Sarah Harry - Jan 1805; min- John Brown

Sly
  Jacob & Lucy Vines 13 Dec 1796; d Thomas who consents s Henry Sligh who consents test- James Kelly b- John Chesnut

Small
  John & Salley Fitzpatrick 9 Dec 1817; min- Wright Burgess

Smallshoffer
  Christian & Elizabeth Leonard 16 Oct 1833; min- George Hildt

Smiley
  Alexander & Margaret Fulton 28 Oct 1842; min- James Morrison
  Alexander & Drusilla Hemp 9 Jan 1845; min- J C Hensell
  Archibald & Mary Hannah 28 Jun 1800; d Robert Archibald from Rockbridge cty s Walter who consents test- James Buchanan & Evan Evans b- James Buchanan Jr
  John & Jane Screle 21 Sep 1809; min- William Bolridge
  Walter & Kitty Kennerly 28 Dec 1816; min- William King
  William M & Jane McCutchen 6 Mar 1834; min- Francis McFarland
  William & Christiana Martin 1 Jan 1840; min- James Morrison

Smiltzer
  Jacob & Catherine Trorabaugh 16 Mar 1797; d Michael Trorobough, dec. Conrad Plum (Blum) swears Katy been married before and is over 21 b- Conrad Plum

Smily
  George & Barbra Ann Landis 16 Feb 1846; min- P Shickel

Smith
  Abel Langddon & Nancy Deam 7 Oct 1816; min- William Wilson
  Andrew & Nancy Ann Brown 25 Mar 1836; min- James Morrison
  Augustin & Dorcus Alexander 17 Dec 1798; Dorcus (of age) d Francis Alexander, dec. Augustin (of age) b- Gabriel Alexander
  Edmund & Catherine Mell 23 Sep 1802; min- William King- 23Sep1802
  Elijah & Lucinda Henderson 16 Jun 1827; min- William C. Morrison
  Francis & ----- ----- - Aug 1761; license only
  Franklin & Sarah Ann Smith 30 Dec 1845; min- Jacob C Spitler
  Fred & ----- ----- 23 Mar 1754; license only
  George & Margaret Beard 5 Oct 1831; min- Francis McFarland
  Harvey F & Hannah E Teter 20 Feb 1848; min- Jacob C Spitler
  Isaac & Polly Young 21 Sep 1809; min- William King
  Jacob & Rebecca Acord 21 Dec 1826; min- John A Gore
  Jacob & Christiana Wiseman 12 May 1796; d Peter b- Peter Wiseman
  James W & Mary B Dobbs 3 Aug 1842; min- Samuel Wagner

Augusta County Marriages -- Man's Name

Smith (cont.)

James & Rebecca Emmett 2 Jun 1803; min- William King
James & Martha A Southwood 3 Sep 1846; min- J A Van Lear
John & Elizabeth Harmon 5 Jul 1810; min- William King
John & Martha Mines 13 Mar 1832; min- James Morrison
John & Barbara Moyer 4 Oct 1821; min- Josiah Cole
John & Eleanor Oakley 6 Apr 1796; b- Alexander Gibson
John & Susanna Reglor 16 Jun 1785; b- Francis Marra
John & Ann Sheets 28 Sep 1818; min- William King
John & Margaret Stuart 26 Mar 1791; s Wm who consents wit- Samuel Hardin & Samuel Camble certificate by Wm & Hannah Bell giving permission wit- Alexander Camble b- Samuel Harding Margaret an orphan
John & Sophia Young 12 Feb 1818; min- William King
John & Nancy Zee 8 Oct 1840; min- J J Reimensnyder
Joseph & Margaret McCutchen 11 Mar 1800; Margaret (of age) d Samuel s John Smith of PA, and of age b- William Smith
Joseph & Susanna Smith 27 Jul 1819; min- William Wilson
Joshua & Elizabeth Henderson 12 Dec 1827; min- William C. Morrison
Matthew & Milly Green 19 Dec 1787; d Edward who consents b- Elihus Green min- William Wilson- 19Dec1787
Mordecai & Henrietta Russell - Aug 1847; min- Stephen Hildebrand
Peter & Rebeccah Hizer 18 Oct 1803; min- John McCue
Philip & Mary Chesnutt 20 Jul 1792; Minister's return spells name as 'Chesnut' d William & Jane who consent b- William Bratton min- John McCue- 21Aug1792
Philip & Anna White 25 May 1819; min- Wright Burgess
Ralph & Barbara Winegardner 26 Jan 1819; min- William King
Richard & Jane Caruthers 13 Apr 1786; b- James Caruthers min- Archibald Scott- 13Apr1786
Robert & Mary Brown 20 Dec 1820; min- Josiah Cole
Solomon & Catherine Hartshooke 4 Jan 1812; min- G H Riemenschneider
Thomas J & Mildred Faundree - Jun 1826; min- Joseph Smith
Thomas P & Peggy Trimble 4 Feb 1808; min- William Calhoon
Thomas & ----- ----- 14 Jul 1771; license only
William D & Frances M Stribling 31 Oct 1839; min- Frederick D Goodwin
William F & Letitia R Randolph 11 Sep 1848; min- Francis McFarland
William R & Mary Jane Pitman 19 Jan 1843; min- James Bunting
William W & Mary S White 20 Mar 1850; min- James Paine
William & ----- ----- 11 Jul 1751; license only
William & ----- ----- 14 Jul 1759; license only
William & Delilah Allen 28 Oct 1828; min- William C. Morrison
William & Nancy Bulcher - May 1814; min- John Brown
William & Barbara Caufman 14 Sep 1837; min- J C Hensell- publication of banns
William & Nelly Johnson 31 Mar 1787; Minister's return spells name as 'Johnston' Nelly gives own consent test- John Killgobbin & James Rapshin b- Francis Mara Nelly widow of Hugh Johnson min- William Wilson- 12Apr1787

Augusta County Marriages -- Man's Name

Smith (cont.)
  William & Margaret King 1 May 1806; min- William Wilson
Snapp
  Robert & Elizabeth Mowry 31 Jan 1821; min- Conrad Speece
  William & Matheras Hogshead 28 May 1822; min- John Hendren
Snedegar
  Isaac & Elenor Story 22 May 1787; Minister's return spells name as 'Snediger' b- James McGavory min- Samuel Shannon- 29May1787
Snedicor
  Christopher & Nancy Hall 15 Nov 1785; d Robert b- John Berry wit- Robert Given
Sneed
  Nicholas & Frances Jane Koogler 13 Apr 1848; min- P Shickel
Snell
  John & Martha Browers 21 Mar 1832; min- Abraham Garber- publication of banns
Snideman
  Henry & Elizabeth Flory 20 Dec 1838; min- John Garber
Snider
  George & Elizabeth Deane 29 Apr 1841; min- George B Rimel
  Henry & Nancy Crist 21 Jun 1802; min- William King- 21Jun1802
  Henry & Jane Donovan 5 Oct 1811; min- A B Davidson
  Joseph & Rosannah Fawber 20 Oct 1831; min- John Hendren
  William & E Jane Palmer 30 Nov 1843; min- D F Bittle
Snodgrass
  James & ----- ----- 14 Jun 1764; license only
Snyder
  Adam & Hannah Hull 19 May 1845; min- D F Bittle
  Daniel & Elizabeth Golladay 17 Feb 1848; min- J C Hensell
  George & Mary Blacker - May 1818; min- John Brown
  Henry & Ann McKenny 10 Sep 1828; min- William C. Morrison
  Jacob & Harriet Jackson 2 Jul 1817; min- William King
  John (Jr) & Sarah Sheets 25 Mar 1849; min Henry Wetzel
  Michael & Eliza Fauber 7 Feb 1828; min- John Hendren
  Peter H & Margaret F Wheeler 21 Feb 1842; min- John W Stine
  Samuel & Mary Jane Howell - --- 1835; min- Wright Burgess- publication of banns
Solleday
  Adam & Polly Leonard 21 Jan 1799; d George Leonard of Shenandoah cty consent before Isaac Goave of Shenandoah Adam (of age) b- Adam Lenert
Somer
  George & Jennetta Davis 25 Nov 1817; min- William King- publication of banns
Sorrels
  Lewis & Elenor Carr 3 May 1792; Elenor an orphan, father died when she was young, mother's whereabouts unknown Elenor raised by Alexander Robertson b- Thomas Clifton min- John McCune- 3May1792
  William & Polly Morriss 12 Nov 1818; min- William King

Augusta County Marriages -- Man's Name

Sours
  J & Ruth Ralston 21 Jan 1836; min- Robert M Lipscomb
  John & Catherine Baylor 17 Nov 1814; min- William King
Southard
  William & Margaret Huff 30 Jan 1829; min- William C. Morrison
Sowers
  George & Elizabeth Haffner - Jun 1817; min- John Brown
Spangler
  George & Polly King 2 May 1801; 'Mary' d Richard b- Richard King min- William King- 2May1801
Spatts
  John & Catherine Imboden 28 Jan 1809; min- William King
Spear
  John & Mary Russell 9 Jun 1801; Minister's return spells name as 'Speer' d John s Samuel who consents test- Samuel Meteers & Thomas Speer b- John Russell min- John Gee- 11Jun1801
Spearing
  Henry & Rebecca Blackamore 21 Sep 1796; widower & widow b- Adam Bickle
  Henry & Jane Price 6 Apr 1795; Minister's return spells name as 'Pearing' widower & widow (of Thomas Price) b- Valentine Sherley min- William Wilson- 9Apr1795
Spears
  Jacob & Sarah Heppard 13 Oct 1835; min- William G Jackson
Speck
  David & Hannah McCray 2 Jan 1821; min- William Calhoon
  Henry & Jane Campbell 29 Sep 1795; d Alexander who consents test- Jacob Coyner, Alexander Campbell Jr & Thomas Turke b- Thomas Turk Jr min- John McCue- 8Oct1795
  Henry & Elizabeth Pepperley 27 Apr 1826; min- William Monroe
  Jacob & Margaret Doom 24 Dec 1847; min- Stephen Hildebrand
Spence
  William & Mary Anderson 25 Jun 1793; Minister's return spells name as 'Polly Anderson' b- James Anderson min- William Wilson- 26May1793
Spencer
  John & Florence Henderson 3 Jun 1801; widower d William Henderson b- John Henderson
  William W & Sarah J Buchanan 28 Mar 1848; min- J C Hensell
Spicer
  Benjamin F & Sarah W Skelton 29 May 1845; min- P Shickel
Spindle
  Adam & Elizabeth Cowman 2 May 1791; d John b- John Cowman
Spinkle
  Adolph & Catherine Ingleman 22 May 1787; min- Archibald Scott- 22May1787
Spitler
  Benjamin F & Lucinda F Spangler 16 Dec 1847; min- John Reubush
  Daniel & Elener Emmery 24 Nov 1806; min- William King
  Jacob (Jr) & Elizabeth Crist 21 Sep 1800; min- Daniel Garber- 21Sep1800

Augusta County Marriages -- Man's Name

Spitler (cont.)
  Jacob C & Amanda Redman 9 May 1833; min- Conrad Speece
  Jacob & Margaret Dunlap 14 Jun 1824; min- Michael Meyerhoeffer
  John & Polly Eccord 22 Feb 1797; d Frantz b- Francis Eccord
  John & Margaret Nichol 21 Dec 1821; min- John Hendren
  William B & Margaret Arehart 9 Nov 1848; min- Alonzo P Ludden

Sponter
  Francis & Catherine Riddle 8 Sep 1791

Spotts
  Jacob & Elizabeth Coiner 23 Jan 1806; min- John McCue

Spring
  Nicholas & Elizabeth Hicks 23 Aug 1796; d Joshua b- Joshua Hicks min- John McCue- 25Aug1796

Sprinkle
  Willson & Martha Patterson 9 Jun 1838; min- James Paine

Sproul
  John & Matilda Scott 13 Sep 1821; min- William W Calhoun
  Samuel B & Margaret Jane Williams 21 Aug 1834; min- Conrad Speece
  William & Janetta Beard 28 Feb 1833; min- James Morrison

Sprouse
  David & Susan Jane Milton 14 Jul 1846; min- John Reubush

Sprowl
  William & ----- ----- - Aug 1757; license only
  William & ----- ----- 23 Jun 1773; license only

StClair
  Alexander R & Mary Jennings 1 Dec 1836; min- B N Brown

Staggs
  George & Jane Evans 13 Apr 1817; min- William King

Stanton
  Clinton & Jacyntha Webb 18 Apr 1825; min- John Hendren

Staples
  Uriah J & Elizabeth Simbro 12 Nov 1846; min- J Montgomery
  William G & Celia A Dyer 6 Sep 1848; min- T T Castleman

Stark
  Thomas & Polly Minick 27 Sep 1807; min- William King

Start
  Garay & Priscilla Herren 25 Jul 1801; Minister's return spells name as 'Geve Stout and Pricilla Herron' widower Priscilla (of age) b- Michael Harmon min- William King- 26Jul1801
  John W & Mary Virginia Hill 29 Feb 1848; 'Rev.' John W min- John Bowen

Staunton
  Thomas & Polly Barns 10 Oct 1800; Polly (of age) d of ----- Barns, dec. b- John Logan
  Thomas & Rody Sprigs 5 May 1797; b- Benjamin Norton

Steel
  John & Elizabeth Burk 4 Jul 1789; d John Burcke, who consents wit- John Christian b- John Christian min- William Wilson- 7Jul1789

Augusta County Marriages -- Man's Name

Steele
Andrew & Elizabeth Tate 10 Jun 1795; d James Tate, dec.
  b- Alexander Hall min- John McCue- 18Jun1795
James & Elizabeth Peck 2 Feb 1815; min- John McCue
John M & Jane Churchman 9 Dec 1843; min- T T Castleman
John & Polly Bush 25 Oct 1800; d Martin s Andrew b- Martin Bush
Nathaniel & Martha McCutchen 23 Nov 1824; min- James Morrison
Robert & Martha M Arbuckle 9 Jun 1829; min- Francis McFarland
William & Mary McChesney 31 Dec 1793; d James who consents test- Adam McChesney s Samuel b- John McDowell no minister listed; clerk's memorandum cites ceremony date as 2Jan1794

Stephen
William & Polly Davis 25 Jun 1804; min- William King

Stephens
John R & Sarah Jane Hendren 15 Jun 1831; min- Conrad Speece
Joseph & Grizel Cumins 28 May 1789; perm- Grizel herself, who test. she is 21 and has no relations in this country wit- John Steven & David Coalter b- John Stevens

Stephenson
Thomas & Eliza Commens 27 Jun 1809; min- William King
William & Sarah Forsythe 13 Mar 1797; d Samuel b- Samuel Forsythe min- William Wilson- 14Mar1797

Sterret
Robert & Isabella Dunlap 8 Dec 1818; min- John D Ewin

Sterritt
Alexander & Mary Hutcheson 6 Jan 1807; min- William King
William & Nancy Bell 3 Feb 1800; Nancy (of age) d James Bell, dec, sis to William Bell b- William Bell

Stevens
Thomas & Polly Beeton 4 Sep 1797; widow d Robert Allison who consents test- Thomas Sawyers b- David Sawyers

Stevenson
Levi L & Elizabeth Dunlap 6 Apr 1815; min- William Calhoon
Robert & ----- ----- 29 Apr 1768; license only
Samuel & ----- ----- 22 May 1771; license only
Thomas & ----- ----- - Sep 1760; license only

Stewart
James & ----- ----- 20 Aug 1766; license only

Sticer
Fielding & Susan Michael 5 Jun 1834; min- Joseph Spriggs

Stickleman
John & Elizabeth Weaver 16 Apr 1787; Minister's return spells name as 'Sickleman' b- John Waid permission by Christiana Weaver (mother), John Waid, Peter Weaver & Philip Steigleman (brothers) min- Archibald Scott- 19Apr178
Philip & Margaret Weaver 31 Jan 1787; d Peter who consents test- William McClure b- William McClure min- Archibald Scott- 2Feb1787

Augusta County Marriages -- Man's Name

Stickley
 William & Sarah Fellers 8 Jan 1835; min- Samuel Kennerly
Stiff
 William W & Elizabeth F Taylor 1 Aug 1845; min- B N Brown
Stodgall
 William & Rebecca Dinsmore 14 Sep 1795; Samuel Dinsmore made oath that Rebecca has lived in the county six months b- Alexander Gibson
Stofer
 Henry & Ellen Humphrey - Jul 1826; min- Joseph Smith
 Simon & Catharine Wyand - Jan 1804; min- John Brown
Stokes
 James & Henrietta Lowrey 21 Dec 1831; min- John Hendren
Stombock
 Martin & Elizabeth Crone 19 Dec 1847; min- Jacob C Spitler
Stone
 Isaac S & Frances Speck 17 Apr 1842; min- Peter Shickel
Stoner
 Abraham & Esther Garber 15 May 1833; min- Abraham Garber- publication of banns
Story
 Thomas & Mary Dixon 15 Jul 1817; min- Wright Burgess
Stoutamire
 Moses & Margaret Michael 10 Oct 1844; min- George B Rimel
Stoutamoyer
 John & Christiana Crum 15 Dec 1842; min- Henry Wetzel
 Reuben & Catharine Michael 23 Feb 1841; min- George Huffman
Stover
 Daniel & Mary Hanah 30 Mar 1803; min- William King
 Daniel & Mary Eliza Swartz 27 Mar 1845; min- T T Castleman
 David & Mary Shelly 15 Jan 1805; min- William King
 Henry & Polly Piper 4 Feb 1814; min- William King
 Jacob & Margaret Towell 26 Aug 1800; Jacob (of age) d John b- John Towell min- William Wilson- 9Sep1800
 Michael & Louisa Stiegle 24 Nov 1842; min- Samuel Wagner
 Samuel (Jr) & Mary Ann Wiseman 9 Nov 1848; min- Alonzo P Ludden
 Samuel D & Catharine Hart 5 Jun 1837; min- George A Leopard
 Samuel & Rachel Frankam 28 Sep 1831; min- William Wilson
 Samuel & Betsey Shelly 26 Apr 1814; min- William King
Strain
 John & Nancy Henderson 22 Nov 1803; min- John McCue
 William & Elizabeth McCutchan 20 Oct 1831; min- Francis McFarland
Strane
 James & Patsey Henderson 13 Nov 1806; min- William King
Street
 Charles H & Catharine J Bowman 9 Mar 1848; min- J C Hensell
Stribling
 Erasmus & Matilda Kinney 23 Apr 1807; min- William Calhoon
 George W & Mary King 8 Dec 1845; min- T T Castleman
Strickland
 Levi & Nancy Harris 23 Nov 1805; min- William King

Augusta County Marriages -- Man's Name

Strickler
  Benjamin & Charlotte Shipton 30 Jul 1840; min- John C Hansell-publication of banns
  Henry & Catharine Arehart 2 Jun 1841; min- John C Hensell-publication of banns
  James & Polly Sensibaugh 26 Oct 1847; min- James Morrison
  John & Katharine Karricofe 8 Jun 1846; min- P Shickel

Strong
  James & Sally Fulton 2 Nov 1798; Sally (of age) d William Fulton, dec. b- Hugh Fulton

Stuart
  Alexander H H & Frances C Baldwin 1 Aug 1833; min- John S Watt
  Archibald P & Josaphine Xaupi 13 Aug 1840; min- Frederick D Goodwin
  Archibald & Polly Alexander 5 Dec 1805; min- John McCue
  Chapman J & Margaret E Baldwin 21 Sep 1842; min- P E Stevenson
  Charles & Elizabeth Risk 15 Mar 1791; wid b- Thomas Mynes
  Charles & Elizabeth Robertson 29 May 1811; min- William Wilson
  Edward & Mary Callaghan 28 Mar 1786; Minister's return spells names as 'Stewart and Calaghan' b- Charles Callaghan min- Samuel Shannon- 4Apr1786
  James & Salley Brockman 1 Jun 1819; min- Wright Burgess
  James & Mary Kinny 21 Apr 1796; d Moses, late of PA Mary born 27Apr1774 and had resided on the Middle River for three months - James Stuart & A Humphreys
  John & Isabella Coalter 1 Apr 1813; min- John McCue
  John & Hannah Hicklin 15 May 1787; b- James McGavory min- Samuel Shannon- 31May1787
  Robert & ----- ----- 18 Aug 1762; license only
  Robert & Polly Armstrong 23 Apr 1792; b- Robert Stuart Sr min- John Brown- 24Apr1792
  Samuel D & Cornelia S Waddell 15 Nov 1838; min- William Calhoon

Stull
  Andrew & Martha Crawford 7 May 1798; Minister's return spells name as 'Andrew Steele' d William b- William Crawford min- William Wilson- 9May1798

Stulzer
  William & Elizabeth Dellon - Jan 1809; min- John Brown

Stunkard
  William & Hanah Erwin 10 Jan 1791; Minister's return spells name as 'William Stockard' orphan sister of Benjamin Erwin b- Benjamin Erwin min- John Montgomery- 13Feb1791

Sturm
  Michael & Elizabeth Hare 6 Sep 1799; Minister's return spells name as 'Sturm' widow b- John Wise & John Hively min- William King- 8Sep1799

Sullivan
  Samuel & Polly Mayfield 27 Nov 1815; min- William King
  Thomas & Peggy Erwin 29 Mar 1790; b- Richard Erwin min- Archibald Scott- 29Mar1790

Augusta County Marriages -- Man's Name

Summers
   Andrew & Margaret Miller 26 Mar 1793; Margaret (of age) sis John b- John Miller
   George W & Eliza Jane Edgar 12 Aug 1847; min- John Bowen
   John (Jr) & Martha Williams 17 Nov 1787; b- John Summers Sr
   John & Catherine Ingleman 3 Oct 1798; d Philip b- Philip Ingleman
   John & Barbary Runkle 29 Oct 1812; min- William King

Supple
   Robert & Mary Shields 7 Nov 1833; min- Francis McFarland

Surber
   Joseph & Rebecca Crawford 27 Jan 1814; min- William Calhoon
   Levi & Sarah Hanger 1 Sep 1831; min- William Calhoon
   William H & Frances W Gibbons 12 Sep 1848; min- J A Van Lear

Surface
   Christian & Florence Crawford 17 Jul 1799; 'Sirfes?' both of age b- Martin Surface, bro of Christian
   John & Easter Rife 1 May 1804; min- William King

Swab
   Henry & Easter Fall - Mar 1805; min- John Brown

Swang
   Joseph & Elizabeth Landes - Nov 1824; min- John Brown

Swank
   Jacob & Anne Culp 15 Aug 1820; min- William Wilson

Swartsley
   Ira & Margaret Teaford 29 Nov 1832; min- Francis McFarland

Swartzel
   Jacob & Elizabeth B Lavel 29 Oct 1844; min- J C Hensell

Swartzley
   John & Catharine Haybarger 1 Apr 1834; min- Augustus Babb

Swats
   Jacob & Nancy Jane Dowell 4 May 1843; min- Peter Miller

Swatsley
   Joseph & Margaret Rough 27 Aug 1835; min- William Calhoon

Swatzel
   Henry & Susana Margaret Bosserman 12 Oct 1837; min- J C Hensell

Swatzley
   John & Susannah Towerman 23 Apr 1805; min- William King

Sweetz
   Jacob & Catherine Smith 3 Jul 1810; min- William King

Swink
   Adam & Latitia Abney 4 Jan 1838; min- John A Steele
   Enos & Rachel Forsythe 9 Jan 1817; min- William King
   Henry P & Sarah Crist 23 Oct 1844; min- T T Castleman
   Henry & Elizabeth Beck 30 Sep 1824; min- Thomas Caldwell
   John & Sarah Brown 17 Sep 1829; min- Francis McFarland
   Lawrence & Patsey Forsythe 30 May 1810; min- William King
   Lawrence & Hetty B Noland 24 Sep 1827; min- Conrad Speece
   Mathias & Sally Wilson 27 Sep 1787; d Robert s Lawrence b- Jacob Swallow wit- William Heart & William Christian min- Archibald Scott- 28Sep1786
   Philip & Piersy L Mizener 3 Feb 1846; min- Jacob C Spitler- publication of banns

Augusta County Marriages -- Man's Name

Swink (cont.)
  Robert & Susannah C Whitsell 30 Aug 1838; min- Thomas Wheeler
  William & Elizabeth Crist 26 Jun 1841; min- John C Hensell

Swisher
  Henry & Julia Ann Daugherty 21 Jan 1847; min- J C Hensell
  Henry & Mary Haffner - Aug 1821; min- John Brown
  Jacob & Jane E Freeman 17 Feb 1842; min- Samuel Wagner
  Jacob & Sarah Swisher 19 Sep 1836; min- James C Wilson
  John (Jr) & Janetta Horne 16 Feb 1837; min- John J Reimensnyder
  John & Priscilla Brian 11 Oct 1842; min- Samuel Wagner
  John & Susan Jarvis 13 Jul 1826; min- James Morrison
  John & Catherine Palmer 27 Oct 1823; 'Jacob Swisher?' min- Josiah Cole
  John & Mary Rader 25 Jan 1841; min- Samuel Wagner
  Washington & Polly Gochenour 18 Sep 1830; min- James Morrison

Switzer
  Abraham & Nancy Rode - Aug 1820; min- John Brown
  Jacob & Jane Graham 29 Jun 1818; min- William King
  John & Frances Hale 6 Aug 1845; min- P Shickel

Swoope
  Jacob & Mary McDowell 2 Jun 1790; d William, who consents wit- Alexander Nelson Jr b- John McDowell
  Reuben & Susan Swank 20 Mar 1834; min- J Hoover

Swope
  George & Martha Armstrong 18 Nov 1837; min- John Hendren

Syford
  Michael & Catherine Tennant 12 Nov 1799; Minister's return spells name as 'Tenant' widower & widow 9of John) b- James McGongal min- William King- 12Nov1799

Symmerman
  Henry & Mary Seftle 18 Jul 1792; d Valentine who consents wit- Jacob Geiger b- Choistion Symerman

Syple
  Conrad & Catharine Landis 29 May 1832; min- John Rhoads

Tacket
  Thomas & Keterenah Dinnison 4 Jul 1785; min- Samuel Shannon- 4Jul1785

Talbert
  Robert & Martha Thompson 26 Mar 1787; d William b- Hugh Talbert (Tarbet?) min- Archibald Scott- 29Mar1787

Taliaferor
  Richard & Frances W Gilmore 29 Mar 1804; min- William Wilson

Taliaferro
  John M & Lucy J Howell - Aug 1847; min- Stephen Hildebrand

Tallman
  Benjamin & Jane Armstrong 20 Aug 1833; min- John Hendren
  James & Nancy Crawford 4 Dec 1790; Bond lists James's name as Tolman d William b- John Armstrong s Benjamin, who consents wit- William Tallman & Thomas Hunter min- Archibald Scott- 10Dec1790

Augusta County Marriages -- Man's Name

Tally
Fleming R & Rebecca Allen 6 Apr 1826; min- Conrad Speece
Gillias N & Mary Ann Hall 20 Nov 1832; min- Samuel Kennerly
William & Catharine Gregory 19 Apr 1825; min- Josiah Cole

Taner
William & Polly Darrow - Oct 1817; min- John Brown

Tankersley
Edmunds & Hanna Hughes 12 Aug 1809; min- John Bell
Obadiah & Elizabeth Davidson 29 Jul 1797; d John b- John Davidson
Reuben & Cynthia Hughes 18 Jan 1798; d John b- John Hughes

Tanner
Abraham & Molly Long 10 Jan 1787; d Mary who consents test- Peter Heiskell & John Thomas s John who consents test- Peter Heiskell & John Thomas b- Jacob Long min- Benjamin Erwin- 16Jan1787
David & Mary Judd 22 May 1800; d Michael who consents test- Lewis Wayland b- George Ailor (Oehler) min- William King- 22May1800
Leonard & Caty Harmon 16 Oct 1798; d Peter con- Johannes Danner & George Danner b- John Towell
Tobias & Elizabeth Wagner - Jun 1804; min- John Brown

Tapp
Walter H & Eliza Jane McCray 2 Apr 1828; min- Joseph Smith

Tate
James & Clorinda Tate 5 Jan 1820; min- Robert H Chapman
John (Jr) & Elizabeth McClenachan 25 Feb 1794; d Elijah McClenachan Sr who consents test- Elijah McClenachan Jr & Lettice Ann McClenachan b- Elijah McClenachan Jr clerk's memorandum cites ceremony date as 27Feb1794
John A & Margaret A Randolph 7 Apr 1836; min- James Morrison
John & Lovey S Gilkeson 16 Apr 1846; min- Francis McFarland
John & Nancy Moffett 22 Apr 1813; min- William Calhoon
Robert & Susan Gold 9 Aug 1837; min- John A Steele
Samuel H & Caroline J Bradshaw 16 Jul 1846; min- Jacob C Spitler- publication of banns
Sturman & Elizabeth McCommis 10 Aug 1795; Elizabeth (of age) Sturman served apprenticeship with Robert McGuffin and was released Dec 1794 b- James King
Thomas & ----- ----- - Oct 1764; license only
William M & Martha E Frazier 14 Nov 1844; min- John Hendren
William P & Sarah Ann Chrisman 5 Jun 1850; min- Francis McFarland

Taylor
Alexander M & Sarah E Mosby 9 Nov 1841; min- P E Stevenson
Charles & Elizabeth E Burgess 4 May 1826; min- Benjamin Denton
Daniel & ----- ----- 17 Mar 1773; license only
David & Mary A C Moffett 8 Sep 1842; min- B M Smith
Edwin M & Jane E Kinney 18 Jun 1839; min- Frederick D Goodwin
Fountain & Jane Stanton 16 Jul 1829; min- John Hendren
George W & Mary J Linn 23 Apr 1840; min- Jacob Killian

Augusta County Marriages -- Man's Name

Taylor (cont.)
George & Susannah Fairburn 15 Jun 1843; min- John A Van Lear
George & Nancy Miller 28 Jul 1823; min- Josiah Cole
George & Elizabeth Stanton 25 Feb 1830; min- John Hendren
Henry & Sarah Dull 8 Mar 1825; min- Josiah Cole
Hezekiah & Elizabeth Swisher 8 Nov 1842; min- John A Van Lear- publication of banns
James W & Martha McMullins 7 Jan 1824; min- John Hendren
John & ----- ----- 24 Jun 1766; license only
John & Sarah Cashaw 6 Oct 1792; d Benoin who consents s Christin Charles Tailor who consents wit- John Cashaw b- Henry Mace
John & Virginia Chapman 29 Oct 1828; min- William C. Morrison
Martin & Catherine Thomas 28 Jan 1791; d Johannes Thommus b- Johannes Thommus (Martin signs his name 'Martin Scheider')
Robert & Agness McCroskey 4 Nov 1796; min- Archibald Scott- 4Nov1796
Theodore & Rebecca Boyer 5 May 1834; min- James C Wilson
William & Nancy Ailor 26 Oct 1821; min- John D Ewin
William & Barbara Tascott 11 Feb 1816; min- William King- publication of banns

Teabo
Abraham R & Catharine Alexander 24 Oct 1841; min- Alfred G Chenowith

Teaford
George & Mary Ann Fleisher 16 Oct 1834; min- William Calhoon
George & Catherine Koontz 2 Aug 1827; min- William Calhoon
George & Polly Palmer 13 Apr 1826; min- William W Calhoun
Henry & Peggy Keller 16 Aug 1804; min- William King
Henry & Julia Ann Seig 2 Nov 1837; min- William Calhoub
John & Polly Geeting 6 Apr 1819; min- William King
S & Mary Moyer 18 Sep 1845; min- J C Hensell

Teagle
John & Mary Edwards 12 Jan 1804; min- John McCue

Tebo
Michael & Elizabeth Jane Clarke 23 Mar 1838; min- John A Steele

Teebo
Abraham & Polly Syford 25 Jun 1796; d Michael b- Michael Syford
Adam & Elizabeth Farrow 3 Aug 1822; min- Josiah Cole

Teeford
George & Mary Spotts 27 Apr 1801; d Jacob b- Jacob Spotts
Henry & Elizabeth Shoultz 22 Oct 1796; d George b- George Shoultz
Jacob & Barbara Gabart 22 Feb 1791; d Jacob b- David Cale
John & Catharine Runkle 12 Mar 1793; d Lewis John (of age) b- Lewis Runkle

Augusta County Marriages -- Man's Name

Tees
  William & ----- ----- 20 Jul 1762; license only
Teese
  Thomas & ----- ----- 24 Oct 1770; license only
Teford
  Lewis & Elizabeth Cook 23 Apr 1840; min- D F Bittle
Teitrick
  John & Mary Krawn 24 Aug 1809; min- William King
Telfair
  Isaac & Jane Mathews 27 Dec 1794; Minister's return spells name as 'Telfare' d George b- Sampson Mathews min- John McCue- 27Dec1794
Telford
  James & Jean McKoskry 13 Jan 1789; Minister's return spells name as 'McCoskrey' d Grizel McKoskey, who consents wit- William McKee & John Hall b- William McKee min- John Brown- 22Jan1789
Templeton
  Alexander & Nancy G Dunlap 25 Nov 1824; min- William W Calhoun
Tennant
  John & Catherine Greiner 13 Jan 1790; widow
Terrell
  J & E Ralston 21 Jan 1836; min- Robert M Lipscomb
Terrill
  Richard & Sarah Reed 2 Jul 1818; min- William King
  Robert & Susan Foutz 31 Mar 1832; min- James C Wilson
Terry
  James & Sarah Loyd 3 Jun 1819; min- William King
Teter
  John (Jr) & Margaret Kershe 5 Mar 1840; min- John J Reimensnyder
Tevenbough
  George & Nancy Mowry 26 Jun 1806; min- William King
Tharp
  Jacob & Nancy Anderson 26 Feb 1801; Minister's return spells name as 'Thorp' d William Anderson, dec. b- William Spence min- William King- 26Feb1801
Thomas
  Abraham & Rebecca Hollis 19 Nov 1835; min- Augustus Babb
  Charles & Polly Bratton 10 Jun 1805; min- William King
  Jacob & Mary Grim 17 Feb 1831; min- Francis McFarland
  Jacob & Elizabeth Hanger 18 Mar 1793; d Frederick b- Frederick Hanger
  John & Jenny Brobeck 12 Apr 1804; min- William King
  John & Susannah Dohine 15 Sep 1814; min- William King
Thompson
  Adam & ----- ----- 13 Mar 1762; license only
  Alexander & Lettice Bell 11 Oct 1790; widow, who gives own consent wit- John & Lina Workman b- Smith Thompson
  Alexander & Jane Thompson 24 May 1799; d Robert who consents test- John Thompson Jean above 21 b- William Blain
  Andrew & Polly Sharp 16 May 1809; min- William McPheeters

Augusta County Marriages -- Man's Name

Thompson (cont.)
  Charles B & Sarah Jane Moffett 5 Feb 1849; min- John Hendren
  John S & Phebe T Pilson 29 May 1838; min- A B McCorkle
  John & ----- ----- 1 May 1765; license only
  John & Jane Blackwood 3 Dec 1793; 'Jenny' d Samuel who consents test- Samuel Blackwood & Joseph Blackwood b- Peter Heiskell no minister listed; clerk's memorandum cites ceremony date as 10Dec1793
  John & Jane Knowles 21 Jun 1790; Minister's return spells name as 'Knowls' d James b- James Knowles min- William Wilson- 22Jun1790
  John & Sarah Miser 1 Sep 1840; min- Peter Shickel
  John & Martha Sawyers 21 Nov 1795; Minister's return spells name as 'Sawyer' d James Sawyers, dec. con- Hannah Sawyers, mother test- D Sawyers & Thomas Sawyers b- David Sawyers min- Archibald Scott- 25Nov1795
  John & Catharine Steele 1 Dec 1787; John from Rockbridge cty d Samuel who consents test- Samuel Steele & Robert Steele b- Robert Steele min- John Brown- 10Dec1787
  John & Elizabeth D Stover 5 Jan 1809; min- John McCue
  Joseph & Isabella Henderson 14 May 1793; d Jones Henderson Isabella born in 1766 b- Philip Dyer no minister listed; clerk's memorandum cites ceremony date as 23May1793
  Mathew & ----- ----- 20 Sep 1763; license only
  Mathew & Sarah Brook 17 Nov 1808; min- William McPheeters
  Matthew & Elizabeth Rutledge 7 Apr 1829; min- Conrad Speece
  Robert & ----- ----- 19 Feb 1759; license only
  Smith & Nancy McCullock 31 Jan 1809; min- Joel Watson
  William & ----- ----- - Jun 1761; license only
  William & Catherine Brooks 25 Oct 1803; min- John McCue
  William & Nancy Francis 26 Nov 1846; min- Francis McFarland
  William & Nancy McGuffin 15 Oct 1830; min- James Morrison
  William & Jane Vanlear 30 Aug 1826; min- John Hendren
  William & Sarah Wilson 29 Dec 1801; Minister's return spells name as 'Willson' d Joseph Mathew Malcolm attests to Sarah's age Jane Cawley attests to William's age b- Michael Cawley min- William King- 29Dec1801

Thornton
  Absalom & Ann Greever 21 Feb 1844; min- D F Bittle
  Coats & Mary King 6 Sep 1787; d Henry who consents (crest on his seal) test- Valentine Jones & John Chrism b- Anthony Mustoe & William Chambers min- James Chambers- 6Oct1787
  David & Mary Reiser 24 Jun 1834; min- Augustus Babb
  John & Nancy Walls 23 Feb 1809; min- William King
  Joseph & Agatha Craig 19 Jan 1816; min- John McCue
  Mordecai & Margaret Hamp 24 Apr 1795; d Stophel who consents test- Jacob Olinger b- James Alderman
  Obediah & Sarah J Almenrode 24 Apr 1845; min- D F Bittle
  Samuel & Patsy Paine 24 Nov 1824; min- Josiah Cole- publication of banns

Augusta County Marriages -- Man's Name

Thorp
Robert & Nancy Pannel 5 Mar 1798; Nancy (of age) b- Samuel Moses
Samuel & Elizabeth Connally 5 Dec 1798; d Thomas Connally, dec. James Patterson swears that Elizabeth is 21 b- Moses Thorp min- William Wilson- 13Dec1798

Throp
Samuel & Elizabeth Connely 13 Dec 1798; min- William Wilson- 13Dec1798

Thurman
Philip & Magdalina Trout 25 May 1825; min- William Wilson

Tiffany
Hugh & Anna Asherd 10 May 1785; widow b- Dennis Callaghan

Tinkle
Henry & Peggy Lamb 5 Nov 1813; min- G H Riemenschneider

Tisdale
Homer & Eliza Martin 17 Aug 1828; min- William Wilson
William & Mary Ann Mildred Small 23 Sep 1834; min- Joseph Spriggs

Todd
James & Catherine Syple 3 Sep 1812; min- William King
John & Sarah Sterrit 13 Aug 1800; d Robert who consents, sis to Charles Sterrett Sarah (of age) b- Charles Sterret (Stenett) min- John McCue- 14Aug1800
Samuel & Susannah Britton 16 Apr 1818; min- Wright Burgess
Samuel & Jane Davis 30 May 1834; min- John Hendren

Toeme
John & Elizabeth Jackson 17 May 1785; d Peter b- John Waddle wit- Thomas Brown & Samuel Blackley

Tole
Joseph & Ketty Krone 28 May 1815; min- Conrad Speece, Jr

Tomblinson
Henry & Polly Evans 21 Aug 1806; min- William King

Tomlinson
James & Madlin Fox 17 Oct 1801; Minister's return spells name as 'Maudline Fox' d Christopher b- Christopher Fox min- William King- 20Oct1801

Toole
Archibald & Barbery Fudge 9 Nov 1791; Minister's return spells name as 'Archibald Sole [Sale?] b- Jacob Peck min- William Wilson- 10Nov1791

Torbet
David & Ann Trimble 9 Sep 1799; d Robert who consents test- George Burwell b- John Evans
Nathaniel & Sarah Philips 3 Jun 1847; min- J C Hensell
Samuel & Jeny Anderson 8 Nov 1790; d Joseph, who consents wit- John Anderson & James Shields b- Hugh Torbet min- Archibald Scott- 10Nov1790

Torbett
Hugh (Jr) & Mary Brawford 30 Jun 1795; Mary (of age) d Samuel Brawford, dec. sis to John Brafford b- Hugh Torbett Sr
Hugh (Jr) & Mary Shannon 4 Jul 1795; 'Mary Brawford?' min- Archibald Scott- 4Jul1795

Augusta County Marriages -- Man's Name

Towel
  John L & Frances P Eskridge 6 May 1836; min- John A Steele
Towell
  John & Sarah Ewing - Dec 1807; min- John Brown
Townsend
  John & Kesiah Tackett 17 Oct 1786; Minister's return spells name as 'Heizia Jacks' d Lewis b- Thomas Galford wit- Charles Hamilton & Solomon Townsend min- Samuel Shannon- 18Oct1786
  Solomon & Elizabeth Allen 8 Aug 1787; d Joshua who consents test- Peter Sanders & Samuel Tompson b- James Townsend min- Archibald Scott- 8Aug1787
Trainer
  James & Sarah Spencer 1 Dec 1825; min- William Wilson
Trainum
  David & Sophronia Bear 24 Oct 1848; min- J McKendree Reiley
Travis
  John & Elizabeth Oliver 11 Aug 1792; d John who consents wit- Sarah Hering b- Leonard Herron
  John & Margaret Ann Trimble 20 Jan 1825; min- William W Calhoun
Trayer
  Daniel & Jane Knowles 20 Dec 1804; min- William King
  William & Nancy E Smith 26 Dec 1827; min- William C. Morrison
Trencher
  Isaac & Margaret McColmick 6 Dec 1785; min- John Brown- 6Dec1785
Trent
  John & Frances Garrison - Sep 1817; min- John Brown
Trimble
  Charles & Sarah Hoover 19 Oct 1830; min- William Calhoon
  Elijah & Jane Bowman 14 Sep 1820; min- William Calhoon
  George & Jane Armstrong 2 Oct 1792; d William b- William Armstrong no minister listed; clerk's memorandum cites ceremony date as 4Oct1792
  James W & Isabella E C Sterrett 9 Nov 1846; min- W W Trimble
  James & ----- ----- 29 Mar 1773; license only
  James & Peggy Wilson 20 Nov 1806; min- William Calhoon
  John (Jr) & Mary Depriest 15 Dec 1794; b- John Trimble Sr
  Moses & Mary Brawley 9 Apr 1793; Mary (of age) b- Patrick Shannon no minister listed; clerk's memorandum cites ceremony date as 9Apr1793
Trobaugh
  George & Barbara Hafner 24 Dec 1801; min- William King- 24Dec1801
Trobough
  Jacob & Catherine Younger 7 Jul 1789; d Maria (German), who consents wit- John Snyder & James Turncuper & William Trobough
Trorobaugh
  George & Barbara Hafner 21 Dec 1801; Minister's return spells name as 'Trobaugh and Hepner' Barbara (of age) d Jacob b- Andrew Haffner min- William King- 24Dec1801

Augusta County Marriages -- Man's Name

Trotter
Archibald D & Eliza Wise 5 Jan 1843; min- A G Chenowith
Archibald & Jane Brown 31 Oct 1839; min- John A Van Lear
Christopher & Prepare McClintick 18 Aug 1786; Minister's
  return spells name as 'McClintock' b- William McClintock
  min- Archibald Scott- 24Aug1786
George & Sarah Scott 9 Jan 1787; b- James Scott min-
  Archibald Scott- 10Jan1787
Isaac & Esther McClure 7 Jul 1807; min- John McCue
Isaac & Catherine Patterson 1 Mar 1832; min- William Wilson
James & Mary Beard 29 Jul 1794; d William who consents
  test- Joseph Beard b- Joseph Beard, James McNutt & John
  Allen min- John Brown- 1Aug1794
James & Martha Bell 7 Jun 1810; min- William Wilson
Richard & Nancy Strain 27 --- 1790; widow b- Daniel Early
William & ----- ----- 16 Sep 1771; license only

Trout
David & Rebecca Blair 14 Jan 1841; min- Wesley H Rohr
David & Susannah Witsel 29 Sep 1787; b- Valentine Forbes
Nicholas K & Matilda K Stribling 8 Jun 1843; min- F D
  Goodwin
Solomon & Hanna Miller 30 Aug 1825; min- William Wilson

Troxall
Abraham & Jane Reed 22 Sep 1812; min- William King

Troxel
David & Anne Miller 10 Dec 1816; min- Conrad Speece, Jr

Troxell
John & Catharine Troxell 25 Apr 1839; min- John C Hensell
Robert & Nancy Cunningham 27 Oct 1831; min- John Howell

Trump
Jacob & Christina Powlas 12 Oct 1799; d Nicholas con-
  George Trump, father of Jacob & Johann test- Samuel Curry
  Jacob (of age) b- Nicholas Powlas min- William King-
  17Oct1799

Tucker
Nathaniel B & Mary Coalter 9 Feb 1809; min- William
  McPheeters

Turk
James & Elizabeth Armstrong 7 Jul 1800; d William
  Armstrong, dec. b- Patrick William Shields Jr min- John
  McCue- 8Jul1800
Rudolph & Ann E Robertson 1 Dec 1842; min- A G Chenowith
Thomas & Elizabeth Barnhart 27 Dec 1832; min- Conrad Speece

Turner
David & Catharine Gregory 8 Feb 1816; min- William King
Elijah & Catherine Peyatt 4 Apr 1830; min- John Hendren
John & E C Baldwin 25 Mar 1833; min- James Kerr-
  publication of banns
Robert & Mary Thompson 5 Mar 1787; b- Andrew Lackey
  (Lenkey?) min- William Wilson- 5Mar1787

Turnipseed
Daniel & Catharine Peters 1 Nov 1816; min- William King
Henry & Elizabeth Deeds 9 Dec 1811; d George min- John
  Bell

Augusta County Marriages -- Man's Name

Tuttle
  Abner & Martha Palmer 17 Jun 1796; Martha (of age) d William Palmer, dec. b- Patterson Thompson min- John McCue- 22Jun1796
  James & Nancy Scribner 2 Aug 1817; min- Wright Burgess
Tutwiler
  Henry & Margaret Lashbaugh 23 Jul 1792; b- Joseph Campbell
Tweedy
  James & Hannah Scott 6 Mar 1806; min- William King
Tyerie
  Alfred & Margaret Ann Scott 12 Sep 1846; free persons of color min- William Calhoon
Ulery
  John & Susana Kerr - Nov 1825; min- John Brown
Ulrick
  John & Sarah Klutz 31 Jan 1817; min- G H Riemenschneider- 1Feb1817
Usher
  James & Catherine Whiteside 6 Dec 1788; d John who consents test- John Whitesides & Alexander Henry b- James Megongal min- James Chambers- 8Dec1788
Ustler
  Madison & Sarah Smith 28 Jan 1844; min- T T Castleman
Utsler
  ----- & Elizabeth Cline 25 Feb 1831; min- Abraham Garber- publication of banns
Utz
  George & Jane H Newton 21 Mar 1833; min- Francis McFarland
Vance
  Samuel & ----- ----- 4 May 1763; license only
  Silas & Barbara Karicofe 27 Jun 1839; min- John A Van Lear
Vanfosen
  Jacob & Sally Lambert 3 Apr 1806; min- William King
Vanfossen
  John & Jane Lambert 19 Feb 1829; min- John Hendren
Vanlear
  Jacob & Nancy Agness Hall 2 Mar 1796; d John b- Andrew Allison min- William Wilson- 3Mar1796
  Jacob & Jane B Tate 27 Jan 1814; min- John D Ewin
  John A & Jane A Bell 2 Nov 1826; min- Conrad Speece
  John H & Jane R Blair 9 Dec 1819; min- Conrad Speece
  Robert & Margaret Ann Mowry 3 Mar 1831; min- Conrad Speece
  William & Letitia Black 28 Nov 1844; min- B M Smith
  William & Elizabeth E Gresham 4 Oct 1827; min- Conrad Speece
Vanosdal
  Cornelius & Jane Wilson 11 Apr 1785; min- Samuel Shannon- 11Apr1785
Vanosdale
  Cornelius & Jane Wilson 2 Apr 1785; Minister's return spells name as 'Vanosdal' d William s of Cornelius b- Elibabb Wilson wit- Ralph & Elibab Wilson min- John Rodgers- 11Apr1785

Augusta County Marriages -- Man's Name

Vanpelt
John & Cordelia H Rankin 18 May 1836; min- William A Coffin
Vansical
Henry & Barbara Myers 24 Feb 1802; min- William King- 24Feb1802
Vanstaven
William & Melinda Walton 5 Feb 1822; min- William W Calhoun
Varley
Samuel & Mary Weaver 28 Mar 1796; d Peter who consents test- Andrew Weaver & John Waid b- Jacob Worley
Varner
Samuel & ----- ----- - Nov 1767; license only
Vaughn
Floyd J & Mary Ann Morrison 17 Aug 1848; min- W T Richardson
Venable
Abraham B & Caroline Britton 7 Jul 1836; min- B N Brown
Vernum
John & Elizabeth Mathews 28 Dec 1797; Minister's return spells name as 'Vernon' d John b- John Mathews min- Archibald Scott- 28Dec1797
Via
James & Pamely Walton 23 Dec 1823; min- William W Calhoun
Jonathan & Elizabeth Powell 16 Jan 1845; min- B M Smith
Vickers
Elias & Tabatha Staunly 25 Nov 1802; min- James Ward- 25Nov1802
Vigar
William A & Hetty Blakemore 26 Nov 1840; min- J A Van Lear
Vines
Abraham & Sarah P Beard 12 Jul 1836; min- B N Brown
John & Jane Brown 1 Mar 1810; min- William Wilson
Major & Margaret Newton 22 Sep 1831; min- Francis McFarland
Waddell
Addison & F A Douglass 4 Jan 1849; min- B M Smith
Jacob & Jane Jackson 19 Jul 1796; Jane (of age) b- Jacob Bumgarner
Livingston & Hannah Estill 8 Feb 1827; min- John Hendren
Waddle
Addison & Catherine Boys 15 Apr 1813; min- William Calhoon
James & Ann Stephenson 27 Jun 1786; d Adam b- Thomas Waddle wit- John Hair & William Stephenson min- Benjamin Erwin- 28Jun1786
John & Philpena Hemp 6 May 1788; b- Daniel Waddle
Wade
Alexander & Sophia Ann Almarode 29 Jun 1847; min- A P Ludden
George & Polly Brobeck 12 Mar 1819; min- William King
John & Peggy Bratton 1 Mar 1808; min- William King
Otho & Catherine Calahan 26 Mar 1788; d Charles, who gives bond
Robert & Catherine McFadden 16 Jan 1823; min- James Morrison
Scott & Jane Byers 27 Dec 1827; min- James Morrison

Augusta County Marriages -- Man's Name

Wadsworth
  Charles Wallace & Sally Callaghan 22 Nov 1797; d Dennis
    b- Alexander Wason
Wagey
  Jacob & Barbara Nebergall 17 Feb 1795; d Jacob b- Jacob
    Nebergall
Waggoner
  George & Elizabeth Delly 25 Jul 1791; d John who consents
    wit- John Snitzer & George Kaelen b- Jacob Balen
  George & Jenny McCannon 8 Nov 1809; min- William Wilson
  George & Polley Painter 30 Jun 1817; min- Wright Burgess
  John & Priscilla Litten 12 Apr 1827; min- William Wilson
  Peter & Margaret Messersmith 6 Apr 1802; min- Benjamin
    Irwin- 6Apr1802
Wagner
  Jacob & Catharine Bander - Nov 1804; min- John Brown
  Joseph & Agnes Jamison - Jan 1819; min- John Brown
Waid
  Isaiah & Susan Troxel 15 Aug 1833; min- John S Watt
  John & Dianah Cale 10 Aug 1837; min- J C Hensell
Waide
  Robert & Catharine M Firebaugh 11 Feb 1845; min- D F Bittle
Wakle
  George & Catherine Harman 1 Jul 1806; min- William King
Walker
  Alexander & Magdalene Hamer 22 Mar 1790; Minister's return
    spells name as 'Harner' b- Joshua Parry ('next friend?')
    min- William Wilson- 22Mar1790
  Alexander & Hannah Hinton 25 Nov 1819; min- Conrad Speece
  Andrew & Elizabeth McKinney 21 Oct 1786; d Alexander wit-
    Alexander McKinney s John wit- William Walker, Arthur
    Graham & William Bell
  David & Jane Holmes 25 Oct 1790; d Samuel, who consents
    wit- James Holmes & Robert Stuart b- John Gothry
  Edward & Catherine Kennedy 28 Feb 1798; Catherine (of age)
    Her parents do not live in Augusta cty b- Benjamin Gregory
    min- John McCue- 1Mar1798
  Ezra & Mary Jane Smith 1 Nov 1832; Ezra from Kanawha cty
    min- Henry Ruffner
  James E & Matilda Henderson 29 Dec 1842; min- James Bunting
  James & Margaret Crawford 8 Aug 1832; min- Samuel Kennerly
  John & Sarah Connelly 8 Sep 1791; Minister's return spells
    name as 'Conaldly' d Arthur who consents wit- Thomas
    Connely & Samuel Frame b- John Connelly min- William
    Wilson- 8Sep1791
  Joseph & Grizzel McCoskey 14 Feb 1791; 'McCrosky' widow
    b- William McPheeters sent to clerk by Samuel Brown and
    dated 22Feb1791
  Robert & Polly Wonderlake 1 Dec 1821; min- Michael
    Meyerhoeffer
  Samuel & Jane Elizabeth Mayes 23 Aug 1838; min- James Paine
  Thomas & Anne Eliza Bourland 2 Dec 1830; min- William
    Wilson

Augusta County Marriages -- Man's Name

Wall
  George W & Eleanor B Eskridge 11 Jan 1820; min- Daniel Stephens

Wallace
  Andrew & Margaret Galbraith 1 Mar 1796; Minister's return spells name as 'Caldbreath' Margaret (of age) d Thomas Galbraith, dec., sis to Thomas Galbreath b- Thomas Galbreath (Colbreath?) 3Mar1796
  James & ----- ----- 21 May 1765; license only
  James & Catherine Newman 23 Jan 1810; min- William Calhoon
  John & Elizabeth Smith 26 Oct 1815; min- John McCue
  Moses & Elizabeth Kerr 2 Jan 1819; bond- 4Jan1819(sic) min- John D Ewin
  Reuben & Annis Lamb 5 Apr 1803; min- James Ward
  Richard & Sarah Christian 11 Oct 1831; min- John S Hall
  Richard & Lavinia Lobban 15 Apr 1817; min- John McCue
  Robert Tate & Caroline M M Humphreys 26 Jan 1832; min- Francis McFarland
  Samuel (Jr) & ----- ----- - Aug 1760; license only
  Samuel & ----- ----- 22 May 1764; license only
  Samuel & Mary Tate 15 Apr 1794; d Robert b- Robert Tate min- John Brown- 24Apr1794
  William & Mary Ellen Shields 30 Nov 1842; min- Francis McFarland

Walls
  James & Elizabeth Watkins 5 Jul 1791; d Christiana Louisa Kidd who consents, along with her guardian Daniel Kidd wit- George White & Mary White b- George White

Walsh
  Edward & Jane Bowman 11 Jun 1807; min- William King

Walters
  John & Jane Tally 1 Mar 1827; min- Conrad Speece

Walton
  John & Sarah Branaman 29 Dec 1842; min- William R Coursey
  Samuel D & Mary Davis 2 Apr 1834; min- George Hildt

Waltz
  Jacob & Winifred Peck 18 Apr 1797; Minister's return spells name as 'Jacob Woltz' b- Jacob Peck

Wandless
  Ralph & Crissey Nickoles 20 Sep 1788; Minister's return spells name as 'Nicolas' d Levan who consents test- Nicholas Doucy (Doncy?) & John White b- John Clayton & John Gorden min- John Brown- 30Sep1788

Wanlis
  Stephen & Catherine Gabhart 3 May 1788; d John Capeheart who consents test- Dorman Laflan, John Capeheart & Ralph Wanlis b- John Geabhart

Ward
  Daniel S & Sarah Ann Hogan 13 Dec 1837; min- John A Steele
  John H & Polly Mines 1 Jul 1819; min- Gerard Morgan
  William & ----- ----- 21 Nov 1761; license only

Wardlaw
  Andrew & Margaret Fulton 31 Jul 1792; d Mary who consents wit- James Fulton & Samuel Fulton b- Samuel Fulton no minister listed; clerk's memorandum cites ceremony date as 5Aug1792

Augusta County Marriages -- Man's Name

Wardlaw (cont.)
  Hugh & ----- ----- 22 Sep 1763; license only
Ware
  Samuel & Nancy Lutz 29 Aug 1839; min- Samuel Wagner
Warley
  John & Magdalena Acker 28 Mar 1796; d Henry Acker, dec.
    b- Daniel Piper
Warner
  William & Polly Halbert 8 Oct 1807; min- William King
Warren
  Uriah & Elizabeth Hampton 5 Aug 1804; min- William King
Warris
  William & Catherine Merrit 20 Jul 1809; min- William King
Wartsook
  Peter & Sally Evilsiser 14 Mar 1809; min- William King
Warwick
  John & ----- ----- 19 Mar 1771; license only
Waserman
  John & Anne Rush 20 Apr 1819; 'Bush?' min- William Calhoon
Washington
  Thomas & Julia Ann Diller 26 Mar 1842; min- Peter Shickel
Wason
  Alexander & Elizabeth Parry 17 Sep 1791; d Joshua who
    consents wit- David & John Parry b- Michael Garber Jr
    min- John Montgomery- 18Sep1791
  Mathew & Rebecca Clemons 22 Nov 1826; min- William Monroe
Waterman
  Asher & Sarah Lockhart 30 Aug 1787; min- John Montgomery-
    30Aug1787
Watkins
  Philip & ----- ----- 16 Nov 1762; license only
Watson
  James & Sarah Bowyer 30 Jun 1836; min- James C Wilson
Watts
  Ebenezer & Mary Adaline Cooper 1 Jan 1828; min- William
    Monroe
  John B & Rebecca Seawright 27 Aug 1834; min- William Wilson
Wayland
  Albert G & Jane L Moffett 7 Jan 1830; min- William Calhoon
  Edwin A & Jane Pearsen 1 Dec 1831; min- John Howell
  Joseph & Polly Rowland 17 May 1810; min- William Wilson
  Lewis & Elizabeth Link 29 Oct 1798; 'Betsey' d Mathias
    b- Mathias Link Sr min- William Wilson- 1Nov1798
Wayt
  John (Jr) & Margaret A Bell 25 May 1820; min- Conrad Speece
  John (Jr) & Sarah A Bell 2 Aug 1826; min- Conrad Speece
  John & Susanah Bell 21 Jun 1790; Minister's return spells
    name as 'John Wayte and Suckey Bell' d Joseph, who consents
    wit- James Bell & Kitty Kennerley b- Jacob Swoope min-
    William Wilson- 22Jun1790
Wead
  Benjamin F & Martha C Dalhouse 24 Jan 1850; min- William T
    Richardson

Augusta County Marriages -- Man's Name

Weathers
  George & Ann Lyburn Newman 18 Dec 1798; d Leroy b- Leroy Newman

Weaver
  Abraham & Sarah Weaver 3 May 1832; min- Henry Brown
  Adam & Elizabeth Fulwider 13 Feb 1840; min- John C Hansell
  Andrew & Rebecca Barley - --- 1794; Rebecca (of age) s Peter test- John Waid b- John Weaver
  George T & Sarah Jane Merritt 30 Sep 1840; min- John C Hensell- publication of banns
  Jacob & Rebecca Bosserman 12 May 1842; min- John C Hensell
  Jacob & Hannah Brosius 12 Mar 1807; min- William McPheeters
  John (Jr) & Rebecca Runkle 23 Nov 1841; min- John C Hensell
  John & Sally Hines 3 Mar 1812; min- William King
  Michael & Margaret Smiley 2 Aug 1848; min- George B Rimel

Webb
  Benjamin & Nancy Bailey 6 Nov 1799; 'Aney?' d Robert wit- Robert Jones b- Henry Swink min- William King- 8Nov1799
  Isaac & Mary Lemmon 15 Sep 1798; Minister's return spells name as 'Mary Lemmons' both of age b- George Compton min- William Wilson- 18Sep1798
  James & Mary Ott 29 Nov 1787; min- Archibald Scott- 29Nov1787
  Jeremiah & Catherine Ailshire 27 Mar 1804; min- William Wilson
  John C & Harriet H Peck 1 Oct 1845; min- G W Israel
  William & Elizabeth S Brown 20 Apr 1837; min- J C Hensell
  William & Catherine Shultz 25 Aug 1819; min- James Morrison

Weer
  John & Jane Sproul 17 Jun 1793; Minister's return spells name as 'Weir' d William who consents test- William Sproul Jr, James Clarck, & James Monce b- William Sproul min- John Brown- 22Jun1793

Wehn
  Henry & Mary Palina Schoue 26 May 1850; min- Z Loyd

Weigant
  Martin & Harriet Woolwine 21 Mar 1842; min- P E Stevenson

Weigle
  Philip & Ann Michael 17 Oct 1797; d Frederick b- George Weigle min- Benjamin Irvin- 31Oct1797

Weikle
  John & Catherine Shyrigh 12 Mar 1798; b- Michael Shyrigh (Schayra)

Weir
  Hugh & Jane S Steele 12 Jun 1834; min- John A Steele

Weirly
  Jacob & Mary Fulwider 1 Jun 1790; d Ulrick, who consents b- John Falwider

Weitzell
  Jacob & Polly Link 17 May 1824; min- Michael Meyerhoeffer
  Peter & Mary Pauff 25 Jul 1792; Minister's return spells name as 'Whitzell' d George Consent by George's son Charles b- Charles Pauff min- John McCue- 26Jul1792

Augusta County Marriages -- Man's Name

Weitzell (cont.)
  Samuel & Elizabeth Moyers 4 Dec 1810; min- John McCue
Welch
  George & Rebecca Fellers 12 Aug 1826; min- Michael Meyerhoeffer
  Henry & Mary T Allen 11 Dec 1823; min- Conrad Speece
  Henry & Betsey Cline 1 Jul 1819; min- Conrad Speece, Jr
  John & Elizabeth Crone 8 Dec 1814; min- William King
  Parkinson & Elizabeth Malcolm 28 Nov 1822; min- William Wilson Jr
Weles
  Thomas & Catrine White 29 Dec 1785; min- John Brown- 29Dec1785
Wenner
  John & Catharine Weast 26 Dec 1847; min- John Reubush
Weri
  Pisant & Jane Astal 22 Mar 1808; min- William King
West
  George & Mary Woodram 30 Aug 1787; Mary gives her own consent test- Joseph Bell & William Bell Jr b- James Lyle Jr
  John & Mary Slusher 30 May 1785; d Henry b- Philip Wolwine (signed in German) wit- Philipp Poman & Christian Bomgertner
Western
  Richard & Rachel Slaten 28 Oct 1816; min- William King
Weston
  Joseph & Elizabeth Slagle 22 Dec 1808; min- John McCue
Wetzel
  Henry & Mary C Staubus 5 Dec 1839; min- Jacob C Killian
Wheelbarger
  Samuel & Catharine Houff 4 Apr 1843; min- Samuel Wagner
Wheeler
  James & Elizabeth Whitesell 26 Dec 1839; min- Frederick D Goodwin
Wherley
  Benjamin & Eliza Kindig 10 Dec 1833; min- Augustus Babb
Whisler
  David & Ann Gochenour 17 May 1842; min- F D Goodwin
Whisman
  Daniel & Julia Fenton 13 Jan 1820; min- Gerard Morgan
  Peter & Francis M Keller 30 Dec 1847; min- George H Martin
  Philip & Mary Ann Cross 7 Jun 1830; min- Hezekiah Best
  Samuel & Nancy Dixon 3 Feb 1829; min- William Wilson
Whist
  James & Mary Sheets - Jun 1824; min- John Brown
Whitaker
  Charles & ----- ----- - Dec 1749; license only
White
  George & Polly Watkins 26 Feb 1791; Polly certifies her own age wit- John Martin & George White b- Smith Thompson
  Gordan & Anna Diddle 25 Jan 1790; Minister's return spells name as 'Gordon White and Ann Duddale' b- John Didel min- Samuel Carrick- 26Jan1790

Augusta County Marriages -- Man's Name

White (cont.)
  Horatio & Elizabeth Trout 15 Sep 1834; min- William Scull
  James N & Mary E Bagby 22 Jun 1848; min- J C Hensell
  James & Mary Campbell 8 Sep 1800; Mary (of age) d
    Alexander who consents test- Alexander Campbell & Andrew
    Campbell b- Alexander Campbell min- John McCue- 9Sep1800
  John & Anne Cooper 20 Mar 1817; min- William King
  Joseph & ----- ----- 2 Jun 1750; license only
  Levi & Patsy Grant 13 Nov 1820; min- Luke Collins
  Robert B & Margaret Donaghe 5 Jul 1843; min- P E Stevenson
  William & Fanny Ballard 11 Feb 1819; min- William King
  William & Eleanor Coalter 24 Jul 1806; min- John McCue
  William & Maria Ann Shelley 30 Jan 1845; min- G W Israel
  William & Frances E Sproul 5 Sep 1844; min- Francis
    McFarland
Whitesell
  Daniel & Barbary Miller 8 Dec 1812; min- Samuel Garber
  John H & Mary M Wright 8 Jun 1843; min- C Parkison
  John & Jane Dunn 10 Jun 1813; min- William King
  John & Sarah Jane Southard 10 Jul 1845; min- T T Castleman
Whitesides
  John & Sally Guiller 6 Jan 1803; min- John McCue
Whitlock
  Jordan & Nancy Eagle 23 Nov 1826; min- William Monroe
  Pleasants & Eliza Miller 24 Feb 1845; min- P Shickel
  Tandy & Susannah Kent 9 Oct 1822; min- William Wilson Jr
  William M & Elizabeth Murray 3 Apr 1831; min- Samuel
    Kennerly
Whitmore
  Christian & Sally Garber 3 Aug 1833; min- Abraham Garber-
    publication of banns
  David & Susannah Cup - Jan 1806; min- John Brown
  Jacob & Polly Cup 29 Dec 1801; d Marcus b- Marcus Cup
    min- John Brown
  Jacob & Polly Swank 18 Oct 1825; min- Michael Meyerhoeffer
  James & Elizabeth Good 14 Jul 1846; widow min- J A Van
    Lear
  Joseph M & Margaret E Cook 29 Oct 1846; min- Stephen
    Hildebrand
  Lewis & Sarah M Sillings 28 May 1846; min- James H Brown
  Samuel & Margaret B Huling 17 Aug 1848; min- J McKendree
    Reiley
  William & Mary Ann Blair 15 Mar 1848; min- Thomas F McClure
Whitsal
  George & Mary Hains 28 Oct 1816; min- Wright Burgess
Whitsel
  Abraham & Catharine Foglesang 24 Dec 1816; min- William
    King
Whitsell
  John P & Nancy Banes 18 Mar 1833; min- James C Wilson
Whitzel
  Benjamin H & Caroline Jackson Lowery 14 Mar 1850; min- J
    Killian
  Peter & Mary Tutwiler 18 Oct 1796; Minister's return
    spells name as 'Whitsel and Mary Fulwiler' d Leonard b-
    Leonard Tutwiler min- John McCue- 19Oct1796

Augusta County Marriages -- Man's Name

Wickle
  Daniel & Catherine Michael 31 May 1803; 'Susannah?' min- William King
  William & Jane Dunlap 16 Oct 1810; min- William King
Wiferd
  Anthoney & Mary Miller 21 Nov 1816; min- William King
Wikel
  George (Jr) & Madelina Michael 30 May 1796; d Frederick b- Frederick Michael
Wilds
  Jacob & Courtney Mood 19 Aug 1828; min- Conrad Speece
Wiles
  Conrad & Rebecka Armstrong 23 Dec 1794; Rebecka (of age) step-daughter of Martin Dixon b- Robert J Kinkead
Wiley
  Alexander & Margaret Callaghan 21 Mar 1786; Minister's return spells name as 'Calaghan' b- Charles Callaghan
  Thomas & Rebecca Harding 23 Jan 1790; b- Edward Harding min- Archibald Scott- 28Jan1790
  William & Anna Harding 7 Sep 1790; Minister's return spells name as 'Wildy and Anne Harding' sis Samuel perm- Esther Harding b- Samuel Harding min- Archibald Scott- 9Sep1790
Wilhelms
  John & Catharine Hanger 4 Jun 1833; min- Francis McFarland
Wilkerson
  Robert & Mary Worth 17 Dec 1793; b- James Brownlee
Will
  John H & Elizabeth A Whitmore 30 Oct 1846; min- Stephen Hildebrand
Willfong
  Henry & Mary Karahoof 26 Aug 1813; min- G H Riemenschneider
Williams
  Andrew J & Mary Ann Thacker 18 May 1843; min- C Parkison
  Benjamin & Susana Collins 17 Oct 1788; widow b- John Stuart min- William Wilson- 17Oct1788
  David & Polly Ruple 23 Jun 1803; min- William King
  Edward C & Mary Ann Welsh 16 Oct 1828; min- Basil Barry
  Elijah & Sally Fulton 4 May 1815; min- John McCue
  Frederick & Peachy Hearn 24 Jul 1822; min- Josiah Cole
  Hezekiah & Elenor Connell 6 Sep 1804; min- William King
  John & Sarah Adams 4 Aug 1791; Certificate that Sarah is of age
  John & Nancy Barker 20 Jul 1795; widow of John b- David Perkins min- John Montgomery- 1Aug1795
  Paschal D & Elizabeth Redner 24 Nov 1845; min- P Shickel
  Robert & ----- ----- 6 Jul 1765; license only
  Thomas & Betsey Robertson 28 Jan 1794; min- William Wilson- 28Jan1794
  William & Ann Lovingood 21 Jun 1785; d Harman b- Samuel Lovingood
Williamson
  Robert & Sarah StClair 21 Jun 1804; min- William Wilson

Augusta County Marriages -- Man's Name

Wills
  Alexander & Margaret Callaghan 4 Apr 1786; min- Samuel Shannon- 4Apr1786

Willson
  Daniel & Betsy Ann Eidson 4 Jan 1827; min- William W Calhoun
  Edward & Elizabeth McGuffin 7 Nov 1827; min- James Morrison
  James T W & Martha J Brown 29 May 1845; min- Francis McFarland
  James & Hetty S Montgomery 2 Dec 1833; min- James Kerr
  John P & Sally Blackwood 30 Oct 1837; min- A B McCorkle
  John & Sally Henry - Jan 1824; min- James Morrison
  Matthew (Jr) & Jane Poage 27 May 1824; min- Conrad Speece
  Thomas P & Hannah Miller 12 Jan 1827; min- John Hendren

Wilson
  Andrew J & Jane Eliza McGuffin 14 Sep 1842; min- James Paine
  Brydon & Rebecca Hamilton 16 Jul 1813; min- Thomas Bourne
  David & Phebe Crathers 30 Apr 1793; min- William Wilson- 30Apr1793
  David & Ellen McClure 15 Feb 1786; d Andrew s John (David over 21) b- William McKee wit- Alex McKiney, Josias McClure & Andrew Wilson
  David & Sarah Steele 17 May 1791; d Samuel who consents wit- John Steele b- John Steele marriage sent to clerk by Samuel Brown and dated 19May1791
  Elibabb & Hanah Hempenstall 22 Oct 1788; d Isaac who consents test- James Wilson & Moses Knap b- William Blagg
  George & ----- ----- - Feb 1749; license only
  George & Isabella Friel 28 Jun 1800; d Daniel Friel, dec. & Agness Friel who consents test- Maurice Friel b- John Trimble
  George & Margaret Wildes 26 Sep 1809; min- Joseph Reid
  George & Margaret Wilds 26 Sep 1809; min- Joseph Reid
  James & Margaret Brown 6 Dec 1827; min- William Calhoon
  James & Elizabeth Hempenstall 29 Mar 1785; min- Samuel Shannon- 29Mar1785
  James & Elizabeth Kenney 6 Apr 1819; min- Conrad Speece, Jr
  James & Debby Patterson 9 Apr 1806; min- William Wilson
  Jamison T & Margaret C Pitman 19 Jan 1843; min- James Bunting
  John & ----- ----- 5 Jul 1769; license only
  John & Sarah Alexander 5 Apr 1786; perm- Sarah herself b- Thomas Hughart wit- Peter Alexander min- Archibald Scott- 6Apr1786
  John & Susanna Craig 30 Sep 1816; min- John McCue
  John & Rebecca Donalson 9 Mar 1809; min- William Calhoon
  John & Martha A Ruff 5 Jun 1850; min- John Hendren
  John & Rachel Wilson 7 Mar 1786; d Robert b- Robert Wilson wit- Robert Wilson Jr & Thomas Wilson min- Archibald Scott- 9Mar1786
  John & Martha Woods 24 Jun 1817; min- John McCue
  Joseph & Rachel Bell 5 Apr 1843; min- S J Love
  Joseph & Salley Friel 28 Mar 1806; min- William Calhoon

Augusta County Marriages -- Man's Name

Wilson (cont.)
  Joseph & Susan E Seig 10 May 1838; min- D F Bittle
  Robert P & Louisa Hamrick 29 Apr 1849; min- William O Lauck
  Robert & ----- ----- 25 Nov 1763; license only
  Robert & Elenor Blackwood 1 Nov 1804; min- John McCue
  Robert & Mary Thompson 8 Jun 1799; d William who consents Mary sis to Matthew and of age b- Matthew Thompson
  Samuel & Eleanor Alexander 26 Jun 1790; b- Hugh Alexander min- Archibald Scott- 1Jul1790
  Samuel & Joanna Hamilton 5 Aug 1813; min- Thomas Bourne
  Samuel & Phebe Tate 26 Oct 1809; min- William McPheeters
  Thomas & ----- ----- 7 Aug 1765; license only
  Thomas & Martha McCune 16 Dec 1801; d John b- John McCune min- John McCue- 16Dec1800
  Thomas & Elizabeth Poage 9 Oct 1826; min- William Wilson
  Thomas & Polly Poage 17 Sep 1792; 'Page?' d Thomas who consents & Agnes who consents wit- William P Skillern & J Cockran b- James Cockran no minister listed; clerk's memorandum cites ceremony date as 20Sep1792
  William (Jr) & Agness Livingston 3 Feb 1789; Minister's return spells name as 'Levingston' b- William Wilson Sr min- Archibald Scott- 5Feb1789
  William & Patience K Brown 23 Mar 1837; min- Isaac Jones
  William & Mary Dick 17 Dec 1793; Minister's return spells name as 'Doak' b- Samuel Dick min- John McCue- 23Dec1793
  William & Susannah McCullock 8 Oct 1812; min- William Calhoon
  William & Betsey McCutchen 21 Dec 1809; min- Joseph Reid
  William & Ann Parks 12 Feb 1802; min- William King- 12Feb1802
  William & Elizabeth Sharp 8 Apr 1795; d Daniel b- Daniel Sharp

Wily
  John & Nancy Lively 18 Dec 1806; min- William King

Wimer
  Philip & Sarah Simmon 31 Mar 1785; d Leonard & Catherine Simmon b- Nicholas Harper (signed in German), from South Branch

Wims
  Samuel & Jinny Patterson 16 Apr 1799; d James Samuel (of age) b- James Patterson

Windle
  Charles & Polly Dennison 1 Nov 1828; min- William Wilson
  Fielding & Nancy Kerr Young 12 Oct 1820; min- William Wilson

Windsor
  Paulus & Elizabeth Siron 26 Sep 1789; (Powells Winsor) b- ----- Millar

Wine
  Daniel & Sarah Miller 17 Oct 1844; min- T T Castleman
  George & Mary Campbell - Mar 1807; min- John Brown
  Jacob & Susanna Smith 2 May 1816; min- William King

Augusta County Marriages -- Man's Name

Winegar
  John & Catherine Hufman   13 Jun 1785; d Jacob b- Nicolas Spring wit- John Banks & William Winegar

Wines
  John & Polly Crumbaker   21 Oct 1815; min- Abraham Garber- publication of banns

Wise
  Adam (Jr) & Elizabeth Roles   17 May 1811; min- G H Riemenschneider
  Adam (Jr) & Amanda Staubus   31 Dec 1846; min- Henry Wetzel
  Adam & Elizabeth Sheetz   - May 1827; min- John Brown
  John & Mary Crawn   9 Jan 1840; min- John J Reimensnyder
  John & Catherine Hanger   12 Oct 1796; d Frederick who consents   b- Henry Harmon

Wiseman
  George & Susan Fix   14 May 1846; min- W G Campbell
  Jacob & Mary Swartzley   29 Dec 1794; d John b- John Swartzley
  John & Loisan Jane Bishop   - Sep 1842; min- D F Bittle- publication of banns
  John & Mary Ann Hollis   3 Nov 1842; min- Henry Wetzel
  John & Lucinda Murray   6 Jul 1824; min- Francis McFarland
  John & Sarah Zimbro   6 Dec 1827; min- James Morrison
  Lewis & Catherine Hull   8 Jan 1799; d Francis who consents Catherine over 25 b- George Dull
  Lewis & Margaret Palmer   9 Mar 1843; min- J C Hensell
  Peter & Sarah Ann Hollis   10 Nov 1836; min- J C Hensell

Witherow
  Samuel & Ellen P Wallace   13 Jun 1839; min- A B McCorkle

Withrow
  Andrew & Margaret McNutt   16 May 1833; min- James Morrison
  John & Sarah L Wright   29 May 1845; min- James Morrison

Witsal
  Anthony & Susannah Earhart   12 Aug 1793; min- John McCue- 12Aug1793

Witts
  Philip & Jemima Revercomb   30 Mar 1847; min- J A Van Lear
  William R & Eveline F Flinn   28 May 1846; min- J A Van Lear

Wolf
  Addison & Barbara Ann Shaver   16 Nov 1848; min Henry Wetzel
  John & Betsey Hapener   14 Oct 1802; min- William King- 14Oct1802
  Martin & Catherine Sharret   9 Jun 1791; d Daniel s Sebastian, who attests to his age b- Daniel Sharret

Woltz
  Jacob & ----- Winefield   18 Apr 1797; min- John McCue- 18Apr1797

Wolwine
  Philip & Elizabeth Harris   27 Apr 1797; Elizabeth (of age) s Elizabeth Wollwine who consents   test- Jacob Woolwin & Thomas Stevens b- Jacob Wolwine

Wombledorf
  Isaac & Mary Croft   23 Oct 1826; min- Michael Meyerhoeffer

Augusta County Marriages -- Man's Name

Wonderlick
David & Nancy Lahman 7 Jan 1816; min- G H Riemenschneider
John & Mary Ann Haffner 30 Apr 1846; min- Henry Wetzel
Philip & Elizabeth Lutz - Feb 1823; min- John Brown
Wood
Alfred P & Mary Koiner 19 May 1846; min- S Wagner
Elisha & Elizabeth Spencer 6 Mar 1823; min- Conrad Speece
George & Anny Beal 7 Jan 1814; min- William King
George & Jenny Curry 20 Jan 1791; min- William Wilson- 20Jan1791
George & Barbara Fry 19 Nov 1826; min- William Monroe
James S & D Brady 21 Dec 1838; min- Thomas Wheeler
Jesse & Nancy Kesterson 25 Feb 1808; min- William King
Joseph & Sarah Gipson 26 Mar 1843; min- Samuel Allenbaugh
Solomon & Rachel Crowbarger 11 Apr 1833; min- Francis McFarland
Stephen & Elizabeth Rhoades 24 Feb 1813; min- William King
Woodall
Thomas & Margaret Erwin 22 Sep 1800; d Edward Erwin, dec. (but Edward gives consent for his daughter Margaret to marry Thomas) test- John Ervine & James Ervine b- John Erwin
Wooddell
Benami & Lydia Michael 23 May 1839; min- John A Van Lear
Woodell
John & Elizabeth Erwin 30 Jan 1792; d Edward who consents wit- Edward Irvine Jr b- Edward Irvine min- Benjamin Irwin- 31Jan1792
Woods
Alexander & Hannah Thompson 7 Aug 1823; min- William W Calhoun
Archibald & Anne Poage 5 Mar 1789; Minister's return spells name as 'Major Archibald Woods' d Thomas, who consents wit- William Wilson b- Robert Poage min- William Wilson- 5Mar1789
George M & Susan Jane Davis 10 May 1848; min- W T Richardson
George & Margaret Ann Fitzpatrick 31 Oct 1830; min- Gerard Morgan
James & Polly Graham 2 Jan 1827; min- William Wilson
Joseph & Elizabeth Collins 5 Apr 1802; min- William King- 5Apr1802
Matthew & Nancy Yorkshire 11 Oct 1810; min- John McCue
Michael & Esther Caruthers 7 Aug 1795; Minister's return spells name as 'Caruthers' con- John Moffett test- Elinor Moffett & John Moffett Jr b- John Moffett Jr min- Archibald Scott- 13Aug1795
Richard & ----- ----- 13 Aug 1770; license only
Samuel & Frances Cason 15 Feb 1816; min- Wright Burgess
Woodward
Ephraim & Nancy Greiner 26 Aug 1817; min- William King
Ephraim & Lydia Sillings 15 Oct 1829; min- William Wilson
Joseph N & Alcinda J Doak 22 Oct 1840; min- James Paine
Luke & Sarah Silling 11 Aug 1828; min- William Wilson
Samuel & Polly Hanger 2 Dec 1819; min- William Wilson

Augusta County Marriages -- Man's Name

Woolard
  John H & Martha G Iseman 8 Feb 1844; min- Samuel Wagner
  Samuel & Elizabeth Giles 18 Feb 1831; min- Samuel Kennerly- publication of banns
Woventuery
  John & Susannah Potter 23 Dec 1806; min- William King
Wright
  Amos & Lavinia Hall 3 Feb 1827; min- William W Calhoun
  George & Nancy Brown 20 Dec 1796; d John b- John Brown min- Archibald Scott- 20Dec1796
  George & Mary Curry 14 Mar 1789; d William, who consents wit- Robert Curry & John Wright b- Robert Curry min- Benjamin Erwin- 18Mar1788
  James & Sarah Gilkeson 28 Sep 1813; min- William Calhoun
  James & Elizabeth Price 15 Feb 1841; min- D F Bittle
  John G & Hester Anne Beeton 28 Mar 1843; min- J C Hensell
  John G & Catharine P Hollaway 23 Mar 1831; min- John Hendren
  Joseph & Eliza J Orebaugh 6 Sep 1846; min- Henry Wetzel
  Joseph & Polly Thompson 26 Jan 1808; min- William Calhoon
  Robert & Rebecca Gardner 17 Jun 1819; min- William Calhoun
Wyan
  David & Mary Watson 3 Nov 1808; min- William McPheeters
Wykle
  David & Susanna Shaver 3 May 1825; min- G H Reimensnyder
Wyms
  Charles & Sally Allison 9 Aug 1810; min- William Wilson
Xaupi
  Joseph E & Frances Ann Mitchell 21 Aug 1833; min- George Hildt
Yager
  Henry & Ellen Spotts 29 Aug 1834; min- James C Wilson
Yancey
  Layton & Fannie Lewis 17 Dec 1788; min- James Chambers- 17Dec1788
Yarberry
  Asberry & Elizabeth Barbour 26 May 1828; min- William C. Morrison
Yates
  Enoch & Sally Wilson 20 Jan 1803; min- William King
  James & Mary Ann Ramsey 3 Sep 1830; min- William Wilson
Yeagly
  Henry & Margaret Snyder - Jan 1803; min- John Brown
Yeaky
  Jacob & Elizabeth Spitler 7 May 1818; min- William King
Yearour
  Charles & Elizabeth Teany 8 Apr 1813; min- William King
Yearout
  Abraham & Susanna Burkart 4 Oct 1794; min- William Wilson- 4Oct1794
  Charles & Anne Early 22 Oct 1802; 'Anne Yearly'? min- William Wilson- 22Oct1802
  Daniel & Elizabeth Hudson 27 Aug 1807; min- William King
  Isaac & Betsy Earley 14 Feb 1801; Betsy (of age) d Daniel who consents b- John Strain min- Daniel Garber- 17Feb1801

Augusta County Marriages -- Man's Name

Yearout (cont.)
Jacob & Nancy Pearson 11 Jan 1802; d George Pearson, dec. Abraham Yearout swears his brother Jacob of age b- Bartholomew Reagen min- William King- 14Jan1802

Yorkshire
John & Margaret Jackson 8 Jan 1808; min- William King

Yost
Charles & Sarah Switzer 26 Apr 1824; min- Michael Meyerhoeffer
Jacob & Esther Slusher 24 Oct 1805; min- William King
John & Christina Woland 3 Jun 1799; d ----- Woland, dec. b- Micajah Coalter min- William King- 6Jun1799
Samuel McPherson & Henrietta Cushing 9 May 1850; min- Thomas M Reese

Youel
John & Nancy McKnight 15 Dec 1808; min- Joseph Reid
John & Nancy McNight 15 Dec 1808; min- Joseph Reid

Youell
James G W & Nancy Gray 21 Feb 1833; min- Francis McFarland
James & Nancy Dunlap 22 Apr 1819; min- John D Ewin
William & Jane Berry 18 Jan 1816; min- John D Ewin

Young
Alexander A & Margaret Dennison 8 Mar 1832; min- Conrad Speece
Andrew & Margaret Garvin 29 Aug 1786; d John b- James Young min- William Wilson- 30Aug1786
Andrew & Margaret Glass 3 Nov 1797; d Isaac b- Isaac Glass min- William Wilson- 7Nov1797
George N & Sarah Hall - Sep 1829; min- William Wilson
James A & Sarah A Griffith 23 Jan 1845; min- John A Van Lear
James H & Mary Brown 28 Jan 1830; min- Conrad Speece
James & ----- ----- - Apr 1750; license only
James & ----- ----- 16 May 1764; license only
James & ----- ----- 19 Mar 1765; license only
James & Polly Burgess 25 Feb 1812; min- Christopher Frye
James & Jane Dickey 17 Feb 1801; Minister's return spells name as 'Deckey' d John b- John Dickey min- Daniel Garber- 17Feb1801
James & Nancy S Griffith 25 Mar 1850; min- John Hendren
John & ----- ----- 7 Sep 1763; license only
John & Ann Hanna 12 May 1814; min- William Calhoon
John & Mary Rankin 5 Sep 1785; b- James Rankin
Robert & Jane Curry 1 Mar 1819; Marriage bond states 'Robert Curry' min- John Hendren
Robert & Sarah Glenn 27 Feb 1792; Minister's return spells name as 'Sarah Green' d George b- William Glenn min- William Wilson- 28Feb1792
Robert & Martha Wallace 24 Feb 1801; Thomas Wallace swears Martha is of age b- Robert Anderson min- John McCue- 26Feb1801
Thomas & Rachel Blair 13 Feb 1807; min- William Wilson
Thomas & Mary Caldwell 7 Dec 1796; d William b- William Caldwell min- John McCue- 8Dec1796

Augusta County Marriages -- Man's Name

Young (cont.)
  Thomas & Rebecca Carson 14 Nov 1833; min- Conrad Speece
  William (Jr) & Rachel Ocheltree 7 Nov 1801; d Michael Ocheltree Sr who consents test- James Young & Michael Ocheltree signed 'Michl. Oughreltree Sr. b- William Young Sr min- William King- 11Nov1801
  William P & Margaret Young 13 Feb 1823; min- William W Calhoun
  William W & Hetty M Griffith 15 Oct 1840; min- John A Van Lear
  William & ----- ----- 11 May 1769; license only
  William & Eleanor Keenon 9 Apr 1787; Minister's return spells name as 'Keenan' Eleanor gives her own consent test- John Keenon & Hugh Keenon b- Alexander Nelson min- William Wilson- 12Apr1787
  William & Polly Trimble 14 Nov 1809; min- William Calhoon
  William & Susanna Young 5 Jan 1796; b- William Young Jr

Yount
  Martin & Nancy Myers 21 Apr 1831; min- William Wilson

Youtzler
  William & Catharine Smith 19 Nov 1840; min- J J Reimensnyder

Zahn
  Joseph & Elizabeth Shindler 14 Oct 1825; min- G H Reimensnyder

Zeller
  Jacob & Barbara Fudge 6 Oct 1794; d John b- John Fudge

Zimbro
  Adam & Mary Crist 6 Sep 1842; min- F D Goodwin
  John & Mary Bailey 27 Nov 1823; min- James Morrison
  William A & Margaret W Swink 24 Aug 1847; min- Francis McFarland

Zimmerman
  Christopher & Catharine Puffenbarger 27 Apr 1826; min- William Monroe
  Johannes & Henrietta Springer 5 Mar 1798; Minister's return spells name as 'John Simmons' Henrietta (of age) b- Baltzer King min- Archibald Scott- 8Mar1798
  Lawrence & Beck Woolf 4 Jun 1792; b- Christopher Zimmerman
  Martin & Sarah Grever 16 Nov 1822; min- Michael Meyerhoeffer

Zink
  Jacob & Catherine Turnins 18 Jun 1818; min- Wright Burgess

Zumbro
  Adam & Jane Wilson 28 Mar 1816; min- John McCue
  John & Polly Moore 5 Aug 1813; min- William King
  John & Frances Yancy 29 Oct 1840; min- Jacob Killian

Augusta County Marriages -- Woman's Name

----- -- ----- & ----- ----- 18 Feb 1794; Rev. Charles O'Neil marriage testimonial bond b- Sampson Mathews & William Forbes
----- & John Abney 10 Jul 1769; license only
----- & ----- Alexander 30 Nov 1772; license only
----- & James Alexander 11 Sep 1759; license only
----- & Hugh Allen 6 Nov 1765; license only
----- & Robert Allen 23 Apr 1762; license only
----- & James Anderson 2 Oct 1764; license only
----- & James Anderson 10 Dec 1771; license only
----- & John Anderson 4 Feb 1774; license only
----- & Robert Anderson 4 Nov 1765; license only
----- & William Anderson 21 May 1763; license only
----- & William Anderson 5 Sep 1774; license only
----- & Christopher Any 20 Mar 1764; license only
----- & James Arbuckle 11 Jan 1762; license only
----- & Charles Baskins 2 Oct 1765; license only
----- & James Baskins 28 Sep 1765; license only
----- & John Baskins 11 Jun 1765; license only
----- & William Bates 15 Jan 1765; license only
----- & Edward Beard 15 Apr 1751; license only
----- & John Beard 16 Jan 1769; license only
----- & James Bell 25 Aug 1759; license only
----- & William Bell 15 Jan 1765; license only
----- & William Black 6 Jan 1764; license only
----- & Joseph Blackwood 18 May 1762; license only
----- & James Bower 16 Aug 1763; license only
----- & John Bowyer 4 Feb 1754; license only
----- & William Bowyer - Aug 1761; license only
----- & Thomas (Jr) Bradshaw 20 Jul 1768; license only
----- & James Bratton 1 May 1754; license only
----- & James Bratton 16 May 1774; license only
----- & Robert Breckinridge - Jul 1758; license only
----- & William Breckinridge Jun 1797; b- Robert McDowell (remainder of bond blank)
----- & Samuel Brown 19 May 1774; license only
----- & Thomas Brown 27 Feb 1765; license only
----- & James Buchanan 23 Aug 1763; license only
----- & Patrick Buchanan 10 Apr 1770; license only
----- & Robert Buchanan - Jun 1761; license only
----- & David Caldwell 18 Nov 1761; license only
----- & John Campbell 8 Aug 1758; license only
----- & John Campbell 7 Sep 1764; license only
----- & Joseph Campbell 16 Apr 1770; license only
----- & Robert Campbell 13 Jun 1766; license only
----- & John Carlile 18 Feb 1762; license only
----- & John Cartmill 29 Jan 1763; license only
----- & Gilbert Christian 14 Jun 1763; license only
----- & Patrick Christian 20 Jun 1766; license only
----- & William Clark - Aug 1760; license only
----- & James Cloyd 20 Nov 1764; license only
----- & Michael Coger 6 Jun 1762; license only
----- & Michael Coulter 21 May 1763; license only

Augusta County Marriages -- Woman's Name

----- (cont.)
- ----- & Samuel Cowdon 25 Feb 1762; license only
- ----- & James Craig 18 Aug 1772; license only
- ----- & John Craig 3 Apr 1771; license only
- ----- & James Crawford 30 Oct 1762; license only
- ----- & William Crow - Apr 1761; license only
- ----- & James Cunningham 24 May 1765; license only
- ----- & Walter Cunningham 4 Jul 1774; license only
- ----- & James Curry 3 Apr 1772; license only
- ----- & Nenian Curry - Jul 1761; license only
- ----- & James Davis 21 Nov 1764; license only
- ----- & Thomas Davis - --- 179-; b- John Crookshank
- ----- & William Davis - Mar 1760; license only
- ----- & John Davison 16 Jan 1763; license only
- ----- & John Dean 26 Dec 1759; license only
- ----- & John Dickinson 7 Nov 1764; license only
- ----- & John Dickson 15 Jun 1763; license only
- ----- & Archibald Dixon 20 Aug 1772; license only
- ----- & Robert Doack 28 Mar 1774; license only
- ----- & David Doage 30 Oct 1762; license only
- ----- & Andrew Donnelly 10 Sep 1766; license only
- ----- & Adam Dunlap 29 Dec 1761; license only
- ----- & Nathaniel Dunlap 30 Sep 1765; license only
- ----- & William Dunlap 21 Feb 1772; license only
- ----- & John Dunlop - May 1761; license only
- ----- & Robert Edmiston 19 Jul 1765; license only
- ----- & James Edmondson - Mar 1749; license only
- ----- & Samuel Erwin 25 Jul 1770; license only
- ----- & Ben Estill - Oct 1764; license only
- ----- & Boyd Estill 16 Nov 1773; license only
- ----- & Solomon Estill 8 May 1773; license only
- ----- & Patrick Evans 28 Aug 1765; license only
- ----- & James Ewing - May 1761; license only
- ----- & Robert Farish - Apr 1760; license only
- ----- & William Fimster 21 Jun 1763; license only
- ----- & Robert Finla 19 Mar 1750; license only
- ----- & William Fleming 6 Apr 1763; license only (listed as 'William Fleming, Gent.')
- ----- & William Foster 14 Dec 1763; license only
- ----- & James Fowler 27 Jan 1764; license only
- ----- & George Francisco - Oct 1761; license only
- ----- & James Frazier 21 Mar 1765; license only
- ----- & John Frogg 16 Oct 1770; license only
- ----- & Henry Fuler 15 Apr 1751; license only
- ----- & Thomas Fulton 4 Apr 1751; license only
- ----- & William Fulton 2 Oct 1759; license only
- ----- & Alexander Galespy 19 Mar 1771; license only
- ----- & Joseph Gamwell 9 Dec 1768; license only
- ----- & Robert Gamwell 23 Aug 1764; license only
- ----- & Thomas Gaugh 1 Oct 1766; license only
- ----- & Robert Gibson 2 Oct 1769; license only
- ----- & Samuel Gibson 3 Jul 1772; license only
- ----- & William Givens 21 Mar 1764; license only
- ----- & Robert Gorrell 18 Aug 1762; license only

Augusta County Marriages -- Woman's Name

----- (cont.)
- ----- & James Graham   12 Feb 1763; license only
- ----- & John Graham   - Apr 1761;   license only
- ----- & Lanty Graham   22 Jun 1763; license only
- ----- & William Graham 24 Mar 1774; license only
- ----- & James Gray   23 May 1765; license only
- ----- & John Gray   26 Feb 1759; license only
- ----- & Alexander Greer 23 Sep 1773; license only
- ----- & John Griffin   30 Aug 1773; license only
- ----- & Alexander Guffy 28 Apr 1763; license only
- ----- & Robert Gwin   20 Feb 1765; license only
- ----- & Henry Hall   25 Feb 1771; license only
- ----- & Alexander Hamilton - Nov 1756; 6
- ----- & Audley Hamilton 18 May 1764; license only
- ----- & Gawin Hamilton 1 Nov 1773; license only
- ----- & Samuel Hamilton 7 Dec 1762; license only
- ----- & William Hamilton 29 May 1771; license only
- ----- & William Hamilton 21 May 1773; license only
- ----- & John Harbison 1 May 1765;   license only
- ----- & Jacob Harman   15 Jun 1751; license only
- ----- & Benjamin Harrison 8 Aug 1763; license only
- ----- & Daniel Harrison - Jul 1761; license only
- ----- & Daniel Harvey 17 Nov 1761; license only
- ----- & John Harvie   3 Jan 1772;   license only
- ----- & Hugh Hays   28 Apr 1763; license only
- ----- & John Head   27 Jul 1774; license only
- ----- & Amos Heaton   20 Nov 1764; license only
- ----- & John Henderson 30 Sep 1765; license only
- ----- & Joseph Henderson 24 Sep 1765; license only
- ---- & William Henderson 1 Apr 1765; license only
- ----- & Leonard Herron - Aug 1761; license only
- ----- & Thomas Hicklin 10 May 1765; license only
- ----- & William Hides 8 Mar 1764;   license only
- ----- & James Hill   25 Mar 1762; license only
- ----- & Michael Hogshead - Nov 1759; license only
- ----- & John Howard   - Oct 1764;   license only
- ----- & Thomas Hugart - Mar 1761;   license only
- ----- & James Huston   - Mar 1749;   license only
- ----- & John Hutcheson 25 Jun 1774; license only
- ----- & Thomas Hutcheson - Apr 1761; license only
- ----- & John Jones   - Feb 1749;   license only
- ----- & Mathew Kenny   3 Oct 1770;   license only
- ----- & James Kerr   13 Jan 1762; license only
- ----- & James Kerr   17 Feb 1764; license only
- ----- & Samuel Kilpatrick 23 Jan 1770; license only
- ----- & Henry King   6 Jul 1768;   license only
- ----- & Robert King   18 Nov 1773; license only
- ----- & John Kirtley   10 Feb 1774; license only
- ----- & David Laird   22 Sep 1763; license only
- ----- & James (Jr) Laird 28 Aug 1769; license only
- ----- & Ralph Laverty 20 Nov 1764; license only
- ----- & Samuel Lawrence 24 Dec 1762; license only
- ----- & Martin Lea   - Jun 1785;   b- Robert McChesney
- ----- & John Van Lear 27 Nov 1772; license only

Augusta County Marriages -- Woman's Name

----- (cont.)
- ----- & Andrew Leeper 4 Sep 1751; license only
- ----- & Charles Lewis 19 Jun 1762; license only
- ----- & David Lewis - Nov 1759; license only
- ----- & John Lewis 12 Mar 1772; license only
- ----- & John Lewis 2 Feb 1773; license only
- ----- & Abraham Lincoln 9 Jun 1770; license only
- ----- & James Littlepage 14 Jul 1759; license only
- ----- & Patrick Lockhart 5 Dec 1770; license only
- ----- & Randall Lockhart - Sep 1760; license only
- ----- & William Lockhart - Jun 1761; license only
- ----- & Andrew Lockridge 6 Apr 1762; license only
- ----- & Edward Long 18 Jan 1762; license only
- ----- & Joseph Looney 25 Jun 1764; license only
- ----- & Samuel Love 3 Jul 1759; license only
- ----- & Robert Lusk 25 Feb 1764; license only
- ----- & John Lyle 29 Dec 1762; license only
- ----- & John Lyle 19 May 1774; license only
- ----- & Nathaniel Lyon 29 Oct 1760; license only
- ----- & Patrick Martin 13 Dec 1762; license only (signed as 'Pat. Martin, Gent.'
- ----- & George Mathews 13 Sep 1762; license only
- ----- & Joshua Mathews - May 1750; license only
- ----- & Sampson Mathews - Sep 1759; license only
- ----- & William Mathews 28 Nov 1763; license only
- ----- & Richard Mays - Sep 1760; license only
- ----- & Joseph Maze 2 Jun 1750; license only
- ----- & James McAfee 25 Sep 1762; license only
- ----- & James McAfee 17 Sep 1765; license only
- ----- & William McBride 17 Oct 1765; license only
- ----- & John McClenachan 24 Jan 1770; license only
- ----- & Robert (Jr) McClenachan 15 May 1770; license only
- ----- & Thomas McClung 24 Jan 1765; license only
- ----- & James McClure 18 May 1773; license only
- ----- & William McClure 26 Dec 1769; license only
- ----- & Edward McCorgar 19 Nov 1763; license only
- ----- & Joshua McCormick 25 Sep 1765; license only
- ----- & Moses McCown 15 Jan 1765; license only
- ----- & John McCreery 20 Nov 1762; license only
- ----- & John McCreery 19 Mar 1771; license only
- ----- & Robert McCreery 21 Nov 1764; license only
- ----- & William McCutchen 2 Aug 1763; license only
- ----- & William McCutchen 10 Sep 1763; license only
- ----- & James McDowell - May 1760; license only
- ----- & John McElwrath 17 May 1763; license only
- ----- & Andrew McFarlane 26 May 1774; license only
- ----- & William McFeeters - Oct 1764; license only
- ----- & James McGaffock - Feb 1760; license only
- ----- & Edward McGarry - Jan 1760; license only
- ----- & Robert McGee 20 Jul 1765; license only
- ----- & John McGill - Feb 1749; license only
- ----- & Samuel McKee 6 Nov 1762; license only
- ----- & Robert McMahon 20 Jul 1758; license only
- ----- & Edward McMullen 16 May 1759; license only

Augusta County Marriages -- Woman's Name

----- (cont.)
- ----- & Samuel McMurtry 30 Sep 1762; license only
- ----- & William McNabb 19 Mar 1750; license only
- ----- & Patrick Miller - Aug 1756; license only
- ----- & Thomas Milsap 10 Sep 1751; license only
- ----- & John Mitchell 30 Apr 1765; license only
- ----- & William Mitchell 18 Feb 1765; license only
- ----- & George Moffett - Apr 1761; license only
- ----- & James Moffett 7 Feb 1762; license only
- ----- & John Moffett - May 1760; license only
- ----- & Robert Moffett 11 Jan 1763; license only
- ----- & John Montgomerie 22 Nov 1753; license only
- ----- & James Montgomery 19 Mar 1765; license only
- ----- & Joseph Montgomery 16 Nov 1762; license only
- ----- & James Moore 26 Aug 1763; license only
- ----- & Jesper Moore 30 Jul 1759; license only
- ----- & Moses Moore 18 Nov 1761; license only
- ----- & Sam Moore 15 Jul 1757; license only
- ----- & William Moore 19 Sep 1763; license only
- ----- & Richard Morris 17 Nov 1761; license only
- ----- & James Morrison 24 Mar 1763; license only
- ----- & Robert Murphy 18 Mar 1762; license only
- ----- & Henry Murray 19 Aug 1758; license only
- ----- & Thomas Nonyer 4 May 1762; license only
- ----- & William Oldham 11 Oct 1769; license only
- ----- & James Patterson 22 Jun 1759; license only
- ----- & James Patterson 23 May 1766; license only
- ----- & John Patterson 17 Feb 1762; license only
- ----- & John Patterson 3 Sep 1770; license only
- ----- & Robert Patterson - Mar 1761; license only
- ----- & John Patton 23 Mar 1754; license only
- ----- & William Paxton 19 Oct 1773; license only
- ----- & John Peerie - Sep 1760; license only
- ----- & Philip Phagan 20 Feb 1763; license only
- ----- & George Poage 23 Jul 1754; license only
- ----- & John Poage 3 Jun 1751; license only
- ----- & Thomas Poage 27 Apr 1762; license only
- ----- & William Poage 17 Apr 1762; license only
- ----- & James Pollock - Jul 1761; license only
- ----- & Thomas Posey 30 Nov 1772; license only
- ----- & Amos Potts 21 Aug 1765; license only
- ----- & Drury Puckett 4 May 1762; license only
- ----- & Thomas Rafferty 6 Jun 1762; license only
- ----- & Jeremiah Ragen - Oct 1764; license only
- ----- & Samuel Ralston 11 Sep 1766; license only
- ----- & William Ralston 1 Nov 1761; license only
- ----- & John Ramsey - Mar 1749; license only
- ----- & John Reaburn 16 Feb 1762; license only
- ----- & Alexander (Jr) Reed 24 Jan 1769; license only
- ----- & Robert Reed - Mar 1758; license only
- ----- & Robert Richey - Oct 1761; license only
- ----- & James Risk 31 Jan 1763; license only
- ----- & James Robertson 3 May 1762; license only
- ----- & James Robinson 21 Aug 1764; license only

Augusta County Marriages -- Woman's Name

----- (cont.)
- ----- & James Robinson 19 Mar 1765; license only
- ----- & John Robinson 6 May 1763; license only
- ----- & Joseph Robinson 8 Apr 1763; license only
- ----- & William Robinson 6 Jun 1762; license only
- ----- & James Rodgers 21 May 1766; license only
- ----- & Andrew Russell 25 May 1762; license only
- ----- & Sampson Sayers - Nov 1759; license only
- ----- & Richard Shankland - Dec 1759; license only
- ----- & Robert Shankland 21 Aug 1764; license only
- ----- & John Shanklin - Nov 1767; license only
- ----- & Thomas Shanklin 6 Nov 1765; license only
- ----- & George Skillern 2 May 1763; license only
- ----- & William Skillern 12 Apr 1763; license only
- ----- & Francis Smith - Aug 1761; license only
- ----- & Fred Smith 23 Mar 1754; license only
- ----- & Thomas Smith 14 Jul 1771; license only
- ----- & William Smith 11 Jul 1751; license only
- ----- & William Smith 14 Jul 1759; license only
- ----- & James Snodgrass 14 Jun 1764; license only
- ----- & William Sprowl - Aug 1757; license only
- ----- & William Sprowl 23 Jun 1773; license only
- ----- & Robert Stevenson 29 Apr 1768; license only
- ----- & Samuel Stevenson 22 May 1771; license only
- ----- & Thomas Stevenson - Sep 1760; license only
- ----- & James Stewart 20 Aug 1766; license only
- ----- & Robert Stuart 18 Aug 1762; license only
- ----- & Thomas Tate - Oct 1764; license only
- ----- & Daniel Taylor 17 Mar 1773; license only
- ----- & John Taylor 24 Jun 1766; license only
- ----- & William Tees 20 Jul 1762; license only
- ----- & Thomas Teese 24 Oct 1770; license only
- ----- & Adam Thompson 13 Mar 1762; license only
- ----- & John Thompson 1 May 1765; license only
- ----- & Mathew Thompson 20 Sep 1763; license only
- ----- & Robert Thompson 19 Feb 1759; license only
- ----- & William Thompson - Jun 1761; license only
- ----- & James Trimble 29 Mar 1773; license only
- ----- & William Trotter 16 Sep 1771; license only
- ----- & Samuel Vance 4 May 1763; license only
- ----- & Samuel Varner - Nov 1767; license only
- ----- & James Wallace 21 May 1765; license only
- ----- & Samuel (Jr) Wallace - Aug 1760; license only
- ----- & Samuel Wallace 22 May 1764; license only
- ----- & William Ward 21 Nov 1761; license only
- ----- & Hugh Wardlaw 22 Sep 1763; license only
- ----- & John Warwick 19 Mar 1771; license only
- ----- & Philip Watkins 16 Nov 1762; license only
- ----- & Charles Whitaker - Dec 1749; license only
- ----- & Joseph White 2 Jun 1750; license only
- ----- & Robert Williams 6 Jul 1765; license only
- ----- & George Wilson - Feb 1749; license only
- ----- & John Wilson 5 Jul 1769; license only
- ----- & Robert Wilson 25 Nov 1763; license only

Augusta County Marriages -- Woman's Name

----- (cont.)
- ----- & Thomas Wilson   7 Aug 1765;   license only
- ----- & Richard Woods   13 Aug 1770;   license only
- ----- & James Young   - Apr 1750;   license only
- ----- & James Young   16 May 1764;   license only
- ----- & James Young   19 Mar 1765;   license only
- ----- & John Young   7 Sep 1763;   license only
- ----- & William Young   11 May 1769;   license only
- Betsy & Frederick Grass   23 Aug 1785;   b- Nicholas Spring
- Diana & Michael Barnet   30 Dec 1786;   bond lists Diana as 'having no relation'

Abney
- Elizabeth & Bird Grill   5 Jan 1820;   min- William Calhoon
- Latitia & Adam Swink   4 Jan 1838;   min- John A Steele
- Margaret & Phillip North   29 Mar 1792;   d John, dec b- David Parry   min- John McCune- 29Mar1792
- Nancy & John Fackler   17 Jul 1798;   d John Abney, dec. b- Robert McClenachan
- Patsy & Peter Hog   18 Sep 1798;   d John Abney, dec. con- Isabella Abney   test- James Hog   b- Robert McClenachan   min- John Montgomery- 18Sep1798
- Sally & Robert McClenachan   4 Jul 1797;   d John Abney, dec. con- Isabella Abney   test- William Abney   b- John McDowell   min- John McCue- 4Jul1797

Acker
- Magdalena & John Warley   28 Mar 1796;   d Henry Acker, dec. b- Daniel Piper

Acord
- Catherine & John Beard   2 Oct 1817;   min- William King
- Elizabeth & Samuel Beard   17 Aug 1822;   min- John Hendren
- Lucy Ann & James Perry   27 Aug 1845;   min- P Shickel
- Nancy & John Fall   17 Mar 1818;   min- William King
- Rebecca & Jacob Smith   21 Dec 1826;   min- John A Gore

Adair
- Polly & Payton Shoemate   11 Feb 1808;   min- John McCue

Adams
- Anne & Mayo Carrington   28 Sep 1789;   Minister's return spells name as 'Carrigton'   b- John Hall   min- John Montgomery- 30Sep1789
- Hannah & Martin Loushback   31 Dec 1791;   b- Michael Fackler
- Margaret & John Bruffey   27 Apr 1785;   d Ann Edgecomb   bond
- Mary Ann & William P Burgentine   15 Jul 1841;   min- Alfred G Chenowith
- Sarah & John Williams   4 Aug 1791;   Certificate that Sarah is of age

Adkins
- Margaret & William Plecker   10 Aug 1845;   min- P Shickel

Aerion
- Ann & Peter Moyers   21 Mar 1850;   min- John Wine

Ailer
- Barbara & John Orbough   19 Dec 1816;   min- G H Riemenschneider
- Elizabeth & Joseph King   1 Oct 1811;   min- John Montgomery
- Mary & Lawrence Crown   3 Jan 1795;   Minister's return spells name as 'Ailor'   b- John Rapp   min- William Wilson- 6Jan1795

Augusta County Marriages -- Woman's Name

Ailor
  Catharine & Frederick Raidner 7 Sep 1817; min- G H Riemenschneider
  Elizabeth & John Rapp 1 Feb 1796; 'Ohler?' d Anthony who consents test- George Oehler b- Lawrence Crown min- William Wilson- 2Feb1796
  Eva & Frederick Karichoff 25 Mar 1823; min- G H Riemenschneider
  Molly & George Crone 1 May 1797; (Crown?) Molly (of age) d Anthony b- Lawrence Crone & Paul Hinckle
  Nancy & William Taylor 26 Oct 1821; min- John D Ewin
  Susan & Michael Orebough 12 Oct 1818; min- Wright Burgess- publication of banns

Ailshire
  Catherine & Jeremiah Webb 27 Mar 1804; min- William Wilson
  Nancy & Thomas Ralston 22 Mar 1810; min- William King

Aistrop
  Jane & James Holmes 22 Nov 1791; b- Philip North min- John McCune- 22Nov1791

Aldoffer
  Magdaline & Henry Dane 25 Jul 1793; min- William Wilson- 25Jul1793

Alexander
  Catharine M & William S Hunter 2 Mar 1848; min- Ro rt L Dabney
  Catharine & Abraham R Teabo 24 Oct 1841; min- Alfred G Chenowith
  Catherine & James Arbuckle 1 Jan 1798; d Andrew Alexander, dec. con- Martha Alexander, mother test- Andrew Hunter & Samuel Hunter Jr b- Samuel Hunter Sr James from Greenbrier cty min- John McCue- 2Jan1798
  Dorcas & Samuel (Jr) Pilson 17 Feb 1795; d James b- James Alexander min- John McCue- 19Feb1795
  Dorcus & Augustin Smith 17 Dec 1798; Dorcus (of age) d Francis Alexander, dec. Augustin (of age) b- Gabriel Alexander
  Eleanor & Samuel Wilson 26 Jun 1790; b- Hugh Alexander min- Archibald Scott- 1Jul1790
  Elizabeth & Samuel Caldwell 11 May 1813; min- John McCue
  Esther L & Andrew Johnson 21 Feb 1828; min- James Morrison
  Jennet & John Alexander 10 Mar 1790; b- Francis Alexander min- William Wilson- 11Mar1790
  Julia S & Cyrus S Larew 17 Dec 1839; min- James Paine
  Martha & Joseph B Scott 5 Feb 1833; min- James C Wilson
  Mary & Charles Campbell 7 Sep 1785; b- Hugh Campbell wit- Samuel McConkey & John Alexander d James min- Benjamin Erwin- 8Sep1785
  Nancy & William R Grass 25 Nov 1823; min- Conrad Speece
  Polly & Archibald Stuart 5 Dec 1805; min- John McCue
  Sarah & John Wilson 5 Apr 1786; perm- Sarah herself b- Thomas Hughart wit- Peter Alexander min- Archibald Scott- 6Apr1786

Augusta County Marriages -- Woman's Name

Alford
   Sally & John Prior 11 Oct 1796; widower & widow John Collins swear Sally of age b- Edmund Wills
Alfred
   Sarah B & Jamison D McGuffin 7 May 1833; min- Conrad Speece
Allbright
   Nancy & Benjamin Houff 10 Dec 1818; min- William King
Allen
   Anne & Robert Crawford 9 Jan 1787; b- Andrew Anderson certificate by William Craig min- William Wilson- 10Jan1788
   Anne & William McClaughlin 2 Jun 1794; 'McLauhgland?' d Ebenezer b- Ebenezer Allen no minister listed; clerk's memorandum cites ceremony date as 3Jun1794
   Betty & David McNair 8 Nov 1786; Minister's return spells name as 'McNare' (Elizabeth'?) d James b- Francis Allen wit- Francis Allen, Rebekah & Poley Allen min- William Wilson- 6Nov1786 (sic)
   Charlotte & John Bateman 19 Aug 1819; min- Wright Burgess
   Delilah & William Smith 28 Oct 1828; min- William C. Morrison
   Elizabeth & William Bateman 2 Jun 1813; min- William Wilson
   Elizabeth & Samuel Dinsmore 29 Aug 1799; d Ebenezer b- Ebenezer Allen min- William King- 27Aug1799
   Elizabeth & Solomon Townsend 8 Aug 1787; d Joshua who consents test- Peter Sanders & Samuel Tompson b- James Townsend min- Archibald Scott- 8Aug1787
   Harriet P & James W Miller 5 Nov 1846; min- Francis McFarland
   Margaret & John Ong 26 Mar 1812; min- William King
   Mary T & Henry Welch 11 Dec 1823; min- Conrad Speece
   Mary & John Hanger 4 Apr 1822; min- Conrad Speece
   Mary & Gabriel Hardwick 10 Jul 1821; min- Daniel Stephens
   Mary & John Miller 30 May 1809; widower min- William Wilson
   Nancy & Samuel Frame 27 Jun 1792; d James, who consents wit- James Allen b- James Allen Jr min- William Wilson- 29Jun1792
   Peggy & William Bell 17 Feb 1790; 'Margaret' d James, who consents b- James Allen wit- David Hanna & James Allen Jr min- Archibald Scott- 27Feb1790
   Peggy & William Poage 23 Jul 1811; min- William Wilson
   Rebecca & John Crawford 5 Jul 1791; d James, who consents wit- David Hanna & Daniel Early b- James Allen min- John McCune- 5Jul1791
   Rebecca & Fleming R Tally 6 Apr 1826; min- Conrad Speece
   Sally & James Bell 27 Apr 1796; 'Sarah' d James who consents test- James Allen & David Hannah b- Jacob Kinney min- William Wilson- 27Apr1796
   Sarah B & George Mays 13 Nov 1823; min- Conrad Speece
   Sarah & William Francis 22 Apr 1801; widower d Ebenezer b- Ebenezer Allen min- William King- 23Apr1801
Allison
   Catherine & Thomas Sawyers 5 Jun 1792; d Robert b- Robert Allison no minister listed; clerk's memorandum cites ceremony date as 9Jun1792

Augusta County Marriages -- Woman's Name

Allison (cont.)
  Darcus & John Mills 2 Sep 1811; min- Wright Burgess
  Elizabeth & John Roland 3 Jan 1809; min- William Wilson
  Fanny & Jonathan Eakle 14 Mar 1820; min- Conrad Speece
  Jane & James Brown 1 Mar 1821; min- Conrad Speece
  Jane & Henry Ralston 28 Sep 1835; min- James C Wilson
  Janet & Samuel Bell 31 Dec 1805; min- William Calhoon
  Mary & David Ross 17 May 1810; min- William Wilson
  Patsy & John Holmes 29 Dec 1828; min- William Wilson
  Phebe & John Early 18 Oct 1809; min- William Wilson
  Sally & Charles Wyms 9 Aug 1810; min- William Wilson

Almarode
  Sophia Ann & Alexander Wade 29 Jun 1847; min- A P Ludden

Almenrode
  Sarah J & Obediah Thornton 24 Apr 1845; min- D F Bittle

Almerode
  Eve & John Lotts 11 Mar 1799; d George who consents test- Richard Hollis b- John Sensebach

Almonroade
  Jane Amanda & Thomas Donoho 11 Sep 1845; min- J C Hensell

Almorode
  Elizabeth & Samuel Minnick 16 Mar 1802; min- William King- 16Mar1802

Alor
  Dianah & John Alexander 5 Feb 1835; min- Samuel Kennerly

Anderson
  Clara & Daniel Robertson 24 Dec 1822; min- Daniel Stephens
  Elizabeth & William Poage 19 Jun 1800; 'Betsey' d Andrew William (of age) and his father living b- William Poage min- William Wilson- 26Jun1800
  Isabella & Thomas Clarke 8 Apr 1828; min- William C. Morrison
  Jane & William Fisher 30 Sep 1817; min- Wright Burgess
  Jane & James Laird 15 Aug 1797; d Andrew b- Andrew Anderson min- William Wilson- 15Aug1797
  Jane & Robert Patterson 30 Jan 1786; d George b- Samuel Armstrong wit- George Anderson, William Brooks s John min- William Wilson- 30Jan1786
  Jeny & Samuel Torbet 8 Nov 1790; d Joseph, who consents wit- John Anderson & James Shields b- Hugh Torbet min- Archibald Scott- 10Nov1790
  Margaret & John McPheeters 22 Dec 1787; (Mary?) b- Robert Donaldson min- Archibald Scott- 25Dec1787
  Mary K & Greenberry Rhodes 3 Nov 1842; min- A G Chenowith
  Mary & Amos Crosby 20 Mar 1813; min- William King
  Mary & Jacob Detrick 21 Dec 1828; min- William Wilson
  Mary & George Glenn 11 Dec 1823; min- Conrad Speece
  Mary & William Lamey 26 Oct 1833; min- George Hildt
  Mary & William Spence 25 Jun 1793; Minister's return spells name as 'Polly Anderson' b- James Anderson min- William Wilson- 26May1793
  Nancy & Jacob Tharp 26 Feb 1801; Minister's return spells name as 'Thorp' d William Anderson, dec. b- William Spence min- William King- 26Feb1801

Augusta County Marriages -- Woman's Name

Anderson (cont.)
  Patsy & George Crosby 28 Dec 1824; min- Josiah Cole
  Polly & Charles Tyree H Brown 8 Jul 1808; min- William Wilson
  Rachel & James Shields 10 Mar 1786; d Joseph b- William Black wit- William Shields min- Archibald Scott- 10Mar1786
  Rebecca & James Curry 1 Jun 1826; min- John Hendren
  Rebecca & Hugh Glenn 13 Nov 1821; min- Conrad Speece
  Rebecca & William A Hanger 17 Jan 1820; min- John Hendren
  Sarah & John Fishburn 3 Jun 1819; min- William King
  Sarah & Jacob Ruff 7 Sep 1819; min- Conrad Speece, Jr

Andrew
  Elizabeth & Washington B Casidy 9 Nov 1845; min- J A Van Lear

Andrews
  Margaret & Jacob Shaffer 16 Jun 1791
  Mary & Christian Lohr 25 Sep 1795; d John who consents test- Mathias Semet & Alexander Scott b- Alexander Scott

Apple
  Betsey & Arthur Bigger 3 Aug 1826; min- Conrad Speece
  Betsey & John Reitenour 16 May 1816; min- William King
  Mary Margaret & Charles H Martin 15 Nov 1849; min- Francis McFarland
  Polly & John King 6 Jul 1820; min- Robert H Chapman

Appleby
  Jane & David Bell 27 May 1801; d Robert Appleby, dec., late of Frederick cty con- Margaret Appleby, mother, from Frederick test-Samuel Calvert & William Bawcutt b- James Edmonston

Arbocast
  Mary & James Mulnix 10 Apr 1785; min- Samuel Shannon- 4Apr1785

Arbuckle
  Martha M & Robert Steele 9 Jun 1829; min- Francis McFarland

Archdaton
  Elizabeth & Jacob Larew 12 Sep 1800; Minister's return spells name as 'Archdain' widow (of Michael Archdalon) Jacob a widower b- Enoch Fenton min- John McCue- 16Sep1800

Arehart
  Catharine & Henry Strickler 2 Jun 1841; min- John C Hensell- publication of banns
  Margaret & William B Spitler 9 Nov 1848; min- Alonzo P Ludden
  Rebecca & Joseph Andrew 9 May 1850; min- Henry Witzel

Arganbright
  Ann & Jacob Ruple 3 Jan 1833; min- William Calhoon

Argebright
  Mary & Nathaniel Long 15 Mar 1824; min- Michael Meyerhoeffer

Argenbright
  Catherine & Fleming Bailey 4 Dec 1834; min- Augustus Babb
  Catherine & George Behler 8 May 1797; 'Bailor?' d Augustine s Jacob and of age b- Augustine Argenbright
  Catherine & George Huffman 17 Aug 1799; Catherine (of age) d John b- John Argenbright

Augusta County Marriages -- Woman's Name

Argenbright (cont.)
  Elizabeth & William Creiner 14 Jan 1802; d Augustine b- John Argenbright
  Mary & Robert McClintick 27 Mar 1834; min- William Calhoon
  Sarah & William Brown 10 Jan 1827; min- John Hendren
  Sarah & Valentine Grever 8 Jan 1829; min- William Calhoon
  Susannah & Jacob Kise 10 Aug 1801; d John who consents test- Wilhem Gruender & Philip Griber b- George Kise

Armentrout
  Catherine & Samuel Johnston 6 Apr 1837; min- John J Reimensnyder

Armintrout
  Sarah & Adam Orebough 26 Jun 1834; min- Joseph Spriggs

Armontrout
  Peggy & George Fridley 4 Sep 1799; Minister's return spells name as 'Armentrot' wit- Will Loving min- William King- 4Sep1799

Armstrong
  Ann & Francis Huff 28 Oct 1824; min- William W Calhoun
  Elizabeth & Benjamin Funkhouser 13 Jul 1826; min- William W Calhoun
  Elizabeth & William Knowles 1 Apr 1841; min- D F Bittle
  Elizabeth & James Turk 7 Jul 1800; d William Armstrong, dec. b- Patrick William Shields Jr min- John McCue- 8Jul1800
  Eveline & Andrew J Acord 28 Mar 1845; min- D F Bittle
  Isabella & Thomas Armstrong 22 Jul 1786; d Archibald bond min- Samuel Carrick- 25Jul1786
  Jane & Samuel McCray 23 Dec 1793; d Archibald who consents test- John Brown & William Armstrong b- William Armstrong min- John Montgomery- 7Jan1794
  Jane & Benjamin Tallman 20 Aug 1833; min- John Hendren
  Jane & George Trimble 2 Oct 1792; d William b- William Armstrong no minister listed; clerk's memorandum cites ceremony date as 4Oct1792
  Margaret J & James Berry 25 Nov 1828; min- James Morrison
  Margaret & George Crosby 17 Jun 1847; min- Stephen Hildebrand
  Margaret & John McGlamery 18 Sep 1827; min- John Hendren
  Martha & William J Newcomb 22 Sep 1825; min- Conrad Speece
  Martha & George Swope 18 Nov 1837; min- John Hendren
  Matilda J & Bennami Armstrong 4 Jan 1849; min- John Bowen
  Nancy & Hugh Means 22 Oct 1785; d Robert b- William Chambers wit- Samuel Armstrong min- Archibald Scott- 26Oct1785
  Nancy & John Riddle 11 Nov 1823; min- John Hendren
  Peggy & James Buchanan 6 Sep 1827; min- William C. Morrison- date of ceremony not listed
  Polly & William Clayton 24 Mar 1818; min- William Calhoon
  Polly & Robert Stuart 23 Apr 1792; b- Robert Stuart Sr min- John Brown- 24Apr1792
  Rachael & Robert W McCutchen 17 Jun 1819; min- John D Ewin
  Rebecka & Conrad Wiles 23 Dec 1794; Rebecka (of age) step-daughter of Martin Dixon b- Robert J Kinkead

Augusta County Marriages -- Woman's Name

Armstrong (cont.)
  Salina & Robert Gray 18 Dec 1828; min- John Hendren
Ashby
  Matilda & Thomas Paul 27 Feb 1812; min- John McCue
Asherd
  Anna & Hugh Tiffany 10 May 1785; widow b- Dennis Callaghan
Askins
  Mary & George Fox 20 Mar 1793; Certificate both parties
    are of age b- John Weaver
Astal
  Jane & Pisant Weri 22 Mar 1808; min- William King
Aston
  Margaret & Daniel Murphy 7 ar 1801; d John b- John Aston
  Mary Ann & George Kirk 26 Dec 1801; d John b- John Aston
Attershall
  Rachel & Frederick Burkett 12 Oct 1786; Minister's return
    spells name as 'Ottershell' d Heinrich Atterschall bond
    min- William Wilson- 13Oct1786
Austin
  Amanda P & John M Fackler 19 Dec 1839; min- Frederick D
    Goodwin
  Betsy & William Harnest 25 Jan 1819; bond- 17Feb1819(sic)
    min- John D Ewin
  Lavenia & Napoleon B Kinsolving 1 Jan 1833; min- Francis
    McFarland
Aylor
  Margaret & David Link 28 May 1829; min- G H Reimensnyder
  Mary & Frederick Kirchkoff 27 Mar 1823; min- G H
    Reimensnyder- publication of banns
Bachelor
  Mary Ann & Alfred Howell 28 Aug 1849; min- John Hendren
Back
  Elizabeth & Charles D Porter 25 Jun 1842; min- Peter
    Shickel
Backenstoe
  Eliza & John Shibley 28 Jul 1823; min- James Sewell
Backley
  Elizabeth & George Russell 6 Apr 1835; min- John A Steele
Bagby
  Mary E & James N White 22 Jun 1848; min- J C Hensell
  Selina M & Hamden Dawson 27 May 1847; min- T T Castleman
Bailey
  Betsey & James Seldomridge 11 May 1826; min- John Hendren
  Mary & John Zimbro 27 Nov 1823; min- James Morrison
  Nancy & Benjamin Webb 6 Nov 1799; 'Aney?' d Robert wit-
    Robert Jones b- Henry Swink min- William King- 8Nov1799
  Sarah & Robert Shields 18 Aug 1812; min- William King
Bailor
  Barbara & Frederick Keller 6 Mar 1787; d Jacob who
    consents test- Samuel Merrit b- Jacob Bailor
  Barbara & Peter Rinehart 22 Dec 1797; d Jacob Behler b-
    Jacob Bailor
  Catherine & Benjamin Dill 9 Mar 1801; Minister's return
    spells name as 'Dile and Baylor' d Jacob b- Jacob Bailor
    min- William King- 12Mar1801

Augusta County Marriages -- Woman's Name

Baily
   Jane & Joseph McClung 13 Feb 1812; min- William King
Bains
   Matilda A & George T Kesterson 30 Jul 1840; min- Frederick D Goodwin
Baker
   Elizabeth & Henry Landes - Mar 1808; min- John Brown
   Elizabeth & George Ransbarger 4 Apr 1796; Minister's return spells name as 'Bambarger' Elizabeth (of age) d Philip Baker, dec. b- John Baker min- William Wilson- 7Apr1796
   Margaret & James Lyle 2 Jun 1789; b- William Lyle
   Susana & Henry Cup - Jan 1806; min- John Brown
Balard
   Martha & John Arisman - Sep 1835; min- Joshua Webb
Balbzell
   Ann & Alexander Drumgold 29 Nov 1809; min- William King
Baldwin
   E C & John Turner 25 Mar 1833; min- James Kerr- publication of banns
   Frances C & Alexander H H Stuart 1 Aug 1833; min- John S Watt
   Margaret E & Chapman J Stuart 21 Sep 1842; min- P E Stevenson
   Margaret S & Henry L Heiskell 11 Nov 1833; min- George Hildt
   Mary E & James M Ranson 1 Jul 1841; min- P E Stevenson
Ballar
   Hannah & Henry A McCormick 7 Jun 1821; 'Ballard?' min- William W Calhoun
Ballard
   Fanny & William White 11 Feb 1819; min- William King
   Patsey & Lewis Harris 6 Nov 1818; min- William King
   Polly & Henry Leddick 4 Apr 1805; min- William King
Balsley
   Elizabeth & Adam Fisher 17 Dec 1811; min- Wright Burgess
Baltzer
   Elizabeth & James Rogers 27 Dec 1827; min- William Wilson
Balzley
   Catherine & Samuel Nickey 30 Jan 1806; min- John McCue
Bander
   Catharine & Jacob Wagner - Nov 1804; min- John Brown
   Sophia & George Price - Aug 1802; min- John Brown
Banes
   Nancy & John P Whitsell 18 Mar 1833; min- James C Wilson
Barbour
   Elizabeth & Asberry Yarberry 26 May 1828; min- William C. Morrison
Bare
   Catherine & Henry Bare 19 Apr 1810; min- William Calhoon
   Elizabeth Ann & Peter Hanger 15 Sep 1834; min- John Hendren
   Elizabeth & John Gladwell 29 Jun 1848; min- Alonzo P Ludden
   Harriet & Alexander Hanger 12 Aug 1833; min- John Hendren

Augusta County Marriages -- Woman's Name

Barger
  Dorcas & Bernard A Garrison 2 Jan 1845; min- T T Castleman
  Elizabeth & John Eagle 26 Jul 1802; min- William Wilson- 26Jul1802
Barker
  Nancy & Henry Sligh 11 Feb 1808; min- William King
  Nancy & John Williams 20 Jul 1795; widow of John b- David Perkins min- John Montgomery- 1Aug1795
Barley
  Rebecca & Andrew Weaver - --- 1794; Rebecca (of age) s Peter test- John Waid b- John Weaver
Barnes
  Eliza & Isaac Golloday 14 Jun 1826; min- Michael Meyerhoeffer
Barnet
  Elizabeth & Thomas Conner 29 Apr 1813; min- Thomas Bourne
  Polly & George Barnhart 27 Jan 1807; min- John McCue
Barnett
  Martha & Daniel Moore 16 Oct 1792; Minister's return spells name as 'Burnett' b- Robert Bailey min- John Brown- 17Feb1793
  Polly & James Cooper 16 Mar 1813; min- William King
  Susan & Amos Martin 27 Aug 1833; min- William Calhoon
Barnhart
  Catharine & William Cullen 7 Nov 1816; min- John McCue
  Elizabeth & Thomas Turk 27 Dec 1832; min- Conrad Speece
  Susan & John Cullen 27 Jan 1814; min- Thomas Bourne
Barns
  Polly & Thomas Staunton 10 Oct 1800; Polly (of age) d of ----- Barns, dec. b- John Logan
Barrett
  Martha & Austin Martin 30 Jul 1835; min- J J Glossbrenner
Barrigar
  Susannah & Jacob Borrigar 15 Dec 1795; Minister's return spells name as 'Susanna Barriger (husband's surname missing) b- Martin Surface min- John McCue- date of ceremony missing
Barry
  Ann & John McCue 20 Apr 1813; min- John McCue
  Rebeckah & Abner Moor 26 Sep 1805; min- William King
Bartley
  Elizabeth B & Henry Rodenheizer 19 May 1840; min- A B McCorkle
  Isabella & Allen Patterson 18 Feb 1847; min- James Paine
Baskins
  Elizabeth M & William H Neal 28 Jun 1836; min- James C Wilson
  Isabella Hellena & William Graham 15 Mar 1788; s John who consents test- John Jamison & Joseph Russell b- Christopher Graham min- William Wilson- 20Mar1788
  Peggy & John Hamilton 12 Mar 1807; min- John McCue
Bateman
  Mary & Alonzo Mills 20 Mar 1845; min- S Wagner

Augusta County Marriages -- Woman's Name

Baties
  Sally & Edward John 20 Jan 1820; 'Batis' min- William Calhoon
Baylor
  Ann & George Slusher 21 Dec 1826; min- William Monroe
  Catharine & Abraham Leedy 1 May 1833; min- William Calhoon
  Catherine & John Sours 17 Nov 1814; min- William King
  Elizabeth & John Acord 20 Jun 1816; min- William Calhoon
  Sarah & Bailey Dunlap 1 Nov 1825; min- William W Calhoun
Baynes
  Susanna & Michael Loudermilk 25 Jul 1836; min- James C Wilson
Bazzle
  Elizabeth & Jacob Leonard 21 Oct 1828; min- William C. Morrison
Beal
  Anny & George Wood 7 Jan 1814; min- William King
Bealy
  Rachel & Francis Cox 23 Aug 1804; min- William Wilson
Beam
  Easter & Jacob Huff 12 Jan 1827; min- John A Gore
  Polly & John M Huff 21 Mar 1822; min- Daniel Stephens
Bear
  Ann & John Huffman 7 Aug 1810; min- William King
  Catherine & Madison Lemon 10 Jul 1827; min- Joseph Smith
  Hetty & Jacob Hanger 6 May 1833; min- William Calhoon
  Polly & David Holton 15 Nov 1804; min- John McCue
  Sophronia & David Trainum 24 Oct 1848; min- J McKendree Reiley
Beard
  Ann & Abraham Lawell 7 Jan 1817; 'Laywell?' min- William King
  Barbara & Michael Apple 16 Feb 1824; min- Francis McFarland
  Catharine & George Kellar - Apr 1822; min- John Brown
  Drucilla Jane & John Bear 13 Oct 1836; min- J C Hensell
  Elizabeth & William Mitchell 25 Feb 1801; d Thomas b- Thomas Beard
  Elizabeth & Frederick Rusmisle 6 Sep 1810; min- William King
  Jane & Robert Alexander 28 Jan 1796; min- Archibald Scott- 28Jan1796
  Janetta & William Sproul 28 Feb 1833; min- James Morrison
  Louisa & George W Baylor 2 Nov 1837; min- D F Bittle
  Margaret & George Smith 5 Oct 1831; min- Francis McFarland
  Martha & Robert Beard 10 Feb 1801; d Thomas b- Thomas Beard
  Mary Ann Eliza & Daniel (Jr) Hull 6 Sep 1832; min- Francis McFarland
  Mary & William Henderson 29 May 1787; d Edward b- Samuel Beard certificate that Mary 21 yrs old or upwards min- William Wilson- 24May1787
  Mary & James Trotter 29 Jul 1794; d William who consents test- Joseph Beard b- Joseph Beard, James McNutt & John Allen min- John Brown- 1Aug1794

Augusta County Marriages -- Woman's Name

Beard (cont.)
  Polly & James Loftus   22 Dec 1807; min- William Calhoon
  Sally & Jacob Red   22 Feb 1804; min- John McCue
  Sarah P & Abraham Vines   12 Jul 1836; min- B N Brown
  Susan R & James A Hall   16 Aug 1831; min- Francis McFarland
  Susan & William Chambers   8 May 1828; min- James Morrison
  Susannah & Joseph Danser   7 Dec 1811; min- G H Riemenschneider
  Susannah & Alexander Seawright   14 Feb 1822; min- James Morrison
Beasley
  Mariann & William Blair   5 Nov 1829; min- William Wilson
Beaty
  Nancy & Harvey Bell   11 Sep 1828; min- James Morrison
  Palina & David Fulwider   3 Feb 1848; min- J C Hensell
Beck
  Elizabeth & Henry Swink   30 Sep 1824; min- Thomas Caldwell
  Mary & Ralph Black   19 Jan 1838; min- John A Steele
Beery
  Catherine & John Andrew   28 Nov 1800; Minister's return spells name as 'Catherine Rury' d Philip b- Philip Peery ('Biry?') min- William King- 2Dec1800
Beeton
  Hester Anne & John G Wright   28 Mar 1843; min- J C Hensell
  Mary Gemima & William L Roberts   13 Feb 1838; min- J C Hensell
  Polly & Thomas Stevens   4 Sep 1797; widow d Robert Allison who consents test- Thomas Sawyers b- David Sawyers
Bell
  Eliza A & William Crawford   8 Mar 1832; min- William Calhoon
  Elizabeth & John Coffman   4 Feb 1806; min- John Bell
  Elizabeth & Bethuel Herring   11 Nov 1822; min- John Hendren
  Elizabeth & John Johnston   16 Sep 1794; 'Dr.' John Johnston d Joseph Bell, Gent. b- William Kennerly min- John Brown- 16Sep1794
  Elizabeth & Joseph Keiser   12 Apr 1808; min- John McCue
  Florence & George Elliott   28 Sep 1785; b- William Bell
  Jane A & John A Vanlear   2 Nov 1826; min- Conrad Speece
  Jane C & Mathew Arbuckle   18 Nov 1834; min- Conrad Speece
  Julia H & Alexander W Arbuckle   2 Dec 1833; min- Conrad Speece
  Lettice & Alexander Thompson   11 Oct 1790; widow, who gives own consent wit- John & Lina Workman b- Smith Thompson
  Lucinda & Isaac C Myers   15 Oct 1840; min- J J Reimensnyder
  Margaret A & John (Jr) Wayt   25 May 1820; min- Conrad Speece
  Margaret P & Ebenezer Christian   14 Aug 1834; min- John Hendren
  Margaret & John Crawford   21 Jan 1819; min- Conrad Speece, Jr
  Margaret & Moses Ralston   21 Feb 1805; min- William Wilson
  Martha K & Jonathan Golladay   2 Jun 1842; min- John C Hensell
  Martha & James Trotter   7 Jun 1810; min- William Wilson
  Mary & Addison Hyde   3 Sep 1812; min- John McCue

Augusta County Marriages -- Woman's Name

Bell (cont.)
  Mary & Archibald McCune 8 Nov 1792; d James b- James Bell min- John McCue- 4Dec1792
  Nancy C & George H Ervine 24 May 1849; min- John A Van Lear
  Nancy & Harvey Bear 2 Dec 1841; min- S J Love
  Nancy & Samuel Bell 20 Jun 1786; Agness? d Nancy bond min- Benjamin Erwin- 22Jun1786
  Nancy & John Brownlee 28 Oct 1819; min- William Calhoon
  Nancy & Zachariah J McChesney 23 Apr 1822; min- Conrad Speece
  Nancy & Isaac Scott 1 Sep 1790; d James, who consents wit- Josias Anderson & James Penmdleton b- James Pendleton min- Archibald Scott- 2Sep1790
  Nancy & William Sterritt 3 Feb 1800; Nancy (of age) d James Bell, dec, sis to William Bell b- William Bell
  Peggy & William McCutchen 4 Jun 1800; d Samuel who consents test- James Bell & John Bell b- Capt. John Bell min- William Wilson- 5Jun1800
  Polly R & Christian Landes 21 Jan 1830; min- Conrad Speece
  Rachel & Israel Patterson 18 Sep 1806; min- William Calhoon
  Rachel & Joseph Wilson 5 Apr 1843; min- S J Love
  Rebecca C & Benjamin S Reid 9 Dec 1830; min- Conrad Speece
  Rebecca G & Benjamin A Curry 21 Jan 1842; min- John A Van Lear
  Sally & Francis Bell 21 Apr 1795; d James, dec. b- Samuel Bell min- John Montgomery- 22Apr1795
  Sally & Robert Christian 18 May 1814; min- William Calhoon
  Sarah A & Davis A Kayser 24 May 1849; min- B M Smith
  Sarah A & John (Jr) Wayt 2 Aug 1826; min- Conrad Speece
  Sarah & Samuel Gardner 19 Feb 1790; d James, who consents b- Robert Bell wit- Robert Bell & Richard Denton min- Archibald Scott- 23Feb1790
  Sarah & Alexander Kerr 23 Nov 1795; d Samuel b- Samuel Bell min- William Wilson- 24Nov1795
  Sarah & James Pendleton 28 Jan 1788; d James b- Robert Bell min- William Wilson- 7Feb1788
  Susan C & Benjamin F Graham 26 Jul 1832; min- Francis McFarland
  Susan & James Craig 4 Jun 1816; min- Conrad Speece, Jr
  Susanah & John Wayt 21 Jun 1790; Minister's return spells name as 'John Wayte and Suckey Bell' d Joseph, who consents wit- James Bell & Kitty Kennerley b- Jacob Swoope min- William Wilson- 22Jun1790

Benson
  Jane & Frederick Almerode 22 Aug 1799; d William who consents and gives bond wit- Charles B Rhoades 'test as to Frederick- John Brown test as to Jane- Andrew Crawford b- John Lotz

Berkeley
  Lavinia H & Absalom Berkeley 4 Dec 1849; min- T T Castleman

Berrier
  Margaret & Gasper Coiner 24 May 1788; d Jacob wit- Samuel McCune & David Vence b- Samuel McCune

Augusta County Marriages -- Woman's Name

Berry
  Ann & John Brown 29 Sep 1841; min- John C Hensell
  Charlotte & John Berry 23 Oct 1823; min- James Morrison
  Charlotte & James McChesney 14 Nov 1797; widower d
    Charles Bery, dec. b- Robert Berry min- Archibald Scott-
    16Nov1797
  Jane Eveline & Robert Hannah 2 Aug 1829; min- Francis
    McFarland
  Jane & John Brawford 2 Dec 1788; d Charles b- John Berry
    min- Archibald Scott- 4Dec1788
  Jane & William Youell 18 Jan 1816; min- John D Ewin
  Mary G & John Harrison 15 Dec 1831; min- James Morrison
  Mary & James Henry 6 Dec 1787; d George who consents
    test- Thomas Freeman & Luis Wiseman b- John Berry min-
    Archibald Scott- 13Dec1787
  Polly & William Bratton 17 Dec 1812; min- I D Irwin
  Rachel & John Porter 21 Dec 1826; min- Alexander Templeton

Best
  Isabella & John Berry 15 Apr 1794; affidavit of John Berry
    that Isabella is over 21 b- James Best min- John McCue-
    17Apr1794
  Isabella & Jacob Clinginpeel 6 Feb 1837; min- James C
    Wilson
  Mary & John Linch 22 Aug 1795; Minister's return spells
    name as 'John Lynch and Mary Risk' b- James Best min- John
    McCue- 3Sep1795
  Nancy & David Doak 11 Feb 1812; min- John McCue

Bibee
  Polly & Johnathan Pickering 16 Sep 1806; min- William King

Biby
  Rebecca & Joseph Miller 1 Jul 1845; min- P Shickel

Bickerton
  Jane & Christopher Hardwick 1 Jun 1820; min- William Wilson

Bickle
  Mary & John Cooper 31 Jan 1801; widow b- Thomas Bell
    min- William King- 1Feb1801

Bilheimer
  Nancy & William Clarke 19 Jan 1832; min- John Howell-
    publication of banns

Billheimer
  Rachel & Jacob Pirkey 13 Aug 1833; min- James C Wilson

Bing
  Margaret & John Nolin 20 Nov 1792; Minister's return
    spells name as 'Mary Bing d John b- John Bing min-
    William Wilson- 22Nov1792

Bird
  Damaris & Nicholas Bookhamer 24 Feb 1845; min- T T
    Castleman
  Eliza & Abraham Michael 8 Aug 1837; min- J C Hensell-
    publication of banns
  Louisa & Peter Dull 15 Mar 1838; min- D F Bittle
  Margaret & Alexander Badger 16 Jul 1787; b- Alexander
    Thompson & William Shields min- Archibald Scott- 17Jul1787
  Sally & Adam Shields 16 Jan 1808; min- William McPheeters

Augusta County Marriages -- Woman's Name

Bird (cont.)
  Susan & Morgan Lamb 5 Mar 1846; min- Jacob Bear
Bishop
  Ann & Taylor Rice 28 Sep 1844; min- G W Israel
  Elizabeth C & Allen Johns 29 Oct 1846; min- William Calhoon
  Elizabeth T & Alexander McClung 12 Jan 1841; min- D F Bittle
  Loisan Jane & John Wiseman - Sep 1842; min- D F Bittle- publication of banns
  Mary L & George L Argenbright 16 Jun 1842; min- D F Bittle
  Mary & Harrison Hazelip 1 Jun 1842; min- F D Goodwin
Bitzell
  Susan & William Harris 24 Sep 1833; min- George Hildt
Black
  Agness & Simon Gillespy - Feb 1810; min- John McCue
  Eleanor & William Shields 4 Dec 1787; Minister's return spells name as 'Sheids' b- John Black min- Archibald Scott- 8Dec1787
  Hanah & John Seldomridge 24 Mar 1814; min- William King
  Jane & Alexander Martin 24 Jun 1788; d Henry who consents test- John Black b- John Johnston min- William Wilson- 25Jun1788
  Letitia & William Vanlear 28 Nov 1844; min- B M Smith
  Margaret & Samuel Bell 23 Sep 1816; min- John D Ewin
  Margaret & Jacob Cline 26 Jan 1790; widow b- Henry Fulwider
  Margaret & Samuel Guinn 29 Mar 1827; min- Alexander Templeton
  Margaret & John McCreery 19 Mar 1787; d William who consents test- John Montgomery & Alexander Black s of Robert who consents b- Charles Donally min- Samuel Shannon- 27Mar1787
  Margaret & Samuel Price 22 Jun 1797; widower d Samuel Black, dec. b- Samuel Black (Jr?) min- John McCue- 22Jun1797
  Margaret & John Roberts 17 Sep 1792; d Rebecca who consents wit- Joanes Henderson & John McCutchan b- Samuel Black no minister listed; clerk's memorandum cites ceremony date as 19Sep1792
  Mary M & William G Shultz 7 May 1840; min- John C Hansell
  Nancy & Thomas McCullock 23 Jun 1824; min- William W Calhoun
Blackamore
  Rebecah & James Brownlee 28 Sep 1796; widower & widow b- John Gates
  Rebecca & Henry Spearing 21 Sep 1796; widower & widow b- Adam Bickle
Blackburn
  Elizabeth & Jacob Shetz 9 Jun 1796; min- William Wilson- 9Jun1796
Blacker
  Elizabeth & Daniel Cupp - Jan 1807; min- John Brown
  Mary & George Snyder - May 1818; min- John Brown

Augusta County Marriages -- Woman's Name

Blackwell
  Jane & John Bowers 7 Sep 1843; min- J C Hensell
  Martha & Adam Propst 27 Aug 1835; min- J J Glossbrenner

Blackwood
  Elenor & Robert Wilson 1 Nov 1804; min- John McCue
  Jane & John Thompson 3 Dec 1793; 'Jenny' d Samuel who consents test- Samuel Blackwood & Joseph Blackwood b- Peter Heiskell no minister listed; clerk's memorandum cites ceremony date as 10Dec1793
  Margaret & William Allison 14 Jun 1790; Margaret gives own consent, stating she has no friends in these parts b- John Steven
  Mary & Robert Scott 29 Oct 1785; d Eleanor Haddan b- Mark Haddan min- Archibald Scott- 1Nov1785
  Rebecca & James Brown 11 May 1798; Rebecca (of age) d William Blackwood, dec. b- William Blackwood (sic) min- John McCue- 17May1798
  Sally & John P Willson 30 Oct 1837; min- A B McCorkle
  Sarah & John McAdams 27 Jun 1786; d Samuel b- William Willson wit- Robert Doneldson & I McClanahan min- Archibald Scott- 28Jun1786
  Tirza & Harry Lambert 29 Oct 1834; min- J Hoover

Blair
  Ann Eliza & James Blair 21 Aug 1828; min- Conrad Speece
  Ann & Michael Archdeacon 1 Oct 1807; min- William McPheeters
  Elizabeth & Joseph Byers 24 Sep 1791; Minister's return spells name as 'Buyers' d Jane, who consents b- Michael Hermon min- William Wilson- 7Oct1791
  Elizabeth & Robert Porter 20 Mar 1790; d John, who consents wit- William Young & John Bell b- John Gamble min- William Wilson- 20Mar1790
  Jane R & John H Vanlear 9 Dec 1819; min- Conrad Speece
  Jane & Henry Reaburn 22 Dec 1814; min- Conrad Speece, Jr
  Jean & Joseph Evans 4 Aug 1797; Jean (of age) d Joseph Blair, dec. b- Joseph Blair min- Archibald Scott- 8Aug1797
  Margaret & Jeremiah W Cullen 28 Mar 1835; min- William A Coffin
  Margaret & Francis Erwin 9 Mar 1801; d John sis to Mathew Blair Margaret (of age) b- Matthew Blair Francis signs as 'Irwin'
  Margaret & Absolem Johnston 8 Nov 1799; Margaret (of age) d W Blair Samuel King swears Margaret of age b- Robert Reed min- William King- 9Nov1799
  Martha & Miles Sims 13 Jul 1826; min- Francis McFarland
  Mary Ann & William Whitmore 15 Mar 1848; min- Thomas F McClure
  Mary & John Hedrick 29 Feb 1792; Minister's return spells name as 'Haduck' d William b- William Blair min- William Wilson- 1Mar1792
  Mary & William Long 23 Sep 1794; Mary gives own consent d James b- John Campbell William affirms he believes himself and Mary both over 21 min- John Brown- 24Sep1794 ('went to Roanoke'?)

Augusta County Marriages -- Woman's Name

Blair (cont.)
Rachel & Thomas Young 13 Feb 1807; min- William Wilson
Rebecca & David Trout 14 Jan 1841; min- Wesley H Rohr
Sally & Robert Griffith 19 Dec 1809; min- William King

Blakely
Agnes & Wilprey Bryant 30 Nov 1791; d Robert, who consents wit- Thomas Call & Lewis Sorrel b- Thomas Call (Caul)
Elizabeth & Joseph Byers 26 Jun 1795; Elizabeth 'Betsey' (of age) d of Thomas who consents b- William Breeze min- William Wilson- 9Jun1795

Blakemore
Catherine & John Beeton 26 Jun 1816; min- William Cravens
Easther & John Shepard 15 Nov 1821; min- Gerard Morgan
Hetty & William A Vigar 26 Nov 1840; min- J A Van Lear
Martha M & James T Clarke 28 Oct 1845; min- S Hildebrand
Mary Jane & Waller Oder 2 Mar 1835; min- William A Coffin
Sally & John Flinn 17 May 1814; min- William Cravens

Blakly
Mary & Garland Higgason - Dec 1817; min- John Brown

Bleaker
Catherine & Peter Etter 14 Jan 1802; d Peter Bleaker, dec. both of age b- John Sheetz

Bleakley
Jenny & George Hook 8 Jan 1789; min- William Wilson- 8Jan1789

Bleakly
Isabella & John Campbell 4 Nov 1789; Minister's return spells name as 'Bleackley' b- Thomas Bleakly min- William Wilson- 12Nov1789
Jane & George Hooke 7 Jan 1789; d Thomas, who consents b- John Campbell

Blear
Becky & Samuel Kirkland 11 Oct 1790; 'Blair' d John, who consents wit- James Black & Wm Johnston s James, who consents wit- Arthur & Thomas Connely b- William Johnston min- Archibald Scott- 12Oct1790

Bohannon
Milly & Burr Harris 18 Oct 1785; d James b- Philemon Bohannon wit- Charles Donnally

Boils
Elizabeth & John Moore 12 Dec 1805; min- William Wilson

Bollar
Susanna & James McCutchen 31 Aug 1803; min- Philip Kennerly

Bolls
Jane & Windle Grove 17 Apr 1806; min- William Calhoon

Bolton
Catherine & Abraham Huffman 18 Sep 1836; min- John Hendren

Boon
Mary & Daniel Murray 10 Oct 1843; min- S Filler

Boone
Anna & James Jordan 31 Dec 1839; min- John J Reimensnyder

Booz
Eliza Jane & John B Duval 20 Jan 1848; min- S Hildebrand

Augusta County Marriages -- Woman's Name

Borland
  Anne & John McClung 6 Dec 1804; min- William Wilson
Bosang
  Elizabeth & Robert Bailey 8 Mar 1792; b- William Scott no minister listed; clerk's memorandum cites ceremony date as 8Mar1792
Bosserman
  Barbara C & David C Arehart 3 Sep 1846; min- J C Hensell
  Elizabeth Ann & Henry N Camper 8 Oct 1834; min- J Hoover
  Mary Ann & John Shannon 31 Aug 1843; min- George H Martin
  Mary Jane & Jacob Holtz 27 May 1841; min- John C Hensell- publication of banns
  Rebecca & Jacob Weaver 12 May 1842; min- John C Hensell
  Sarah & John Almarode 6 Nov 1837; min- J C Hensell
  Sarah & Robert C Hall 31 Jan 1839; min- John C Hensell
  Susana Margaret & Henry Swatzel 12 Oct 1837; min- J C Hensell
Botkin
  Euphemia & William Botkin 29 Sep 1786; b- Andrew Jordan d John s James min- Samuel Shannon- 3Oct1786
  Isabella & William Botkin 1 Sep 1789; d Hugh, who consents wit- Richard Botkin & Alexander McQuain s of John, who consents wit- Andrew Jordan & Moses Knapp, who gives surety
  Jane & Richard Botkin 13 Aug 1789; d John Sr, who consents wit- William Botkin & Andrew Jordan Richard is son of Hugh
Botram
  Elizabeth & John Beal 27 Oct 1811; min- G H Riemenschneider
Bott
  Nancy & Nicholas Fulks 28 Sep 1790; b- Erasmus Jones, who made his mark because of a hurt arm
Bouler
  Patsey & John Houseright 25 Jun 1793; d James who consents (Patsey under age) test- J Brooks & Thomas Pannell b- Benjamin Pannell
Bourland
  Anne Eliza & Thomas Walker 2 Dec 1830; min- William Wilson
Bowen
  Frances & Henry Sisler 2 Nov 1848; min- John A Van Lear
  Margaret & Ephraim Orebaugh 7 Jul 1847; min- J A Van Lear
Bowers
  Edith J & George W Graham 14 Apr 1840; min- John J Reimensnyder
  Margaret & Michael Kanely - Jun 1803; min- John Brown
Bowls
  Catharine & David Grove 15 Feb 1844; min- T T Castleman- publication of banns
Bowman
  Ann & Jacob Acord 29 Mar 1821; min- William W Calhoun
  Betsy & Charles Collins 22 Dec 1814; min- William Wilson
  Catharine J & Charles H Street 9 Mar 1848; min- J C Hensell
  Elizabeth Ann & James Jackson 11 Sep 1845; min- W G Campbell
  Elizabeth & William Armstrong 15 Jun 1822; min- John Hendren

243

Augusta County Marriages -- Woman's Name

Bowman (cont.)
  Jane & Elijah Trimble 14 Sep 1820; min- William Calhoon
  Jane & Edward Walsh 11 Jun 1807; min- William King
  Margaret & Jeremiah Showalter 11 Mar 1841; min- J J Reimensnyder
  Mary E & William Glover 13 May 1847; min- J C Hensell
  Sally & Samuel N Bell 26 Dec 1822; min- James Morrison

Bowyer
  Mary & Leonard Israel Fleming 20 Jun 1787; d William who consents test- William Neeley b- Richard Mathews min- Archibald Scott- 21Jun1787
  Sarah & James Watson 30 Jun 1836; min- James C Wilson

Boyd
  Ann & John Shannon 30 Mar 1815; min- John McCue
  Cynthia & Joshua R Brooks 17 Feb 1834; min- James C Wilson
  Elizabeth & Robert Shaw 30 May 1799; widower & widow (of John) b- Michael Garber Sr
  Jane & William Hapener 19 Jun 1806; min- William King
  Nancy & James Brown 6 Feb 1827; widower min- Michael Meyerhoeffer
  Peggy & James Brown 9 Feb 1815; min- John McCue
  Polly & Joseph Harrison 18 Dec 1806; min- John McCue

Boyer
  Elizabeth & John New 10 Jun 1807; min- William King
  Rebecca & Theodore Taylor 5 May 1834; min- James C Wilson

Boyles
  Margaret & William Jackson 26 Mar 1785; d Thomas b- Benjamin Yardley

Boys
  Catherine & Addison Waddle 15 Apr 1813; min- William Calhoon

Braden
  Anny & John Buckley 17 Jun 1799; d Edward b- Edward Braden

Bradshaw
  Caroline J & Samuel H Tate 16 Jul 1846; min- Jacob C Spitler- publication of banns

Brady
  Cynthia & David C Braneman 18 Aug 1838; min- J Killian
  D & James S Wood 21 Dec 1838; min- Thomas Wheeler
  Elizabeth & Philip Heisey - Mar 1827; min- Joseph Smith
  Martha & John Clinedinst 21 Apr 1835; min- John A Steele

Brafford
  Rebecca & William Hall 11 Jun 1787; widow b- Robert McChesney min- Archibald Scott- 16Jun1787

Braford
  Ann & Samuel Miller 6 Jun 1786; Minister's return spells names 'Millar & Brawford' d Samuel b- John Braford min- Archibald Scott- 13Jun1786

Bragg
  Diana W & Samuel G Coleman 4 Nov 1824; min- Francis McFarland
  Eliza B & Williamson Kelly 20 Nov 1832; min- Francis McFarland
  Martha & John O'Kane 1 Dec 1840; min- P E Stevenson

Augusta County Marriages -- Woman's Name

Branaman
  Elizabeth & Isaac Garmon 29 Mar 1804; min- John McCue
  Nancy & John Garmen 26 Oct 1802; min- John McCue- 26Oct1802
  Sarah & John Walton 29 Dec 1842; min- William R Coursey

Brand
  Frances & Richard Brand 3 Apr 1827; min- Francis McFarland
  Peggy & Henry Russell 26 May 1810; min- William King
  Sarah & William Breeze 11 Jun 1794; d James b- Robert Stevenson affidavit that Sarah is 21

Branen
  Susanah & John Patterson 2 Jan 1806; min- William King

Branham
  Mary Ann & William Likes 11 Jun 1812; min- William King

Bratten
  Elizabeth & John Alison 9 Mar 1807; min- William King

Bratton
  Elizabeth & Samuel Craig 6 Feb 1821; min- John D Ewin
  Elizabeth & William Huston 26 Aug 1790; d-in-law of John Burk, who consents wit- Hance Herron & John Gregory min- Archibald Scott- 2Sep1790
  Peggy & William Crawford 19 Dec 1805; min- John Montgomery
  Peggy & John Wade 1 Mar 1808; min- William King
  Polly & Charles Thomas 10 Jun 1805; min- William King

Brawford
  Mary & Hugh (Jr) Torbett 30 Jun 1795; Mary (of age) d Samuel Brawford, dec. sis to John Brafford b- Hugh Torbett Sr
  Polly & Benjamin K Bryan 20 Sep 1819; min- William Calhoon
  Polly & Zachariah Johnston 3 Dec 1822; min- James Morrison

Brawley
  Mary & Moses Trimble 9 Apr 1793; Mary (of age) b- Patrick Shannon no minister listed; clerk's memorandum cites ceremony date as 9Apr1793

Bray
  Peggy & Winstead Litteral 27 Aug 1804; min- William King

Breckenridge
  Margaret Sarah & William B Johnson 24 Sep 1846; min- T T Castleman

Breckinridge
  Lettice & Elijah McClenachan - Sep 1749; license only

Breden
  Hannah & Henry Headrick 11 Mar 1802; min- William King- 11Mar1802
  Martha & Peter Jones 1 Dec 1792; 'Bredon?' d Edward b- Edward Breden no minister listed; clerk's memorandum cites ceremony date as 5Dec1792

Bredin
  Mary & George Anderson 11 Feb 1789; Minister's return spells name as 'Breedon' b- Edward Bredin min- William Wilson- 12Feb1789
  Sarah & Joseph Russell 13 Feb 1797; d Edward b- Edward Bredin

Augusta County Marriages -- Woman's Name

Breesland
　Polley & William Fairbairn 25 Sep 1806; min- William McPheeters
Breezeley
　Mary & Robert Bruntain 16 Apr 1791; widow b- Isaac Beal
Brian
　Priscilla & John Swisher 11 Oct 1842; min- Samuel Wagner
Brice
　Elizabeth & Isaac W Day 11 Jun 1800; Elizabeth 28 Isaac belongs to Capt. Grayson's Company and over 21 according to Richard Rowland min- William King- 11Jun1800
Bridge
　Ann Maria & Enoch H Hensley 5 Aug 1845; min- G W Israel
　Elizabeth D & Joseph B Rife 13 Sep 1842; min- Samuel Wagner
　Mary Ann & Nicholas Demasters 23 Jun 1837; min- E Joshua Webb
　Mary & Joshua Foster 8 Aug 1836; min- James C Wilson
Bridger
　Mary & William Dougherty 30 Jan 1786; min- Samuel Shannon- 30Jan1786
Bright
　Elizabeth & Henry Fizar 10 Oct 1808; min- William King
　Elizabeth & George (Jr) Lott 9 Mar 1795; d George Adam Bright who consents test- John Bright b- John Bright
　Mary & Isaac Liptrap 28 Jun 1785; d George b- John Bright wit- Henry Lawrence & Elijah Brumfield min- Archibald Scott- 29Jul1785
　Sarah & Augustine Kaufelt 10 Mar 1794; 'Coffeld?' d George Bright Sr who consents test- George Bright Jr b- George Bright Jr
　Susannah & Martin Miller 6 Mar 1823; min- James Morrison
Brisco
　Mary & William Ryder 2 Feb 1786; widow b- David Gregory min- Samuel Shannon- 21Feb1786
Brittain
　Polly & James Paine 12 Jun 1828; min- John Hendren
Britton
　Caroline & Abraham B Venable 7 Jul 1836; min- B N Brown
　Elizabeth & George Rumbough 5 Sep 18--; min- A B Davidson
　Martha A & Richard W Hardy 20 Feb 1849; min- T T Castleman
　Susannah & Samuel Todd 16 Apr 1818; min- Wright Burgess
Brobeck
　Jenny & John Thomas 12 Apr 1804; min- William King
　Polly & George Wade 12 Mar 1819; min- William King
Brockman
　Salley & James Stuart 1 Jun 1819; min- Wright Burgess
Brooback
　Elizabeth & Jacob Morrell 26 Oct 1785; b- Lewis Geldmecher min- John Brown- 9Nov1785
Brook
　Sarah & Mathew Thompson 17 Nov 1808; min- William McPheeters

Augusta County Marriages -- Woman's Name

Brooke
  Helen W & Thomas M Foreman 30 Aug 1849; min- T T Castleman
Brooking
  Mary & James Corry 18 Feb 1795; Minister's return spells name as 'Curry' d Charles Brooking & Ann Brooking who consent test- Robert Curry s Samuel Corry who consents b- William Curry min- William Wilson- 19Feb1795
Brooks
  Amelia & Henry Rowe 2 Dec 1822; 'Rau' min- Josiah Cole
  Catherine & William Thompson 25 Oct 1803; min- John McCue
  Martha P & James Caruthers 20 Dec 1830; min- James C Wilson
  Mary & Stephen Ruddle 6 Oct 1808; min- John McCue
  Sarah & Jacob Acord 25 Dec 1823; min- Josiah Cole
  Susannah & Robert Knowls 13 Feb 1811; min- Regin Hammond
Brosius
  Hannah & Jacob Weaver 12 Mar 1807; min- William McPheeters
  Susannah & Jacob Cline 6 Apr 1803; min- William King
Brothers
  Rebecca & Michael Forbes 18 Feb 1819; min- William King
Brower
  Catharine & Samuel Gochenauer 1 Jul 1835; min- John Gotber
  Elizabeth & Martin Garber 16 Nov 1842; min- Peter Miller
  Fanny & John Miller 10 Sep 1840; min- Peter Miller
  Hannah & Samuel Croft 26 Oct 1825; min- Josiah Cole
  Nancy & Joseph Grove 5 Sep 1833; min- Abraham Garber- publication of banns
Browers
  Lidda & Jacob Croft 7 Jan 1833; min- Abraham Garber- publication of banns
  Martha & John Snell 21 Mar 1832; min- Abraham Garber- publication of banns
Brown
  Arabella & John Black 23 Dec 1841; min- James Paine
  Betsey & John Huff 23 Mar 1813; min- William King
  Catherine & Joseph Helms 19 Jul 1822; min- Daniel Stephens
  Elizabeth S & William Webb 20 Apr 1837; min- J C Hensell
  Elizabeth & John Bell 19 Jan 1797; Elizabeth (of age) d James Brown, dec con- Jane Brown b- John Brown min- Archibald Scott- 20Jul1797
  Isabella & George L Kennedy 29 Apr 1828; min- William Calhoon
  Jane D & Thomas Lyons 15 Dec 1825; Bond gives name as 'Beam' min- Francis McFarland
  Jane & Patrick Hayes 25 Jan 1802; d William b- William Brown
  Jane & Archibald Trotter 31 Oct 1839; min- John A Van Lear
  Jane & John Vines 1 Mar 1810; min- William Wilson
  Jannet & John Risk 23 Aug 1786; 'Jannett?' d John b- James Moore wit- James Risk John Brown's wife listed as Frankie min- John Brown- 26Aug1786 (in another document date listed as 17Aug1786)
  Juliann & William Kennedy 10 Jun 1801; d William who consents sis to John Brown Juliann (of age) b- John Brown min- William King- 11Jun1801

Augusta County Marriages -- Woman's Name

Brown (cont.)
Margaret & John G Allison 20 May 1823; min- John Hendren
Margaret & John Fisher 29 Apr 1806; min- William King
Margaret & Walter Heron 14 May 1798; wit- Benjamin Burgher b- Jacob Kinney
Margaret & James Wilson 6 Dec 1827; min- William Calhoon
Martha J & James T W Willson 29 May 1845; min- Francis McFarland
Martha & William Berry 2 Mar 1845; min- S Wagner
Mary Ann & John Helms 2 May 1822; min- Conrad Speece
Mary Jane & Archibald A McPheeters 25 Oct 1838; min- A B McCorkle
Mary & John Browning 11 Jul 1832; min- James C Wilson
Mary & George H Conklin 27 Dec 1842; min- James Bunting
Mary & William Hart 18 May 1789; widow b- Andrew Scott min- Archibald Scott- 19May1789
Mary & John B Lavel 2 Mar 1843; min- J C Hensell
Mary & John Miller 2 May 1820; min- Abraham Garber- publication of banns
Mary & James Mitchell 23 Jun 1806; min- William McPheeters
Mary & John Perry 29 Dec 1818; min- William King
Mary & Robert Smith 20 Dec 1820; min- Josiah Cole
Mary & James H Young 28 Jan 1830; min- Conrad Speece
Nancy Ann & Andrew Smith 25 Mar 1836; min- James Morrison
Nancy & John Daniels 24 Jan 1825; min- John Hendren
Nancy & James Hogshead 20 Mar 1809; min- William Calhoon
Nancy & James Poage 31 Aug 1837; min- William Calhoub
Nancy & George Wright 20 Dec 1796; d John b- John Brown min- Archibald Scott- 20Dec1796
Patience K & William Wilson 23 Mar 1837; min- Isaac Jones
Peggy & Alexander Campbell 20 May 1797; Peggy (of age) d Thomas Brown, dec. con- Elizabeth Brown b- Hugh Paul min- John Montgomery- 22May1797
Phebe B & Thomas L Henry 1 Feb 1846; min- J C Hensell
Rebecca A S & John D Hamilton 25 Nov 1834; min- E R Veitch
Rebecca & William B Helms 13 Jan 1820; min- Daniel Stephens
Rebeccah & George King 27 Dec 1790; b- Hugh Brown wit- J Beal min- William Wilson- 29Dec1790
Rhoda & Daniel Harrison 14 Apr 1834; min- John Hendren
Sally & Robert Graham 11 May 1790; d Thomas b- Stephen Graham
Sarah J & John Robertson 26 Oct 1843; min- James Paine
Sarah Jane & James Heizer 19 Jun 1834; min- William Calhoon
Sarah & William Bridge 18 Jan 1816; min- John McCue
Sarah & John (Jr) Brown 7 Nov 1798; d Benjamin b- Benjamin Brown min- Archibald Scott- 10Nov1798
Sarah & Robert G Poage 24 Mar 1831; min- William Calhoon
Sarah & John Swink 17 Sep 1829; min- Francis McFarland
Susan & Stephen Fitch 20 Mar 1825; min- William C. Morrison

Brownlee
Agness & William Mitchell 15 Sep 1785; min- Archibald Scott- 15Sep1785
Ann & Robert Kinkead 12 Jun 1792; b- Robert Rennick no minister listed; clerk's memorandum cites ceremony date as 12Jun1792

Augusta County Marriages -- Woman's Name

Brownlee (cont.)
  Isabella & Robert Fulton 29 Jan 1799; Isabella (of age) d John b- Alexander Brownlee
  Jane & John Gilkeson 6 Aug 1809; min- William McPheeters
  Mary Jane & James R Bell 7 Apr 1842; min- Francis McFarland
  Sarah & Joseph Houston 21 Mar 1805; min- John McCue
  Sarah & James Murry 19 Dec 1829; min- Francis McFarland
  Susan & William Heizer 8 Mar 1832; min- Francis McFarland
Brubeck
  Barbara & James Armstrong 17 Nov 1831; min- Francis McFarland
Bruce
  Sarah J & John H Fravel 4 Jul 1848; min- D W Arnold
Brunk
  Hannah & Reuben Evy 10 Jan 1843; min- Samuel Wagner
Bryans
  Elizabeth & Thomas (Jr) Chambers 13 May 1795; Elizabeth (of age) b- Thomas Chambers Sr min- John McCue- 14May1795
Bryant
  Sally & David McKesson 27 May 1801; d Anderson Bryant, dec., late of Albemarle cty b- William Chambers min- John McCue- 27Mar1801
  Susan M & John J Reimensnyder 3 May 1838; min- D F Bittle
Buchanan
  Ann K & Addison McCutchen 22 Aug 1833; min- James Morrison
  Ann & John McCampbell 4 Oct 1797; d William b- William Buchanan
  Elizabeth & William Roach 3 Nov 1836; min- James Morrison- publication of banns
  Esther & William Caldwell 4 Sep 1787; Minister's return spells name as 'Buchanon d William who consents wit- David Wilson & John Bell b- Alexander Hindman min- John Brown- 10Sep1787
  Nancy & John R Berry 21 Oct 1829; min- James Morrison
  Polly & William Hanna 13 Mar 1797; Minister's return spells name as 'Hannah' d David Buchanan (Buckwhanen) who consents test- James Hanna b- James Buchanan Jr min- Archibald Scott- 16Mar1797
  Polly & Daniel Paine 1 Feb 1827; min- William Monroe
  Rebecca K & James Berry 22 Dec 1836; min- James Morrison
  Sarah J & William W Spencer 28 Mar 1848; min- J C Hensell
Buckley
  Lydia & Adam Sansebough 1 Apr 1802; min- William King- 1Apr1802
Buckner
  Sally & James Patterson 23 Sep 1827; min- William Wilson
Bulcher
  Nancy & William Smith - May 1814; min- John Brown
Bull
  Lavina & Samuel W Burnsides 24 May 1849; min- T A Morgan
Bumgardner
  Julianna & John Life 24 Feb 1823; min- Josiah Cole
  Sally & Alexander McGilvray 16 Mar 1820; min- Robert H Chapman

Augusta County Marriages -- Woman's Name

Bunch
Jane & Alexander Parr 11 Jan 1816; min- William King
Lucy Jane & Wheeler Minnis 5 Aug 1834; min- Samuel Kennerly

Burch
Catherine & John Ray 4 Feb 1800; d William Burch, dec. b- James Buchanan min- John McCue- date of ceremony missing
Sarah E & Erasmus A Cease 26 Nov 1844; min- G W Israel

Burges
Molly & William Page 25 Oct 1798; Molly (of age) Tamor Elliott swears Molly is of age b- Hance Calvert

Burgess
Elizabeth E & Charles Taylor 4 May 1826; min- Benjamin Denton
Elizabeth & George Fox 9 Jun 1831; min- William Calhoon
Elizabeth & John Mays - Jun 1832; min- Samuel Kennerly- publication of banns
Frances M & George Shaver 15 Sep 1841; min- Alfred G Chenowith
Jane & Thomas Armstrong 27 Nov 1815; min- Wright Burgess
Lucinda Virginia & Isaiah Baker 18 Jul 1848; min- J McKendree Reiley
Magdelen O & James A Hamrick 5 Oct 1848; min- J McKendree Reiley
Mariah A & James W Patterson 10 Nov 1842; min- A G Chenowith
Nancy & David Gabhart 1 Nov 1834; min- Augustus Babb
Polly & James Young 25 Feb 1812; min- Christopher Frye

Burk
Elizabeth & John Steel 4 Jul 1789; d John Burcke, who consents wit- John Christian b- John Christian min- William Wilson- 7Jul1789
Nancy & John M D Nichol 4 Sep 1837; min- Stephen Smith

Burkart
Susanna & Abraham Yearout 4 Oct 1794; min- William Wilson- 4Oct1794

Burke
Susan E & Nicholas Kyger 15 Nov 1845; min- P Shickel

Burket
Polly & Hays Coffey 7 Feb 1815; min- William King
Sally & Jacob Long 28 Feb 1791; Minister's return spells name as 'Burkitt' d Nathaniel b- Nathaniel Burket min- William Wilson- 28Feb1791
Tina & John Argenbright 28 Jun 1827; min- Joseph Smith

Burkett
Eliza Jane & Solomon Coffman 3 Dec 1846; min- J A Van Lear
India & Peter Link 10 Mar 1788; Minister's return spells name as 'Judy Burkitt' d Daniel who consents test- Alexander Moore & John Brumfill b- Dieter Fishborn min- William Wilson- 11Mar1788
Nancy & Daniel Crist 18 Jun 1802; min- William King- 18Jun1802

Burkhart
Susana & Abraham Earhart 2 Oct 1794; Minister's return spells name as 'Abraham Yeorhouse and Susanna Burkett' d Nathaniel b- Peter Link min- John Brown- 4Oct1794

Augusta County Marriages -- Woman's Name

Burkholder
  Francis & Peter Reubush 30 Mar 1836; min- John Hendren
Burner
  Franny & John Lantin 2 Mar 1824; min- Abraham Garber
Burnes
  Ellen & Solomon Clide 23 Jun 1801; d Richard who consents test- Thomas Burnes & James Burns b- Thomas Bevens Bond signed Solomon Cloyde & Thomas Burns
Burnett
  Jane & John Driskell - Aug 1749; license only
Burns
  Eve & John Miller 17 May 1791; min- John Montgomery- 17May1791
  Letticia & William Gibson 17 Nov 1808; min- William McPheeters
Burton
  Columbia Jane & William Morris 14 Jun 1849; min- T A Morgan
  Sarah & John Craig 17 Jul 1787; b- John Burton min- William Wilson- 17Jul1787
Bush
  Asenath & Andrew B Riddle 23 Apr 1835; min- Samuel Kennerly
  Catherine & Ralph Dudleston 16 Jun 1792; Minister's return spells name as 'Duddleson' d Nicholas b- Nicholas Bush (German) min- John McCue- 19Jun1792
  Hanah & David W Davis 23 Feb 1809; min- John McCue
  Margaret D & Leonard Farr 22 Feb 1848; min- J C Hensell
  Mary L & Elijah D Brown 8 Nov 1832; min- John S Watt
  Peggy & Frederick Carey 18 Apr 1816; min- William King
  Polly & John Steele 25 Oct 1800; d Martin s Andrew b- Martin Bush
  Rachel J & Thomas S Baskin 12 Nov 1840; min- Benjamin M Smith
Bushong
  Catharine & George Cox 7 Feb 1839; min- John C Hensell
  Susannah & Henry Eccord 1 Feb 1803; min- William King
Butt
  Barbary & Christian Huffman 19 Jul 1790; d Henry, who consents (in German) b- Jacob Sheetz wit- Jacob Sheets (signs in German) & Adam Butt
  Elizabeth & Adam May 11 Feb 1791; d Henry Bott who consents b- Chaistain Huffman wit- William Patterson
  Elizabeth & Jacob Sheets 2 Jul 1788; Elizabeth gives her own consent test- John Lanahan & Thomas Leanch b- John Heizer
Byerley
  Madeline & John Early 1 Aug 1820; min- Abraham Garber- publication of banns
Byers
  Elizabeth & John Daugherty 10 Oct 1798; d David b- David Byers
  Elizabeth & John Dougherty 10 Oct 1796; Elizabeth Burris? min- Archibald Scott- 10Oct1796
  Jane & Scott Wade 27 Dec 1827; min- James Morrison
  Mary & Jacob Coiner 18 Aug 1795; d Joseph b- Joseph Byers min- William Wilson- 20Aug1795

Augusta County Marriages -- Woman's Name

Byers (cont.)
  Rosanna & Jacob Crick 17 Dec 1829; min- James Morrison
  Sarah & Samuel Myers 17 Aug 1844; min- John Hendren
Bywaters
  Frances O & William Pearey 20 Oct 1845; min- P Shickel
Cail
  Mary & John Crouse 4 Jul 1816; min- William King
Calahan
  Catherine & Otho Wade 26 Mar 1788; d Charles, who gives bond
Calbraith
  Mary & George Rutledge 7 May 1800; Minister's return spells name as 'Caldbreath' Mary (of age) d Thomas Calbraith, dec., sis to Thomas Calbraith b- Thomas Calbraith min- John McCue- 8May1800
Calbreath
  Margaret J & Thomas J Kerr 22 Apr 1823; min- James C Willson
  Martha B & Andrew Allison 19 Apr 1823; min- James C Willson
  Sarah & Henry Crist 10 Oct 1848; min- Robert L Dabney
Caldbreath
  Jane & William Alison 9 Oct 1816; min- Wright Burgess
Caldwell
  Anis & William Davis 4 Apr 1791; William the father of the late Walter Davis d William b- John Caldwell marriage sent to clerk by Samuel Borwn and dated 5Apr1791
  Ann & James Henderson 1 Mar 1792; d William b- John Caldwell min- John McCune- 1Mar1792
  Annas & William Buchanan 12 Aug 1795; Annas (of age) d of John, dec. sis to John Caldwell who consents b- Alexander Buchanan min- John McCue- 24Aug1795
  Catherine & James Marshall 7 Feb 1805; min- John McCue
  Celestine & David D Coiner 11 Oct 1836; min- James C Wilson
  Elizabeth & John Marshall 12 Jun 1799; Elizabeth (of age) d John Caldwell, dec., sis to Samuel Caldwell b- Samuel Caldwell
  Margerate & George Marshall 27 Feb 1812; min- John McCue
  Mary & Hugh Linch 10 Sep 1794; Minister's return spells name as 'Lynch' widow who consents for herself test- William Wilson & John Caldwell b- William Wilson & John Caldwell min- John McCue- 10Sep1794
  Mary & Thomas Young 7 Dec 1796; d William b- William Caldwell min- John McCue- 8Dec1796
  Sarah & David Buchanan 13 Apr 1789; d John b- John Caldwell
Cale
  Dianah & John Waid 10 Aug 1837; min- J C Hensell
  Elizabeth & David Hanger 12 Feb 1846; min- J C Hensell
  Sarah Ann & Elijah Hunter 27 Mar 1849; min- Alonzo P Ludder
  Sarah & Jacob (Jr) Kyle 6 Aug 1840; min- D F Bittle
Cales
  Elizabeth & Samuel Nutty 6 Feb 1845; min- J C Hensell
  Isabella & John McClintick 16 Nov 1820; min- Robert H Chapman

Augusta County Marriages -- Woman's Name

Calhoon
Eliza & John Edmundson 10 Dec 1822; min- Conrad Speece

Call
Betsy & Thomas Clifton 1 Jan 1789; Minister's return spells name as 'Caul' d Timothy Caul, who consents wit- Jeremiah Washington & James Rutledge b- Thomas Story min- William Wilson- 1Jan1789

Callaghan
Margaret & Alexander Wiley 21 Mar 1786; Minister's return spells name as 'Calaghan' b- Charles Callaghan
Margaret & Alexander Wills 4 Apr 1786; min- Samuel Shannon- 4Apr1786
Mary & Edward Stuart 28 Mar 1786; Minister's return spells names as 'Stewart and Calaghan' b- Charles Callaghan min- Samuel Shannon- 4Apr1786
Sally & Charles Wallace Wadsworth 22 Nov 1797; d Dennis b- Alexander Wason

Calleson
Margaret & Thomas Mitchell 28 Mar 1786; Minister's return spells name as 'Margaret Callison' d James s James b- Robert Calleson wit- W Cunningham & William Mitchell min- Archibald Scott- 4Apr1786

Callison
Isabella & Joseph Evans 25 Feb 1801; widower Isabella (of age) d John b- Robert Callison

Calvert
Susan & James Bare - --- 182-; min- William C. Morrison

Cambden
Elenor E A & John Palmer 28 Aug 1848; min- Alonzo P Ludden

Cambell
Sarah & Robert Blakely - Oct 1817; min- John Brown

Campbell
Ann & Robert Scott 17 Mar 1785; perm- Ann herself b- James Anderson wit- Samuel Black, James O'Neal
Diana & Michael Barnett 4 Jan 1787; min- William Wilson- 4Jan1787
Eliza N & George H Mitchell 26 Feb 1839; min- Frederick D Goodwin
Elizabeth N & Joseph C Brown 27 May 1847; min- J C Hensell
Jane & Thomas Riddle 23 Jul 1791; d George wit- Philip Hull & George Kuhn b- Philip Hull
Jane & Henry Speck 29 Sep 1795; d Alexander who consents test- Jacob Coyner, Alexander Campbell Jr & Thomas Turke b- Thomas Turk Jr min- John McCue- 8Oct1795
Lucy A & William H Shelton 27 Jul 1847; min- J C Hensell
Margaret & Michael Goodlink 30 Apr 1791; Minister's return spells name as 'Goldlink' d Alexander, who consents wit- Robert Porterfield b- John Campbell min- William Wilson- 11May1791
Mary Jane & Samuel Golladay 27 May 1837; min- James Paine
Mary & George Hutchenson 7 Jan 1786; Minister's return spells name as 'Hutcheson' George from Greenbrier cty d James b- W. Urquhart wit- Samuel Strong min- William Wilson- 2Jan1786

Augusta County Marriages -- Woman's Name

Campbell (cont.)
  Mary & James White 8 Sep 1800; Mary (of age) d Alexander who consents test- Alexander Campbell & Andrew Campbell b- Alexander Campbell min- John McCue- 9Sep1800
  Mary & George Wine - Mar 1807; min- John Brown
  Nancy & Alexander Elliott 19 Dec 1786; Alexander from Rockingham cty d Andrew b- John Didall & Alex, son of George Elliott wit- Moras Loyd, Wm Elliott, John Camel min- William Wilson- 20Dec1786
  Nancy & Samuel Reid 30 Nov 1801; widower & widow (of George) b- James Foster
  Rebecca & Andrew Campbell 28 Jan 1793; d John b- Alexander Humphreys affidavit of age of Rebecca no minister listed; clerk's memorandum cites ceremony date as 28Jan1793
  Rebecca & Samuel Early 12 Jul 1804; min- William Wilson
  Sally & Jonathan Dunbar 5 May 1790; Minister's return spells name as 'Peggy Campbell' d James, who consents wit- William Burgess & James Essex b- William Dunbar min- Archibald Scott- 6May1790

Cannady
  Margaret & William Black 16 Dec 1809; min- John McCue

Canole
  Polly & George Pifer 22 Mar 1804; min- William King

Canote
  Rosannah & Christian Shally 28 Nov 1796; d John b- John Canote

Carcofe
  Elizabeth Jane & Joseph Rader 25 Mar 1833; min- John Hendren

Cargo
  Peggy & James Criswell 13 Dec 1794; Minister's return spells name as 'Chriswell and Mary Carge' b- Jacob Kinney min- John McCue- 24Dec1794

Carhart
  Sophia & Anthony Oehler 3 Apr 1797; widower & widow b- Deter Fischborn

Caricofe
  Hannah & Peter Fifer 17 Mar 1831; min- John Hendren

Carlyle
  Rachel & Robert Peebles 29 Aug 1786; Minister's return spells names as 'Peples' and 'Carlile' d Robert b- John Carlyle s John wit- Robert Peebles, George Carlyle, Robert Carlyle Jr min- Samuel Shannon- 5Sep1786

Carnal
  Elizabeth & Daniel Fisher 25 Feb 1806; min- William Wilson

Carpenter
  Elizabeth & John Kiplinger 8 Aug 1788; b- John Pence
  Sally & Peter Kiplinger 18 Jun 1791; Minister's return spells name as 'Hiplinger and Mary Carpenter d Mary who consents b- Frederick Myers wit- Frederick Myers & John Kiplinger min- William Wilson- 20Jun1791

Augusta County Marriages -- Woman's Name

Carr
  Catherine & George Fallwider 25 Oct 1791; b- Valentine
    Carr (German)
  Elenor & Lewis Sorrels 3 May 1792; Elenor an orphan,
    father died when she was young, mother's whereabouts unknown
    Elenor raised by Alexander Robertson b- Thomas Clifton
    min- John McCune- 3May1792
Carrico
  Christina & Jacob Price 25 Jan 1811; min- G H
    Riemenschneider
Carricof
  Catharine & Samuel Hufford 12 Jan 1827; min- John Hendren
Carrol
  Harriet & Valentine Bare 1 Oct 1840; min- Samuel Wagner
Carroll
  Margaret A & Benjamin Larew 12 Nov 1840; min- Frederick D
    Goodwin
Carson
  Elizabeth & John (Jr) Brown 22 Sep 1801; d David Adam
    Palmer swears Elizabeth of age b- George Palmer John Brown
    swears as to his age min- William King- 22Sep1801
  Jane & Robert (Jr) McCawley 29 Mar 1794; Jane (of age) b-
    Robert McCawley Sr min- John Brown- 5Apr1794
  Mary & Abraham Hanna 9 Mar 1793; b- John Mills min-
    William Wilson- 15Mar1793
  Rebecca & Thomas Young 14 Nov 1833; min- Conrad Speece
Carter
  Jane & Peter Grigsby 31 May 1808; min- William King
  Polly & William Ramsey 26 Jul 1798; Polly (of age) b-
    Samuel Gibson (signed: Sammy Gibson) min- William Wilson-
    31Jul1798
Caruthers
  Esther & Michael Woods 7 Aug 1795; Minister's return
    spells name as 'Carothers' con- John Moffett test- Elinor
    Moffett & John Moffett Jr b- John Moffett Jr min-
    Archibald Scott- 13Aug1795
  Jane & Richard Smith 13 Apr 1786; b- James Caruthers min-
    Archibald Scott- 13Apr1786
  Rachel P & William Browning 16 Jul 1832; min- James C
    Wilson
Cary
  Sarah Ann & Anderson Scott 8 Dec 1824; min- Luke Collins
Cashaw
  Esther & Thomas Scott 6 Oct 1792; d Benoni Cashaw who
    consents wit- John Cashaw & John Taylor b- Henry Mace
  Sarah & John Taylor 6 Oct 1792; d Benoin who consents s
    Christin Charles Tailor who consents wit- John Cashaw b-
    Henry Mace
Cason
  Frances & Samuel Woods 15 Feb 1816; min- Wright Burgess
  Mary & Joseph Beaty 7 Apr 1824; min- Josiah Cole
Casper
  Catherine & Andrew F Hatfield 12 Nov 1827; min- William C.
    Morrison

Augusta County Marriages -- Woman's Name

Cassady
  Margaret & Ephraim Hulvey 8 Oct 1834; min- William Wilson
  Mary & Samuel Hoover 23 Jun 1840; min- J J Reimensnyder
  Nancy & John Parry 11 Apr 1822; min- William Wilson Jr
Castleman
  Hannah E & William T Mount 27 Sep 1848; min- T T Castleman
Caufman
  Barbara & William Smith 14 Sep 1837; min- J C Hensell-
    publication of banns
Caul
  Agness & John Holmes 16 Jan 1792; d Timothy, dec. con-
    Elizabeth Caul wit- H Caul, John Campbell, Thomas Caul b-
    Thomas Story & Hugh Caul min- William Wilson- 17Jan1792
Cave
  Elizabeth B & John H Bell 24 Jun 1822; min- John Hendren
  Jane S & Benami Ervin 5 Dec 1821; min- John Hendren
  Margaret & Charles Anderson 5 Nov 1792; d Elizabeth, who
    consents wit- Thomas Story, Agnes Holmes & William Caul b-
    John Holmes min- John McCue- 8Nov1792
Cawly
  Fanny & Elijah Churchman 2 Jun 1814; min- John McCue
Cawthron
  Anna & Patrick Cribbins 4 Aug 1840; min- J J Reimensnyder
  Charlotte & Thornton Paul 12 Oct 1840; min- J J
    Reimensnyder
Cease
  Caroline & John C Henn 31 Mar 1845; min- T T Castleman
  Elizabeth & John M Houghobout 1 Nov 1838; min- Thomas
    Wheeler
  Mary & Garland Eubank 17 May 1806; min- William King
Cesterson
  Juliana & William Grass 27 Feb 1834; min- William G Jackson
Chambers
  Catherine & Washington Sevier 6 Oct 1807; min- William
    Calhoon
  Peggy & George Buchanan 3 Feb 1818; min- John D Ewin
  Rachael & William Lockridge 1 Jun 1815; min- John D Ewin
Chaplain
  Lucy & Zephaniah H Ballard 27 Dec 1832; min- Samuel
    Kennerly
Chaplin
  Matilda & William Claytor 29 Dec 1842; min- Samuel Wagner
  Polly & Richard Mooney 17 Jan 1828; min- William C.
    Morrison
  Susan & Jacob Messmaker 20 Mar 1828; min- William C.
    Morrison
Chapman
  Elizabeth & Jesse Greogry 3 Jan 1822; min- James C Willson
  Polly & Robert Grooms 9 May 1814; min- Thomas Bourne
  Rosanah & Anderson Moony 24 Jul 1829; min- William C.
    Morrison
  Virginia & John Taylor 29 Oct 1828; min- William C.
    Morrison

Augusta County Marriages -- Woman's Name

Cheatham
  Nancy & Valentine Bird 29 Sep 1829; min- Francis McFarland
  Patsy & Peter Good 22 Dec 1821; min- James Sewell
Chesnut
  Agnes & Augustine Harlow 17 Jul 1798; Agnes (of age) d
    William b- William Chesnut
  Ann & Thomas Duffield 23 Jan 1789; b- John Chesnut, who
    also consents
  Isabella & Jacob Moore 21 Sep 1809; min- William King
  Martha & Joshua Hyden 26 Jan 1796; Minister's return
    spells name as 'Chesnutt' Martha (of age) d William who
    consents test- Daniel Good b- Robert Bailey min- John
    McCue- 2Feb1796
Chesnutt
  Jenny & William (Jr) Palmer 12 Jan 1790; Minister's return
    spells name as 'Chestnut' b- John Chesnutt min- William
    Wilson- 12Jan1790
  Mary & Philip Smith 20 Jul 1792; Minister's return spells
    name as 'Chesnut' d William & Jane who consent b- William
    Bratton min- John McCue- 21Aug1792
Childers
  Martha Ann & Vincent Huff 6 Jan 1825; min- Josiah Cole
Chrisman
  Anna & Noah Ramsbottom 30 Jul 1846; min- Jacob Bear
  Elizabeth & Garland R Eubank 11 Jan 1844; min- Jacob Baer
  Jane & Isaac Ramsbottom 11 Mar 1847; min- Jacob Bear
  Sarah Ann & William P Tate 5 Jun 1850; min- Francis
    McFarland
Christian
  Isabella & Edward Mulholland 5 Jan 1822; min- John Brown
  Margaret & Robert (Sr) Christian 22 Feb 1790; s Robert
    sis Robert Christian Jr (both parents deceased) b- Robert
    Christian Jr min- Archibald Scott- 23Feb1790
  Martha & Philemon (Jr) Richards 7 Mar 1793; Martha (of
    age) d Patrick b- Gilbert Christian min- John McCue-
    21Mar1793
  Mary & David Bell 18 Feb 1796; d Patrick Christian who
    consents test- James Christian b- Alexander Robertson
    min- William Wilson- 19Feb1796
  Nancy B & Robert P Brown 4 Oct 1842; min- S J Love
  Rachel & Nicholas Hope 21 Apr 1796; widow b- Joseph Burk
  Sarah & Richard Wallace 11 Oct 1831; min- John S Hall
Churchman
  Abigail & James Allison 23 Mar 1812; min- Wright Burgess
  Jane & John M Steele 9 Dec 1843; min- T T Castleman
Clark
  Mary & James Perry 11 Mar 1841; min- J J Reimensnyder
  Nancy & George H Shewy 24 Mar 1836; min- John A Steele
  Sarah W & John G Hogshead 1 Dec 1842; min- James Bunting
  Sarah & Archibald Elliott - Feb 1858; license only
Clarke
  Deborah & Samuel Faucet 23 Feb 1809; min- John McCue
  Elizabeth Jane & Michael Tebo 23 Mar 1838; min- John A
    Steele

Augusta County Marriages -- Woman's Name

Clarke (cont.)
Elizabeth & Hugh Hamilton 18 Feb 1813; min- William Calhoon
Lucy M & James H Baskins 24 Apr 1838; min- John A Steele
Margaret & Joseph Grove 29 May 1817; min- William Calhoon
Polly & Henry Harman 4 Oct 1825; min- Conrad Speece
Sally & John Houff 15 Mar 1821; min- Conrad Speece

Clayton
Hetty A M & Cyrus A McCutchan 29 Dec 1846; min- W G Campbell

Clemants
Jane & Johnson Elliot 24 Aug 1815; min- William King

Clemens
Nancey & George Crawford 9 Sep 1812; min- William Wilson

Clemer
Ann C & John Crick 9 Feb 1826; min- James Morrison
Elizabeth & William McKensey 14 Aug 1834; min- Cornelius Gates
Fanny DLiza & Jacob Bowman 6 Aug 1829; min- James Morrison
Polly & David Palmer 21 Feb 1822; min- James Morrison

Clemmons
Frances & John Bell 22 Apr 1833; min- Wright Burgess

Clemons
Rebecca & Mathew Wason 22 Nov 1826; min- William Monroe

Clifton
Elizabeth & James Moore 21 Aug 1794; Woman's name blank on bond b- Richard Clifton min- John Brown- 21Aug1794

Cline
Ann & Henry Fulwider 6 Jun 1789; d Jacob, who consents wit- Jacob Gochnouer & Jacob Cline Jr
Betsey & Henry Welch 1 Jul 1819; min- Conrad Speece, Jr
Catharine & Jacob Bushong - Apr 1810; min- John Brown
Christian & Michael Miller 25 Mar 1791; d Jacob Cline Sr who consents wit- Peter Cline & Jacob Kockanorer b- Jacob Cline marriage sent to clerk by Samuel Brown and dated 7Apr1791
Elizabeth & ----- Utsler 25 Feb 1831; min- Abraham Garber- publication of banns

Clinebill
Catharine & John Barkley 3 Sep 1829; min- Francis McFarland
Jane & Alexander Eakin 18 May 1829; min- Francis McFarland
Mary & Robert Carden 18 Sep 1813; min- Wright Burgess
Mary & Samuel Runnolds 18 Nov 1847; min- James Morrison

Clinetinch
Elizabeth & William D Morrison 19 Apr 1830; min- William Wilson

Clinon
Jane & James Logan 23 Jun 1796; b- Thomas Simpson affidavit by Jane that she is 21, has no residence, and is a seamstress

Cloverfield
Catherine & John Gibson 1 Mar 1796; Catherine (of age) d of ----- Cloverfield, dec. b- James King min- William Wilson- 3Mar1796
Mary & John Crookshanks 27 Aug 1787; b- John Kirk min- Archibald Scott- 30Aug1787

Augusta County Marriages -- Woman's Name

Clynes
  Elizabeth & Joseph Rankin 5 Oct 1804; min- William King
Coalter
  Eleanor & William White 24 Jul 1806; min- John McCue
  Elizabeth & James McPheeters 23 May 1791; James from Botetourt cty d Michael who consents b- John Coalter no minister listed; clerk's memorandum cites ceremony date as 25May1791
  Isabella & John Stuart 1 Apr 1813; min- John McCue
  Margaret & Alexander Brown 19 Jul 1799; d David Alexander of age b- David Coalter
  Mary & Nathaniel B Tucker 9 Feb 1809; min- William McPheeters
  Nancy J & William B Crawford 17 May 1849; min- B M Smith
Cochran
  Jane St Clair & Henry Harrison 28 Nov 1844; min- T T Castleman
  Magdelin & Benjamin Crawford 20 Oct 1829; min- John Hendren
Coffey
  Elizabeth J & Matthew W Robertson 3 Sep 1846; min- James Paine
Coffman
  Ann Eliza & Lindsay Morris 17 Mar 1846; min- T T Castleman
  Catharine & Thomas Scott 25 Dec 1845; min- T T Castleman
  Elizabeth & John W Depriest 21 Mar 1850; min- John Garber
  Elizabeth & Thomas F Payne 12 Nov 1846; min- J C Hensell
  Frances & Henry A Johnson 15 Sep 1842; min- Samuel Wagner
  Margaret & George Hanger 22 Feb 1844; min- J C Hensell
  Martha & James Borden 5 Jan 1847; min- J A Van Lear
  Rebecca & David Meyers 13 Aug 1840; min- J J Reimensnyder
Cofney
  Betsy & Dennis Donavan 30 Apr 1787; Minister's return spells name as 'Dannavan and Betty Cofney' b- James McGonagal min- William Wilson- 30Apr1787
Coiner
  Catharine & Adam Hawp 18 Nov 1794; Minister's return spells name as 'Haup and Corrier'd George b- George Coiner min- John McCue- 27Nov1794
  Catharine & Joseph L Rupert 3 Nov 1831; min- Ambrose Henkel
  Elizabeth & Jacob Spotts 23 Jan 1806; min- John McCue
  Jane & Peter Engleman 11 Apr 1821; min- G H Riemenschneider
  Jane & Henry Imboden 14 Apr 1800; Minister's return spells name as 'Impoten' Signed 'Heinrich Imboden' Henry (of age) d George b- George Coiner min- John McCue- 17Apr1800
  Margaret & William Bradshaw 15 Oct 1820; min- John Hendren
  Margaret & Martin Grove 7 Feb 1813; min- G H Riemenschneider
  Margaret & Samuel Leonard 17 Oct 1833; min- William G Jackson
  Margaret & Lewis (Jr) Mowry 9 Jun 1800; b- George Koiner min- William Wilson- 15Jun1800
  Nancy & Clinton G Miller 25 May 1831; min- Samuel Kennerly
  Peggy & James Kilkenny 22 Apr 1801; 'Comer?' d Michael Coiner, dec. Sarah Kilkenny, mother, attests to James's age b- Samuel Long

Augusta County Marriages -- Woman's Name

Coiner (cont.)
Polly & Daniel Kiser 26 Apr 1804; min- John McCue
Susan & Samuel G Henkel 1 Dec 1832; min- Ambrose Henkel
Coldbreath
Elizabeth & John Gold 26 Mar 1798; Minister's return spells name as 'Galbreath' d Thomas Coldbreath, dec. John of age b- Nicholas Spring Jr min- William Wilson- 27Mar1798
Cole
Jane R & Thomas Rankin 21 Sep 1815; min- William Calhoon
Coley
Elizabeth & Marshall E Panzle 30 May 1850; min- Daniel Brower
Louisa & Jacob Long 17 Jun 1819; min- William Wilson
Collins
Clarinda & Fountain Campbell 16 Oct 1826; min- Francis McFarland
Elizabeth & Thomas Bishop 23 May 1811; min- John McCue
Elizabeth & Joseph Woods 5 Apr 1802; min- William King- 5Apr1802
Matilda & Jacob Carricofe 17 Jan 1850; min- Peter Miller
Sarah & Philip Earhart 8 Jun 1843; min- John A Van Lear
Sarah & Samuel C Morrison 16 Feb 1846; min- John Paine
Susana & Benjamin Williams 17 Oct 1788; widow b- John Stuart min- William Wilson- 17Oct1788
Coltrider
Sarah & John Johnson 15 Sep 1807; min- William King
Comerford
Catherine & Thomas Elsey 19 Jun 1797; d Patrick b- Patrick Comerford Thomas a widower
Commens
Eliza & Thomas Stephenson 27 Jun 1809; min- William King
Conell
Margaret & Robert Bruffey 1 Apr 1813; min- William Cravens
Connally
Elizabeth & Samuel Thorp 5 Dec 1798; d Thomas Connally, dec. James Patterson swears that Elizabeth is 21 b- Moses Thorp min- William Wilson- 13Dec1798
Connaway
Elizabeth & Henry Clarke 30 Jul 1812; min- William King
Rosannah & John Brown 15 Sep 1800; d Lawrence Connaway, dec. & Elizabeth Connaway who consents test- Moses Rusil & James Allison b- James Allison min- William Wilson- 16Sep1800
Connell
Elenor & Hezekiah Williams 6 Sep 1804; min- William King
Patsy & William Revercomb 19 Feb 1816; min- William Cravens
Polly & Joseph Blakemore 18 May 1814; min- William Cravens
Connelly
Aggy & John Goin 21 Jan 1815; min- Wright Burgess
Polly & George Berry 18 Sep 1792; d Thomas, who consents wit- Alexander & John Connelly, James Crawford b- Thomas Connelly min- James Johnston- 24Sep1792
Sarah & John Walker 8 Sep 1791; Minister's return spells name as 'Conaldly' d Arthur who consents wit- Thomas Connely & Samuel Frame b- John Connelly min- William Wilson- 8Sep1791

Augusta County Marriages -- Woman's Name

Connely
  Elizabeth & Samuel Throp 13 Dec 1798; min- William Wilson- 13Dec1798
  Mary & Joseph McColley 20 Aug 1789; Minister's return spells name as 'McCauley and Connelly' d Arthur wit- James & Robert Connely b- Robert Connely min- William Wilson- 20Aug1789

Conner
  Nancy & Samuel Shaver 23 Aug 1827; min- Conrad Speece
  Rachel & Daniel Shaver 13 May 1834; min- Conrad Speece
  Rebecca & Robert Reed 19 Apr 1823; min- William Wilson Jr

Conova
  Aribella & Henry Anderson 24 Jul 1828; min- Francis McFarland

Conway
  Peggy & William Jackson 27 Nov 1817; min- William King

Cook
  Betsy & Henry Lotz 20 Oct 1798; d Jacob Cook (Koch) b- Jacob Cook
  Catharine & John Rubush 12 Jun 1835; min- Francis McFarland
  Christina & Christian Eagle - Oct 1800; min- John Brown
  Elizabeth & Henry Doom 31 Jan 1850; min- William T Richardson
  Elizabeth & Lewis Teford 23 Apr 1840; min- D F Bittle
  Jane & Christian Eagle 20 Oct 1800; Signed Christian Ekel, Paulus Koch & Christian Ekell, the latter two giving surety
  Margaret Ann & Isaac Hoover 13 Feb 1845; min- Jacob Baer
  Margaret E & Joseph M Whitmore 29 Oct 1846; min- Stephen Hildebrand
  Margaret & David Houdishell 26 Dec 1827; min- G H Reimensnyder
  Mary A & Adam A Kiblinger 24 Sep 1846; min- Stephen Hildebrand
  Peggy & Frederick Hanger 23 Mar 1815; min- William King

Cooke
  Elizabeth & Jacob Coffman 16 Apr 1800; min- William Wilson- 16Apr1800

Cooper
  Anne & John White 20 Mar 1817; min- William King
  Eliza Ann & William J Potter 23 Apr 1849; min- B M Smith
  Isabella & William B Henry 17 Aug 1833; min- James Morrison
  Isabella & Christian Nickey 15 Jul 1830; min- Gerard Morgan
  Margaret & William McCutchen 5 Apr 1827; min- James Morrison
  Martha & William Crawford 16 Jun 1786; min- Samuel Shannon- 16Jun1786
  Mary Adaline & Ebenezer Watts 1 Jan 1828; min- William Monroe
  Rebecca Jane & Samuel C Hickok 8 Oct 1833; min- George Hildt
  Sally & John McCutchen 30 Oct 1823; min- James Morrison

Coorsy
  Winny & James Fraser 10 May 1785; d James

Augusta County Marriages -- Woman's Name

Corby
  Nancy & John Grose 25 Apr 1842; min- James Morrison
Cord
  Jean & Alexander Robertson 10 Apr 1786; b- James Robertson
    min- William Wilson- 10Apr1786
Coughenour
  Caty & John Alfort 4 Oct 1830; min- Abraham Garber-
    publication of banns
Coursey
  Caroline & George M Blakemore 3 Apr 1850; min- George B
    Rimel
  E M & Oliver Rinehart 28 Feb 1850; min- D W Arnold
  Elizabeth & John Cooper 30 Jun 1814; min- John McCue
  Elizabeth & Lewis Keller 24 Aug 1846; min- James H Brown
  Mary & Henry Gilkeson 30 Jan 1806; min- John McCue
  Rebecca & David Roads 8 Nov 1821; min- Daniel Stephens
Cowan
  Eleanor B & Jacob S Brown 16 Sep 1837; min- John A Steele
  Mary & Mathew Blair 28 Jul 1836; min- John A Steele
Cowman
  Catherine & John Sensebough 25 Feb 1793; d John b- John
    Cowman
  Elizabeth & Adam Spindle 2 May 1791; d John b- John Cowman
  Eve & Peter Clyne 25 Feb 1793; d John b- John Cowman
  Susan & Philip Loots 29 Nov 1821; 'Lutz' min- Daniel
    Stephens
Cox
  Amanda J & Thomas Cross 27 May 1845; min- E G Jamison
  Catherine & John Shuby 7 Sep 1837; min- James Paine
  Eliza A & James McCamey 1 Nov 1822; min- John Hendren
  Eliza & Samuel Brown 14 Aug 1810; min- William King
  Elizabeth & Abraham Bushong 20 Feb 1845; min- J C Hensell
  Julia Ann & John Grass 20 Jan 1842; min- F D Goodwin
  Mary & Jacob Bowers 28 Jun 1821; min- James Morrison
  Polly & William Brown 14 Oct 1811; min- William King
  Sally & John Lottz 8 Jan 1824; min- James Morrison
Coyner
  Elizabeth & Jacob Coyner 21 Dec 1815; min- John McCue
  Elizabeth & Robert Coyner 25 Dec 1841; min- John A Van
    Lear- publication of banns
  Lucy Ann & George W Allen 10 Sep 1835; min- William Scull
  Sarah & James Bell 11 Aug 1831; min- John Hendren
Craig
  Agatha & Joseph Thornton 19 Jan 1816; min- John McCue
  Ann & Joseph Harvey 30 Aug 1791; d Robert (dec) b- Robert
    Craig min- William Wilson- 1Sep1791
  Bell & Samuel McDaniel 29 Jan 1811; min- Joseph Reid
  Betsy & Braxton Davis 31 Jan 1822; min- James C Willson
  Elizabeth & Charles Berry 28 Jul 1819; min- John D Ewin
  Elizabeth & Samuel Crawford 9 Oct 1790; d Margaret, who
    consents wit- Alexander & James Craig b- William Crawford
    min- Archibald Scott- 12Oct1790
  Elizabeth & Charles C McCutchen 18 Mar 1819; min- William
    Calhoon

Augusta County Marriages -- Woman's Name

Craig (cont.)
  Jane & John Bekane 27 Dec 1827; min- William Wilson
  Jenney & James Patterson 24 Jun 1799; d William b- William Craig
  Julia Ann & Robert Dickenson 12 Sep 1832; min- Samuel Kennerly
  Lucinda & John Fulwider 4 May 1843; min- J C Hensell
  Margaret & James Bell 1 Sep 1807; min- William Wilson
  Margaret & William Jameson 2 May 1789; d Samuel, who consents wit- James Craig & Samuel Crawford b- James Craig min- John Montgomery- 12May1789
  Margaret & Samuel Patterson 12 Nov 1816; min- Conrad Speece, Jr
  Maria & Samuel Paine 7 May 1840; min- D F Bittle
  Mary & William Gay 24 Sep 1785; d Alexander b- William Armstrong wit- John Elliott min- Archibald Scott- 27Sep1785
  Mary & Robert McGill 16 Dec 1797; d James b- James Craig min- William Wilson- --Dec1797
  Nancy & Andrew Hamilton 14 Aug 1816; min- William Wilson
  Polly & John Cooper 22 Sep 1808; min- Joseph Reid
  Rebecca & Henry Platt 3 Jun 1793; b- Robert Craig min- John McCue- 20Jun1793
  Sarah & John Hamilton 3 Mar 1808; min- William Wilson
  Susanna & John Wilson 30 Sep 1816; min- John McCue

Crane
  Barbara & John Hunter 29 Jan 1805; min- William Wilson
  Elizabeth & Henry Amen 24 Feb 1795; min- William Wilson- 24Feb1795
  Mary & John McKensey 22 Apr 1800; Mary (of age) b- Cornelius O'dair min- John McCue- 24Apr1800

Crathers
  Phebe & David Wilson 30 Apr 1793; min- William Wilson- 30Apr1793

Craun
  Catharine & Daniel W Link 7 Nov 1847; min- P Shickel
  Sarah & Daniel Krickenbarger 8 Feb 1849; min Henry Wetzel

Crawford
  Ann & John Erwin 13 Sep 1821; min- Conrad Speece
  Ann & William Robertson 2 Jun 1788; b- John Crawford min- William Wilson- 3Jun1788
  Betsy & William Ingles 22 Sep 1818; min- Conrad Speece, Jr
  Betsy & Samuel McClung 29 Jan 1818; min- Conrad Speece, Jr
  Elizabeth & James (Jr) Craig 6 May 1813; min- Thomas Bourne
  Florence & Christian Surface 17 Jul 1799; 'Sirfes?' both of age b- Martin Surface, bro of Christian
  Isabella & James Ritchey 16 Feb 1798; d James Crawford, dec. con- Hugh Fulton test- Robert Fulton James Ritchey from Rockbridge b- John Fulton min- Archibald Scott- 22Feb1798
  Jane & John Gillaspie 2 Jun 1807; min- William Calhoon
  Jane & Franklin McCue 16 Sep 1819; min- Conrad Speece, Jr
  Margaret A & Cyrus Hyde 27 Dec 1820; min- Conrad Speece
  Margaret & James Crawford 12 Apr 1823; min- Conrad Speece
  Margaret & Daniel Fall 30 Aug 1797; d John who consents test- John Rees b- James Brown min- William Wilson- 31Aug1797

Augusta County Marriages -- Woman's Name

Crawford (cont.)
  Margaret & James Walker 8 Aug 1832; min- Samuel Kennerly
  Martha & Andrew Anderson 12 Mar 1788; b- John Miller min- William Wilson- 13Mar1788
  Martha & William Hogshead 5 Nov 1807; min- William Wilson
  Martha & Robert Poage 16 Sep 1791; d James who consents b- Robert Crawford & John Robertson b- William Crawford min- William Wilson- 15Sep1791
  Martha & Andrew Stull 7 May 1798; Minister's return spells name as 'Andrew Steele' d William b- William Crawford min- William Wilson- 9May1798
  Mary L & Edward G Moorman 19 Mar 1835; min- Conrad Speece
  Mary & William Bell 1 Mar 1796; Mary (of age) d James Crawford, dec. b- Alexander StClair Approbation of Jane Crawford min- William Wilson- 3Mar1796
  Mary & James Borland 17 Sep 1812; min- William Wilson
  Mary & James Crawford 27 Dec 1786; b- George Crawford wit- ----- Urquhart min- Archibald Scott- 18Mar1786 min- Archibald Scott- 30Dec1786
  Nancy A & Franklin McCue 19 Oct 1830; min- Conrad Speece
  Nancy & John Miller 7 Aug 1817; min- Conrad Speece, Jr
  Nancy & Leroy Newman 15 Sep 1825; min- Francis McFarland
  Nancy & James Tallman 4 Dec 1790; Bond lists James's name as Tolman d William b- John Armstrong s Benjamin, who consents wit- William Tallman & Thomas Hunter min- Archibald Scott- 10Dec1790
  Patsy & Peter Hanger 24 Nov 1818; min- Conrad Speece, Jr
  Polley & Samuel P V Gillespie 4 Apr 1815; min- William Calhoon
  Polly & John Armstrong 4 Dec 1790; d William b- James Tallman min- Archibald Scott- 10Dec1790
  Polly & James Lessley 7 Sep 1817; min- William Calhoon
  Rachel & John M Bare 3 Aug 1829; min- William Calhoon
  Rachel & William Bell 17 Sep 1799; widower & widow (of Charles) b- Alexander Crawford
  Rachel & John Poage 26 Nov 1792; b- Thomas Wilson min- William Wilson- 27Nov1792
  Rebecca Ann & Robert McClung 6 Nov 1828; min- Conrad Speece
  Rebecca & Joseph Surber 27 Jan 1814; min- William Calhoon
  Rebeccah & James Bell 19 Feb 1818; min- William Calhoon
  Sally & John Hyde 9 May 1811; min- John McCue
  Sally & Charles McClung 12 Oct 1815; min- Conrad Speece, Jr
  Sarah & Theobald John Campbell 7 Aug 1792; Minister's return spells name as 'Polly' b- John Campbell Sr min- William Wilson- 9Aug1792
  Violet & David Gwinn 11 Nov 1790; Minister's return spells name as 'Grim or Ginn' d William, who consents b- J Lyle Jr min- John Montgomery- 11Nov1790

Crawn
  Eliza & John Plecker 3 Oct 1839; min- John J Reimensnyder
  Mary & John Wise 9 Jan 1840; min- John J Reimensnyder

Creek
  Sarah & Jacob Dice 8 Aug 1829; min- James Morrison

Augusta County Marriages -- Woman's Name

Crick
  Catherine & John McKenzie 27 Dec 1827; min- James Morrison
Crips
  Elizabeth & Christian Faber 29 May 1821; min- Josiah Cole
Criser
  Susan Ann & George W Barger 5 Oct 1847; min- G W Israel
Crist
  Barbara & Thomas Sheets 5 Nov 1805; min- John McCue
  Catharine & David Fauber 24 Feb 1831; min- Francis McFarland
  Elizabeth & Jacob (Jr) Spitler 21 Sep 1800; min- Daniel Garber- 21Sep1800
  Elizabeth & William Swink 26 Jun 1841; min- John C Hensell
  Fanny & John Rife 28 Feb 1803; min- William King
  Hetty & Christopher Burkholder 25 Feb 1808; min- William McPheeters
  Margaret E & Thomas E Euritt 23 Nov 1846; min- Jacob C Spitler
  Mary S & Benjamin Lewis - --- 1834; min- Luke Collins
  Mary & Adam Zimbro 6 Sep 1842; min- F D Goodwin
  Nancy & Henry Snider 21 Jun 1802; min- William King- 21Jun1802
  Polly & Thomas Frazer 5 Dec 1797; d Andrew John Crist swears to Polly's age b- William Breeze min- Archibald Scott- 7Dec1797
  Rebecca & Philip Coiner 16 Mar 1826; min- William Wilson
  Sarah & Henry P Swink 23 Oct 1844; min- T T Castleman
  Susan Jane & David Clinebill 2 Aug 1827; min- James Morrison
  Susan & Reuben Lambert 10 Sep 1839; min- A B McCorkle
Croan
  Elizabeth & Samuel Hamaker - Sep 1813; min- John Brown
Crobarger
  Elizabeth & John Coffman 6 Jun 1815; min- William King
Croft
  Hetty & Samuel Cox 23 Jun 1837; min- Fred D Goodwin
  Julia Ann & John H Batis 26 Oct 1846; min- J A Van Lear
  Mary & Isaac Wombledorf 23 Oct 1826; min- Michael Meyerhoeffer
  Sarah & George Doom 5 May 1835; min- Robert M Lipscomb
Crombaker
  Elizabeth & Daniel Myers 13 Sep 1806; min- Samuel Garber
  Hannah & Isaac Myers 13 Sep 1806; min- Samuel Garber
Crombick
  Sarah & John Shown 16 Jan 1786; Minister's return spells name as 'Grombick' d George b- Andrew Shown wit- John Donald & William Gregory min- William Wilson- 31Jan1786
Crone
  Elizabeth & John Berry 19 Jan 1832; min- William Wilson
  Elizabeth & Martin Stombock 19 Dec 1847; min- Jacob C Spitler
  Elizabeth & John Welch 8 Dec 1814; min- William King

Augusta County Marriages -- Woman's Name

Croom
  May & Adam Daggy 23 May 1839; min- George Huffman
Croome
  Elizabeth & Isaac Foley 28 Sep 1841; min- J A Van Lear
Crosby
  Betsey & Sanders Reed 25 Dec 1803; min- Philip Kennerly
  Esther & Alexander Anderson 26 Feb 1811; min- William Calhoon
  Rebecca & John S Lambert 10 May 1849; min- J McKendree Reiley
  Sarah & David Hanger 15 Sep 1807; min- William Wilson
  Susan & John C Armstrong 21 Jul 1836; min- Stephen Smith
Cross
  Elizabeth & Thomas Cross 12 Oct 1834; min- George Hildt
  Mary Ann & Philip Whisman 7 Jun 1830; min- Hezekiah Best
Crossin
  Peggy & James Crist 6 Jan 1820; min- Luke Collins
Crouch
  Polly & James P Beard 13 Apr 1820; min- Robert Boyd
Crow
  Catherine & Nelson Hall 26 Nov 1828; min- William C. Morrison
Crowbarger
  Catharine & John Hawpe 17 Mar 1831; min- Francis McFarland
  Rachel & Solomon Wood 11 Apr 1833; min- Francis McFarland
  Susannah & John Shields 23 Apr 1835; min- Cornelius Gates
Crum
  Catharine & William Sheffer 25 Sep 1832; min- G H Reimensnyder
  Christiana & John Stoutamoyer 15 Dec 1842; min- Henry Wetzel
  Margaret & Jacob (Jr) Huffer 26 Aug 1847; min Henry Wetzel
Crumbacker
  Rebecca & Samuel (Jr) Leedy 21 Oct 1824; min- Abraham Garber- publication of banns
Crumbaker
  Polly & John Wines 21 Oct 1815; min- Abraham Garber- publication of banns
Crump
  Mary G & William Christian 6 Sep 1843; min- J C Hensell
Crumpecker
  Elizabeth & Benjamin Garber 14 May 1846; min- T T Castleman
Cullen
  Catharine & Thomas Cress 2 Oct 1834; min- William Scull
  Dorcas & George Brocius 27 Jun 1822; min- James C Willson
  Nancy & Jacob Barger 30 Jan 1812; min- John McCue
Cullon
  Elizabeth & John Bush 24 May 1803; 'Elizabeth Collins?' min- John McCue
Culp
  Anne & Jacob Swank 15 Aug 1820; min- William Wilson
  Polly & Henry Fisher 1 Dec 1825; min- Conrad Speece
  Sarah Ellen & Nathaniel Groves 3 Mar 1836; min- Joshua Webb

Augusta County Marriages -- Woman's Name

Culpt
Elizabeth & Jacob Aukes   21 Nov 1805;   min- William King
Cumins
Grizel & Joseph Stephens   28 May 1789;   perm- Grizel herself, who test. she is 21 and has no relations in this country   wit- John Steven & David Coalter   b- John Stevens
Cummins
Elizabeth & John Cummins   25 Sep 1803;   min- Philip Kennerly
Nancy & John Allison   15 Apr 1799;   d Charles   b- Charles Cummins   John of age
Cunningham
Fanny & Ezekiel Hopping   24 Jun 1795;   Minister's return spells name as 'Hoffing'   d John who consents test- David Cunningham Jr & James Ewing   b- John Diddey   min- John McCue- 24Jul1795
Margaret & Robert Ewing   31 Dec 1816;   min- William Calhoun
Mary & George Burwell   6 Jun 1805;   min- William King
Nancy & Robert Troxell   27 Oct 1831;   min- John Howell
Sarah & Samuel Bell   28 Aug 1804;   min- Benjamin Irwin
Sarah & John McChesney   30 Jul 1803;   min- William King
Cup
Catherine & Philip Sheets   27 May 1791;   d Marcus Kopp   b- Marcus Kopp
Polly & Jacob Whitmore   29 Dec 1801;   d Marcus   b- Marcus Cup   min- John Brown
Susannah & David Whitmore   - Jan 1806;   min- John Brown
Cupp
Catharine & William S Miller   29 Feb 1844;   min- Jacob Baer
Margaret A & James M Cambell   4 Aug 1845;   min- S Hildebrand
Margaret & Thomas Chrisman   19 Feb 1846;   min- Jacob Bear
Peggy & Conrad Noll   29 Aug 1826;   min- Daniel Stephens
Cupps
Dolly & John Moyers   4 Mar 1810;   min- William King
Sarah Jane & Samuel Parent   10 Nov 1841;   min- Peter Shickel
Curry
Ann & William Glenn   14 Jun 1791;   d Robert, who consents wit- Samuel & James Curry   bride & groom both of age   b- Samuel Curry   min- William Wilson- 15Jun1791
Ann & Samuel Rolston   10 Sep 1811;   min- Wright Burgess
Elizabeth & Alexander Curry   6 Oct 1795;   Elizabeth (of age) d William   b- Benjamin Curry   no minister listed; clerk's memorandum cites ceremony date as 9Oct1795
Elizabeth & Richard Dickson   27 Mar 1828;   min- John Hendren
Elizabeth & John Sharp   30 Sep 1797;   Minister's return spells name as 'John Thorp'   d Richard   b- Richard Curry   min- Archibald Scott- 30Sep1797
Jane & Mordecai Bean   17 Oct 1795;   Jane nicknamed 'Jenny' d William who consents   test- Benjamin Curry & Alexander Curry   b- Benjamin Curry   no minister listed; clerk's memorandum cites ceremony date as 20Oct1795
Jane & Benjamin Erwin   28 Apr 1806;   min- William King
Jane & George Hood   17 Jan 1791;   'Jenney'   b- Robert Curry min- William Wilson- 20Jan1791
Jane & John Hueston   23 Apr 1807;   min- William King

Augusta County Marriages -- Woman's Name

Curry (cont.)
  Jane & Robert Young 1 Mar 1819; Marriage bond states
    'Robert Curry' min- John Hendren
  Janetta & Robert C Glenn 30 Nov 1826; min- Conrad Speece
  Jenny & George Wood 20 Jan 1791; min- William Wilson-
    20Jan1791
  Julia A & Andrew H Ross 8 Mar 1832; min- Conrad Speece
  Lydia & John Burdett 16 Aug 1816; min- William Wilson
  Margaret & James Bell 14 Sep 1785; d Robert bond min-
    Benjamin Erwin- 15Sep1785
  Margaret & Samuel Curry 26 May 1802; min- Benjamin Irwin-
    26May1802
  Mary & Richard Brown 12 Apr 1798; Mary (of age) d Samuel
    b- Isaac Hanna
  Mary & James Oliver 10 Oct 1788; ni Robert Curry who
    consents test- James King & William Betman b- Andrew
    Thompson
  Mary & Thomas Reed 2 Dec 1799; Thomas (of age) d Richard
    b- Richard Curry min- William King- 2May1799
  Mary & James E Ross 29 Nov 1836; min- Stephen Smith
  Mary & George Wright 14 Mar 1789; d William, who consents
    wit- Robert Curry & John Wright b- Robert Curry min-
    Benjamin Erwin- 18Mar1788
  Melvina & William Dunlap 9 Nov 1849; min- John Hendren
  Polly & John Curry 28 Jun 1819; min- John Hendren
  Rebecca & John Erwin - Feb 1792; d James, who consents
    wit- Polly & John Curry b- John Curry
  Sally & James Curry 8 Oct 1821; min- John Hendren
  Sarah & Robert Black 9 Sep 1833; min- Conrad Speece
  Shelly & ----- Brown - Sep 1830; min- Gerard Morgan
  Susanah & William Erwin 4 Jul 1785; d James b- Andrew
    Erwin min- Benjamin Erwin- 7Jul1785
Cury
  Ann & John Lambert 24 Mar 1808; min- William King
Cushing
  Henrietta & Samuel McPherson Yost 9 May 1850; min- Thomas
    M Reese
Cusin
  Sally & Woodson Martin 17 Sep 1821; min- Josiah Cole
Dachen
  Elizabeth & Jacob Peck 9 Mar 1789; Minister's return
    spells name as 'Daken' d Windel Butt, who consents b-
    Henry Dill wit- John Clark & Samuel Jimeson min- William
    Wilson- 9Mar1789
Dack
  Catharine & John Kessecker 26 Dec 1791; d John, dec. b-
    Henry Deck
Daggy
  Betsy & John Hiney 17 Jan 1823; min- G H Reimensnyder
  Betsy & John Hiney 18 Jan 1823; min- G H Riemenschneider
  Catharine & Samuel Props 30 Nov 1819; min- G H
    Riemenschneider
  Elizabeth & John Botram 21 Mar 1823; min- G H
    Riemenschneider

Augusta County Marriages -- Woman's Name

Daggy (cont.)
  Polly & John Huffman - Oct 1825; min- John Brown
  Susan & John Baylor 24 Mar 1817; 'Aylor?' min- John McCue

Dale
  Jane & Arthur Connelly 23 Nov 1785; b- William Johnston d John min- John Brown- 6Dec1785

Dalhouse
  Jane & Samuel McAlery 22 Aug 1805; min- John McCue
  Juliet L & Thomas Montgomery 22 Apr 1811; min- John Montgomery
  Martha C & Benjamin F Wead 24 Jan 1850; min- William T Richardson

Dalton
  Letty & Robert Rennick 17 Nov 1794; Letty (of age) b- Francis Gardiner

Daniels
  Mary & John Fifer 15 Jan 1827; min- John Hendren

Danner
  Catherine & John Miller 9 Mar 1802; min- William King- 9Mar1802

Darrow
  Polly & William Taner - Oct 1817; min- John Brown

Darst
  Lucy Ann & Samuel Lightner 7 Feb 1839; min- A B McCorkle

Daugherty
  Julia Ann & Henry Swisher 21 Jan 1847; min- J C Hensell
  Sasannah & John Goodwin 27 Dec 1808; min- William King
  Susannah & Robert Powers 20 Nov 1834; min- William Calhoun

Davidson
  Agnes & John Dougherty 28 Jul 1790; Minister's return spells name as 'Doughady' d John & Sarah, who consent b- John Davidson wit- Benjamin Kilborn & James Dougherty (return sent by Samuel Brown and dated 31Jul1790)
  Elizabeth & Obadiah Tankersley 29 Jul 1797; d John b- John Davidson

Davies
  Sarah & John Ewing 22 May 1787; min- Archibald Scott- 22May1787

Davis
  Betsy & Joseph Parks 24 Jul 1795; Betsy 'Elizabeth' d Walter who consents test- John Brown b- John Davis min- John McCue- 13Aug1795
  Elizabeth & Joshua R Brooks 20 May 1845; min- G W Israel
  Elizabeth & John Kennedy 29 Oct 1846; min- James H Brown
  Fanny & John Caldwell 1 Dec 1789; Minister's return spells name as 'Nancy Davis' b- Zachariah Estill min- Archibald Scott- 2Dec1789
  Frances & William H Groom 29 Dec 1842; min- Samuel Wagner
  Genetta & John Fleming 26 Jul 1827; min- John Hendren
  Jane Annis & Thomas R Blair 10 May 1838; min- John A Van Lear
  Jane & Samuel Todd 30 May 1834; min- John Hendren
  Jennetta & George Somer 25 Nov 1817; min- William King- publication of banns

Augusta County Marriages -- Woman's Name

Davis (cont.)
Juda & Samuel Keller 13 Dec 1828; min- William C. Morrison
Martha Jane & Shelton R Abney 3 Dec 1835; min- William G Jackson
Mary & Samuel D Walton 2 Apr 1834; min- George Hildt
Polly & William Stephen 25 Jun 1804; min- William King
Rebecca & Zephaniah Nichols 30 Oct 1790; d James, who consents wit- Osborn Hamilton & Roger Heckman b- Joseph Davis
Ruth & William Lockridge 18 Apr 1820; min- John Hendren
Susan Jane & George M Woods 10 May 1848; min- W T Richardson

Dawson
Ann & James Barnet 10 Jun 1817; min- Wright Burgess

Deal
Ellen Ann & Lyman Harvey 26 Sep 1844; min- T T Castleman
Margaret & George Roberts 3 Feb 1848; min- Thomas H Busey
Mary J & John C Pockrott 24 Aug 1846; min- S Wagner
Sarah R & Thomas B Crigler 25 Jul 1839; min- Samuel Wagner

Deam
Nancy & Abel Langddon Smith 7 Oct 1816; min- William Wilson

Dean
Ferlisha & Benjamin Ervin 16 Jul 1835; min- Wright Burgess
Harriet & Alexander Ervin 19 Nov 1835; min- Wright Burgess
Mary & William Boreland 14 Feb 1786; bond
Sarah & William Borland 15 Feb 1786; 'Mary Dean'? min- William Wilson- 15Feb1786

Deane
Elizabeth & George Snider 29 Apr 1841; min- George B Rimel
Sarah & Isaac Felps 23 Sep 1788; b- Jacob Warwick

Deary
Barbara & Jacob Creek 28 Mar 1797; d Ustena b- Jacob Deary
Diannah & John Cook 6 Aug 1829; min- William Wilson
Elizabeth & Balser W Lutz 11 Aug 1831; min- William Wilson
Mary Jane & Nathan Fenton 5 Apr 1832; min- William Wilson

Decker
Margaret & Peter Burkhart 28 Jul 1794; b- Christian Bomgardner con- Jacob Kinney
Rebecca Ann & Calison Evans 31 Jan 1832; min- Francis McFarland

Deeds
Elizabeth & Henry Turnipseed 9 Dec 1811; d George min- John Bell

Dellon
Elizabeth & William Stulzer - Jan 1809; min- John Brown

Delly
Elizabeth & George Waggoner 25 Jul 1791; d John who consents wit- John Snitzer & George Kaelen b- Jacob Balen

Denison
Isabella & John Hyland 19 Feb 1835; min- Conrad Speece

Dennis
Elizabeth & Joseph Clarke 28 Jan 1817; min- William King

Augusta County Marriages -- Woman's Name

Dennison
  Margaret & Alexander A Young 8 Mar 1832; min- Conrad Speece
  Polly & Charles Windle 1 Nov 1828; min- William Wilson
Denny
  Sarah & Thomas McCaleb 4 Dec 1804; min- William King
Depriest
  Jane & David Moore 13 Aug 1788; d Ann who consents test-
    William Sterrett & James Elliott b- William Sterratt min-
    Archibald Scott- 14Aug1788
  Mary & John (Jr) Trimble 15 Dec 1794; b- John Trimble Sr
Dequeza
  Polly & Charles Clark 4 Nov 1807; min- John McCue
Derrough
  Elizabeth & John Apley - Sep 1817; min- John Brown
Despar
  Mary Ellen & Benjamin Davis 1 Feb 1849; min- D W Arnold
Detamore
  Elizabeth & Solomon Landes 22 Jan 1829; min- John Hendren
Dettemore
  Sara & Samuel Skyles 19 Mar 1827; min- G H Reimensnyder
Devenbough
  Mary & John Blackwell 15 Jan 1835; min- J J Glossbrenner
Devericks
  Margaret & Thomas Botkin 20 Apr 1786; d Thomas bond min-
    Samuel Shannon- 24Apr1786
Devine
  Bridget & James Campbell 21 Dec 1792; Minister's return
    spells name as 'Divine' widow consent signed by Thomas
    Greene & Bridget Devin, widow b- John Price min- William
    Wilson- 24Dec1792
Dick
  Mary & William Wilson 17 Dec 1793; Minister's return
    spells name as 'Doak' b- Samuel Dick min- John McCue-
    23Dec1793
Dickenson
  Elizabeth & Hugh Crawford 25 May 1820; min- William Wilson
Dickerson
  Lydia & Addison Fifer 13 Sep 1834; min- John Hendren
Dickey
  Ellen & Abraham LaRue 30 Mar 1809; min- William Wilson
  Jane & James Young 17 Feb 1801; Minister's return spells
    name as 'Deckey' d John b- John Dickey min- Daniel
    Garber- 17Feb1801
  Mary & Richard Johnston 23 Dec 1806; min- William Wilson
  Sarah & Henry Cooper 5 Aug 1804; min- William King
Dicky
  Margaret & Thomas Rankin 26 May 1807; min- William Wilson
Diddle
  Anna & Gordan White 25 Jan 1790; Minister's return spells
    name as 'Gordon White and Ann Duddale' b- John Didel min-
    Samuel Carrick- 26Jan1790
Didell
  Jane & James Hunter 19 May 1808; min- William King

Dietrick
Susannah & Henry Hiestand 12 Jun 1812; min- William Cravens

Diller
Julia Ann & Thomas Washington 26 Mar 1842; min- Peter Shickel

Dillon
Polly & Adam Neighborrgall 22 Oct 1802; min- William Wilson- 22Oct1802

Dinkle
Eliza & James F Davis 28 Jul 1848; min- D W Arnold
Rebecca & David Shover 26 Dec 1847; min- D W Arnold
Rebecca & Oliver Henry Perry Silings 25 Jan 1849; min- P Shickel

Dinnison
Keterenah & Thomas Tacket 4 Jul 1785; min- Samuel Shannon- 4Jul1785
Sarah & James Davison 4 Jul 1785; min- Samuel Shannon- 4Jul1785

Dinsmore
Judith & David Bright 6 Jun 1799; s James Dinsmore, dec. of Amherst George Bright, bro of David, attests to age Samuel Dinsmore, bro of Judith attests to age b- George Bright min- William King- 6Jun1799
Rebecca & William Stodgall 14 Sep 1795; Samuel Dinsmore made oath that Rebecca has lived in the county six months b- Alexander Gibson

Dixon
Ann & James McIntire 27 Aug 1827; min- Conrad Speece
Hariet & Jacob Griner 1 Nov 1825; min- William Wilson
Letty & James Byers 29 Apr 1817; min- Conrad Speece, Jr
Mary & Thomas Story 15 Jul 1817; min- Wright Burgess
Nancy & Samuel Whisman 3 Feb 1829; min- William Wilson
Sally & William Bawcutt 29 Apr 1803; min- William King

Doak
Alcinda J & Joseph N Woodward 22 Oct 1840; min- James Paine
Catherine & Alexander Brownlee 19 Jan 1829; min- Francis McFarland
Elizabeth & Henry Haupe 7 Feb 1828; min- Francis McFarland
Elizabeth & John Lilley 10 Apr 1797; d Robert John Doak swears John Lilley over 21 b- Robert Doak & Alexander StClair min- Archibald Scott- 11Apr1797
Isabella & John Milliken 27 Sep 1786; Minister's return spells name as 'Millihen' b- Robert Torbet min- Archibald Scott- 28Sep1786
Jennie & James Berry 6 Jan 1787; d David & Jannet who consent wit- Robert Doak & John Doak b- John Berry min- Archibald Scott- 10Jan1787

Doake
Sarah T & James L Cunningham 3 Mar 1825; min- Francis McFarland

Dobage
Hannah & Joseph Hooke 4 Jan 1790; Minister's return spells name as 'Hook' widow b- Isaac Beal min- Benjamin Erwin- 19Jan1790

Augusta County Marriages -- Woman's Name

Dobbs
  Elizabeth & Thomas Pickering 31 Dec 1831; min- Samuel Kennerly
  Mary B & James W Smith 3 Aug 1842; min- Samuel Wagner
  Melvina & John B Eagle 4 Aug 1835; min- Samuel Kennerly
Dohine
  Susannah & John Thomas 15 Sep 1814; min- William King
Doke
  Elizabeth & John Lerew 11 Mar 1799; d David sis to Samuel Elizabeth (of age) s Jacob who consents test- Benjamin Larew b- Samuel Doke & John McClelland
Dold
  Catherine & John Lawrence 24 Nov 1798; d Philip who consents test- William Dold b- Jesse Dold
  Eliza & Frederick Burns 10 Mar 1834; min- James C Wilson
  Elizabeth & William Donaldson 22 May 1795; d Philip b- Philip Dold min- John McCue- 26May1795
  Nancy & Luther Morgan 31 Jan 1798; d Philip who consents test- Gideon Morgan b- Robert McDowell min- John McCue- 1Feb1798
  Patsey & Robert McDowell 28 Feb 1798; d Philip b- Philip Dold min- John McCue- 1Mar1798
Dollen
  Letty & Robert Ranicks 18 Nov 1794
Dollhouse
  Sally & Samuel Hunter 7 Jan 1808; min- John McCue
Donaghe
  Ann & Valentine Meritt 3 Sep 1812; min- William King
  Elizabeth & John Nichol 9 Dec 1802; Minister's return spells name as 'Donaho' min- William Wilson- 9Dec1802
  Jane & Hatch Clark 22 Dec 1817; min- William King
  Margaret & Robert B White 5 Jul 1843; min- P E Stevenson
  Nancy & John Rankin 20 Oct 1800; Minister's return spells name as 'Runkel' Nancy (of age) d William Jeremiah Runkle swears his brother, John, is of age b- John Roberts & Jeremiah Runkle min- William King- 22Oct1800
  Peggy & John Keys 18 Apr 1796; Peggy (of age) d William b- James McGongal
Donahe
  Polly & John Coursey 29 Dec 1814; min- William Wilson
Donaho
  Matty & William Mardis 4 Nov 1813; min- William King
Donaldson
  Margaret & Stephen Cocke 9 Sep 1794; 'Donnaldson' d Robert b- Robert Donaldson no minister listed; clerk's memorandum cites ceremony date as 11Sep1794
Donally
  Nancy & Thomas (Jr) Crow 13 Mar 1789; d Charles & Mary, who consent wit- John Wayt & Stephen Smith b- Alexander Lewis
Donalson
  Rebecca & John Wilson 9 Mar 1809; min- William Calhoun

Augusta County Marriages -- Woman's Name

Donefin
  Elizabeth & Isaac Blackwood 22 Jun 1818; min- William King

Donnally
  Mary & Reuben Slaughter 8 Apr 1791; Minister's return spells name as 'Donally' d Andrew who consents wit- Samuel Merritt b- William Chambers min- John Montgomery- 14Apr1791

Donovan
  Jane & Henry Snider 5 Oct 1811; min- A B Davidson

Doom
  Elizabeth & Solomon Reece 17 Sep 1840; min- Samuel Wagner
  Margaret Ann & David R Blackburn 19 Apr 1843; min- E R Veitch
  Margaret & Jacob Speck 24 Dec 1847; min- Stephen Hildebrand

Doren
  Elizabeth & James Gray 6 Jun 1787; Minister's return spells name as 'Dooran' b- Abraham McFarland min- Samuel Shannon- 14Jun1787

Dougherty
  Peggy & John Risk 6 Nov 1806; min- William McPheeters

Douglas
  Ellen S & John McCue 5 Dec 1849; min- B M Smith
  Nancy & John Ransbarger 26 Aug 1793; Minister's return spells name as 'Douglass' b- Garsper Clements min- William Wilson- 19Aug1793

Douglass
  F A & Addison Waddell 4 Jan 1849; min- B M Smith

Douthat
  Anne & Hugh French 14 Jan 1797; widow of William b- Robert McClenachan min- John McCue- 15Jan1797

Dowell
  Darcas & John Dunlap 24 Sep 1802; min- John McCue- 24Sep1802
  Milley & Robert McAlary 24 Sep 1805; min- John McCue
  Nancy Jane & Jacob Swats 4 May 1843; min- Peter Miller

Downey
  Barbara & Jacob Olinger 1 Jun 1785; d George b- William Cale wit- Thomas Gwin
  Elizabeth & John Ramsey 2 Dec 1793; Request by John for license test- James Hodge & James Guy b- Adam Bratton
  Jane & Joseph Bell 26 Mar 1798; Jane (of age) d Philip Downey, dec. b- John Donnelly min- William Wilson- 27Mar1798
  Mary & Nathan Hall 2 Jan 1800; widow (of William) b- William Short & Judy Price min- William King- 2Jan1800

Driver
  Anna & Joseph Click 25 Mar 1845; min- T T Castleman

Dudley
  Martha Ann & Lorenzo (Jr) Houdashell 3 Apr 1849; min Henry Wetzel

Dull
  Catherine & George Cox 31 Jan 1828; min- James Morrison
  Elizabeth & David Andrews 12 May 1825; min- Josiah Cole
  Elizabeth & Christopher Palmer 11 Mar 1801; d George b- George Dull

Augusta County Marriages -- Woman's Name

Dull (cont.)
  Sarah & Henry Taylor 8 Mar 1825; min- Josiah Cole
Dunbar
  Elizabeth & Jeremiah Donovan 29 Sep 1790; d Francis, who
    consents wit- William Dunbar & Leroy Newman min- Archibald
    Scott- 16Oct1790
Dunlap
  Elizabeth & John Ailshire 2 Nov 1809; min- William King
  Elizabeth & Philip O Palmer 8 Mar 1827; min- Francis
    McFarland
  Elizabeth & Levi L Stevenson 6 Apr 1815; min- William
    Calhoun
  Isabella & Thomas Harris 31 Oct 1841; min- D F Bittle
  Isabella & Robert Sterret 8 Dec 1818; min- John D Ewin
  Jane & Augustus Argenbright 16 Sep 1833; min- Augustus Babb
  Jane & David Kerr 29 Mar 1824; min- Francis McFarland
  Jane & William Wickle 16 Oct 1810; min- William King
  Margaret & Jacob Spitler 14 Jun 1824; min- Michael
    Meyerhoeffer
  Martha & William Buchanan 5 Mar 1835; min- Francis
    McFarland
  Mary & Alexander Crosby 10 Jun 1813; min- William King
  Mary & John Kendle 30 Apr 1818; min- William King
  Nancy G & Alexander Templeton 25 Nov 1824; min- William W
    Calhoun
  Nancy & James Youell 22 Apr 1819; min- John D Ewin
Dunn
  Eleanor & Benjamin Pursell 10 Dec 1798; Minister's return
    spells name as 'Pursel' Eleanor (of age) d Walter Dunn,
    dec. b- John Trimble min- Archibald Scott- 13Dec1798
  Jane & John Whitesell 10 Jun 1813; min- William King
  Nancy & Edward Barker 6 Feb 1786; widow bond
  Peggy & William Quick 12 Jun 1811; min- William King
Dunwiddie
  Mary & John Kincaid 7 Jan 1786; Minister's return spells
    name as 'Dinwiddie' d Robert Dunwoody b- William Dickey
    min- Samuel Shannon- 17Jan1786
Dyer
  Celia A & William G Staples 6 Sep 1848; min- T T Castleman
  Mary & John Sheets 22 Feb 1827; min- John Hendren
Eagal
  Elizabeth & John Clements 10 Jul 1790; d Christian Eckell,
    who consents wit- Alexander Stuart & J Beal b- Christian
    Eckell
Eagle
  Catherine & Peter Sheets 16 Feb 1796; d Christian Ekel b-
    Christian Eagle
  Magdalena & Henry Eagle 20 Jun 1799; d Christian b-
    Christian Eagle
  Nancy & Jordan Whitlock 23 Nov 1826; min- William Monroe
Eagon
  Sally & William Lowman 19 Feb 1835; min- George Hildt

Augusta County Marriages -- Woman's Name

Eakle
  Elizabeth & Jacob Slagle 10 Jan 1822; min- James C Willson
  Margaret & William Allison 30 Oct 1828; min- Conrad Speece
  Mary & John H Newcomb 10 Nov 1825; min- Josiah Cole
  Mary & Isaac Peters 9 Oct 1828; min- William C. Morrison
  Polly & Daniel Miller 20 Jan 1823; min- James C Willson
  Sarah & Jesse Hart 20 Apr 1819; min- Conrad Speece, Jr
Earhart
  Catherine & Christopher Bartley 20 Apr 1805; min- Samuel Monett
  Elizabeth & Benjamin Karicofe 29 Nov 1838; min- John A Van Lear
  Katharine & Henry Puls 17 Aug 1846; min- P Shickel
  Mary & Jacob Haldeman 7 Jun 1791; d Nicholas, who consents b- Jacob Eversole
  Sarah Ann & John B Hess 30 Mar 1848; min Henry Wetzel
  Sarah & Abraham Holderman 7 Jan 1794; d Nicholas Affidavit of full age of Sarah b- Thomas Turk Jr min- John McCue- 9Jan1794
  Sophia & Anthony Ailor 4 Apr 1797; min- William Wilson- 4Apr1797
  Susannah & Anthony Witsal 12 Aug 1793; min- John McCue- 12Aug1793
Earley
  Betsy & Isaac Yearout 14 Feb 1801; Betsy (of age) d Daniel who consents b- John Strain min- Daniel Garber- 17Feb1801
  Elizabeth & Isaac Moses 30 May 1823; min- William Wilson Jr
Early
  Anne & Charles Yearout 22 Oct 1802; 'Anne Yearly'? min- William Wilson- 22Oct1802
  Mary & John Campbell 5 Feb 1795; 'Polly?' d Daniel b- Daniel Early min- William Wilson- 5Feb1795
East
  Elizabeth & William King 5 Oct 1826; min- William Monroe
  Mary & John Beard 11 Sep 1828; min- James Morrison
  Nancy & Timothy Hartigan 9 Jan 1798; d James b- James East
Eastham
  Sarah & Abraham Halderman 9 Jan 1794; min- John McCue- 9Jan1794
Eccord
  Mary & John Lowtermilk 23 May 1795; d Francis b- Christian Eccord
  Polly & John Spitler 22 Feb 1797; d Frantz b- Francis Eccord
Edde
  Margaret & John Cooper 16 Apr 1791; d John, of Cowpasture, who consents b- I Beal
Edgar
  Eliza Jane & George W Summers 12 Aug 1847; min- John Bowen
Edgecomb
  Ann & Jeremiah Dowling 7 Mar 1795; widow who gives her own consent test-John Bruffey & Margaret Bruffey b- John Bruffey min- John McCue- 12Mar1795

Augusta County Marriages -- Woman's Name

Edmiston
  Jane & John McGill 5 Oct 1785; Edmondson? d Mathew b-
    William Shires wit- Richard Jones & James McCann min-
    Archibald Scott- 6Oct1785
Edmonds
  Ann & John Morgan 12 Jul 1792; Minister's return spells
    name as 'Edmunds' d George, dec.& Nelly Fillis, who
    consents b- Benjamin Johnston min- John McCue- 12Jun1792
  Lucy A & Charles T Cameron 12 May 1840; min- Frederick D
    Goodwin
Edmunds
  Helen & John McLeer 4 Sep 1837; min- Fred D Goodwin
Edson
  Jane A & John Moffett 21 Feb 1822; min- William W Calhoun
Edwards
  Mary & John Teagle 12 Jan 1804; min- John McCue
Eeast
  Mary & Peter Repetoe 22 Jun 1811; min- Wright Burgess
Eidsell
  Harriet & Waddle Burch 26 Mar 1817; min- Wright Burgess
Eidson
  Betsy Ann & Daniel Willson 4 Jan 1827; min- William W
    Calhoun
  Margaret S & William S Hanger 2 Sep 1834; min- William
    Calhoun
  Mary Catharine & Jessee Hoover 15 May 1834; min- William
    Calhoun
Ekerson
  Christiana & John Farmer 10 Feb 1796; widow sis of Jacob
    Minnick b- Jacob Minnick
Ellery
  Eliza & Balser W Lutz 14 Apr 1840; min- Jacob Stirewalt
Ellet
  Eliza & Noah Shaver 17 Apr 1850; min- George B Rimel
Ellinger
  Elizabeth & George Gabhart 24 Aug 1799; d Stoaks b-
    Stoaks Ellinger s Jacob Gabert who consents test- Philip
    Palmer & Peter Gabert
Elliott
  Amelia & William Page 31 Jul 1800; widower Amelia not yet
    20 d Peter who consents b- David Greiner
  Julia Ann & Eli Shelly 17 Mar 1845; min- Jacob Baer
  Margaret Ann & Joel Garrison 16 Jun 1823; min- John Hendren
  Margaret & Robert Givens 17 May 1785; Margaret of age d
    William b- George Bratton min- Samuel Shannon- 2Jun1785
  Mary & Audley Campbell 26 Oct 1791; b- James Elliott no
    minister listed; clerk's memorandum cites ceremony date as
    28Oct1791
  Mary & John Coruthers 14 Aug 1795; Mary (of age) d
    William Elliott, dec. b- John Gordan
  Sarah & Morris Friel 1 Aug 1797; 'Freel?' d John who
    consents test- Reuben Sursell & Joseph Wilson con- Daniel
    Friel test- Robert Armstrong & James Ross b- James Ross
    min- Archibald Scott- 3Aug1797

Augusta County Marriages -- Woman's Name

Ellis
Susan & William Caldwell 23 Dec 1844; min- B M Smith
Elstock
Mary & Moses Hugghart 5 Sep 1799; Mary (of age) d Joseph Elstock of Louisa, and a free mulatto woman b- John McCutchen
Emmery
Elener & Daniel Spitler 24 Nov 1806; min- William King
Emmett
Anna & John Lee 2 Jun 1803; min- William King
Rebecca & James Smith 2 Jun 1803; min- William King
Emmitt
Polly & Robert Mills 24 Mar 1807; min- William King
Engleman
Catharine G & William B Lavell 6 Aug 1842; min- D F Bittle
Catharine & Samuel Kellar 2 Oct 1821; min- Michael Meyerhoeffer
Elizabeth & Peter Engleman 11 Aug 1842; min- D F Bittle
Elizabeth & Eleazer Fenton 3 Aug 1809; min- William King
Mary & Joseph Heyden 30 Sep 1828; min- William C. Morrison
Mary & Andrew Sheets 11 Oct 1841; min- John C Hensell
Rachel & John C Barger 15 Dec 1842; min- J C Hensell
Rebecca & George W Keller 15 Dec 1842; min- J C Hensell
Susannah & Harman D Keller 27 Jul 1847; min- J C Hensell
English
Acheas & Nehemiah Armstrong 2 Jun 1815; min- William King
Ergebright
Susana & John Sheetz - May 1810; min- John Brown
Erwin
Eliza & John Lockridge 29 May 1821; min- John Hendren
Elizabeth & William Armstrong 1 Apr 1788; d Jarred who consents wit- John Armstrong & Andrew Jordan b- John Armstrong min- Archibald Scott- 1Apr1788
Elizabeth & Edward Brady 29 Mar 1791; d Richard b- Richard Erwin min- John Montgomery- 4Apr1791
Elizabeth & Charles Hambleton 7 Apr 1809; min- William King
Elizabeth & James McGuffin 19 Apr 1803; min- William King
Elizabeth & John Woodell 30 Jan 1792; d Edward who consents wit- Edward Irvine Jr b- Edward Irvine min- Benjamin Irwin- 31Jan1792
Frances & James Allen 1 Apr 1793; sis to John Erwin who consents, and affirms Frances over 21 b- David McNair min- William Wilson- 2Apr1793
Hanah & William Stunkard 10 Jan 1791; Minister's return spells name as 'William Stockard' orphan sister of Benjamin Erwin b- Benjamin Erwin min- John Montgomery- 13Feb1791
Jane & John Burges 15 Jun 1796; 'Burgess?' d Samuel s Thomas (con) test- Elisha Price & Robert Gamble Consent before William Price, magistrate of Henrico cty b- Samuel Erwin min- William Wilson- 16Jun1796
Jane & James (Jr) Curry 3 Feb 1801; d Edward b- Edward Erwin min- Daniel Garber- 5Feb1801
Jenney & Christian Coiner 3 Aug 1802; min- William King- 3Aug1802

Augusta County Marriages -- Woman's Name

Erwin (cont.)
Jenny & John Erwin 22 Feb 1791; Minister's return spells name as 'Jane' d Francis, who consents wit- William Erwin & John Bell b- William Irwin min- Benjamin Irvin- 22Feb1791
Margaret & Hugh Campbell 14 Jun 1796; d Samuel Hugh (of age) b- Samuel Erwin min- William Wilson- 16Jun1796
Margaret & Bethuel Herring 11 Oct 1800; widower Margaret (of age) d John, sis to Thomas Erwin Margaret gives own consent b- Thomas Erwin
Margaret & Thomas Woodall 22 Sep 1800; d Edward Erwin, dec. (but Edward gives consent for his daughter Margaret to marry Thomas) test- John Ervine & James Ervine b- John Erwin
Mary Ann & Jesse Scott 19 Nov 1816; min- William Wilson
Mary & James Curry 27 Mar 1786; min- William Wilson- 27Mar1786
Mary & John Guy 19 Nov 1785; d Edward (dec) b- James Guy
Peggy & John Slagle 24 Dec 1810; min- William King
Peggy & Thomas Sullivan 29 Mar 1790; b- Richard Erwin min- Archibald Scott- 29Mar1790
Polly & Francis Bell 25 Jan 1802; d John wit- Charles Penn b- John Erwin min- Benjamin Irwin- 26Jan1802
Polly & James Hamilton 18 Nov 1806; min- William Wilson
Rebecca & William McKee 12 Aug 1789; orphan, granddaughter of Jane Erwin, who consents wit- Robert Grattan & Mary Erwin b- John Young min- William Wilson- 13Aug1789

Erwine
Ann & James Rayburn 2 Jul 1807; min- William King

Eskridge
Eleanor B & George W Wall 11 Jan 1820; min- Daniel Stephens
Frances P & John L Towel 6 May 1836; min- John A Steele

Estill
Catherine & Robert M Kule 6 Mar 1819; min- John Hendren
Elizabeth & John Ervin 9 Jul 1835; min- John Hendren
Hannah & Livingston Waddell 8 Feb 1827; min- John Hendren
Mary Ann & Joseph Davies 17 Oct 1786; Davis? b- Zachary Estill wit- Hugh Campbell min- Archibald Scott- 15Oct1786
Nancy & Thomas M McClintic 14 Feb 1843; min- John A Van Lear
Rebecca & Zachariah Fort Estill 4 May 1785; widow of John Estill b- George Hudson
Sarah & William Shields 23 Jun 1792; d John b- James Aston no minister listed; clerk's memorandum cites ceremony date as 28Jun1792

Etter
Mary & John Carothers 13 Aug 1795; 'Mary Elliott?' min- Archibald Scott- 13Aug1795

Eurick
Mary M & William H Marshall 21 Jan 1847; min- J A Van Lear

Euritt
Nancy B & Edward P Coatney 23 Feb 1843; min- John A Van Lear
Sarah J & James R Lamb 7 Sep 1843; min- John A Van Lear

<u>Augusta County Marriages -- Woman's Name</u>

Evan
   Sarah &   James Robertson   12 Oct 1837;   min- James Paine
Evans
   Elizabeth G &   James Beard   7 Mar 1833;   min- Francis
      McFarland
   Elizabeth &   George Craig   16 Dec 1790;   'Betsy'   d Griffin
      b- James Craig   min- William Wilson- 19Dec1790
   Grizey &   Robert Brooks   24 Sep 1794;   Affidavit by Robert
      that Grisez (Crisey?) is over 21   b- William Bell   min- John
      Brown- 26Sep1794
   Jane &   George Staggs   13 Apr 1817;   min- William King
   Nancy &   William Engard   26 Nov 1799;   d David Evans, dec.
      b- Jacob Gregory   min- William King- 28Nov1799
   Polly &   George Rankin   7 Feb 1829;   min- William C. Morrison
   Polly &   Henry Tomblinson   21 Aug 1806;   min- William King
   Sally &   James Campbell   7 Jan 1800;   d Griffin   b- John
      Campbell   min- William Wilson- 7Jan1800
Eve
   Mary &   James Brownlee   28 Jan 1825;   min- Josiah Cole
Evelsizer
   Mary &   William Hamd   25 Dec 1799;   Minister's return spells
      name as 'Ham'   d Jacob Evilsizer (Ubelsaueftzer)   test- John
      Lee   b- John Armstrong   min- William King- 27Dec1799
Eversole
   Catharine &   William Fifer   23 Jan 1845;   min- S Wagner
   Polly &   Spicer Humphreys   26 May 1817;   min- William King
Evilsiser
   Sally &   Peter Wartsook   14 Mar 1809;   min- William King
Ewell
   Jennett &   Robert Miller   8 Jul 1793;   Minister's return
      spells name as 'Youel'   d William Youel   b- William Ewell
      min- John Montgomery- 16Jul1793
Ewin
   Betsy &   Joseph Boyers   30 Jul 1818;   min- William King
   Martha &   John Riner   14 Apr 1800;   Minister's return spells
      name as 'Erwin'   John (of age)   d Henry   b- Henry Ervin
      min- William Wilson- 14Apr1800
   Mary &   George H Harris   3 Jul 1820;   min- Gerard Morgan
Ewing
   Jane &   William Beard   8 Mar 1821;   min- James Morrison
   Jane &   Moses Moore   22 Mar 1786;   d James   wit- William
      Rankin & Alexander Gibson   min- Samuel Shannon- 11Apr1786
   Sarah &   John Towell   - Dec 1807;   min- John Brown
Ewings
   Margaret &   Peter Long   28 Jul 1800;   Minister's return
      spells name as 'Peggy Erwin'   d Henry   b- Henry Ewing, John
      Allison & Jacob Coyner   min- William Wilson- 29Jul1800
Fackler
   Ann &   Samuel Gardner   20 Oct 1814;   min- William Calhoun
   Eleanor &   Hugh Paul   22 Dec 1794;   Eleanor nicknamed 'Ally'
      d Michael, merchant in Staunton who consents   test- G
      Christian & Phill North   b- Philip North
   Sally &   Calvin Morgan   20 Jan 1801;   d Michael who consents
      test- H Paul   b- John Bowyer

280

Augusta County Marriages -- Woman's Name

Fadely
   Polly & Anderson Furr 9 Sep 1833; min- George Hildt
Faegely
   Elizabeth & Thomas Brownfield 19 Dec 1819; min- G H
      Riemenschneider
Faidley
   Catharine & William Cox 5 Mar 1834; min- Augustus Babb
Fairburn
   Isabella & James Back 25 Sep 1834; min- John A Steele
   Mary & John Ramsey 5 Jan 1830; min- William Wilson
   Susannah & George Taylor 15 Jun 1843; min- John A Van Lear
Fall
   Catharine & Lewis Keller 16 Apr 1818; min- William Calhoun
   Easter & Henry Swab - Mar 1805; min- John Brown
   Elizabeth & John Brown 8 Jun 1801; Elizabeth (of age) d
      George b- Daniel Fall
   Hannah & Patrick Mellen 25 Jun 1807; min- William King
   Magdalene & Frederick Keller 24 Feb 1818; min- William King
Falls
   Anna & David Mays 6 Aug 1828; min- John Hendren
   Mary & Valentine Cup 21 Dec 1793; 'Valentine Crop?'d
      George b- George Falls no minister listed; clerk's
      memorandum cites ceremony date as Jan1794
   Nancy & Samuel Baylor 10 Apr 1828; min- William Calhoun
Farrow
   Elizabeth & Adam Teebo 3 Aug 1822; min- Josiah Cole
   Martha Jane & Francis Huff 21 Dec 1848; min- J McKendree
      Reiley
Fauber
   Barbara & Pleasant Ewell 27 Jan 1814; min- William King
   Barbara & Samuel McClure 14 Feb 1805; min- John McCue
   Catherine & Daniel Shelley 15 Jan 1817; min- William King
   Eliza & Michael Snyder 7 Feb 1828; min- John Hendren
   Elizabeth & Henry Harner 22 Apr 1823; min- James C Willson
   Elizabeth & Thomas James 30 Jun 1819; min- G H
      Riemenschneider
   Elizabeth & Philip Reeser 15 Jan 1839; min- Isaac Jones
   Kitty & John Brownfield 14 Jul 1792; Minister's return
      spells name as 'Fauver' d Christian, who consents wit-
      John Stout & Timothy Turner b- James Johnston, Jacob Kinney
      & Patrick Ryan min- John McCue- 14Jul1792
   Mary Ann & David Sink 11 Apr 1822; min- John Brown
   Matilda & William Shelton 30 Dec 1837; min- J C Hensell
   Polly & George Resley 24 Sep 1811; min- William King
   Sarah & Daniel Leonard 15 Jan 1822; min- James C Willson
Faucet
   Elizabeth W J & William Nales 23 Sep 1808; min- Joel Watson
Faundree
   Mildred & Thomas J Smith - Jun 1826; min- Joseph Smith
Fauver
   Margaret & Ezra G Huffman 29 Oct 1839; min- George B Rimel
   Margret & John Crist 14 Jun 1837; min- James Paine

Augusta County Marriages -- Woman's Name

Fawber
  Anne & Jacob Ruple 20 Mar 1815; min- Wright Burgess
  Catherine & Philip Coiner 5 Mar 1798; d Valentine wit-
    William Sterrett b- Jacob Swoope min- John McCue- 8Mar1798
  Rosannah & Joseph Snider 20 Oct 1831; min- John Hendren
  Sally & John Cash 18 Nov 1824; min- Luke Collins
Fawner
  Madlena & Frederick Hoof 4 Jun 1799; d Christian b-
    Christian Fawner
Feamster
  Elizabeth & Adam Bratton 4 Jul 1788; Minister's return
    spells name as 'Feemster' d Thomas who consents wit-
    William Black & John McGummery b- James Lyle Jr min-
    Archibald Scott- 9Jul1788
Fellers
  Catharine & William Armstrong 26 Dec 1833; min- Samuel
    Kennerly
  Polly & David Rinehart 14 Oct 1813; min- William King
  Rebecca & George Welch 12 Aug 1826; min- Michael
    Meyerhoeffer
  Sarah & William Stickley 8 Jan 1835; min- Samuel Kennerly
Fellows
  Sally & Joseph Fellows 26 Aug 1820; min- Daniel Stephens
Fennel
  Kitty & John Beck 23 Nov 1826; min- Alexander Templeton
Fenton
  Elizabeth & Samuel Fackler 23 Jul 1801; Minister's return
    spells name as 'Fackar' d Enoch b- Enoch Fenton min- John
    McCue- 23Jul1801
  Julia & Daniel Whisman 13 Jan 1820; min- Gerard Morgan
  Matilda & Enos Jones 23 Aug 1822; min- Josiah Cole
  Rebecca & Enos Jones 26 Nov 1827; min- William Wilson
Fertig
  Sarah L & Jacob Perkey 16 Feb 1837; min- Stephen Smith
Fielding
  Jane & Richard Graves 28 Feb 1799; widower & widow b-
    William King min- William King- 28Feb1799
Fife
  Jane & William Ingleton 7 Aug 1806; min- William King
Fifer
  Elizabeth & Jacob Shalley 11 Nov 1820; min- Daniel Stephens
  Margaret & Henry Kiracofe 15 Apr 1841; min- Peter Shickel
    Jr
  Mary & William Fisher 12 Oct 1809; min- William King
  Peggy & John Rusmisle 27 Sep 1804; min- William King
  Prudence & Reuben Curry 5 Sep 1823; min- John Hendren
Finely
  Jean & William Frazer 1 Apr 1794; Minister's return spells
    name as 'Finley' d John who consents test- Samuel Finly &
    John McClure b- Samuel Finley min- John McCue- 1Apr1794
  Jean & William McCutchen 13 May 1794; d Robert who
    consents b- Alexander St. Clair Jean of age min- John
    McCue- 20May1794

Augusta County Marriages -- Woman's Name

Finley
  Anne & James Shannon 18 Jan 1802; d John who consents
    Anne (of age) b- Samuel Finley min- John McCue- 21Jan1802
  Caroline E & James Harper 29 Aug 1833; min- Francis
    McFarland
  Eleanor & Samuel Lyle 18 Sep 1801; d William b- William
    Finley min- John McCue- 10Sep1801
  Jane & John B Christian 26 Jul 1820; min- John D Ewin
  Jane & James Rutledge 27 Mar 1786; b- Robert Finley min-
    Samuel Carrick- 28Mar1786
  Lavinia E & Matthew Pilson 5 Nov 1834; min- Francis
    McFarland
  Margaret & John Hutcheson 19 Mar 1793; d John b- George
    Hutcheson min- John McCue- 2Jun1793
  Maria W & Isaac Jones 9 Nov 1837; min- A B McCorkle
  Martha Ann & William S Ramsay 19 Mar 1832; min- James C
    Wilson
  Nancy M & Abraham Hall 29 Nov 1827; min- Francis McFarland

Firebaugh
  Catharine M & Robert Waide 11 Feb 1845; min- D F Bittle

Firebough
  Margaret & Archibald Resors 14 Sep 1826; min- John Hendren

Fishburn
  Elizabeth & John Greiner 18 Mar 1817; min- William King
  Polley & Jonathan Hains 17 Sep 1816; min- William King

Fisher
  Ann & Abner G Rankin 2 Nov 1826; min- James Watts
  Barbara & Jacob Eversole 25 Nov 1812; min- William King
  Dorcas & Andrew Holt 22 Apr 1830; min- William Hank
  Dorcas & William Phillips 10 Jan 1843; min- D F Bittle
  Elizabeth C & Adam R Melrose 11 Jun 1846; min- James H
    Brown
  Mary Ann & ----- Peters 15 Feb 1831; min- Gerard Morgan
  Nancy & John Britton 18 Jun 1800; b- Hance Calvert min-
    William King- 18Jun1800
  Nancy & Richard King 9 Mar 1793; 'Margaret Fisher?' b-
    William Preston Skillern no minister listed; clerk's
    memorandum cites ceremony date as 18Apr1793
  Nancy & Robert Langford 7 May 1846; min- T T Castleman
  Polly & John Henry 1 Jul 1797; d James Fisher, dec. b-
    Richard King min- Archibald Scott- 1Jul1797
  Polly & Jacob Mohler 18 Apr 1822; min- Josiah Cole
  Polly & Samuel Sheetz - Jul 1826; min- John Brown
  Rebecca & Elias Sheets 25 May 1827; min- Michael
    Meyerhoeffer
  Sally & Archibald Dixon 13 Mar 1810; min- William King
  Sally & Abraham Freed 22 Dec 1823; min- Josiah Cole

Fitch
  Amanda & William Leckie 24 Aug 1831; min- Samuel Kennerly
  Mary Ann & Cyrus Grove 5 Sep 1849; min- William T
    Richardson

Fitz
  Mary & Barnabas Newlen 6 Dec 1804; min- William King

Augusta County Marriages -- Woman's Name

Fitzgerald
  Nancy & Isaiah Elmore 15 Jan 1822; min- Josiah Cole
Fitzpatrick
  Ann & Francis Brown 16 Dec 1830; min- William Calhoon- publication of banns
  Ann & George Groah 23 Apr 1822; min- James C Willson
  Margaret Ann & George Woods 31 Oct 1830; min- Gerard Morgan
  Polly & James Frazer 3 Nov 1814; min- John McCue
  Rachel A & William Merit 1 Jan 1838; min- Isaac Jones- publication of banns
  Rebecca & William Johns 27 Jan 1825; min- Josiah Cole
  Salley & John Small 9 Dec 1817; min- Wright Burgess
Fix
  Hanna & Job Hart 4 Jan 1794; 'Hannah Swinks?' d Jacob b- Jacob Fix (Swinks?) no minister listed; clerk's memorandum cites ceremony date as 7Jan1794
  Margaret & George M Apple 23 Dec 1847; min- J C Hensell
  Margaret & John H B Shultz 21 Oct 1841; min- John C Hensell
  Naomi E & John R Robertson 3 Jun 1847; min- J C Hensell
  Susan & George Wiseman 14 May 1846; min- W G Campbell
Flack
  Elizabeth & Samuel McCune 26 May 1808; min- William King
  Isabella & Pleasant A Clarke 5 Oct 1815; min- William King
  Mary Ann & Samuel Brown 25 Dec 1834; min- William Scull
  Matilda & Abraham Lynn 20 Feb 1835; min- William Scull
Fleiger
  Catharine & Amos Hook 21 Mar 1801; Marriage bond lists groom's name as John Fleiger' d John b- John Fleiger min- William King- 22Mar1801
  Christiana & Isaac Ong 2 Jul 1789; d John, who consents wit- W Chambers b- John Bosang & Henry Hall
  Elizabeth & George Rhodes 29 May 1792; Minister's return spells name as 'Rodes' d John who consents b- Isaac Ong min- John Montgomery- 29May1792
  Polly & John Backenstoe 22 Dec 1790; d John b- John Fleiger min- William Wilson- 23Dec1790
Fleisher
  Elizabeth & David Arbogast 4 Jul 1785; d Peter Flaisher bond
  Mary Ann & George Teaford 16 Oct 1834; min- William Calhoon
Flinn
  Eliza A & William Morgan 29 May 1835; min- Augustus Babb
  Eveline F & William R Witts 28 May 1846; min- J A Van Lear
Flory
  Catharine & George Fairberman 9 Oct 1845; min- T T Castleman
  Elizabeth & Henry Snideman 20 Dec 1838; min- John Garber
Flowers
  Elizabeth & John Overshiner 5 Apr 1804; min- William King
Fogel
  Catherine & Jacob Cain 6 Jun 1785; b- Samuel Runkle wit- Samuel McConkey Jr d Anthony

Augusta County Marriages -- Woman's Name

Foglesang
  Catharine & Abraham Whitsel 24 Dec 1816; min- William King
Forber
  Susanah & John Brownfield 13 Dec 1814; min- William King
Forbes
  Lavina & Solomon Gray 23 Dec 1839; min- John C Hensell
Forbush
  Sally & Harrison Furr 30 May 1831; min- Conrad Speece-
    publication of banns
  Susan & James Helms 1 Nov 1831; min- Conrad Speece
Forrest
  Elizabeth & Robert McCorkle 12 May 1785; d James
  Lidia & John McCorkle 12 May 1790; d James, who consents
    b- Benjamin Chapman wit- John Bossard & Benjamin Chapman
    min- Archibald Scott- 12May1790
Forsythe
  Catherine & Enos Jones 31 Oct 1805; min- William King
  Elizabeth & William C Curry 25 Aug 1818; min- William King
  Esther & Abraham Litten 9 Jan 1805; min- William King
  Jane & Elisha Hook 9 Apr 1820; min- John Hendren
  Nancy & Alexander Curry 16 Nov 1814; min- William King
  Patsey & Lawrence Swink 30 May 1810; min- William King
  Rachel & Enos Swink 9 Jan 1817; min- William King
  Sarah & William Stephenson 13 Mar 1797; d Samuel b-
    Samuel Forsythe min- William Wilson- 14Mar1797
Fortune
  Catherine & Anderson Lavender 11 Sep 1826; min- Daniel
    Stephens
Foster
  Rachel & John Bell 2 Apr 1791; orphan of Andrew Campbell
    b- by next friends, Thomas Carruthers & Andrew Campbell
    marriage sent to clerk by Samuel Brown and dated 5Apr1791
  Sarah & Peter Bumgarner 9 Nov 1806; min- William King-
    publication of banns
Fouber
  Nancy & Jacob Link 7 May 1811; min- William King
Fourber
  Elizabeth & John Hupman 4 Mar 1813; min- William King
Foutz
  Sarah & William Ramsey 17 Mar 1836; min- William Scull
  Susan & Robert Terrill 31 Mar 1832; min- James C Wilson
Fowler
  Peggy & George Campbell 22 Jun 1791; d Andrew Certificate
    that Peggy is over 21 b- James Curtis
Fox
  Madlin & James Tomlinson 17 Oct 1801; Minister's return
    spells name as 'Maudline Fox' d Christopher b- Christopher
    Fox min- William King- 20Oct1801
  Margaret & John Goins 6 Mar 1841; min- D F Bittle-
    publication of banns
  Margaret & Joseph Rednour 17 Apr 1793; d Christopher b-
    Christopher Fox
  Rachel & David Glassburn 5 Sep 1805; min- John Montgomery
  Sally & Daniel Burgess 21 Jul 1808; min- William King

Augusta County Marriages -- Woman's Name

Fox (cont.)
  Susannah & John Fletcher 7 Oct 1813; min- William King
Fraim
  Elizabeth & John Duffield 1 Dec 1790; d David, who
    consents b- Thomas Duffield wit- Thomas Duffield & Andrew
    Jordan
Frainer
  Sarah E & Benjamin D Morris 10 Jan 1850; min- William T
    Richardson
Frame
  Betsy & Henry Benner 8 Oct 1798; d John Fream who consents
    test- William Shields & William Fream b- Archibald Frame
  Elizabeth & John Duffield 9 Dec 1790; min- John
    Montgomery- 9Dec1790
  Margaret & John Robertson 26 Jan 1793; d John Fream who
    consents test- Peter Killy & Henry Kelly b- Andrew Cutler
    min- John McCue- 26Feb1793
  Nancy & Thomas Poage 6 Mar 1817; min- Conrad Speece, Jr
  Polly & John Allison 4 Sep 1806; min- John McCue
  Polly & James McMahon 20 Feb 1806; min- William Wilson
France
  Eve & Valentine Miller 9 Jan 1794; Eve (of age) b-
    William Sansebaugh
  Martha & Alexander Hind 23 Aug 1787; Minister's return
    spells name as 'Francis' d Mary Francy who consents test-
    William Alexander & Charles Campbell b- John Allison min-
    William Wilson- 23Aug1787
Frances
  Jane & Samuel Hind 7 Aug 1787; Minister's return spells
    name as 'Francis' d Mary who consents test- Robert
    Alexander & Hugh Campbell b- John Alexander min- Benjamin
    Erwin- 7Aug1788
Francis
  Margaret & James Curry 21 Oct 1788; b- James McKenny min-
    Benjamin Erwin- 28Oct1788
  Margaret & John Hogshead 20 Jun 1786; d Mary b- John Bell
    wit- Thomas Bradshaw min- Benjamin Erwin- 22Jun1786
  Nancy & William Thompson 26 Nov 1846; min- Francis
    McFarland
Francisco
  Sally & George Frazer 29 Sep 1786; Minister's return
    spells name as 'Freyer' 'Capt' George Frazer Sarah? d
    George b- John Francisco min- Samuel Carrick- 14Oct1786
    (Rev. Samuel Shannon also lists marriage on 5Oct1786)
Frankam
  Elizabeth & John Painter - Mar 1828; min- William Monroe
  Rachel & Samuel Stover 28 Sep 1831; min- William Wilson
Frankum
  Catharine & John Cain 2 Mar 1814; min- William Cravens
Franzman
  Susan C & Jacob Ringuson - Nov 1824; min- John Brown
Frazer
  Isabella Hillanah & James Paul 20 Jul 1801; widower &
    widow (of Samuel) b- James Frazer min- John McCue-
    23Jul1801

Augusta County Marriages -- Woman's Name

Frazer (cont.)
  Issabella & William Hillis 25 Oct 1810; min- John McCue
  Mary A & John King 15 Sep 1808; min- John McCue
  Winniford & Andrew Early 26 Jul 1808; min- John McCue
Frazier
  Amanda C & Adam H Kurtz 16 Jun 1836; min- John A Steele
  Angelina M & Addison Dold 30 Jul 1834; min- John Hendren
  Margaret & John Harris 4 Feb 1829; min- William C. Morrison
  Martha E & William M Tate 14 Nov 1844; min- John Hendren
  Mary Jane & John Randolph 4 Jun 1818; min- Wright Burgess
  Melvina L & James P Frazier 21 Dec 1831; min- John Hendren
Fream
  Rachel & Joseph Shields 24 Nov 1800; Minister's return
    spells name as 'Frame' widower d John who consents test-
    William Fream b- Archibald Fream min- John McCue- 27Nov1800
Freed
  Mary Ann & John Dooms 20 Nov 1845; min- S Wagner
Freeland
  Nancy & John Day 17 Nov 1795; Nancy (of age) b- Andrew
    Jordan
Freeman
  Jane E & Jacob Swisher 17 Feb 1842; min- Samuel Wagner
  Peggy & William Shepherd 14 Jan 1808; min- John McCue
Frenger
  Betsey & George Hite 2 Aug 1808; min- William McPheeters
  Elizabeth & George Reubush 10 Mar 1829; min- Francis
    McFarland
Fridley
  Barbara & Michael Jackson 18 Feb 1817; min- William King
Friel
  Catherine & William (Jr) Armstrong 23 Feb 1793; 'Catherine
    Price?' d Daniel who consents test- James Ross & John Friel
    b- William Armstrong Sr no minister listed; clerk's
    memorandum cites ceremony date as 26Feb1793
  Isabella & George Wilson 28 Jun 1800; d Daniel Friel, dec.
    & Agness Friel who consents test- Maurice Friel b- John
    Trimble
  Jane & Robert Armstrong 15 Apr 1794; d Daniel, who gives
    bond
  Salley & Joseph Wilson 28 Mar 1806; min- William Calhoon
Fry
  Barbara & Andrew Slone 11 Jan 1817; 'Sloan?' min- William
    King
  Barbara & George Wood 19 Nov 1826; min- William Monroe
  Hannah C & James A Gardner 15 Sep 1846; min- S Wagner
Fudge
  Barbara & Jacob Zeller 6 Oct 1794; d John b- John Fudge
  Barbery & Archibald Toole 9 Nov 1791; Minister's return
    spells name as 'Archibald Sole [Sale?] b- Jacob Peck min-
    William Wilson- 10Nov1791
  Elizabeth & Samuel Miller 3 Jun 1785; d John b- George
    Craig wit- William Chambers, Francis Huff, John Black

Augusta County Marriages -- Woman's Name

Fuller
  Emila G & John Ellis 2 May 1850; min- J Killian
Fulton
  Eleanor & Robert Hunter 22 Dec 1803; min- John McCue
  Eleanor & John (Jr) Shannon 26 May 1800; d James Fulton, dec. b- John Shannon Sr
  Eliza S & Charles Patton 5 Sep 1822; min- Michael Meyerhoeffer
  Elizabeth & Alexander Brownlee 4 Mar 1800; d Hugh who consents Elizabeth (of age) test- Robert Fulton & John Fulton b- John Fulton
  Elizabeth & John Caldwell 1 Dec 1801; d Mary b- William Fulton min- John McCue- 3Dec1801
  Elizabeth & William Patterson 1 Dec 1832; min- Francis McFarland
  Margaret & Ferdinand Kinkead 19 Mar 1799; d James b- James Fulton
  Margaret & Alexander Smiley 28 Oct 1842; min- James Morrison
  Margaret & Andrew Wardlaw 31 Jul 1792; d Mary who consents wit- James Fulton & Samuel Fulton b- Samuel Fulton no minister listed; clerk's memorandum cites ceremony date as 5Aug1792
  Martha & James Delzell 16 Nov 1796; d Hugh who consents test- Archibald Murray b- Robert Fulton
  Mary Ann & Thomas A Clayton 10 Oct 1844; min- James Morrison
  Mary & Samuel Bing 18 Jul 1797; d James b- James Fulton min- John Montgomery- 3Aug1797
  Mary & William Brownlee 10 Nov 1795; d Hugh who consents test- Robert Fulton & John Fulton b- Robert Fulton min- Archibald Scott- 12Nov1795
  Nancy Ann & John Rutledge 17 Mar 1829; min- Francis McFarland
  Sally & James Strong 2 Nov 1798; Sally (of age) d William Fulton, dec. b- Hugh Fulton
  Sally & Elijah Williams 4 May 1815; min- John McCue
  Sarah & David Gunning 17 Sep 1807; min- William McPheeters
  Sarah & Archibald Murray 11 Jan 1792; d Hugh b- Robert Fulton min- John Brown- 12Jan1791
  Sarah & William Ramsey 18 Dec 1794; Sarah (Sally) (of age) sis to William Fulton b- William Fulton no minister listed; clerk's memorandum cites ceremony date as 18Dec1794
  Virginia & Hugh G Kennedy 16 Mar 1848; min- J C Hensell
Fultz
  Margaret Ann & John O Lewis 7 Oct 1847; min- B M Smith
Fulweider
  Catharine & Philip Haffner 9 Mar 1793; d Ulerick Fulwyder Affidavit of Philip that he is 21 b- Ulerick Fulwider
Fulwider
  Catherine & John Fulwider 23 Feb 1829; min- Francis McFarland
  Elizabeth & Adam Weaver 13 Feb 1840; min- John C Hansell
  Hannah & Jacob Hanger 21 May 1835; min- Cornelius Gates

Augusta County Marriages -- Woman's Name

Fulwider (cont.)
 Margaret & John Gall 10 Mar 1798; John from Rockbridge cty
  d Jacob Fulwider, dec. b- John Ott
 Mary & George Cox 18 Jun 1846; min- J C Hensell
 Mary & Jacob Weirly 1 Jun 1790; d Ulrick, who consents b-
  John Falwider
 Sally & Kilkenney Klingenpeel 27 Jul 1826; min- Francis
  McFarland
 Susan & John Lowman 15 Dec 1831; min- Francis McFarland
Funkhoser
 Catherine & John Shewy 31 Aug 1809; min- William King
Funkhouser
 Elizabeth & Daniel Shearley 15 Oct 1824; min- William W
  Calhoun
 Lidey & George Baylor 12 Aug 1824; min- William W Calhoun
 Mary M & Preston B Cale 15 Nov 1827; min- William Calhoon
 Peggy & George Hansel 10 Sep 1812; min- William King
 Sally & Jacob Gabbert 16 May 1826; min- William W Calhoun
Fur
 Martha L & William McGuffin 27 Sep 1834; min- Samuel
  Kennerly- publication of banns
Gabart
 Barbara & Jacob Teeford 22 Feb 1791; d Jacob b- David Cale
 Hannah & Lewis Mines 13 Feb 1810; min- William King
Gabbert
 Elizabeth & Joseph Heise 29 Oct 1798; Elizabeth (of age) d
  Jacob who consents test- Jacob Palmer b- John Gabbert
Gabert
 Peggy & Jacob Kershner 14 Apr 1801; d Jacob who consents
  test- George Hanger s David b- John Gabert
Gabhart
 Barbara & Jacob Palmer 21 Feb 1791; d Jacob who consents
  b- John Sharp Jr
 Barbarah & William Forbish 10 Nov 1787; b- Anthony Mustor
  & William Chambers
 Catharine & Philip Dull 7 Apr 1794; d Jacob b- Jacob
  Gabhart
 Catherine & Stephen Wanlis 3 May 1788; d John Capeheart
  who consents test- Dorman Laflan, John Capeheart & Ralph
  Wanlis b- John Geabhart
 Sarah & Charles McClung 7 Aug 1834; min- Augustus Babb
Gaines
 Ann Pollard & James Mathews 5 Jul 1796; d James Gaines,
  dec. of Orange cty con- Mildred Gains, mother test- Abner &
  Elizabeth Gains b- Abner Gains
Galbraith
 Ann & Thomas Mitchell 9 Jan 1798; Minister's return spells
  name as 'Caldbreath' d Thomas Galbraith, dec. b- Thomas
  Galbraith (Coldbreath) min- John McCue- 11Jan1798
 Margaret & Andrew Wallace 1 Mar 1796; Minister's return
  spells name as 'Caldbreath' Margaret (of age) d Thomas
  Galbraith, dec., sis to Thomas Galbreath b- Thomas
  Galbreath (Colbreath?) 3Mar1796

Augusta County Marriages -- Woman's Name

Galen
  Sara & Thomas Broom 28 Jan 1786; min- John Brown- 28Jan1786
Gamble
  Elizabeth & William Moffett 28 Jun 1785; b- Robert Gamble
  Esther & John Bell 23 Jul 1800; widower d James Gamble, dec. b- John Gamble min- William Wilson- 24Jul1800
  Polly & William Ramsay 6 Jan 1824; min- Conrad Speece
  Rebecca B & Robertson Ervine 14 May 1835; min- Conrad Speece
Garber
  Ann & Christian Coffman 19 Oct 1819; min- Abraham Garber- publication of banns
  Anne & Windle Sites 10 Mar 1846; min- T T Castleman
  Barbara & William Forbes 10 Nov 1787; min- James Chambers- 10Nov1787
  Barbara & Jacob Garhenour 17 Nov 1836; min- Peter Miller
  Elizabeth & John Brower 4 Nov 1841; min- Peter Miller
  Elizabeth & William A Menzies 17 Oct 1809; min- William Calhoon
  Esther & Abraham Stoner 15 May 1833; min- Abraham Garber- publication of banns
  Frances & Joseph Berry 15 Nov 1831; min- Abraham Garber- publication of banns
  Laney & Rice Morris 8 Jan 1807; min- William Calhoon
  Magdaline & Emmanuel Arnold 19 Oct 1819; min- Abraham Garber- publication of banns
  Margaret R & Thomas J Michie - Nov 1826; min- Joseph Smith
  Mary & John Arion 15 Dec 1831; min- Abraham Garber- publication of banns
  Rebecca & Daniel Miller 1 Oct 1846; min- Peter Miller
  Sally & Christian Whitmore 3 Aug 1833; min- Abraham Garber- publication of banns
Gardner
  Martha S & James P Barger 20 Aug 1846; min- J A Van Lear
  Nancy & Obediah Curby 1 Aug 1844; min- Samuel Wagner- publication of banns
  Rebecca & Abel Carson 17 Oct 1832; min- Francis McFarland
  Rebecca & Robert Wright 17 Jun 1819; min- William Calhoon
  Sarah A B & Alexander B Lightner 15 Nov 1844; min- Francis McFarland
  Sarah & James Brownlee 14 Apr 1825; min- Francis McFarland
Garmen
  Elizabeth & Adam Fudge 1 Sep 1795; Minister's return spells name as 'Garman' d Adam b- Adam Garmen min- John McCue- 10ct1795
Garmon
  Eve & John Hart 17 Feb 1800; 'John Horb?' d Adam who consents test- John Drumm & John Gorman b- John Garmon & John Drum min- John McCue- 20Feb1800
Garnes
  ----- & Samuel King 3 May 1797; d Adam b- Adam Garnes
Garnett
  Fanny & David Leonard 28 Aug 1817; min- William King

Augusta County Marriages -- Woman's Name

Garretson
  Elizabeth & William Miller 12 Jan 1821; min- Robert Boyd- publication of banns
Garrison
  Frances & John Trent - Sep 1817; min- John Brown
Garton
  Phaney & Joseph Shanklin 13 Jun 1792; 'Garlon?' daughter in law of John Brown who consents d of Phaney Brown who consents wit- Joseph Douglas b- Joseph Douglass of Rockingham cty marriage dated 23Jun1791
Garvin
  Margaret & Andrew Young 29 Aug 1786; d John b- James Young min- William Wilson- 30Aug1786
  Rebecca & William Donaghe 16 Jan 1810; min- William Calhoon
Gates
  Nancy & William King 8 Jun 1830; min- William Wilson
Gatewood
  Elizabeth A & Clement R Harris 16 Mar 1845; min- John A Van Lear
Gayhart
  Elizabeth & Philip Engleman 31 Dec 1842; min- J B Houck- publication of banns
Geating
  Rebecca & Washington H Dennison - Dec 1826; min- Joseph Smith
Geeding
  Catherine & Christian Shuey 6 Sep 1814; min- William King
Geeting
  Polly & John Teaford 6 Apr 1819; min- William King
Geralds
  Nancy E & John Painter 25 Jan 1849; min- James Paine
Gibbons
  Amanda & John H Brown 27 Jun 1844; min- Francis McFarland
  Eliza Ann & Daniel M Harden 15 Sep 1836; min- J C Hensell
  Evalina & Andrew Bear 23 Jan 1834; min- Francis McFarland
  Frances W & William H Surber 12 Sep 1848; min- J A Van Lear
  Susan & Joseph F Hottle 30 Aug 1842; min- John C Hensell
Gibson
  Alcinda & David Shaffer 4 Jul 1841; min- George Huffman
  Ann & Jesse Davis 9 Oct 1827; min- Conrad Speece
  Ann & William Ralston 13 May 1796; Minister's return spells name as 'William Wilson' d David b- David Gibson min- William Wilson- 4May1796
  Betsy & William Slaven 2 Oct 1826; min- Conrad Speece
  Elizabeth & John Mahan 3 Mar 1787; min- William Wilson- 3Mar1787
  Elizabeth & Alexander Moss 20 Jun 1836; min- John A Steele
  Fanny & Joshua Russell 20 Aug 1804; min- William Wilson
  Jane & George W Bain 13 Jul 1833; min- George Hildt
  Margaret & William Beard - Apr 1827; min- Joseph Smith
  Margaret & Samuel Brown 26 Aug 1797; 'Elizabeth?' d Samuel Joseph Shields swears that Samuel Brown, s William, is of age b- Samuel Gibson min- Archibald Scott- 31Aug1797
  Margret & James Hall 30 Jun 1836; min- William Calhoon

Augusta County Marriages -- Woman's Name

Gibson (cont.)
  Mary & Adam Bumgarner 29 May 1800; d David both of age s
    Balzer b- John Sheetz min- William King- 29May1801
  Mary & Samuel Given 18 Mar 1823; min- Conrad Speece
  Mary & Henry Mowry 8 Jun 1791; d Alexander b- Alexander
    Gibson, Jr no minister listed; clerk's memorandum cites
    ceremony date as 10Jun1791
  Sarah & John Alexander 27 Nov 1789; min- Benjamin Erwin-
    27Nov1789
Giles
  Elizabeth & Samuel Woolard 18 Feb 1831; min- Samuel
    Kennerly- publication of banns
Gilkerson
  Margaret & Elijah McClenachan 21 Aug 1799; widower d
    William b- William Gilkerson
  Susan & William Marshall 15 May 1823; min- James C Willson
Gilkeson
  Ann & James Craig 26 Jan 1800; d Hugh Archibald Dixon
    swears James of age b- Hugh Gilkeson min- John McCue-
    29Jan1801
  Elizabeth E & Hugh G Guthrie 31 May 1849; min- Robert L
    Dabney
  Elizabeth & David Gilkeson 7 Jul 1808; min- John McCue
  Gracey & Thomas C Poage 28 Aug 1828; min- John Hendren
  Jane B & Silas Hogshead 7 Feb 1845; min- John Hendren
  Jane & Robert Herron 5 Dec 1820; min- William Calhoon
  Lovey S & John Tate 16 Apr 1846; min- Francis McFarland
  Margaret & John Guthrey 14 May 1794; Minister's return
    spells name as 'Guthery & Gilkerson' d Hugh b- Hugh
    Gilkeson min- John McCue- 15May1794
  Nancy & Andrew Irvine 28 Sep 1830; min- John Hendren
  Rebecca & George Moffett 25 Oct 1797; Rebecca (of age) d
    Archibald Gilkeson, dec. b- Francis Gilkison
  Sarah & James Wright 28 Sep 1813; min- William Calhoon
Gillaspie
  Barbara & Calvin Davis 25 Aug 1842; min- F D Goodwin
Gillaspy
  Martha & Joseph McCoskey 19 Mar 1790; Minister's return
    spells name as 'McCoskrey and Gilaspey' d John b- wit-
    Samuel Bleak & John Thompson b- James Telford min- John
    Montgomery- 25Mar1790
Gilliam
  Mary C & Frederick Fridley 14 Jan 1836; min- Francis A C
    Mills
Gilliat
  Amanda & Jacob Bruback 11 Feb 1834; min- Augustus Babb
Gillis
  Hannah & John Poage 9 Oct 1798; d Joseph b- Joseph Gillis
Gilmore
  Eliza & John Dun - May 1820; min- John Brown
  Frances W & Richard Taliaferor 29 Mar 1804; min- William
    Wilson

Augusta County Marriages -- Woman's Name

Gipson
  Sarah & Joseph Wood 26 Mar 1843; min- Samuel Allenbaugh
Given
  Jennat & John Berry 25 Nov 1790; Minister's return spells
    name as 'Jannet Givens' d William, who consents b- Samuel
    McClintick wit- J Beal & Robert Given min- John
    Montgomery- 9Dec1790
Givens
  Eliza A & James A Fitch 12 Dec 1842; min- William H Laney
  Margaret & James Egnew 21 Apr 1788; d John who consents
    wit- William Patton, Thomas Givens & James Givens b- Thomas
    Givens
  Margaret & Samuel Fulton 2 Oct 1795; d John b- John
    Givens min- John McCue- 13Oct1795
  Mary & James Allison 4 Jun 1798; d John Givens, dec. b-
    James Givens min- William Wilson- 6Jun1798
  Sarah & Isaac Gregory 16 Mar 1790; Minister's return
    spells name as 'Givins' d William, who consents b- Robert
    Givin wit- Robert Eastham & John Berry min- Samuel
    Houston- 25Mar1790
Givins
  Margaret & James Agnue 22 Apr 1788; min- William Wilson-
    22Apr1788
Gladden
  Nancy & Richard Reed 28 Jan 1829; min- William Wilson
Glass
  Fanny Ann & Adam King 3 Oct 1805; min- William Wilson
  Margaret & Andrew Young 3 Nov 1797; d Isaac b- Isaac
    Glass min- William Wilson- 7Nov1797
Glenn
  Martha & John Meade 22 Nov 1798; Minister's return spells
    name as 'Mead' widower Martha (of age) d George William
    Glenn swears that his sister of age b- William Morrison
    min- William King- 28Nov1798
  Mary & Samuel Curry 25 Mar 1800; Minister's return spells
    name as 'Glen' Mary (of age) d George b- Hugh Glenn min-
    William Wilson- 3Apr1800
  Mary & Andrew B McCausland 16 Jul 1822; min- Conrad Speece
  Patsy & Henry B Roland 18 Mar 1819; min- Conrad Speece, Jr
  Sarah & Robert Young 27 Feb 1792; Minister's return spells
    name as 'Sarah Green' d George b- William Glenn min-
    William Wilson- 28Feb1792
Glutz
  Susan Ann & Jacob Barger 29 Aug 1836; min- Ambrose Henkle
Gochenour
  Ann & David Whisler 17 May 1842; min- F D Goodwin
  Catherine & George Bright 11 Feb 1802; min- William King-
    11Feb1802
  Lidia & Solomon R Peters 4 Mar 1847; min- J A Van Lear
  Magdalene & Jacob (Jr) Hiltebrand 22 Aug 1839; min- John J
    Reimensnyder
  Polly & Washington Swisher 18 Sep 1830; min- James Morrison

Augusta County Marriages -- Woman's Name

Goff
  Margaret & Samuel Hudlow 20 Aug 1835; min- Conrad Speece- publication of banns
Goings
  Frances & Thomas Goings 20 Sep 1839; coloured min- Samuel Wagner
  Keziah & Mathew Goings 5 Mar 1834; coloured persons min- James C Wilson
Gold
  Jane & Gimpsey Caruthers 3 Dec 1792; 'Carothers?' d Robert b- Samuel Gould no minister listed; clerk's memorandum cites ceremony date as 5Dec1792
  Mary & William Chesnut 23 Mar 1801; 'Chestnut' d Robert Gold & Esther Gold Mary (of age) b- Vincent Tapp min- John McCue- 26Mar1801
  Susan & Robert Tate 9 Aug 1837; min- John A Steele
Golladay
  Betsy & Abraham Crist 21 Nov 1822; min- John Brown
  Elizabeth J & Martim Cromer 14 Nov 1848; min- W Lee Spotswood
  Elizabeth & Daniel Snyder 17 Feb 1848; min- J C Hensell
  Polly & Joseph Eikord 17 Feb 1826; min- Daniel Stephens
Golloday
  Sally & Henry Hansbarger - Jun 1814; min- John Brown
Gonwer
  Margaret & Samuel Washington Patterson 10 Feb 1850; min- J Killian
Good
  Catharine & John Shull 27 Jun 1850; min- Henry Witzel
  Catherine & Peter Shaffer - Mar 1825; min- John Brown
  Elizabeth & John Gordon 23 Dec 1838; min- P E Stevenson
  Elizabeth & James Whitmore 14 Jul 1846; widow min- J A Van Lear
  Margaret & Daniel Shull 25 Aug 1828; min- G H Reimensnyder
  Martha M & Samuel G Jones 1 Dec 1842; min- F D Goodwin
  Mary A & John Risk 19 Apr 1845; min- D F Bittle
  Mary & Stephen Roadcap 20 Jul 1840; min- J J Reimensnyder
Goodnight
  Catherine & Jacob Seylor 3 Mar 1814; min- William King
Goodwin
  Catherine & John Leffley 17 Jun 1799; d Joseph Goodwin ('Gooden?') John (of age) b- Joseph Goodwin
  Jane & Lewis Runkle 17 Nov 1805; min- John Emmill
  Sarah & Theophilus Leopard 16 Mar 1826; min- Francis McFarland
Gordan
  Malinda & Andrew Lamb 28 Feb 1845; min- P Shickel
Gorden
  Mary Ann & Nathaniel L Long 24 Dec 1833; min- William G Jackson
Gordon
  Amanda K & Emanuel Long 24 Oct 1839; min- P E Stevenson
  Frances E & Amos R Ball 24 Dec 1846; min- James H Brown
  Martha Ann & Harris Sites 11 Jun 1834; min- Samuel Kennerly

Augusta County Marriages -- Woman's Name

Gragg
  Polly & William Hays 26 Jul 1804; min- William King
Graham
  Betsy B & John Flesher 11 Jul 1831; min- James Kerr
  Catherine & David Hogshead 16 Nov 1790; b- Thomas Graham
    min- William Wilson- 19Nov1790
  Diannah & Andrew Koogler 1 Aug 1837; min- John A Van Lear
  Elizabeth & Andrew Russell 2 May 1815; min- William King
  Isabella & Alexander Boyd 22 Jun 1793; b- Samuel Wilson
    min- John McCue- 27Jun1793
  Isabella & William Gibson 15 Apr 1821; min- Conrad Speece
  Jane & Samuel Neill 14 Jan 1793; Minister's return spells
    name as 'Neal' Jane (of age) b- John Cooper min- John
    Montgomery- 15Jan1793
  Jane & Jacob Switzer 29 Jun 1818; min- William King
  Mary & John Boyd 2 Nov 1790; Mary 22, d Thomas Sr, who
    consents b- Solomon Johnson wit- Thomas & Catty Greham
  Mary & James McCulloch 8 Feb 1805; min- John McCue
  Nancy & Daniel Hine 16 Sep 1824; min- James Morrison
  Patsey & Robert Dunlap 10 May 1793; d John who consents
    test- James Fulton b- Adam Bratton min- John Montgomery-
    14May1793
  Polly & James Woods 2 Jan 1827; min- William Wilson
  Rebecca & John Bell 3 Jan 1787; d Elizabeth who consents
    wit- William Yoall & Robert McDowell b- William Yoall (date
    of bond uncertain - 1786? 1787?) min- Samuel Carrick-
    9Jan1787
  Sally & Samuel Litten 2 Nov 1826; min- William Wilson
  Sarah & John Cooper 10 Sep 1793; 'Robert Cooper?'
    Affidavit of Sarah's full age b- John Lockridge no
    minister listed; clerk's memorandum cites ceremony date as
    12Sep1793
  Winey & John Ryan 8 Jul 1824; min- William W Calhoun
Grant
  Ann Eliza & James Bridget 22 Jan 1834; min- Augustus Babb
  Isabella & John Craine 15 Nov 1788; b- James Lyle Jr
    Permission from Bull Pasture by Thomas Green & Eleander
    McQuin attesting that they are free people and can marry
  Margret & William Knowls 3 Jan 1839; min- D F Bittle-
    publication of banns
  Patsy & Levi White 13 Nov 1820; min- Luke Collins
  Sarah & Henry Allinger 23 Aug 1834; min- Augustus Babb
  Susan Jane & Jacob C Carson 14 Sep 1848; min- Alonzo P
    Ludden
Grass
  Caroline M & George W Lee 25 Sep 1834; min- Francis
    McFarland
  Elizabeth & Henry Fagus 5 Oct 1785; (Fogas?) widow d
    Henry Hawk b- Frederick Hawk min- Archibald Scott- 6Oct1785
  Elizabeth & Hazard Hesterson 6 Mar 1807; min- William King
  Elizabeth & John Shuey 12 Dec 1835; min- J J Glossbrenner
  Mary & George Brooks 16 Mar 1786; bond (ministers return
    lists names as Robert Brooks and Polly Grass) min-
    Archibald Scott- 16Mar1786

Augusta County Marriages -- Woman's Name

Grass (cont.)
    Sarah & William Rediford 30 Dec 1799; Minister's return spells name as 'Rodeford' d Frederick b- Frederick Grass min- William King- 31Dec1799

Gratton
    Mary & Samuel Miller 29 Nov 1791
    Nancy & Elijah Poage 31 Jul 1787; min- William Wilson- 31Jul1787

Graves
    Jane & John Dohm 20 Jun 1806; min- William King
    Sarah & James Siddons 16 Oct 1798; d Richard b- Richard Graves James (of age)

Gray
    Amelia & William Hanna 22 Dec 1831; min- John Hendren
    Martha & Samuel Gelston 8 Feb 1787; b- James McGonagal min- Archibald Scott- 8Feb1787
    Nancy & James G W Youell 21 Feb 1833; min- Francis McFarland

Greaver
    Elizabeth & John Reed - --- 1835; min- Augustus Babb- publication of banns
    Jane & David Palmer 1 Jun 1837; min- William Calhoub

Green
    Judith & George Pugh 20 Oct 1798; b- Thomas Chinn
    Lucy & John Kersner 1 Apr 1824; min- Francis McFarland
    Milly & Matthew Smith 19 Dec 1787; d Edward who consents b- Elihus Green min- William Wilson- 19Dec1787

Greenwood
    Rebecca & Archibald Gay 29 Nov 1798; d ----- Greenwood, dec. James Frasure, gdn, swears Rebecca of age b- James Frazer

Greever
    Ann & Absalom Thornton 21 Feb 1844; min- D F Bittle

Gregery
    Sarah & James Hutcheson 9 Sep 1802; min- William King- 9Sep1802

Gregory
    Amy & James Hogg 20 Aug 1798; Minister's return spells name as 'Hog' 'Ann' con- James Edmondson, gdn of Amy James Edmundson from Staunton test- A Stuart min- William Wilson- 20Aug1798
    Catharine & William Tally 19 Apr 1825; min- Josiah Cole
    Catharine & David Turner 8 Feb 1816; min- William King
    Catherine & Isom Johnson 12 May 1800; d John Gregory, dec. sis to Benjamin Gregory b- Benjamin Gregory min- William King- 12May1800
    Caty & Willis Hasterson 9 Oct 1808; min- William King
    Elenor & John Middleton 24 Oct 1833; min- George Hildt
    Elizabeth & John Patton 17 Sep 1816; min- Wright Burgess
    Katurah & James S Rankin 14 Feb 1837; min- Stephen Smith
    Mary & James Hutcheson 1 Mar 1804; min- William King
    Polly & Archibald Campbell 21 Aug 1806; min- William King
    Sarah Scott & Washington Clinedinst 7 Feb 1828; min- William Monroe

Augusta County Marriages -- Woman's Name

Greiner
  Catherine & John Tennant 13 Jan 1790; widow
  Dianna & Thomas Ballew 27 Oct 1842; min- A G Chenowith
  Elizabeth & Henry Fishburne 1 Dec 1812; min- Wright Burgess
  Feliska & Daniel Beard 12 Jan 1832; min- John Howell-
    publication of banns
  Mary & John Johnston 3 May 1797; Mary (of age) sis to
    David Greiner b- David Greiner
  Nancy & Ephraim Woodward 26 Aug 1817; min- William King
  Sarah & Joseph Points 3 May 1798; d Samuel Greiner Sr,
    dec. con- Catherine Tennant test- John Johnson & David
    Greiner b- David Greiner min- John McCue- 3May1798

Gresham
  Elizabeth E & William Vanlear 4 Oct 1827; min- Conrad
    Speece

Grever
  Sarah & Martin Zimmerman 16 Nov 1822; min- Michael
    Meyerhoeffer

Griever
  Catherine & George (Jr) Elinger 20 Apr 1797; d Philip who
    consents test- Philip Griever b- Andrew Cutler

Griffeth
  Elizabeth & John Bell 1 Dec 1812; min- William King

Griffin
  Elizabeth & Green McClanahan 10 Jun 1808; min- William
    Calhoon
  Mary & Joseph Cowan 26 Sep 1799; Mary (of age) b- Thomas
    Barry

Griffith
  Catherine & Abraham Carson 2 Jun 1802; min- William
    Wilson- 2Jun1802
  Hetty M & William W Young 15 Oct 1840; min- John A Van Lear
  Jane Elizabeth & Addison H Campbell 30 Aug 1849; min- W G
    Campbell
  Nancy S & James Young 25 Mar 1850; min- John Hendren
  Peggy & Cornelious Donaphan 26 Oct 1807; min- William King
  Rebecca E & David K Orebaugh 27 May 1850; min- John Hendren
  Rebecca & George Revercomb 25 Sep 1822; min- John Hendren
  Ruth & Robert Jones 9 Apr 1812; min- William King
  Sarah A & James A Young 23 Jan 1845; min- John A Van Lear

Grim
  Mary & Jacob Thomas 17 Feb 1831; min- Francis McFarland
  Sally & William Link 21 Aug 1801; s John Nicholas Link s
    Jacob Grim, dec, of Shenandoah cty Christian Beard ('Bart')
    swears Sally is of age b- John Nicholas Link

Grimm
  Polly & Jacob Bright 23 Jun 1810; min- William King
  Susan & Silas Hinton 15 Oct 1824; min- John Hendren

Grips
  Elizabeth & Vincent G Newman 14 Apr 1836; min- William
    Calhoon
  Mary & John Hansell 28 Apr 1835; min- William Calhoon
  Sarah & William Funkhouser 1 Oct 1835; min- William Calhoon

Augusta County Marriages -- Woman's Name

Groah
  Mary K & Christian Palmer 26 Aug 1843; min- James Paine
Grooms
  Judy & Hugh Hillis 31 Dec 1812; min- William King
  Mary & Andrew J Decker 1 Apr 1840; min- Samuel Wagner
  Sarah & Pleasant Brooks 1 Apr 1840; min- Samuel Wagner
  Susan & Robert Grass 22 Feb 1816; min- John McCue
Grove
  Ann & David Grove 24 Jun 1813; min- William King
  Catharine & David Fishburn 3 Jun 1830; min- William Wilson
  Catherine Susan & Fountain T Paine 17 Dec 1827; min- William C. Morrison
  Eliza B & James C Miller 9 Feb 1832; min- Francis McFarland
  Elizabeth A & Jonathan Besse 26 Apr 1848; min- W T Richardson
  Elizabeth Ann & Jacob N Rodes 14 Oct 1835; min- John A Steele
  Elizabeth & Henry Amon 21 Feb 1795; Minister's return spells name as 'Grone' b- Michael Grove
  Margaret & Samuel Bell 17 Nov 1791; d David, who consents wit- John Black & John Hay b- Samuel Miller
  Mary C & David C Noffinger 4 Apr 1839; min- A B McCorkle
  Mary Elizabeth & Robert McClune 30 Mar 1848; min- P Shickel
  Mary & William Kerr 20 Dec 1796; Minister's return spells name as 'Mary Windlegrove(?)' d Windle who consents test- Henry Grove b- John Grove min- Archibald Scott- 22Dec1796
  Nancy & Kyle B Klingenpeel 21 Jul 1842; min- James Bunting
  Susan & Henry Hiltebrand 9 Jun 1814; min- William King
  Susannah & Peter (Jr) Hanger 26 Feb 1800; d Windle who consents test- Windle Grove Jr b- John Wise & Henry Grove
Groves
  Martha & Jacob Miller 23 May 1830; min- Abraham Garber
  Sarah & Andrew Donaghe 24 Nov 1823; min- John Hendren
Grub
  Elizabeth & James (Jr) Kirkland 11 Oct 1787; Minister's return spells name as 'Mary Grub' s James Sr who consents test- James Runken & Thomas Peterson b- William Johnston min- William Wilson- 15Oct1787
Guffy
  Elizabeth & William Brown 27 Mar 1804; min- William King
Guiller
  Sally & John Whitesides 6 Jan 1803; min- John McCue
Guin
  Elizabeth & Frederick Hanger 11 Apr 1826; min- William Monroe
  Martha & William F Baker 22 Oct 1846; min- Jacob Montgomery
Guinn
  Jane & Alexander Hawkins 30 Aug 1832; min- William Calhoon
  Jane & James Kinkaid 3 Dec 1829; min- Henry S Kepler
Gully
  Mary E & James B Culton 25 Sep 1849; min- William T Richardson

Augusta County Marriages -- Woman's Name

Gutherie
Ann & Isaac Blain 9 Apr 1795; Ann (of age) d William sis to Daniel b- Daniel Gutherie min- John McCue- 9Apr1795

Guthrey
Ann & Isaac Blane 9 Apr 1794; min- John McCue- 9Apr1794
Nancy & Isaiah Roberts 11 Jan 1794; Minister's return spells name as 'Guthery' Nancy (of age) d William Guthery b- John Guthery min- John McCue- 14Jan1794

Guthrie
Elizabeth & Charles Henderson 18 Sep 1817; 'Harrison?' min- John McCue
Margaret & Daniel Fishburn 19 Oct 1841; min- Samuel Wagner

Gutshall
Mary Jane & Charles C Shirer 30 Apr 1840; min- John J Reimensnyder

Guy
Jane & James Lockridge 22 Mar 1791; b- James Guy min- John Montgomery- 5Apr1791

Gwin
Eleanor Tate & Cyrus McKemy 8 Oct 1834; min- George Hildt

Gwinn
Jane & John Law 15 Dec 1795; Jane (of age) b- John Erwin min- William Wilson- 29Dec1795

Haffner
Betsy & Frederick Karikoff 18 Jan 1820; min- G H Riemenschneider
Elizabeth & George Sowers - Jun 1817; min- John Brown
Mary Ann & John Wonderlick 30 Apr 1846; min- Henry Wetzel
Mary & Samuel McClung 11 Jun 1840; min- J J Reimensnyder
Mary & Henry Swisher - Aug 1821; min- John Brown

Hafner
Barbara & George Trobaugh 24 Dec 1801; min- William King- 24Dec1801
Barbara & George Trorobaugh 21 Dec 1801; Minister's return spells name as 'Trobaugh and Hepner' Barbara (of age) d Jacob b- Andrew Haffner min- William King- 24Dec1801
Catherine & Daniel Michael 16 Sep 1813; min- G H Riemenschneider
Magdalene & Christian Lambert 20 May 1795; d Jacob b- Adam Lambert
Margaret & Samuel McClung 9 Jun 1840; min- John J Reimensnyder

Hagarty
Hannah & Leonard Lootz 25 Jan 1802; d John b- John Cooper

Hagerty
Hannah & Leonard Lutz 25 Jan 1802; min- William King- 25Jan1802
Margaret & John Brown 1 Apr 1795; Minister's return spells name as 'Hagarty' d John who consents test- Vincent Tapp & Hannah Hagerty b- Vincent Tapp
Margaret & Oliver Miller 9 Feb 1799; Also known as Margaret Brown (See description of this unusual bond in the Introduction)

Augusta County Marriages -- Woman's Name

Hain
  Nancy & William Palmer 31 Dec 1818; min- William King
Haines
  Catharine & Ward McNair 14 Dec 1826; min- John A Gore
Hains
  Elizabeth & Paul Seig 27 Aug 1816; min- William King
  Julianna & Edward Keenan 6 May 1814; min- William Calhoon
  Lydia & Jacob Seig 3 May 1810; min- William Calhoon
  Mary & George Whitsal 28 Oct 1816; min- Wright Burgess
Halbert
  Esther & Jacob Richeson 10 Dec 1807; min- William King
  Polly & William Warner 8 Oct 1807; min- William King
Halderman
  Catherine & Solomon Bushong 13 May 1829; min- William C. Morrison
  Fanny & Thomas Price 22 Dec 1803; min- Philip Kennerly
  Mary & David Branaman 17 Dec 1816; min- William King
Hale
  Frances & John Switzer 6 Aug 1845; min- P Shickel
  Mary & Philip Echord 10 Aug 1841; min- George B Rimel
Hall
  Anne & James Patterson 16 Sep 1786; d Susannah b- Alexander Gibson Jr
  Catharine & John Newton 23 Jul 1829; min- Francis McFarland
  E & W B Kayser 17 Nov 1847; min- B M Smith
  Eleanor & John H Greiner 9 Sep 1828; min- William C. Morrison
  Elizabeth & Andrew Allison 21 Mar 1786; Minister's return spells name as 'Holt' bond min- William Wilson- 26Mar1786
  Francis D & William Breeze 16 Oct 1827; min- William Monroe
  Harriett & Jacob Coffman 14 Sep 1834; min- Wright Burgess
  Jane & James Boyd 13 Mar 1823; min- John Brown
  Jane & Robert Hutchison 8 Apr 1786; Minister's return spells name as 'Hutcheson' d Robert b- W Urquhart wit- John Berry, Robert Ramsey & James Hall min- Samuel Shannon- 11Apr1786
  Joanna & Wilson Brown 5 Sep 1821; min- John Brown
  Lavinia & Amos Wright 3 Feb 1827; min- William W Calhoun
  Malinda & James McCutcheon 12 Jun 1823; min- William W Calhoun
  Margaret & Samuel Jackson 16 Jan 1797; d William Hall, dec. con- Fanny Allison, mother of Margaret test- Isabella Sterrett & William Sterrett b- William Sterritt min- Archibald Scott- 24Jan1797
  Mary Ann & Gillias N Tally 20 Nov 1832; min- Samuel Kennerly
  Mary Jane & Francis Johnson 4 Jul 1825; min- Josiah Cole
  Mary & John Plunkett 26 Mar 1798; widower & widow Mary gives own consent b- James Lowe & Jeremiah Dowling
  Matilda & Robert Lynch 15 Feb 1827; min- Francis McFarland
  Nancy Agness & Jacob Vanlear 2 Mar 1796; d John b- Andrew Allison min- William Wilson- 3Mar1796
  Nancy & Christopher Snedicor 15 Nov 1785; d Robert b- John Berry wit- Robert Given

Augusta County Marriages -- Woman's Name

Hall (cont.)
Polly & Benjamin Harrison 19 Mar 1791; d John b- John Hall min- William Wilson- 22Mar1791
Sarah & Cyrus Ramsey 2 Jan 1842; min- Samuel Wagner
Sarah & George N Young - Sep 1829; min- William Wilson

Ham
Mary Ann & Alexander Black 17 Sep 1793; b- Samuel Miller min- John McCue- 17Sep1793

Hamer
Magdalene & Alexander Walker 22 Mar 1790; Minister's return spells name as 'Harner' b- Joshua Parry ('next friend?') min- William Wilson- 22Mar1790

Hamilton
Belenah & James Hamilton 26 Mar 1794; min- John McCue?- 26Mar1794
Belenah & James Hamilton 24 Mar 1795; d William Hamilton, dec. b- Charles Baskin min- John McCue- 26Mar1795
Charity & Edward Brison 21 Aug 1787; widow b- Samuel Gray min- James Chambers- 8Jul1788
Elizabeth & John Colbreth 18 Apr 1785; Minister's return spells name as 'Calbreth' b- James Johnston d John min- John Rodgers- 4Apr1785
Fanny & Robert Neal 23 Jan 1799; Fanny (of age) d William Hamilton, dec., and Patience Hamilton who consents test- John C Hamilton & Hugh Hamilton b- John Hamilton
Jane & John Hamilton 16 Apr 1800; d William Hamilton, dec. & Patience Hamilton who consents test- Fanny Neel b- John Craig Hamilton min- John McCue- date of ceremony missing
Joanna & Samuel Wilson 5 Aug 1813; min- Thomas Bourne
Margaret & James Gardiner 27 Nov 1787; Minister's return spells name as 'Gardner' widow b- Anthony Mustoe min- James Chambers- 27Nov1787
Mary A E & Andrew B Cowan 23 Aug 1838; min- William Calhoon
Mary & William Britten 24 Dec 1801; Mary (of age) d Arthur b- John Hamilton
Mary & William Colbreath 20 Aug 1787; d John who consents wit- Alexander Kelly & William Gillespie b- John Johnston
Mary & Cyrus Poage 8 Mar 1832; min- Conrad Speece
Mary & Charles Reaburn 7 Nov 1805; min- John McCue
Nancy & Andrew Alexander 16 Sep 1788; d John who consents wit- William Stoner & Philip Brown b- Francis Alexander min- William Wilson- 16Sep1788
Nancy & Moses L Alexander 25 Jun 1835; min- Samuel Kennerly
Perrina & William K Golladay 5 Oct 1848; min- W T Richardson
Rebecca & Brydon Wilson 16 Jul 1813; min- Thomas Bourne

Hamm
Patsy & James Mathews 3 Jul 1827; min- William Monroe

Hammaker
Barbara & Abraham Lambard 26 Dec 1795; d David of Shenandoah cty who consents test- John Gets b- Christian Lambard

Augusta County Marriages -- Woman's Name

Hamp
  Margaret & Mordecai Thornton 24 Apr 1795; d Stophel who consents test- Jacob Olinger b- James Alderman
Hampton
  Elizabeth & Uriah Warren 5 Aug 1804; min- William King
Hamrick
  Louisa & Robert P Wilson 29 Apr 1849; min- William O Lauck
Hanah
  Mary & Daniel Stover 30 Mar 1803; min- William King
Hance
  Ann & Charles Lewis 15 Mar 1792; Minister's return spells name as 'Ann Hann' b- John Mackall min- William Wilson- 18Mar1792
Hanger
  Annette & Peter Eagle 17 Feb 1789; Minister's return spells name as 'Agness' d Frederick, who consents b- Augustine Argenbright min- Archibald Scott- 21Feb1788
  Barbara & Peter Rush 19 Jun 1789; Minister's return spells Peter's name 'Rusk' Peter from Rockingham cty d Peter Henger Sr b- Carl Rusch min- Archibald Scott- 20Jun1786
  Catharine & John Wilhelms 4 Jun 1833; min- Francis McFarland
  Catherine & Henry Eidson 17 May 1803; min- William King
  Catherine & James Fennel 11 Jan 1827; min- Alexander Templeton
  Catherine & William Mills 19 Aug 1822; min- John Hendren
  Catherine & John Ross 12 Dec 1821; min- William W Calhoun
  Catherine & John Wise 12 Oct 1796; d Frederick who consents b- Henry Harmon
  Elizabeth & Joshua Evans 29 Apr 1806; min- William Wilson
  Elizabeth & James Nutty 13 May 1841; min- James Morrison
  Elizabeth & Jacob Thomas 18 Mar 1793; d Frederick b- Frederick Hanger
  Eveline E & Jacob Baylor 2 Oct 1826; min- Michael Meyerhoeffer
  Hanah & Jacob Fridley 26 Apr 1786; d Frederick b- George Hanger (See 'Olinger, Hanah' under Women's listing?) min- Archibald Scott- 27Apr1786
  Hannah A & Peter Palmer 11 Oct 1825; min- Michael Meyerhoeffer
  Hannah & James Allen 10 Nov 1808; min- William Wilson
  Hannah & Frederick Fultz 9 May 1795; d Peter b- Peter Hanger
  Hannah & Moses Gwinn 23 Apr 1829; min- Henry S Kepler
  Hannah & George W Miller 22 May 1845; min- G W Israel- publication of banns
  Isabella & William Cale 8 Jan 1846; min- J C Hensell
  Jane & Mathias Link 23 Jan 1826; min- Michael Meyerhoeffer
  Margaret & William Dull 7 Feb 1837; min- J C Hensell
  Margaret & Andrew Lucas 24 Mar 1842; min- John C Hensell
  Margaret & George Shirey 24 Apr 1817; min- William King
  Mary Ann & Jacob Dull 8 Mar 1832; min- Francis McFarland
  Polly & Hugh Daugherty 16 Apr 1827; min- James Morrison

Augusta County Marriages -- Woman's Name

Hanger (cont.)
 Polly & Samuel Woodward 2 Dec 1819; min- William Wilson
 Sarah & Enos Dull 7 Sep 1843; min- J C Hensell
 Sarah & Levi Surber 1 Sep 1831; min- William Calhoon
Hanke
 Susan & Henry Doom 14 Aug 1842; min- John C Hensell-
   publication of banns
Hankie
 Elizabeth & Jacob Fowtick 14 Oct 1786; d Simon b- Thomas
   Johnson min- Samuel Carrick- 14Oct1786
Hanna
 Ann & John Young 12 May 1814; min- William Calhoon
 Isabella H & William Nest 9 Dec 1824; min- Francis
   McFarland
 Isabella & Robert King 30 Nov 1793; b- William King min-
   William Wilson- 3Dec1793
 Nancy & Joseph Heizer 2 Sep 1824; min- Francis McFarland
 Sarah & John Dinkle 24 Jan 1849; min- John A Van Lear
Hannah
 Mary & Archibald Smiley 28 Jun 1800; d Robert Archibald
   from Rockbridge cty s Walter who consents test- James
   Buchanan & Evan Evans b- James Buchanan Jr
 Susan & John Kerr 23 Nov 1815; min- William Calhoon
Hansbarger
 Barbara Jane & John Hamilton 11 Oct 1827; min- William
   Monroe
 Elizabeth & Jacob Peck 14 Oct 1811; min- Wright Burgess
 Mary J & John C McCue 27 Oct 1842; min- A G Chenowith
 Mary & Matthew Hunter 18 Nov 1830; min- Gerard Morgan
Hansel
 Dorothy & Charles Caphart 31 Mar 1785; b- Adam Calbscop d
   Philip
 Elizabeth & Jacob Shull 27 Jan 1806; min- William King
 Sally & John Harris 7 Aug 1806; min- William King
Hansell
 Catherine & Richard Armstrong 7 Sep 1815; min- William King
Hanzele
 Magdalena & Lewis Scholl - Oct 1808; min- John Brown
Hapener
 Betsey & John Wolf 14 Oct 1802; min- William King-
   14Oct1802
Hapner
 Mary & Peter Fultz 5 Feb 1801; Minister's return spells
   name as 'Hepner' d Casper Hepner b- Casper Hapner min-
   William King- 5Feb1801
Harbarger
 Anzaleah & Henry Harris - --- 183-; min- Conrad Speece
Harberger
 Susana & William Dalton 3 Aug 1795; d Frederick b-
   Frederick Harbarger
Hardbarger
 Catherine & Zachariah Pennell 9 Jun 1813; min- William King
 Elizabeth & Stephen Mayfield 5 Jan 1819; min- William King

Augusta County Marriages -- Woman's Name

Harding
  Anna & William Wiley 7 Sep 1790; Minister's return spells name as 'Wildy and Anne Harding' sis Samuel perm- Esther Harding b- Samuel Harding min- Archibald Scott- 9Sep1790
  Elizabeth & Christian Frely 20 Sep 1787; Minister's return spells name as 'Freley' b- Samuel Harding min- Archibald Scott- 22Sep1787
  Rebecca & Thomas Wiley 23 Jan 1790; b- Edward Harding min- Archibald Scott- 28Jan1790

Hardshell
  Mary Margaret & John M Liggett 26 Nov 1847; min- J A Van Lear

Hare
  Elizabeth & Michael Sturm 6 Sep 1799; Minister's return spells name as 'Sturm' widow b- John Wise & John Hively min- William King- 8Sep1799
  Mary & Henry Miller 26 Mar 1827; min- Michael Meyerhoeffer

Haring
  Nancy & James Davies 8 Jun 1808; min- William Wilson

Harman
  Catherine & George Wakle 1 Jul 1806; min- William King

Harmon
  Caty & Leonard Tanner 16 Oct 1798; d Peter con- Johannes Danner & George Danner b- John Towell
  Elizabeth & John Smith 5 Jul 1810; min- William King
  Polly & John Flack 29 Apr 1806; min- William King

Harner
  Betsey & John Ramsey 12 Oct 1807; min- William King

Harness
  Mary & Peter Michel - Jun 1817; min- John Brown

Harnest
  Elizabeth L & Samuel Finley 16 Nov 1841; min- Francis McFarland
  Margaret L & Jacob Pitman 16 May 1848; min- James Paine

Harnsbarger
  Ann & George C Robertson 23 May 1814; min- Wright Burgess
  Sarah & William Clarke 1 Nov 1821; min- Gerard Morgan

Harouff
  Rebecca & Samuel Kellar 31 Jul 1828; min- William Calhoon

Harper
  Susanah & James Murphy 16 Mar 1785; min- Samuel Shannon- 16Mar1785

Harris
  Amelia & David McCrery 3 Sep 1829; min- James Morrison
  Catherine & William Blackmore 23 Feb 1804; min- William Wilson
  Elizabeth & Thomas Bibe 6 Mar 1817; min- William King
  Elizabeth & Joseph Blair 29 Apr 1794; d Robert who consents and gives bond no minister listed; clerk's memorandum cites ceremony date as 1May1794
  Elizabeth & David W Hutchens 13 Nov 1832; min- William Wilson
  Elizabeth & Robert Scott 22 Nov 1820; min- Luke Collins
  Elizabeth & Philip Wolwine 27 Apr 1797; Elizabeth (of age) s Elizabeth Wollwine who consents test- Jacob Woolwin & Thomas Stevens b- Jacob Wolwine

Augusta County Marriages -- Woman's Name

Harris (cont.)
 Isabella & William Callison 12 Apr 1821; min- John Brown
 Mary F & William David 25 Dec 1839; min- John J
   Reimensnyder
 Nancy & Levi Strickland 23 Nov 1805; min- William King
 Sarah & Samuel Carson 28 Feb 1828; min- James Morrison
 Susan & William Hart 14 Dec 1826; min- James Morrison
 Susanna & Joseph Cooper 30 Dec 1802; min- James Harper-
   30Dec1802
 Susannah & James McCutchen 16 Jan 1836; min- James Morrison
Harrison
 Edith & Mefford Hannah 10 Dec 1823; min- Michael
   Meyerhoeffer
 Elizabeth M & John Clarkson 6 Aug 1816; min- William
   Cravens
 Elizabeth & Elijah McClenachan 31 Mar 1803; min- John McCue
 Lucretia & Abraham Leonard 11 Jun 1822; min- Michael
   Meyerhoeffer
Harrow
 Susan & Charles McLeas 4 Dec 1837; min- John A Steele
Harry
 Sarah & Jacob Slusher - Jan 1805; min- John Brown
Harsbarger
 Lydia & Jacob Landes 14 Dec 1843; min- John A Van Lear
Harshaw
 Catherine & George Greiver 16 Feb 1832; min- William
   Calhoon
Harshman
 Mary & Henry Pence - Dec 1812; min- G H Riemenschneider
Hart
 Catharine & Samuel D Stover 5 Jun 1837; min- George A
   Leopard
 Elizabeth & John Grim 9 Nov 1789; d William b- William
   Heart min- Archibald Scott- 11Nov1789
 Polley & William Robertson 20 Jun 1816; min- William King
Hartigan
 Elizabeth & Richard Crosen 16 Aug 1832; min- James Morrison
 Mary & Ready Cash 29 Aug 1823; min- Tobias Riley
 Patsey E & Thomas M Pryor 16 Aug 1832; min- James Morrison
Hartman
 Sarah & Joseph Cline - Mar 1807; min- John Brown
Hartshooke
 Catherine & Solomon Smith 4 Jan 1812; min- G H
   Riemenschneider
 Margaret & John Glenn 29 Oct 1819; min- G H Riemenschneider
Hartsook
 Catharine & John Lambert - Jun 1826; min- Joseph Smith
Hartzo
 Elizabeth & Anthony King 3 Aug 1795; d Engelbert b-
   Engelbert Hartzo
Harzog
 Elizabeth & Henry Baumgartner - Sep 1804; min- John Brown

Augusta County Marriages -- Woman's Name

Hashaw
  Ann & Daniel Andrew 1 Nov 1811; min- Wright Burgess
Haskins
  Esther & Patrick Mares 10 Mar 1798; Esther (of age)
Haslet
  Jane & William Cawly 16 Aug 1808; min- William King
  Mary & Lewis Matheny 5 Jun 1814; min- William Wilson
Hassafluck
  Catherine & Isaiah Russel 2 Jun 1808; min- William McPheeters
Hatfield
  Sarah & Robert Beard 16 Aug 1790; d Hanah, who consents b- William Richardson wit- John Hatfield & John Gregg min- William Wilson- 17Aug1790
Hatten
  Jane & James Aston 15 Dec 1825; Bond gives name as 'Staton' min- Francis McFarland
Haup
  Catherine & William Lyons 9 May 1805; min- John McCue
  Elizabeth & Henry Shields 14 Nov 1822; min- John Brown
  Mary & Jacob Kershner 10 Nov 1840; min- John C Hensell- publication of banns
Hawk
  Catherine & Valentine Shoults 17 Jun 1799; d Henry wit- John Hawk b- Henry Hawk
  Polly & Thomas Gregory 4 Jan 1800; d Henry & Catherine Hawk and of age b- William Redford min- William King- 9Jan1800
  Rachel & Samuel Gregory 8 Sep 1798; Minister's return spells name as 'Hauk' Rachel (of age) d Henry Jacob Gregory swears Samuel of age b- Thomas Gregory min- Archibald Scott- 15Sep1798
Hawp
  Betsy & Christian Mummer 21 Apr 1790; d Rudolph, who consents wit- John & Susanna Hawp b- Walter Herrin
  Susanna & George Coiner 3 Jun 1794; d Rudolph who consents test- George Almeroth & John Hawpe b- John Hawpe
Hawpe
  Jane & George Dice 17 Feb 1820; min- James Morrison
  Sarah & Joseph Miller 13 Nov 1813; min- William King
Haybarger
  Catharine & John Swartzley 1 Apr 1834; min- Augustus Babb
  Mary & Henry Kice 23 Mar 1820; min- Robert H Chapman
  Sally & John Grass 30 Jun 1814; min- Conrad Speece, Jr
Hays
  Catherine & Edward Mooney 23 Dec 1789; Catherine recently from Ireland b- James Curtis
  Harriet G & John Crobarger 17 Nov 1845; min- T T Castleman
  Jane & Thomas Kirkpatrick 31 Jun 1810; min- William Calhoon
  Sally & John (Jr) Moffett 8 Jan 1799; Sally (of age) sis to Patrick Hays b- Patrick Hays
Headly
  Mary & George Goah 19 Dec 1809; min- William King

Augusta County Marriages -- Woman's Name

Hearn
  Peachy & Frederick Williams 24 Jul 1822; min- Josiah Cole
Heatherley
  Ann & William Chambers 23 Mar 1786; b- Anthony Mustoe
    min- James Waddle- 26Mar1786
Heaton
  Susan & William L Davis 25 May 1847; min- D W Arnold
Hedebough
  Polly & Thomas Denney 16 Jan 1806; min- John Emmill
Heiden
  Jane & Adam Fix 20 Dec 1827; min- William Monroe
Heiskell
  Amelia & James R Riddle 21 Jul 1807; min- William Calhoon
  Julia W & John W Miller 28 Aug 1810; min- William Calhoon
  Sarah D & Jehab Graham 20 May 1813; min- Thomas Bourne
Heizer
  Polly & Jacob Rapp 7 May 1807; min- William King
  Ruth E & James Brownlee 24 Oct 1833; min- William Calhoon
Helm
  Margaret & Roland Rittenhouse 28 Apr 1822; min- Conrad
    Speece
Helmick
  Elizabeth & William Anderson 8 Feb 1831; min- James
    Morrison
Helms
  Elizabeth & Micajah McCollins 1 Oct 1809; min- William King
Hemp
  Catherine & Jeremiah Grant 31 Aug 1813; min- William King
  Drusilla & Alexander Smiley 9 Jan 1845; min- J C Hensell
  Margaret Ann & Allison Ransbarger 30 Mar 1837; min- J C
    Hensell
  Philpena & John Waddle 6 May 1788; b- Daniel Waddle
Hempenstall
  Elizabeth & James Wilson 29 Mar 1785; min- Samuel Shannon-
    29Mar1785
  Hanah & Elibabb Wilson 22 Oct 1788; d Isaac who consents
    test- James Wilson & Moses Knap b- William Blagg
Henderson
  A M & W W Peaco 26 Dec 1839; min- P E Stevenson
  Anny & Morgan Kinkaid 14 Mar 1839; min- William Calhoon
  Betsy & John Burkentine 22 Feb 1816; min- William King
  Betsy & Samuel Guinn 1 Dec 1831; min- James Kerr
  Elizabeth & Samuel Guinn 15 Dec 1831; min- James Kerr
  Elizabeth & Joshua Smith 12 Dec 1827; min- William C.
    Morrison
  Florence & John Spencer 3 Jun 1801; widower d William
    Henderson b- John Henderson
  Hannah & John (Jr) Dennison 23 May 1800; d Jones Henderson
    b- John Dennison Sr & James Henderson
  Isabella & James C Graham 27 Dec 1820; min- John D Ewin
  Isabella & Joseph Thompson 14 May 1793; d Jones Henderson
    Isabella born in 1766 b- Philip Dyer no minister listed;
    clerk's memorandum cites ceremony date as 23May1793
  Jane & Henry Gay 15 Apr 1785; d Joanes b- William Galloway

Augusta County Marriages -- Woman's Name

Henderson (cont.)
  Lucinda & Elijah Smith 16 Jun 1827; min- William C. Morrison
  Mary & James McMullan 4 Mar 1800; Minister's return spells name as 'McMillan' d Valentine who consents James (of age) b- James Cochran min- William Wilson- 6Mar1800
  Matilda & James E Walker 29 Dec 1842; min- James Bunting
  Nancy C & John Parris 12 Sep 1839; min- Isaac Jones
  Nancy & David Beck 14 Nov 1833; min- James Kerr
  Nancy & John Strain 22 Nov 1803; min- John McCue
  Patsey & James Strane 13 Nov 1806; min- William King
  Rebeccah & James Risk 23 May 1799; No bond consent of father, Jones Henderson test- Joseph Henderson John Risk swears James of age
  Sarah & Addison Gregory 31 Mar 1842; min- P E Stevenson
  Sarah & John Risk 13 Jun 1796; s Robert d Jones Henderson who consents Sarah (of age) John Risk swears that his cousin, John is past 21 b- Joseph Henderson min- John Montgomery- 16Jun1796
  Susana & James McComb 9 Jan 1793; Susana (of age) d William sis David b- David Henderson min- John McCue- 29Jan1793

Hendren
  Sarah Jane & John R Stephens 15 Jun 1831; min- Conrad Speece

Henry
  Agnes & Charles Henry 23 Jul 1798; Agnes (of age) d James Charles (of age) b- James Henry
  Agness & James Nelson 14 Aug 1787; Minister's return spells name as 'Neilson' d James who consents test- Joseph Nilson & Robert Henery b- James Henry min- Archibald Scott- 16Aug1787
  Ann & James Harris 15 Mar 1822; min- John Brown
  Drusilla & Elijah Patterson 13 Dec 1827; min- James Morrison
  Elizabeth & Thomas McElwee 9 Feb 1797; d Samuel b- Samuel Henry
  Jane B & William W Alexander 7 May 1833; min- James Morrison
  Margaret & George Cochran 30 Sep 1790; d James, who consents wit- David Humphreys & John McCutchan b- Samuel McCutchan
  Mary & Joseph Nelson 4 Dec 1786; d James b- Robert Blair wit- Alexander Ramsey
  Polly A & Andrew Poage 22 Feb 1827; min- James Morrison
  Sally & John Willson - Jan 1824; min- James Morrison
  Sarah & William Alexander 19 Nov 1794; min- John Brown- 19Nov1794
  Sarah & James Fulton 19 May 1836; min- James Morrison
  Sarah & James Poage 3 Aug 1793; Minister's return spells name as 'Poake' d James b- James Henry min- John Brown- 5Sep1793

Augusta County Marriages -- Woman's Name

Heppard
  Sarah & Jacob Spears 13 Oct 1835; min- William G Jackson
Herndon
  Mildred & Joseph R Beaty 1 Jan 1843; min- D F Bittle
Herpine
  Catherine & John Kennerly 13 Aug 1796; d Thomas Herpine, dec. of shenandoah cty Catherine not of age con- Mary Kennerly, mother & James Kennerly test- Catherine Kennerly b- Mathew Robertson
Herren
  Priscilla & Garay Start 25 Jul 1801; Minister's return spells name as 'Geve Stout and Pricilla Herron' widower Priscilla (of age) b- Michael Harmon min- William King- 26Jul1801
Herring
  Margaret C & John Hendren Ervin 30 Dec 1845; min- J A Van Lear
  Merry & John Lamb 19 Nov 1846; min- Jacob C Spitler
Herron
  Betsey & Garrett McCauley - May 1828; min- William Wilson
Heslet
  Sarah & John Garvin 14 Aug 1808; min- William Wilson
Hess
  Rebecca & James H Rhodes 23 Feb 1841; min- John C Hensell- publication of banns
  Sarah & William Lange 1 Aug 1839; min- John C Hansell
Hibbert
  Betsey & Adam Leonard 17 Sep 1816; min- William King
Hickell
  Elizabeth & James Guy 10 Oct 1809; min- John Montgomery
Hicklin
  Agness & Joseph Maze 14 Jun 1787; Minister's return spells name as 'Mays' d Hugh who consents test- Samuel McDonnald & Hugh McDonnald b- John Bosang & James Culbertson min- Samuel Shannon- 18Jun1787
  Hannah & John Stuart 15 May 1787; b- James McGavory min- Samuel Shannon- 31May1787
  Jane & James Gwinn 13 Jan 1792; d John, who consents b- John Hicklin min- John Montgomery- 24Jan1792
  Nancy & James Hall 15 Nov 1785; d Thomas Hickland b- John Berry wit- Robert Givens
  Ruth & Isaac Maze 6 Sep 1788; d Hugh who consents test- Valentine White b- Joseph Maze
  Sarah & John Montgomery 2 Mar 1785; min- Samuel Shannon- 2Mar1785
Hicks
  Elizabeth & Nicholas Spring 23 Aug 1796; d Joshua b- Joshua Hicks min- John McCue- 25Aug1796
  Jane & John Gay 13 Mar 1817; min- William King
  Lucy & David Henderson 30 Mar 1809; min- John McCue
Hide
  Margarett & Jacob Roler 22 May 1835; min- Samuel Kennerly

Augusta County Marriages -- Woman's Name

Higs
  Elizabeth & John (Jr) Dull 7 Mar 1832; min- Francis McFarland
Hildebrand
  Ann & Peyton Carson 20 Jan 1834; min- John Hendren- publication of banns
  Magdaline & John Rader 16 Apr 1816; 'Rider?' min- William King
Hill
  Catherine & John Crouse 18 Oct 1814; min- William King
  Eleanor & James Searaight 26 Nov 1802; min- William King- 26Nov1802
  Lydia & David Keizer 6 Mar 1801; Lydia (of age) sis to Eleanor Hill b- James Rankin
  Mary Virginia & John W Start 29 Feb 1848; 'Rev.' John W min- John Bowen
  Mary & James Baker 28 Sep 1785; min- Archibald Scott- 28Sep1785
  Pauline C & Alexander B Campbell 16 Sep 1829; min- Conrad Speece
Hillis
  Martha & William Brown 25 Apr 1811; min- John McCue
Hines
  Catherine & Frederick Sheets 20 Feb 1812; min- William King
  Fanny & John Kilkenny 9 Jul 1812; min- William King
  Sally & John Weaver 3 Mar 1812; min- William King
Hinkle
  Elizabeth & William Hart 19 Mar 1798; d John b- John Hinkle & Stuart Kennedy wit- William Sterritt
Hinton
  Elizabeth & John Sites 29 May 1816; bond min- Conrad Speece, Jr--May1816
  Hannah & Alexander Walker 25 Nov 1819; min- Conrad Speece
Hipard
  Polly & Benjamin Arisman 1 Apr 1833; min- James C Wilson
Hipes
  Hetty & John Armstrong 21 Oct 1823; min- James Morrison
Hite
  Lucinda & John Rankin 27 May 1813; min- William King
  Nancy & Jacob Fridley 3 Feb 1818; min- John D Ewin
Hizer
  Rebeccah & Peter Smith 18 Oct 1803; min- John McCue
Hodge
  Elizabeth & John McIlvain 28 Jul 1789; b- John Hodge
  Elizabeth & John Slaven 30 Jul 1789; min- John Montgomery- 30Jul1789
  Margaret & Charles Fawcet 25 Aug 1805; min- John Montgomery
  Margaret & Thomas Ruddle 13 Oct 1825; min- Josiah Cole
  Sally & David Kinkead 14 Oct 1800; d John Hodge, dec. sis to William Hodge, and of age b- William Hodge
Hodges
  Betsy & Lewis Pauley 6 Jul 1824; min- William W Calhoun

Augusta County Marriages -- Woman's Name

Hofert
   Susana & Jonas Michel - Mar 1806; min- John Brown
Hog
   Elizabeth & Jesse Bennett 6 Apr 1793; Minister's return
      spells name as 'Betsy Hogg of Rockbridge' Dr. Jesse Bennett
      Elizabeth gives her own consent test- B Kennerly b- James
      Hogg min- William Wilson- 8Apr1793
Hogan
   Sarah Ann & Daniel S Ward 13 Dec 1837; min- John A Steele
Hogg
   Ann & Joseph S Effinger 14 May 1833; min- Conrad Speece
   Elizabeth & John Blair 14 Oct 1823; min- Conrad Speece
   Margaret P & George Blackeley 17 Feb 1835; min- John A
      Steele
   Nancy & William Hawkins 22 Feb 1787; d Elizabeth Hogge who
      consents test- Thomas Smythe & Patrick Sharkey b- Patrick
      Shirkey of Botetourt cty min- William Wilson- 23Feb1787
Hogsett
   Elizabeth & John Nichol 14 May 1798; Minister's return
      spells name as 'Hogshead' d Robert Hogsett, dec. con-
      Nancy Hogsett test- William Hogsett & James Hogsett b-
      John McDowell min- Benjamin Irvin- 15May1798
   Manda J & Thomas H Dryden - Aug 1847; min- Stephen
      Hildebrand
   Peggy & Thomas Hogsett 19 Mar 1811; min- William Calhoon
Hogshead
   Ann & John McNair 29 Aug 1825; min- John Hendren
   Ann & Michael (Jr) Shuey 11 Jan 1821; min- William Calhoon
   Betsy & Jacob Pfifer - Oct 1821; min- John Brown
   Eliza Ann & Alexander Bell 21 Nov 1831; min- John Hendren
   Eliza & William Hanger 11 Oct 1825; min- John Hendren
   Elizabeth & John Kerr 3 Sep 1792; Minister's return spells
      name as 'John Then' d James b- Thomas Rutledge & John Watt
      min- William Wilson- 4Sep1792
   Isabella & Robert Graham 5 Mar 1793; d David sis of David
      and above 21 b- David Hogshead Jr min- William Wilson-
      6Mar1793
   Margaret & James Armstrong 7 Apr 1808; min- William Calhoon
   Margaret & Alexander Malcolm 28 Dec 1798; Minister's
      return spells name as 'Malcom' d John Hogshead, dec. b-
      John Hogshead (Jr?) min- William Wilson- 1Jan1799
   Martha & William Hinds 3 May 1819; min- John Hendren
   Mary & John Black 17 Oct 1812; min- William Wilson
   Mary & Dorman Lafland 29 Feb 1788; Minister's return
      spells name as 'Laughlin' b- John McKittrick min- Benjamin
      Erwin- 10Mar1788
   Matheras & William Snapp 28 May 1822; min- John Hendren
   Matilda & Hugh Gilkerson 27 Oct 1825; min- William Wilson
   Nancy & John Elliot 8 Mar 1829; min- John Hendren
   Patsey & John Roberts 8 Feb 1793; Patsey (Polly?) (of
      age) d John sis of John b- John Hogshead no minister
      listed; clerk's memorandum cites ceremony date as 8Feb1793
   Polly & Francis Gilkeson 1 Oct 1799; d James b- James
      Hogshead

Augusta County Marriages -- Woman's Name

Hogshead (cont.)
Polly & John Hogshead 22 Jan 1829; min- John Hendren
Rachel & John Frame 10 Mar 1814; min- William Wilson
Rebecca & James Brown 14 Mar 1805; min- Benjamin Irwin
Rebecca & David Hogshead 27 Nov 1799; Rebecca (of age) d Michael who consents   b- Thomas Hogshead
Rebekah & Isaac Hanna 10 Nov 1786; Minister's return spells name as 'Hanah' b- John Mills min- Archibald Scott- 9Nov1786
Sarah C & Richard J C Dudley 26 Mar 1838; min- John Hendren

Holladay
Polly & John J T Mills 15 Nov 1814; min- Conrad Speece, Jr

Hollaway
Catharine P & John G Wright 23 Mar 1831; min- John Hendren

Hollis
Emily A & James Gray 9 Jan 1845; min- J C Hensell
Mary Ann & John Wiseman 3 Nov 1842; min- Henry Wetzel
Rebecca & Abraham Thomas 19 Nov 1835; min- Augustus Babb
Sarah Ann & Peter Wiseman 10 Nov 1836; min- J C Hensell

Holmes
Elizabeth & James Long 2 Nov 1810; min- William King
Elizabeth & David McClure 29 Sep 1795; Minister's return omits David's surname d Samuel of Shenandoah cty who consents test- Hugh Stuart & James Walker b- David Parry min- Archibald Scott- 29Sep1795
Jane & David Walker 25 Oct 1790; d Samuel, who consents wit- James Holmes & Robert Stuart b- John Gothry
Mary & William Blair 26 Sep 1793; d John who consents test- Hugh Caul & John Holme b- Hugh Caul min- John McCue- 26Sep1793
Nancy & David Bell 2 Mar 1809; min- John McCue

Holt
Maria F & Frederick Berlin 1 Sep 1844; min- G W Israel

Holton
Martha & Nathaniel Heizer 22 Nov 1804; min- John McCue

Homes
Mary & William Davis 24 Jul 1789; Minister's return spells name as 'Holms' d Joseph, who consents b- John Craig wit- John Craig & George Davis min- William Wilson- 24Jul1789

Hoof
Catherine & John Brilhart 24 Mar 1801; min- Samuel Garber- 24Mar1801

Hook
Katty & John Lyon 7 Jan 1794; min- William Wilson- 7Jan1794
Nancy & Joseph (Sr) Peck 18 Nov 1824; min- Josiah Cole- publication of banns

Hooks
Nancy & Daniel Propst 21 May 1846; min- J A Van Lear

Hoopman
Catherine & Conrad Peters 1 May 1806; min- William King
Elizabeth & John Devenbough 23 Feb 1804; min- William King

Hoover
Catherine Jane & John B Fairburn 9 Nov 1837; min- J C Hensell

Augusta County Marriages -- Woman's Name

Hoover (cont.)
  Eliza & David Baylor 22 Oct 1834; min- George Hildt
  Elizabeth & Henry Grove 8 Aug 1825; min- Michael
    Meyerhoeffer
  Eve Margaret & Adam Rusmisel 13 May 1841; min- John C
    Hensell- publication of banns
  Margaret & Jacob Grove - Oct 1828; min- William Calhoon
  Sarah E & Michael Engleman 22 May 1845; min- J C Hensell
  Sarah & Charles Trimble 19 Oct 1830; min- William Calhoon

Hopewell
  Maria & William Jordan 30 Apr 1843; min- John A Van Lear

Hopkins
  Sarah & William Blain 2 Dec 1799; d Samuel who consents
    test- P Thompson b- John Henry

Hopper
  Evaline & Samuel Blewitt 6 Mar 1829; min- William Wilson

Horn
  Elizabeth & John Ellis 9 Dec 1806; min- William King
  Elizabeth & James F Huffman 29 Jul 1849; min- George B
    Rimel
  Rebecca & Andrew Perry 6 Aug 1848; min- P Shickel

Horne
  Elizabeth & David Byers 10 Apr 1827; min- James Morrison
  Janetta & John (Jr) Swisher 16 Feb 1837; min- John J
    Reimensnyder

Hortshough
  Mary & John Pauf 10 Jan 1798; Mary (of age) d Englebert
    b- Englebert Hartshough

Hottle
  Margaret S & Lewis Dinkle 18 Oct 1838; min- John A Van Lear
  Mary & Alexander Crawford 3 Aug 1830; min- William Calhoon
  Rebecca Ann & John C Revercomb 2 Jun 1845; min- P Shickel

Houchins
  Sarah & John Kiger 28 Feb 1812; min- William Wilson

Houf
  Anne & Henry S Shaver 28 Jan 1828; min- William Wilson
  Lydia & Samuel Lowman 10 Jun 1834; min- William Wilson
  Sarah & Joseph Fulwider 10 Apr 1834; min- William Wilson

Houff
  Catharine & Samuel Wheelbarger 4 Apr 1843; min- Samuel
    Wagner

Houston
  Anna & John Miller 13 Jan 1810; min- William King
  Nancy & Henry Madison Graham 10 Jan 1833; min- James Kerr
  Patience & James Kerr 18 Jan 1786; Minister's return
    spells name as 'Huston' d James Huston s James b- Matthew
    Kenny wit- Walter Boil, John Mison, John Lewis & John
    Dogherty min- William Wilson- 16Jan1786

Howdasher
  Susannah & Jacob Detamore 28 Sep 1846; min- P Shickel

Howdeshell
  Anney & Vincent Sandy - Sep 1842; min- John Brower-
    publication of banns

Augusta County Marriages -- Woman's Name

Howell
  Lettice & Dennis Mahony 5 Jun 1793; Minister's return spells name as 'Mehony and Nowell' b- John Campbell min- William Wilson- 24Apr1793
  Lucy J & John M Taliaferro - Aug 1847; min- Stephen Hildebrand
  Mary Jane & Samuel Snyder - --- 1835; min- Wright Burgess- publication of banns

Hubard
  Elizabeth & John Bowyer 26 Feb 1801; Elizabeth (of age) d Francis b- Jacob Kinney

Hubbard
  Charlotte & Thomas Griggs 15 Jul 1801; Minister's return spells name as 'Hubbord' b- John Bowyer min- John McCue- 16Jul1801

Hudlaw
  Catherine & John Kiplinger 1 Jan 1788; Minister's return spells name as 'Catherine Carpenter' min- William Wilson- 1Jan1788

Hudson
  Elizabeth & Daniel Yearout 27 Aug 1807; min- William King
  Hannah & William M Logan 16 May 1827; min- William Calhoon
  Mary & Thomas Parris 8 Jul 1800; s John Mary (of age) d George Hudson, dec. b- Charles Hudson
  Sarah & Philip F Shepherd 2 Dec 1824; min- William W Calhoun

Huff
  Caroline Amanda & Alexander Roudabush 5 Apr 1849; min- George H Martin
  Elizabeth M & Peter Crickenbarger 29 Aug 1841; min- Samuel Wagner
  Elizabeth & Robert Sanders 15 Jan 1835; min- Samuel Kennerly
  Margaret & William Southard 30 Jan 1829; min- William C. Morrison
  Mary & John Childers 9 Jun 1825; min- Josiah Cole
  Polly & Anthoney Fisher 5 Feb 1807; min- William King
  Sarah & John S Kesterson 27 Mar 1835; min- Samuel Kennerly
  Sarah & James McBride 30 May 1827; min- William Wilson
  Susan & Benjamin Lamb 6 Aug 1818; min- William King

Huffer
  Ann & Christian Daggy 18 Jan 1847; min- George Huffman
  Susanna & Jonathan Michael 28 Jan 1830; min- G H Reimensnyder

Huffert
  Catherine & Henry Naher 17 Nov 1827; min- G H Reimensnyder

Huffman
  Margaret & Ludwick Haroff 6 Feb 1818; min- William King
  Rosey & George Lowdermilk 23 Dec 1800; Minister's return spells name as 'Loudermilk and Huff' George (of age) d George b- George Huffman min- John McCue- 25Dec1800

Hufman
  Catherine & John Winegar 13 Jun 1785; d Jacob b- Nicolas Spring wit- John Banks & William Winegar

Augusta County Marriages -- Woman's Name

Hufman (cont.)
Rebeca & Samuel Roudenbush 15 May 1844; min- D F Bittle
Hughes
Agness & Edward Sims 7 Sep 1785; min- Archibald Scott- 7Sep1785
Cynthia & Reuben Tankersley 18 Jan 1798; d John b- John Hughes
Hanna & Edmunds Tankersley 12 Aug 1809; min- John Bell
Hughs
Sophia & William Patterson 15 Jun 1848; min- J C Hensell
Susan & James L Alexander 24 Nov 1842; min- A G Chenowith
Hulett
Elizabeth & James Black 26 Apr 1787; min- Archibald Scott- 26Apr1787
Huling
Margaret B & Samuel Whitmore 17 Aug 1848; min- J McKendree Reiley
Hull
Barbary & Jacob Cook 29 Dec 1795; d Francis b- Francis Hull
Catherine & Lewis Wiseman 8 Jan 1799; d Francis who consents Catherine over 25 b- George Dull
Hannah & Adam Snyder 19 May 1845; min- D F Bittle
Mary & David Argenbright 6 Apr 1848; min- J C Hensell
Mary & Frederick Hanger 4 May 1785; d Francis b- Anthony Mustoe wit- Robert Campbell & Samuel Black
Susannah & John Shultz 12 Jan 1829; min- Francis McFarland
Humbert
Elizabeth & Jacob Humbert 7 Sep 1837; min- John Garber
Humes
Jane & Peter Moore 8 May 1827; min- James Watts- publication of banns
Humphrey
----- & William Bowen 27 Jul 1835; min- William G Jackson
Ellen & Henry Stofer - Jul 1826; min- Joseph Smith
Mary & Joseph Fix 30 Mar 1848; min- J C Hensell
Patsey & John (Jr) Risk 21 Nov 1831; min- Conrad Speece
Sarah & David Kyle 27 Nov 1835; min- Augustus Babb
Humphreys
Ann & Archibald Rhea 16 Oct 1798; d David b- David Humphreys min- Archibald Scott- 26Oct1798
Caroline M M & Robert Tate Wallace 26 Jan 1832; min- Francis McFarland
Elizabeth & Samuel McCutcheon 16 Feb 1801; d David s Capt. Samuel McCutcheon b- David Humphreys & Capt. Samuel McCutcheon
Margaret & Samuel Blackwood 21 Nov 1797; 'Peggy?' d David b- John Davis min- Archibald Scott- 24Nov1797
Polly & David Gilkeson 25 May 1809; min- William McPheeters
Hunley
Mildred & Christian Hupman 16 Mar 1833; min- William Calhoon

Augusta County Marriages -- Woman's Name

Hunter
Amanda & Elijah Ewin 11 Nov 1830; min- Hezekiah Best
Catherine & Mathew Hunter 8 Dec 1790; d Samuel, who consents b- John Hunter min- Archibald Scott- 9Dec1790
Dicy & John Giles 11 Nov 1809; min- William King
Eliza & Jeremiah Cross 15 Apr 1841; min- James Gamble
Elizabeth & Jeremiah Cross 16 Mar 1809; min- William King
Elizabeth & James McCutchen 15 Nov 1786; d William s Ellenor McCutchan b- David Cale wit- Margrit Hunter & Sarah Hunter, John & James McCutchan min- Archibald Scott- 15Nov1786
Jane & James Cross 19 Nov 1835; min- Francis A C Mills
Margaret & William Benson 6 Aug 1795; Margaret (of age) d William b- James Rollins min- Archibald Scott- 11Aug1795
Martha & David Beard 17 Jun 1795; d John b- John Hunter
Mary L & Alexander M Austin 4 Mar 1829; min- William Wilson
Mary & James Ewing 15 Dec 1795; b- William Patterson min- John McCue- 15Dec1795
Rachel & Andrew Crawford 22 Aug 1799; d William who consents & Mary Hunter who consents test- William Crawford Andrew of age b- William Benson
Sarah J & Thomas S Sitlington 26 Aug 1840; min- Benjamin M Smith
Sarah & John Harland 23 May 1837; min- Zach Jordan
Sarah & John Nesbet 24 Aug 1787; Minister's return spells name as 'Neisbet' consent for both- Samuel Neisbitt & William Hunter test- John Yeager & James McCutchan b- James McCutchan min- Archibald Scott- 26Aug1787
Susannah & Andrew A Alexander 11 Feb 1833; min- James C Wilson

Hurst
Margaret & James Gilbert 4 Jan 1827; min- William Monroe

Hushour
Elizabeth & Frederick Michael - Dec 1826; min- Joseph Smith

Husk
Elizabeth & Solomon Danner 23 Mar 1801; Minister's return spells name as 'Hink' s Solomon who consents test- George Danner & Leonard Danner b- John Towell min- John McCue- 23Mar1801

Huston
Elizabeth & Thomas Boyd 5 Oct 1795; d Mary who consents test- John Burk b- James Houston min- Archibald Scott- 5Oct1795
Mary & Robert Christian 2 Sep 1789; d Wm, who consents wit- G Christian Jr & Frances Long b- Gilbert Christian min- Archibald Scott- 3Sep1789
Mary & Humphrey Ellis 2 Dec 1799; Humphrey from Wythe cty widower & widow (of William) b- Joseph Burke

Hutchens
Catharine & John Fauver 20 Apr 1826; min- William W Calhoun
Cyntha & Valentine Hupman 29 May 1834; min- Cornelius Gates

Hutcheson
Amanda T & John Newton 4 Mar 1835; min- George Hildt
Eleanor & Joseph Henderson 1 Apr 1794; d George b- George Hutchison min- John McCue- 3Apr1794

<u>Augusta County Marriages -- Woman's Name</u>

Hutcheson (cont.)
   Jane & Thomas Coldbreath 26 Nov 1801; Minister's return spells name as 'Caldbreath' d James b- James Hutcheson min- John McCue- 26Nov1801
   Margaret & Isaac Hutcheson 10 Nov 1807; min- John McCue
   Mary & Alexander Sterritt 6 Jan 1807; min- William King
Hutchins
   Jane & Samuel Garvin 4 Mar 1833; min- John S Watt
Hyatt
   Sarah & Cornelius Cain 17 Aug 1790; min- William Wilson- 17Aug1790
Hycarser
   Betsy & Felly Argenbright 2 Dec 1802; min- William King- 2Dec1802
Hynes
   Elizabeth & Philip Byer 17 Jun 1806; min- William King
Imboden
   Catherine & John Spatts 28 Jan 1809; min- William King
   Eleanor & John Deal 13 Sep 1810; min- William King
   Elizabeth & James Kilkenny 22 Feb 1820; min- Daniel Stephens
   Jane & Abraham Aughe 20 Mar 1806; min- John McCue
   Polly & David Foutz 9 Dec 1813; min- William King
Ingleman
   Catherine & Adolph Spinkle 22 May 1787; min- Archibald Scott- 22May1787
   Catherine & John Summers 3 Oct 1798; d Philip b- Philip Ingleman
Ingleton
   Hannah & Christian Lightner 20 Jun 1805; min- William King
Ingram
   Nisy & Thomas Redmond 4 Mar 1786; 'Nancy'? d Joshua b- Robert Wilson wit- Robert Wilson, James McGengal, Joseph Willson min- William Wilson- 4Mar1786
Insle
   Rebecca & Christian Mesner 15 Jun 1793; Rebecca (of age) b- George Bernard
Irvine
   Ann & David Sheets 28 Jan 1826; min- John Hendren
   Elizabeth G & Theophilus Gamble 31 Mar 1834; min- John Hendren
   Elizabeth & Simon Sheetz 11 Mar 1841; min- J J Reimensnyder
   Jane & John Hopkins 11 Jan 1820; min- John Hendren
   Margaret & Francis Allen 7 Dec 1826; min- John Hendren
   Mary & Josiah Hogshead - Mar 1827; min- John Hendren
   Sophia & John Bell 19 Apr 1827; min- John Hendren
Irwin
   Susanna & George A Bolsley 19 Apr 1808; min- William Wilson
Iseman
   Martha G & John H Woolard 8 Feb 1844; min- Samuel Wagner
Isenhouser
   Mary & James Shepherd 15 Apr 1794; d Michael b- Michael Isenhouser

Augusta County Marriages -- Woman's Name

Jackson
Ally & Jeremiah Hook 19 Apr 1810; min- William King
Annis & Daniel Joseph 24 Feb 1817; min- William King
Elizabeth & David Caruthers 14 Mar 1786; (Coruthers?) d David min- Archibald Scott- 18Mar1786
Elizabeth & George W Miller 7 Oct 1847; min- W G Campbell
Elizabeth & William Rodchers - Feb 1808; min- John Brown
Elizabeth & John Toeme 17 May 1785; d Peter b- John Waddle wit- Thomas Brown & Samuel Blackley
Harriet & Jacob Snyder 2 Jul 1817; min- William King
Jane & Jacob Waddell 19 Jul 1796; Jane (of age) b- Jacob Bumgarner
Margaret & James Carrethers 17 Dec 1805; min- John McCue
Margaret & John Evans 18 Oct 1796; widower & widow b- John Evans Jr min- John McCue- 20Oct1796
Margaret & John Yorkshire 8 Jan 1808; min- William King
Mary A & Martin Johnson 24 Mar 1843; min- Samuel Wagner- publication of banns
Mary L & Pleasant G Gillum 24 Jun 1841; min- P E Stevenson
Nancy & Alexander Connelly 3 Jan 1801; Margaret?' d ----- Jackson, dec. John Walker swears that Nancy lived with him for eight years since she was fourteen b- John Walker min- Daniel Garber- 5Jan1801
Sarah & James Gaines 28 Mar 1805; min- William Wilson
Sidney & Jacob Argenbright 10 Sep 1829; min- Francis McFarland

James
Anna & Thomas King 1 Apr 1806; min- William King
Elizabeth & George Rabb 26 Nov 1799; d Thomas b- Thomas James min- William King- 1Dec1799

Jameson
Sarah & Thomas Beard 16 Apr 1785; d George bond

Jamison
Agnes & Joseph Wagner - Jan 1819; min- John Brown
Ann & David McCormick 8 Sep 1794; 'McCormack' d John b- James Jamison no minister listed; clerk's memorandum cites ceremony date as 9Sep1794
Eleanor & John Berry 17 Oct 1797; Minister's return spells name as 'Jameson' Eleanor (of age) d John b- Matthew Jamison min- Archibald Scott- 19Oct1797
Eliza Matilda & George Lynch 24 Jan 1825; min- Thomas Caldwell
Elizabeth & Elijah Griffith 2 Oct 1805; min- William King
Patsey & George Parr 5 Dec 1815; min- William King

Jarvis
Mary Jane & Andrew H Black 15 Jun 1848; min- J C Hensell
Susan & John Swisher 13 Jul 1826; min- James Morrison

Jenkins
Isabella & James Johnson 3 Jan 1792; Minister's return spells name as 'Joseph Johnson b- John Gorden min- William Wilson- 5Jan1792

Jennings
Betsey & Robert Johnson 11 May 1831; min- John Howell
Letitia & Francis Huff 23 Dec 1841; min- F D Goodwin

Augusta County Marriages -- Woman's Name

Jennings (cont.)
 Martha Jane & David Pecot 26 Feb 1846; min- T T Castleman
 Mary & Alexander R StClair 1 Dec 1836; min- B N Brown
 Sarah A & Adison K Fisher 27 Feb 1844; min- T T Castleman- publication of banns
 Susan C & Peter Row 7 Apr 1840; min- D F Bittle- publication of banns

Jewell
 Polly & Samuel Bailey 9 Mar 1799; 'Mary' d Joseph who consents & Susanna Jewell who consents test- Catherine Lynch both of age b- Ambrose Lee Tinsley & James Lowe min- William King- 9Mar1799

Johns
 Polly & John Gowing 25 Feb 1836; min- William Calhoon

Johnson
 Ann & Zachariah S Gibson 27 Oct 1808; min- William King
 Duretta Ann & Robert H Grooms 20 Jul 1848; min- J McKendree Reiley
 Elizabeth & William Nabours 27 Apr 1803; min- William King
 Margaret & Henry Goodrich 22 May 1821; 'Hezekiah?' min- Josiah Cole
 Mary Ann & Josiah Batcheller 15 Nov 1821; min- Daniel Stephens
 Nelly & William Smith 31 Mar 1787; Minister's return spells name as 'Johnston' Nelly gives own consent test- John Killgobbin & James Rapshin b- Francis Mara Nelly widow of Hugh Johnson min- William Wilson- 12Apr1787
 Rebecca & James W Davis 14 Mar 1839; min- Frederick D Goodwin

Johnston
 Caroline C & Erasmus R Showalter 21 Apr 1835; min- Conrad Speece- publication of banns
 Elenor & Hugh Hannah 22 Nov 1788; Minister's return spells name as 'Hanna' d James who consents test- William Wilson b- Thomas Frame Hugh lists trade as shoemaker min- William Wilson- 22Dec1788
 Elizabeth & Wilson Mills 23 Jul 1818; min- Conrad Speece, Jr
 Hester & Stephen S Moore 28 Sep 1847; min- T H Busey
 Jane & Thomas Baskin 10 Apr 1815; min- William King
 Margaret & Malachi Licks 25 Dec 1793; Minister's return spells name as 'Malika Lucke' d William b- Andrew Allison min- John McCue- 26Dec1793
 Margaret & William Scott 26 Jul 1827; min- William Wilson
 Mary Ann & John Evy 14 Oct 1847; min- Jacob Bear
 Mary & Edward McCan 16 Jun 1790; widow b- William Downey
 Nancy & Robert Cantley 18 Jul 1796; Minister's return spells name as 'Cantly' Nancy (of age) d Robert b- Thomas Turk min- John McCue- 20Jul1796
 Nancy & William Pearce 8 Jan 1833; min- James C Wilson
 Rebecca & Dabney Maupin 1 Feb 1827; min- James Watts
 Rebecca & Reuben Shackelford 6 Jan 1790; d Eleanor, who consents wit- James Rutledge & Andrew Allison & William Shackelford b- Andrew Allison min- William Wilson- 8Jan1790

Augusta County Marriages -- Woman's Name

Johnston (cont.)
  Sarah & John Garvin 25 Nov 1785; d William b- Joseph
    Garvin wit- Thomas Poage
Jonas
  Margaret & Nicholas Lingsweiler 9 Jan 1797; Margaret (of
    age) d Daniel b- John Winiger Nicholas a widower
Jones
  Ann & Andrew Silling 4 Jan 1796; d Enos b- Enos Jones
  Anna & Daniel Rine 20 Oct 1803; min- John McCue
  Catherine & Joshua Crosby 12 Apr 1827; min- William Wilson
  Elizabeth & James Brown 22 Aug 1816; min- William King
  Elizabeth & Peter Kuhns 2 Dec 1793; d Enos b- Enos Jones
  Hannah & George Crosby 27 Mar 1817; min- William King
  Jane & William Rader 13 Jan 1794; Minister's return spells
    name as 'Redder' d William who consents test- John
    Lockridge b- James Trimble min- Bennett Maxey- 16Jan1794
  Jemima & William Griffith 29 Jan 1805; min- William King
  Jemima & Michael Hite 11 Aug 1798; 'Hight?' d Robert b-
    Robert Jones min- Archibald Scott- 14Aug1798
  Lydia & William Selling 26 Apr 1804; min- William King
  Malinda & Ptolemy Brightwell 26 Jul 1837; min- Stephen
    Smith
  Martha & Jacob Canote 6 Jan 1798; d Joshua b- Joshua Jones
  Martha & James R Curry 29 Mar 1828; min- John Hendren
  Mary & William Moffett 28 Feb 1820; min- John Hendren
  Nancy & James Craig 6 Aug 1822; min- Michael Meyerhoeffer
  Nancy & Elisha H Gentry 20 May 1834; min- George Hildt
  Priscilla & Abraham Silling 3 Apr 1790; Minister's return
    spells name as 'Selling' b- Enos Jones perm-Enos Jones,
    father & Gasper Seiling (father?) min- William Wilson-
    6Apr1790
  Sophia & Adam Patterson 26 Mar 1796; d Enos b- Enos Jones
    Adam is 22 years old in January 1796 min- William Wilson-
    25Mar1796
  Winifred & Kinney Sillings 19 Nov 1829; min- John Hendren
Jordan
  Nancy & George Drummond 20 Dec 1786; widow b- Thomas
    Davis min- Archibald Scott- 20Dec1786
Joseph
  Eve & John Gilleat 5 Jan 1809; min- William King
  Peggy & David Lowman 7 Apr 1812; min- William King
Jourdan
  Sarah & George Dameron 17 Aug 1838; min- George A Leopard
Journal
  Elizabeth & Thomas Dickson 24 Dec 1818; min- Conrad
    Speece, Jr
Judd
  Mary & David Tanner 22 May 1800; d Michael who consents
    test- Lewis Wayland b- George Ailor (Oehler) min- William
    King- 22May1800
Jurtz
  Sarah & Robert Grove 12 Dec 1833; min- William G Jackson

Augusta County Marriages -- Woman's Name

Karahoof
  Mary & Henry Willfong 26 Aug 1813; min- G H Riemenschneider
Karichoof
  Anna & Elijah Messersmith 16 Oct 1818; min- G H
    Riemenschneider
  Susanna & Jacob Huffer 27 Apr 1820; min- Daniel Stephens
Karicofe
  Barbara & James Flemming 4 Nov 1830; min- Benjamin Denton
  Barbara & Silas Vance 27 Jun 1839; min- John A Van Lear
  Catharine & Joshua Cupp 12 Aug 1841; min- J A Van Lear
  Margaret & Simon Cupp 29 Aug 1838; min- John A Van Lear
  Martha Jane & George McQuain 29 Aug 1844; min- John A Van
    Lear
Karracofe
  Elizabeth & George Bailey 5 Oct 1848; min- John A Van Lear
Karricofe
  Katharine & John Strickler 8 Jun 1846; min- P Shickel
Kasterson
  Mary & James Lamay 21 Aug 1827; min- William C. Morrison
Keener
  Ann & John Brown 20 Apr 1791; John from Shenandoah cty d
    David b- David Keener
Keenon
  Eleanor & William Young 9 Apr 1787; Minister's return
    spells name as 'Keenan' Eleanor gives her own consent
    test- John Keenon & Hugh Keenon b- Alexander Nelson min-
    William Wilson- 12Apr1787
Keeth
  Kathorine & Lawrence Lynch 1 Oct 1794; widow who consents
    for herself test- James Welsh & Richard Trater b- Richard
    Trotter min- John Brown- 5Oct1794
Keiser
  Julia A & Peter Shirey 11 Sep 1834; min- William Scull
Keith
  Mary & James Lowe 23 Jan 1798; d Andrew Keith, dec. b-
    Lawrence Lynch & Arthur Ringland
Kellar
  Barbara & George Fall - Apr 1806; min- John Brown
  Eve & Peter Baldwin 12 Sep 1826; min- William Monroe
  Jane & Martin Hanger 27 Aug 1827; min- William C. Morrison
  Polly & David Moyers 11 Mar 1824; min- Josiah Cole
Keller
  Ann & Jacob Baylor 28 Mar 1789; b- George Keller
  Barbara & Daniel Moyers 16 Sep 1819; min- William Calhoon
  Catharine B & Daniel Fall 3 Oct 1844; min- J C Hensell
  Catharine & Andrew Lynch 12 Aug 1836; min- J C Hensell
  Eliza & James M Peaco 24 Dec 1846; min- George H Martin
  Francis M & Peter Whisman 30 Dec 1847; min- George H Martin
  Janetta C & Samuel (Jr) Peaco 9 Jan 1843; min- J C Hensell
  Peggy & Jacob Harouf 12 Mar 1829; min- William Calhoon
  Peggy & Henry Teaford 16 Aug 1804; min- William King
Kellor
  Barbara & Charles Shafer 7 Jun 1808; min- Z Emmerson

Augusta County Marriages -- Woman's Name

Kelly
  Mary & Jeremiah Salvage 18 Oct 1788; min- Benjamin Erwin- 18Oct1788
  Mary & Jeremiah Savage 16 Oct 1787; Mary gives own consent, having neither parents not guardian test- Henry Black & Thomas Fulton b- John Black of Rockingham cty

Kelsey
  Abigail & Alexander Cummins 18 Apr 1789; widow b- William Knowles

Kennaday
  Elizabeth & Jacob Klingingpeel 16 Dec 1806; min- John McCue
  Mary & William Black 20 Nov 1810; min- John McCue

Kennady
  Abigail & John Shields 10 Mar 1810; min- John McCue

Kennedy
  Catherine & John B Eakle 6 Mar 1818; min- William King
  Catherine & Edward Walker 28 Feb 1798; Catherine (of age) Her parents do not live in Augusta cty b- Benjamin Gregory min- John McCue- 1Mar1798
  Martha & Robert Curry 15 Apr 1788; Minister's return spells name as 'Martha Kenedy' b- John Stuart min- William Wilson- 15Apr1788
  Sarah & Michael Coiner 12 Sep 1844; min- George H Martin

Kennerley
  Dorinda & James L Maupin 26 Dec 1827; min- Gerard Morgan
  Jane & Henry Bare 28 Sep 1820; min- Robert Boyd
  Lucy & James Kennerley 3 Apr 1806; min- Philip Kennerly
  Susannah & James Clemmons 17 Jan 1809; min- William Wilson

Kennerly
  Catherine & Matthew Robertson 19 May 1803; min- William King
  Harriet S & Henry G George 13 Jun 1834; min- Samuel Kennerly
  Kitty & George Craig - Feb 1792; d James b- A Mustoe min- John McCune- 1Mar1792
  Kitty & Walter Smiley 28 Dec 1816; min- William King
  Mary & John Ewell 25 Feb 1801; Minister's return spells name as 'Kennerley' John from Albemarle cty d James who consents test- Philip & Kitty Kennerly b- Philip Kennerly min- John McCue- 3Mar1801

Kenney
  Elizabeth & James Wilson 6 Apr 1819; min- Conrad Speece, Jr
  Rebecca & William Givens 9 Mar 1789; Minister's return spells name as 'Givins and Kennedy' d Matthew, who consents b- Robert Kenny wit- Robert Kenney & William Robertson min- William Wilson- 9Mar1789

Kent
  Susannah & Tandy Whitlock 9 Oct 1822; min- William Wilson Jr

Kerr
  Betsy & Thomas Givens 6 May 1789; Minister's return spells name as 'Givins' d James b- James Kerr min- William Wilson- 8May1789
  Elizabeth & Isaac Gray 23 Aug 1796; d Robert who consents test- William Koons & David Koons b- William Kerr

322

Augusta County Marriages -- Woman's Name

Kerr (cont.)
  Elizabeth & Moses Wallace 2 Jan 1819; bond- 4Jan1819(sic)
    min- John D Ewin
  Jane & James Laird 4 Dec 1799; d James who consents test-
    Alexander Kerr & Jacob Hershaw b- James McGongal
  Jean & John Hinds 28 Jun 1749; license only
  Margaret & Robert Dunlap 29 Oct 1792; 'Kern?' d Robert
    b- Daniel Kerr no minister listed; clerk's memorandum cites
    ceremony date as 1Nov1792
  Margaret & Charles Hogshead 22 Mar 1828; min- John Hendren
  Margaret & James Ramsey 17 Oct 1794; Minister's return
    spells name as 'Ramsay and Mary Kerr' d James b- James
    Kerr min- John Brown- 25Oct1794
  Margaret & Charles Scantland 25 Mar 1817; min- William King
  Mary Jane & W N Anderson 9 May 1838; 'Dr.' W N Anderson
    min- John A Steele
  Mary & James Kerr 24 Nov 1803; min- John McCue
  Sarah & Peter E Hogg 2 Mar 1829; min- Francis McFarland
  Susana & John Ulery - Nov 1825; min- John Brown
  Susanna & John Donaldson 11 Jun 1805; min- John McCue
Kershe
  Margaret & John (Jr) Teter 5 Mar 1840; min- John J
    Reimensnyder
Kershner
  Christiana & Adam Palmer 6 Oct 1795; Christiana (of age) d
    David who consents con- Elizabeth Kershner b- Christian
    Olinger
  Margaret A & William S D Rodgers 7 Jun 1842; min- Samuel C
    Waters
Kesterson
  Clary & Isaac Moore 28 Aug 1833; min- George Hildt
  Ellen & John H Miller 26 Jan 1836; min- Francis A C Mills
  Nancy & Jesse Wood 25 Feb 1808; min- William King
  Sallie & John A Desper 22 Feb 1849; min- J McKendree Reiley
Keyser
  Ann & David Coiner 6 Feb 1829; min- William Wilson
  Polly & John B Brown 7 Feb 1822; min- Conrad Speece
Kilkenny
  Sarah & Enos Jones 26 Mar 1805; min- William King
  Sarah & John Klingingpeal 13 Mar 1804; min- William King
Kilpatrick
  Agnes & Jacob Martin 21 Mar 1787; b- John Kirkpatrick
    min- Archibald Scott- 5Apr1787
Kincaid
  Isabella & James Gordan 18 Jan 1838; min- Zach Jordan
  Martha & Samuel Gorden 26 Jan 1836; min- William Calhoon
Kinder
  Elizabeth & John Hight 27 Sep 1810; min- William King
Kindig
  Eliza & Benjamin Wherley 10 Dec 1833; min- Augustus Babb
  Mary & John Reubush 7 Mar 1848; min- B M Smith
  Mary & J Robinson 22 Sep 1842; min- James Morrison

Augusta County Marriages -- Woman's Name

Kindred
  Jane & Mark Hatton 22 Dec 1792; Minister's return spells name as 'Renaered' b- Jacob Swallow no minister listed; clerk's memorandum cites ceremony date as 29Dec1791

King
  Charity & John Diddle 29 Dec 1814; min- John McCue
  Eleanor & John Fennel 19 Jul 1796; b- John Montgomery min- John Montgomery- 3Aug1796
  Elizabeth & John C Clemons 3 Mar 1827; widow min- William W Calhoun
  Elizabeth & David Mynes 12 Mar 1796; d William who consents test- Adam King & Robert King b- Thomas Mynes
  Ellen & James A Mines 16 Aug 1832; min- William Calhoun
  Margaret & John Balsley 29 May 1818; min- William King
  Margaret & William Smith 1 May 1806; min- William Wilson
  Mary & Ezekiel Cooper 28 Apr 1790; d John, who consents wit- Wm Anderson & Isaac White & Wm Bratton b- John Didell & Wm Anderson min- William Wilson- 29Apr1790
  Mary & George W Stribling 8 Dec 1845; min- T T Castleman
  Mary & Coats Thornton 6 Sep 1787; d Henry who consents (crest on his seal) test- Valentine Jones & John Chrism b- Anthony Mustoe & William Chambers min- James Chambers- 6Oct1787
  Polly & John Going 14 Apr 1823; min- John Brown
  Polly & George Spangler 2 May 1801; 'Mary' d Richard b- Richard King min- William King- 2May1801
  Sally & Samuel Cramer 15 Jun 1809; min- William Calhoun
  Susanna & Samuel McClentock 22 Nov 1793; Minister's return spells name as 'McClintock' d Adam b- Adam King min- John Brown- 23Nov1793

Kinkaid
  Mary & Paul Bear 30 Jan 1832; min- William Wilson

Kinkead
  Betsy & Moses Guin 21 May 1821; min- John D Ewin
  Nancy & Thomas Clayton 17 Oct 1820; min- John D Ewin
  Nancy & Charles Kinkead 26 Feb 1807; min- John Montgomery

Kinney
  Jane E & Edwin M Taylor 18 Jun 1839; min- Frederick D Goodwin
  Mary E & Alfred Chapman 1 Dec 1837; min- Fred D Goodwin
  Matilda & Erasmus Stribling 23 Apr 1807; min- William Calhoon

Kinny
  Mary & James Stuart 21 Apr 1796; d Moses, late of PA Mary born 27Apr1774 and had resided on the Middle River for three months - James Stuart & A Humphreys

Kiplinger
  Mary & Frederick Miser 17 Nov 1790; min- William Wilson- 17Nov1790
  Nancy & Lewis Kellar 20 Dec 1810; min- William King

Kiracofe
  Elizabeth & Reuben Rawley 30 Nov 1846; min- P Shickel
  Rebecca G & William Grim 14 Jan 1841; min- Peter Shickel Jr

Augusta County Marriages -- Woman's Name

Kirchoff
  Elizabeth & Adam Firebough - Apr 1808; min- John Brown
Kirk
  Agnes & David Bratton 14 Dec 1799; d John David of age b- John Kirk
  Jane & Robert Cunningham 12 Mar 1812; min- William Calhoon
  Rachel & John Cunningham 6 Feb 1796; d John b- John Kirk min- Archibald Scott- 9Feb1796
  Sophia & William Beith 25 Jun 1807; min- William King
Kirkland
  Esther & Alexander Anderson 26 Apr 1786; d James bond min- William Wilson- 27Apr1786
  Jenny & William Johnston 29 Dec 1786; d James b- Arthur Connelly wit- Samuel & James Kirkland min- William Wilson- 4Jan1787
Kirkpatrick
  Elizabeth & James McCutchen 2 Jul 1811; min- William Calhoon
  Jane & James McKemy 6 Feb 1810; min- William McPheeters
  Margaret & William Armstrong 20 Apr 1809; min- William Calhoon
  Mary & Daniel Kerr 29 Jun 1790; d John, who consents b- John Kirkpatrick min- Archibald Scott- 1Jul1790
Kiser
  Elizabeth & Michael A Coiner 17 Jan 1839; min- John J Reimensnyder
Kisner
  Mary & John Collins 6 Aug 1788; Minister's return spells name as 'Kizner' b- Martin Miller wit- John Hall min- John Brown- 14Aug1788
Kitch
  Susan & Abraham Landes 26 Jun 1834; min- William Wilson
Klutz
  Sarah & John Ulrick 31 Jan 1817; min- G H Riemenschneider- 1Feb1817
Knave
  Catherine & Gordon Hogshead 16 Dec 1810; min- William King
Knowles
  Amanda M & Anton Miely 27 Feb 1845; min- W Kirby
  Elianor & George Gordon 13 May 1807; min- William King
  Isabella & Paul Apple 27 Apr 1803; min- William King
  Jane & John Thompson 21 Jun 1790; Minister's return spells name as 'Knowls' d James b- James Knowles min- William Wilson- 22Jun1790
  Jane & Daniel Trayer 20 Dec 1804; min- William King
  Margaret & Robert F Bibb 21 Aug 1841; min- J A Van Lear- publication of banns
Knowls
  Elizabeth & Archibald McDonald 31 Dec 1795; d John b- John Knowls
  Mary & Michael Hays 26 Jul 1825; min- Josiah Cole
Koiner
  Jane & Hiram Faber 3 Dec 1840; min- Benjamin Kendig
  Jane & James Moore 17 Apr 1823; min- James C Willson

Augusta County Marriages -- Woman's Name

Koiner (cont.)
  Julian & Jacob Killian 4 Feb 1840; min- Ambrose Henkel
  Margaret & Absalom Koiner 16 Apr 1850; min- J Killian
  Mary M & Paul N Rupert 28 Apr 1838; min- J Killian
  Mary & Alfred P Wood 19 May 1846; min- S Wagner
  Maryan & Abraham Henkel 30 Jun 1835; min- Ambrose Henkel
  Rebecca & George M Deal 4 Feb 1836; min- William Scull
Koogler
  Frances Jane & Nicholas Sneed 13 Apr 1848; min- P Shickel
Koontz
  Catherine & George Teaford 2 Aug 1827; min- William Calhoon
  Mary J & Joseph Muck 6 Sep 1837; min- James Morrison
Kootz
  Molly & Jacob Beard 9 Apr 1811; min- William King
Krawn
  Mary & John Teitrick 24 Aug 1809; min- William King
Krickenbarger
  Catherine & Joseph Erinaund 30 Nov 1813; min- William Wilson
Krizer
  Elizabeth & Andrew Shriver 25 Dec 1810; min- John McCue
Krone
  Ketty & Joseph Tole 28 May 1815; min- Conrad Speece, Jr
Kurtz
  Susan & George Fetzer 17 Aug 1837; min- William G Jackson
  Susanna & William Jones 12 Feb 1807; min- William King
Kyger
  Sally & Peter Kohler - Oct 1820; min- John Brown
Lahman
  Nancy & David Wonderlick 7 Jan 1816; min- G H Riemenschneider
Laird
  Amy & Samuel Garber 18 Aug 1812; min- Samuel Garber
  Barbary & Peter Miller 17 Mar 1812; min- Samuel Garber
  Jane & Robert Cochran 17 Dec 1787; d David who consents b- John Campbell min- William Wilson- 17Dec1787
Lamb
  Ann V & Harrison D Lively 4 Feb 1840; min- John A Van Lear
  Annis & Reuben Wallace 5 Apr 1803; min- James Ward
  Catherine & Matthew Lainey 6 Jun 1795; Minister's return spells name as 'Laney' d Peter b- Peter Lamb min- William Wilson- 9Jun1795
  Catherine & Andrew McCreery 1 Jun 1795; Minister's return spells name as 'McCreary' d John b- John Lamb min- William Wilson- 4Jun1795
  Elizabeth & David Conrod 5 Nov 1811; min- William King
  Mary & Jacob Crawn 12 May 1840; min- John A Van Lear
  Mary & George Sively 26 Nov 1799; George from Rockingham cty d John b- John Lamb
  Peggy & Henry Tinkle 5 Nov 1813; min- G H Riemenschneider
Lambert
  Esther & George Hizer 27 Mar 1817; min- William King
  Jane & John Vanfossen 19 Feb 1829; min- John Hendren
  Mary & Samuel A Burgess 18 Feb 1847; min- Stephen Hildebrand

Augusta County Marriages -- Woman's Name

Lambert (cont.)
  Mary & Philip Nebergall 25 Mar 1802; min- William King- 25Mar1802
  Sally & Jacob Vanfosen 3 Apr 1806; min- William King
Lamme
  Margaret & Abraham McNeil 3 Feb 1795; d James b- James Lamme min- William Wilson- 5Feb1795
Lanack
  Julian & John Hanger 25 Mar 1825; min- Josiah Cole
Lancaster
  Sarah & William Pearson 5 Jan 1802; widower Sarah (of age) b- George Craig min- John McCue- 7Jan1802
Lance
  Mary & Cunrad Burke 19 Apr 1787; d Mary who consents wit- John Bowman & Absalom Sprun b- John Bowman min- Archibald Scott- 19Apr1787
Lanckton
  Eave & Julius Bertrum 9 Jul 1792; b- Christopher Mantel
Landes
  Catharine & Josiah Andrew 21 Dec 1832; min- G H Reimensnyder
  Catharine & Enoch Brower 30 Nov 1848; min- Daniel Brower
  Catharine & Jonathan Landes 20 Dec 1838; min- John J Reimensnyder
  Elizabeth & John Miller 26 Mar 1811; min- Samuel Garber- publication of banns
  Elizabeth & Joseph Swang - Nov 1824; min- John Brown
  Lydia & John Ruff 1 Sep 1846; min- P Shickel
  Malinda & George Coley - --- 182-; min- Benjamin Denton
  Mary & Jacob Good 21 Mar 1826; min- Abraham Garber- publication of banns
  Sarah & John Denizen 10 Dec 1840; min- J J Reimensnyder
  Susan & Lewis Keller 27 Sep 1832; min- John Haney
Landis
  Barbra Ann & George Smily 16 Feb 1846; min- P Shickel
  Catharine & Conrad Syple 29 May 1832; min- John Rhoads
  Elizabeth Ann & Washington Casady 2 Feb 1837; min- John J Riemensnyder
  Mary & Peter Link 26 Oct 1817; min- William King- publication of banns
  Nancy & William Bittle 19 Oct 1826; min- John Hendren
  Polly & Peter Michael 12 Nov 1818; min- Wright Burgess
Landiss
  Anna & Godfrey Bolton 13 Mar 1817; min- G H Riemenschneider
  Elizabeth & John Eppard 28 Aug 1811; min- G H Riemenschneider
Lange
  Nancy & John Balmer 22 Jan 1838; min- Robert Beers
Langford
  Lucinda Jane & Isaac Battow 16 Dec 1845; min- G W Israel
Lantern
  Nancy & John George Offlider 21 Jan 1793; b- William Chambers

Augusta County Marriages -- Woman's Name

Laporte
  Victoire & James Campbell 14 Oct 1795; Victoire (of age) gives her own consent dated 'Calf Pasture' b- Robert Gamble min- John Montgomery- 19Oct1795

Larew
  Ann & Daniel Ray 29 Aug 1816; min- John McCue
  Elizabeth & Jonathan Brooks 23 Oct 1792; d Jacob wit- Peter Larew & P Brown min- John McCue- 6Nov1792
  Polly W & John Glendy 2 Jan 1827; min- Francis McFarland
  Sally & John Best 19 Feb 1807; min- John McCue

Larner
  Julia A & George Hodge 12 May 1835; min- Robert M Lipscomb

Larrick
  Sally & John Pointer - Aug 1815; min- John Brown

Lashbaugh
  Margaret & Henry Tutwiler 23 Jul 1792; b- Joseph Campbell

Lavel
  Elizabeth B & Jacob Swartzel 29 Oct 1844; min- J C Hensell

Laverty
  Rebecca & John Hamilton 10 Aug 1786; min- Samuel Shannon- 10Aug1786

Law
  Jenny & James Black 21 Jul 1803; min- William King

Lawrence
  Frances A & George G Bunch 2 Sep 1841; min- Alfred G Chenowith
  Nancy A & Archibald Davis 1 Apr 1841; min- Alfred G Chenowith

Lawson
  Ann Eliza & Adam Hippard 30 Mar 1837; min- E Joshua Webb

Laymore
  Mary & Lewis Myers 23 Nov 1791; b- Michael Garber

Laywell
  Elizabeth & Jacob Dohm 24 Jun 1801; widow of Abraham b- Robert McClenachan
  Hanna & John Coiner 19 Jun 1793; Minister's return spells name as 'Cryner' d Andrew b- Philip Ingleman min- John McCue- 20Jun1793

Leas
  Margaret & David Fultz 5 Apr 1825; min- William W Calhoun
  Sarah & John Kennerley 4 Aug 1808; min- William Calhoon

Ledegay
  Catharine & Abraham Hedwick 24 Nov 1800; d George b- George Ledegay Signed 'Hetwich' in German Abraham (of age)

Leedy
  Elizabeth & Cyrus Crumpacker 17 Mar 1825; min- Abraham Garber- publication of banns

Leeser
  Keziah & Mathias (Jr) Meek 4 Sep 1786; d Joseph b- Mathias Meek Sr wit- Richard Cain

Lefler
  Polly & John McMillen 7 Mar 1791; Minister's return spells name as 'McMellan [McMiller?] and Leflar' d Jacob who consents b- William Brine & John Hale b- Joseph Lefter min- William Wilson- 7Mar1791

Augusta County Marriages -- Woman's Name

Lehman
  Isabella & Jacob S Carrol 18 May 1826; min- William Monroe
Lemmon
  Mary & Isaac Webb 15 Sep 1798; Minister's return spells
    name as 'Mary Lemmons' both of age b- George Compton min-
    William Wilson- 18Sep1798
Lemmy
  Susanna & Henry Eagle 24 Jul 1807; min- William King
Lemon
  Mary & John Mefford 8 Jan 1787; d George who consents
    test- John Cofman & Thomas Hannah s Gasper who consents b-
    Jacob Lemon
Leonard
  Catherine & Peter Armentrout 8 May 1804; min- William King
  Elizabeth & Christian Smallshoffer 16 Oct 1833; min-
    George Hildt
  Margaret & Ezekiel Cooper 26 Oct 1826; min- John A Gore
  Polly & Adam Solleday 21 Jan 1799; d George Leonard of
    Shenandoah cty consent before Isaac Goave of Shenandoah
    Adam (of age) b- Adam Lenert
  Sarah & Williamson Burton 25 Jan 1837; min- James C Wilson
  Susannah & John Hildebrand 24 Sep 1816; min- William King
Leopard
  Elizabeth & James Duke 7 Jun 1810; min- William King
Lesley
  Polly & David Hanger 4 Jun 1818; min- William Calhoon
Lessley
  Agness & Morgan Evans 22 Sep 1792; d James (dec) consent
    by John & Sarah Lessley wit- William Johnston & William
    Gamble min- John McCue- 23Oct1792
  Catharine Jane & Richard Humphrey 9 Feb 1844; min- J C
    Hensell
  Hannah & Abner Dyer 7 Dec 1789; sis of Thomas Lessley, who
    also gives surety
  Malinda & John Humphrey 11 Apr 1844; min- J C Hensell
  Margaret B & Andrew Huling 4 Sep 1834; min- Samuel Kennerly
  Mary & Robert Bell 7 Aug 1793; Certificate of A.
    Humphreys, A J.P., that Mary over 21 consent by Samuel
    McCune Sr, John McCune 7 James McCune b- Archibald McCune
    min- John McCue- 8Aug1793
  Rachel & Alexander Crawford 20 Feb 1793; 'Lesley?' con-
    William Bell affidavit of Rachel's full age b- Phillip
    Dyer no minister listed; clerk's memorandum cites ceremony
    date as 21Feb1793
  Sarah & John Henderson 3 Jan 1792; Minister's return
    spells name as 'Betsy Lofly' d James (dec) b- Alexander
    Buchanan wit- John McClenachan no minister listed; clerk's
    memorandum cites ceremony date as 3Jan1792
Lessly
  Mary & James Calhoon 8 Feb 1792; Minister's return spells
    name as 'Lessley' d Thomas b- David Steel min- John
    Brown- 8Feb1792

Augusta County Marriages -- Woman's Name

Levingston
  Elizabeth & Arthur Connally 6 Jan 1787; b- James Levingston
  Peggy & Abraham Root 24 Feb 1825; min- Conrad Speece
Lewis
  Anna & William Douthat 10 Jun 1790; b- Samuel Boys min- John Brown- 10Jun1790
  Evalina T & Robert A Miller 6 Dec 1827; min- Francis McFarland
  Fannie & Layton Yancey 17 Dec 1788; min- James Chambers- 17Dec1788
  Jinney & Isham Cooper 24 Oct 1816; min- Wright Burgess
  Margaret Linn & John Cochran 28 Sep 1826; min- Daniel Stephens
  Polly & James Hook 20 Jan 1798; Polly gives own consent d Anthony Lewis, dec. test- Thomas Bleakly b- George Hook min- William Wilson- 25Jan1798
  Rachel & Peyton Isaacs 26 Sep 1816; min- William King
  Sarah & George Compton 5 Sep 1794; Minister's return spells name as 'Mary' Affidavit of Sarah's full age b- James Laird min- John McCue- 10Sep1794
Lightner
  Eliza & John T Haupe 8 Oct 1840; min- John C Hensell- publication of banns
  Sarah & William H Pollard 26 Sep 1833; min- Francis McFarland
Likes
  Margaret & Solomon Sheets 13 May 1834; min- George Hildt
Lilley
  Isabella Ann & Thomas C Mitchell 25 May 1837; min- William Calhoon
  Mary Ann & Joshua (Jr) Reynolds 25 Dec 1845; min- G W Israel
  Mary & Robert Christopher 22 Mar 1838; min- John A Steele
  Sarah & Samuel Keran 2 Nov 1822; min- Josiah Cole
Linck
  Elizabeth & Joseph McMinn 28 Feb 1825; min- Josiah Cole
Lindel
  Elizabeth & Nicholas Redder 29 Jul 1793; Elizabeth (of age) b- Thomas Liggett
Link
  Catharine & Peter Beard 1 Sep 1808; min- William Wilson
  Catharine & John Redman 9 Mar 1843; min- Samuel Wagner
  Cathorine & Peter (Jr) Hanger 8 Apr 1785; d Mathias b- Peter Hanger Sr
  Elizabeth & Joseph Miller 26 Nov 1827; min- Joseph Smith
  Elizabeth & Lewis Wayland 29 Oct 1798; 'Betsey' d Mathias b- Mathias Link Sr min- William Wilson- 1Nov1798
  Louisa C & Samuel Lambert 18 Dec 1845; min- P Shickel
  Polly & Moses Gresham 7 May 1807; min- William Wilson
  Polly & Jacob Weitzell 17 May 1824; min- Michael Meyerhoeffer
  Rebecca & Peter E Houff 11 Apr 1845; min- P Shickel
  Sarah & Calvin Collins 6 Dec 1827; min- William Monroe
  Susan C R & William W Houf 11 Jan 1846; min- Jacob C Spitler

Augusta County Marriages -- Woman's Name

Linn
Mary J & George W Taylor 23 Apr 1840; min- Jacob Killian
Litten
Elizabeth & Preston Jones 28 Apr 1831; min- William Wilson
Priscilla & John Waggoner 12 Apr 1827; min- William Wilson
Sarah Jane & Joshua Kidd 18 Jun 1846; min- James H Brown
Lively
Nancy & John Wily 18 Dec 1806; min- William King
Livick
Catherine & Jacob Harshall 9 Dec 1820; 'Harshaw' min- Josiah Cole
Katy & Jacob Roots 1 Aug 1816; min- G H Riemenschneider
Mary & Daniel Adkins 7 Jun 1849; min- Samuel Martin
Mary & Peter Jones 18 Apr 1833; min- William Calhoon
Livingston
Agness & William (Jr) Wilson 3 Feb 1789; Minister's return spells name as 'Levingston' b- William Wilson Sr min- Archibald Scott- 5Feb1789
Harriett L & Porterfield B Rippetoe 13 Oct 1835; min- William Scull
Lobban
Lavinia & Richard Wallace 15 Apr 1817; min- John McCue
Lockbridge
Ann & James Lockbridge 22 Aug 1788; min- Archibald Scott- 22Aug1788
Lockhart
Sarah & Asher Waterman 30 Aug 1787; min- John Montgomery- 30Aug1787
Lockridge
Ann & James Lockridge 18 Aug 1788; d Robert who consents b- Arthur Walkup min- Archibald Scott- 22Aug1788
Catherine & William Ptomey 22 Sep 1825; min- Alexander Templeton
Christiana & Robert Anderson 24 Mar 1808; min- Joseph Reid
Eleanor & Jacob Daggy 29 Oct 1818; min- William Calhoon
Elizabeth & Thomas Gwinn 8 Apr 1800; d Samuel who consents wit- James Graham test- James Gwinn b- Joseph Gwinn
Ellenor & James Dinwiddie 16 Aug 1785; d Andrew
Mary & Michael Ptomy 21 Oct 1824; min- Thomas Caldwell
Peggy & Robert Kinkead 22 Apr 1806; min- John Montgomery
Rebecca & Robert Gay 18 Nov 1788; b- Robert Lockridge min- Archibald Scott- 20Nov1788
Rebecca & William Kinkead 11 Mar 1806; min- John Montgomery
Savanna & Hugh McAlary 7 Jun 1831; min- James Kerr
Sophia Jane & George W McCutchen 25 Oct 1849; min- W G Campbell
Loeffler
Olivia & Lewis Fisher 4 Apr 1843; min- F D Goodwin
Loetz
Barbara & Peter Menker 7 Mar 1796; d George who consents b- John Loetz
Loffties
Margaret & Alexander Sanders 25 Nov 1794; Minister's return spells name as 'Saunders and Peggy Lofftes' d Ralph of Rockingham Cty who consents test- James Givens & Thomas Givens b- Andrew Moody min- John Brown- 3Dec1794

Augusta County Marriages -- Woman's Name

Logan
 Lavinia & John Abernathy 17 Apr 1823; min- James Morrison
Lohr
 Catherine & Francis Conal 8 Oct 1837; min- John A Steele
 Elizabeth & John Kelly 6 May 1803; min- William King
 Margaret & Jacob (Jr) Doom 8 Feb 1842; min- P E Stevenson
 Polly & George Osborne 19 Sep 1807; min- William King
Long
 Barbary & Solomon Garber 23 Oct 1805; min- Samuel Garber
 Betsey & George Fry 31 May 1791; sis Joseph & orphan of Isaac Long (dec) b- Joseph Long min- William Wilson- 1Jun1791
 Betsy & John W Miller 27 Oct 1825; min- William Wilson
 Elizabeth & Caleb Perry 3 Dec 1807; min- John McCue
 Eve & George Baker 7 Feb 1797; widower d Henry Long, dec. Alexander Zallinger swears Eve of age, but has not resided in county for six months b- Nicholas Echus
 Frances & Hiatt Cain 23 Mar 1830; min- William Wilson
 Maria & David C Koiner 13 Sep 1842; min- James Bunting
 Mary & David Jackson 8 Apr 1824; min- Josiah Cole
 Molly & Abraham Tanner 10 Jan 1787; d Mary who consents test- Peter Heiskell & John Thomas s John who consents test- Peter Heiskell & John Thomas b- Jacob Long min- Benjamin Erwin- 16Jan1787
 Peggy & William Clifton 3 Apr 1800; widow and of age b- Lawrence Lynch min- William King- 3Apr1800
 Polly & John Fisher - Aug 1823; min- John Brown
 Rebecca & Sampson Pelter 2 May 1822; min- James C Willson
 Sarah & Alexander B Davidson 23 Mar 1838; min- John A Steele
 Sarah & Abraham May 20 Jan 1820; min- William Wilson
 Susanah & Michael Dull 23 Jan 1845; min- Jacob Baer
 Susannah & David Lair 4 Oct 1818; min- Abraham Garber- publication of banns
Lookelbough
 Polly & Leonard Sheets 2 May 1805; min- William King
Loop
 Sarah & Jacob Bowman 3 Apr 1828; min- James Morrison
 Susanna & George Hanger 24 Aug 1822; min- John Brown
Lotts
 Catherine & John Liptrap 16 Dec 1828; min- James Morrison
 Mary & Christian Hearse 20 Mar 1797; d George Lotts (Loetz) b- Henry Lotts
 Polly & Washington Helmick 18 Jun 1829; min- James Morrison
 Sarah & Benjamin Clinebill 29 Jun 1837; min- J C Hensell
Lotz
 Barbara & Isaac Liptrap 13 Jan 1839; min- John C Hensell
Loucks
 Susanah & Jacob Pickle 5 Apr 1794; d George b- John Allison
Louney
 Jenny & John Seawright 3 Jan 1804; min- William Wilson

Augusta County Marriages -- Woman's Name

Love
  Sarah & Isaac Hudson 18 Aug 1789; s George, who consents
    b- John Emmitt wit- William Gilkeson & David Williams
Lovel
  Caty & John Quick 28 Feb 1826; min- Abraham Garber-
    publication of banns
Lovell
  Sophia & William Davis 24 Apr 1834; min- Joseph Spriggs
Lovingood
  Ann & William Williams 21 Jun 1785; d Harman b- Samuel
    Lovingood
  Barbara & John Beard 14 Nov 1787; Minister's return spells
    name as 'Baird' d Hermon b- Hermon Lovingood min- James
    Chambers- 14Nov1787
Lowdermilk
  Elizabeth & Charles East 12 Feb 1791; d Mickle, who
    consents wit- Isaac White, Balcher Seldoneridge b- John
    Diddle
Lowery
  Caroline Jackson & Benjamin H Whitzel 14 Mar 1850; min- J
    Killian
Lowman
  Betsey & Jacob Lucas 6 Mar 1832; min- Francis McFarland
  Catherine & Robert Russell 8 Dec 1817; min- Wright Burgess
  Eliza Jane & Pollard Jennings 4 Mar 1838; min- Stephen
    Smith
  Lydia & Joseph Pifer 1 Apr 1812; d Bardhard min- John
    Bell- 24Jun1812
  Mary & Samuel Elliott 29 Dec 1840; min- D F Bittle
  Mary & William Fulwider 6 Oct 1831; min- Francis McFarland
  Sarah & George Hippart 22 Jan 1828; min- William Monroe
Lowrey
  Henrietta & James Stokes 21 Dec 1831; min- John Hendren
Lowry
  Eazy & John Riddle 4 Jun 1792; b- Matthew Gambill
Loyd
  Sarah & James Terry 3 Jun 1819; min- William King
Lucas
  Ann & James Crosby 2 Feb 1826; min- Francis McFarland
  Catharine E & James F Hite 2 Mar 1848; min- J C Hensell
  Mary & Anderson Robertson 9 Apr 1840; min- John C Hansell
Luck
  Lucinda & Young Hill 2 Dec 1823; min- Josiah Cole
Lukeden
  Louisa & Jacob Keller 1 Sep 1831; min- Samuel Kennerly
Lunsford
  Polly & George Meddings 9 Mar 1837; min- J C Hensell
Lushbough
  Polly & Calib Fitzpatrick 20 Feb 1810; min- William King
Lutz
  Catharine & Abraham Billhymer 28 Mar 1839; min- John J
    Reimensnyder
  Diana & Daniel Haffner 24 Sep 1839; min- John J
    Reimensnyder

Augusta County Marriages -- Woman's Name

Lutz (cont.)
  Elizabeth & Philip Wonderlick - Feb 1823; min- John Brown
  Mary A & George W Gongwer 8 Jun 1846; min- P Shickel
  Nancy & Samuel Ware 29 Aug 1839; min- Samuel Wagner
  Rosanah & Adam Nebergall 28 May 1827; min- Michael Meyerhoeffer
Lyle
  Isabella & John McDowell 17 Feb 1798; d John Lyle, dec. con- Archibald Stuart b- John Bowyer min- John McCue- 17Feb1798
  Lucinda H & William McCurdy 7 Dec 1837; min- Enoch Thomas
  Rosanna & William McCutchan 11 Nov 1830; min- Francis McFarland
Lynn
  Jane & James Givens 16 Feb 1804; min- Philip Kennerly
Madison
  Priscilla & John Miller 21 May 1788; Priscilla gives her own consent test- James Hogge con- Thomas Miller test- James Anderson, David Anderson, & Phi. Finkle b- Peter Heiskill min- Benjamin Erwin- 21May1788
Mahon
  Margaret & Robert McCoy 29 Nov 1791; min- Benjamin Irwin- 29Nov1791
Mahoney
  Margaret & Ambrose Clark 25 Sep 1820; min- Josiah Cole
  Susannah & David Coffman 17 Apr 1820; min- John Hendren
Malcolm
  Elizabeth & Parkinson Welch 28 Nov 1822; min- William Wilson Jr
  Sally & Samuel Cargo 22 Nov 1814; min- William King
Malcom
  Elizabeth & Frederick Backenstoe 13 Feb 1812; min- William King
Mandele
  Elizabeth & Paul Beard - Apr 1809; min- John Brown
Manuell
  Elizabeth & James Hogsett 13 Feb 1815; min- Wright Burgess
Marks
  Jane & James Balman - Nov 1812; min- John Brown
Markwood
  Elizabeth & Hering Brown 28 Feb 1826; min- Abraham Garber- publication of banns
  Nancy & John D D Ragland 15 Jan 1844; min- C Parkison
Marshall
  Catherine & William Morris 26 Jan 1809; min- John McCue
  Polly & David Moore 26 Dec 1812; min- Wright Burgess
Martin
  Christiana & William Smiley 1 Jan 1840; min- James Morrison
  Eliza & Homer Tisdale 17 Aug 1828; min- William Wilson
  Elizabeth & John Day 8 Jan 1800; d David Martin, dec. b- William Allison John swears he is of age min- William Wilson- 9Jan1800
  Elizabeth & Paul Roller - Feb 1808; min- John Brown
  Hannah & Edward Luffler 17 Jan 1792; b- Stephen Martin min- John McCune- 17Jan1792

Augusta County Marriages -- Woman's Name

Martin (cont.)
  Jane & William Allason 29 Nov 1797; Minister's return
    spells name as 'Allison' widower & widow (of David) b-
    Andrew Alloson min- William Wilson- 30Nov1797
  Nancy & Thomas R Hall 11 Aug 1846; min- P Shickel
  Polly & John Funkhouser 15 Jun 1826; min- William W Calhoun
  Sarah & Robert Moore 23 Jul 1828; min- William Calhoon
Masincup
  Jane & William Redifer 4 Apr 1844; min- Jacob Baer
Mason
  Elizabeth & Peter Baird 23 May 1816; min- Wright Burgess
Masoncup
  Polly & John Grass 26 Jan 1802; Minister's return spells
    name as 'Masincupp' d Jacob Frederick Wear ('Wehr') swears
    Polly of age John also of age b- Abraham Hawk min-
    William King- 26Jan1802
Massey
  Salley & Thomas Layton 24 Apr 1790; b- Smith Thompson
    wit- James Guy & Isham Ready (note attached:'a girl who has
    served her time with me- Thomas Smyth') min- John
    Montgomery- 27Apr1790
Massie
  Hetty C & William Patrick 18 Oct 1849; min- William T
    Richardson
  Mary B & Robert B Moon 29 Oct 1846; min- Joseph H Fox
Masters
  Jane D & James W Grant 10 Feb 1848; min- J C Hensell
Mateer
  Eliza & David Hanna 24 Oct 1826; min- Francis McFarland
Matheny
  Nelly & John Keller 13 Nov 1790; Minister's return spells
    name as 'Kellar' widow b- Jacob Faulkner (note attached
    that John Keller is a free person & has no relation in this
    State) min- William Wilson- 19Nov1790
Mathews
  Anna & Samuel Blackburn 17 Aug 1785; 'Ann?' d George
    bond min- Archibald Scott- 18Aug1785
  Elizabeth & Abner Gaines 8 Dec 1792; d William, who
    consents wit- William Mathews Jr & Ed Rankin b- Joseph
    Rankin
  Elizabeth & John Vernum 28 Dec 1797; Minister's return
    spells name as 'Vernon' d John b- John Mathews min-
    Archibald Scott- 28Dec1797
  Jane & Samuel Clark 30 Oct 1790; d Sampson, who consents
    wit- John Cooper & Minton Collins b- A Nelson Jr min- John
    Montgomery- 2Nov1790
  Jane & Isaac Telfair 27 Dec 1794; Minister's return spells
    name as 'Telfare' d George b- Sampson Mathews min- John
    McCue- 27Dec1794
  Mary & George Fauber 27 May 1833; min- Conrad Speece
  Polly & Richard Rankin 10 Jun 1789; d William, who
    consents wit- George Rankin & John Campbell b- John
    Campbell min- William Wilson- 11Jun1789

Augusta County Marriages -- Woman's Name

Maupin
  Derky & John Gillespy 11 Sep 1805; min- John McCue
Maury
  Martha M & John G Potter 7 Jun 1849; min- T T Castleman
May
  Maria A & John G McClanahan 26 Sep 1843; min- P E Stevenson
Mayes
  Jane Elizabeth & Samuel Walker 23 Aug 1838; min- James Paine
Mayfield
  Matilda & Charles East 11 May 1826; min- John Hendren
  Polly & Samuel Sullivan 27 Nov 1815; min- William King
Mays
  Nancy & George Shaw 6 Mar 1787; Minister's return spells name as 'Maiss' d Rebecca who consents test- Charles Stewart & Charles Donnelly b- John Griffin min- Samuel Shannon- 16Mar1787
McAlary
  Julia & Andrew Beck 24 Oct 1831; min- James Kerr
McAlear
  Peggy & Madison Doom 1 Dec 1836; min- B N Brown
McCLure
  Margaret & Andrew Henderson 5 Apr 1796; d John who consents test- James Hutcheson b- George Hutcheson min- John McCue- 7Apr1796
McCaaley
  Margaret & Francis Hunter 24 Mar 1787; Minister's return spells name as 'McCawley' d Margaret McCaly test- William Brown & David McCaly b- James Coulter min- Samuel Carrick- 21Apr1787
McCabe
  Polly & Andrew Robertson 14 Feb 1832; min- John Howell- publication of banns
McCadden
  Elizabeth & Robert McCleland 3 Feb 1825; min- Francis McFarland
McCaferty
  Ellen & Michael Kenady 12 Jan 1786; min- John Brown- 12Jan1786
McCames
  Nancy & Henry Nebergall 17 Feb 1795; 'McKemy?' b- Jacob Nebergall
McCamey
  Jane & Robert Corby 14 May 1820; min- John Hendren
McCampbell
  Nancy & William Elliott 10 Dec 1785; 'Agness'? d Samuel wit- John Bosang min- Archibald Scott- 12Dec1785
McCann
  Agnes & Edward Burrus 15 Nov 1798; Minister's return spells name as 'Barras' widow James McCann b- Isaac Hays min- Archibald Scott- 15Nov1798
McCannon
  Jenny & George Waggoner 8 Nov 1809; min- William Wilson

Augusta County Marriages -- Woman's Name

McCaslin
  Mary & Sampson Sawyers 17 Nov 1790; d John, who consents wit- James Crow b- James Crow of Botetourt Cty min- John Montgomery- 22Nov1790

McCauley
  Ardemisia & John Long 2 Feb 1831; min- John Hendren

McCausland
  Elizabeth & Hugh Glenn 1 Aug 1801; d John b- John McCausland min- Daniel Garber- 28Jul1801

McChesney
  Betsy Ann & Robert Hunter 31 Aug 1799; d James who consents test- James McClung s Samuel b- Adam McChesney
  Ebby & John Sharp 19 Aug 1796; d James Adam McChesney testifies that his sister, Ebby, is over 21 b- John McDowell
  Eleanor & John Coalter 28 Jan 1808; min- John McCue
  Jane & Nathan McClure 15 Feb 1821; min- John Brown
  Jane & Thomas J Patton 28 Mar 1844; min- J C Hensell
  Margaret W & John Armstrong 18 Jan 1844; min- J C Hensell
  Mary & James McClung 23 Aug 1799; d Robert b- Robert McChesney
  Mary & William Steele 31 Dec 1793; d James who consents test- Adam McChesney s Samuel b- John McDowell no minister listed; clerk's memorandum cites ceremony date as 2Jan1794
  Salley & William Moffette 23 Dec 1806; min- William McPheeters
  Susan Jane & David B Hogshead 11 Jun 1846; min- W G Campbell

McCleland
  Polly & William McCormick 1 Sep 1807; min- William McPheeters

McClelland
  Elizabeth & James Mines 21 Feb 1828; min- James Morrison

McClenachan
  Elizabeth & William Abney 23 Dec 1794; d Alexander who consents test- John McDowell b- John McDowell min- John McCue- 23Dec1794
  Elizabeth & John (Jr) Tate 25 Feb 1794; d Elijah McClenachan Sr who consents test- Elijah McClenachan Jr & Lettice Ann McClenachan b- Elijah McClenachan Jr clerk's memorandum cites ceremony date as 27Feb1794
  Lettice Ann & Thomas Caldwell 29 Jan 1800; d Elijah Mrs. Margaret McClenachan swears Letice Ann is of age test- Isaac Tate b- John Tate min- John McCue- 6Feb1800
  Lettitia W & Morris Austin 5 Oct 1797; d Alexander McClenachan, dec con- William Chambers, gdn b- Chesley Kinney min- Archibald Scott- 7Oct1797
  Margaret & Robert Mays 2 Dec 1790; min- Archibald Scott- 2Dec1790
  Mary & William Moffet 11 May 1791; Minister's return spells name as 'Moffett' d Elijah b- James Moffett wit- David Coalter & Elijah McClenachan Jr min- Benjamin Irvin- 11May1791

Augusta County Marriages -- Woman's Name

McClintick
Prepare & Christopher Trotter 18 Aug 1786; Minister's return spells name as 'McClintock' b- William McClintock min- Archibald Scott- 24Aug1786

McClung
Isabella & Simeon E Gordon 12 Nov 1844; min- T T Castleman
Janetta W & William L Kyle 31 Oct 1832; min- Nathaniel W Calhoon

McClure
Elizabeth & Francis Alexander 28 Dec 1790; b- Josias McClure min- William Wilson- 29Dec1790
Elizabeth & Jacob Shreckhise 24 Oct 1836; min- James C Wilson
Ellen & Joseph Peck 3 Mar 1814; min- Thomas Bourne
Ellen & David Wilson 15 Feb 1786; d Andrew s John (David over 21) b- William McKee wit- Alex McKiney, Josias McClure & Andrew Wilson
Esther & Isaac Trotter 7 Jul 1807; min- John McCue
Frances & William Seldomridge 29 May 1832; min- James C Wilson
Mary & Thomas Harris 16 Jan 1840; min- A B McCorkle
Mary & David Kennady 27 Mar 1817; min- John McCue
Mary & Alexander McKenny 27 Dec 1785; 'McKenney?' d Andrew b- William Bell wit- Alexander Stewart & Josias McClure min- Archibald Scott- 27Dec1785

McColmick
Margaret & Isaac Trencher 6 Dec 1785; min- John Brown- 6Dec1785

McComb
Mary Susan & Alexander Long 18 Feb 1845; min- B M Smith

McCommis
Elizabeth & Sturman Tate 10 Aug 1795; Elizabeth (of age) Sturman served apprenticeship with Robert McGuffin and was released Dec 1794 b- James King

McCorkell
Mary & John McWhorter 4 Nov 1791; b- John McCorkell no minister listed; clerk's memorandum cites ceremony date as 5Nov1791

McCorkle
Elizabeth & James Hulet 21 Apr 1787; d Samuel who consents test- John McCorkell, Benjamin Chapman & Samuel McCorkell b- Jacob Swallow Elizabeth 22 yrs old min- Archibald Scott- 22 Apr1787

McCormick
Eliza & William Cochran 3 Nov 1824; min- William W Calhoun
Mary Ann & William Martin 27 Jul 1795; b- George Givens
Polly S & Jacob Crist 10 Feb 1825; min- Francis McFarland

McCoskey
Grizzel & Joseph Walker 14 Feb 1791; 'McCrosky' widow b- William McPheeters sent to clerk by Samuel Brown and dated 22Feb1791

McCray
Eliza Jane & Walter H Tapp 2 Apr 1828; min- Joseph Smith
Hannah & David Speck 2 Jan 1821; min- William Calhoon

Augusta County Marriages -- Woman's Name

McCroskey
  Agness & Robert Taylor 4 Nov 1796; min- Archibald Scott- 4Nov1796
  Elizabeth & Enoch Bogas 3 Dec 1790; d Grizel, who consents b- John McCrosky s Thomas Baggess wit- Thomas Hinds, Henry Venis & Robert Cooper (return sent in by Samuel Brown and dated 8Dec1790)

McCue
  Ann & John Allen 5 Jun 1821; min- John Hendren
  Betsey & Thomas Catling 24 Mar 1814; min- Thomas Bourne
  Eliza & Andrew M Gatewood 24 Nov 1830; min- John Hendren
  Eliza & John D Imboden 26 Jun 1845; min- B M Smith
  Margaret & George Miller 27 Dec 1819; min- John Hendren
  Mary & Jacob Ruff 12 Nov 1811; min- John McCue
  Nancy & David S Bell 25 Aug 1842; min- B M Smith
  Polly & Andrew Barry 18 Aug 1807; min- William Calhoon
  Sarah Jane & Cyrus Alexander 5 Aug 1848; min- Robert L Dabney
  Sarah & Joseph McDowell 17 Apr 1822; min- James C Willson

McCullock
  Nancy & Smith Thompson 31 Jan 1809; min- Joel Watson
  Susannah & William Wilson 8 Oct 1812; min- William Calhoon

McCullough
  Jane & Armstead Mosby 29 Mar 1810; min- William Calhoon

McCune
  Deborah & Robert C Harris 9 Aug 1810; min- John McCue
  Elizabeth & William Henry 21 Nov 1787; d Samuel & Elizabeth who consents test- James McCune & Samuel Henry b- Samuel Henry min- James Chambers- 21Nov1787
  Elizabeth & John Kinnear 16 Aug 1793; Minister's return spells name as 'Keaner' d John b- John McCue min- John McCue- 27Aug1793
  Martha & Thomas Wilson 16 Dec 1801; d John b- John McCune min- John McCue- 16Dec1800
  Mary G & David Henkle 24 Oct 1839; min- John A Van Lear
  Peggy & Thomas Harris 10 Jun 1814; min- John McCue
  Polly & Thomas McCulloch 5 Apr 1808; min- John McCue
  Sarah & Joseph McCune 27 May 1813; min- Thomas Bourne

McCurdy
  Elizabeth & Robert McCutchen 28 Mar 1844; min- W G Campbell
  Rebecca & John C McCutchan 5 Sep 1844; min- W G Campbell

McCutchan
  Adaline V & Lewis T K McCutchan 23 May 1844; min- W G Campbell
  Cassandra D & Robert Grove Kerr 26 Apr 1830; min- Francis McFarland
  Catharine & Edward Heizer 1 Apr 1847; min- J C Hensell
  Elizabeth & Samuel C Harris 9 Sep 1847; min- W G Campbell
  Elizabeth & William Strain 20 Oct 1831; min- Francis McFarland
  Isabella P & James H Callison 15 Dec 1853; min- Luther Emmerson
  Mary Jane & James Buchanan 12 Mar 1846; min- W G Campbell
  Rebecca & Philander McCutchen 22 May 1844; min- W G Campbell

Augusta County Marriages -- Woman's Name

McCutchan (cont.)
   Sarah & Joseph Pinkerton 27 Apr 1787; d Samuel who
   consents test- John McCutchan & John Logan b- John Logan

McCutchen
   Betsey & William Wilson 21 Dec 1809; min- Joseph Reid
   Eleanor & Robert Dunlap 2 Sep 1828; min- Alexander
   Templeton
   Elenor & Jabin B Corby 16 Jan 1840; min- John C
   Hansell-publication of banns
   Elizabeth & Archibald Armstrong 23 Nov 1824; min- William
   W Calhoun
   Elizabeth & Andrew McCurdy 28 Jun 1849; min- W G Campbell
   Francis & Samuel McCutchen 9 Oct 1804; min- John McCue
   Hannah & William Bell 12 Oct 1837; min- Enoch Thomas
   Hannah & Joseph Henderson 2 Feb 1799; d Robert Consent
   test- John Risk b- Jones McCutchen
   Jane Amanda & Thompson Edmonson 8 Apr 1828; min- Alexander
   Templeton
   Jane & James Furr 9 Sep 1841; min- John C Hensell
   Jane & William M Smiley 6 Mar 1834; min- Francis McFarland
   Margaret A & William Kunkel 25 Feb 1833; min- William
   Calhoun
   Margaret & Robert Jamison 28 Oct 1795; d John of
   Calfpasture test- John Meek b- Samuel McCutchen Jr min-
   John Montgomery- 3Nov1795
   Margaret & Joseph Smith 11 Mar 1800; Margaret (of age) d
   Samuel s John Smith of PA, and of age b- William Smith
   Martha & Nathaniel Steele 23 Nov 1824; min- James Morrison
   Mary Steele & William Cooper 25 Nov 1833; min- Francis
   McFarland
   Polly & William Edmondson 18 Aug 1831; min- Francis
   McFarland
   Rebecca & John Black 19 Mar 1788; d Robert who consents
   wit- John McCutchen & John Meek b- James McCutchan min-
   Archibald Scott- 19Mar1788
   Sarah & John Bell 25 Aug 1800; d Samuel Joseph Bell, s of
   Samuel, swears that his brother, John, is over 21 b- Samuel
   McCutchen
   Sarah & Albert A McCutchen 18 May 1839; min- John C Hensell
   Sophronia & John Carwell 21 Dec 1843; min- J C Hensell

McCutcheon
   Mary P & William J Armstrong 8 Jan 1823; min- William W
   Calhoun

McDaniel
   Lucy & Jacob Herrin 31 Oct 1832; min- James C Wilson

McDead
   Jinny & Samuel Hutchison 24 Sep 1807; min- John McCue

McDowell
   Ann & Willis Hering 31 Mar 1835; min- Samuel Kennerly-
   publication of banns
   Mary & Jacob Swoope 2 Jun 1790; d William, who consents
   wit- Alexander Nelson Jr b- John McDowell
   Peggy & John McCleland 20 Jan 1806; min- William Calhoon
   Peggy & John McClelland 20 Jan 1806; min- William Calhoon

Augusta County Marriages -- Woman's Name

McElroy
  Peggy & Thompson Patterson 5 Jan 1808; min- John McCue
McFadden
  Catherine & Robert Wade 16 Jan 1823; min- James Morrison
McFaddin
  Margaret & Jacob Caulk 23 May 1792; Bond spells name as
    'McFarren' b- John McFaddin min- John Brown- 29May1792
  Sarah & James Hay 12 Feb 1829; min- James Morrison
McFall
  Betcey & Thomas Bleakly 28 Nov 1805; min- William Wilson
  Mary Jane & James Dolton 4 Oct 1849; min- Peter Miller
  Nancy & Daniel Dennison 30 Jun 1813; min- William Wilson
McFarland
  Francis & George Frenger 6 Jan 1848; George a merchant
    min- J C Hensell
  Zaday & John Acord 27 Jan 1823; min- Michael Meyerhoeffer
McGlaflin
  Sally & John Fox 22 Nov 1827; min- William Calhoon
McGlammery
  Jane & Charles Hogshead 28 Jan 1801; Jane (of age) d John
    b- John McGlammery
McGraw
  Nancy & Christian Shoemaker 27 May 1788; Martin Wolff &
    Daniel Shirey attest Nancy single and has no relations in
    this country b- Martin Wolff
McGuffin
  Elizabeth & Edward Willson 7 Nov 1827; min- James Morrison
  Jane Eliza & Andrew J Wilson 14 Sep 1842; min- James Paine
  Lavinia B & Martin Nevins 24 Nov 1842; min- James Paine
  Martha S & Abraham B Roadcap 10 Feb 1847; min- J C Hensell
  Nancy & William Thompson 15 Oct 1830; min- James Morrison
  Polly & Jacob Hart 10 Nov 1825; min- James Morrison
McIntire
  Anne & John Cummins 24 Jul 1811; widower min- John Bell
  Jane & Jacob Miller 6 Jun 1820; min- Daniel Stephens
McIntosh
  Matilda & Samuel D Morgan 2 Nov 1819; min- William Calhoon
McKamy
  Isabella & William Kenedy 21 May 1828; min- James Morrison
McKee
  Grizel & William Dyer 2 Mar 1803; min- William King
McKemy
  Margaret & William Corby 18 Oct 1797; d John McKemy, dec.
    b- Robert Harris
  Margaret & Andrew McKemy 27 Oct 1795; d William b-
    William McKemy no minister listed; clerk's memorandum cites
    ceremony date as 5Nov1795
  Mary & John McKemy 27 Oct 1795; d William b- William
    McKemy no minister listed; clerk's memorandum cites
    ceremony date as 5Nov1795
  Polly & George Herdman 15 Jan 1802; Minister's return
    spells name as 'McKerny' d James b- James McKemy min-
    Benjamin Irwin- 26Jan1802

Augusta County Marriages -- Woman's Name

McKenny
Ann & Henry Snyder 10 Sep 1828; min- William C. Morrison

McKinney
Elizabeth & Andrew Walker 21 Oct 1786; d Alexander wit- Alexander McKinney s John wit- William Walker, Arthur Graham & William Bell

McKitrick
Rachael & George Silknitter 24 Sep 1807; min- William Calhoon

McKnight
Elizabeth & John Adair 10 Jan 1791; Minister's return spells name as 'Addair and McNight' d-in-law of William Burgess b- William Burgess min- Archibald Scott- 11Jun1791
Margaret & Martin Dixon 14 Nov 1785; (McNight?) b- William Burgess, father in law of Margaret min- Archibald Scott- 15Nov1785
Nancy & John Youel 15 Dec 1808; min- Joseph Reid

McKoskry
Jean & James Telford 13 Jan 1789; Minister's return spells name as 'McCoskrey' d Grizel McKoskey, who consents wit- William McKee & John Hall b- William McKee min- John Brown- 22Jan1789

McMahon
Elizabeth & Hugh Donaghe 7 Mar 1791; d Debora, who consents wit- William Richardson b- James McGongal min- William Wilson- 8Mar1791
Margaret & Thomas Noland 13 May 1794; Minister's return spells name as 'Nowland & McMahan' Thomas was 21 in October, 1793 b- Moses Russell 15May1794
Mary & Peter Blake 3 Sep 1792; d Deborah, who consents wit- George Farrel & John Baxter b- John Donaghe min- William Wilson- 6Sep1792

McMullen
Christiana & Thomas Ruket 19 Nov 1792; b- Nicholas Reader
Polly & John Fisher 30 Nov 1801; 'Mary' d Michael Jane Davey, sis of Polly, swears as to her age b- Charles Page min- William King- 30Nov1801

McMullin
Jenny & John Deary 30 Oct 1799; d Michael McMullin b- Chesley Kinney

McMullins
Martha & James W Taylor 7 Jan 1824; min- John Hendren

McNair
Eleanor & Felix Sheltman 30 Jul 1814; min- John Bell
Elizabeth O & John Sheets 4 Sep 1849; min- John Hendren
Hanah & John Burgess 27 Jul 1820; min- Josiah Cole
Mary & James Brooks 15 Jan 1827; min- John A Gore

McNight
Abigail & Dabney Fretwell 25 Jun 1840; min- Jacob Killian
Jane & Dudley Jones 28 Sep 1801; d Timothy b- Timothy McNight
Mary & William Jameson 24 Mar 1800; d Timothy b- Timothy McNight min- Robert Wilson- 3Apr1800
Mary & Robert McCutchen 11 Mar 1799; d Timothy s John McCutchan b- William Morrison

Augusta County Marriages -- Woman's Name

McNight (cont.)
Nancy & John Youel 15 Dec 1808; min- Joseph Reid
McNutt
Apalenah & George Eubank 21 Jun 1832; min- William
 Calhoon- publication of banns
Margaret & William Beard 10 Jun 1793; d James who consents
 test- William Sproul & James McNutt Jr b- William Sproul
 min- John Brown- 15Jun1793
Margaret & Andrew Withrow 16 May 1833; min- James Morrison
Mary Jane & David Mines 22 Oct 1844; min- J C Hensell
Mary S & Henry Brown 10 Feb 1831; min- James Morrison
McPheeters
Ann & William Downey 19 May 1791; d Alexander b-
 Alexander McPheeters no minister listed; clerk's
 memorandum cites ceremony date as 24May1791
Elizabeth & William Campbell 9 Aug 1800; d William b-
 William McPheeters
Elizabeth & James McClung 21 Feb 1791; d John b- William
 McPheeters min- Archibald Scott- 8Mar1791
May & Charles Kelso 6 Jun 1794; 'Polly?' d William b-
 William McPheeters no minister listed; clerk's memorandum
 cites ceremony date as 13Jun1794
Rachel & John Logan 25 Aug 1797; d William b- John
 Coalter min- Archibald Scott- 30Aug1797
Rebecca & Robert Culton 27 Jun 1796; Minister's return
 spells name as 'Cullen' d Alexander b- Alexander
 McPheeters min- Archibald Scott- 31Mar1796
Rebecca & John Gamble 7 Jun 1785; d William b- James
 Buchanan wit- George Lyburn & John McPheeters
McQueen
Frankey & John Krown 28 Jul 1810; min- William King
McTear
Isabella & Andrew Hodge 5 Sep 1791; Bond spells name as
 'Meteer' d William who consents b- John Hodge, father of
 Andrew min- John Montgomery- 6Sep1791
McWilliams
Eliza & Andrew Anderson 10 Sep 1828; min- John Hendren
Nancy & Samuel Mines 30 Oct 1821; min- John Brown
Susannah & John Farrow 24 Jun 1822; min- John Hendren
Virginia & Jacob Bell 10 Apr 1839; min- D F Bittle
Meek
Lavinia & John Rowh 31 Jan 1839; min- William Calhoon
Martha & Lewis Johnson 26 Mar 1826; min- Daniel Stephens
Sarah & William McKnight 28 Feb 1801; d Daniel who
 consents test- Agness Meek b- Robert McCutchen
Meeks
Eliza & Joseph Ross 14 Aug 1845; min- S Wagner
Elizabeth & Jesse Kendall 19 Feb 1819; min- William Calhoon
Lavina & Edward Douglas 17 Sep 1829; min- Henry S Kepler-
 publication of banns
Margaret & George Ham 8 Sep 1844; min- James Paine
Mary & John Ham 8 Sep 1844; min- James Paine

Augusta County Marriages -- Woman's Name

Mell
  Barbara & George Silling 1 Mar 1804; min- William King
  Catherine & Edmund Smith 23 Sep 1802; min- William King- 23Sep1802
  Polly & Jacob Miller 5 Sep 1805; min- William King

Menker
  Mary & George Ruhl 25 Mar 1799; d Henry Menker who consents b- Henry Rhinehart
  Mary & George Rule 26 Mar 1799; 'Minker?' min- William King- 26Mar1799

Merrit
  Catherine & William Warris 20 Jul 1809; min- William King

Merritt
  Catharine & John Harrigan 18 Nov 1825; min- Josiah Cole
  Margaret A & Robert Doyle 8 Sep 1836; min- James Morrison
  Margaret & Clove L Fitzpatrick 12 Nov 1835; min- J J Glossbrenner
  Mary & Valentine Hunley 12 Nov 1835; min- J J Glossbrenner
  Sarah Jane & George T Weaver 30 Sep 1840; min- John C Hensell- publication of banns

Messersmith
  Anne & Richard S Jones 19 Nov 1846; min- J A Van Lear
  Catharine & Jesse Kiser 20 Jun 1844; min- John A Van Lear
  Catherine & Christian Michael 11 Sep 1799; d Henry Messersmith, dec. Both of age Christian's mother is Elizabeth Michael b- George Messersmith
  Lucy Ann & George Kiracofe 8 Jan 1839; min- Peter Shickle
  Margaret & Peter Waggoner 6 Apr 1802; min- Benjamin Irwin- 6Apr1802

Messmaker
  Mary A & John Giles 8 Feb 1844; min- Samuel Wagner

Michael
  Ann & Philip Weigle 17 Oct 1797; d Frederick b- George Weigle min- Benjamin Irvin- 31Oct1797
  Anna & John Huffert 17 Nov 1829; min- G H Reimensnyder
  Betsy & William Myers 15 Apr 1835; min- Wright Burgess
  Catharine & Reuben Stoutamoyer 23 Feb 1841; min- George Huffman
  Catherine & Daniel Wickle 31 May 1803; 'Susannah?' min- William King
  Christiena & Samuel Hiner 29 Dec 1839; min- George Huffman
  Deliley & Abraham Kershner 29 Mar 1849; min- George B Rimel
  Elizabeth & Jacob Daggey 16 Nov 1790; d Frederick Michael, who consents b- Richard Roach wit- Terrence Swiney
  Elizabeth & Jacob Moyers 24 Jul 1848; min- George Huffman
  Eve & Jacob Huffert 28 Aug 1839; min- George Huffman
  Hannah & Abraham Landis 23 Sep 1830; min- John Hendren
  Hannah & Lewis Moyers 2 May 1843; min- George B Rimel
  Lydia & Benami Wooddell 23 May 1839; min- John A Van Lear
  Madelina & George (Jr) Wikel 30 May 1796; d Frederick b- Frederick Michael
  Margaret & George Moirs 22 Sep 1800; Minister's return spells name as 'George Morris' d Frederick Michael, dec. b- John Michael min- John McCue- 23Sep1800

Augusta County Marriages -- Woman's Name

Michael (cont.)
  Margaret & Moses Stoutamire 10 Oct 1844; min- George B Rimel
  Polly & John Aylor 17 Jun 1825; min- G H Reimensnyder
  Sarah & John Moyers 28 Nov 1833; min- John S Watt
  Susan & Fielding Sticer 5 Jun 1834; min- Joseph Spriggs
Michel
  Elizabeth & Henry Hoffert - Aug 1806; min- John Brown
Miller
  Anne & William Risk 20 Apr 1820; min- William Calhoon
  Anne & David Troxel 10 Dec 1816; min- Conrad Speece, Jr
  Barbary & Daniel Whitesell 8 Dec 1812; min- Samuel Garber
  Catherine & William Lilley 31 Jul 1815; min- Wright Burgess
  Catherine & John Miller 19 Nov 1798; d John (Adam? Miller)
    b- Adam Miller
  Caty & John Hilberd 24 Dec 1833; min- Abraham Garber-
    publication of banns
  Christinah & Jacob Orner 24 May 1806; min- Samuel Garber
  Deborah & James Davis 31 Dec 1787; 'Millar'? d Abraham
    b- Cornelius Ruddle min- Archibald Scott- 3Jan1786
  Easter & John Roop 16 Sep 1828; min- John Hendren
  Eliza & Pleasants Whitlock 24 Feb 1845; min- P Shickel
  Elizabeth & John Bear 27 Feb 1844; min- D F Bittle
  Elizabeth & Thomas Bingham 26 Oct 1818; min- Wright Burgess
  Elizabeth & William Lewis 11 May 1820; min- John Hendren
  Frances & John Reid 22 Jul 1796; widow William late of
    Rockbridge cty b- John Kilkainey
  Hanna & Solomon Trout 30 Aug 1825; min- William Wilson
  Hannah & James Moffett 19 Sep 1797; d Henry Miller, dec.
    b- Chesley Kinney
  Hannah & John Prewer 8 Dec 1812; min- Samuel Garber
  Hannah & Thomas P Willson 12 Jan 1827; min- John Hendren
  Jane & Peter Burns 21 Nov 1789; Minister's return spells
    name as 'Burnes' d James, who consents b- Francis Huff
    wit- Robert McClery & William Black min- John Brown-
    27Nov1789
  Kitty & John Garber 9 Apr 1816; min- Abraham Garber-
    publication of banns
  Margaret & John Arbast 6 Jan 1844; min- D F Bittle
  Margaret & A Warrick Cameron - Jan 1828; min- Gerard Morgan
  Margaret & Simon Coiner 2 Jan 1834; min- Ambrose Henkel
  Margaret & Daniel Rezer 16 Jun 1796; Margaret (of age) d
    Jacob Miller, dec., late of PA b- Francis Miller
  Margaret & Andrew Summers 26 Mar 1793; Margaret (of age)
    sis John b- John Miller
  Martha & Peter Sheetz 12 Mar 1840; min- Peter Miller
  Mary & Benjamin Coiner 28 Feb 1833; min- John S Watt
  Mary & John Crist 15 Jan 1807; min- William McPheeters
  Mary & Robert Martin 26 Dec 1791; b- John Huggins min-
    John Brown- 29Dec1791
  Mary & Robert Morton 21 Jun 1792; Cited in bond as 'Robert
    Merton & Mary Motes' b- James Crawford min- Benjamin
    Irwin- 21Jun1792
  Mary & Anthoney Wiferd 21 Nov 1816; min- William King

Augusta County Marriages -- Woman's Name

Miller (cont.)
Matilda & Daniel Funkhouser 27 Apr 1818; min- William King
Nancy & Charles Francisco 29 Mar 1814; min- Conrad Speece, Jr
Nancy & George W McCullock 9 Apr 1835; min- Samuel Kennerly
Nancy & James C Shipman 28 Mar 1832; min- John Hendren
Nancy & George Taylor 28 Jul 1823; min- Josiah Cole
Peggy & Joel Saxon 27 Jul 1804; min- William King
Polly & William Bowman 26 May 1842; min- Alfred G Chenowith
Polly & John Potter 23 Apr 1811; min- William King
Rachel & John Alexander 12 Feb 1791; widow b- George Harding min- John Montgomery- 13Feb1791
Rachel & John Lewis 31 Mar 1789; b- Robert Douthat min- Benjamin Erwin- 1Apr1789
Rebecca & William Sensebaugh 25 Apr 1791; d George who consents wit- William Sensebaugh & J Beal b- Valentine Miller
Sally & Paul Akerly 27 Nov 1788; b- Stephen Miller (Paul signs as 'Paul Akerlein')
Sally & Christian Browers 21 Feb 1832; min- Abraham Garber- publication of banns
Sally & James Dixon 19 Jul 1814; min- William Wilson
Sally & Peter Reed 5 Sep 1799; d William Miller, dec. b- John Moore & John Reed min- William King- 5Sep1799
Sarah Ann & George P Allen 18 May 1847; min- J A Van Lear
Sarah & Luke Collins 7 Aug 1790; Sarah nearly of age d Worttri Moller & Caterine Miller, who consent wit- Alex & James Stuart b- John Collins (return sent by Samuel Brown and dated 9Aug1790)
Sarah & Daniel Wine 17 Oct 1844; min- T T Castleman
Sicily & Joseph Risk 30 Apr 1829; min- William C. Morrison
Susan & Peter Hofe 22 Apr 1806; min- Samuel Garber

Mills
Ann & Rufus M Markwood 20 Nov 1845; min- T T Castleman
Elizabeth & James Craig 9 Mar 1804; min- William Wilson
Hester T & Jacob P Effinger 4 May 1847; min- Thomas D Bell
Mary McC. & William Beard 9 Dec 1841; min- Samuel Wagner
Obediance & Robert Hogsett 20 May 1847; min- J A Van Lear
Sarah & James P Sims 7 Nov 1841; min- Samuel Wagner

Milton
Susan Jane & David Sprouse 14 Jul 1846; min- John Reubush

Mims
Sarah & Andrew Hays 19 Sep 1809; min- John Montgomery

Mines
Martha & John Smith 13 Mar 1832; min- James Morrison
Polly & John H Ward 1 Jul 1819; min- Gerard Morgan

Minga
Margaret & Ulrick Rhinehart 6 Mar 1797; d Henry b- Henry Minga

Mingo
Elizabeth & Jacob Cline 15 Jan 1822; min- James Morrison

Minick
Margaret & Archibald Dunlap 31 Aug 1830; min- Francis McFarland

Augusta County Marriages -- Woman's Name

Minick (cont.)
  Polly & Thomas Stark 27 Sep 1807; min- William King
Minnick
  Elizabeth & George Brosius 25 Sep 1806; min- William McPheeters
  Margaret & Samuel McCleland 23 Apr 1807; min- William McPheeters
  Susannah & David Kroll 22 Jul 1797; 'Crall?' d Jacob b- Jacob Minnick
Miser
  Barbara & Martin Bailor 1 Nov 1796; d Adam b- Adam Miser
  Sarah & John Thompson 1 Sep 1840; min- Peter Shickel
  Sophia & Jacob Argenbright 10 Aug 1846; min- P Shickel
Mitchel
  Betsy & James Fulton 27 Sep 1809; min- William McPheeters
  Elizabeth & Robert Callison 16 Feb 1793; d James who consents b- Thomas Mitchell affidavit of age of Elizabeth no minister listed; clerk's memorandum cites ceremony date as 19Feb1793
Mitchell
  Cynthia & William Moffett 27 Dec 1827; min- Francis McFarland
  Elizabeth M & Henry Perkins 8 Mar 1827; min- Francis McFarland
  Elizabeth & John W Cockrell 25 Jan 1825; min- Josiah Cole
  Elizabeth & Henry Shields 29 Jan 1790; Minister's return spells name as 'Sheids' d William, who consents wit- Christian Mummer & James Henry b- A Mustae min- Archibald Scott- 4Feb1790
  Frances Ann & Joseph E Xaupi 21 Aug 1833; min- George Hildt
  Isabella & John Doak 16 Dec 1807; min- William McPheeters
  Mary Archer & Hall Neilson 26 Feb 1839; min- Frederick D Goodwin
  Mary & Fountain Estis 26 Apr 1831; min- John Howell
  Mary & Andrew McClure 13 Jan 1789; b- Thomas Hall min- Archibald Scott- 15Jan1789
  Sally & Henry Hawpe 30 Nov 1847; min- J C Hensell
  Sally & Leonard Hays 14 Aug 1823; min- Francis McFarland
  Sarah & Robert Beard 30 May 1785; d James bond
  Sarah & James Moffett 31 Mar 1831; min- Francis McFarland
Mizener
  Piersy L & Philip Swink 3 Feb 1846; min- Jacob C Spitler- publication of banns
Mizer
  Elizabeth & George Shue 14 Nov 1823; min- Michael Meyerhoeffer
  Julia Ann & Peter (Jr) Shickel 28 Feb 1839; min- D F Bittle
Moffett
  Betty S & Alexander T Barclay 21 Nov 1826; min- Francis McFarland
  Eleanor R & Peter Eidson 29 Sep 1842; min- S J Love
  Eleanor & James C Moore 6 Nov 1823; min- Francis McFarland
  Elizabeth M & James Miller 30 Apr 1836; min- James C Wilson
  Elizabeth & James Miller 7 Jan 1799; d George who consents b- James Cochran

Augusta County Marriages -- Woman's Name

Moffett (cont.)
  Evelina & George W McChesney 21 Dec 1826; min- John Hendren
  Hannah & John McCue 22 Sep 1819; min- John Hendren
  Jane L & Albert G Wayland 7 Jan 1830; min- William Calhoon
  Jane & Joseph Culton 29 Mar 1796; Minister's return spells name as 'Cullen' d James b- James Moffett min- Archibald Scott- 21Mar1796
  Julia A L & William Peyton 3 May 1836; min- James Morrison
  Magdalin & James Cockran 4 Dec 1792; Minister's return spells name as 'Cochran' d George, who consents b- Matthew Gambill min- John McCue- 10Jan1793
  Martha & William W King 8 Feb 1827; min- John Hendren
  Martha & Robert Kirk 16 Aug 1786; d George b- James Lyle Jr min- William Wilson- 16Aug1786
  Mary A C & David Taylor 8 Sep 1842; min- B M Smith
  Mary & Joseph McDowell 25 Apr 1786; b- Robert Kirk min- William Wilson- 27Apr1786
  Nancy & Elijah (Jr) McClenachan 11 Apr 1792; d John, who consents b- Jacob Kinney, who also is witness no minister listed; clerk's memorandum cites ceremony date as 13Apr1792
  Nancy & John Tate 22 Apr 1813; min- William Calhoon
  Sarah Jane & Charles B Thompson 5 Feb 1849; min- John Hendren
  Sarah & John Brown 17 May 1836; min- Isaac Jones
  Sarah & Andrew Gatewood 12 Aug 1822; min- John Hendren
Moffette
  Sally & John (Jr) Asten 3 Jun 1806; min- William McPheeters
Mohler
  Magdalin & Martin Garber - Sep 1816; min- Abraham Garber- publication of banns
  Mary Ann & John Hawkins 12 Mar 1846; min- T T Castleman
  Sarah & Martin Carlos 5 Jul 1841; min- S J Love
Mohr
  Rebeckah & Adam Patterson 12 Nov 1805; min- William King
Moneymaker
  Dolly Ann & Samuel Parmer 30 Dec 1843; min- James Paine
  Nancy & George W Scott 19 Jul 1849; min W W Trimble
Monroe
  Elizabeth & William Greer 11 Oct 1821; min- Josiah Cole
Montgomery
  Agnes & Isaac Miller 27 Apr 1802; min- William King- 27Apr1802
  Anne & John Ingram 23 Dec 1841; min- James Paine
  Hetty S & James Willson 2 Dec 1833; min- James Kerr
  Isabella & Eugenio Irvine 11 Oct 1821; min- John D Ewin
  Peggy & Joseph Erwin 15 May 1810; min- S Montgomery
  Peggy & Lewis Johnson 17 Aug 1826; min- William Monroe
Mood
  Courtney & Jacob Wilds 19 Aug 1828; min- Conrad Speece
Moore
  Catharine Ann & George B Shaner 5 Feb 1846; min- S Wagner
  Elizabeth & George D Harshaw 25 Mar 1823; min- Josiah Cole
  Elizabeth & James Hume 24 Aug 1834; min- William Calhoon
  Elizabeth & John Shettman 14 Jan 1796; 'Skellman?' 'Mohr?' d John b- John Mohr

Augusta County Marriages -- Woman's Name

Moore (cont.)
  Fanny & Jacob Lynn 22 Aug 1815; min- Wright Burgess
  Frances E & John Curry 2 Jan 1845; min- D F Bittle
  Margaret & John Moore 29 Mar 1788; d Moses who consents
    test- John McCutchan & John Black b- James Reaugh min-
    John Brown- 17Jun1787
  Martha Poague & Samuel Frame 25 Jan 1802; widower & widow
    b- James Bell min- John McCue- 26Jan1802
  Polly & Henry Huff - --- 179-; d John b- John Moore
  Polly & John Zumbro 5 Aug 1813; min- William King
  Prudence & James Finley 29 Aug 1785; d Samuel who consents
    test- Arthur Glasgow & Samuel McCorkle b- James Sproul
    min- Archibald Scott- 30Aug1785
  Sally & Henry Morel 5 Sep 1785; d Benjamin b- Samuel
    Moore wit- Henry Jones & Samuel Moore
  Susan & David B Grice 2 Jun 1831; min- William Calhoon
  Susanna & Peter Lowery 19 Dec 1811; min- William King
Morgan
  Margaret C & Edmund H Lewis 14 Apr 1847; min- B M Smith
Morris
  Josephine & John W Doyle 9 Feb 1843; min- F D Goodwin
Morrison
  Mary Ann & Floyd J Vaughn 17 Aug 1848; min- W T Richardson
  Mary Jane & Jeremiah Fuller 4 Jan 1848; min- John Bowen
Morriss
  Polly & William Sorrels 12 Nov 1818; min- William King
Mosby
  Sarah E & Alexander M Taylor 9 Nov 1841; min- P E Stevenson
Moses
  Charlotte & John Decrisen 10 Jun 1813; min- William King
  Nancy & Abram Miller 13 Apr 1815; min- Conrad Speece, Jr
Mowbray
  Elizabeth & Henry Brooks 19 Sep 1825; min- Josiah Cole
Mowrer
  Rebecca & Ephraim Harnsberger - Sep 1808; min- John Brown
Mowrey
  Mary & John Kline 30 Dec 1793; Minister's return spells
    name as 'Clyne' d Lewis b- Lewis Mowrey min- William
    Wilson- 30Dec1793
Mowry
  Catherine & Samuel Hoff 20 Sep 1788; b- Lutwig Maurer
  Christena & Jacob (Jr) Argenbright 26 Mar 1798; d Lewis
    Maurer b- Lewis Mowry
  Elizabeth & David Painter 17 Mar 1828; min- Joseph Smith
  Elizabeth & Robert Snapp 31 Jan 1821; min- Conrad Speece
  Hannah & David Link 20 Nov 1817; min- William King
  Jane & John Coiner 4 Dec 1817; min- William King
  Lydia & Jacob Crist 14 Apr 1800; d Lewis b- Lewis Mowry
    ('Maurer?') min- William Wilson- 14Apr1800
  Margaret Ann & Robert Vanlear 3 Mar 1831; min- Conrad
    Speece
  Nancy & George Tevenbough 26 Jun 1806; min- William King
  Polly & John Dixon 25 May 1804; min- William King
  Sophia & George Kellor 5 May 1786; Minister's return
    spells name as 'Kellar' d Lewis b- Lutwig Mawrer 'consent
    personally?' min- William Wilson- 7May1786

Augusta County Marriages -- Woman's Name

Mowry (cont.)
  Susanna & Samuel McCutchan 20 Nov 1817; min- William King
Moyer
  Barbara & John Smith 4 Oct 1821; min- Josiah Cole
  Mary & S Teaford 18 Sep 1845; min- J C Hensell
Moyers
  Ann & John Keller 15 Apr 1818; min- William King
  Elizabeth & Samuel Weitzell 4 Dec 1810; min- John McCue
  Polly & Jonas (Jr) Michael 23 Jul 1846; min- Henry Wetzel
  Sarah Ann & William Crosby 25 May 1848; min- J McKendree Reiley
  Susan & Joseph Michael 22 May 1849; min Henry Wetzel
Muchmore
  Mary & Benjamin Johnston 8 Oct 1788; min- William Wilson- 8Oct1788
Murray
  Caroline M & James A Austin 22 Feb 1846; min- William Calhoon
  Elizabeth & William M Whitlock 3 Apr 1831; min- Samuel Kennerly
  Lovinah & Henry Brew 26 Sep 1829; min- William Wilson
  Lucinda & John Wiseman 6 Jul 1824; min- Francis McFarland
Murry
  Catharine & Adam (Sr) Long 12 May 1840; min- John J Reimensnyder
  Harriet & A H Price 23 Jun 1835; min- Robert M Lipscomb
  Jenetta & William Anderson 21 Apr 1836; min- John A Steele
  Mariah & Jacob Long 1 Jan 1843; min- A G Chenowith
Myers
  Ann & George Puff 3 Dec 1791; b- George Barnhart min- John McCune- 25Dec1791
  Barbara & Henry Vansical 24 Feb 1802; min- William King- 24Feb1802
  Elizabeth & Benjamin Kerr 24 Jun 1796; d Michael b- Michael Myers min- William Wilson- 26Jun1796
  Lucinda & Henry K Myers 28 Mar 1850; min- B M Smith
  Margaret & Jacob Jones 8 Aug 1797; d Frederick Mauers b- Frederick Myers
  Nancy & Martin Yount 21 Apr 1831; min- William Wilson
  Rebecca & Christian Cline 11 May 1832; min- William Wilson
  Rosannah & Jeremiah Davis 8 Dec 1808; min- William McPheeters
  Susan & Jacob Davis 26 Jan 1809; min- William McPheeters
Myres
  Catherine & John Gillespie 6 Jan 1810; min- William McPheeters
  Peggy & Jacob Hawk 8 Oct 1792; d Stophel Myers (German), who consents b- Michael Garber
Nair
  Susan & Reuben Shirfey 3 Feb 1835; min- Wright Burgess
Neal
  Susanah & Silvans Odell 7 Feb 1788; Minister's return spells names as 'Silvias O'Dell and Neil' d William Neal (Neill) test- J Underwood & J Slavens b- John Underwood min- Archibald Scott- 10Feb1788

Augusta County Marriages -- Woman's Name

Near
  Susanna & William Michael 18 Aug 1818; min- Daniel Garber- publication of banns
Nebergall
  Barbara & Jacob Wagey 17 Feb 1795; d Jacob b- Jacob Nebergall
  Catherine & William Cromer 22 May 1800; Minister's return spells name as 'Cronser and Nebergale' d Jacob b- Jacob Nebergall min- William Wilson- 25May1800
Neere
  Sarah & Henry Michael 22 Aug 1819; min- Daniel Garber- publication of banns
Neighbourgall
  Mary & Jacob Day 22 Jan 1802; d Jacob s George who consents test- William Cromer, John Cromer, & Jacob Livergall b- Jacob Neighbourgall
Neizer
  Pally & John Hawp 23 Apr 1791; d Adam who consents wit- Adam Hawp b- Jacob Tieport
Nelson
  Elizabeth & John (Jr) Montgomery 19 Nov 1813; min- Conrad Speece, Jr
  Jerutia & John Breverd 6 Dec 1788; Minister's return spells name as 'Beverd' 'McClung informs that Miss Nelson is aged about 30 and about one year from Jersays' b- Thomas McClung min- William Wilson- 7Dec1788
  Mary Anna & David Bell 18 Jun 1800; Minister's return spells name as 'Joseph Bell Jr' 'Polly' d Alexander b- Alexander Nelson min- William Wilson- 22Jun1800
Newell
  Mahal & Milton Parsons 22 Jan 1832; min- Samuel Kennerly- publication of banns
Newman
  Ann Lyburn & George Weathers 18 Dec 1798; d Leroy b- Leroy Newman
  Catherine & James Wallace 23 Jan 1810; min- William Calhoon
  Fanny & James Brown 11 Jun 1807; min- William Calhoon
  Sally & John Crawford 11 Feb 1797; widower Sally (of age) d Leavy b- Joshua Parry min- Archibald Scott- 24Feb1797
Newton
  Jane H & George Utz 21 Mar 1833; min- Francis McFarland
  Margaret & Major Vines 22 Sep 1831; min- Francis McFarland
  Mary S & John T Hawpe 19 Dec 1832; min- Francis McFarland
  Sarah & William Mitchell 16 Feb 1826; min- Francis McFarland
Nichol
  Margaret & John Spitler 21 Dec 1821; min- John Hendren
  Sally & William Hogshead 24 Nov 1823; min- John Hendren
Nicholas
  Lydia & Joseph Ray 14 Oct 1791; b- Gilbert Christian certificate by Daniel Friel & John sutton that Lydia of age, her parents dead, and no other relatives in the area
  Margaret & David Hepler 2 Apr 1818; min- John D Ewin

Augusta County Marriages -- Woman's Name

Nicholson
　Antoinetta A & Smith Caldwell 5 Nov 1840; min- Frederick D Goodwin
　Sarah Ann & Andrew H Brady 10 Apr 1834; min- William G Jackson

Nickel
　Polly & Joseph Cravens 26 Nov 1790; Minister's return spells name as 'Nickle' d John, who consents wit- Wm Lang & W Chambers b- W Chambers min- Benjamin Irvin- 30Nov1790

Nickle
　Elizabeth & Alexander Blair 18 Feb 1792; d John, who consents wit- William Curry & Matthew Gambell b- John Nichol min- William Wilson- 19Feb1792
　Nancy & John Nickle 18 Apr 1803; min- William King

Nickoles
　Crissey & Ralph Wandless 20 Sep 1788; Minister's return spells name as 'Nicolas' d Levan who consents test- Nicholas Doucy (Doncy?) & John White b- John Clayton & John Gorden min- John Brown- 30Sep1788

Nigle
　Mary & Christopher Clemans 7 Sep 1815; min- John McCue

Nimerick
　Mary & William Buks 27 Oct 1808; min- William Wilson

Nixon
　Ann J & Henry Morris 8 Oct 1815; min- William King

Noland
　Hetty B & Lawrence Swink 24 Sep 1827; min- Conrad Speece
　Sarah & Archibald Kinkade 21 Aug 1798; Minister's return spells name as 'Kinkead' d John b- Moses Russell min- John Montgomery- 28Aug1798

Norton
　Phebe & John Hopping 14 Jan 1812; min- William King

Nutty
　Elizabeth & John Gregory 27 Sep 1833; min- George Hildt
　Sally & Charles Batis 28 Jan 1819; min- William King

Nyman
　Elizabeth & Jacob Shoults 15 Mar 1804; min- William King

Oakley
　Eleanor & John Smith 6 Apr 1796; b- Alexander Gibson

Ocheltree
　Margaret & Jonathan Flory 4 Mar 1841; min- J J Reimensnyder
　Mary & Samuel Fauver 29 Mar 1833; min- John Hendren
　Rachel & William (Jr) Young 7 Nov 1801; d Michael Ocheltree Sr who consents test- James Young & Michael Ocheltree signed 'Michl. Ougheltree Sr. b- William Young Sr min- William King- 11Nov1801

Offord
　Ann & Mathew Orrele 16 Nov 1826; min- Benjamin Denton

Olinger
　Hanah & Jacob Fridley 27 Apr 1786; min- Archibald Scott- 27Apr1786

Oliver
　Elizabeth & John Travis 11 Aug 1792; d John who consents wit- Sarah Hering b- Leonard Herron

Augusta County Marriages -- Woman's Name

Olves
  Polly & William Linsey 24 Dec 1802; min- John McCue- 24Dec1802
Ong
  Jane & Willis Copeland 7 Nov 1795; Minister's return spells names as 'Wellcome Copland and Jane Ongg' widow of Isaac Jane gives her own consent dated Staunton b- William Throckmorton min- Archibald Scott- 6Nov1795
Orbison
  Casandra P & Thomas M Mansfield 1 Jan 1827; min- William Wilson
Orebaugh
  Eliza J & Joseph Wright 6 Sep 1846; min- Henry Wetzel
  Margaret Ann & John Crum 28 Jun 1842; min- Henry Wetzel
Orebough
  Elizabeth & John Rusmisel 31 Oct 1835; min- John Hendren
  Margaret & Levi Crone 16 Jan 1840; min- A B McCorkle
  Maria & John Michael 21 Jan 1837; min- John J Riemensnyder
  Nancy & William Shiplet 9 Nov 1837; min- John J Reimensnyder
Orr
  Mary & John Hobock 11 May 1815; min- William King
Ott
  Anna Maria & Adam King 31 May 1796; d John who consents (in German) b- Henry Huffman
  Eliza & James Cooper 31 May 1838; min- John C Hensell
  Mary & James Webb 29 Nov 1787; min- Archibald Scott- 29Nov1787
  Sarah J & Noah A Dove 18 Jun 1846; min- J C Hensell
Ougheltree
  Ann & Joseph Lowry 24 Aug 1798; Minister's return spells name as 'Augheltree' Ann (of age) d Michael b- James Lowry min- Benjamin Irvin- 28Aug1798
Overshiner
  Catherine & Henry Coltrider 26 Aug 1807; min- William King
  Eliza & James Bryan 20 Feb 1809; min- William King
  Margaret & William Merritt 10 Jul 1796; widower & widow (of John) b- George Wiford (Weifford)
Owens
  Hardenia W & Benjamin K Bryant 2 Jul 1833; min- Samuel Kennerly
Owie
  Catherine & Michael Cowger 18 Mar 1788; b- Stophel Owie
Padget
  Elizabeth & Martin E Shreve 11 Feb 1850; min- J Killian
Paine
  Patsy & Samuel Thornton 24 Nov 1824; min- Josiah Cole- publication of banns
  Susannah & William Buchanan 2 Aug 1827; min- James Morrison
Painter
  Eliza Ann & Henry Lewis 13 Aug 1794; Minister's return spells name as 'Elizabeth Ann' d John con- Nicholas Spring b- Joseph Bell & Nicholas Spring min- John McCue- 14Aug1794

Augusta County Marriages -- Woman's Name

Painter (cont.)
  Elizabeth & William Grips 20 Aug 1812; min- William King
  Phebe & John Patterson 21 Dec 1848; min- James Paine
  Polley & George Waggoner 30 Jun 1817; min- Wright Burgess

Palmer
  Amanda & William Cox 1 Dec 1836; min- N B Brown- publication of banns
  Anne & John Chesnutt 19 May 1790; Minister's return spells name as 'Chestnut' d William b- James Spence min- William Wilson- 22May1790
  Barbara & David Faulber 27 Jun 1816; min- William King
  Catherine & John Swisher 27 Oct 1823; 'Jacob Swisher?' min- Josiah Cole
  E Jane & William Snider 30 Nov 1843; min- D F Bittle
  Eliza Jane & John Anderson 10 Apr 1845; min- B M Smith
  Eliza & William Morris - May 1820; min- John Brown
  Elizabeth & James Coursey 31 May 1831; min- Francis McFarland
  Elizabeth & Jacob Ellinger 24 Mar 1835; min- Cornelius Gates
  Elizabeth & Peter Koontz 28 Sep 1824; min- James Morrison
  Margaret & Lewis Wiseman 9 Mar 1843; min- J C Hensell
  Martha & Abner Tuttle 17 Jun 1796; Martha (of age) d William Palmer, dec. b- Patterson Thompson min- John McCue- 22Jun1796
  Mary & William Moore 25 Feb 1793; d William b- John Hamilton Hodge & John McDowell min- John McCue- 4Mar1793
  Peggy & Jacob Rozen 2 Nov 1829; min- William Calhoon
  Polly & George Teaford 13 Apr 1826; min- William W Calhoun
  Sarah & John Gordon 5 Jan 1843; min- J C Hensell

Pannel
  Nancy & Robert Thorp 5 Mar 1798; Nancy (of age) b- Samuel Moses

Papper
  Nancy & John Crane 10 Feb 1790; Minister's return spells name as 'Pepper' b- James Pepper wit- Samuel Merrit min- John Montgomery- 11Feb1790

Parent
  Jane & Richard Murry 18 Dec 1823; min- William Wilson Jr
  Mary & Perry Lankford 30 Nov 1815; min- William King

Paris
  Matilda Jane & James McClung 12 Jan 1837; min- Isaac Jones
  Sarah & James Hutchens 17 Sep 1835; min- Isaac Jones

Parks
  Ann & William Wilson 12 Feb 1802; min- William King- 12Feb1802
  Nancy & Jacob Dull 28 Dec 1826; min- Francis McFarland

Parratt
  Mary & John Buckman 1 May 1789; d Henry, who consents b- John Mifferd wit- John & Mary Cofman

Parrent
  Mary & George Peters 2 Dec 1840; min- Samuel Wagner

Augusta County Marriages -- Woman's Name

Parris
  Betsy & Samuel Dennison 10 Oct 1816; min- William Calhoon
  Martha & John Dennison 27 Jun 1811; min- William Calhoon
  Martha & William McNight 18 Oct 1832; min- William Calhoon
  Mary & Charles Hudson 17 Dec 1800; d John b- John Parris
  Nancy & Charles McClung 4 Aug 1836; min- Isaac Jones
Parry
  Elizabeth & Alexander Wason 17 Sep 1791; d Joshua who
    consents wit- David & John Parry b- Michael Garber Jr
    min- John Montgomery- 18Sep1791
  Nancy & James Brown 18 Apr 1826; min- William Monroe
  Nancy & Samuel Denison 18 Jun 1828; min- John Hendren
Parsons
  Hannah & Samuel Coffman 27 Dec 1832; min- Samuel Kennerly
  Sarah & Mansfield Marshall 14 Jun 1842; min- Samuel Wagner
Pary
  Susan E & Allen Pollock 14 Jan 1850; min- William T
    Richardson
Patrick
  Isabella & John McCutchen 11 Nov 1797; Isabella (of age) d
    John sis William b- William Patrick min- John McCue-
    16Nov1797
  Mary Jane & Henry M Estill 6 Dec 1833; min- James C Wilson
  Mary & Samuel McCutchen 16 Jun 1792; d John b- John
    Patrick min- John McCune- 19Jun1792
  Rebeccah & David Bell 20 Aug 1800; d John who consents
    test- William Patrick & James Gwinn b- William Patrick
  Sarah J & William T Richardson 16 May 1850; min- B M Smith
Patterson
  Betsey & Nathaniel Gunnell 31 Mar 1808; min- William Wilson
  Caroline & Peter Bright 24 Aug 1843; min- Samuel Wagner
  Catherine & Isaac Trotter 1 Mar 1832; min- William Wilson
  Debby & James Wilson 9 Apr 1806; min- William Wilson
  Elizabeth & Levi Parent 30 Dec 1830; min- Gerard Morgan
  Frances & Peter Bratton 22 Sep 1795; d Thomas, dec. b-
    Mary Patterson min- William Wilson- 24Sep1795
  Isabella & John (Jr) Dixon 24 Dec 1794; d Thomas b- John
    Dixon Sr min- William Wilson- 24Dec1794
  Isabella & William Graham 6 Jun 1791; d Robert b- Robert
    Patterson
  Jane & Joseph Gongwer 26 Feb 1829; min- William Wilson
  Jane & John Patterson 31 Oct 1794; d John b- John
    Patterson & William Moffett min- William Wilson- 3Nov1794
  Jinny & Samuel Wims 16 Apr 1799; d James Samuel (of age)
    b- James Patterson
  Keziah & John Fadely 25 Sep 1837; min- William G Jackson
  Margaret & Edward Harding 28 Jun 1790; d Robert, who
    consents b- George Kirkpatrick wit- William Scott & Thomas
    Sharp
  Margaret & Jacob Heiser 23 Jun 1842; min- Samuel Wagner
  Martha & William Baird 4 Jan 1786; d James bond min-
    William Wilson- 5Jan1786
  Martha & Willson Sprinkle 9 Jun 1838; min- James Paine
  Mary A & James A Patterson 25 Dec 1839; min- Jacob C
    Killian

Augusta County Marriages -- Woman's Name

Patterson (cont.)
  Nancy & Samuel Byers 29 Oct 1823; min- William Wilson Jr
  Nancy & John McCulloch 9 Feb 1804; min- William Wilson
  Polly & John (Jr) Mohr 3 Feb 1807; min- William King
  Rebecca & Jacob Bumgarner - Apr 1812; min- I D Irwin
  Sally & John Craig 23 Jun 1795; d James who consents
    test- William Patterson & William Beard b- William
    Patterson min- John McCue- 24Jun1795
  Sally & John Silling 27 Oct 1798; d John b- John
    Patterson min- William Wilson- 30Oct1798
  Sarah & Christian Echard 13 Dec 1831; min- John Howell
  Susannah & Caleb Crow 21 Feb 1837; min- B N Brown
Patton
  Margaret & John Buchanan 17 Jun 1749; license only
Pauff
  Mary & Peter Weitzell 25 Jul 1792; Minister's return
    spells name as 'Whitzell' d George Consent by George's son
    Charles b- Charles Pauff min- John McCue- 26Jul1792
Paul
  Elenor & Claudius Buster 28 Nov 1815; min- John McCue
  Elizabeth & John Adam Peck 23 Jan 1823; min- William W
    Calhoun
  Hannah & John Bazzle 5 May 1829; min- William Wilson
  Margaret & John Frazer 24 May 1803; min- John McCue
  Nancy & David Peer 30 Jan 1817; min- William King
Pauley
  Ambrosia & Alexander Laporte 6 Jun 1826; min- Alexander
    Templeton
Paulus
  Elizabeth & Jacob Foreman 14 Jul 1800; 'Fuehrman?' d
    Nicholas b- Nicholas Paulus
Paxton
  Elizabeth & William Melton 23 Dec 1817; min- William King
  Hetty & Robert Sampson 10 Jan 1835; min- Joshua Webb
Peaco
  Elizabeth & David Nimmo 28 May 1844; min- Francis McFarland
  Harriet W & John Beard 9 Nov 1831; min- John Howell
  Mary Margaret & James Powers 7 Nov 1844; min- Francis
    McFarland
Pearsen
  Jane & Edwin A Wayland 1 Dec 1831; min- John Howell
Pearson
  Margaret & Bartholomew Ragan 28 Dec 1793; b- Philip Dyer
  Nancy & Jacob Yearout 11 Jan 1802; d George Pearson, dec.
    Abraham Yearout swears his brother Jacob of age b-
    Bartholomew Reagen min- William King- 14Jan1802
Peatt
  Isabella & John McWilliams 3 Aug 1826; min- John Hendren
Peck
  Barbara & Jacob Eccard 14 Oct 1790; Minister's return
    spells name as 'Eccord' d Andrew, who also consents b-
    Henry Hull min- William Wilson- 14Oct1790
  Catherine Ann & Robertus Henderson 18 Oct 1849; Ceremony
    performed at the home of Chesley Kinney min- S J Love

Augusta County Marriages -- Woman's Name

Peck (cont.)
Elizabeth & Franklin L Marshall 2 Feb 1842; min- Alfred G Chenowith
Elizabeth & James Steele 2 Feb 1815; min- John McCue
Ellen & Abraham Shephard 10 Feb 1813; min- William Calhoon
Harriet H & John C Webb 1 Oct 1845; min- G W Israel
Hester Q & Robert Scott 30 Nov 1843; min- C Parkison
Maria P & Alexander Gilliam 8 Mar 1836; min- John Hendren
Mary Ann & James M Dunn 19 Aug 1837; min- Stephen Smith
Nancy & Isaac Gray 11 Jun 1835; min- J J Glossbrenner
Nancy & George Savage 2 Apr 1834; min- William Calhoon
Winifred & Jacob Waltz 18 Apr 1797; Minister's return spells name as 'Jacob Woltz' b- Jacob Peck

Peebles
Mary & John Deverix 16 Apr 1787; d John wit- John Graham & William Stuart b- Thomas Deverix
Mary & Nathaniel A McKenny 29 Apr 1830; min- Gerard Morgan

Peer
Alizabeth & Michael Levick 4 Aug 1837; min- John A Steele
Catharine A & Henry StJ. Davis 23 Feb 1848; min- John Bowen
Sarah B & George W May 12 Jul 1848; min- D W Arnold

Peery
Elizabeth & George Andrews 27 Dec 1790; b- Joseph Lang
Margaret & William Owens 2 Apr 1795; b- Chesley Kinney

Pelter
Mary Jane & John W C Newham 18 Jul 1843; min- C Parkison

Pence
Margaret & William King 26 Sep 1792; d Jacob Bentz, who consents wit- Thomas & Robert Poage b- Michael Garber

Penrose
Mary & Samuel Brooks 9 May 1789; gdn & next friend (?), John Emmitt, who consents and gives surety min- Archibald Scott- 9May1789

Peples
Mary & John Devericks 24 Apr 1787; Minister's return spells name as 'Peebles' min- Samuel Shannon- 24Apr1787

Pepperley
Elizabeth & Henry Speck 27 Apr 1826; min- William Monroe

Percy
Hannah & John Gragg 8 Nov 1792; Minister's return spells name as 'Hannah Perey' d John, who consents wit- Christian & John Percy Jr b- Alexander Robertson min- Benjamin Irwin- 13Nov1792
Sarah & Edward Erwin 31 May 1808; min- William Wilson

Perkey
Margaret & Jacob ----- 17 Sep 1804; min- John McCue

Perkins
Julia Ann & Abraham Brubeck 2 Jul 1835; min- Henry Brown

Perry
Hamilton & Thomas Gay 28 Jan 1840; min- A B McCorkle
Mary & George Mines 27 Dec 1827; min- William Calhoon

Peters
Ann & Samuel Garber 21 Jun 1838; min- Thomas Wheeler
Catharine & Jacob Hoover 2 Dec 1834; min- George Hildt

Augusta County Marriages -- Woman's Name

Peters (cont.)
  Catharine & Daniel Turnipseed 1 Nov 1816; min- William King
  Catherine & Balser Sherly 26 Apr 1808; min- William Calhoon
  Elizabeth & John Merritt 15 Feb 1816; min- William King
  Elizabeth & Joseph Pateson 28 Aug 1835; min- Samuel Kennerly
  Lydia & John Roades 17 Mar 1814; min- William Wilson
  Melinda & Simeon Fitch 15 Jan 1834; min- Samuel Kennerly
Peterson
  Mary Catharine & Samuel Showalter 29 Jan 1846; min- J A Van Lear
Petty
  Agness & James McCann 5 Sep 1785; min- Archibald Scott- 5Sep1785
Peyatt
  Catherine & Elijah Turner 4 Apr 1830; min- John Hendren
Peyton
  Susan M & John B Baldwin 20 Sep 1842; min- F D Goodwin
Philips
  Agnes & John H Dunlap 23 Feb 1832; min- John Hendren
  Catherine & Thomas Meck 31 Oct 1807; min- John Montgomery
  Demima & Samuel V Bare 6 Apr 1845; min- B M Smith
  Jane & Eugenio Anderson 14 Feb 1830; min- John Hendren
  Mary & George Messersmith 22 Jun 1826; min- John Hendren
  Peggy & David Lambert 9 Feb 1802; min- William King- 9Feb1802
  Sarah & James Conner 3 Aug 1802; 'James Coiner'? min- William Wilson- 3Aug1802
  Sarah & Nathaniel Torbet 3 Jun 1847; min- J C Hensell
Phillips
  Fanny & James Cundiff 8 Dec 1809; min- William King
  Margaret & Shadrach Samuels 20 Sep 1824; min- John Hendren
  Mary C & John Barnett 6 Jul 1826; min- Daniel Stephens
  Polly & Emmanuel Long 9 Feb 1809; min- William King
Pickering
  Polly & David Huffer 16 Apr 1830; min- William Wilson
Pickral
  Nancy & Addison Carson 7 Jun 1832; min- William Wilson
Pillson
  Mary W & Jacob Lightner 18 May 1837; min- William Calhoon
Pilson
  Phebe T & John S Thompson 29 May 1838; min- A B McCorkle
Pine
  Julia A C & Samuel McCutchen 13 Nov 1837; min- Enoch Thomas
Piper
  Polly & Henry Stover 4 Feb 1814; min- William King
  Sarah & Isaac Craun 6 Jul 1826; min- William Monroe
Pitman
  Margaret C & Jamison T Wilson 19 Jan 1843; min- James Bunting
  Mary Jane & William R Smith 19 Jan 1843; min- James Bunting
Plecker
  Margaret & William Livick 22 Jul 1849; min- Samuel Martin

Augusta County Marriages -- Woman's Name

Poage
Agnes & William Eidson 14 Jan 1832; min- William Wilson
Ann & Andrew Kinkead 22 Jun 1786; Minister's return spells name as 'Kinkade' d John b- Robert Gamble min- William Wilson- 22Jun1786
Ann & James Scott 20 Nov 1834; min- Conrad Speece
Anne & Archibald Woods 5 Mar 1789; Minister's return spells name as 'Major Archibald Woods' d Thomas, who consents wit- William Wilson b- Robert Poage min- William Wilson- 5Mar1789
Elizabeth & James G Patterson 22 Dec 1842; min- P E Stevenson
Elizabeth & Thomas Wilson 9 Oct 1826; min- William Wilson
Jane & Matthew (Jr) Willson 27 May 1824; min- Conrad Speece
Margaret & Peter (Jr) Hanger 22 Aug 1850; min- W G Campbell
Mary E & Archer M Moore 1 Dec 1833; min- James Morrison
Polly & William Gamble 15 Jun 1815; min- Conrad Speece, Jr
Polly & Thomas Wilson 17 Sep 1792; 'Page?' d Thomas who consents & Agnes who consents wit- William P Skillern & J Cockran b- James Cockran no minister listed; clerk's memorandum cites ceremony date as 20Sep1792
Priscilla & Samuel (Jr) Miller 22 Mar 1828; min- Gerard Morgan
Sally & Robert Carson 9 Dec 1799; d William s Samuel who consents and states Robert of age last spring test- David Carson Sally also of age b- William Carson

Poindexter
Frances & James Edgar 25 May 1826; min- William Monroe

Points
Anna Maria & John P Michie 13 Oct 1847; min- T T Castleman
Felicia G & William Kyle 13 Oct 1846; min- James H Brown
Rosa E & Robert Nelson 6 Oct 1848; min- T T Castleman

Pool
Elizabeth & William Lovegrove 14 Oct 1834; min- Peter Miller- publication of banns

Porter
Amanda & Peter D Dillan 29 Jan 1850; min- William T Richardson
Mary & Edward Bickerstoff 4 Dec 1791; b- William Shields wit- Matthew Gambill no minister listed; clerk's memorandum cites ceremony date as 9Dec1791

Porterfield
Eleanor & Robert Boyd - Jul 1749; license only

Potter
Susannah & John Woventuery 23 Dec 1806; min- William King

Poulas
Catharina & Henry Ohrbough - Nov 1810; min- John Brown

Powell
Elizabeth & Jonathan Via 16 Jan 1845; min- B M Smith
Jane & James Kirk 18 Jan 1810; min- William Calhoon
Mary & Archibald Mulinx 5 Feb 1786; d Thomas b- William Urquhart wit- John Mulinx & Thomas Cox

Augusta County Marriages -- Woman's Name

Powers
  Amanda & Isaac Collins 2 Sep 1847; min- George Huffman
  Elizabeth & Anthony Engleton 19 Jan 1809; min- William King
  Elizabeth & Samuel Peaco 11 Sep 1810; min- William King
  Fanny & James Miller 4 Nov 1797; widow William b- Thomas Painter
  Harriet & William Livick 21 May 1835; min- Isaac Jones
  Jenetta & David Baylor 24 Apr 1828; min- William Calhoon
  Margaret & David Fitzpatrick 11 Jan 1827; min- John A Gore
  Mary Ann & Elijah Blackwell 18 Jan 1849; min- George H Martin
  Sarah & James Frazier 10 Sep 1827; min- William C. Morrison

Powlas
  Christina & Jacob Trump 12 Oct 1799; d Nicholas con- George Trump, father of Jacob & Johann test- Samuel Curry Jacob (of age) b- Nicholas Powlas min- William King- 17Oct1799
  Mary & Christopher McElvanny 2 Nov 1796; d Nicholas (Paulus) who consents b- Jacob Powlas

Price
  Ann & John Runkle 25 Jan 1838; min- D F Bittle
  Elizabeth & James Wright 15 Feb 1841; min- D F Bittle
  Frances & Adam Long 5 Oct 1843; min- E R Veitch
  Gerdrant & Henry Dacke 2 May 1785; d Daniel b- Gasper Snider wit- James Preis
  Jane & Henry Spearing 6 Apr 1795; Minister's return spells name as 'Pearing' widower & widow (of Thomas Price) b- Valentine Sherley min- William Wilson- 9Apr1795
  Jean & Thomas Douthat 1 Jun 1793; 'Jane?' con- Lewis Price (Staunton) wit- Robert Douthat & James Bradshaw min- John Brown- 4Jun1793
  Mary & John Silor 20 Apr 1843; min- J C Hensell
  Polly & Robert Douthat 26 May 1791; Minister's return spells name as 'Dowthat' sis Peter, who consents wit- William Austin b- Philip North min- William Wilson- 27May1791

Printz
  Susannah & Henry Harmon 20 Jan 1801; Susannah (of age) sis to Peter Printz b- John McCausland min- William King- 20Jan1801

Probst
  Elizabeth & Jacob Probst 20 Jul 1823; min- G H Reimensnyder

Propst
  Ann & Jacob Karricoff 10 Jan 1835; min- John Hendren
  Mary & Samuel H Lambert 5 Oct 1848; min- George H Martin

Ptomey
  Mary & John Kinkaid 30 Sep 1824; min- Thomas Caldwell
  Nancy & William R Black 27 Sep 1825; min- Alexander Templeton

Pue
  Catharine & David Diddle 5 Jan 1815; min- John McCue

Puffenbarger
  Catharine & Christopher Zimmerman 27 Apr 1826; min- William Monroe

Augusta County Marriages -- Woman's Name

Puffinbarger
   Catherine & William Donaghe 23 Aug 1821; min- Gerard Morgan
Pugh
   Hannah & Jesse Balsley 5 Jan 1832; min- John Howell- publication of banns
   Mary & John Letcher 3 Dec 1818; min- William King
Quick
   Polly & Charles Carrol 22 Aug 1811; min- John McCue
Rabern
   Sarah & Patrick Rady 15 Nov 1791; d John Raberen who consents wit- David Fane & Edward Day b- Daniel Fane
Rader
   Elizabeth & Richard Hudson 5 Sep 1795; 'Reading?' Minister's return spells name as 'Ridden' Elizabeth (of age) d James Raiden b- James Elliott min- Archibald Scott- 6Sep1795
   Mary & John Swisher 25 Jan 1841; min- Samuel Wagner
Radner
   Mary Ann & Nicholas Croushorn 17 Jan 1839; min- John J Reimensnyder
Raines
   Betsy & Jacob Epply 19 Nov 1824; min- Michael Meyerhoeffer
Ralston
   E & J Terrell 21 Jan 1836; min- Robert M Lipscomb
   Eleanor & Richard Rankin 11 Jan 1820; min- John Hendren
   Elenor & James Rutledge 7 Jul 1788; Minister's return spells name as 'Rutlidge' d William who consents test- George Rutledge & James Ralston b- Matthew Ralston min- William Wilson- 14Jul1788
   Polly & Armstrong Rankin 15 Dec 1801; d Samuel b- Samuel Ralston min- William King- 17Dec1801
   Ruth & J Sours 21 Jan 1836; min- Robert M Lipscomb
   Ruthey & John Johnston 20 Dec 1804; min- William King
Ramsay
   Janetta M & Michael Dickson 31 Aug 1821; min- John D Ewin
   Jemima & Robert Depriest 1 Oct 1816; min- William King
   Peggy & William Hart 6 Mar 1829; min- William Wilson
   Peggy & Thomas Perkins 25 May 1815; min- John McCue
   Salley & James Gamble 7 Jun 1815; min- John McCue
Ramsbottom
   Mary A & John C Armstrong 17 Feb 1842; min- Jacob Bachtel
Ramsey
   Mary Ann & James Yates 3 Sep 1830; min- William Wilson
   Mary & John Brown 5 Apr 1804; min- John McCue
   Salley & James Gambell 6 Jun 1815; 'Rev.' James Gambell min- John D Ewin
   Sally & William Finley 15 Jun 1801; d Andrew who consents test- William & Charles Patrick Samuel & William Finley are cousins William (of age) b- Samuel Finley min- John McCue- 16Jun1801
Ramsy
   Patsy & James Finly 2 Oct 1811; min- John McCue
   Polly & James Finley 16 Jul 1813; min- Thomas Bourne

Augusta County Marriages -- Woman's Name

Randal
  Emely & Jacob Roach 11 Nov 1841; min- Benjamin W Kindig- publication of banns

Randolph
  Hesther Ann & John F W Shaver 30 Mar 1846; min- P Shickel
  Letitia R & William F Smith 11 Sep 1848; min- Francis McFarland
  Margaret A & John A Tate 7 Apr 1836; min- James Morrison

Rankin
  Ann & Isaac Farrow 11 Jan 1820; min- John Hendren
  Betsy & Matthew Blair 23 Sep 1797; d Thomas Rankin, dec. b- William Robertson min- William Wilson- 21Sep1797
  Cordelia H & John Vanpelt 18 May 1836; min- William A Coffin
  Eliza & William Golladay 23 Oct 1827; min- Gerard Morgan
  Margaret & Absolem Fisher 1 Nov 1826; min- James Watts
  Margaret & George Poage 9 Apr 1800; George from Bath Cty d Thomas Rankin, dec. perm- Robert Crawford, gdn of Margaret test- Robert Poage & William Poage Jr b- Robert Crawford s William of Bath cty
  Martha Adline & Thomas C Coursey 20 Sep 1847; min- John L Blakemore
  Martha & John Poage 26 Nov 1798; con- William Crawford, gdn test- Alexander Poage John Poage swears he was 21 last May b- William Poage min- William Wilson- 27Nov1798
  Mary & Gabriel Hite 19 Jun 1820; min- John Hendren
  Mary & John Young 5 Sep 1785; b- James Rankin
  Nancy & Edward Mooney 11 Jul 1816; min- William King
  Patsey & James A Frazer 12 Feb 1809; min- John Montgomery
  Polly & William Gibson 23 Nov 1813; min- William Calhoon
  Polly & George Rankin 24 Sep 1806; min- William Wilson
  Polly & William Silling 30 Oct 1820; min- Daniel Stephens

Ransbarger
  Elizabeth & George M Helms 27 Oct 1830; min- Gerard Morgan

Ransberger
  Mary & Jacob G Shutler 23 Dec 1834; min- Samuel Kennerly

Rapp
  Elizabeth & Richard E Johnston 17 Nov 1840; min- John C Hensell- publication of banns
  Mary C & George W Burgess 25 May 1843; min- J C Hensell
  Polly & George Bittle 12 Feb 1798; d Michael Rapp, dec. b- John Fleiger

Rauch
  Peggy & Mathias Fuchs 27 Nov 1799; d Peter Rauch (consent given in German) test- John Rauch b- John Mount

Rauly
  Anne & John Andrew 25 Nov 1841; min- John Brower
  Sarah & Lewis Sandy 13 Sep 1841; min- John Brower

Rawley
  Susanna & William Sandy 17 Nov 1836; min- John J Riemensnyder

Ray
  Sally & David Bare 10 May 1810; min- John McCue

Augusta County Marriages -- Woman's Name

Rayburn
  Martha & Samuel Campbell 9 Sep 1806; min- William McPheeters
Reah
  Elizabeth & Martin Koiner 14 Apr 1792; b- Thomas Turke min- John McCune- 20Apr1792
Reburne
  Sarah & Patrick Ready 18 Nov 1791; min- William Wilson- 18Nov1791
Redman
  Amanda & Jacob C Spitler 9 May 1833; min- Conrad Speece
Redner
  Elizabeth & Paschal D Williams 24 Nov 1845; min- P Shickel
Reed
  Catherine D & John (Jr) Hanger 18 Mar 1830; min- Francis McFarland
  Catherine & Jacob Runkel 23 Apr 1800; d Christopher & Barbara Reed Barbara consents test- Peter Reed ('Rhead?, Read?') b- Lewis Runkle min- William King- 30Apr1800
  Elizabeth & Thomas L Allison 3 Mar 1831; min- Conrad Speece
  Elizabeth & James (Jr) Gardner 23 Jul 1792; Minister's return spells name as 'Joseph Gardner and Betsey Reed' d Robert, who consents wit- John Gardiner & Alexander Reed b- Jacob Kinney min- William Wilson- 24Jul1792
  Jane & Septimus Goodwin 6 Feb 1806; min- William Wilson
  Jane & Abraham Troxall 22 Sep 1812; min- William King
  M M & John Eakerman 1 Feb 1841; min- Benjamin M Smith
  Margaret & George Mathews 28 Sep 1790; Minister's return spells name as 'Reid' widow b- Robert Gamble min- Archibald Scott- 29Sep1790
  Mary Elizabeth & George T Myers 23 Apr 1850; min- James Morrison
  Rebecca & George Sheigis 28 Mar 1811; min- William Wilson
  Sally & Patrick Humphrey 26 Dec 1805; min- John McCue
  Sarah & John Johnson 28 Dec 1826; min- William Monroe
  Sarah & Richard Terrill 2 Jul 1818; min- William King
Reese
  Elizabeth & James M Davis 20 Sep 1845; min- S Wagner
Reeves
  Catharine A & David Landes 17 Dec 1840; min- J A Van Lear
  Martha Jane & Samuel Near 27 Dec 1849; min- John Harshbarger
  Polly & Elijah Grandie 8 Nov 1826; min- Daniel Stephens
Reglor
  Susanna & John Smith 16 Jun 1785; b- Francis Marra
Regon
  Betty & Samuel Rankin 12 Oct 1794; min- William Wilson- 12Oct1794
Reid
  Nancy Ann & Robert Hanger 20 Sep 1828; min- James Morrison
  Polly & Robert Heslet 5 Feb 1807; min- William Wilson
Reif
  Barbara & Andrew Crist 31 Jan 1795; d John b- John Reif

Augusta County Marriages -- Woman's Name

Reiff
Nancy & Jonathan Shirley 14 Apr 1801; Minister's return spells name as 'Nancy Ruph (Rife?) and omits Jonathan's surname' d John, who signs 'Johann Reiff' as surety min- William King- 9Apr1801 (sic)

Reignheart
Hanna & George Houser 13 Aug 1792; d Owen b- Henry Rinehart

Reiser
Mary & David Thornton 24 Jun 1834; min- Augustus Babb

Revercomb
Jemima & Philip Witts 30 Mar 1847; min- J A Van Lear

Reyburn
Margaret & Samuel Samuels 19 Mar 1785; stepdaughter of John Harper b- Hugh Brown

Reynolds
Mary Ellen & John E Harris 22 Feb 1849; min- J McKendree Reiley
Sarah Austin & William Donnell 4 Dec 1833; min- William G Jackson

Rhinehart
Mary & Jacob Miller 1 Oct 1794; Mary of age b- George Houser

Rhoades
Elizabeth & Stephen Wood 24 Feb 1813; min- William King
Mary & Joseph Mathews 22 Sep 1787; b- Asher Waterman min- James Chambers- 22Sep1787

Rhyan
Lucy & Cyrus Fry 3 Apr 1845; min- T T Castleman

Rice
Betsy & James Black 9 Jun 1800; Betsy (of age) d Margaret who consents b- John Clayton
Margaret & John Clayton 20 Dec 1785; widow b- Andrew Hamilton min- Samuel Shannon- 2Jan1786
Polly & Henry Sheetz - May 1804; min- John Brown

Richey
Mary & Joseph Brown 19 Jan 1804; min- William King

Riddle
----- & George Campbell 14 Nov 1789; min- William Wilson- 14Nov1789
Catherine & Francis Sponter 8 Sep 1791
Jane & Peter Hughs 14 Nov 1809; min- John McCue
Martha Jane & John M Perry 31 Apr 1845; min- P Shickel

Rife
Easter & John Surface 1 May 1804; min- William King
Polly & Thomas Edmunds 10 Mar 1803; min- William King

Rigby
Mary & Peter Kelly 26 Nov 1788; Minister's return spells name as 'Mary Reyburn' widow b- Robert Burges min- James Chambers- 26Nov1788

Riley
Polly & Alfred Howell 18 Sep 1821; min- John Hendren

Augusta County Marriages -- Woman's Name

Rinehart
  Betsey & James S Connoway 19 Jan 1815; min- William King
  Hannah & Christian Bowman 19 May 1815; min- William King
  Lydia & John Shuey 2 Jan 1835; min- Henry Brown
  Rebecca & Jacob Bailor 19 Apr 1822; min- Daniel Stephens

Risk
  Elizabeth & James Risk 14 Dec 1785; d John Risk of Rockbridge who consents b- David Risk min- John Brown- 19Dec1785
  Elizabeth & Charles Stuart 15 Mar 1791; wid b- Thomas Mynes
  Peggy & James Dillan 29 Oct 1801; Minister's return spells name as 'Dillen' 'Margaret' d William Sarah Guffie, of lawful age and Augusta resident, swears Peggy of age b- Govey Stuart min- William King- 29Oct1801
  Rachel & Richard Hays 27 Dec 1792; d Elizabeth Stuart, who consents wit- Charles Stuart (Stewart) & John Risk b- John Risk min- John Brown- 24Jan1793

Rittenhouse
  Catherine & Edward Law 8 Jan 1799; Catherine (of age) b- Richard Roach ('Roche, Rotch?')

Ritter
  Elizabeth & Christian Grow 26 Jun 1787; Minister's return spells name as 'Groff' b- John Moore min- Archibald Scott- 27Jun1787
  Jane C & William Bible 15 Sep 1831; min- Benjamin Denton

Roach
  Frances & William Shiflett 24 Jul 1820; bond- 27Jul1820 min- Josiah Cole

Roberts
  Anne & John Alexander 6 Nov 1823; min- William Wilson Jr
  Elisabeth & Michael Apple 21 Jun 1786; min- Archibald Scott- 21Jun1786
  Jane & Andrew B Acord 11 Jan 1843; min- James Bunting
  Mary & William A Cale 4 Oct 1825; min- William W Calhoun
  Mary & Selden Harrison 9 Jun 1835; min- Conrad Speece- publication of banns

Robertson
  Ann Archer & Joseph Wayt Bell 25 Sep 1845; min- B M Smith
  Ann E & Rudolph Turk 1 Dec 1842; min- A G Chenowith
  Betsey & Thomas Williams 28 Jan 1794; min- William Wilson- 28Jan1794
  Catherine & William Beard 1 Jan 1793; min- William Wilson- 1Jan1793
  Elizabeth & Samuel Givens 19 Mar 1785; b- Alexander Robertson
  Elizabeth & Charles Stuart 29 May 1811; min- William Wilson
  Hannah & William Herring 28 Dec 1786; d Peter b- Randall Givens wit- Thomas & John Robertson William son of Leonard wit- Sarah Herring min- Benjamin Erwin- 8Jan1787
  Jane & Silas Hart - Sep 1749; license only
  Margaret & Peter H Hanger 25 Jan 1838; min- J C Hensell
  Mary & Thomas Downey 21 Apr 1798; Minister's return spells name as 'Downing' Mary (of age) d William b- Matthew Robertson min- John McCue- 3Apr1798

Augusta County Marriages -- Woman's Name

Robertson (cont.)
  Nancy & William Johnson 10 May 1828; min- William C. Morrison
  Sarah Jane & George W Mowry 23 Dec 1847; min- S Hildebrand
Robinson
  Margaret & Robert Givens 29 Mar 1785; d William b- Alexander Robinson wit- Mathew Mathewson & Alexander Robertson
  Milly & Jacob Raab 6 May 1806; min- William King
Rode
  Nancy & Abraham Switzer - Aug 1820; min- John Brown
Rodgers
  Fanny & George Morrow 30 Aug 1787; Minister's return spells name as 'George Muncy & Nanney Rodgers' b- John Elliott min- James Chambers- 30Aug1787
  Mary & John Hardwick 19 Jan 1830; min- Henry S Kepler- publication of banns
  Nancy & George Muncy 30 Aug 1787; Minister's return spells name as 'George Morrow & Fanny Rodgers' min- Archibald Scott- 30Aug1787
Rogers
  Elizabeth J & Matthew Reeves 27 Jan 1848; min- J A Van Lear
  Elizabeth & Levi L Moses 22 Aug 1822; min- William Wilson Jr
  Melvina & Robert Alford 26 Feb 1850; min- John Garber
Roland
  Diana & Daniel Lootz - Oct 1818; min- John Brown
Roles
  Elizabeth & Adam (Jr) Wise 17 May 1811; min- G H Riemenschneider
Roller
  Sarah Elizabeth & William F Detrick 18 Mar 1849; min- George Huffman
Roop
  Catherine & Samuel Martin 5 Jun 1827; min- William Monroe
  Christiana & John Martin 26 Aug 1823; min- Josiah Cole
  Elizabeth & Archibald Elliott 30 Jan 1840; min- William Calhoon
  Margaret & Oliver Cromwell 16 Nov 1829; min- John Hendren
Roople
  Elizabeth & Robert Campbell 9 Aug 1813; min- Wright Burgess
Root
  Catharine & Lewis Bailey 4 Jun 1835; min- Samuel Kennerly
  Mary Ann & William F Crouse 1 Apr 1848; min- W T Richardson
  Nancy & George H Miller 19 Jul 1848; min- T T Castleman
Rosenbarger
  Mary & William H Martin 24 Sep 1840; min- Benjamin M Kindig
Ross
  Ann & William Lively 26 Oct 1790; b- Robert Craig Ann served her time with Miss Craig and is now free
  Catherine & Charles L Marshall 19 May 1828; min- William C. Morrison
  Margaret & Daniel Green 15 Nov 1793; d William who consents test- James McGummery & Henry Laywell b- John McClure min- John McCue- 19Nov1793

Augusta County Marriages -- Woman's Name

Ross (cont.)
  Polly & Adam Russell 13 May 1799; d William Ross, sis to
    John Ross, and of age b- John Ross
  Ruthey & Robert McKee 18 Feb 1794; Minister's return
    spells name as 'Betsey Ross' b- John Alexander min- John
    McCue- 25Feb1794
Rough
  Lucinda & John S Robertson 2 Sep 1847; min- J C Hensell
  Malinda & David H Davis 10 Mar 1840; min- John C Hansell
  Margaret & Henry S Gregory 22 Jan 1846; min- J C Hensell
  Margaret & Joseph Swatsley 27 Aug 1835; min- William
    Calhoon
  Nancy & Joseph H Miller 14 May 1846; min- James Paine
  Susannah & Edward McFadden 16 Oct 1798; d Peter who
    consents b- Christian Lukenbill
Row
  Esabella & John Row 16 Aug 1832; min- William Calhoon
Rowh
  Catharine & John Fry 9 Sep 1841; min- John C Hensell
Rowland
  Polly & Joseph Wayland 17 May 1810; min- William Wilson
Rowler
  Mary & Adam Lauks 15 Dec 1795; b- Martin Surface
  Mary & Adam Louks 15 Dec 1795; 'Mary Brownlee?' min- John
    McCue- 15Dec1795
Ruff
  Lucinda & James Moredock 28 Apr 1850; min- Henry Witzel
  Margaret & James Blakely 21 Apr 1789; Minister's return
    spells name as 'Bleakley' b- Smith Thompson min- Archibald
    Scott- 22Apr1789
  Martha A & John Wilson 5 Jun 1850; min- John Hendren
Runkle
  Barbary & John Summers 29 Oct 1812; min- William King
  Betsy & Jacob Joh 24 Jan 1804; min- William King
  Catharine & John Patterson 16 Jan 1845; min- W G Campbell
  Catharine & John Teeford 12 Mar 1793; d Lewis John (of
    age) b- Lewis Runkle
  Catherine & John Cale - May 1827; min- Joseph Smith
  Catherine & John Cale 17 May 1827; min- Joseph Smith
  Christiana & Jeremiah Runkle 16 Feb 1796; d Lewis b-
    Lewis Runkle
  Dorothy & George Cups 6 Jul 1789; b- Samuel Runkle
  Rebecca & John (Jr) Weaver 23 Nov 1841; min- John C Hensell
Runnels
  Sarah & George Simmerman 4 Aug 1842; min- P E Stevenson
Rupe
  Hannah & Samuel Collins 9 Sep 1841; min- William Calhoon
Ruple
  Peggy & George Palmer 15 Mar 1816; min- William Calhoon
  Polly & David Williams 23 Jun 1803; min- William King
  Sally & Henry Shelton 15 Feb 1824; min- Michael
    Meyerhoeffer

Augusta County Marriages -- Woman's Name

Rush
Anne & John Waserman 20 Apr 1819; 'Bush?' min- William Calhoon
Hannah & Robert Beaten 1 Aug 1811; min- Wright Burgess
Julia Ann & William Scull 6 Nov 1833; 'Rev.' Scull min- Augustus Babb
Mary Jane & Robert G Bickle 26 Oct 1842; min- James Paine

Rusmisel
Eliza Jane & William Hall 25 May 1842; min- John C Hensell
Mary A & John Bosserman 12 Mar 1840; min- John C Hansell
Mary Ann & Simeon Cupp 19 Oct 1848; min- George H Martin
Mary & William Letshew 19 May 1842; min- D F Bittle
Mary & Daniel McMullen 8 Jun 1826; min- John Hendren
Sarah & Peter Alinger 24 Mar 1842; min- D F Bittle
Sarah & Asher Argenbright 29 Mar 1839; min- John A Van Lear
Sarah & Joseph Hodge 22 Nov 1832; min- John Hendren- publication of banns

Russel
Mary A & George W Shultz 20 May 1841; min- John C Hensell- publication of banns

Russell
Elizabeth Margaret & John Bosserman 8 Nov 1837; min- J C Hensell
Elizabeth & Adam Gardner 23 Jan 1788; con- Robert Russell wit- A Stuart & William Skillern b- Nicholas Spring & Thomas Scott min- James Chambers- 7Jan1788
Elizabeth & Benjamin Plunket 25 Jun 1835; min- Augustus Babb
Elizabeth & Robert Rankin 12 Sep 1805; min- John McCue
Elmira & George Breeze 19 Oct 1845; min- J C Hensell
Florence & William Brooks 29 Mar 1798; d Joshua Russell, dec., sis of Adam Russell b- Adam Russell min- Archibald Scott- 29Mar1798
Henrietta & Mordecai Smith - Aug 1847; min- Stephen Hildebrand
Jane & Isiah Jones 17 Nov 1789; d John, who consents wit- Robert Jones & Henry Swink b- Griffith Evans
Jinny & James Ranken 17 Sep 1807; min- John McCue
Martha & James Brown 15 Nov 1786; d Joshua bond min- Archibald Scott- 15Nov1786
Mary M & Philip Fauver 11 Apr 1842; min- John C Hensell
Mary & James Robertson 2 Feb 1789; b- Andrew Russell min- William Wilson- 12Feb1789
Mary & John Spear 9 Jun 1801; Minister's return spells name as 'Speer' d John s Samuel who consents test- Samuel Meteers & Thomas Speer b- John Russell min- John Gee- 11Jun1801
Nancy & David Ott 6 Jun 1827; min- Joseph Smith
Sarah Ann & George W Campbell 17 Dec 1835; min- Francis A C Mills
Susannah & Jacob Argenbright 25 Aug 1803; min- William King

Rutledge
Elizabeth & Matthew Thompson 7 Apr 1829; min- Conrad Speece
Jane & George Brand 26 Mar 1816; min- William King

Augusta County Marriages -- Woman's Name

Rutledge (cont.)
  Jane & Amaziah Kerr 11 Mar 1825; min- William Wilson
  Margaret & Hiram Deary 3 May 1831; min- Samuel Kennerly
  Rosanna & Elijah Rutledge 30 Jul 1822; min- Conrad Speece
Rutlidge
  Catherine & Stephen Riddle 10 Oct 1789; d Thomas, who
    consents wit- Samuel Prier & John Reader b- Jonathan
    Brooks min- William Wilson- 10Oct1789
Ryan
  Elleanor & James Brodhurst 30 Jan 1798; widow John Ryan
    b- Smith Thompson & William Short
  Polly & Philip Rodgers 28 Dec 1819; min- Daniel Stephens
Ryanhart
  Magdalena & John Mohler 16 Apr 1799; min- Daniel Garber-
    16Apr1799
Safley
  Elizabeth & Adam Orbough 3 Jan 1811; min- William Wilson
Salvage
  Anne & Garland McCauley 10 Feb 1822; min- William Wilson Jr
Sandy
  Mary & Joseph Rader 21 Oct 1830; min- John Hendren
Saufley
  Susanna & Daniel Pickering 19 Feb 1811; min- William Wilson
Saunders
  Sarah & Andrew Karikoff 1 Dec 1831; min- John Hendren
Savage
  Mary & Frederick Ript 7 Jun 1786; b- Dennis Callaghan
    min- Archibald Scott- 14Jun1786
Sawyers
  Martha & John Thompson 21 Nov 1795; Minister's return
    spells name as 'Sawyer' d James Sawyers, dec. con- Hannah
    Sawyers, mother test- D Sawyers & Thomas Sawyers b- David
    Sawyers min- Archibald Scott- 25Nov1795
  Nancy & James Crawford 28 Jan 1797; d James Sawyers, dec.
    con- Hannah Sawyers test- John Thompson b- Thomas Sawyers
    min- Archibald Scott- 31Jan1797
  Rachel & John Glass 12 Aug 1797; d James Sawyers, dec. b-
    Hannah Sawyers & John Thompson
  Rebecca & Samuel Buchanan 25 Dec 1790; b- Philip North
    min- Archibald Scott- 30Dec1790
Schooler
  Sylvia & Valentine Miller 22 Aug 1786; Minister's return
    spells name 'Millar' d Zachariah min- Archibald Scott-
    29Aug1786
Schoue
  Mary Palina & Henry Wehn 26 May 1850; min- Z Loyd
Scott
  Ann & Jacob Larew 3 Oct 1815; min- John McCue
  Elenor & John Caldwell 27 Feb 1806; min- John McCue
  Elizabeth & Joseph Larew 21 Jan 1808; min- John McCue
  Elizabeth & Jeremiah Molds 20 Jun 1801; Elizabeth (of age)
    d Joseph b- Joseph Paxton min- William King- 20Jun1801
  Esther & Thomas Rice 25 May 1797; Esther from Rockingham
    cty min- William Wilson- 25May1797

Augusta County Marriages -- Woman's Name

Scott (cont.)
  Hannah & James Tweedy 6 Mar 1806; min- William King
  Jane & John W Davison 29 May 1828; min- William Calhoon
  Jane & Robert McPheeters 24 Feb 1814; min- William Calhoon
  Janetta & Robert Alexander 14 Nov 1831; min- James C Wilson
  Julianna & Joseph Sharp 23 Jan 1812; min- William Calhoon
  Margaret Ann & Alfred Tyerie 12 Sep 1846; free persons of color min- William Calhoon
  Mary Jane & William H Boyd 6 Mar 1849; min- Robert L Dabney
  Mary & James McNight 17 Oct 1810; min- John Montgomery
  Matilda & John Sproul 13 Sep 1821; min- William W Calhoun
  Polly & John Campbell 25 May 1797; Polly from Rockingham cty min- William Wilson- 25May1797
  Rebecca & John Bare 6 Oct 1825; min- Francis McFarland
  Sarah & George Trotter 9 Jan 1787; b- James Scott min- Archibald Scott- 10Jan1787

Screle
  Jane & John Smiley 21 Sep 1809; min- William Bolridge

Scribner
  Nancy & James Tuttle 2 Aug 1817; min- Wright Burgess

Scylor
  Mary & James Newton 11 Oct 1797; d Philip Scylor, late of Augusta sis Jacob Scylor b- Jacob Scylor (Silor)

Searight
  Anne & Isaac Rankin 1 Jun 1789; Minister's return spells name as 'Seawright' b- James Searight wit- John Hall min- William Wilson- 2Jun1789
  Jane & Joseph McCutchen 5 Sep 1785; widow of George Searight b- John King d John King wit- James Larid, James Miller, Samuel King min- Archibald Scott- 6Sep1785

Sears
  Molley & Michael Miller 25 Mar 1817; min- Abraham Garber- publication of banns

Seawright
  Anna & Joshua E Myers 26 May 1829; min- William Wilson
  Elizabeth Ann & Samuel McCutchen 24 Oct 1844; min- J C Hensell
  Mary & David B Landis 12 Oct 1826; min- William Wilson
  Rebecca & John B Watts 27 Aug 1834; min- William Wilson

Seftle
  Mary & Henry Symmerman 18 Jul 1792; d Valentine who consents wit- Jacob Geiger b- Choistion Symerman

Seig
  Ann Caroline & John B Davis 20 Apr 1848; 'Rev.' John B min- P Shickel
  Julia Ann & Henry Teaford 2 Nov 1837; min- William Calhoun
  Susan E & Joseph Wilson 10 May 1838; min- D F Bittle

Seldomredg
  Margret & William Dice 26 Dec 1811; min- William King

Seldomridge
  Elizabeth & John Crow 10 Mar 1814; min- William King

Sellers
  Elizabeth M & Jacob Shirey 21 Nov 1843; min- Samuel Wagner
  Mary Ann & Thomas P Crawford 30 Mar 1848; min- George H Martin

Augusta County Marriages -- Woman's Name

Sensabaugh
Rebecca & Archibald Martin 2 Jun 1825; min- James Morrison

Sensebaugh
Mary & John Hess 1 Sep 1791; d John s of Christian who consents wit- John Ewing & Jacob Sensibaugh b- John Sensebaugh

Sensebough
Catherine & Andrew Sheetz 23 Sep 1799; d John b- Jacob Sheetz & John Sensibough

Sensibaugh
Elizabeth & John Buchanan 27 Apr 1848; min- J C Hensell
Polly & James Strickler 26 Oct 1847; min- James Morrison

Sewall
Elizabeth & Jacob Dolino 24 Jun 1801; min- William King- 24Jun1801

Shackelford
Sarah & Hugh Keenon 11 Mar 1789; Minister's return spells name as 'Shackleford' d James, who consents wit- James Megongal & Samuel Forsythe min- William Wilson- 12Mar1789

Shafer
Caty & George Lovel 28 Feb 1826; min- Abraham Garber- publication of banns

Shaffer
Elizabeth & David Good - Aug 1825; min- John Brown
Elizabeth & John Michael 10 May 1803; min- William King

Shannon
Jane & Michael Cawley 24 May 1785; b- Robert McClenachan
Jane & Christian Gregory 21 Jul 1797; 'Jean?' Jane (of age) d ----- Shannon, dec. b- Jacob Gregory min- Archibald Scott- 23Jul1797
Mary Jane & David Palmer 21 Jan 1847; min- J C Hensell
Mary & Hugh (Jr) Torbett 4 Jul 1795; 'Mary Brawford?' min- Archibald Scott- 4Jul1795
Polly & William Higginbotham 16 Mar 1790; b- John Shannon min- John Brown- 16Mar1790

Sharp
Amy & John Henry 14 Feb 1800; d John Sharp Sr who consents test- Thomas Sharp b- Joseph Sharp
Elizabeth & William Wilson 8 Apr 1795; d Daniel b- Daniel Sharp
Fanny & William Porter 30 Sep 1796; Minister's return spells name as 'Fanny Thorp' d John Sharp Sr who consents test- John Sharp Jr b- Joseph Sharp min- Archibald Scott- 5Oct1796
Jane & James Black 4 Jan 1799; d John Sharp Sr who consents test- Joseph Sharp b- Robert Sharp
Polly & Andrew Thompson 16 May 1809; min- William McPheeters

Sharret
Catherine & Martin Wolf 9 Jun 1791; d Daniel s Sebastian, who attests to his age b- Daniel Sharret

Shaver
Barbara Ann & Addison Wolf 16 Nov 1848; min Henry Wetzel
Elizabeth & Isaac Carson 2 Jan 1828; min- John Hendren

Augusta County Marriages -- Woman's Name

Shaver (cont.)
  Elizabeth & Thomas Cook 5 Oct 1843; min- Henry Wetzel
  Elizabeth & Andrew Lowrets 20 Dec 1787; widow b- William Trorback
  Hannah & John Huffer 18 Dec 1845; min- Henry Wetzel
  Jane & John Claytor 12 Jun 1828; min- William C. Morrison
  Margaret & Jacob Andrew 5 Jun 1839; min- John A Van Lear
  Margaret & Samuel Landes 3 Jun 1845; min- Daniel Brower
  Mary & Philip Sheets 21 Feb 1827; min- G H Reimensnyder
  Molly & Philip Rusht 2 Aug 1791; wid b- Valentine Sherley
  Phebe & Jacob Dedamore 26 Jul 1827; min- John Hendren
  Rachel & David Sheffer 28 Jun 1833; min- George Hildt
  Susanna & David Wykle 3 May 1825; min- G H Reimensnyder

Sheaffer
  Sarah & George Miller 22 Mar 1816; min- William King

Shedden
  Mary & James Grinstead 7 Nov 1787; widow b- Nicholas Spring

Sheets
  Ann & John Smith 28 Sep 1818; min- William King
  Catharine & John Connor 2 Dec 1831; min- William Wilson
  Cynthia & Jacob Palmer 6 Feb 1840; min- D F Bittle
  Harriet D & Charles A Laporte 15 Nov 1842; min- Samuel Wagner
  Julia A F & William Ocheltree 24 Jan 1843; min- Samuel Wagner- publication of banns
  Mary & Martin Fitzpatrick 8 Dec 1836; min- B N Brown
  Mary & James Whist - Jun 1824; min- John Brown
  Peggy & William Brooks 2 Jan 1822; min- Josiah Cole
  Sarah & William Donaho 4 Dec 1828; min- John Hendren
  Sarah & John (Jr) Snyder 25 Mar 1849; min Henry Wetzel
  Susannah & Jacob Brooks 23 Sep 1833; min- William Calhoon

Sheetz
  Catherine & Peter Rolestone 25 Mar 1824; min- Josiah Cole
  Elizabeth & Henry Keneday - Dec 1818; min- John Brown
  Elizabeth & Samuel Landess 28 May 1816; min- G H Riemenschneider
  Elizabeth & George Livick 28 May 1823; min- Josiah Cole
  Elizabeth & John Long - Jul 1818; min- John Brown
  Elizabeth & John Rankin 7 Feb 1820; min- John Hendren
  Elizabeth & Adam Wise - May 1827; min- John Brown
  Frany & Joseph Long 6 Jan 1818; min- G H Riemenschneider
  Mary & William Johnston - Oct 1825; min- John Brown
  Polly & Matthias Simmons 17 Nov 1825; min- Josiah Cole
  Susana & Kirkley Loyd 24 Mar 1825; min- Josiah Cole

Sheffer
  Catharine & Samuel Sheets 22 Jan 1834; min- John Hendren

Shell
  Maria & David Engleman 21 Oct 1833; min- Augustus Babb

Shelley
  Maria Ann & William White 30 Jan 1845; min- G W Israel

Shelly
  Ann & Christian Rusmissel 26 Jan 1808; min- William King
  Betsey & Samuel Stover 26 Apr 1814; min- William King

Augusta County Marriages -- Woman's Name

Shelly (cont.)
  Elizabeth & Jacob Jordan 3 Sep 1845; min- P Shickel
  Frances & James Runkle 17 May 1796; Minister's return
    spells name as 'Frances Sherley' d Peter Shally b- Peter
    Shelly min- William Wilson- 26May1796
  Mary & David Stover 15 Jan 1805; min- William King
Shelman
  Cathorine & Peter Bowyer 16 Aug 1793; d Lewis, who gives
    bond
Shelton
  Sarah & Richard Helms 17 Apr 1834; min- Conrad Speece
Shempe
  Catherine & Dabney Shelton 26 Dec 1810; min- John McCue
Shepherd
  Susan Caroline & Henry Berry 4 Mar 1845; min- P Shickel
Sherley
  Barbara & Samuel Pecker 24 Sep 1791; d Valentine b-
    Valentine Sherley
Sherman
  Sally & Adam Russmassell 30 Aug 1808; min- William King
Sherrets
  Elizabeth & William Lansaw - --- 179-; 'Landsaw' d Daniel
    Sharrets b- Daniel Sharrets no minister listed; clerk's
    memorandum cites ceremony date as 20Jun1792
Shewe
  Christian & Andrew Rinehart 29 May 1803; min- William King
Shields
  Ann & Peter Lerew 21 Nov 1795; Minister's return spells
    name as 'Larew' b- William Wilson min- Archibald Scott-
    24Nov1795
  Elizabeth & James Craig 13 Mar 1792; d Robert b- Robert
    Shields min- John Montgomery- 20Mar1792
  Eveline & Samuel Black 2 Dec 1830; min- William Wilson
  Margaret T & Robert G Gilkeson 11 Nov 1845; min- B M Smith
  Margaret & William Craig 23 Aug 1800; d Robert b- Robert
    Shields
  Mary Ellen & William Wallace 30 Nov 1842; min- Francis
    McFarland
  Mary & William McClure 20 Jan 1790; d Jane, widow, who
    consents b- Peter Waddel wit- Peter Waddel & John Delacy
  Mary & Robert Supple 7 Nov 1833; min- Francis McFarland
  Nancy A & Henry L Crowbarger 9 Apr 1835; min- Cornelius
    Gates
  Polly & John Brown 16 Oct 1823; min- Francis McFarland
  Polly & John Buster 2 Mar 1820; min- Robert H Chapman
Shiflet
  Rhoday Ann & Abraham Shiflett 8 Nov 1842; min- B M Smith-
    publication of banns
Shiflett
  Frankey Jane & Henry Ross 17 May 1842; min- F D Goodwin
  Winny & Chilles Herring 13 Feb 1837; min- B N Brown
Shindler
  Catharine & David Dorman 16 Apr 1817; min- G H
    Riemenschneider

Augusta County Marriages -- Woman's Name

Shindler (cont.)
  Elizabeth & Joseph Zahn 14 Oct 1825; min- G H Reimensnyder
  Ester Charlott & Will Link 10 Jun 1818; min- G H Riemenschneider
  Susannah & John Link 5 Nov 1813; min- G H Riemenschneider
Ship
  Betsy & French S Johnson 29 Jun 1841; min- P E Stevenson
  Lucy A F & W J L Bell 27 May 1834; min- John A Vanlear
Shipman
  Jane & George Cliff 10 Apr 1803; min- William King
Shipton
  Charlotte & Benjamin Strickler 30 Jul 1840; min- John C Hansell-publication of banns
Shirey
  Sarah & James (Jr) Alexander 11 May 1843; min- B M Smith
Shirley
  Anne & Thomas Sewell 6 Oct 1814; min- Wright Burgess
  Susannah & William McFall 16 Mar 1843; min- S J Love
Shoemate
  Polly & Henry Campbell 28 Jul 1814; min- William Wilson
Shonk
  Elizabeth & Philip Kister 2 Feb 1795; b- Henry Deck
Shore
  Barbara & George Faysnight 27 Oct 1790; b- Frederick Shore min- William Wilson- 27Oct1790
  Evy M & Monticue Allen 10 Oct 1795; Minister's return spells name as 'Montique' Evy (of age) b- Francis Huff min- John McCue- 13Oct1795
  Polly & George Groff 2 Feb 1790; b- Francis Huff min- William Wilson- 3Feb1790
Shoritz
  Cathorine & Daniel Shirey 12 Sep 1793; d Daniel b- Daniel Sheretz
Short
  Catherine & John McDade 10 Aug 1811; d William min- John Bell
Shott
  Kitty & John Bright 26 May 1816; min- G H Riemenschneider
Shotts
  Sally & John Sheetz 24 Feb 1814; min- G H Riemenschneider
Shotwell
  Delilah & Benjamin G Kindig 21 Oct 1841; min- Benjamin W Kindig
Shoue
  Susannah & Nathaniel Mathews 28 Dec 1835; min- Joshua Webb
Shoultz
  Elizabeth & Henry Teeford 22 Oct 1796; d George b- George Shoultz
Shover
  Catherine & John Brownfield 22 Oct 1829; min- William Wilson
  Elizabeth & Jacob Haybarger 17 Aug 1815; min- William King

Augusta County Marriages -- Woman's Name

Showalter
  Sarah & James H Huffman 22 Feb 1838; min- William R Coursey
Shown
  Sally & James Bryan 16 Aug 1815; min- G H Riemenschneider
Shreckhise
  Catharine & Robert Carson 24 Feb 1839; min- John J Reimensnyder
Shroader
  Ann Mary & John Hager 22 Oct 1785; Minister's return spells name as 'Stroader' d George b- James Basset min- Archibald Scott- 28Oct1785
Shropshire
  Margaret & Lewis Bailey 22 Nov 1822; min- Josiah Cole
  Sarah & Thomas Chandler 18 Nov 1805; min- William King
Shuey
  Catherine & George Crone 22 Apr 1817; min- William King
  Charlotte & Joseph Rapp 26 Sep 1806; min- William King
  Lydia & David Baylor 10 May 1831; min- Francis McFarland
  Margaret & William Botkins 12 Aug 1834; min- E R Veitch
  Margaret & Henry Rhyan 15 Dec 1828; min- William C. Morrison
  Polly & James Armantrout 1 Sep 1835; min- William Calhoon
  Susanah & John Ott 24 Sep 1835; min- Cornelius Gates
Shull
  Polly & William Harris 25 Jul 1830; min- Gerard Morgan
Shultz
  Catherine & William Webb 25 Aug 1819; min- James Morrison
  Eve Elizabeth & Thomas H McGuffin 24 Apr 1845; min- J C Hensell
  Margaret & Joseph Delter 13 Oct 1829; min- James Morrison
  Maria Jane & William Hawpe 15 Feb 1841; min- D F Bittle
  Peggy & Mathew Robertson 5 Oct 1809; min- William McPheeters
  Sarah M & William S Hiser 11 Jun 1845; min- P Shickel
  Susan & James Harrison 21 Jan 1841; min- John C Hensell- publication of banns
  Susan & Jacob Michael 24 Apr 1839; min- George Huffman
Shumate
  Lucy & Joseph Henry 8 Sep 1802; min- John McCue- 8Sep1802
Shura
  Eliza & Francis M Finley 3 Dec 1840; min- Benjamin M Smith
Shyrigh
  Catherine & John Weikle 12 Mar 1798; b- Michael Shyrigh (Schayra)
  Polly & Andrew Robertson 7 Jan 1700; d Jacob Shyrigh, dec, sis to Jacob Shirigh b- Jacob Shyrey
Sieg
  Susannah & Michael Bear 4 Feb 1808; min- William Calhoon
Silknatre
  Dolly & John Peters 23 Mar 1798; d Jacob b- Jacob Silknatre
Silling
  Ann & Isaiah Jones 21 Jan 1797; widower d Gasper Silling b- Gasper Silling

Augusta County Marriages -- Woman's Name

Silling (cont.)
  Barbara & George Patterson 20 Jan 1798; d Gasper b- Gasper Silling
  Catherine & George Crosby 24 May 1814; min- William King
  Catherine & William Fishburn 29 May 1820; min- Daniel Stephens
  Lydia & Philip Fishburn 4 Jun 1812; min- William King
  Sarah & Luke Woodward 11 Aug 1828; min- William Wilson

Sillings
  Lydia & Ephraim Woodward 15 Oct 1829; min- William Wilson
  Rebecca & William Hanger 19 Feb 1829; min- John Hendren
  Sarah M & Lewis Whitmore 28 May 1846; min- James H Brown

Silor
  Peggy & John Kee 24 Sep 1799; Minister's return spells name as 'Silar' Peggy from Augusta her father, Philip Silor Jr, from Rockbridge Philip consents test- Sarah Silers b- John Acker min- William King- 26Sep1799

Simbro
  Elizabeth & Uriah J Staples 12 Nov 1846; min- J Montgomery

Simmerman
  Barbara & Daniel Sanders 2 Dec 1800; Minister's return spells name as 'Landus' Daniel swears he is of age d John b- John Simmerman min- William King- 2Dec1800
  Elizabeth & John Loudermilk 29 Sep 1831; min- William Calhoon
  Sarah & David Arginbright 29 Nov 1844; min- William Calhoon
  Susannah & David Loudermilk 17 Nov 1831; min- William Calhoon

Simmon
  Sarah & Philip Wimer 31 Mar 1785; d Leonard & Catherine Simmon b- Nicholas Harper (signed in German), from South Branch

Simmons
  Sarah & Christian Michael 19 Sep 1816; min- Wright Burgess

Simpson
  Mary & Abraham Nickenson 4 Nov 1791; Mary a free mulatto b- James Patterson

Siron
  Elizabeth & Paulus Windsor 26 Sep 1789; (Powells Winsor) b- ----- Millar

Sitlington
  Agness & Andrew Betty 15 Dec 1786; d John bond
  Betsy & James Kelso 24 Aug 1789; d John, who consents wit- Alexander Crawford & Andrew Sitlington s Hugh, who consents wit- John Walker, John Moore & John Stewart b- Alexander McPheeters min- John Brown- 1Sep1789

Skelton
  Delilah & John Landes 11 Feb 1841; min- J J Reimensnyder
  Sarah W & Benjamin F Spicer 29 May 1845; min- P Shickel

Slagel
  Rachael & George Grimm 24 May 1827; min- Michael Meyerhoeffer

Augusta County Marriages -- Woman's Name

Slagle
  Catharine & Jacob C Kite 25 Jun 1817; min- Wright Burgess
  Elizabeth & Joseph Weston 22 Dec 1808; min- John McCue
  Margaret & Jonathan G Fellows 8 Jan 1822; min- James C Willson
  Mary & George Engleman 10 Dec 1812; min- John McCue
  Rachel & David Dixon 26 Feb 1830; min- William Wilson
  Susanah & John Clemmens 16 Oct 1815; min- William King

Slanker
  Mary C & George H Hudson 28 Jun 1848; min- T T Castleman

Slaten
  Rachel & Richard Western 28 Oct 1816; min- William King

Sligh
  Fanny & George Riddle 5 Aug 1805; min- William King

Sloane
  Elizabeth & David Burket 30 May 1813; min- William King

Slusher
  Barba & John Kale 26 Jul 1804; min- William King
  Esther & Jacob Yost 24 Oct 1805; min- William King
  Lidia & John Boswell 24 May 1790; d Coonrod b- George Slusher
  Mary & John West 30 May 1785; d Henry b- Philip Wolwine (signed in German) wit- Philipp Poman & Christian Bomgertner

Slye
  Polly & Peter Seal 1 Oct 1807; min- William King

Small
  Jane & William Pannell 3 Dec 1836; min- E Joshua Webb
  Mary Ann Mildred & William Tisdale 23 Sep 1834; min- Joseph Spriggs

Smallshoffer
  Catherine & J Leonard 24 Sep 1835; min- Robert M Lipscomb

Smiley
  Ellen & Harvey Fulton 1 Dec 1825; min- James Morrison
  Margaret & Michael Weaver 2 Aug 1848; min- George B Rimel

Smith
  Ann & John Golladay 27 Apr 1818; min- William King
  Ann & Thomas McFall 12 Jan 1832; min- William Wilson
  Barbara & Charles Caler 20 Apr 1789; (Koehler?) Minister's return spells name as 'Kaylor' b- Michael Apple min- William Wilson- 20Mar1789
  Betsey & James Donaho 15 Aug 1816; min- William King
  Caroline & William Barnett 24 Nov 1836; free persons of color min- Isaac Jones
  Catharine & John Montgomery 22 May 1834; min- Joseph Spriggs
  Catharine & William Youtzler 19 Nov 1840; min- J J Reimensnyder
  Catherine & Andrew Anderson 6 Feb 1812; min- William King
  Catherine & Jacob Sweetz 3 Jul 1810; min- William King
  Cornelia & John Q James 18 Oct 1842; min- P E Stevenson
  Elizabeth & John Bailey 27 Dec 1848; min- B M Smith
  Elizabeth & John Ballard 10 Nov 1794; 'Eliza'? Own consent test- Thomas Wilson J McCue affirms she lived with his family for many years and is over 21 test- Jacob Kemp min- John McCue- 11Nov1794

Augusta County Marriages -- Woman's Name

Smith (cont.)
  Elizabeth & John Jones 25 Jun 1799; d Thomas Smith, dec. & Elizabeth Smith, his wife who consents test- William Bell Jr b- Micael Garber Jr
  Elizabeth & James Lohr 19 Oct 1848; min- John Bowen
  Elizabeth & John Wallace 26 Oct 1815; min- John McCue
  Fanny & Robert Bell 4 Jan 1798; Fanny (of age) d John Smith, dec. Joseph Smith swears to Fanny's age b- Andrew Mines
  Hetty & Arthur Connelly 27 Aug 1818; min- William King
  Isabella & William Jones 27 Nov 1787; Isabella gives her own consent test- William Henery & William Restill b- Adam Bickel min- James Chambers- 27Nov1787
  Jane & Mathew Kinney 28 Jun 1809; min- William Wilson
  Juliana & Abraham Golloday 28 Mar 1822; min- William Wilson Jr
  Margaret S & Robert S Brook 24 Nov 1835; min- John A Steele
  Margaret & Michael (Jr) Garber 11 Oct 1792; d Thomas (dec) & Elizabeth, who consents wit- Sally Smith & Bettey Smith b- Vincent Tapp min- John Montgomery- 11Oct1792
  Martha A R & James G Hamilton 17 May 1842; min- F D Goodwin
  Mary Ann E & Henry Coiner 4 Aug 1846; min- James H Brown
  Mary Jane & Ezra Walker 1 Nov 1832; Ezra from Kanawha cty min- Henry Ruffner
  Mary & George Deeds 10 May 1788; b- Ludwick Smith min- William Wilson- 11May1788
  Mary & Samuel Donaghe 9 Mar 1810; min- William King
  Mary & Leonard Gerhart 10 Mar 1787; d Ludwick b- Ludwick Smith
  Mary & William Peatt 17 Nov 1814; min- William King
  Mildred Ann & Samuel J Davis 2 Sep 1847; min- John Bowen
  Nancy E & William Trayer 26 Dec 1827; min- William C. Morrison
  Polly & Thomas Elliott 25 Aug 1803; min- William King
  Polly & John Lambert 13 Jan 1825; min- Josiah Cole
  Rebecca & John Sheets - Aug 1825; min- John Brown
  Rosanna & Samuel Bell 3 Jan 1787; b- David Byers min- William Wilson- 4Jan1787
  Sally & Jonathan Life 10 Feb 1815; min- Abraham Garber- publication of banns
  Sally & Moses McCue 17 Apr 1800; Moses from Staunton d Thomas Smith, dec. b- William Chambers of Staunton min- John McCue- 17Apr1800
  Sarah Ann & Franklin Smith 30 Dec 1845; min- Jacob C Spitler
  Sarah J & William Rhodes 24 Oct 1830; min- Francis McFarland
  Sarah & Alexander Coly 7 Jan 1834; min- Samuel Kennerly- publication of banns
  Sarah & Madison Ustler 28 Jan 1844; min- T T Castleman
  Susan C & James R Bell 22 Nov 1827; min- Francis McFarland
  Susan & Cary A B Calvert 15 Jan 1844; min- E R Veitch
  Susanna & Joseph Smith 27 Jul 1819; min- William Wilson
  Susanna & Jacob Wine 2 May 1816; min- William King

Augusta County Marriages -- Woman's Name

Smith (cont.)
  Virginia W & N L Price   21 May 1835;   min- Robert M Lipscomb
Sneders
  Jenny & Robert McCullough 28 Jan 1789;   b- John Hall
Snider
  Fanny & William Powers 3 Feb 1791; b- James Rutledge
  Nancy & Samuel Fairburn 6 Jun 1841; min- George B Rimel-
    publication of banns
  Polly & David Silling 7 Aug 1806; min- William King
  Sarah & Nimrod S Showalter 20 Sep 1846; min- Jacob C
    Spitler
Snyder
  Betsy & Enos Silling 28 Dec 1826; min- John Hendren
  Caroline & Michael Roop 12 Nov 1829; min- John Hendren
  Larina & Thomas Brians 5 Mar 1828; min- William C. Morrison
  Margaret & Henry Yeagly - Jan 1803; min- John Brown
  Martha A & John W Sandy 24 Sep 1845; min- P Shickel
  Polly & Benjamin Curry 20 Dec 1827; min- John Hendren
  Rebecca & James H Curry 10 May 1830; min- Conrad Speece
  Rosannah & Robert Graham 10 Oct 1826; min- William Monroe
Sorrells
  Polly & Andrew Fisher 8 Aug 1822; min- Conrad Speece
Sorrels
  Keziah & Mathew Lamb 8 Oct 1795; d Joseph, late of Augusta
    cty, sis to Lewis Sorrels b- Lewis Sorrels
  Merney & John Fisher 27 Jan 1803; 'Nancy Sorrells?' min-
    John McCue
  Sarah & Robert Morton 29 Dec 1792; d Joseph, who consents
    wit- Thomas Beard & Kezzeyar Beard b- Nathaniel Kelley
    min- William Wilson- 1Jan1793
Sours
  Margaret & Henry Haffner - Jun 1818; min- John Brown
Southard
  Sarah Jane & John Whitesell 10 Jul 1845; min- T T Castleman
Southwood
  Martha A & James Smith 3 Sep 1846; min- J A Van Lear
Sowers
  Caroline Sidney & Hugh John Crawford 20 Aug 1841; min- S J
    Love
  Mary & Joseph Davis - Nov 1818; min- John Brown
  Susan E & Wade H Heiskell - Sep 1826; min- Joseph Smith
  Susannah & John Kellar - May 1805; min- John Brown
Spangler
  Lucinda F & Benjamin F Spitler 16 Dec 1847; min- John
    Reubush
Spear
  Rachel & Thomas Hardbarger 3 Jan 1822; min- James C Willson
Spears
  Nancy & John Lemon 19 Nov 1807; min- William King
Speck
  Frances & Isaac S Stone 17 Apr 1842; min- Peter Shickel
  Lettitia J & Robert S Baldwin 4 Aug 1846; min- T T
    Castleman

Augusta County Marriages -- Woman's Name

Speers
Susan Jane & Jacob Hippard 12 Oct 1831; min- John Howell
Spencer
Elizabeth & Elisha Wood 6 Mar 1823; min- Conrad Speece
Liza & John K Reed 16 Jun 1842; min- James Morrison-
 publication of banns
Sarah & James Trainer 1 Dec 1825; min- William Wilson
Sperry
Margaret S & George A Anderson 5 Dec 1839; min- P E
 Stevenson
Spitler
Eliza Jane & William W Joseph 26 Oct 1848; min- J Markwood
Elizabeth & Henry J Deal 2 Apr 1840; min- Jacob Bachtel
Elizabeth & Daniel Delman 28 Jul 1799; min- Daniel Garber-
 28Jul1799
Elizabeth & Jacob Yeaky 7 May 1818; min- William King
Frances & George L Arehart 5 Oct 1848; min- J McKendree
 Reiley
Hannah & John Myers 2 Oct 1810; min- Samuel Garber-
 publication of banns
Sarah & John Mizer 10 May 1831; min- William Calhoon
Spotts
Catherine & John Coiner 2 Feb 1804; min- William King
Elizabeth & Parker Bush - Jun 1814; bond- 2Jun1814 min-
 William Wilson
Ellen & Henry Yager 29 Aug 1834; min- James C Wilson
Mary & George Teeford 27 Apr 1801; d Jacob b- Jacob Spotts
Sprigs
Rody & Thomas Staunton 5 May 1797; b- Benjamin Norton
Spring
Catherine & Augustine Kaiger 2 Jan 1786; Minister's return
 spells name as 'Keiger' d Nicholas b- Samuel Merrit min-
 William Wilson- 2Jan1786
Springer
Henrietta & Johannes Zimmerman 5 Mar 1798; Minister's
 return spells name as 'John Simmons' Henrietta (of age) b-
 Baltzer King min- Archibald Scott- 8Mar1798
Sproul
Dorthula & John McCutchen 13 Oct 1834; min- William Calhoon
Frances E & William White 5 Sep 1844; min- Francis
 McFarland
Jane & John Weer 17 Jun 1793; Minister's return spells
 name as 'Weir' d William who consents test- William Sproul
 Jr, James Clarck, & James Monce b- William Sproul min-
 John Brown- 22Jun1793
Nancy & Jacob Hull 19 Apr 1827; min- James Morrison
Sprouse
Martha Jane & Thomas Chrisman 11 Mar 1847; min- Jacob Bear
Sprowl
Sidney & Joseph Beard 21 Jan 1799; Sidney (of age) d
 William who consents test- James Clarke b- William Sprowl
 Jr

Augusta County Marriages -- Woman's Name

StClair
  Anna & John Boys 18 Jan 1790; d Alexander, who consents
    b- Robert Douthat min- William Wilson- 18Jan1790
  Jane & William Boys 9 Jul 1800; d Alexander b- Alexander
    StClair
  Sarah & Robert Williamson 21 Jun 1804; min- William Wilson
StJohn
  Mary & Thomas Rickett 11 Jan 1794; Mary (of age) b-
    William Ridder min- Bennett Maxey- 16Jan1794
Standforth
  Nancy & John Armstrong 10 Oct 1821; min- Daniel Stephens
Stanton
  Catharine W & Joseph Peterson 18 Jan 1849; min- John A Van
    Lear
  Elizabeth & George Taylor 25 Feb 1830; min- John Hendren
  Jane & Fountain Taylor 16 Jul 1829; min- John Hendren
  July & Peachy Matheny 17 Oct 1825; min- John Hendren
  Sarah Nancy & David A Hemp 5 Apr 1849; min- Alonzo P Ludden
Starks
  Nancy & George Cox 9 Dec 1834; min- Conrad Speece
Staubus
  Amanda & Adam (Jr) Wise 31 Dec 1846; min- Henry Wetzel
  Elizabeth & John Earhart 25 Dec 1839; min- Jacob C Killian
  Louisa & Abraham A Lamb 12 Mar 1846; min- Henry Wetzel
  Mary C & Henry Wetzel 5 Dec 1839; min- Jacob C Killian
Stauffer
  Angeline & Enos Dull 17 Aug 1848; min- Alonzo P Ludden
Staunly
  Tabatha & Elias Vickers 25 Nov 1802; min- James Ward-
    25Nov1802
Steel
  Charlotte & James P Davis 21 Jul 1836; min- James Paine
  Jane & John McClure 18 Aug 1808; min- John McCue
  Jane & George McCormack 21 Jan 1796; d David b- David
    Steele
  Martha & Robert Cooper 2 Oct 1789; Minister's return
    spells name as 'Steele' b- Robert McCullough min- John
    Brown- 6Oct1789
  Rebecca & John Elliott 22 Mar 1827; min- Francis McFarland
Steele
  Catharine & John Thompson 1 Dec 1787; John from Rockbridge
    cty d Samuel who consents test- Samuel Steele & Robert
    Steele b- Robert Steele min- John Brown- 10Dec1787
  Catherine & William (Jr) Handly 18 Dec 1799; d Samuel
    Steele, dec. William Steele swears Kitty of age b- John
    Handly
  Catherine & Thomas Jackson 10 Apr 1807; min- William
    McPheeters
  Eleanor & John Allen 29 Sep 1790; d Robert b- Robert
    Steele min- Archibald Scott- 16Oct1790
  Elizabeth & John T Arnall 10 Oct 1836; min- James C Wilson
  Elizabeth & John Marton 13 Dec 1798; Minister's return
    spells name as 'John Martin' widow of John b- William
    Sterrett min- Archibald Scott- 13Dec1798

Augusta County Marriages -- Woman's Name

Steele (cont.)
  Jane Ann & John A Brown 21 Aug 1842; min- James Morrison
  Jane S & Hugh Weir 12 Jun 1834; min- John A Steele
  Janet & Robert Carden 17 Dec 1799; d James who consents test- William & Polly Steele Robert of age b- Thomas Fulton min- William King- 19Dec1799
  Jenny & John Moore 14 Dec 1785; min- John Brown- 14Dec1785
  Jinny & Peter Alexander 24 Mar 1787; d Samuel who consents wit- Samuel Steele & Robert Steele b- Samuel Steele min- Archibald Scott- 27Mar1787
  Margaret & Peter Houser 28 May 1829; min- Francis McFarland
  Martha & Daniel Henderson 18 Feb 1802; min- John McCue- 18Feb1802
  Martha & Thomas Paxton 19 Apr 1791; d Robert b- Robert Steele marriage sent to clerk by Samuel Brown and dated 28Apr1791
  Mary & Samuel Hunter 24 Apr 1804; min- John McCue
  Mary & William McCormack 30 Jan 1801; William from Rockbridge cty d Robert Steele, dec. Both (of age) b- David Steele
  Nancy & Joseph Evans 17 Aug 1799; both of age d Samuel Steele, dec, sis to William Steele b- William Steele
  Nancy & Samuel Hanger 15 Mar 1832; min- Francis McFarland
  Polly & Andrew (Jr) McClure 25 Oct 1800; d Andrew who consents test- John McClure & Martin Bush s James b- John Steele, son of Andrew Steele
  Sally & Adam Campbell 19 Dec 1805; min- William Calhoon
  Sarah F & Moses H McCue 6 Sep 1838; min- John A Van Lear
  Sarah & John Bush 3 Nov 1803; min- John McCue
  Sarah & David Wilson 17 May 1791; d Samuel who consents wit- John Steele b- John Steele marriage sent to clerk by Samuel Brown and dated 19May1791
Steigle
  Elizabeth & William Quick 12 Oct 1837; min- John J Reimensnyder
Stephen
  Nancy & Christian Hincey 5 Jun 1795; widower & widow (of Robert Stephen b- George Craig
Stephenson
  Ann & James Waddle 27 Jun 1786; d Adam b- Thomas Waddle wit- John Hair & William Stephenson min- Benjamin Erwin- 28Jun1786
Sterlinger
  Polly & Daniel Burkhart 20 Jan 1801; Also called Polly Heddebach George Heddebaugh swears Polly of age b- Jacob Bealer ('Behler?')
Sterret
  Isabella & Isaac Funston 5 Oct 1807; min- John McCue
  Jane & John Allen 16 Mar 1815; min- John D Ewin
  Salley & Alexander Johnson 10 Dec 1818; min- John D Ewin
Sterrett
  Evelina Ann & Thomas M Hite 14 Mar 1836; min- John Hendren
  Henrietta & Edwin H Gooch 25 Aug 1849; min- John Hendren
  Isabella E C & James W Trimble 9 Nov 1846; min- W W Trimble

Augusta County Marriages -- Woman's Name

Sterrett (cont.)
  Nancy R & John Humphreys 4 Oct 1827; min- William Calhoon
Sterrit
  Rebecca & Spotswood Brawford 13 Aug 1819; min- John D Ewin
  Sarah & John Todd 13 Aug 1800; d Robert who consents , sis to Charles Sterrett Sarah (of age) b- Charles Sterret (Stenett) min- John McCue- 14Aug1800
Stevenson
  Caroline P & Michael G Harman - --- 184-; min- T T Castleman
  Elizabeth G & George W Gette 19 Dec 1848; min- Robert Nelson
  Isabella & Robert P Kinney 6 Jun 1844; min- T T Castleman
  Margaret & William McNutt 3 Aug 1843; min- James Morrison
  Mary & Archibald Huston 20 Jun 1749; license only
Steward
  Patty & Isaiah Slaven 22 Feb 1786; Minister's return spells name as 'Stuart' b- Abraham Ingram min- William Wilson- 22Feb1786
Stickley
  Elizabeth & Peter Kennedy 25 Mar 1847; min- George H Martin
  Mary Ann & John Craig 19 Dec 1833; min- Samuel Kennerly
Stiegle
  Louisa & Michael Stover 24 Nov 1842; min- Samuel Wagner
Stiles
  Elizabeth & William Francis 24 Oct 1786; Minister's return spells name as 'Stile' widow b- John Jenkins min- William Wilson- 25Oct1786
Stockdale
  Fanny & Martin E Edwards 8 Nov 1808; min- John McCue
  Margaret & Isaac Collins 16 May 1826; min- John Hendren- publication of banns
Stofer
  Amelia V & Slyvester Huffman 11 Nov 1847; min- John Bowen
Stoffer
  Susannah & George Painter 26 Jan 1814; min- William King
Stombock
  Catharine & Grandison Lee 18 Apr 1847; min- Jacob C Spitler
Stone
  Ann & Urbane J Poe 16 Aug 1827; min- Michael Meyerhoeffer
  Elizabeth & David Andrew 25 Apr 1809; min- William King.
Story
  Elenor & Isaac Snedegar 22 May 1787; Minister's return spells name as 'Snediger' b- James McGavory min- Samuel Shannon- 29May1787
Stoudamire
  Elizabeth & George A Orebaugh 20 Feb 1845; min- John A Van Lear
Stoutamoyer
  Ann & Fielding Jollett - Dec 1822; min- John Brown
  Pheby & Jacob Skyles 15 Jun 1826; min- G H Reimensnyder
  Sara & John Probst 29 Mar 1830; min- G H Reimensnyder

Augusta County Marriages -- Woman's Name

Stover
  Catharine & Frederick Rodes 7 Sep 1835; min- John Hendren
  Elizabeth D & John Thompson 5 Jan 1809; min- John McCue
  Elizabeth & Abraham Garber 7 Sep 1830; min- Abraham Garber
  Elizabeth & Elias Sheets 11 Mar 1837; min- George A Leopard
  Elizabeth & John Shelly 17 Dec 1804; min- William King
  Margaret C & William M Althaffer 23 Sep 1847; min- G W Israel
  Mary & Noah Beard 15 Jan 1844; min- C Parkison
  Mary & Christian Groff 3 Feb 1825; min- Josiah Cole
  Nancy & Benjamin Garber - --- 182-; min- Abraham Garber- publication of banns
  Polly & Jacob Shank 5 Sep 1837; min- Fred D Goodwin
  Sarah & John Beam 25 May 1826; min- John Hendren

Strain
  Eliza & Samuel Heizer 4 Sep 1828; min- Francis McFarland
  Mary Jane & James Cochran 30 Dec 1834; min- Conrad Speece
  Mary & David Connelly 4 Dec 1799; Mary (of age) d James Strain, dec. b- John Strain
  Nancy & Richard Trotter 27 --- 1790; widow b- Daniel Early

Stribling
  Frances M & William D Smith 31 Oct 1839; min- Frederick D Goodwin
  Mary T & John S Lewis 6 Aug 1837; min- Fred D Goodwin
  Matilda K & Nicholas K Trout 8 Jun 1843; min- F D Goodwin

Strickland
  Sarah & William Johnston 27 Jul 1801; d John b- John Strickland

Strickler
  Mary & William Carpenter 9 Jan 1786; min- John Brown- 9Jan1786
  Rebecca & Richard Anderson 20 Oct 1836; min- James Morrison
  Rebecca & John Engleman 13 Jan 1842; min- John C Hensell

Strine
  Elizabeth & David Lucas 29 Nov 1832; min- Francis McFarland

Stroader
  Ann & George Hagar 28 Oct 1785; min- Archibald Scott- 28Oct1785

Strong
  Betty & James McClure 26 Mar 1807; min- John McCue
  Margaret L & William Haines 4 Nov 1834; min- Conrad Speece
  Rachel & William Hays 16 Jun 1841; min- John C Hensell

Stuart
  Casindanete & Andrew J Redifer 17 Apr 1845; min- S Wagner
  Eleanor T & James M Brooks 7 Aug 1832; min- James C Wilson
  Elizabeth & George (Jr) Hutchison 4 Dec 1798; d Benjamin wit- Benjamin Stuart, Chesley Kinney & John Fackler b- George Hutchison Sr
  Elizabeth & Samuel Lessley 24 Jul 1792; Minister's return spells name as 'Lesley' d John, dec. b- Matthew Gambill perm- Arch & Mary Dickson, parents of Elizabeth min- William Wilson- 4Aug1792
  Frances & Joseph Moore 11 May 1802; min- William Wilson- 11May1802

Augusta County Marriages -- Woman's Name

Stuart (cont.)
  Jane & James Hicklin 30 Nov 1790; Minister's return spells name as 'Jane Stewart' d William, who consents b- John Stuart min- John Montgomery- 28Dec1790
  Malinda & Jacob Eckard 22 Dec 1828; min- William C. Morrison
  Margaret & John Smith 26 Mar 1791; s Wm who consents wit- Samuel Hardin & Samuel Camble certificate by Wm & Hannah Bell giving permission wit- Alexander Camble b- Samuel Harding Margaret an orphan
  Mary & John McClung 5 Nov 1788; d Benjamin wit- George Moore b- Benjamin Stuart min- William Wilson- 12Nov1788
  Mary & James McLaughlin 30 May 1787; b- Robert Stuart min- Samuel Shannon- 7Jun1787
  Mary & James Moffett 26 Dec 1789; b- Archibald Stuart min- Samuel Carrick- 29Dec1789
  Nancy & John Alexander 19 Jan 1809; min- John McCue
  Peggy & James Sims 11 Nov 1808; min- Joseph Reid
  Polly & Edward Hall 20 Jul 1790; b- John Burnsides min- William Wilson- 22Jul1790
  Sally & William Diddle 5 Dec 1805; min- John McCue
  Sarah & James Ailer 2 Aug 1831; min- William Calhoon
  Seelia & Francis Acord 27 Jan 1823; min- Josiah Cole
Stull
  Charity & Henry Funk 17 Jul 1787; 'Steell?' b- George Givens
Suddarth
  Ann S & James Matheny 4 Feb 1847; min- W G Campbell
Sullivan
  Julian & David Curren 20 Dec 1827; min- Joseph Smith
Sumner
  Barbara & David Sanders 2 Dec 1800; min- William Wilson- 2Dec1800
Summers
  Barbara & Daniel Hull 15 Feb 1796; d John b- John Summers
  Christiana & Philip Ling 11 Jun 1791; d John, who consents b- John Summers
  Elizabeth & Daniel Beck 9 Dec 1799; d John b- John Summers
  Elizabeth & Samuel A Keen 25 Apr 1837; min- J C Hensell
  Mary & Joseph Dohm 8 Apr 1797; d John b- John Summers
  Sally & John Porter 27 May 1806; min- William King
  Sarah & Jacob Beck 22 Dec 1834; min- Augustus Babb
Surface
  Catherine & William Fisher 21 Apr 1803; min- William King
  Rosanna & Martin Fisher 2 Sep 1805; min- William King
  Susannah & Adam Fisher 7 Dec 1801; Minister's return spells name as 'Surfis' d Martin William Fisher, bro of Adam swears latter is of age b- Martin Surface min- William King- 17Dec1801
Swank
  Frances & Larkin Pumphrey 25 Jan 1834; min- J Hoover
  Lydia & Slorum Roller 2 Jan 1834; min- Augustus Babb
  Polly & Jacob Whitmore 18 Oct 1825; min- Michael Meyerhoeffer

Augusta County Marriages -- Woman's Name

Swank (cont.)
  Susan & Reuben Swoope 20 Mar 1834; min- J Hoover
Swartz
  Mary Eliza & Daniel Stover 27 Mar 1845; min- T T Castleman
Swartzley
  Mary & Jacob Wiseman 29 Dec 1794; d John b- John Swartzley
Swatzel
  Mary Ann & James W Sheets 23 Dec 1847; min- Francis McFarland
Swearingen
  Mary & Thomas Guy 14 Feb 1791; Minister's return spells name as 'Swerengin' d Van Robert Guy affirms that Mary is 'reputed' to be 21 b- Robert Guy min- John Montgomery- 23Feb1791
Sweed
  Catharine & Joseph Evy 22 Feb 1844; min- T T Castleman
Swick
  Elizabeth & William Row 30 Jan 1840; min- D F Bittle
  Margaret & John Lilley 12 Oct 1848; min- J McKendree Reiley
Swink
  Barbara & Jacob Fix 4 Dec 1786; d Lawrence b- Henry Swink min- Archibald Scott- 4Dec1786
  Betsy & Spencer Goin 1 Dec 1825; min- Francis McFarland
  Caroline & Reuben Bryan 2 Sep 1845; min- Francis McFarland
  Deniza Jane & Elijah Hunter 22 Feb 1842; min- James Gamble
  Elizabeth & Bestor B Corby 21 Dec 1840; min- John C Hensell- publication of banns
  Margaret W & William A Zimbro 24 Aug 1847; min- Francis McFarland
  Mary Jane & Harvey Lambert 27 Dec 1844; min- Francis McFarland
  Nancy & Joseph Guin 8 Sep 1821; min- John D Ewin
  Rebecca H & Alexander Gardner 4 Jan 1844; min- Francis McFarland
Swisher
  Elizabeth & Joseph Fawber 28 Jul 1798; d John who consents b- John Kaylor test- John Kaler & John Sweitzer
  Elizabeth & William Henderson 9 Sep 1834; min- Joseph Spriggs
  Elizabeth & Hezekiah Taylor 8 Nov 1842; min- John A Van Lear- publication of banns
  Margaret & George Craun 10 Sep 1845; min- P Shickel
  Mary & Jonathan Coiner 7 Apr 1829; min- William Wilson
  Mary & John Hale 19 Jan 1842; min- George B Rimel
  Nancy & John Rimel 23 Dec 1833; min- J Hoover
  Sarah & Jacob Swisher 19 Sep 1836; min- James C Wilson
Switzer
  Elizabeth & Jacob Bosserman 22 Sep 1836; min- J C Hensell
  Frances & Henry Cups 13 Feb 1834; min- William Wilson
  Mary & David Nebergall 10 Apr 1827; min- Michael Meyerhoeffer
  Sarah & Charles Yost 26 Apr 1824; min- Michael Meyerhoeffer
  Susanna & John Donahugh 14 Jun 1849; min- Jacob Bare

Augusta County Marriages -- Woman's Name

Swoope
  Catherine & Peter Paulus 3 Mar 1798; d Peter Schwoop who
    consents   b- Jacob Paulus
  Mary M & William P Kyle 5 Oct 1843; min- S J Love
Swords
  Jane & Thomas Patton 16 May 1811; min- William King
Syford
  Eve & Abraham Leedy 20 May 1803; min- William King
  Polly & Abraham Teebo 25 Jun 1796; d Michael b- Michael
    Syford
Syfort
  Catherine & John Rutherford 10 Apr 1789; d Michael, who
    consents wit- Michael Garber Jr & Thomas Bratton b-
    Michael Garber Jr
Syler
  Margaret & William Carrol 24 Jun 1794; Minister's return
    spells name as 'Carrel' d of Jacob Margaret gives own
    consent test- Daniel Thorp affidavit of Margaret's full
    age b- Hugh Paul min- John McCue- 24Jun1794
Sylor
  Elizabeth & Abraham Laywell 29 Jan 1791; b- John Tennant
Syple
  Catherine & Jacob Michael 15 Apr 1813; min- G H
    Riemenschneider
  Catherine & James Todd 3 Sep 1812; min- William King
  Hana & Jacob Daggy 30 Oct 1816; min- G H Riemenschneider
  Magdalina & Michael Sheetz 25 Nov 1822; min- G H
    Riemenschneider
  Sybill & Michael Daggy 21 Dec 1818; min- G H
    Riemenschneider
Syrcle
  Lydia & George Scrogden 14 Jan 1834; min- Samuel Kennerly
Tackett
  Kesiah & John Townsend 17 Oct 1786; Minister's return
    spells name as 'Heizia Jacks' d Lewis b- Thomas Galford
    wit- Charles Hamilton & Solomon Townsend min- Samuel
    Shannon- 18Oct1786
Talley
  Salley M & Jacob N Fronsman 6 Apr 1826; min- Daniel
    Stephens
Tally
  Jane & John Walters 1 Mar 1827; min- Conrad Speece
  Martha Ann & Arthur Grooms 28 Oct 1824; min- Josiah Cole
Tankesley
  Nancy & William Black 21 Sep 1826; min- Benjamin Denton
Tanner
  Eve & Henry Amend - Sep 1813; min- John Brown
  Mary & George Ailer 22 Apr 1791; d John (German) b- John
    Tanner
Tapp
  Fanny & Dabney Cosley 5 Mar 1801; d Vincent b- Vincent
    Tapp

Augusta County Marriages -- Woman's Name

Tarbert
  Polly & John Darst 9 Jan 1823; min- A B Davidson
Tascott
  Barbara & William Taylor 11 Feb 1816; min- William King-
    publication of banns
Tate
  Catherine & Benjamin Newlan 29 Mar 1787; d Samuel who
    consents test- James Beard & James Sprowl b- Samuel Sprowl
    min- John Brown- 29Mar1787
  Clorinda & James Tate 5 Jan 1820; min- Robert H Chapman
  Elenor & John Finley 21 Apr 1807; min- William McPheeters
  Elenor & Samuel Patterson 6 Dec 1808; min- William
    McPheeters
  Elizabeth M & John Moffett 5 Nov 1823; min- Francis
    McFarland
  Elizabeth & James Allen 3 Sep 1793; d Robert & Margret
    Tate who consents test- Ibby McClung & Polly Tate b- Peter
    Hanger Jr min- John McCue- 5Sep1793
  Elizabeth & Andrew Steele 10 Jun 1795; d James Tate, dec.
    b- Alexander Hall min- John McCue- 18Jun1795
  Fanny & James Hoye 5 Jun 1800; Fanny (of age) sis to Mary
    Shepherd, late Mary Tate James (of age) b- George Grant
    Mcintosh & David Parry
  Jane B & Jacob Vanlear 27 Jan 1814; min- John D Ewin
  Margaret A & Charles L Peyton 9 Jul 1835; min- Francis
    McFarland
  Margaret & Joseph Reidenour 18 Apr 1793
  Mary & Samuel Finley 20 Sep 1796; d John b- John Tate
    min- John Brown- 22Sep1796
  Mary & Samuel Wallace 15 Apr 1794; d Robert b- Robert
    Tate min- John Brown- 24Apr1794
  Nancy & Adam McChesney 10 Jan 1800; d John who consents
    test- Polly Finley b- Isaac Tate
  Phebe & Samuel Wilson 26 Oct 1809; min- William McPheeters
  Sarah & Hugh Fulton 4 May 1785; widow of James Tate b-
    John Tate wit- Anthony Mustoe
Taylor
  Ann & John Royer 16 Jun 1792; d Charles of Augusta con-
    John Taylor Jr b- Dietre Fishburne & John Taylor
  Catharine & John Grooms 12 Apr 1847; min- T T Castleman
  Eliza Ann & David Fox 28 Oct 1841; min- Alfred G Chenowith
  Eliza Jane & Daniel Beard 14 Nov 1839; min- Jacob Bachtel
  Elizabeth F & William W Stiff 1 Aug 1845; min- B N Brown
  Elizabeth & Joseph H Bell 22 Aug 1844; min- G W Israel
  Harriet Ann & John Pitzer 9 Oct 1834; min- George Hildt
  Lovey & James Daft 24 Oct 1811; min- John McCue
  Mary E & James Foster 18 Dec 1849; min- B M Smith
  Mary & Philip Reed 17 Sep 1812; min- William King
  Nancy & Baird Gladwell 27 Jan 1823; min- Josiah Cole
  Patsey & Christian Rusmisel 6 Oct 1831; min- John Hendren
  Rebecca Ann & John S Brown 9 Oct 1849; min- Francis
    McFarland
  Sarah F & David S Bear 2 Dec 1847; min- John Bowen

Augusta County Marriages -- Woman's Name

Teabo
  Elizabeth & Francis Cushingberry 31 Oct 1833; min- George Hildt
Teaford
  Eliza Ann & Jackson Cox 10 Aug 1844; min- D F Bittle
  Jane & John W Brown 11 Sep 1837; min- J C Hensell
  Margaret & Ira Swartsley 29 Nov 1832; min- Francis McFarland
  Mary & William Gilliat 21 Apr 1834; min- Augustus Babb
  Sarah & Arioine McIlree 3 Jun 1828; min- William Calhoon
  Sophanna & Samuel Fletcher 12 Jan 1832; min- William Calhoon
Teany
  Elizabeth & Charles Yearour 8 Apr 1813; min- William King
Tebo
  Mary J & Philip P Pitman 29 Nov 1838; min- Thomas Wheeler
Teebo
  Catherine & Frederick Kurtz 1 Oct 1820; min- Josiah Cole
Teeford
  Elizabeth & Henry Hawp 8 Mar 1790; b- Jacob Teeford
Telfair
  Ann & Robert D Lilley 15 Jun 1824; min- William W Calhoun
Temereman
  Caty & Joseph Sheets 25 Jul 1808; min- William King
Teney
  Margaret P & John Jones 27 May 1828; min- William Wilson
Tennant
  Catherine & Michael Syford 12 Nov 1799; Minister's return spells name as 'Tenant' widower & widow 9of John) b- James McGongal min- William King- 12Nov1799
Tenton
  Polly & Philip Eakel 15 Jun 1809; min- William King
Terrill
  Jane & John D Greiner 29 Feb 1820; min- Robert H Chapman
  Kitty & Joseph Brown 14 Jul 1814; min- John McCue
  Martha Ann & George B Cullen 26 Nov 1846; min- S Wagner
  Martha & Benjamin Reese 23 Jun 1823; min- Francis McFarland
  Sarah W & Robert J Bennett 12 Nov 1845; min- B M Smith
Teter
  Hannah E & Harvey F Smith 20 Feb 1848; min- Jacob C Spitler
  Rebecca Jane & E A Perkey 1 Oct 1845; min- P Shickel
Tetrick
  Elizabeth & George Kraun 15 Aug 1809; min- William King
Tevenbaugh
  Catherine & Christopher Karichoff 21 Dec 1795; Minister's return omits Christopher's surname d Baltzer b- Baltzer Tevenbaugh min- William Wilson- 21Dec1795
Thacker
  Mary Ann & Andrew J Williams 18 May 1843; min- C Parkison
  Sarah & James Hardwick 24 Nov 1828; min- William Wilson
Tharp
  Georgiana & John Givens 8 Sep 1835; min- Samuel Kennerly
  Phebe & Henry Crone 9 Apr 1806; min- William Wilson

Augusta County Marriages -- Woman's Name

Thomas

Barbara & Christian Eakard 2 Jun 1792; d John b- John Thomas

Catherine & Martin Taylor 28 Jan 1791; d Johannes Thommus b- Johannes Thommus (Martin signs his name 'Martin Scheider')

Elizabeth & John Cooke 7 Apr 1812; min- William King

Elizabeth & William Greaver 23 Oct 1826; min- Daniel Stephens

Hannah & Joseph Beck 28 Dec 1785; bond lists 'next friend'(?) as Gilbert Christian min- Archibald Scott- 30Dec1785

Mary & Levi Goodwin 19 Jan 1802; min- William King- 19Jan1802

Peggy & Joseph Brobeck 25 Aug 1808; min- William King

Thomason

Mary & Luke Collins - --- 183-; min- Cornelius Gates- publication of banns

Thompson

Betsey L & James Shields 2 May 1822; min- James C Willson

Eliza Jane & James M Calhoon 9 May 1837; min- William Calhoon

Elizabeth & Abraham Kearns 19 Sep 1795; Minister's return spells name as 'Abraham Coiner' d Andrew b- Andrew Thompson min- Archibald Scott- 29Sep1795

Elizabeth & George Pilson 4 Jan 1795; d Mathew who consents test- John Pilson b- Alexander StClair min- John McCue- 5Jan1796

Elizabeth & William B Porter 28 Oct 1829; min- William Calhoon

Elizabeth & John Scott 5 Jun 1823; min- William W Calhoun

Elizabeth & Matthew Shields 20 Jan 1822; min- John Brown

Hannah & Alexander Woods 7 Aug 1823; min- William W Calhoun

Jane B & John (Jr) Brownlee 12 Jan 1842; min- Francis McFarland

Jane & William McCurdy 25 Dec 1806; min- William Calhoon

Jane & Alexander Thompson 24 May 1799; d Robert who consents test- John Thompson Jean above 21 b- William Blain

Jean & Thomas Brown 21 Aug 1792; Minister's return spells name as 'Mary Thompson' d William b- Robert Wilson Jr min- John McCue- 4Oct1792

Jean & Andrew Hunter 27 Dec 1791

Jenny & John Hughart 30 Jul 1789; d Edward & Jean , who consents b- Daniel Friel min- John Montgomery- 3Aug1789

Margaret Augusta & Paul J Carrington 11 Nov 1845; min- T T Castleman

Martha & Robert Talbert 26 Mar 1787; d William b- Hugh Talbert (Tarbet?) min- Archibald Scott- 29Mar1787

Mary & William Blair 20 Dec 1796; Minister's return spells name as 'Blane' d Alexander who consents test- Alexander Thompson & Peterson Thompson b- Alexander Thompson min- John McCue- 20Dec1796

Mary & John Garvey 10 Mar 1788; b- John Lockridge min- John Brown- 13Mar1788

Augusta County Marriages -- Woman's Name

Thompson (cont.)
  Mary & William Shields 10 Oct 1797; d Mathew who consents
    test- William Thompson & William Marshall b- Walter Herring
    min- John McCue- 12Oct1797
  Mary & Robert Turner 5 Mar 1787; b- Andrew Lackey
    (Lenkey?) min- William Wilson- 5Mar1787
  Mary & Robert Wilson 8 Jun 1799; d William who consents
    Mary sis to Matthew and of age b- Matthew Thompson
  Nancy & Archibald Shields 7 Nov 1805; min- John McCue
  Polly & Joseph Wright 26 Jan 1808; min- William Calhoon
  Rachel & Alexander Berryhill 31 Mar 1786; d William bond
    min- Archibald Scott- 5Apr1786
Thomson
  Isabell & Robert Haslett 2 Oct 1786; Minister's return
    spells names as 'Haslett' and 'Thompson' d William min-
    Archibald Scott- 2Oct1786
Thornton
  Nancy & James Kerr 17 Dec 1818; min- William King
Tiefenbach
  Mary & Abraham Mowry 19 Mar 1798; d Baltzer b- Baltzer
    Tevenbaugh
Tisdale
  Mary & Henry Kirby 19 Aug 1830; min- Gerard Morgan
Todd
  Catharine & David McFall 23 Jul 1842; min- John A Van Lear
  Elizabeth & George Brittain 23 Jul 1823; min- John Hendren
Tolmink
  Ann Catharine & Henry Everhart 19 Jun 1845; min- T T
    Castleman
Tomblinson
  Jane & John Sheetz 20 Jan 1831; min- William Calhoon
Toms
  Margaret & William Baxter 24 Aug 1788; b- John Dickinson
Torbet
  Catherine & Anthony Black 6 Nov 1798; d Robert con- Hugh
    Torbet b- John Torbet Catherine (of age) min- Archibald
    Scott- 10Nov1798
Towberman
  Elizabeth & George Bengas 31 Dec 1816; 'Banjay?' min-
    William King
Towell
  Margaret & Jacob Stover 26 Aug 1800; Jacob (of age) d
    John b- John Towell min- William Wilson- 9Sep1800
  Sally & Thomas Cassady 26 Jan 1813; min- William Wilson
Towerman
  Susannah & John Swatzley 23 Apr 1805; min- William King
Trainer
  Mary & James Shiflett 26 Oct 1825; min- William Wilson
Travis
  Phebe & John Nesbit 10 Nov 1820; min- John D Ewin
Trayer
  Sally Ann & Alexander French 20 Jan 1835; min- George Hildt

Augusta County Marriages -- Woman's Name

Tremper
 Maria H & James F Patterson 4 Mar 1828; min- Joseph Smith
Trible
 Mary & Lewis Jordan 10 Nov 1785; min- John Brown- 10Nov1785
Trimble
 Ann & David Torbet 9 Sep 1799; d Robert who consents test- George Burwell b- John Evans
 Elizabeth & Fergus Graham 8 Mar 1787; d David s Arthur of Rockbridge cty who consents test- John Stuart & Alexander Hindman b- David Trimble min- Archibald Scott- 13Mar1787
 Jane & John Evans 16 Mar 1793; 'Jean?' d Robert b- Robert Trimble no minister listed; clerk's memorandum cites ceremony date as 19Mar1793
 Jane & David McCutchen 17 Dec 1836; min- Isaac Jones (Clerk records another return from Isaac Jones for same couple dated 17Dec1835)
 Jane & Adam Shultz 23 Oct 1838; min- Isaac Jones- publication of banns
 Margaret Ann & John Travis 20 Jan 1825; min- William W Calhoun
 Margaret & Christian Bear 15 Sep 1842; min- S J Love
 Margaret & James McCue 12 Apr 1808; min- John McCue
 Mart & Samuel Jamison 15 Feb 1821; min- William W Calhoun
 Mary & Ephraim Geeding 27 Mar 1828; min- William Calhoon
 Mary & John McKinney 8 Sep 1785; d David min- Archibald Scott- 20Sep1785
 Mary & John Nelson 10 Dec 1813; min- John McCue
 Mary & Moses Powers 29 Apr 1803; min- William King
 Peggy & Thomas P Smith 4 Feb 1808; min- William Calhoon
 Polly & William Young 14 Nov 1809; min- William Calhoon
 Rebecca & James Gilkerson 16 Feb 1833; min- William Calhoon
Trorabaugh
 Catherine & Jacob Smiltzer 16 Mar 1797; d Michael Trorobough, dec. Conrad Plum (Blum) swears Katy been married before and is over 21 b- Conrad Plum
Trorebach
 Mary & Andrew Hafner 6 Jun 1795; d Nicholas b- Nicholas Trorebach
Trorobaugh
 Elizabeth & Henry Myers 16 Oct 1799; d Nicholas b- Nicholas Trorabaugh Henry was apprenticed until he was of age a year before
 Montelany & John Roller 21 Jun 1799; d Nicholas b- Nicholas Trorabaugh
Trotter
 Rebecca & John Dixon 22 May 1810; min- William Wilson
Troughrobaugh
 Catherine & John Daggy 20 May 1794; b- Nicholas Troughrobaugh
Trout
 Elizabeth & Horatio White 15 Sep 1834; min- William Scull
 Jane & Samuel Fawber 14 Jan 1819; min- William King
 Magdalina & Philip Thurman 25 May 1825; min- William Wilson
 Mary & John Armstrong 3 Feb 1820; min- William Calhoon

Augusta County Marriages -- Woman's Name

Trout (cont.)
  Sarah & James Desper 12 Jul 1826; min- William Wilson
Troxal
  Susanna & George Olinger 13 Sep 1810; min- William Calhoon
Troxall
  Catherine & Michaes Rodgers 24 Jun 1791; sis of Peter who
    consents (Catherine's parents both deceased) wit- John
    Moore & Peter Wilson b- Valentine Miller
Troxel
  Polly & Samuel Cunningham 15 Jun 1826; min- James Morrison
  Rachel & David Buchanan 8 Feb 1827; min- James Morrison
  Rachel & David Hemp 28 Nov 1844; min- J C Hensell
  Susan & Isaiah Waid 15 Aug 1833; min- John S Watt
Troxell
  Catharine & John Troxell 25 Apr 1839; min- John C Hensell
  Nancy & Amos Jarvis 11 Dec 1834; min- Conrad Speece
Trump
  Agnes & John Phifer 5 Apr 1803; min- William King
  Catherine & Isaiah Curry 24 Jan 1803; min- William King
Tuening
  Elizabeth & Jeremiah Jarvis 27 Mar 1834; min- Conrad Speece
Tumbleston
  Peggy & John (Jr) Canote 7 Jun 1798; d Thomas b- Thomas
    Tumbleston min- John McCue- 7Jun1798
Tumblin
  Catherine & Jesse Evans 8 Mar 1810; min- Joseph Reid
  Elizabeth & Daniel Rutt 22 Jul 1799; Minister's return
    spells names as 'Daniel Rule and Elizabeth Tumbling' d
    Thomas b- Henry Huff min- William King- 1Aug1799
Tummins
  Elizabeth & Cyrus Brown 22 Aug 1843; min- B M Smith
Turk
  Elizabeth & James Coger 19 Jul 1797; Minister's return
    spells name as 'James Conger' d Thomas Turk Sr who consents
    test- James Turk b- James Johnston min- William Wilson-
    20Jul1797
  Elizabeth & Thomas Harris 20 Jun 1814; min- Wright Burgess
  Esther & James Johnston 19 Dec 1786; d Thomas Sr b-
    William Robertson s Zachariah min- William Wilson-
    19Dec1786
  Peggy & William Robertson 16 Mar 1808; min- William King
  Polly & Thomas McCulloch 31 Aug 1802; min- John McCue-
    31Aug1802
Turner
  Martha & John McMullen 16 May 1788; Minister's return
    spells name as 'McMullon' b- James Frazer min- Archibald
    Scott- 16May1788
  Matilda & Austin Hunley 12 Mar 1835; min- John Hendren
Turnins
  Catherine & Jacob Zink 18 Jun 1818; min- Wright Burgess
Turnipseed
  Janetta & George Patton 22 Oct 1835; min- William Calhoon
  Margaret & Thomas J Patton 26 Sep 1839; min- Isaac Jones

Augusta County Marriages -- Woman's Name

Tuttle
Sarah S & David J Kenny 28 Mar 1832; min- Samuel Kennerly
Tutwiler
Mary & Peter Whitzel 18 Oct 1796; Minister's return spells name as 'Whitsel and Mary Fulwiler' d Leonard b- Leonard Tutwiler min- John McCue- 19Oct1796
Underwood
Elenor & John Skiner 22 Jan 1788; min- William Wilson- 22Jan1788
Usher
Ann & Hugh Donaghe 19 Aug 1795; d Robert b- Archibald Stuart min- William Wilson- 21Aug1795
Jenny & Gersham Clements 22 Apr 1791; d Robert, who consents wit- David & Francis Bell b- David Bell min- William Wilson- 22Apr1791
Polly & John Link 31 Oct 1805; min- William Wilson
Vachub
Isbell & David Chambers 18 Oct 1794; d John who consents test- William McKee & William Dunlap b- William McKee min- John Montgomery- 23Oct1794
Jane & Alexander Dunlap 20 Jun 1791; d John Vachub, who consents wit- Alexander Dod & Joseph Vachub b- William McPheeters min- John Montgomery- 21Jun1791
Valentine
Mary E & John W Jones 19 Nov 1840; min- Frederick D Goodwin
Vance
Elizabeth & James Long 24 Jan 1839; min- George Huffman
Rachel & James Hamilton 16 Sep 1786; d Samuel b- William Armstrong of Back Creek min- Samuel Shannon- 21Sep1786
Vancent
Derthy & Joseph Dannell 24 Sep 1804; min- William King
Vanfossen
Elizabeth & Francis Lambert 21 Nov 1801; Minister's return spells name as 'Vanfasson' d Jacob b- Jacob Vanfossen min- William King- 26Nov1801
Margaret & Henry Puffenbarger 24 Aug 1815; min- William King
Susanna & William Anderson 1 Jul 1817; min- William King
Vanlear
Arabella & David Caldwell 7 Aug 1806; min- John McCue
Elizabeth G & Charles A Baskins 6 Mar 1827; min- Conrad Speece
Jane & William Thompson 30 Aug 1826; min- John Hendren
Peggy & William McKee 1 Feb 1803; min- John McCue
Sally & William Davis 30 Nov 1813; min- Thomas Bourne
Sarah & William Baskins 16 Jan 1829; min- Conrad Speece
Vantrump
Mary & Joseph Mathews 12 Oct 1811; min- William King
Varner
Elizabeth & Samuel McCullock 4 Feb 1793; d Henry who consents test- John Copenhaver & Andrew Wallace b- Cornelius Odear no minister listed; clerk's memorandum cites ceremony date as 5Feb1793
Peggy & John Copehaver 29 Jul 1789; b- Henry Verner

Augusta County Marriages -- Woman's Name

Varnum
  Lidia & Lawson McCullough 7 Jan 1790; Minister's return
    spells name as 'Vernum' d Elizabeth, widow wit- John
    Varnum b- John Varnum min- John Brown- 11Jan1790
Vauchob
  Jane & William Deitz 20 Jul 1796; Minister's return spells
    name as 'William Dietz & Jane Vachub' d Robert b- Robert
    Wahob min- John Montgomery- 26Jul1796
Vernon
  Elizabeth & John Boyd 18 Jun 1787; Minister's return
    spells name as 'Vernom' b- George Campbell min- John
    Brown- 26Jun1787
Vernum
  July Ann & Martin Holmes 3 Mar 1797; d Daniel b- Daniel
    Vernum
  Rebecca & Jameston Patterson 12 May 1796; d Abrahaim sis
    to John Vernum b- John Vernum
Vians
  Jenney & Thomas Gregory 21 Nov 1818; 'Fanny Vines' min-
    William King
Vines
  Jane & Abraham Harbarger 3 Aug 1795; d Thomas Thomas
    Masterson affirm that Jane above 21 and has lived in the
    county about 12 months b- Roger Sullivan
  Lucy & Jacob Sly 13 Dec 1796; d Thomas who consents   s
    Henry Sligh who consents test- James Kelly b- John Chesnut
Waddell
  Cornelia S & Samuel D Stuart 15 Nov 1838; min- William
    Calhoon
  Lucy Ann & William D Cooke 27 Sep 1834; min- William
    Calhoon
Waddle
  Jane & Edward Erwin 2 Apr 1792; Minister's return spells
    name as 'Wooddell' b- Thomas Wooddell min- Benjamin Irwin-
    3Apr1792
  Mary & Jacob Bumgarner 28 Jun 1785; d John bond
  Susan & John Carico 3 Aug 1810; min- William King
Waddy
  Elizabeth B & Jonathan Brewer 8 Oct 1840; min- John C
    Hensell- publication of banns
  Sarah & Edward Cason 10 Jun 1824; min- Josiah Cole
Wade
  Margaret & William McFadden 13 Aug 1821; min- Daniel
    Stephens
  Martha & John Armstrong 29 Aug 1822; min- John Brown
  Priscilla & Abraham Gum 8 Jun 1785; d John b- William
    Slaven wit- William Slaven & John Gum min- Samuel Shannon-
    20Apr1785
Waggener
  Peggy & Silas Hogshead 7 Nov 1816; min- William King
Waggy
  Elizabeth & Adam Lamb 18 Oct 1803; min- William King

Augusta County Marriages -- Woman's Name

Wagner
  Catharine & Peter Lambert 29 Jul 1831; min- John Hendren- publication of banns
  Elizabeth & Tobias Tanner - Jun 1804; min- John Brown
  Eve & Jacob Shue - Mar 1806; min- John Brown

Wagoner
  Mary & Jacob Nebergall 17 Nov 1824; min- Michael Meyerhoeffer

Wakely
  Margret & David Alexander 21 Mar 1839; min- J Killian

Walace
  Elizabeth & Archibald McClung 27 Jan 1825; min- Francis McFarland

Walch
  Sophia & John Doom 5 Dec 1809; min- William King

Walker
  Barbara & William Donaldson 6 Sep 1792; wrd of Elizabeth Walker, who consents wit- Robert & John Reed, Hugh & Elizabeth Donaghe, Wm McMahon b- Robert Reed min- William Wilson- 6Sep1792
  Elizabeth & Robert Hook 1 May 1817; min- Conrad Speece, Jr
  Isabella & Robert Reed 19 Jan 1790; d Elizabeth, widow, who consents b- John Walker min- William Wilson- 19Jan1790
  Mary & Thomas Frame 3 Jun 1819; min- Conrad Speece, Jr
  Patsey & John Johnston 29 Dec 1837; min- John J Reimensnyder
  Rebecca & Charles McClung 4 Dec 1834; min- Samuel Kennerly
  Sarah & Alben W Eaton 20 Aug 1835; min- Samuel Kennerly- publication of banns
  Sarah & Zachariah Johnston 23 Dec 1823; min- Conrad Speece

Walkup
  Rebecca & John Sims 6 Jan 1806; min- William King

Wallace
  Betsey & David Griffith 6 Jan 1815; min- William Calhoon
  Cinderella & James (Jr) Mays 6 Nov 1839; min- A B McCorkle
  Eleanor & John Cooper 21 May 1832; min- James Kerr
  Ellen P & Samuel Witherow 13 Jun 1839; min- A B McCorkle
  Margaret & Benjamin Erwin 24 Sep 1793; d Robert b- Robert Wallace no minister listed; clerk's memorandum cites ceremony date as 26Sep1793
  Margaret & David McKinny 26 Sep 1785; McKenny? d James min- Archibald Scott- 26Sep1785
  Maria & Benjamin S McClung 29 Dec 1825; min- Francis McFarland
  Martha & John Ruff 5 Oct 1804; min- William King
  Martha & Robert Young 24 Feb 1801; Thomas Wallace swears Martha is of age b- Robert Anderson min- John McCue- 26Feb1801

Walls
  Nancy & John Thornton 23 Feb 1809; min- William King
  Sally & George Mines 25 Mar 1839; min- John C Hensell

Walters
  Jane & Joseph Allen 6 Feb 1845; min- T T Castleman

Augusta County Marriages -- Woman's Name

Walton
  Catherine & Charles Bruce 15 Oct 1793; Minister's return spells name as 'Catherine Walters' b- Moses Jackson min- William Wilson- 17Oct1793
  Melinda & William Vanstaven 5 Feb 1822; min- William W Calhoun
  Pamely & James Via 23 Dec 1823; min- William W Calhoun
Ward
  Betsy & John Scott 25 Aug 1808; min- Joel Watson
  Elizabeth & Jacob Rush - May 1811; min- John Brown
Ware
  Nancy & David Hays 5 Apr 1824; Free persons of color min- John Hendren
Warner
  Catherine & James Alderman 8 Jun 1795; d Henry who consents test- John Boswell b- John Boswell
  Elizabeth & Jacob Faber - Sep 1809; min- John Brown
  Mary & George Hook 22 Jun 1791; 'Mary Weaver?' min- William Wilson- 22Jun1791
Warrenburgh
  Mary & William Shepard 11 Mar 1802; min- William King- 11Mar1802
Warrick
  Margaret & David Gregory 2 Feb 1786; s of Mary d of William b- William Rider wit- John Slavins min- Samuel Shannon- 9Feb1786
Waseman
  Polley & Henry Sheets 15 Jun 1815; min- William King
  Susan & David Rusk 5 Jan 1815; min- William King
Waters
  Priscilla & Elijah Moore 22 Apr 1822; min- John Hendren
Watkins
  Elizabeth & James Walls 5 Jul 1791; d Christiana Louisa Kidd who consents, along with her guardian Daniel Kidd wit- George White & Mary White b- George White
  Martha & John Robison 8 Nov 1832; min- William Calhoon
  Polly & George White 26 Feb 1791; Polly certifies her own age wit- John Martin & George White b- Smith Thompson
Watson
  Mary & David Wyan 3 Nov 1808; min- William McPheeters
Way
  Susanna & Cornelius Hall 13 Dec 1810; min- William Calhoon
Wayland
  Rebecca R & Robert H Kinney 20 May 1841; min- Benjamin M Smith
Wayt
  Sarah A & Robert Porterfield 17 Nov 1842; min- B M Smith
Weade
  Martha Ann & Gideon Barnhart 13 Mar 1845; min- S Wagner
Weast
  Catharine & John Wenner 26 Dec 1847; min- John Reubush
  Sarah & William Fort 8 Oct 1835; min- William G Jackson

Augusta County Marriages -- Woman's Name

Weathers
  Polly & John Martin 28 Dec 1820; min- William Calhoon
Weaver
  Betsy & David Bowers 25 Sep 1826; min- Daniel Stephens
  Betsy & John Goodnight - Aug 1825; min- John Brown
  Charity & Robert Donaldson 9 Jun 1831; min- Francis
    McFarland
  Charity & William Grow 7 Sep 1837; min- J C Hensell
  Chatrine & Valentine Carell 25 Aug 1808; min- William King
  Elizabeth & Jacob (Jr) Brosius 16 Nov 1833; min- James
    Morrison
  Elizabeth & Henry Miller 8 Jun 1797; d John Peter Weaver
    who consents test- William Sterritt & Thomas Douthat s
    Martin Moller who consents test- Luke Collins & John Kisner
    b- John Kesner
  Elizabeth & John Stickleman 16 Apr 1787; Minister's return
    spells name as 'Sickleman' b- John Waid permission by
    Christiana Weaver (mother), John Waid, Peter Weaver & Philip
    Steigleman (brothers) min- Archibald Scott- 19Apr178
  Jane & Mahlon Armstrong 29 Jan 1829; min- John Hendren
  Margaret & Philip Stickleman 31 Jan 1787; d Peter who
    consents test- William McClure b- William McClure min-
    Archibald Scott- 2Feb1787
  Mary & Samuel Varley 28 Mar 1796; d Peter who consents
    test- Andrew Weaver & John Waid b- Jacob Worley
  Polly & Joseph Hess 11 Aug 1826; min- Daniel Stephens
  Polly & Thompson Owens 20 Sep 1830; min- John Hendren
  Rachel & John Kisner 22 Mar 1794; d Peter who consents
    test- Philip Steigleman & Rebecka Weaver b- Philip
    Stickleman no minister listed; clerk's memorandum cites
    ceremony date as 26Mar1794
  Rebecca Ann & Hugh L Risk 27 Aug 1835; min- Henry Brown
  Rebecca & David M Greiner 26 May 1848; min- D W Arnold
  Sarah & Abraham Weaver 3 May 1832; min- Henry Brown
Web
  Hannah M & Jefferson Hall 11 Apr 1832; min- John Hendren
Webb
  Elizabeth & William Harris 18 Dec 1792; b- Thomas
    Tombleston
  Jacyntha & Clinton Stanton 18 Apr 1825; min- John Hendren
  Mary & John Miller 19 Jul 1827; min- James Morrison
  Rachel & William F Black 13 Mar 1834; min- Francis
    McFarland
Weckle
  Elizabeth & John Sherror 14 Jan 1805; min- Benjamin Irwin
Weed
  Elizabeth & John Carpenter 27 Mar 1815; min- Wright Burgess
Weeks
  Martha & William Patterson 8 Jan 1846; min- James Paine
Weickel
  Sarah Jane & John Casady 27 Nov 1845; min- P Shickel
Weiford
  Elizabeth & John Gilbraith 7 Nov 1826; min- Daniel Stephens
  Peggy & David Redifer 2 May 1799; Minister's return spells
    name as 'David Rodefer and Margaret Werferd' d George
    Wayford b- George Weiford

Augusta County Marriages -- Woman's Name

Weiford (cont.)
  Polly & William Caslen 26 Sep 1806; min- William King
Weigle
  Elizabeth & John Mackaby 10 Mar 1803; min- William King
  Margaret & Samuel Andrew 9 Apr 1800; d Philip b- Philip Weigle min- William Wilson- 14Apr1800
Weikle
  Mary & Henry Harmon 20 Feb 1799; d Philip b- Philip Weikle
Weitzel
  Elizabeth F & Andrew H Clinedinst 11 May 1843; min- Samuel Wagner
  Jane & Jacob Fawner 30 Jan 1799; d Anthony Weitzel, dec. b- John Fawner Jacob was 21 on 10Mar1798 Jane also of age
  Sarah Jane & James Murry 10 Sep 1840; min- Samuel Wagner
Welch
  Ellen & James E Crawford 19 Apr 1831; min- William Calhoon
  Polly & John Patterson 8 Feb 1820; min- Daniel Stephens
Weller
  Eliza & Philip C Linn 23 Dec 1847; min- S Hildebrand
  Margaret & Christian Eakle 18 Nov 1845; min- G W Israel
Welsh
  Elizabeth & William Ness - Jan 1809; min- John Brown
  Mary Ann & Edward C Williams 16 Oct 1828; min- Basil Barry
Wenger
  Elizabeth & Abraham Kindig 5 Nov 1846; min- J A Van Lear
  Polley & Peter Cline 16 Apr 1816; min- William King
Werley
  Lea & Henry Clinebill 28 Mar 1833; min- Francis McFarland
Wesit
  Hannah & Christian Iseman 4 Feb 1826; min- Michael Meyerhoeffer
West
  Susanna & James Brownlee 11 Jul 1816; min- William Wilson
Western
  Eliza Ann & William Peters 14 Sep 1843; min- Samuel Wagner
  Margaret Jane & John G Forbes 17 Jul 1845; min- T T Castleman
Wheeler
  Margaret F & Peter H Snyder 21 Feb 1842; min- John W Stine
Wheeling
  Nancy & James Hanlen 30 Dec 1788; b- John Rhea (Reaugh) min- James Chambers- 30Dec1788
Whetesel
  Frances C & Daniel Goin 11 Mar 1845; min- P Shickel
Whisman
  Nancy & John Ryan 14 May 1838; min- Z Freeman
  Sarah A & B H Morris 9 Mar 1843; min- P E Stevenson
White
  Anna & Philip Smith 25 May 1819; min- Wright Burgess
  Anne & John Coiner 21 Sep 1823; min- John Watson
  Catrine & Thomas Weles 29 Dec 1785; min- John Brown- 29Dec1785
  Elizabeth F & Harrison Keeran 8 Jun 1848; min- J C Hensell
  Isabella & William Hutcheson 14 May 1812; min- John McCue

Augusta County Marriages -- Woman's Name

White (cont.)
Margaret & John Russell 14 Aug 1797; Margaret (of age) d Isaac White, dec. b- James White min- John McCue- 14Aug1797
Mary Jane & Cyrus Shultz 3 Jan 1837; min- Stephen Smith
Mary S & William W Smith 20 Mar 1850; min- James Paine
Mary & William Plumb 24 Apr 1821; min- William W Calhoun

Whitemore
Elizabeth & Daniel Sheets 27 Mar 1790; min- William Wilson- 27Mar1790

Whitesell
Elizabeth & James Wheeler 26 Dec 1839; min- Frederick D Goodwin
Mary M & William T Cooper 5 Jul 1838; min- Thomas Wheeler
Mary W & James A Kelly 19 Mar 1840; min- P E Stevenson
Sarah A & Hamson Offlighter 5 Nov 1840; min- Frederick D Goodwin

Whiteside
Catherine & James Usher 6 Dec 1788; d John who consents test- John Whitesides & Alexander Henry b- James Megongal min- James Chambers- 8Dec1788

Whitlock
Mary Jain & Noah J Minnick 22 Apr 1845; min- Jacob Baer
Susan C & George W Hanger 30 Aug 1849; min- Samuel Martin

Whitmore
Elizabeth A & John H Will 30 Oct 1846; min- Stephen Hildebrand
Nancy & John McCausland 9 Jul 1835; min- William Scull
Polly & Philip Coiner 25 Mar 1819; min- William King
Rebecca & George Hernsberger 21 May 1846; min- J A Van Lear
Susannah & Jacob Forer 4 Sep 1840; min- Jacob Killian

Whitsel
Catherine & John Schnebly 7 Jan 1808; min- William Calhoon

Whitsell
Barbara & John Eagle 27 Jun 1803; min- William King
Mary & John H East 27 Dec 1849; min- T T Castleman
Sally & George Grant McIntosh 17 Sep 1796; Sally (of age) d Christopher Whitsell b- Peter Heiskell min- John McCue- 19Sep1797
Susannah C & Robert Swink 30 Aug 1838; min- Thomas Wheeler

Whitzel
Cathorine & George Greiner 31 Aug 1797; Cathorine (of age) d ----- Whitzel, dec. b- Abraham Garber

Wicle
Maria & John G Naher 17 Jan 1834; min- John Hendren

Wiekle
Peggy & William Dodson 9 Jun 1813; bond- 29Jun1813(sic) min- William Cravens

Wilds
Margaret & George Wilson 26 Sep 1809; min- Joseph Reid

Wilen
Anna & John Gates 6 Nov 1786; b- John Ritter min- William Wilson- 6Nov1786

Augusta County Marriages -- Woman's Name

Wiley
  Ann & John McGlaughlin 27 Oct 1790; d Robert, who consents wit- Thomas Stinson & John McIntire b- Robert Wiley

Wilfong
  Ann & George Pumphrey - --- 183-; min- John Hendren- publication of banns

Williams
  Catherine & John McCarty 6 Sep 1808; min- William McPheeters
  Elizabeth & Wesley Scott 25 Jan 1825; min- Luke Collins- publication of banns
  Margaret Jane & Samuel B Sproul 21 Aug 1834; min- Conrad Speece
  Margaret & Gabriel Pendell 16 May 1786; Minister's return spells name as 'Pendleton' d Moses b- Zachariah Estill wit- George Hudson, David Williams min- William Wilson- 16May1786
  Martha & John (Jr) Summers 17 Nov 1787; b- John Summers Sr
  Mary Ann & George W Bridgett 15 Apr 1841; min- J J Reimensnyder
  Rachel & Joseph Henry 30 Sep 1800; d John who consents test- William whitesides b- George Williams
  Susannah & Jesse Ailstrop 14 Jan 1802; d John wit- John Williams b- Alexander StClair

Willis
  Frances & John Miller 4 May 1842; min- Alfred G Chenowith

Willson
  Julia Ann & John L McCune 2 May 1832; min- James C Wilson
  Lucy & George Parson 9 Apr 1829; min- Conrad Speece
  Margaret A B & John J Larew 15 Feb 1844; min- Francis McFarland
  Nancy & William Hamilton 7 Jun 1832; min- William Calhoon
  Susan & Robert Hanna 6 Sep 1825; min- Francis McFarland

Wilson
  Eliza Jane & John H Brown 28 Jun 1849; min- Francis McFarland
  Elizabeth & Thomas Cooper 5 Mar 1798; d Robert b- James McKemy & Robert Wilson min- William Wilson- 7Mar1798
  Elizabeth & Andrew Dixon 19 Mar 1799; widow of Thomas b- George Borrel & John Jones s Martin (Morton) Dixon signed - 'George Burwell' min- William King- 19Mar1799
  Elizabeth & David Finley 9 Mar 1791; d Joseph, who consents wit- Alexander Gibson Jr b- Alexander Gibson Jr min- Archibald Scott- 10Mar1791
  Elizabeth & David Hart 29 Jan 1798; Elizabeth (of age) d William Wilson Sr, sis William Wilson Jr b- William Wilson Jr
  Fanny & Samuel Skelton 6 Jan 1807; min- William King
  Isabella Jane & John Shaver 10 May 1842; min- S J Love
  Jane & Cornelius Vanosdal 11 Apr 1785; min- Samuel Shannon- 11Apr1785
  Jane & Cornelius Vanosdale 2 Apr 1785; Minister's return spells name as 'Vanosdal' d William s of Cornelius b- Elibabb Wilson wit- Ralph & Elibab Wilson min- John Rodgers- 11Apr1785

Augusta County Marriages -- Woman's Name

Wilson (cont.)
  Jane & Adam Zumbro 28 Mar 1816; min- John McCue
  Jean & Thomas Sharp 20 Nov 1794; 'Mary Willson?' d Mathew b- John Sharp no minister listed; clerk's memorandum cites ceremony date as 3Dec1794
  Margaret Ann & William W Baskin 14 May 1832; min- James C Wilson
  Margaret & George Danner 11 Aug 1798; Margaret (of age) d James b- Henry Amon min- William Wilson- 16Aug1798
  Mary J L & Robert S Larew 14 Dec 1837; min- A B McCorkle
  Mary & Thomas Harris 25 Jan 1816; min- John McCue
  Mary & Thomas W Shelton 1 Apr 1842; min- B M Smith
  Nancy & Samuel Crawford 21 May 1805; min- Benjamin Irwin
  Peggy & James Trimble 20 Nov 1806; min- William Calhoon
  Polly & Samuel Erwin 10 Jun 1806; min- William Calhoon
  Rachel & John Gardiner 20 Jul 1789; Minister's return spells name as 'Gardner' d Rachel Willson, who consents b- James Gardiner wit- William Willson & James Willson min- Archibald Scott- 20Jul1789
  Rachel & John Wilson 7 Mar 1786; d Robert b- Robert Wilson wit- Robert Wilson Jr & Thomas Wilson min- Archibald Scott- 9Mar1786
  Rebecca & James Bush 30 Nov 1815; min- John McCue
  Sally & Mathias Swink 27 Sep 1787; d Robert s Lawrence b- Jacob Swallow wit- William Heart & William Christian min- Archibald Scott- 28Sep1786
  Sally & Enoch Yates 20 Jan 1803; min- William King
  Sarah & William Logan 22 Nov 1792; Hugh Wilson certifies before Robert Douthat that Sarah of age and lives in Augusta cty b- Hugh Wilson & Robert Bailey
  Sarah & William Thompson 29 Dec 1801; Minister's return spells name as 'Willson' d Joseph Mathew Malcolm attests to Sarah's age Jane Cawley attests to William's age b- Michael Cawley min- William King- 29Dec1801

Wine
  Barbara & Thomas Leaguet 20 Feb 1817; 'League?' min- William King
  Catharine & Samuel Miller 28 Nov 1844; min- T T Castleman
  Elizabeth & Elias Kindig 6 Sep 1838; min- John Garber
  Susanna & Christley Brown 12 Dec 1815; min- Abraham Garber- publication of banns

Winefield
  ----- & Jacob Woltz 18 Apr 1797; min- John McCue- 18Apr1797

Winegardner
  Barbara & Ralph Smith 26 Jan 1819; min- William King

Wineinger
  Peggy & George Sluser 18 May 1795; d John who consents & Caty Wineinger who consents test- Peter Troxell b- David Kershner

Wingfield
  Betsy & John Hays 20 Jan 1807; min- Benjamin Brughes
  Dolly & John Silvers 7 Dec 1804; min- John McCue
  Maria & William Ancell 30 Mar 1809; min- William King

Augusta County Marriages -- Woman's Name

Winters
  Nancy & George Crawford 22 Jun 1789; b- Robert Gamble
    min- Benjamin Erwin- 23Jun1789
Wise
  Eliza & Archibald D Trotter 5 Jan 1843; min- A G Chenowith
  Susana & Jacob Lamb - Apr 1806; min- John Brown
Wisehart
  Polly & Philip Rust 12 Mar 1800; widower min- William
    Wilson- 12Mar1800
Wiseman
  Catherine & George Dull 28 Mar 1798; d Peter b- Peter
    Wiseman
  Christiana & Jacob Smith 12 May 1796; d Peter b- Peter
    Wiseman
  Elizabeth & Peter Cale 22 Nov 1838; min- John C Hensell
  Margaret & Henry J Bowers 21 Jan 1847; min- J C Hensell
  Mary Ann & Samuel (Jr) Stover 9 Nov 1848; min- Alonzo P
    Ludden
  Susan & John Craig 11 Oct 1828; min- James Morrison
  Susan & David Lortz 28 Mar 1844; min- J C Hensell
Wishart
  Polly & Philip Rush 10 Mar 1800; 'Weisshart?' d Nicholas
    b- Nicholas Weisshart
Withrow
  Elizabeth & William Beard 13 Aug 1837; min- James Morrison
  Sarah & John McDowell 13 Aug 1788; John from Staunton d
    William consent for Sarah by Robert Withrow of Mossy Creek
    b- Griffith Evans of Staunton min- Benjamin Erwin- 16Aug1788
Witsel
  Susannah & David Trout 29 Sep 1787; b- Valentine Forbes
Witts
  Sarah & William Frey 12 Feb 1829; min- John Hendren
Woland
  Christina & John Yost 3 Jun 1799; d ----- Woland, dec. b-
    Micajah Coalter min- William King- 6Jun1799
  Mary & Thomas Bell 18 Apr 1798; d Jacob b- Adam Bickle
Wolf
  Elizabeth & Christopher Moeler 29 Nov 1809; min- William
    King
Wolfe
  Fanny & Nicolas Pauss 25 Oct 1786; sis Andrew b- Andrew
    Wolfe
Wonderlake
  Isabella & George Imboden 21 May 1822; min- Michael
    Meyerhoeffer
  Polly & Robert Walker 1 Dec 1821; min- Michael Meyerhoeffer
Wonderlick
  Eliza & Paul Rosenbarger 29 Jul 1833; min- J Hoover
  Rosana & Enos Dunahugh 7 Oct 1847; min- John Reubush
Wood
  J R & J Maupin 10 Sep 1835; min- Robert M Lipscomb
  Jane & Gabriel Cross 11 Dec 1838; min- Robert Beers
  Jinney & Joseph Blair 20 Nov 1816; min- Wright Burgess
  Malinda & Shepherd H Hite 11 May 1839; min- James Paine

Augusta County Marriages -- Woman's Name

Wood (cont.)
Sarah & William Jones 30 May 1787; 'Johns?' d James who consents test- Thomas Duglas & William Killpatrick Wm Jordan swears Sarah 18 on Jan 29 last and Wm is 21 b- William Jordan min- Samuel Shannon- 5Jun1787

Woodram
Mary & George West 30 Aug 1787; Mary gives her own consent test- Joseph Bell & William Bell Jr b- James Lyle Jr

Woods
Amanda W & James Brady 20 Nov 1834; min- George Hildt
Catharine & Michael Crone 1 Nov 1816; min- William King
Elizabeth & Daniel Donavin 19 Aug 1794; Affidavit as to Elizabeth's full age b- Jacob Woods
Martha & John Wilson 24 Jun 1817; min- John McCue
Mary & Charles Brown 28 Nov 1786; d Mary bond min- Archibald Scott- 30Nov1786
Polly & John Ballard 21 Sep 1809; min- William King
Sally & Samuel McComb 22 Oct 1817; min- William King

Woodson
Emily & James Alexander 16 Feb 1843; min- B M Smith

Woodward
Eveline H & Caleb Crone 2 Jan 1849; min- John Bowen
Lucy & James Cain 28 Apr 1812; bond min- Ezra Grover- 30Apr1812
Mary G & Hamilton E Ocheltree 13 Dec 1832; min- William Wilson
Mary Jane & Albert G McCutchen 21 Jun 1836; min- Isaac Jones
Rebecca & Okey Quick 27 Feb 1832; min- William Wilson

Woolf
Beck & Lawrence Zimmerman 4 Jun 1792; b- Christopher Zimmerman

Woolwine
Elizabeth & James McLaughlin 1 Feb 1787; Minister's return spells name as 'Laughlin' d Elizabeth Wolvine who consents test- G Cordell & John Gorden b- John Moore min- Archibald Scott- 2Feb1787
Harriet & Martin Weigant 21 Mar 1842; min- P E Stevenson
Susanna & John Hively 20 May 1800; d Philip Woolwine, dec. & Edward Woolwine who consents Both (of age) b- Jacob Woolwine min- William King- 20May1800

Worth
Mary & Robert Wilkerson 17 Dec 1793; b- James Brownlee

Wright
Agness & John Heitzer 22 Apr 1800; d Joseph b- Joseph Wright
Betsy & Gilbert Deemster 30 Nov 1826; min- William W Calhoun
Catherine & Thomas Griffey 28 Mar 1786; d William b- John Andiddie wit- Robert Caldwall min- Samuel Carrick- 28Mar1786
Mary Ann & Abraham Rinehart 30 Jun 1814; min- William Wilson
Mary M & John H Whitesell 8 Jun 1843; min- C Parkison

Augusta County Marriages -- Woman's Name

Wright (cont.)
Nancy & William Jenkins 30 May 1810; min- William King
Polly & William Poage 3 Nov 1800; d William s William
    (see Introduction for complete information on this bond)
Rosanna & Samuel Black 23 Apr 1787; Minister's return
    spells name as 'Rosana' b- Alexander Wright
Ruth Ann & Rodney B Henderson 21 Oct 1847; min- Francis
    McFarland
Ruth Ann & James J Martin 13 Jan 1848; min- James Morrison
Sarah Jane & John H Fix 11 Nov 1847; min- Francis McFarland
Sarah L & John Withrow 29 May 1845; min- James Morrison
Wyand
Catharine & Simon Stofer - Jan 1804; min- John Brown
Wyatt
Mary A & Joseph A Hillary 11 Apr 1822; min- Josiah Cole
Xaupi
Josaphine & Archibald P Stuart 13 Aug 1840; min- Frederick
    D Goodwin
Louisa Virginia & Abel G Bell 24 Nov 1846; min- J A Van
    Lear
Yancy
Frances & John Zumbro 29 Oct 1840; min- Jacob Killian
Yearouse
Catharine & Michael Puffenberry 4 Nov 1793; Minister's
    return spells name as 'Yearhouse' d Charles b- Charles
    Yearouse min- William Wilson- 5Nov1793
Yearout
Dolly & Frederick A Mayo 29 May 1810; min- William King
Elizabeth & George Pepperley 21 Feb 1801; Minister's
    return spells name as 'Pepperly' d Charles ('Jahrous?') b-
    Charles Yearout min- William King- 26Feb1801
Susanah & David McCarty 30 Jan 1806; min- William King
Yonas
Sophia & William Brukmann 26 Apr 1806; min- William King
Yorkshire
Nancy & Matthew Woods 11 Oct 1810; min- John McCue
Yost
Elizabeth & John David Greiner 23 May 1793; d Henry who
    consents test- John Garber & Edward Burk con- A Mustoe
    test- Phill North & Charles O'Neil b- Adam Bickle
Elizabeth & Morris Jones 31 Jan 1828; min- John Hendren
Polly & Robert Douthat 6 Nov 1800; d Henry, sis of Polly
    (?), who swears Polly is of age b- David Greiner
Rebecca & Sampson Eagan 1 Jun 1796; d Henry b- Henry Yost
    min- John McCue- 22Jun1796
Youel
Christena & Andrew Lockridge 20 Mar 1797; Minister's
    return spells name as 'Christiana Youel' d William b-
    William Youel min- John Montgomery- 23Mar1797
Polly & Robert ----- 6 Nov 1800; min- William Wilson-
    6Nov1800
Young
Agnes & James Graham 12 Jun 1804; min- William King
Agness & William Cunningham 5 Apr 1825; min- William W
    Calhoun

Augusta County Marriages -- Woman's Name

Young (cont.)
Elizabeth & Thomas Garvin 21 Apr 1789; d James, who consents b- Andrew Young wit- John Dickey & William Hook
Elizabeth & Hugh Kennedy 25 Nov 1802; min- James Harper- 25Nov1802
Elizabeth & Abraham McNeil 20 Dec 1834; min- George Hildt
Jane & Hugh Daugherty 15 Sep 1808; min- William McPheeters
Jane & William Harrison 25 Aug 1801; d William s Benjamin who consents test- Christopher Carman b- Robert Anderson min- William King- 25Aug1801
Jean & William Allison 9 Feb 1788; d James who consents b- William Anderson min- Archibald Scott- 21Apr1788
Lydia & John Reed 30 Sep 1800; d Robert Young, dec. sis to Andrew of Naked Creek, Augusta cty, who swears Lydia of age b- Andrew Young min- William Wilson- 2Oct1800
Margaret & Robert Anderson 11 Sep 1786; d William bond min- William Wilson- 13Sep1786
Margaret & James Glenn 27 Nov 1785; d Robert b- James Young min- William Wilson- 28Dec1785
Margaret & John Ocheltree 29 Aug 1836; min- John Hendren
Margaret & William P Young 13 Feb 1823; min- William W Calhoun
Mary ann & William Seawright 6 Jul 1820; min- James Morrison
Mary & John Bell 25 Dec 1787; Minister's return spells name as 'Margaret Young' widow b- James McGonagal min- William Wilson- 27Dec1787
Mary & Francis Brown 17 Jun 1794; d James b- James Young min- John Brown- 19Jun1794
Nancy Kerr & Fielding Windle 12 Oct 1820; min- William Wilson
Peggy & Michael Ocheltree 2 Apr 1807; min- William Wilson
Polley & Darby Downey 21 Jul 1817; min- Wright Burgess
Polly & James Allen 21 Feb 1788; min- William Wilson- 21Feb1788]
Polly & John Fry 8 Dec 1815; min- William King
Polly & William Kirk 31 Aug 1809; min- William Calhoon
Polly & Isaac Smith 21 Sep 1809; min- William King
Sarah & Robert Curry 19 Mar 1791; d Robert, who consents wit- Andrew & Robert Young b- Robert Young min- William Wilson- 22Apr1791
Sophia & John Smith 12 Feb 1818; min- William King
Susana & Edward Brien 12 Oct 1795; Minister's return spells name as 'Bryan' widow, d of Michael Fackler who consents b- Hugh Paul min- Archibald Scott- 12Oct1795
Susanna & William Young 5 Jan 1796; b- William Young Jr
Virginia & Fountain May 26 Jul 1848; min- D W Arnold

Younger
Catherine & Jacob Trobough 7 Jul 1789; d Maria (German), who consents wit- John Snyder & James Turncuper & William Trobough

Younkard
Easther & John Drum 26 May 1800; Minister's return omits bride's name b- James Williams min- William King- 26May1800

Augusta County Marriages -- Woman's Name

Youstler
  Columbia & John Foley 9 Jan 1845; min- T T Castleman
Zahn
  Sally & John Bowman 14 Jan 1824; min- Josiah Cole
  Susan & Benjamin Demasters 25 Feb 1840; min- D F Bittle
Zahns
  Nancy & Peter Jackson 26 Mar 1846; min- W G Campbell
Zee
  Nancy & John Smith 8 Oct 1840; min- J J Reimensnyder
Zimbro
  Catherine & Daniel Grow 16 Sep 1813; min- William King
  Sarah & John Wiseman 6 Dec 1827; min- James Morrison
Zimmerman
  Catharine & Jacob M Palmer 12 Aug 1841; min- John C Hensell
  Margaret S & Philip G Almonroade 22 Mar 1849; min- Alonzo P Ludden
  Mary A & James A Brown 15 Sep 1841; min- Samuel Wagner
  Mary A & James A Brown 16 Sep 1841; min- Benjamin M Smith
  Mary Jane & John B Shultz 8 Feb 1843; min- D F Bittle
  Matilda & Peter Livick 6 Dec 1832; min- William Calhoon
  Rachel & John Shaver 3 Dec 1822; min- G H Riemenschneider
Zwitchel
  Eleanor & Thomas Curry - Sep 1806; min- John Brown

Appendix 1.
MINISTERS PERFORMING MARRIAGE CEREMONIES AS RECORDED IN AUGUSTA CLERK'S RETURNS

Allenbaugh, Samuel	(United Brethren: Became a Lutheran in 1842)
Arnold, D.W.	(Methodist)
Babb, Augustus	(Lutheran)- Mt. Tabor
Bachtel, Jacob	(United Brethren)
Baer, Jacob	(United Brethren)- Churchville
Baldridge, William	(Associate Reformed Presbyterian)- Rockbridge County
Barry, Basil	(Methodist)- Staunton
Beers, Robert	(Methodist)- Deerfield
Bell, John	(Methodist)- Rockbridge County
Bell, Thomas D.	(Presbyterian)- Cook's Creek {Rockingham County}; Harrisonburg
Best, Hezekiah	(Methodist)- Rockingham District; Warm Springs
Bittle, D.E.	(Lutheran)- Mt. Tabor; St. Peter's
Blakemore, John L.	(Methodist [Note: John Blakemore was a former Lutheran who converted to Methodism])- Rockingham County
Bourne, Thomas	(Presbyterian)- South River {Rockingham County}
Bowen, John	(Methodist)- Pendleton (1828-1829); Staunton (1847-1848)
Boyd, Robert	(minister's denomination unidentified)
Brower, Daniel	(Church of the Brethren)
Brown, B.H.	(Methodist)- Staunton (1836); Rockingham (1842-1843), Presiding Elder (1847-1849)
Brown, Henry	(Presbyterian)- Shemariah
Brown, James	(minister's denomination unidentified)
Brown, John	(Lutheran)- Friedens {Rockingham County}; St. Michael's; McGaheysville
Brown, John	(Presbyterian)- New Providence
Brughes, Benjamin	(minister's denomination unidentified)
Bunting, James	(Methodist)- Augusta County (1842)
Burgess, Wright	(Methodist)
Busey, Thomas H.	(Methodist)- Franklin {Pendleton Circuit} (1842-1843); East Rockingham (1846-1847)
Caldwell, Thomas	(Presbyterian)- Rocky Spring
Calhoon, Nathaniel W.	(Presbyterian)- Augusta Stone
Calhoon, William	(Presbyterian)- First Presbyterian {Staunton}; Hebron
Calhoun, Nathaniel W.	(See Calhoon, Nathaniel W.)
Calhoun, William	(See Calhoon, William)
Campbell, W.G.	(Presbyterian)- Shemariah
Carrick, Samuel	(Presbyterian)- Lebanon; Rocky Spring
Castleman, T.G.	(Episcopal)- Trinity {Staunton}
Chambers, James	(Episcopal)
Chapman, Robert H.	(Presbyterian)- Bethel

Appendix

Chenowith, Alfred .G.	(Methodist)- Augusta (1841-1842)
Cole, Josiah	(minister's denomination unidentified)
Collins, Luke	(Methodist)- Augusta
Coursey, William R.	(United Brethren)
Cravens, William	(Methodist)- Rockbridge County
Dabney, Robert L.	(Presbyterian)- Tinkling Spring
Davidson, A.B.	(Presbyterian)- Mossy Creek
Denton, Benjamin	(United Brethren)- Rockingham County
Emmerson, Luther	(Presbyterian)- Shemariah
Emmitt, John	(minister's denomination unidentified)
Erwin, Benjamin	(Presbyterian)- Cook's Creek; Mossy Creek
Ewin, John D.	(Presbyterian)- Rocky Spring
Filler, Samuel	(Lutheran) (no particular church cited); Rockingham & Rockbridge Counties
Fox, Joseph H.	(minister's denomination unidentified)
Frye, Christopher	(Methodist)
Gamble, James	(Methodist)- Deerfield (1841)
Garber, Abraham	(Church of the Brethren)- Middle River
Garber, Daniel	(Church of the Brethren)
Garber, John	(Church of the Brethren)
Garber, Samuel	(Church of the Brethren)
Gates, Cornelius	(minister's denomination unidentified)
Gee, John	(Methodist) (M'Gee; McGee?)
Glossbrenner, J.J.	(United Brethren)- Churchville (Note: minister's name frequently recorded in returns as 'Glassbrenner')
Goodwin, Fred D.	(Episcopal)- Trinity {Staunton}
Gore, John A.	(minister's denomination unidentified)
Gotber, John	(minister's denomination unidentified) (Garber?)
Grover, Ezra	(Methodist)- Rockingham County
Guffin, William A.	(minister's denomination unidentified) (Coffin?)
Hall, John S.	(Methodist)- Augusta County (1839)
Hammond, Rezin	(Methodist)
Haney, John	(minister's denomination unidentified)
Hank, William	(Methodist)- Rockingham (1829-1830); Pendleton (1831)
Harper, James	(Associate Reformed Presbyterian)- Timber Ridge; Old Providence
Harshbarger, John	(Church of the Brethren)
Hendren, John	(Presbyterian)- Mossy Creek; Union
Henkle, Ambrose	(Lutheran)- Trinity {Koiner's}
Hensell, John C.	(Reformed Lutheran)- Mt. Crawford; St. Michael's; Friedens; St. John's
Hildebrand, Stephen	(Methodist)- Rockingham (1844-1845); Augusta (1846-1847)
Hildt, George	(Methodist)- Staunton (1833-1834)

Appendix

Hoover, Jesse	(Lutheran)- Salem {Mt. Sidney}; Friedens
Houston, Samuel	(Presbyterian)- High Bridge; Oxford {Rockbridge County}
Howell, John	(Methodist)- Warm Springs (1827-1828); Staunton (1831)
Huffman, George	(United Brethren)- Mt. Zion {Mt. Solon}
Irvin, Benjamin	(See Erwin, Benjamin)
Irvine, Benjamin	(See Erwin, Benjamin)
Irwin, Benjamin	(See Erwin, Benjamin)
Irwin, I.D.	(minister's denomination unidentifi
Israel, G.W.	(Methodist)- Augusta (1844-1845); Rockingham (1846-1847); East Rock ingham (1848)
Jackson, William G.	(Episcopal)- Trinity {Staunton}
Jamison, Enoch G.	(Methodist)- Deerfield (1845); High land (1848-1849)
Johnston, James	(minister's denomination unidentif
Jones, Isaac	(Presbyterian)- Hebron
Jordan, Zach(ariah)	(Methodist)- Rocky Spring (1837)
Kennerley, Philip	(Methodist)
Kennerley, Samuel	(Methodist)- Augusta
Kepler, Henry S.	(Methodist)- Rockingham (1828); Wa Springs (1829)
Kerr, James	(Presbyterian)- Rocky Spring
Killian, Jacob	(Lutheran)- Trinity {Koiner's}; Be lehem; St. Paul {Mt. Solon}; McG heysville
Kindig, Benajmin W.	(Church of the Brethren)
King, William	(Episcopal)- Trinity {Staunton}
Kirby, W.	(minister's denomination unidentif
Laney, William H.	(Methodist)- Rockingham (1842)
Lauck, William O.	(minister's denomination unidentif
Leopard, George A.	(minister's denomination unidentif
Lipscomb, Robert M.	(Methodist)- Staunton (1835)
Love, Solomon J.	(Presbyterian)- Hebron
Loyd, John	(Methodist)- Deerfield
Ludden, Alonzo P.	(Lutheran)- Salem; Middlebrook; Mt Tabor
Martin, George H.	(minister's denomination unidentif
Martin, Samuel	(minister's denomination unidentif
Maxey, Bennett	(Methodist)- Cumberland
McClure, Thomas F.	(Methodist)- Augusta (1845)
McCorkle, A.B.	(Presbyterian)- Bethel; Shemariah
McCue, John	(Presbyterian)- Tinkling Spring (N minister's name sometimes found register as 'J. McCune')
McFarland, Francis	(Presbyterian)- Bethel
McPheeters, William	(Presbyterian)- Bethel; Windy Cove

Appendix

...yerhoeffer, Michael	(Lutheran)- Mt. Tabor; Salem; Zion {Waynesboro}
...ller, Peter	(Lutheran)- Rockingham County
...lls, Francis A.	(Methodist)- Franklin (Pendleton Circuit)(1836-1837)
...nnett, Samuel	(minister's denomination unidentified)
...nroe, William	(Methodist)- Staunton (1826-1827)
...ntgomery, Jacob	(Methodist)- Deerfield (1846-1847); Highland (1850)
...ntgomery, John	(Presbyterian)- Windy Cove {Bath County}; Williamsville {Bath County}
...ntgomery, S.	(minister's denomination unidentified)
...organ, Gerard	(Methodist)- Presiding Elder, Rockingham (1826-1827); Staunton (1829-1830)
...organ, Tillotson A.	(Methodist)- Lexington (1842); East Rockingham (1849)
...orrison, James	(Presbyterian)- New Providence
...orrison, William C.	(Methodist)- Pendleton (1814)
...aine, James	(Presbyterian)- Mount Carmel
...aine, John	(minister's denomination unidentified)
...arkison, C.	(minister's denomination unidentified)
...eese, Thomas M.	(Methodist)- Staunton (1849-1850)
...eid, Joseph	(Presbyterian)- Windy Cove; Lebanon
...eiley, J. McKendree	(Methodist)- Augusta (1848-1849)
...eubush, John	(United Brethren)
...ichardson, William T.	(Presbyterian)- First Presbyterian {Waynesboro}
...iley, Tobias	(Methodist)- Rockingham (1818); Staunton (1823-1824)
...iemensnyder, John J.	(Lutheran)- Trinity {Koiner's}; Zion; Salem; Friedens
...iemensnyder, G.H.	(Lutheran)- Trinity {Koiner's}; Rockingham County
...imel, George B.	(United Brethren)
Rodgers, John	(Associate Reformed Presbyterian)- Timber Ridge; Old Providence
...ohr, Wesley H.	(Methodist)- Lexington (1839-1840)
Ruffner, Henry	(Presbyterian)- Timber Ridge {Rockbridge}
Scott, Archibald	(Presbyterian)- Bethel
Scull, William	(Lutheran)- Zion {Waynesboro}
Sewall, James	(Methodist)- Staunton (1821-1822)
Shannan, Samuel	(Presbyterian)- Windy Cove
Shannon, Samuel	(See Shannan, Samuel)
Shickel, Peter	(Lutheran)- St. Peter's {Churchville}; Salem {Mt. Sidney}
Shickel Jr., Peter	(Lutheran)
Smith, Benjamin M.	(Presbyterian)- First Presbyterian {Staunton}
Smith, Joseph	(Presbyterian)- First Presbyterian {Staunton}

Appendix

Smith, Stephen	(Methodist)- Augusta (1836-1837); Franklin (Pendleton Circuit)(1838-1839); Lexington (1842)
Speece, Conrad	(Presbyterian)- Augusta Stone
Spitler, Jacob C.	(United Brethren)- Bethlehem
Spotswood, W. Lee	(Methodist)- Rockingham (1848-1849); Lexington (1850)
Spriggs, Joseph	(Methodist)- Lexington (1832); Rockingham (1833); Augusta (1834) (Superintendent- 1845); Staunton Superintendent (1848-1849)
Steele, John A.	(Presbyterian)- First Presbyterian {Staunton}
Stephens, Daniel	(Episcopal)- Trinity {Staunton}
Stevenson, P.E.	(Presbyterian)- First Presbyterian {Staunton}
Stine, John W.	(Methodist)- Lexington (1818); Deerfield (1840); Rockingham (1841)
Stirewalt, Jacob	(Lutheran)- Trinity {Koiner's}
Templeton, Alexander	(Presbyterian)- Rocky Spring
Thomas, Enoch	(Presbyterian)- Shemariah
Trimble, W.W.	(Presbyterian)- Bethesda {Rockbridge}
Vanlear, John A.	(Presbyterian)- Mossy Creek
Veitch, E.R.	(Methodist)- Franklin (Pendleton Circuit)(1833-1834); Staunton (1843-1844)
Waddell, James	(See Waddle, James)
Waddle, James	(Presbyterian)- Tinkling Spring
Wagner, Samuel	(Lutheran)- Zion {Waynesboro}; Salem {Mt. Sidney}
Ward, James	(Methodist)- Rockbridge County
Waters, Samuel C.	(minister's denomination unidentified)
Watson, Joal	(Methodist)- Staunton
Watson, John	(Methodist)- Pendleton (1818); Rockingham (1823)
Watt, John S.	(Presbyterian)- First Presbyterian {Staunton}
Watts, James	(minister's denomination unidentified)
Webb, E. Joshua	(minister's denomination unidentified)
Welly, Bernard	(Reformed Church)- Woodstock; Shenandoah County
Wetzel, Henry	(Lutheran)- St. Paul {Mt. Solon}; Zion {Waynesboro}
Wheeler, Thomas	(Methodist)- Pendleton (1832); Augusta (1838); Rockingham (1839)
Willson, William	(Presbyterian)- Augusta Stone (Old Stone?) (Note: minister's name frequently found as 'William Wilson': 'Willson' appears to be the correct spelling)

Appendix

Wilson, James C.   (Presbyterian)- Tinkling Spring
Wilson, Robert   (Presbyterian)- Rocky Spring; Windy Cove; Lebanon
Wilson, William C.   (minister's denomination unidentified) (William Willson?)
Wine, John   (Church of the Brethren)
Zenas, Freeman   (Missionary Baptist)- Waynesboro (1834)

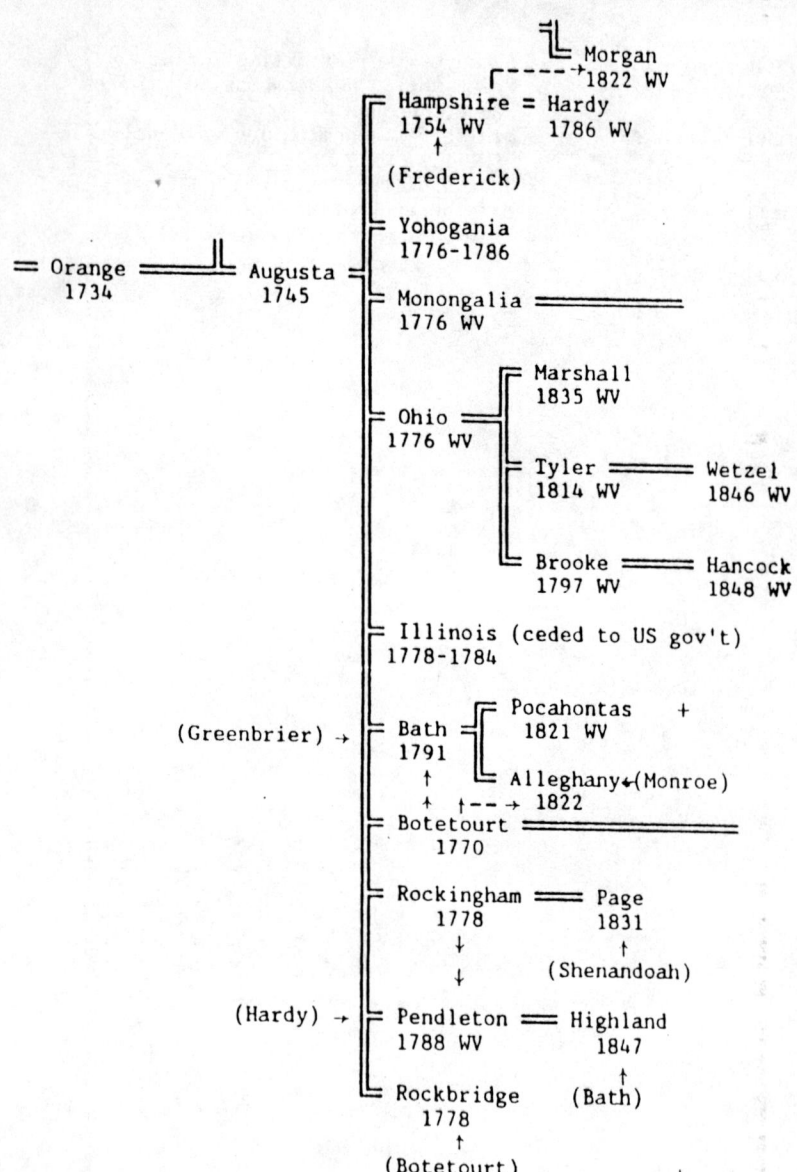

Figure 1. Origin of Augusta County, Virginia & some derivative counties formed from it.

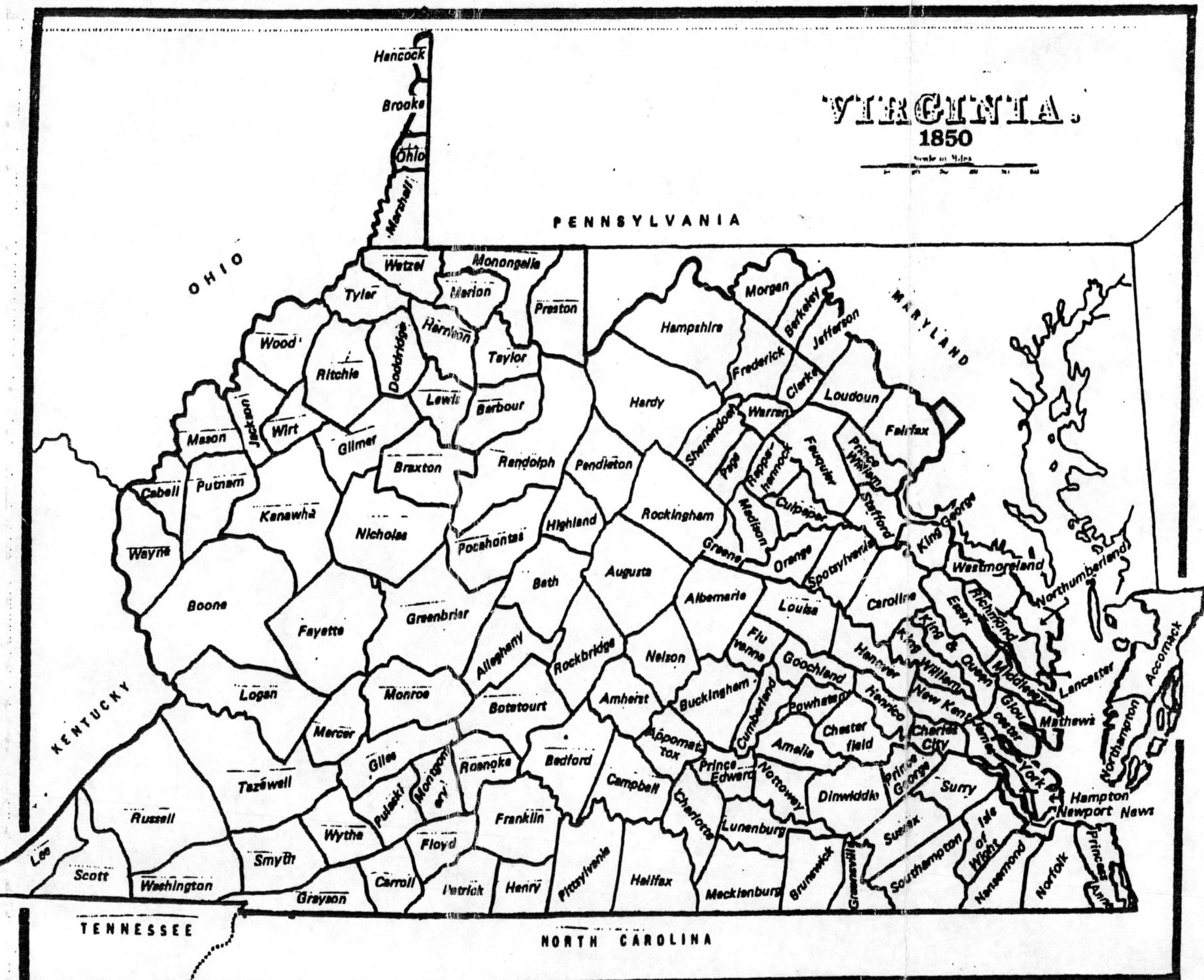